NATURALISM
WITHOUT
FOUNDATIONS

NATURALISM
WITHOUT
FOUNDATIONS

KAI
NIELSEN

THE PROMETHEUS LECTURES

 **Prometheus Books**

59 John Glenn Drive
Amherst, New York 14228-2197

Published 1996 by Prometheus Books

00 99 98 97 96   5 4 3 2 1

Library of Congress Cataloging-in-Publication Data

Nielsen, Kai, 1926–
    Naturalism without foundations / Kai Nielsen.
        p.   cm.
    Includes bibliographical references and index.
    ISBN 1–57392–076–2
    1. Naturalism. 2. Atheism. 3. Ethics. 4. Political science—Philosophy.
I. Title.
B828.2.N54   1996
146—dc20   96–8794
                                                          CIP

Printed in the United States of America on acid-free paper

For Rodger Beehler, Andrew Lugg, and Bob Ware

Contents

Preface

I

Substantial portions of part 1 of *Naturalism Without Foundations* were given as my Prometheus Lectures at the State University of New York at Buffalo in March 1995. I am grateful for the insightful and penetrating questions put to me by those who had to endure those lectures. I am grateful, as well, for the hospitality afforded to me by my hosts. Stimulating conversations were a rich part of that. Particular thanks go to Paul Kurtz and Timothy J. Madigan for good cheer and good conversation and for shepherding me around and looking after my needs so well. It was good humanist fraternity.

Antony Flew made a strong case for atheism in his "Fundamentals of Unbelief." (Delivered at the University of Buffalo in November of 1991 and subsequently published as part 1 of his *Atheistic Humanism*. They were the first Prometheus Lectures.[1] Following Flew here, I, too, seek to make a strong case for atheism in a world awash with religion.

It is also a world of widespread passive acceptance of the (at least sociologically speaking) legitimacy of religion even by those—indeed, most particularly by those—who do not have much, if anything at all, in the way of religious belief. Among the intelligentsia when they die there not infrequently is an elaborate church funeral even though most of the parties involved are quite without religious belief. People sit and passively listen to the clergy go on about the resurrection and the life beyond the grave even though they do not have the slightest temptation to believe a word of it. In some instances, they may even think such beliefs childish or at least so utterly credulous such that they could in no way be live options for them. Hypocrisy and/or simply an acceptance of convention here is pervasive. Unlike what was thought by progressive intellectuals of the nineteenth century or the first half of our waning century, it is often thought now by our intelligentsia to be just too *vulgaire* to be critical of religion, let alone to attack it. This leads to a widespread ignoring on the part of many (perhaps most) intellectuals of the role religion plays in the world. Moreover, sometimes—and here it is particularly humanly damaging—the religion in question is of a thoroughly Neanderthal sort. It is not only Islamic fundamentalism which has this feature, but our own homegrown Christian and Jewish fundamentalisms and near fundamentalisms as well. In such a world atheism should not be taken for granted as simply one comprehensive worldview among others, but needs to be vigorously argued for in all sorts of public forums in the hope that we can through careful reflective discussion and a setting out clearly of the relevant facts, nudge, by the force of the better deliberation, our world in a more secular direction.

Such an endeavor is always close to Flew's heart, and Flew and I (whatever our differences over politics) are at one about this. However, as a matter of background and theoretical articulation, as a comparison of part 1 of my book with part 1 of his will reveal, I proceed in a much more contextualist, historicist, and pragmatist fashion. That notwithstanding, in much of chapter 3, where part of the time I rehearse and critique traditional defenses of religious belief, I stand on his shoulders as we both, in these respects, stand on the sturdy shoulders of David Hume. We both share the belief—indeed, a belief common to all secular humanists—that there is no establishing or reasonably postulating, presupposing, or even taking on faith that there is "an omnipotent, just, and omnibeneficent person God"—the longed for "something, not ourselves, which makes for righteousness."[2] I argue in the body of the text that we not only have no sound reasons for believing in such a reality, we have very good reasons for (a) believing that there is no such supernatural reality and (b) for rejecting the claim, popular in some religious circles, including among certain Christian philosophers (e.g., Alvin Plantinga), that, groundless or not, we can reasonably and responsibly accept such a belief on faith.[3]

However, before engaging in that nay-saying, I engage in a little yea-saying. In chapter 1 I give a characterization, together with an elucidation, more historicized than is usual, of what I think naturalism should be and in chapter 2 I set out what I take to be its proper method.

Part 2 turns to issues, including central methodological issues, in ethical theory and in normative social and political philosophy. This, as I hope will become clear, is closely linked to what I defend as a central method of naturalism in part 1. Part 3, building on those discussions, turns to what are essentially metaphilosophical discussions: discussions about the nature and proper office, to use John Dewey's phrase, of philosophy. There I defend pragmatism against the challenge—a challenge that is deeper and more troubling than most secular humanists realize—of postmodernism (so-called postmodernism, if you will). Here a central element is a discussion of Charles Saunders Peirce's pragmatism in relation to his critical commonsensism and to how his thought bears on this postmodernist challenge. Building on that, I pursue metaphilosophical themes—all in the service of a naturalism without foundations—in a discussion of Richard Rorty, Jürgen Habermas, and Michel Foucault and to how they stand to each other and to the tradition of the Enlightenment. Like Foucault and Rorty, I, though not without some reconceptualization, defend the tradition of the Enlightenment, while, as they do as well, eschewing Enlightenment *rationalism.*

Finally in part 4, I return, but now from a series of quite different angles, to a discussion of religion. In responding to some critiques of my account of religious beliefs—critiques that broadly speaking would be extended to atheistic humanism generally—I try to show how there is no good reason to believe that atheism need take the fanatical and unreasonable form of an inverted Platonism: a dogmatic response to religious dogmas. Indeed, I show that it should not and need not take any unreasonable or fanatical form at all. This should be obvious, but, given what is not infrequently said about atheists and atheism, I fear that, culturally speaking, it is not.

Concerning militancy and atheism—to continue with this a bit and to give it a historical reference point—there is a considerable distance between d'Holbach and Hume, even though they were contemporaries who knew each other and they were both thorough secularizers.[4] The former was a dogmatic militant atheist, the latter was not. Not a few religious apologists console themselves with the belief that atheism must be fanatical, thinking that atheists must go the way of d'Holbach or, closer to home, Lenin, but that is simply false.

In part 4, I explore, free from fanaticism and dogmatism, what an atheism should look like when it is a key element in a naturalism without foundations. I also engage in an examination of the social and psychological functions of religion: its role in the lives of human beings.[5] I discuss, in this connection, the plausibility of secular replacements of what, historically and culturally speaking, has been, and still continues to be, a pervasive and persistent religious answering to our needs. Here Feuerbach, Marx, Freud, and Durkheim are good supplements to Bayle and Hume, though supplements that take into consideration very different matters than was taken into consideration by the classical secularizers of the eighteenth century. I try to show that there is a good division of labor between these different kinds of secularizers. Taken together, they provide, I argue, a powerful elucidation and critique of religion. I also, in this context, return to some themes from my *Ethics Without God,* though this time without even an echo of foundationalism. I end with a consideration of both the very possibility and, given the possibility, a consideration of the desirability, everything considered, of our living as secularists in an utterly secular world. If the springs of social wealth can come to flow more fully and more evenly and the general level of education rises, can we, at least in those parts of the world where this obtains, reasonably hope that such a world will be ours? Will be, that is, both thoroughly secular and humanistic. And can we rightly struggle to bring such a world into being and to sustain it? Or should we simply let things be? Moreover, would such an utterly secular world, everything considered, be a good thing? I engage these issues.

Some of the chapters in parts 2, 3, and 4 have had previous incarnations, though, as they appear here, they have, like incarnations tend to be, been extensively transformed. I would like to thank the editors of the journals and books in which they, in rather different forms, first appeared for permission to reprint them here.

Finally, I would like to close by thanking those who in various ways have been of a very considerable help to me in the writing and preparation of this book. First thanks go to Andrew Lugg and Hendrick Hart for their perceptive criticisms of an earlier version of part 1. I hope I have done something in the version that appears here to address their concerns. Thanks also go to Merlette Schnell for her conscientious preparation of earlier versions of parts 2 and 3 and to Elisabeth Landry for her meticulous preparation of the final version of the whole manuscript. This is all the more remarkable in that she did it in a language that is not her mother tongue and that she does not daily live with. And last, but certainly not least, I would like to thank Jocelyne Couture for helping me in various ways in the preparation of the text and more importantly—incommensurably more importantly—for her persistent skeptical and critical scrutinizing of my philosophical ideas and ways, including her not infrequently finding them obscure and wrongheaded: wrongheaded down to the very way I go about things. I only *hope* that in the form they appear here they are neither.

II

So much for prolegomena. I will in this section make only two connected substantive points. In this volume what I call, following Norman Daniels and John Rawls, *wide reflective equilibrium* gets a lot of play, as it does in their work as well.[6] It is the core method—or if "method" is too highfalutin a word here, "a way of doing things"—of my moral and social thinking. It also plays an important role in *some* of what I say about religion and it is the distinctive method (way of doing things) of my form of naturalism. It is not an extravagant hyperbole to say I do philosophy within the limits of wide reflective equilibrium alone. However, it is a method, like other methods or conceptions at the cutting edge of philosophy, that has had both considerable acceptance and considerable, sometimes even extravagant, rejection. It has also, as is invariably the case with such philosophical conceptions, generated considerable perplexity as to just what it is. However, I do not think it is problematical. I think *au contraire* that it should be seen as a rather more precise and somewhat more pedantic articulation of a commonsense way of going about things that we all pervasively and indeed rather routinely employ in a less explicit form, though typically unself-consciously and without conscious articulation. Indeed, in my way of viewing things, being such a pervasive bit of common sense—if indeed that is what it is—is something which counts in its favor, particularly when it gets extended in good pragmatist fashion to some scientific ways of going about things as well and is seen to have a cross-cultural basis. But it has not commonly been seen in this way and has remained— rightly or wrongly—a matter of extensive controversy.

Given the strategic role it plays in my thought, I want in most of the rest of this preface to show in as simple and direct a way as I can something of what it is, so that readers not familiar with that lay of the land here can come to have a reasonable sense of what this method is and some sense of what is controversial about it.

Reflective equilibrium (whether wide or narrow) is a coherentist method of explanation and justification used in ethical theory, social and political philosophy, philosophy of science, philosophy of mind, and epistemology. Its initial articulation was made by Nelson Goodman.[7] But its more familiar and extensive utilization is in moral and social philosophy where it was initiated by John Rawls and Stuart Hampshire and was later amplified by Norman Daniels, Richard Rorty, and myself.[8] Its most forceful critics are Richard Brandt, David Copp, Joseph Raz, Jean Hampton, and Simon Blackburn.[9]

As a method of justification in ethics, it starts with a society's, or a cluster of similar societies', most firmly held *considered judgments (convictions)*, principally their considered moral judgments or convictions, and seeks to *forge* them into a consistent and coherent whole that squares with the other relevantly related things that are reasonably believed and generally and uncontroversially accepted in the society, or cluster of similar societies, in question. The considered judgments (convictions) appealed to can be, and should be, at all levels of generality, though the point of departure in rationalizing moral matters would usually be from specific considered judgments, which in turn will be placed in a comprehensive pattern with more general moral principles, middle-level moral rules, and moral practices. (More strictly with the verbal articulations of the practices.) Suppose, for example, a particular moral belief fails to be compatible with a moral principle in turn supported by many other firmly held particular considered judgments, other general moral principles, and middle-level moral rules. That being so, then that particular considered judgment should either be modified until it is consistent with the other principles, practices, beliefs, judgments, and the like or be excised from the corpus of considered moral judgments and the moral repertoire of that society or those societies. The way of modification here, as elsewhere, would usually, but not invariably, be the first step. Only if repeated attempts here failed should we turn to excisement. It should be plain here that we will have nothing like an algorithm or mechanical decision procedures. Such notions are—or at least should be—remote from the domains of the moral, social, and political theory. But, to continue with my description of how the method works, if, in contrast with my first description, a general moral principle (say, the principle of utility) is incompatible with a considerable number of firmly held considered judgments, then it should also be either similarly modified or rejected.

The general idea is to shuttle back and forth between particular moral judgments, general principles, medium-level moral rules, and moral practices, modifying and pruning, until we have gained what we have good reason to believe is the most consistent and coherent pattern achievable at the time. By the metaphor of "shuttling back and forth" I mean we attend, for example, to particular judgments relating them to and comparing them with other particular judgments, general moral principles, and middle-level moral rules, and we in turn ascertain what particular moral judgments and middle-level rules are either derivable from or are compatible with the general moral principles. We try clearly to display these principles, middle-level moral rules, particular moral judgments, and verbal articulations of practices and to discern how they relate to each other. We try to ascertain if from this mélange of moral elements we can create a consistent and coherent whole which we then seek perspicuously to display. When this is attained, a reflective equilibrium has been attained.

The idea is to seek to maximize the coherence of our moral beliefs and practices: to get them, in an ever-widening circle, into the most coherent pattern we can for the time manage. But there is no assumption that any reflective equilibrium that may have been attained, or that can be attained, will be *final* or even complete and will not in time be upset.[10] It will actually be upset (and this is something we should expect to happen, historically speaking, repeatedly) if either we come to gain a still more coherent pattern or because, as the situation changes, new moral judgments enter the scene which conflict with some of the beliefs in the reflective equilibrium which has been established. When the latter is so, we need to forge a new consistent cluster of beliefs and practices. So, in such a situation, the extant reflective equilibrium is upset. In that case, a new, more adequate one has, if we can manage it, to be wrought which will contain either a larger circle of coherent related beliefs

and practices or will instead, while not enlarging very much the circle of belief, articulate a more coherent package of beliefs and practices more perspicuously displayed. The expectation is that this pattern of self-correcting
reasoning will continue indefinitely and, in doing so, yield, if it is pursued diligently and intelligently, and if things go reasonably well in the society, ever
more coherent conceptions of moral belief and practice, while never attaining anything even like a final closure.[11] (There is no Absolute, not even a 'relative Absolute'.)

Fallibilism is the name of the game. No *ultimate* critical standards are
sought, no Archimedean point (let alone an ahistorical one) is expected, and
no principles or beliefs or convictions, not even the most firmly held, are, in
principle at least, free from the possibility of being modified or even set
aside, though some moral truisms may always *in fact* be unquestionably accepted. But this non-Absolutism is not skepticism, for, if a reflective equilibrium is for a time achieved, or, more realistically, approximated, we will
have found a rationale for our moral beliefs and practices by seeing how they
are in what we have good reason to believe is a consistent and coherent pattern. Justification, on this conception, is attained in this way. And objectivity
is obtained, as well, in such an extensive and coherent intersubjectivity. (Here
we should also recognize that things are always more or less objective. After
all, objectivity is something that admits of degrees. Without an Absolute we
will have no 'complete objectivity'. But that is a will-o'-the wisp anyway.)

The coherentist pattern of explanation and justification described above
is still a pattern that might just be a narrow (partial) reflective equilibrium. It
collects together moral and like particular considered judgments, articulations
of moral practices, medium-level moral rules, and moral principles, including very general ones. But this would simply be a limited coherentism that
does not take into consideration facts about the functioning of economies or
indeed even of morality and of other parts of the social structure, conceptions
of human nature, social and psychological facts, political realities, and scientific developments. Following Rawls and Daniels in this respect, I seek to
set out and defend a *wide* reflective equilibrium that takes these matters into
consideration as well as what is taken into consideration in narrow reflective
equilibrium. Besides seeking to forge a coherent pattern of the moral matters
mentioned above, it seeks—continuing to work to maximize coherence—an
equilibrium that takes into account our best corroborated social scientific
theories and theories of human nature, firmly established social and psychological facts and political realities, such as the extent and intractability of pluralism (reasonable or otherwise) in the society or cluster of societies where
the reflective equilibrium is sought. It also should take into consideration what
it is reasonable to believe in the society or societies in question and whether
the *de facto* pluralism in question is a reasonable pluralism or whether it is

plausible to believe that things could so change that we would come to have a reasonable pluralism. The thing is, considering all these matters, to achieve a consistent cluster of moral, factual, and theoretical beliefs that would yield the best available account of what the social situation is, what possibilities obtain in the society or societies, and what it is reasonable and desirable to do. Such an account is both descriptive and normative and it is through and through coherentist and holistic, justifying our beliefs and practices by showing the consistency and coherency of their fit with each other, if they can be seen to have it, or, what is more likely, by forging one if they do not. If such a fit is either discovered or forged, the beliefs and practices will be justified.

In taking one account of such beliefs and practices to be superior to another and thus being more justified than the others (justification like objectivity admitting of degrees), we do so by ascertaining which account makes the superior fit of our beliefs and practices. That is to say, the superior one is the account that constructs a pattern of the widest circle of beliefs, convictions, and verbal articulations of practices, generally believed to be relevant, into what is most plausibly taken to be the most clearly consistent and coherent pattern displayed with the greatest perspicuity among the, at the time, available rival accounts seeking to articulate such patterns.

Wide reflective equilibrium accounts do not suffer from the defects of pure coherentist theories where any set of consistent beliefs, no matter how unrealistic—say, Christian Science—is justified simply in virtue of the fact of forming a consistent system. But in reflective equilibrium, we seek to get a cluster of *considered judgments* into wide reflective equilibrium. We do not seek just any consistent cluster of beliefs, for we start with *considered judgments* (judgments we take to have an initial credibility) and return to them as well in the testing of our accounts. (This is not to give to understand that appeal to them is ever a *decisive* test. The account, after all, is holistic and fallibilistic.)

Some critics of reflective equilibrium have argued that there is no coherent system of moral beliefs and practices there to be *discovered* by careful reflection, analysis, and investigation.[12] Instead, we have inherited a mass of conflicting views, unreflectively come by, held, and persisted in. They are beliefs, which are just psychologically speaking, stamped in by arbitrary social conditioning. They are our tribal mores drilled into us in our infancy and vulnerable youth. Moreover, these views are views which are not infrequently ideological. They often are the nonprincipled result of brute compromises between contending parties with conflicting interests or the result of religious biases and/or of class, ethnic, racial, or gender prejudice. This unrationalized mélange is not supportive of, the objection goes, the idea of there being an underlying coherent whole, whose deep underlying structure is to be unearthed by careful investigation, but is simply a cluster of conflicting beliefs and practices *revealing a jumble rather than a coherent pattern.*

To this, it can and should, in turn, be responded that philosophers who are defenders of reflective equilibrium are also *constructivists*. The pattern of consistent beliefs, including very centrally moral beliefs, is not a structure to be discovered or unearthed, as if it were analogous to the deep underlying "depth grammar" of language (if indeed there is any such a thing), but something to be *forged*—constructed—by a careful and resolute use of the method of reflective equilibrium. We start from our considered judgments (convictions), however culturally and historically skewed. This involves—indeed, inescapably involves—seeing things by our own lights. Where else could we start? We can hardly jump out of our cultural and historical skins. And talk of an appeal to pure reason here—pure theoretical reason or pure practical reason—is just arm waving. (What is it, after all, in such a context, to appeal to reason?) But that we cannot overleap culture and history is no justification or excuse for *remaining uncritically* with our initial convictions, convictions that we cannot avoid *starting* with. We should go on, and will go on, if we are reasonable, bootstrapping our way through the world. If we use the method of wide reflective equilibrium, we will, after careful examination, reflection, and the taking of the relevant moral considerations *to heart,* come to modify or even excise some considered judgments, persistently seeking a wider and a more coherent web of beliefs and practices, gaining, as we go along, increasingly, a more adequate understanding of things. (It is in this way in which there can be, its unfashionable ring to the contrary notwithstanding, progress in morality.) We will, if we are reasonable, so proceed until we have constructed a consistent and relevantly inclusive cluster of beliefs and practices. But it is not a question of discovering some underlying moral structure that has always been there. Such 'moral realism' is mythical. (Moreover, even *if* such a method is larger than life and we can never achieve anything like this, it remains a *heuristic* to be approximated.[13])

Other critics of reflective equilibrium have argued that reflective equilibrium, both narrow and wide, is ethnocentric, relativist, and conservative.[14] Similar responses to those made to the previous criticism can be relevantly made here. There is no escaping starting with our considered judgments. But the very fact of such a starting point is not a manifestation of ethnocentrism. In seeking to maximize coherence and to get the full range of relevant considerations into as coherent and inclusive a pattern as we can manage, the moral and empirical beliefs and conceptions of others, sometimes, culturally speaking, very different 'others', need to be taken into consideration. If our particular considered judgments (more realistically some of them) are in conflict with either well-established factual claims, well-grounded and established social theories, or carefully articulated moral theories, they must, if we will be reasonable, be up for critical inspection and for at least possible rejection. If they conflict with the considered judgments of other peoples whose considered judgments square better with a careful appraisal of the facts or the most carefully articulated social, biological, and natural scientific theories as well as with reflectively articulated general moral principles, then we have good reason to accept these considered judgments rather than our own. This is true even of our more general considered judgments—if you will, our 'fundamental' moral principles—where they conflict with such massively supported considered judgments.

The method of reflective equilibrium is a *self-correcting* method which gives us, as we repair or rebuild the ship at sea, a *critical* morality. So, though we start, and inescapably, with our considered judgments, if we apply reflective equilibrium resolutely and intelligently, our account will not, or at least need not, be ethnocentric. Similar considerations obtain against the claim that wide reflective equilibrium is relativistic or inherently conservative.

A somewhat different criticism of reflective equilibrium claims that it, even when it is a *wide* reflective equilibrium, does not push questions of justification far enough.[15] It does not come to grips with the foundational issues, or at least the foundational epistemological issues, that would show us what moral knowledge really is or what warranted moral beliefs really are, so that we could defeat a determined global ethical skepticism. An underlying *assumption* of reflective equilibrium is that our considered judgments have an *initial credibility*. But unless we can show how we could establish these considered judgments to be true or warranted, that assumption will not be justified and we will not really have faced the epistemological questions that need to be faced if we are to come to have a genuinely objective ethical theory philosophically defended. Defenders of reflective equilibrium will in turn respond that such a foundationalist quest is both impossible and unnecessary. (Rawls, at least as a methodological stance, more cautiously, will only commit himself to saying such a quest is unnecessary to establish a political conception of justice with its allied principles and conceptions.) There is no just knowing moral propositions to be true or warranted. There is no just noting that there is some direct correspondence of moral propositions to the facts (moral or otherwise). There are no such factlike entities for moral propositions to correspond to. But the recognition of this should not lead to the abandonment of an idea of objectivity in morality. Cross-culturally agreed-on considered judgments (convictions) set in a wide reflective equilibrium (the widest and most perspicuously displayed that we can muster at any given time) give us an intersubjectivity that is reflectively sustainable. That is all the moral or political objectivity that we can get—and it is all we need.

The method of wide reflective equilibrium, as the above gestures at, and as this book argues in detail, and, as has been argued in somewhat different ways by Richard Rorty and Hilary Putnam, enables us—to turn now to my second substantive point—to dispense with a search for Absolutes—a hopeless, not altogether coherent, search, I think—without ending up with relativism, subjectivism, nihilism, or skepticism.[16] The very extensive intersubjective agreement it can yield concerning the coherent weaving together of our beliefs gives us a perfectly reasonable sense of objectivity without even the ghost of an Absolute or of objectivism or any other reification of reason. Richard Rorty puts the point well when he remarks:

> Socrates and Plato suggested that if we tried hard enough we should find beliefs which *everybody* found intuitively plausible, and that among these would be moral beliefs whose implications, when clearly realized, would make us virtuous as well as knowledgeable. To thinkers like Allan Bloom (on the Straussian side) and Terry Eagleton (on the Marxist side), there just *must* be such beliefs—unwobbling pivots that determine the answer to the question "Which moral or political alternative is *objectively* valid?" For Deweyan pragmatists like me, history and anthropology are enough to show that there are no unwobbling pivots, and that seeking objectivity is just a matter of getting as much intersubjective agreement as you can manage.[17]

A core argument of this book is that we can get along perfectly well without, and indeed are well off without, allegedly unwobbling pivots, certainty, unquestionable foundations, the Truth, timeless warrants, and the like—all the obscure trappings of theology or traditional metaphysics that cannot accept the through and through contingency and historicity of our existence. The method of wide reflective equilibrium will yield us all the objectivity and reasonability we can have or need. Rawls puts the matter succinctly, but aptly: "The overall criterion of the reasonable is general and wide reflective equilibrium."[18]

NOTES

1. Antony Flew, *Atheistic Humanism* (Amherst, N.Y.: Prometheus Books, 1993).
2. Ibid., 10. The second quotation, cited by Flew, is, of course, from Matthew Arnold.
3. These Christian philosophers—the so-called reform epistemologists, with their basic belief apologetic (the most visible being William Alston, Alvin Plantinga, and Nicholas Woltersrtorff)—are discussed extensively in the text.
4. See Richard Wollheim's introduction to his selections from Hume on religion. Richard Wollheim, ed., *Hume on Religion* (London: Fontana Library, 1963), 29–30. See also Bernard Williams, "Hume on Religion," in *David Hume: A Symposium,* ed. D. F. Pears (London: Macmillan and Co. Ltd., 1963), 77–88; and J. C. A. Gaskin, "Hume on Religion," in *The Cambridge Companion to Hume,* ed. David Fate Norton (Cambridge, England: Cambridge University Press, 1993), 313–44.
5. This, as I remember, was the subject of my first published article on religion. Kai Nielsen, "Religion and the Modern Predicament," *Humanist* 18 (Fall 1958).

6. Norman Daniels, *Justice and Justification: Reflective Equilibrium in Theory and Practice* (Cambridge, England: Cambridge University Press, 1996); John Rawls, *A Theory of Justice* (Cambridge, Mass.: Harvard University Press, 1971), 20, 48–51, 120, 432; John Rawls, "The Independence of Moral Theory," *Proceedings and Addresses of the American Philosophical Association* 48 (1974): 5–22; John Rawls, *Political Liberalism* (New York: Columbia University Press, 1993), 8, 28, 45, 72, 95–97; and John Rawls, "Reply to Habermas," *Journal of Philosophy* 92, no. 3 (March 1995): 141–42. See also my *After the Demise of the Tradition: Rorty, Critical Theory and the Fate of Philosophy* (Boulder, Colo.: Westview Press, 1991), 195–248.

7. Nelson Goodman, *Fact, Fiction and Forecast,* 2d ed. (Indianapolis, Ind.: Bobbs-Merrill, 1965), 63–64. See here as well Marsha Hanen's perceptive discussion of Goodman's views about these matters in relation to mine in her "Reflections on Contemporary Metaphilosophy," in Rodger Beehler et al., eds., *On the Track of Reason: Essays in Honor of Kai Nielsen* (Boulder, Colo.: Westview Press, 1992), 197–202.

8. See the references to Rawls in note 6. Stuart Hampshire, *Morality and Conflict* (Cambridge, Mass.: Harvard University Press, 1983), 82–125; and Hampshire, "A New Philosophy of the Just Society," *New York Review of Books* 18, no. 3 (February 24, 1972): 34–39. Richard Rorty, *Objectivity, Relativism and Truth* (Cambridge, England: Cambridge University Press, 1991), 175–96. See note 5 for references to Daniels and myself.

9. Richard Brandt, *A Theory of the Good and the Right* (Oxford, England: Clarendon Press, 1979), 16–22, 151, 163, 186, 235–36, 289–90; David Copp, "Considered Judgments and Moral Justification: Conservatism in Moral Theory," in *Morality, Reason and Truth: New Essays on the Foundations of Ethics,* ed. David Copp and David Zimmerman (Totowa, N.J.: Rowman and Allanheld, 1985), 141–68; Joseph Raz, "The Claims of Reflective Equilibrium," *Inquiry* 25 (1982): 307–30; Joseph Raz, "Facing Diversity: The Case of Epistemic Abstinence," *Philosophy and Public Affairs* 19, no. 1 (Winter 1990): 3–46; Jean Hampton, "Should Political Philosophy Be Done Without Metaphysics?" *Ethics* 99 (July 1989): 791–814; and Jean Hampton, "The Moral Commitments of Liberalism," in *The Idea of Democracy,* ed. David Copp, Jean Hampton, and John Roemer (Cambridge, England: Cambridge University Press, 1993), 292–313. (I respond to Hampton in my "Rawls and the Socratic Ideal," *Analyse and Kritik* 13, no. 1 [July 1991]: 67–93.) Simon Blackburn, "Can Philosophy Exist?" in *Méta-Philosophie: Reconstructing Philosophy?* ed. Jocelyne Couture and Kai Nielsen (Calgary, Alberta: University of Calgary Press, 1993), 83–105.

10. Rawls remarks: "Reflective equilibrium is a point at infinity we can never reach, though we may get closer to it in the sense that through discussion our ideals, principles, and judgments seem more reasonable to us and we regard them as better founded than they were before." Rawls, "Reply to Habermas," 142. See the references in note 6. As Rawls stresses himself, here his views and Habermas's are very similar.

11. Suppose someone, skeptically inclined or just wishing to avoid rationalism over moral matters, asks (the question coming as a kind of challenge): "Why do we need, or even want, a more coherent conception of moral belief?" Several answers come trippingly to the tongue only one of which I shall consider here. We want (where "we" is meant to range over every normal adult or near adult) to make sense of our tangled lives and of the political order and social world in which we live. Just doing, and passively accepting doing, the thing done, hardly suffices for that. We want to make sense of our lives; we do not want, if we can help it, our lives to be a jumble without rhyme or reason. Getting a more coherent conception of our moral beliefs is surely not all of that making sense of our lives, but it is some of it—an important some of it—so, given those interests of ours, we

very much want, if it can be had and if we are reasonable, a more coherent conception of our moral beliefs. Suppose, *pace* the above, and as may be the case, that some of that "we" do not care about making sense of their lives, do not care, in that sense, about "being reasonable," but just want to do the thing done in order to get on in the world and to keep out of trouble so that they can live an easy life. They do not want to be puzzling their heads about how they should live, about how they should relate to other people beyond what is minimally necessary to have a quiet life. Moreover, they do not want to think about what sort of social order we should have beyond thinking about what is necessary for them to be tolerably confident of having an easy life. We can moralistically, though I think also correctly, say to that extent—to the extent, that is, that they are not morally reflective—they will lead lives that are more impoverished than they need be. Still, such people (if there really are any) neither want nor arguably need a more coherent conception of moral belief and we *may* beg some questions by saying they, if they go that way, will lead lives that are more impoverished than the lives of those who are reflective—but, not infrequently, also more anguished—and who try to make sense of their lives and the world they live in. Some implicit *persuasive* definitions of "impoverished lives" *may* be at play here, though without anything like a clear awareness that that is what is going on. Kant's man of good morals, complacently but prudently doing the thing done, must, on such a conception, by *persuasive* definition be living an impoverished life. Moralistically inclined intellectuals *may* be carrying around with them a kind of Dostoyevskian syndrome. But, then again, it may be no bad thing to be so moralistically inclined. Kai Nielsen, *Why Be Moral?* (Amherst, N.Y.: Prometheus Books, 1989).

12. Blackburn, "Can Philosophy Exist?" 89–105.

13. Note, in this context, the quotation from Rawls given in note 10.

14. See references to Copp and Hampton in note 9.

15. See the references to Brandt, Copp, Hampton, and Raz in note 9. See my responses in *After the Demise of the Tradition,* 195–204; in "Rawls and the Socratic Ideal," in part 3 of my *On Transforming Philosophy: A Metaphilosophical Inquiry* (Boulder, Colo.: Westview Press, 1995), as well as my arguments about this in this volume.

16. Rorty, *Objectivity, Relativism and Truth*; Hilary Putnam, *Realism With a Human Face* (Cambridge, Mass.: Harvard University Press, 1990); and Hilary Putnam, *Words and Life* (Cambridge, Mass.: Harvard University Press, 1994).

17. Richard Rorty, "Trotsky and the Wild Orchids," in *Challenges to the Enlightenment,* ed. Paul Kurtz and Timothy J. Madigan (Amherst, N.Y.: Prometheus Books, 1994), 96.

18. Rawls, "Reply to Habermas," 141.

Part One

Laying the Nonfoundations

Chapter One

Nonscientistic
Historicized Naturalism

I

I want to articulate and defend a naturalism without foundations. The naturalism I have in mind will be a nonscientistic, contextualist, and historicist naturalism without being subjectivist, relativistic, or nihilistic. As a consistent naturalism, it should be a materialism or what is nowadays called physicalism, but it is of a nonreductive variety. A fully coherent naturalism should also be a form of atheism or at least an agnosticism. However, though not very plausibly, an atheist could, as far as logical possibilities are concerned, be a dualist or even an idealist.[1] But there is, those anomalies notwithstanding, a close affinity between naturalism and atheism and the naturalism I shall defend will also be an atheism.[2]

Some explanations are in order. Naturalism denies that there are any supernatural or spiritual realities. There are, naturalists claim, no purely mental substances and there are no supernatural realities beyond nature or transcendent to the world or anything of the sort or at least we have no sound reasons for believing that there are such realities or perhaps even that there can be such realities. Physical realities, or perhaps as well realities dependent on physical realities, are the only kind of realities there are. This makes, as I have already remarked, naturalism also some kind of a physicalism or a materialism. These are but different terms for the same conception. But it is, as I have already remarked, a nonreductive naturalism for it does not claim that all talk of the mental can be translated into purely physicalist terms, such as neurophysiological terms or behaviorist terms or macroscopic descriptions of bodily movements. Very frequently mentalistic talk in terms of feelings, thoughts, beliefs, desires, and the like is not only useful, but indispensable if we are to make sense of human life and of the interactions between people.[3] But there we are talking about the same physical things under different descriptions, as, for example, when we give a mentalistic description rather than a purely physicalistic description. We are talking about the same thing, though we, in using mental terms, are talking for a different purpose. These descriptions are different and usefully so, but only one kind of reality is being referred to, namely, physical reality.

Besides being nonreductionistic, it is also nonscientistic. By *scientism* I mean the belief that what cannot be known by science—and particularly by the "hard" sciences—cannot be known. This view was famously held by Bertrand Russell and W. V. O. Quine, but not by other naturalists such as Donald Davidson, Richard Rorty, Hilary Putnam, or P. F. Strawson. My nonscientistic naturalism is, of course, not antiscientific and it full well recognizes the enormous importance of science in our lives and in any coherent modern view of the world. Moreover, I think, as I also believe any naturalist should, that when we come to make claims about what things, processes, states of affairs there are in the world, it is to science that we should turn for our best answers. And when we make claims about what are the best candidates for fundamental particles—the basic building blocks of our world—it is to physics that we should turn. Neither philosophy, theology, nor common sense can gainsay science here. Of course physics will change over time. What physics said two hundred years ago, or even fifty years ago, is not what, or not all of what, physicists are saying now. And very likely they will say different things in fifty years, to say nothing of what they will say in two hundred years if physics is still around then. But still, if, at any given time, where physics is a going concern, we want the best answers we can get to what these fundamental particles are, to what processes there are in the world, in short, knowledge as to what nature is like, then we should go to the hard sciences. This does not mean that science can save us or even give us an important social empowerment. Michel Foucault may very well be right and it may do just the opposite.[4] But that notwithstanding, if we want the best answers to what things there are, it is to science that we should turn. But saying this is not to take a scientistic worshipful attitude toward science. We will not attain certainty here or a "final theory," anymore than we will attain either any place else. Fallibilism is the name of the game. There is no more in science, even natural science, an overleaping history than anywhere else. But, nonetheless, our best answers to such questions come from science. Here it is science which yields our most reliable knowledge. But this does not at all mean that what science cannot tell us we cannot know. Science does not tell us that it is wrong to exploit people, that we should keep faith with our friends, that knowing the truth about our situation is often a good thing, that the choice between socialism and capitalism is a momentous choice, that women have a right to the control over their own bodies, and the like. Our moral knowledge is not scientific knowledge, and it often does not wait on science for its validation, though sometimes scientific knowledge is very relevant to ascertaining what we should believe and do. But before the rise of science people had moral knowledge and were sometimes able to justify some of their moral beliefs. Moral beliefs are not a subspecies of scientific beliefs, but they are none the worse for all of that. They are not antiscientific beliefs, but just non-scientific beliefs. Similar things should be said for many of our aesthetic beliefs. The claims literary critics make about literary works are also not—or at least not typically—scientific claims, but they very frequently are none the worse for that. Similar things can be said for all the arts.

Certain commonsense beliefs are also not scientific beliefs and are not overthrown by scientific beliefs nor are they in conflict with them. Thus when I say "The table I am typing on is solid," that remark could very well be true and would not be gainsaid by anything that we could learn from particle physics. And when I stroll along during a warm and hazy autumn's evening and remark, looking up at the moon, that it is pink tonight, that remark could very well be true, though it is certainly not a scientific remark. But it is also not gainsaid by anything that science tells us about the moon. *The belief that all our knowledge is scientific knowledge is just a dogma that no naturalist should accept.* My commonsense observation about the moon being pink is not a scientific observation, but it could very well yield reliable information. Some of the things I know commonsensically science could also tell me. But my knowledge that in Ontario it gets dark at night and the sun comes up in the morning, that people are born and that after a time they die, that sometimes people are miserable and sometimes they are happy are all things that I firmly know. And you firmly know them, too. Moreover, this is knowledge that could be had by someone without any scientific knowledge at all. Things like that were known by people just as firmly as we know them now who lived in prescientific cultures. Moreover, some bits of firm knowledge such as that pain is bad and pleasure is good, that promises should be kept and truth told are things that we know independently of what science tells us and there is very little reason to think that science could establish that they are true or that they really need a scientific backing. The belief that what science cannot tell us humankind cannot know is an utterly unwarranted dogma. Russell and Quine to the contrary notwithstanding, a sound naturalism should eschew scientism.

I also said that the naturalism I shall articulate is fallibilist, contextualistic, and historicist. By *fallibilistic* I mean that my naturalism takes it that all reasonably specific substantive claims are at least revisable in principle and that over matters of substance there can be no absolute certainty. In reliably fixing belief, as Charles Peirce and John Dewey argued, we must eschew the quest for certainty.[5] Reliable beliefs, for matters of substance, will always be less than certain. The very idea of a "final theory" is a Holmesless Watson.

In saying that my naturalism is *contextualistic* I mean that it takes our knowledge to be practice and context dependent. Reliable knowledge claims, a few truisms aside, cannot be made without reference to some determinate situation or context. When I spoke of the moon being pink it was of an utterance being made in and for a certain context. If I were doing physics, I would, while doing physics, not make such assertions. They would be at best pointless. Similarly it was only by failing to pay attention to context that made the physicists A. S. Eddington and J. H. Jeans believe that tables and chairs were not really solid or led Bertrand Russell to believe that we only really see our own brains. Similarly in certain circumstances I may be justified in saying that the use of dialysis machines needs to be carefully rationed and only those whose need is gravest and chances for cure reasonable should have access to them, while in other contexts such a claim would be outrageously wrong. To just say, *sans* context, that dialysis machines should be rationed makes very little sense.

My claim that naturalism should also be a form of historicism is a little more problematic. It may suggest to some a form of relativism or even nihilism that I do not intend.[6] To be a historicist is to believe that the warrant for interesting and at least potentially controversial knowledge claims is always historical-epoch dependent. There is no ahistorical, society-independent criteria or standards by which we can assess such beliefs. It is not (*pace* Nicholas Wolterstorff) a denial of the rationality of belief, but it is a claim that standards of rationality with much substance will be, at least in part, historical-epoch and cultural-context dependent.[7] In that way Hegel was right, no one can overleap history. But this does not imply relativism or subjectivism.[8] In the first place, an historicist can, and most do, recognize that knowledge is cumulative. Concerning many things, we know more than what people knew in the nineteenth century and they in turn knew more than people knew in the Middle Ages. We, standing where we are in history, can see how certain things were mistakenly believed in the nineteenth century. But we can have no such a comprehensive knowledge of our own mistakes, but it is plausible to believe that people in the twenty-first century, barring some great catastrophe, will come to know some things that we do not know and will have, in certain respects, a more adequate grasp of things than we have. With that they will sometimes be able, quite uncontroversially and with a firm objectivity, to specify some of our mistakes, just as we can specify some of the things that were erroneously believed in the nineteenth century. But people in the twenty-first century will be in the same pickle about their own knowledge that we are in about ours. And so on throughout history.

Historicism goes well with fallibilism. But it is not saying that everything is relative or subjective or that no view can be any better than any other view or more adequately grounded. It is surely not saying that anything goes. It is saying just the opposite, namely, that knowledge is often cumulative, but still is always incomplete and always, where issues of substance are concerned, less than certain. But this is not to say that all is relative or subjective or that all views are equally adequate or equally valid (whatever that means) or anything of the kind. Historicism is, however, the denial of Absolutism and of the claim to certain knowledge at least for matters of significant substance.

Fallibilism, contextualism, and historicism mesh well together and they seem to me to be views which go with a steady and informed acceptance of modernity, the view of the world stemming from the Enlightenment. My naturalism embraces all three. It should also be a corollary to say that it is antifoundationalist. But that, too, takes a little explaining. In speaking of foundationalism I have principally in mind classical foundationalism, a view held by the British empiricists and later by C. I. Lewis and A. J. Ayer, among others, and held, in a significantly different form, by Descartes. I shall state it in its empiricist form where it has been the most influential and the most persuasive. Foundationalists believe that there are basic beliefs, which are, as we go in the search for knowledge, terminating judgments. By that I mean that all knowledge and justified beliefs are suppose to be based on them or justified by reference to them, while they themselves in turn do not rest on any other beliefs, but their truth is supposedly immediately evident. They are primitive sense certainties the truth of which the individual having the experience is supposedly immediately aware of as I am aware that I have a headache or an itch. Our knowledge here is supposed to be immediate and absolutely certain and all our other substantive knowledge is supposed to be based on these sense certainties: these pure givens. Presently, many, perhaps most, philosophers think this view has very little to recommend it and it is indeed an expression of what has been called 'the myth of the given'. My fallibilistic, contextualistic naturalism is far more holistic and in that respect is more like the naturalism of Dewey, Quine, and Davidson. But a naturalist could consistently be a foundationalist as in our time Russell, Ayer, and Lewis were. But that is not the naturalism I propose to articulate and defend.[9]

II

Naturalism Without Foundations will also defend a naturalism that in a broad sense is a pragmatism and that is as well resolutely antimetaphysical. In saying that it is antifoundationalist and holistic as well as being contextualist and historicist, it might be thought I was already giving to understand that it is a pragmatism. But, while all pragmatists, on my reading, are those things, some people who firmly accept those things are not pragmatists. Hermeneutical philosophers such as Hans Gadamer and some of the Frankfurt School critical theorists, Theodor Adorno being a prominent example, are both historicists and contextualists.[10] So what do we have to add to these things to make a philosopher a pragmatist, at least in my books?

I think we must add three things. The first is the hardest to characterize succinctly without in one way or another being misleading. Let me put it this way. A pragmatist's holism takes the form of making a close link between language, thought, belief, and action.[11] Actions are not merely bodily movements, but are always in a broad sense intentional. "He moved his arm" as distinct from "His arm went up" or "He crossed his legs" as distinct from "His leg moved in a patellar reflex" are examples of actions and they, as all actions, are intentional. Actions are always thought-embedded (which, of course, does not mean that they are always, or even typically, thoughtful or that they are never habitual). For human beings, this means that they are also always language-embedded. They are a part of linguistic practices that are also social practices. Language on such a conception is not a formal structure (though it may have one), but crucially a connected cluster of doings and interactions of people engaged in these practices. Our rationality comes in some considerable measure from in practice mastering and integrating these elements and with that, acting intelligently in life. There is no coherent possibility of setting these elements aside and seeing if, or how, the world matches with them; there is no just seeing, or somehow just apprehending, the world, just as it is in itself, and then seeing whether it is adequately, or for that matter inadequately, represented by our thoughts and language. We cannot so stand free of our social practices. There is no way of making such comparisons or even of understanding what it would be like to have such a correspondence.

It is not that pragmatists are in spite of themselves really idealists, for language, thought, or action only exceptionally create such structures and never from whole cloth. Moreover, there are events and objects there in the world, some of which occurred or, as in the case of objects, were there in the world before there were any human beings or even sentient life. The pragmatist is not denying, or even questioning, that banality. And even actions (as particular doings) are events, particular things happening in the world. It would be absurdly silly not to believe that that world which is the field of such actions did not antedate any of these actions or indeed any human actions. But that not withstanding, any event, action, or object can have an indefinitely large number of alternative descriptions made sometimes for quite different purposes and there is no way of shedding our belief system or language (our particular way of looking at and acting in the world) and just seeing or apprehending which description gives us the one true description of the world.

Indeed, there is no such thing as the one true description of the world. Such talk makes no sense. Moreover, the pragmatist stresses that there is not only no possibility of, but no point in, such a metaphysical endeavor.

Our language, thoughts, and beliefs (all something that go together) are better viewed as instruments for coping with the various problems that beset us and as answering to, though also being partly constitutive of, our interests. Sometimes intelligently using our language will enable us to predict more adequately; other times it will enable us to interpret a text or someone's remarks more adequately; sometimes it will enable us to communicate and act more effectively in political life. Language is a form of linguistic behavior and thoughts and beliefs are always language dependent and they are all used to make interventions in the world. Indeed, they themselves are bits of the world and not something "standing apart from the world," as if we could even understand what that could mean. We use our language in this way as a tool for various kinds of coping. We do not use it, and have no intelligible idea how to use it, to give "the one true description of the world as it is in itself apart from human devising." In this way pragmatists have an instrumentalist conception of thought, belief, and language, and can rightly be called linguistic behaviorists.[12]

The second feature characteristic of pragmatism can, for present purposes, be more briefly characterized. Pragmatists, as C. S. Peirce put it, have a distinctive method for fixing belief and they are concerned to argue for and to clearly articulate that conception. This has been variously called the pragmatic method, the method of intelligence, the experimental method, or most frequently the scientific method. It has sometimes been mistakenly thought that this commits pragmatists to scientism, which is something that I, like Richard Rorty and Hilary Putnam, am anxious to keep out of naturalism. But this fixing belief by the scientific method is not a scientism for two reasons. Firstly, it is not to the results of science or to scientific theories that the pragmatists are appealing, but rather to the use of the scientific method in fixing belief. They are not, as we have seen, claiming that what science, meaning one or another of the established sciences, cannot know, humankind cannot know. Rather, they are claiming that a method, continuous with commonsense problem-oriented reasoning, namely, trial-and-error experimental reasoning, most exemplarily developed so far in the hard sciences, is the best way, the most reliable way, of going about fixing belief.

However, what Dewey repeatedly, almost obsessionally, argued must be done is to find ways of utilizing this very general method in politics, morals, and the other domains of life where we are concerned with coping with the world.[13] It is not that we should appeal to some science to find out how we ought to act—though sometimes this is useful—but more fundamentally we should learn how to use this method in resolving moral and political problems. It is not that we bring science to morals, but that we use the general methods found useful in science, but adopted and adjusted to a new context, namely, in this instance to morality or to politics. This is not at all like saying that if the hard sciences cannot solve it, it cannot be solved, for what these established sciences cannot know cannot be known or that what they do not at a given time know is not known at that time.[14] The naturalism I defend is not saying that at all.

Secondly, it is not scientism because the scientific method is construed very broadly by the pragmatists. It is a very general method. Some positivists might even say it is a platitudinous method, so broad that (*pace* Peirce) it cannot be used to fix any determinate belief. Indeed, if we get more precise, we discover that there is no such a thing as *the* scientific method but a cluster of different methods developed by various scientific disciplines for their various purposes and answering to their often quite different interests. The pragmatist's conception of scientific method, it is not infrequently thought, is so vague and general as to be useless. It is not only useless, but it is as well a form of methodolatry. Moreover, it conspicuously fails where pragmatists most want it to apply, namely, in the domain of the social. In the next chapter I shall argue that *au contraire,* its very generality is a virtue and that it can well be meshed with what John Rawls and others have called the method of wide reflective equilibrium in giving us a useful method for fixing belief, not only as a general guide in the sciences, but, as well, and for my purposes more interestingly, in the domain of the social, including the moral and political. But my concern at this point has only been to point out that this experimentalism—this use of the scientific method—is a characteristic feature of pragmatism and that there are good reasons for thinking that it is not scientistic.

Thirdly, and lastly, there is another feature in the pragmatism that I would defend and, as well, a feature that I pick out as distinctive of the pragmatism of John Dewey. It is the claim that philosophy should transform itself by setting aside the perennial problems of philosophers—problems (so-called problems) like the problem of the external world or of other minds—and concern itself instead with the live context-dependent, epoch-dependent problems of human beings: centrally political, social problems; religious problems; and live moral problems that beset human beings. Philosophy will be creatively renewed when it does this and treats with benign neglect the traditional problems, metaphysical, epistemological, foundationalist normative ethical, and meta-ethical. (I shall illustrate and defend this in the second and third parts of this book.) The standard objection to this is that these human problems cannot have anything but an ideological or rhetorical solution unless these more fundamental traditionally philosophical issues can first be resolved or in some other way adequately attended to. But with them there are issues which are thought to be deep and intractable and there is little consensus concerning either their proper resolution or how to go about gaining such a resolution. But nonetheless the belief persists with many nonpragmatist philosophers that rational progress with the problems of human beings awaits their resolution, for the various solutions to these practical problems presuppose different positions concerning some of these perennial problems of philosophy.

It is often thought by philosophers that whatever we say about specific moral issues that when we say anything that is the least bit controversial, that claim will presuppose some position at the foundational level, though often inarticulately and confusedly held. Consider, for example, what gets said about abortion or euthanasia and the sharp differences we have in practical life concerning them. But, the claim goes, we simply, or at least largely, mirror in these disputes the differences that exist at this deeper, more abstract and foundational level of general principles and conceptions and of the appropriate methods to be used in resolving these problems of life. In trying to do the very thing that Dewey wanted to do, we cannot set aside these traditional problems of philosophy.[15] This challenge to pragmatism cannot be lightly set aside. It has been put with vigor by Alasdair MacIntyre and Charles Taylor.[16] It is, I believe, something that it is very plausible to believe, particularly if one has had a certain sort of philosophical education. Still notwithstanding that, it is, I shall argue, fundamentally mistaken. (I shall say something about it in the last two sections of this chapter and, returning to it from another perspective, I shall give it careful consideration in the second part of this book.) But for now I simply want to note that this Deweyan problems-of-life conception of philosophy is a crucial feature of the pragmatism I wish to defend and comports well with its contextualism and historicism.

III

My naturalism is not only modestly pragmatic but it is also resolutely antimetaphysical. I want now to give some explanation and defense of that and to consider a certain fairly obvious problem it has for my naturalism and indeed for any naturalism.[17] In saying that it is antimetaphysical I am saying that it rejects the idea that there can be any substantive truth that is *a priori* establishable. There are, in fine, no synthetic *a priori* truths neither about the world—about what there is—nor about what ought to be or about what it would be a good thing to be the case. No such truths have been established, let alone a grounding system of such truths, and it has not been shown that we must presuppose some such truths to make sense of the world or of our lives or to ground our moralities or scientific or commonsense knowledge claims. The whole category of the synthetic *a priori* is of doubtful coherence and we have no understanding of how to establish such truths or how just to be directly aware that there are any such self-evident timeless truths about what there is or about what the good life for human beings consists in. Such a metaphysics has come to seem increasingly problematic. It has few takers today. Indeed, some will believe that criticizing it is like flogging a dead horse.

Alternatively, we might have a scientistic metaphysics, what Putnam mockingly calls "metaphysics within the limits of science alone." This is a metaphysics which regards itself as part of science, and is usually taken to be continuous with the most abstract side of physics and mathematics.[18] It will eschew the *a priori* and provide us with very general claims concerning what is taken to be "the system of the world." This is the kind of metaphysics espoused by W. V. O. Quine, David Armstrong, and J. J. C. Smart. It is a form of naturalism, though a scientific one. If it would set aside its imperialistic conception of reality such that moral and political realities were not banished by implicit persuasive definition, I would not have any *principled* objections to such metaphysics, though it seems to me that when it comes to making empirical claims (the only kind of claims it can, on its own conception of things, make) it yields only substantive platitudes. And I can accordingly see little point in it beyond articulating some counter to some wild metaphysical claim such as an Absolute Idealist or Thomist might make.[19] But what it does do, engaging in semantic ascent, is sometimes to make insightful analyses of terms such as *event, object, fact, reference, truth,* and the like and to show how they are perspicuously arranged in our discourses and thus in our life. Here they are in effect, though not in programmatic intent, doing what linguistic philosophers of the analytical tradition have been doing in giving us an elucidation of our fundamental concepts, including a showing of how they hang together. I think this is *sometimes* a valuable activity and I have no reservations about their doing it. But I see no reason to regard it as metaphysics and I do not see how it gives us any *first-order* knowledge of the world, though it does sometimes give us—going *second-order*—a perspicuous representation of the functions of our language. But, however, this activity is to be characterized, it is not metaphysics in the traditional and straightforward sense with its claims to synthetic *a priori* knowledge, yielding the fundamental self-evident truths of a First Philosophy, a philosophy which will be the grounding for everything else that we can know. It is such claims that I am rejecting when I say my account is antimetaphysical.

IV

However, as I remarked, this poses a problem for my naturalism. It might be claimed that my naturalism is metaphysical in just the sense I characterized, for my naturalism yields statements that are neither, on the one hand, empirical statements (synthetic *a posteriori* statements), such as "Puppies are hard to train," nor, on the other, analytic truths such as "Puppies are young dogs." Note below the set of sentences giving a characterization of naturalism and ask yourself concerning these sentences how their truth would be ascertained. Do we know what it would be like to establish them empirically? To say that we do seems at best implausible. Still, they do not seem to be true by definition or plausibly to be taken as true by stipulation. But how then would we or could we vouch for their truth? Do they not have a rather anomalous status? Indeed, is not naturalism unwittingly metaphysical in the very traditional sense to which I have objected? My very characterization of naturalism brings this to the fore.

To see at least the plausibility of this, consider the following seven sentences which in part characterize my naturalism and would be assented to by many naturalists, though perhaps not in quite that form.

1. There is nothing beyond nature.

2. All reality is physical reality or at least are realities which are dependent on physical realities.

3. There is no supernatural reality, spiritual beings, or any purely mental realities.

4. Events are particular occurrences in the world.

5. All objects are physical objects.

6. Human actions are particular doings (events) which, in being actions, are in at least some broad sense intentional, but where the reason for doing them, under a different description, is also the cause of their occurring.

7. There are only particulars with their relational properties (properties which have no independent existence apart from particulars).

These statements are all core claims of my naturalism. But, as I remarked above, they do not appear to be analytic truths and I certainly do not want them to be and they are not intended by me to be true by stipulation. We all can make our own stipulations. My intentions aside, they do not appear to be analytic or stipulative truths. Moreover, if these naturalistic theses were such, then they would then be utterly trivial. They also surely do not have the look of empirical hypotheses or any plainly identifiable kind of empirical statement. We have no idea how to confirm them or disconfirm or perhaps even to infirm them. We do not know, or so it at least seems, what to look for to establish either their truth or their falsity. Compare "There are only brown trout in this pond" with "There is nothing beyond nature." We know how to go about establishing the truth of the statement about trout, but not the statement about there being nothing beyond nature. What experiment would we have to set up to establish that there is nothing beyond nature or that there are no supernatural realities? Or how would we set about verifying or disverifying (or even infirming) the claim that all reality is physical reality? If someone responds that there plainly are mental realities—thoughts, feelings, sensations, and the like—the naturalist could respond that thoughts are brain processes or dispositions to behave in certain ways. We, he could add, are not disputing that there are thoughts, but we are disputing traditional accounts (say, dualist accounts) of how they are to be classified. Similar things will be said for feelings and sensations. And the truth of the matter concerning these issues is not going to be established by experiment or by observation. But then how are we going to establish who is right or is the more likely to be right concerning such things? Are sensations brain processes or aren't they and how would we find out, even fallibilistically? And so we can go down the list. None of them (to state it conservatively) appear to be analytic truths; they all appear at least to be substantive claims about what is the case. But the established and clear way of establishing such at least apparently substantive claims about the world to be either true or false, namely, by appeal to empirical evidence (perhaps a pleonasm), seems to be of no avail here.[20] The very logical status of these claims seems at least to be anomalous. Yet they are central claims of naturalism. A critic could claim that they are, the naturalist's beliefs about them to the contrary notwithstanding, indeed metaphysical claims: unwitting claims to synthetic *a priori* truth. We have no idea how to even fallibilistically establish or disestablish their truth. This being so, are they not just dogmas of naturalism?

I shall argue that they are not. The dogma that is causing the trouble here is the dogma exposed by Quine that every intelligible declarative sentence must be either analytic or empirical.[21] It is the mistake of believing that we have two bins in which to place sentences: an analytic bin and an empirical bin and whatever does not fit in one or the other of these bins is to be discarded as something of very dubious intelligibility. I shall call this the *dualism* of the *a priori* and the empirical, and I shall argue that this is an utterly unrealistic picture of how language works. When this is clearly seen and the implications of this are thought through, those core statements of naturalism should not be seen as unwitting pieces of metaphysics—as synthetic *a priori* principles which are there to be simply accepted or rejected—or should be regarded as some mysterious principles just "seen" to be true—or, for that matter, false— by some flash of *a priori* insight. There is nothing like this to be had anywhere at least in any substantive domain. Moreover, I am not claiming or presupposing anything like this for the core statements of naturalism that I stated or indeed for any part of my naturalism. Rather, when we see how these statements are embedded in a complicated interconnected cluster of practices, containing a host of other statements interlocked with these core statements, and when we get this cluster of practice-embedded statements into the most coherent pattern we can now achieve, and in doing so come to see how all of them hang together in the most reasonable manner we can articulate for now, and situated as we are, we will, I shall argue, assent to these core statements of naturalism. We will see how central and strategic they are and how, given the other things we know or reasonably believe, they are to be assented to. Indeed, I am tempted to say that they are rationally inescapable. But that, though it still seems to me to be appropriate, may be too strong, perhaps more of a rhetorical flourish than anything else. We should not take any of these core statements as *foundational* principles of our naturalism. No principles have that status for us. Moreover, we do not have a *system* of beliefs but a rather large, but still indefinite, cluster of beliefs that we seek to arrange in a coherent pattern. My naturalism is, through and through, anti-foundationalist.

To see how the dichotomy either analytic or empirical or the related dichotomy either *a priori* or *a posteriori* is indeed an unjustified dualism, I want—roughly following the line of argument of a set of brilliantly reasoned papers by Hilary Putnam, and oversimplifying, but I hope not by way of distortion—to show how, if we look at the things we do with our language with a realistic eye, we will come to see how many very different types of utterance are made for very different purposes: purposes that answer to a wide range of different human interests.[22] They are a heterogeneous lot that do not fit into the supposedly neat dualism of either *a priori* or empirical. Indeed, they are in a kind of shifting continuum. At the one extreme we have statements that are our candidates for—indeed, are paradigms of—purely *a priori* statements such as "Bachelors are unmarried males," "Vixens are foxes," "Two plus two equal four," and "No statement is both true and false." The latter, put more cautiously, as Putnam puts it, reads: "Not every statement is both true and false" and this, of course, is a minimal statement of the law of noncontradiction. It may very well be, as Putnam once thought, "an example of an absolutely, unconditionally, truly, actually *a priori* truth."[23] However, near the purely (allegedly purely) *a priori* end, other propositions are included, such as geometrical ones, that we are also loath to abandon. Indeed, it may be the case that they would never be abandoned. Still, they are not so plainly and utterly unrevisable as the law of noncontradiction at least appears to be. Indeed, some of them we no longer think are unrevisable. But during certain periods of history they seemed to be unrevisable. In this way they are what Putnam calls contextual *a priori* statements or principles. But he agrees with Quine that many principles of logic and mathematics *seem* at least to be utterly unrevisable. But this is not true, or as true, of others. We have a *contin-*

uum here with gradations. Putnam has argued that for a select few they seem at least to stand fast against any apparently recalcitrant experience or theory development. Quine sometimes, and some Quineans more unreservedly, took it to be the case that not even these statements are unrevisable in principle.[24] We have no *utterly certain* grounds for thinking that they must hold come what may. They are just some of the most centrally located beliefs in our web of the belief and they would not readily be abandoned.

Sometimes Quine believes, and many Quineans believe, that not even the beliefs expressed in the paradigm *a priori* statements I listed above are unrevisable in principle. And this being so, they are not really *a priori*. The thought is that the very notion of being "a real *a priori* statement" is a mistaken conception, for all that is involved with such beliefs is that they are the most deeply embedded beliefs in our web of belief and as such they would be the last to be abandoned in the face of recalcitrant experience or some other challenge to our web of belief. We should, if we are reasoning carefully, not try to take them to be beliefs that are absolutely, unconditionally unrevisable. We should not try to rule out the *possibility* that they could stand in need of revision, but simply observe in good fallibilist fashion that there is no actual or reasonably foreseeable reason to think they would ever need to be revised or that there could be any real question of their needing to be revised. Indeed, we might go on to say that we have no very clear idea of what it would be like to revise them. No provision seems to have been made for that in our language-games. But we should not go on to make the unnecessary claim that it is *a priori* certain that no question of their revisability could ever arise. No such claim should be made; there is no such need to give such hostages to fortune, to ban, or more accurately, try to ban, the very possibility of their revision.

Putnam thinks this is generally a good strategy to take, with respect to the *a priori* and *a posteriori*, or the analytic and empirical, so that with Einstein and Reichenbach it became rational to take our geometrical principles to be empirical principles of a very theoretical abstract sort. While remaining empirical, still, these principles were very unlike ordinary empirical generalizations, e.g., "Brown trout are more wary than rainbow trout." They are more like, though still different from, laws of nature. But Putnam thinks it is very counterintuitive to regard the principle of noncontradiction as being even in principle rejectable or even revisable. It is, he once thought, fully and absolutely *a priori*.[25]

For our purposes, the dispute between Quine and Putnam need not be resolved, for Putnam agrees that Quine's pragmatist and fallibilist reading of the history of science, logic, and mathematics is the right way to go, given the development of non-Euclidean geometries, the actual working them out and applying of them, and given, as well, the development of relativity theory and quantum theory in physics. To take these geometrical principles as unconditionally *a priori* is a mistake. We have again and again revised principles all through these domains, which were once thought to be immune from the very possibility of revision. During Newton's and Hume's time, it was rational to believe that of the principles of Euclidean geometry. These principles were mistakenly *thought* by them to be unconditionally (absolutely) *a priori*, while *actually* for them—that is, in the way in which they actually employed them—they were contextually *a priori*. For Einstein and Reichenbach, by contrast, they are abstract empirical principles. Even these things—things we traditionally have thought to be part of a Platonic heaven—shift with history. Even they do not provide us with unwobbling pivots. So contextually and historically viewing things fits well with fallibilism. With fallibilism, Putnam points out, we are never *totally* sure that any belief of ours is true even if we believe it to be an *a priori* belief. But that still seems to cut in Quine's favor, for if we can never be absolutely sure that a principle we think is unconditionally *a priori* actually is, we cannot go on to claim that we can be certain that we could never have a reason for believing it to be revisable as distinct from saying that as things stand we have no idea at all about what it would be like to revise it.

However, to repeat, for our purposes that issue between Quine and Putnam need not be resolved. They both agree that, between "Bachelors are unmarried males," on one end of the continuum, on the one hand, and "The bread is on the table" at the other end of the continuum, on the other, there is a heterogeneous mélange of sentences (and of the beliefs that go with them). Some of these sentences are used in certain contexts to make statements which are contextually *a priori* statements (that is, they are relatively immune from revision), and in other contexts these very same sentences are used to make theoretical empirical statements. The principles of Euclidean geometry are good examples. As we have already observed, during Hume's and Newton's time, in relation to what they knew or reasonably could have known, the principles of Euclidean geometry were for all practical purposes to be viewed as unconditionally *a priori*. With the actual working out and the application of non-Euclidean geometries and the development of relativity theory, the principles of Euclidean geometry came to be viewed by Einstein and Reichenbach as very abstract and general empirical principles, though certainly not as straightforward empirical generalizations such as "All swans are white," which was (and quite appropriately so) simply disconfirmed by observing a black swan in Australia. The principles of Euclidean geometry were only seen to be *non-a priori,* or perhaps only came to so function, with the development of alternative geometrical theories and with the showing that they could be applied to the world. Disconfirming experience was not irrelevant, but it was entirely subservient to the development of such an alternative theory. So, alternatively, with them we can say, as Putnam does, that they are contextually *a priori*. Relative to certain background beliefs, to a certain development of science at a certain historical period, they were plausibly regarded as *a priori* and unrevisable, but with the development of science they ceased to be taken to be *a priori* statements, analyticities, true of all possible worlds (all consistently thinkable worlds).

What is true for the principles of Euclidean geometry is true for at least much of mathematics and at least for large areas of logic as well. With the development of quantum mechanics and intuitionist logic, even the law of the excluded middle lost its former seemingly unconditional *a priori* status. Quantum mechanics may very well require a distinct logic of its own that sets aside certain classical principles of logic in the sense that they no longer have their formerly supposed unconditional *a priori* status. Logic, even in parts of the propositional calculus, is now seen to be revisable and hence has lost its *a priori* status. Putnam, as we have seen, at one time thought that that is not so for a streamlined statement of the law of noncontradiction, namely, the statement that no statement is both true and false.[26] This, he thought, has an unconditional *a priori* status. But, given the fact that the law of the excluded middle does not have that status, though until very recently it was thought by logicians to have that status, how can we now be absolutely certain that with the development of science or logic that a similar thing will not happen to the law of noncontradiction? That that seems to us now to be absurd—indeed, as something we can make no sense of—does not settle the matter. It seems that the lesson of fallibilism and of pragmatism is that we should not make such strong claims about propositions being unconditionally *a priori*. Moreover, it is an unnecessary and gratuitous claim as well. We have every good reason for going on relying on the principle of noncontradiction and no reason at all for thinking it is the least bit problematic, perhaps requiring revision. Indeed, we do often take certain propositions to be *a priori*; in doing so, we take them, as relative to the practices that they go with, as analyticities, as the principles of Euclidean geometry were for Newton and Hume. As the principles of analytic geometry were for them, so some of these contextual *a priori* propositions for us seem at least to be presupposed in all our thinking and reasoning. Moreover, we see the point in so reasoning and acting in accordance with our reasoning. Why isn't this justificatory rationalization enough? What do we gain by saying that any such proposition is an absolutely unconditional *a priori*? Isn't this arm waving?

However, even if we do go on saying this, and insist that at one end of the continuum there are some absolutely unrevisable principles, my main point about the *a priori*/empirical distinction remains intact. We *at best* have a rather small class of absolutely unrevisable statements all of which are analyticities, i.e., principles whose denials are self-contradictions. But none of them has a synthetic status. "Brothers are male siblings" does not tell us anything about the world beyond something about the uses of our concepts. Where we get something that we might think is synthetic *a priori* and thus some kind of metaphysical principle, we get a contextual *a priori* proposition. It is from not keeping firmly in mind the sometimes historical shift in the use of sentences expressing such propositions that we mistakenly think that we have some synthetic *a priori* propositions. But we have no reason at all to think that we have some unconditional *a priori* propositions, some absolutely unrevisable propositions, which are also synthetic, which also tell us what the world is like or what we ought to do or be. Propositions relative to some background practice, which are also theoretical propositions or sometimes practical principles deeply embedded in that practice, still can function very like *a priori* propositions, e.g., "Parallel lines will not meet in space" or "Thoughts to be thoughts must be conscious." But against another background of belief and practice, the same sentences are used to express empirically false propositions or at least propositions which are good candidates for empirical falsehoods.

There are as well, as Putnam stresses, a host of other sorts of sentences that are neither *a priori* nor empirical. "Orthodox Jews fast on the Day of Atonement" is neither true by definition nor is it falsified by what some Orthodox Jews upon occasion might fail to do. Or take the following cluster of absurd, but, for all of that, meaningful and indeed true statements: "Live human beings have heads," "Watches do not just disappear without cause," "A human being cannot change into a grasshopper," "Worms cannot speak." They are all plainly true, though people do not go around uttering such absurdly true utterances. But when we hear them, we confidently take them to be true. We think someone would have to be crazy to deny them. We might, as well, also think they would have to be a bit odd to go around asserting them, unless we knew that they were just doing philosophy. But we also realize that they are not true by definition. "Worms cannot speak" is not like "Bachelors cannot be married" or "Triangles cannot be four-sided" true by definition.

The above absurdities have the superficial look of empirical propositions. But, as Wittgenstein argued in *On Certainty,* they are not. If I held a worm in my hand and from the vicinity of the worm, seemingly coming right from it, perfect BBC English flowed, where it looked like it was coming right out of its skin and where as well I "put questions to the worm" and the worm "replied," I still would not think that the worm was actually speaking. I would conclude instead that some trick had been played on me or that I was dreaming or that I had gone mad or something of the sort, but I would not conclude that the worm was talking. Even if I did, I would be mistaken. And nothing would change if instead of a worm, a frog or mouse were in my hand and it "behaved" like that. It is not at all like the proposition that chimpanzees cannot speak which is an empirical proposition that we—or at least some us— have good theoretical reasons for thinking to be true. But if some Nim Chimpsky were placed before us and, in suitably controlled circumstances, spoke, then, though thoroughly baffled, we would reluctantly conclude that after all we were mistaken in thinking that chimps cannot speak and we would have to go back to the drawing board and rework our theories. But not so with "The worm talked" or "The frog talked." But the denial of these bizarre statements is also not self-contradictory and they are not unintelligible like "Procrastination drinks melancholy" or at least like "Gavgfigrtik grinkley." We *in some way* understand them well enough, but do not even entertain the *possibility* of their being true. Indeed, more strongly, gesturing at the slipperiness in saying we understand them, we are baffled by what this could possibly come to.

Compare "Live human beings have heads" with "Live human beings have livers." Though I think, perhaps in ignorance on my part, that we have good empirical-theoretical reasons for believing that all live human beings have livers, still it is an empirical proposition that can rather straightforwardly be disconfirmed, though we, or at least I, never expect it to be disconfirmed. Similarly we surely can describe a situation in which something without a head looked, and in certain ways acted, very much like a live human being. But—and here comes the difference—if something like this actually came to pass, we would not know what to say. Such things cannot happen, we rightly say. But the "cannot" here is not a logical or clearly a conceptual "cannot" like the "cannot" in "Bachelors cannot be married"; but it is also not clearly a physical (empirical) "cannot" as in "A person cannot live without a liver." If we saw, when there were many others making the same observations, and sometimes under controlled conditions, beings walking around dressed like we are with English, French, or German coming from the hole in the neck where we expect a head to rest, we would not know what to say. We would not know whether to say they were human beings or not; nothing in our language or system of thought would settle that for us. Similar things should be said for "Watches do not just disappear without cause" or "A human being cannot change into a grasshopper."[27]

There is a continuum between what is plainly, or not so *plainly*, empirical, but still possibly so and what seems at least to be neither empirical nor *a priori* at all. Consider the following three sentences: (1) "People cannot walk over a bed of burning coals barefooted," (2) "People cannot levitate," and (3) "A crow cannot do calculus." All three sentences are intelligible. They are not like "Nothing noughts nonbeing." We, or at least some of us, are inclined to think that statement one is true. But we have also heard it said that in India some people can do it. We are inclined to think that that must be a trick or a fabrication. (Most of us have been fooled by adroit magicians.) But, if under suitable conditions, we actually saw it happening, we would say that we were mistaken in thinking it impossible. Statement one clearly is an empirical proposition. We are even more skeptical about statement two. Again we understand the sentence all right, but we also believe we have very good reasons indeed for believing that that cannot happen. We know that people cannot levitate. This is firmer with us than statement one, though the difference here is a matter of degree. But, as before, if many of us, in suitably controlled situations, saw "the impossible" happening, again we would take it that we had been mistaken in thinking people cannot levitate. We would firmly assert that even without having an account of *how* it could happen. We would say and believe that sometimes some people can levitate. But with statement three we are in a different ball game. We just do not understand what it would be for a crow to do, or try and fail, or never try at all, to do calculus. With statement three we do not have an empirical utterance, but it is not self-contradictory, or at least not obviously and unproblematically so, or in some other way (if there is any other way) *a priori* false either, and it is not, or at least not plainly so, a meaningless utterance like "Nights knightly telephone bluely." Again what we need to see is that we have a heterogeneous bunch of sentences, many of indeterminate status, which, when employed in many contexts, cannot be plausibly said to be either *a priori* or empirical. It is a great mistake to try to force our language or our thought into such a straitjacket: into such a dualism of the *a priori* and the empirical.

It might be countered that these are absurd utterances that no one other than a philosopher would utter and they should therefore be ignored. I think that is a perfectly irrelevant remark, for we, even if we are not philosophers, understand them well enough and in understanding them also recognize that they do not naturally, or in some instances clearly at all, go in either the *a priori* or the empirical bin. Moreover, as we have seen, even with several straightforward sentences from science and from mathematics and logic, they did not go into either bin. So it certainly looks as if the claim I made about the heterogeneous continuum stands.

In concluding my remarks on this topic, I shall throw in some, at least apparently, straightforwardly intelligible sentences which cannot be placed, without some arbitrary pushing, into either bin: "The meter stick in Paris is a meter long," "Peano arithmetic is consistent," "An electron is a particle," "An electron is a wave," "In particle physics they have found a final theory," "The Higgs particle is the ultimate particle," "The three-dimensional world is finite and unbounded," and "Every number has a successor." With the possible exception of the last sentence, which may somehow, in some unspecified way, be *a priori,* none of the sentences mentioned above—important and intelligible as they are, or at least seem to be—nonarbitrarily go in either the *a priori* or the empirical bin. (Some of them, the first one, for example, *may* turn out to be disguised bits of nonsense, but clearly most of them are not.)

Let me now, perhaps at long last, apply the lessons learned above about the untenable dualism of the *a priori* and the empirical to my fundamental naturalist statements, the seven statements I listed in the previous section. They were felt to be problematical, for they seemed to be neither empirical hypotheses, straightforwardly confirmable or infirmable, that is, plainly testable empirical statements, nor *a priori* statements. It is plain enough, for example, that the seven propositions listed are not analytic, for their negations are not self-contradictory. Moreover, they are not statements which are unrevisable. They are not statements such that no matter what, a rational being must accept them.[28] This led to the worry that the naturalist in asserting them, as at least seemingly he must, was abandoning his commitment to being empirical: was, that is, abandoning his empiricism. (For me, as for Quine, there is no conflict between a proper naturalism and a proper empiricism, though what we will take to be "a proper" of either will in certain respects differ.) So it seemed, at least, that he is in a pickle no matter what he does. Either he abandons the very statement of his naturalism (the seven statements listed a few pages back or something very like them) or he ends up making, or at least presupposing, the very synthetic *a priori* statements of an *a priori* metaphysics that his naturalism commits him to eschewing. Either way he is in the mud.

It should be clear from my undermining of the *dualism* of the analytic and the empirical that the naturalist is not so stuck.[29] Not *all* intelligible statements, including plainly nonmetaphysical statements, can be put in either bin. So why cannot this be true of my seven statements of naturalism and statements like them? Consider: "There is nothing beyond nature," "All reality is physical reality or at least are realities which are dependent on physical realities," "There is no supernatural reality," and "All objects are physical objects." Such conceptions are deeply embedded in modern secular thought: a thought growing out of the Enlightenment. They are like some deeply embedded scientific statements which cannot be overthrown by observation alone, but require as well for their overthrowing an alternative and better account, though still an account to which empirical observation is not irrelevant. But what is crucial to see for these deeply embedded scientific statements, and as well for the naturalistic statements that I have given, is that they can only be overthrown after, and with reference to, an alternative theory or an account which is more adequate. What is required for their overthrow, both for deeply embedded theoretical propositions in a developed science and for these seven propositions central to naturalism, is both the articulation of a more adequate theory or account *and* the relevant observations. Neither alone suffices. Neither in the scientific case nor in the case for naturalism is experience or observation irrelevant; in neither case can we establish anything *by pure reason alone.* Rationalism with its metaphysical outlook is out.

Here, as elsewhere, my moderate holism comes into play. I shall argue— and this surely has to be argued and not just asserted—that, considering everything we know or plausibly believe, or can be reasonably expected to know or plausibly believe, in the attempt to make sense of our lives, morally, politically, and as persons trying to live nonevasively, we, with that end in view, in considering how things hang together, should go naturalistic. In trying to gain a little better sense of how things hang together, we seek (among other things), perspicuously to conceptualize things so as to avoid incoherence and problematical conceptions. But, in the very doing of this, we will come to recognize that the acceptance of naturalistic beliefs is our best bet, our best hunch, about how we should view the way things hang together. These claims are, and should be, made in an utterly fallibilistic spirit with the recognition that such an account may be mistaken and some nonnaturalistic, nonmaterialistic account may be more adequate.

We need to also nonevasively face the possibility that no such account— neither naturalist nor nonnaturalist—*at such a level of generality* can yield a reasonable account of how things hang together. Perhaps no plausible articulation of worldviews of any sort can be given? Perhaps all we have are incommensurable *Weltanschauungen*? Perhaps particular, and in part variable, cultural socialization calls the tune here? Perhaps we just have various *Weltanschauungen* without grounds for even fallibilistically choosing between them? If we would be reasonable and reflective we cannot reasonably just dismiss that possibility. The thought that this may be so is part of what gives fuel to postmodernism.

I shall be concerned to resist the claims of incommensurability and will argue that on the contrary we can reasonably and perhaps even persuasively argue the case for naturalism against supernaturalistic and other nonnaturalistic alternatives. But my immediate point was a more modest one. I sought, by undermining the dualism of the analytic and empirical, in a *roughly* Quinean way, and by showing how some scientific statements functioned in that respect, to free the fundamental naturalistic statements I articulated from the charge that they were synthetic *a priori* principles as vulnerable as the supernaturalistic avowedly metaphysical principles and the other transcendental principles that naturalism criticizes and is concerned to reject. Metaphysicians of The Tradition, including Thomists and the like, want, and indeed need, synthetic *a priori* propositions. Naturalists, by contrast, neither want them nor need them. I have, against what is often believed, shown how they need not be understood to be unwittingly assuming them either and thus, in spite of themselves, are really metaphysicians in disguise.

V

I want now to consider, as a kind of coda to this first chapter, two very different kinds of objection that can be made to naturalism. The first is Alasdair

MacIntyre's objection, running against what I have claimed above. Contrary to what I have maintained, MacIntyre claims that naturalism has metaphysical presuppositions that it does not justify, or sometimes even recognize, presuppositions which perhaps cannot be justified and which it just dogmatically sets in opposition to a theistic view of the world. The second, and very different kind of objection, is a Wittgensteinian one aiming at a minimalist strategy in philosophy. It is the objection that one need not, and indeed should not, defend naturalism as a *positive* philosophical position, but rather content oneself with pointing to the endemic confusions that hove into view when philosophers try to go beyond naturalism: to assert, for example, that there is something beyond nature or that there is something supernatural. We do not have to, and indeed should not, assent to such philosophical theses, but we do not have to assent to their denials either, i.e., some positive statement of naturalism. We should avoid all such philosophical entanglement. Why put oneself unnecessarily at risk?

Let us turn to MacIntyre's argument first. "Naturalism," he remarks, "has to be rejected as in error not only about theology . . . but also about natural science."[30] Naturalism, he takes it, is an expression of the "presently dominant view of the natural sciences," a view which is in reality, MacIntyre has it, a scientistic dogma, imposed by naturalistic philosophers "upon the findings of the sciences, rather than being part of what natural scientists discover by observation and experiment."[31] He might have added, to strengthen his case, that it is also not a view that would simply emerge from a neutral elucidation of the language of science or the sciences. What this dominant view of the natural sciences simply presupposes is a naturalistic *Weltanschauung* with, in its developed forms, an unfalsifiable physicalism: a materialism that is pure dogma.[32]

The first dogma, on MacIntyre's understanding of this naturalistic worldview, is the characterization of the natural sciences in terms of necessary and invariant laws. "The physical sciences so construed purport to tell us not how nature generally and characteristically is, but how, necessarily and universally, it must be."[33] We have, MacIntyre believes, both dogma and myth here. The scientific aim, on such a conception, is to progressively move toward a *final* theory, articulated in a systematic account of a unified science. "Natural science, thus envisaged, is understood as progress towards a complete account not only of the laws governing nature, but also of the phenomena of nature."[34] On such a conception of science every "event and state of affairs must be characterizable as the outcome of some antecedent physical event or state of affairs, whether it is itself characterized in physical terms, or in some other terms, biological or psychological or social."[35] The claim is that "given the way things are physically, there is one and only one way they can be nonphysically."[36] This has been called by one naturalist "the Principle of the determination of all truth by physical truth."[37]

MacIntyre's point is that this naturalism, this, as he has it, presently dominant view of science, has not been established either by science itself or by science and logic working in tandem. Moreover, it has not been established by the scientific method as a set of falsifiable truths and it has not been shown that rationality requires such naturalistic beliefs. It has not been shown that if we proceed dialectically in a careful and judicious manner we will end up with such a naturalistic view. Rather, we have what in effect is an *a priori* metaphysical view dogmatically imposed on the findings of science. It is, in reality, but one perspective among others. It is not just a record of what science really and truly is or even would be if it were done perfectly. There are alternative metaphysical perspectives and what we need, but do not get from naturalists, is some argument for the adoption of their distinctive perspective, some argument for the acceptance of their metaphysical principles. We get nothing like that, let alone sound arguments for their position.

What should be apparent from the very articulation of my fallibilistic, pragmatic, nonscientistic, contextualist, historicized naturalism is that I am neither asserting nor presupposing any of these things that MacIntyre says are constitutive of naturalism. I do not think, and neither do such fellow naturalists as Putnam, Davidson, Rorty, Flew, and Strawson think, that everything has to be explained in terms of physics; I do not think that there is, or even can be, one true description of the world; I do not think that there is such a thing as a final theory and with that I do not think natural science, or anything else, is to be understood (to quote MacIntyre on this again) "as in progress towards a complete account not only of the laws governing nature, but also of the phenomena of nature."[38] Moreover, I do not even think that chemistry or physics should be, or even can be, characterized in terms of necessary and invariant laws; I do not think, if we conclude that things are in a certain way physically, that then we can conclude that that determines just how they are nonphysically (e.g., psychologically or socially as understood by a nonreductive physicalist) and I do not think that what science cannot tell us we cannot know. This is not just an eccentric form of naturalism, on my part, but is, in essentials, also the type of the naturalism defended by Putnam, Davidson, Rorty, and Strawson. "Scientistic naturalism" is not pleonastic. The naturalism MacIntyre describes is indeed a scientistic metaphysics and should be rejected along with all other metaphysical views, including Thomistic-Aristotelian ones.[39]

My naturalism, by contrast, is resolutely antimetaphysical and is without the kind of metaphysical presuppositions taken by MacIntyre to be constitutive of naturalism or, for that matter, any other *metaphysical* presuppositions. MacIntyre takes one species of naturalism, the *scientistic* naturalism stated most forcefully by Quine, to be naturalism *sans phrase*, as if Putnam, Rorty, or Strawson had never written.

VI

I turn now to the quite different Wittgensteinian objection, an objection I am much more ambivalent about, feeling the force of its anti-Philosophy *philosophy* claims myself. Why, a Wittgensteinian therapeutic analyst might ask, defend naturalism as a *philosophical position* or as any kind of articulated worldview?[40] When we start defending and articulating worldviews, we invariably get into trouble. Why talk of naturalism as a *positive philosophical view*? Why defend any philosophical position here? Why take any positive philosophical stance at all? Why not take your main point, the Wittgensteinian could be construed as saying to me, to be (what it seems to come to in any event) the purely *negative* one of giving to understand that we do not *have to go* (try to go) beyond nature, that we do not *have to* assume that reality is anything other than physical (in some broad sense), that we do not *have to* assume that there is anything other than particulars or that events are anything other than particular occurrences in the world? Why not stick with this more guarded way of putting things, giving fewer hostages to fortune? When some metaphysician comes along and asserts that there are supernatural realities, a teleology in or of nature, or that there are Platonic universals, the thing is to show him that we do not have to say any of these strange things to make sense of our world, that neither logic or otherwise careful reasoning nor the facts or some combination thereof give us good reasons for having such beliefs, let alone compel us to assert them (try to assert them). We can with greater simplicity and more plausibility simply stick with a more modest, purely *negative* naturalism. Indeed, you can, if you wish, to avoid labels altogether, drop the talk of naturalism and simply take what I am saying as just the negative view that we do not have to say any of these metaphysical things, e.g., that there are Platonic forms or that God exists. *Perhaps* we can go on to show that these metaphysical claims make no sense. But, even without that rather risky enterprise, we can show that we do not have to say or think, let alone believe, any of these obscure metaphysical things: that, even if we are being maximally reasonable, or perhaps because we are being maximally reasonable, we do not need to be nudged in a metaphysical direction. Stick, such a Wittgensteinian injunction goes, with conceptual therapy and do not respond to, try to answer, a metaphysical thesis with what may turn out to be another equally objectionable, or at least nearly as objectionable, metaphysical thesis or even with any metaphysical thesis at all.

Do not, the Wittgensteinian could continue, by making positive naturalistic claims, make yourself vulnerable to what at least looks like commonsensical objections such as "How do you know that all objects are physical objects?" Your naturalism, if that is what it is, should be articulated *utterly negatively* rather than being a naturalism which proffers another alternative philosophical theory to set in contestation with a long and varied tradition of antinaturalistic philosophical theories. In science and everyday life, we can get along very well without any of these philosophical theories. They are obscure enough in any event and they always raise more problems than they solve. Just completely keep your head free of metaphysics and other bits of philosophical theory construction.

If my naturalism—say, the seven theses stated by me—turns out, as I do not believe it will, to have metaphysical presuppositions, then, if my account cannot be modified so that they are excised, then I will drop my naturalism, my antimetaphysics being stronger than my naturalism: my belief that we can and should get along without rationalistic synthetic *a priori* principles being more deep-seated than my acceptance of propositions like the seven principles of naturalism that I stated. However, I think, perhaps with a good bit of self-deception, that that is a choice that does not have to be made; a good consistent nonscientistic naturalism will be antimetaphysical both in intent and in reality.

The Wittgensteinian, as we have just seen, being reluctant to talk in any accepting way of naturalism as a positive view, sticks with saying that we do not have to go beyond nature or have to assume that reality is anything other than physical (in some broad sense). But to that it can in turn be responded, as some will indeed respond, "Well, we do not have to, but we just might. It might be a more reasonable, a more intellectually satisfying thing to do." The kind of naturalist that I am will, in turn, respond that we do not understand, and we do not think that our metaphysical interlocutor understands either, what it *means* to go "beyond nature" or for "reality to be other than physical." We have strings of words here that have no determinate use in any language-game, in any established practice. (Don't talk of the language and social practice of metaphysics; there isn't such a thing.) Such strange strings of words only occur when some people are just doing philosophy and everything is free spinning. It isn't that we do not have to go beyond nature, but that we do not understand what such talk comes to. We have no idea of what it would be like to go beyond nature. We can, of course, just stick with nature, physical reality, particulars (after all, what else could we do?), operating on the principle of not multiplying conceptions beyond need. But, fortunately or not, things go deeper than that, blocking the need to get into perplexity about how we determine "beyond need" in the above methodological maxim and as used in such a context. Things go deeper, allowing us to go around such questions, because we are at a loss to understand what we are talking about in speaking of going "beyond nature" and the like. (But then are we not at a loss to understand what it means to be "sticking with nature" as well?)

Still, naturalistic talk, such as my seven theses, just seems to be a relatively straightforward way we can talk without involving ourselves in nonsense or very obscure claims. But, with these seven theses and with their elaboration and elucidation, we have a positive view, a positive philosophical view of a kind. It will be important to get clear about *what kind of philosophical view* it is. I shall argue later in this book, as I have elsewhere, that it is not the *a priori* philosophical view of traditional philosophy. Toward such a traditional view we should take a resolutely Wittgenstein-Deweyan-Rortyan anti-Philosophy *philosophy* line.[41]

To the point about "All objects are physical objects," "There are only particulars," "There is nothing beyond nature" being both nonanalytic and unfalsifiable and thereby metaphysical, it should be said that the same thing, vis-à-vis falsifiability, obtains for "An electron is a wave," "The Higgs particle is the ultimate particle," and "The three-dimensional world is finite and unbounded." They, on the very same grounds, could be said to be metaphysical propositions. But such a claim is problematical, for they (or at least some of them) are at least arguably not metaphysical propositions, but, at least putatively, scientific ones. What this straightforward statement by statement unverifiability in reality attests to is the soundness of Quinean holism as over against a positivism of an atomistic sort, though it does not count against positivists such as Otto Neurath who were both resolutely antimetaphysical and as holistic as Quine. Quine's talk of ontological commitment is, to say the least, unfortunate.[42] Deeply embedded statements are not falsifiable *one by one*. They do not, in Quine's famous phrase, meet the tribunal of experience individually. Still, evidence is not irrelevant to establishing their truth or their justifiability, but they are so deeply a strategic part of a theory, a whole way of conceptualizing the world, that it is evidence in conjunction with a whole lot of other interconnected propositions that is required in testing them. And indeed, it is only in very exceptional circumstances that they even come up for test.

Even more broadly, we sometimes need to call on a whole theory and as well consider it against the possibility of a competing alternative theory being a more coherent way of viewing what is the case. If it is, then that would falsify, or at least infirm, the proposition or propositions in question, if it, or they, is/are not accommodatable by the alternative theory or come out as false on that theory. So the propositions in question remain testable, but they are not straightforwardly testable in the way "All swans are white" or "Brown trout are more wary than rainbow trout" are testable. To ask if you have observed that the three-dimensional world is finite and unbounded makes no more sense than to ask about checking—somehow just looking and seeing—whether there are some nonphysical objects. The propositions in question are too deeply embedded in our web of belief for that. They are too far from the experiential periphery, and too presupposed in, and central to, a lot of other things we believe, for observational checkings, *just taken by themselves,* to be in order. Evidence here is much more indirect and much less straightforward. They are what Wittgenstein called "hinge propositions" and they are not directly falsifiable as are claims such as "I left the keys in the car" or "There was a frost last night." Yet, for all of that, they are not utterly untestable metaphysical propositions. To think that they are is to miss the Quine-Putnam point, and, I think, the Wittgensteinian point as well, that between the *a priori* and the empirical there are all kinds of propositions, which are neither clearly *a priori*, nor straightforwardly empirical, that nonetheless are plainly meaningful sentences which have a use in our language, that are working elements in our social practices, including sometimes our scientific practices. Some of these propositions are not falsifiable in the unproblematic way that "There are only brown trout in the pond" or "There is more crime in Russia now than in the days of the Soviet Union" are falsifiable. But, as we have seen, this does not mean that in indirect ways evidence (empirical evidence) is not relevant to establishing their truth on falsity. "An electron is a wave," "The three-dimensional world is finite and unbounded," as well as "Live human beings must have heads" and "Dogs cannot converse," are such propositions. It is only by accepting a *dualism* of the analytic and the empirical—the belief that all meaningful declarative sentences must be either analytic or empirical—that we come to have trouble with the above sentences (some of which are at least putatively scientific) or come to think my naturalism is, in spite of itself, metaphysical. But this dualism is very unrealistic.[43] Both MacIntyre and such a Wittgensteinian (but not Wittgenstein himself), their good intentions to the contrary notwithstanding, are held, vis-à-vis this alleged dualism, captive to standard, but by now discredited, positivist conceptions.[44]

NOTES

1. C. D. Broad was an atheist but also a dualist, and J. T. E. McTaggart, surprisingly for an atheist, was an uncompromising idealist. Still, most particularly, in the case of McTaggart, that is certainly an anomaly.

2. Kai Nielsen, *Philosophy and Atheism: In Defense of Atheism* (Amherst, N.Y.: Prometheus Press, 1985), 9–31, 55–106.

3. P. F. Strawson, *Skepticism and Naturalism* (London: Metheun, 1985), 51–68; Richard Rorty, *Objectivity, Relativism and Truth* (Cambridge, England: Cambridge University Press, 1991), 113–25; Donald Davidson, *Essays on Actions and Events* (Oxford, England: Clarendon Press, 1980), 207–59; and Simon Evinine, *Donald Davidson* (Stanford, Calif.: Stanford University Press), 7–71.

4. Michel Foucault, *Power/Knowledge* (New York: Pantheon Books, 1980); and Paul Rabinow, ed., *The Foucault Reader* (New York: Pantheon Books, 1984), part 11.

5. Charles Sanders Peirce, *Collected Papers*, vol. 5 (Cambridge, Mass.: Harvard University Press, 1934), 223–92; John Dewey, *The Quest for Certainty* (New York: G. P. Putnam's Sons, 1929).

6. Sometimes it seems to me that Richard Rorty says just the right things about historicism, and about how it need not be relativistic, as in, for example, his "Putnam and the Relativist Menace," *Journal of Philosophy* 90, no. 9 (September 1993): 443–61. But then at other times he seems at least to be backsliding into thinking that historicism must be a form of relativism. See, for example, his "Dewey between Hegel and Darwin," in *Modernist Impulses in the Human Sciences*, ed. Dorothy Ross (Baltimore, Md.: The Johns Hopkins University Press, 1994), 54–68. See, on the general issue of a relativism-free Rorty, Barry Allen, "Atheism, Relativism, Enlightenment and Truth," *Studies in Religion* 23, no. 2 (1944): 172–76. For an insightful way of bringing out the import of historicism without any commitments to relativism, see Rorty, "Should Hume Be Answered or Bypassed?" in *Human Nature and Natural Knowledge*, ed. A. Donagan et al. (Dordrecht, Holland: D. Reidel Publishing Co., 1986), 346–52.

7. Nicholas Wolterstorff badly misunderstands historicism when he thinks that for a historicist rationality must be discarded. Nicholas Wolterstorff, "Can Belief in God Be Rational If It Has No Foundations?" in *Perspectives in Philosophy*, ed. Michael Boylan (Fort Worth, Tex.: Harcourt Brace Jovanovich, 1993), 444–45. For what should be said concerning this, see Stephen Toulmin, *Cosmopolis* (Chicago: University of Chicago Press, 1990), 198–201.

8. See my entry under "Historicism" in *The Cambridge Dictionary of Philosophy*, ed. Robert Audi (Cambridge, England: Cambridge University Press, 1996).

9 I criticize foundationalism in my *After the Demise of the Tradition* (Boulder, Colo.: Westview Press, 1991), and in my *Transforming Philosophy: A Metaphilosophical Inquiry* (Boulder, Colo.: Westview Press, 1995).

10. Raymond Geuss sees very well how, and properly how, critical theory in some of its forms takes a historicist form. Raymond Geuss, *The Idea of a Critical Theory* (Cambridge, England: Cambridge University Press, 1981), 62–64, 94–95. See, as well, my "The Very Idea of a Critical Theory," *Ratio* (Fall 1991); my "On the Status of Critical Theory," *Interchange* 23, no. 3 (1992): 265–84; and my "The Confirmation of Critical Theory: The Role of Reflectiveness," *Human Studies* 16 (1993): 381–97.

11. Richard Rorty, "Epistemological Behaviorism and De-Transcendatalization of Analytic Philosophy," in *Hermeneutics and Praxis*, ed. Robert Hollinger (Notre Dame, Ind.: University of Notre Dame Press, 1985), 89–121; and John P. Murphy, *Pragmatism from Peirce to Davidson* (Boulder, Colo.: Westview Press, 1990). Note, as well, Rorty's introduction.

12. Rorty, "Epistemological Behaviorism and the De-Transcendentalization of Analytic Philosophy," 89–121; and his *Objectivity, Relativism and Truth*, 1–20.

13. See John Dewey, "Logical Conditions of a Scientific Treatment of Morality" (1903), reprinted in his *Problems of Men* (New York: Philosophical Library, 1946), 211–49. See also his *The Quest for Certainty*, chapter 10.

14. Hilary Putnam, *Realism With a Human Face* (Cambridge, Mass.: Harvard University Press, 1990), 135–200; and Putnam, *Words and Life* (Cambridge, Mass.: Harvard University Press, 1994), 151–97.

15. E. W. Hall, "Metaphysics," in *Living Schools of Philosophy*, ed. Dagobert D. Runes (Ames, Iowa: Littlefield, Adams and Co., 1956), 129–39. See also his *Philosophical Systems* (Chicago: University of Chicago Press, 1960), 72–79.

16. Alasdair MacIntyre, *Whose Justice? Which Rationality?* (Notre Dame, Ind.: University of Notre Dame Press, 1988); and MacIntyre, *Three Versions of Moral Enquiry* (Notre Dame, Ind.: University of Notre Dame Press, 1990); and Charles Taylor, *Sources of the Self* (Cambridge, Mass.: Harvard University Press, 1989).

17. O. K. Bousma, *Philosophical Essays* (Lincoln: University of Nebraska Press, 1965), 71–83. See also Raphael Demos, "Naturalism and Values," in *The Student Seeks an Answer,* ed. John A. Clark (Waterville, Maine: Colby College Press, 1960), 163–79.

18. Quine's scientism is expressed succinctly in his claim "that it is within science itself, and not in some prior philosophy, that reality is to be identified and described." W. V. Quine, *Theories and Things* (Cambridge, Mass.: Belknap Press, 1981), 21. Contextualist naturalists will agree with Quine that there is no prior or First philosophy that will identify and describe reality. But they will not accept his *persuasive* definition of "reality." There are legal, moral, political realities, and otherwise commonsense realities, e.g., "The moon is pink tonight," which do not need, let alone require, science for their identification and description or to establish that they really are realities. They certainly are not supernatural realities, and we do not require a "superscience" to know them, but they are not scientific realities either and science does not show them to be nonrealities or illusions. See also Brian Magee, "Dialogue With W. V. Quine," in Magee's *Men of Ideas* (Oxford, England: Oxford University Press, 1982), 143–55. See the discussion of Quine by Couture and Nielsen, "On Construing Philosophy," in Couture and Nielsen, eds., *Méta-Philosophie: Reconstructing Philosophy?* (Calgary, Alberta: Calgary University Press, 1993), 31–51.

19. See my "Jolting the Career of Reason: Absolute Idealism and Other Rationalisms Reconsidered," *Journal of Speculative Philosophy* 8, no. 2 (1994): 113–40; and my "Reconsidering the Platonic Conception of Philosophy," *International Studies in Philosophy* 26, no. 1/2 (1994): 51–71.

20. A. J. Ayer, "A Defense of Empiricism," in *A. J. Ayer: Memorial Essays,* ed. A. Phillips Griffiths (Cambridge, England: Cambridge University Press, 1991),1–16. See also in the same volume Ted Honderich's "An Interview with A. J. Ayer," 209–26. Isaiah Berlin, *Concepts and Categories: Philosophical Essays* (Oxford, England: Oxford University Press, 1980), vii–viii, 1–11, 143–72. See the discussion of these issues by Couture and Nielsen, "On Construing Philosophy," 7–12.

21. Willard Van Orman Quine, "Two Dogmas of Empiricism," in his *From a Logical Point of View* (Cambridge, Mass.: Harvard University Press, 1953), 320–46. Quine, "Two Dogmas in Retrospect," *Canadian Journal of Philosophy* 21, no. 3 (September 1991): 265–74.

22. Putnam has discussed the analytic and the synthetic in a series of brilliant papers. See Hilary Putnam, *Mind, Language and Reality: Philosophical Papers*, vol. 2 (Cambridge, England: Cambridge University Press, 1975), 33–69; and Hilary Putnam, *Realism and Reason: Philosophical Papers,* vol. 3 (Cambridge University Press, 1983), 87–138. But Putnam, never one to stand still philosophically, has increasingly distanced himself from Quine and increasingly taken a more Wittgensteinian turning. But, for the theses *contra* a dualism of the analytic and the empirical, Putnam's shift in position, even if well taken, as I am inclined to think that it is, will not affect what I claim above. There is, moreover, no turn here, or even temptation to turn, to claiming that there are any absolute, unconditional *a priori* truths. In this respect his thinking is even more fallibilistic and metaphysics-free than before. Hilary Putnam, *Words and Life* (Cambridge, Mass.: Harvard University Press, 1994), 245–63.

23. Putnam, *Realism and Reason*, 101. He abandons this view in *Words and Life*. We can make no sense of saying such a principle is revisable, but then we can make no sense of saying it is unrevisable either. They take in each other's dirty linen.

24. Quine, "Two Dogmas of Empiricism," 20–46. Morton White, "The Analytic and the Synthetic: An Untenable Dualism," in *Semantics and the Philosophy of Language,* ed. Leonard Linsky (Urbana: University of Illinois Press, 1952), 272–330.

25. Putnam, *Realism and Reason*, 100–104.

26. Ibid., 100–102.

27. Norman Malcolm, "The Groundlessness of Belief," in *Reason and Religion*, ed. Stuart Brown (Ithaca, N.Y.: Cornell University Press, 1977), 141–57, 185–90; and Norman Malcolm, *Wittgenstein: A Religious Point of View?* (Ithaca, N.Y.: Cornell University Press, 1994).

28. It is not that I can state clearly, or sometimes even unclearly, the circumstances under which they would, or at least should, be abandoned. They are too deeply embedded for that. But I do not set up (try to set up) either *a priori* or methodological roadblocks to their possible abandonment. If putatively disconfirming evidence builds up, too many strange things happen that are anomalies, at least given the acceptance of these propositions, then it would be reasonable to abandon them, if some plausible alternative account is available. (We should not beg questions by insisting that it be some form of naturalism. But we should also not underestimate the difficulty in gaining some consensus on what will even count as a "plausible alternative.") No algorithm can be given here, but that is true as well for many areas in science. But these naturalistic propositions are not *synthetic a priori* propositions chiseled in stone.

29. It is the undermining of the *dualism* that is crucial—the undermining, that is, of the claim that all meaningful declarative sentences must be one or the other—and not the undermining of the claim that there can be conceptual propositions (including analytic ones) which are not empirical truth-claims. We can remain agnostic about that second claim. In short, what I say here is perfectly compatible with Wittgenstein's remarks about grammatical remarks.

30. Alasdair MacIntyre, "Hume, Testimony to Miracles, the Order of Nature, and Jansenism," in *Faith, Scepticism and Personal Identity*, ed. J. J. MacIntosh and H. A. Meynell (Calgary, Alberta: University of Calgary Press, 1994), 95. But see here, as well, Terence Penelhum's discussion in the same volume, pp. 257–63.

31. MacIntyre, "Hume, Testimony to Miracles," 96.

32. Ibid., 97–98.

33. Ibid., 96.

34. Ibid., 97.

35. Ibid.

36. Ibid. See John F. Post, *The Faces of Existence: An Essay in Non-reductive Metaphysics* (Ithaca, N.Y.: Cornell University Press, 1987), 184–85.

37. MacIntyre, "Hume, Testimony to Miracles," 97; and Post, *The Faces of Existence*, 184–85.

38. MacIntyre, "Hume, Testimony to Miracles," 97.

39. I argue against such metaphysical views in my *Transforming Philosophy: A Metaphilosophical Inquiry*, part 1. Henry Sidgwick, defining *metaphysics* uncontroversially as The Tradition has defined it, just remarks that metaphysics inquires into "what, if anything, can be known *a priori*." Henry Sidgwick, *Philosophy: Its Scope and Relations* (London: Macmillan and Co., 1902), xi, 87–91. This is just what has been metaphysics and it is very distant from the way Quine, Armstrong, Nussbaum, and Smart think of the subject. They turn the subject into something which is not metaphysics at all, but very general and systematic *conceptual* analysis, if you will, categorial analysis, but, as second-order, as any other conceptual analysis. They, for example, analyze *cause,* but do not tell us what the causes of so and so, say alienation or inflation or social strife, or anything you like, are. The word *cause,* when doing any work in their accounts, occurs in mention and not in use. See, in this connection, Couture and Nielsen, "On Construing Philosophy," 31–51.

40. For the issues and the argument that follow I am much indebted to the searching comments of Andrew Lugg on an earlier draft of this chapter. I hope I do something to address his Wittgensteinian unease about my very project. Note here, as well, my "Anti-Philosophy philosophy: Some Programmatic Remarks," *Diàlogos* 64 (1994): 149–58.

41. See my *Transforming Philosophy: A Metaphilosophical Inquiry* and my "Transforming Philosophy," *Soundings* (1991).

42. W. V. O. Quine, *Ontological Relativity and Other Essays* (New York: Columbia University Press, 1969), 26–68. Contrast Otto Neurath's firm and sensible antimetaphysics along with a holism and an antifoundationalism that is as thorough as Quine's or, for that matter, as Davidson's. Otto Neurath, *Philosophical Papers: 1913–1946* (Dordrecht, Holland: D. Reidel, 1983). For a useful discussion of Neurath's views see Jordi Cat, Hasok Chang and Nancy Cartwright, "Otto Neurath: Unification as the Way to Socialism," in *Einheit der Wissenchaften,* ed. J. Mittelstrass (Berlin: *Akademic der Wissenchaften,* 1991), 91–110.

43. Rejecting that dualism need not lead to a denial that there is an important distinction between the conceptual and the empirical and that it is sometimes crucial to recognize it and to recognize the role that conceptual remarks play in our language-games. This remains true even after we recognize that whether a given sentence functions as a conceptual remark or not depends on the context of its use. The sort of considerations stressed by Wittgenstein in *On Certainty* (Oxford, England: Basil Blackwell, 1959) are crucial here. We can, perhaps, consistently have both Quine and Wittgenstein.

44. There is a lot of patronizing denigration of positivism nowadays and I do not wish the above remark to be taken as adding to it. The denigration is not the old-fashioned, alarmed sort which regarded positivism as an irrationalist and nihilistic threat (e.g., Freddie Ayer fiddles while Rome burns), but instead the patronizing sort that just blandly has it that positivism is a confused, hopelessly antiquated, superficial scientistic philosophy. What is regarded as revolutionary in one epoch is thought to be reactionary in the next. I think this reaction to positivism, to put it minimally, is just too strong. Putnam, one of positivism's acutest critics, has also pointed to some of its virtues in his *Words and Life*, 85–148. I would also claim, making a rather different point than Putnam's, that its critique of metaphysics, something that present-day systematic analytical philosophy hardly even recognizes, let alone dreams that it may have some force, is essentially sound. (Logical positivism is deeply antimetaphysical while contemporary systematic analytic philosophy is uncritically metaphysical.) In this I am joined, perhaps surprisingly, by Richard Rorty, who remarks in his *Philosophy and the Mirror of Nature* (Princeton, N.J.: Princeton University Press, 1979), that "the positivists were absolutely right in thinking it imperative to extirpate metaphysics when "metaphysics" means the attempt to give knowledge of what science cannot know" (384). Rorty is very distant from Carnap's and Quine's scientism, but *here* he recognizes that all is not dross in scientism.

Chapter Two

A Naturalistic Method

I

I want to articulate in this chapter how a naturalist should proceed in doing philosophy. I first characterize a method and then defend the use of such a method against the claim that we are better off without method just as I think we are better off without foundations.

C. S. Peirce and John Dewey set forth and defend a method for fixing belief that, as I remarked in the previous chapter, was both contextualistic and fallibilistic. The method I shall elucidate and defend is a generalization and extension of that, though I shall start from considered judgments—considered judgments in all sorts of domains—and sometimes, more standardly for a pragmatist, from experience or from experimental data without a simultaneous appeal to considered judgments. But, like Dewey, I also take a problem-oriented, situation-structured approach. Philosophical inquiry should start from specific, or relatively specific, real live doubts and not à la Descartes from mere methodological doubt: what Peirce called paper doubts. Welling up from the stream of life come real problems, political, economic, scientific, religious, moral, personal, aesthetic, and the like. We do not, for example, know in certain circumstances what role an anthropologist should play when living with the primitive society he studies. Suppose that they, as part of their very way of life, do what he regards as horrendous things. When, if ever, where he is able to, should he intervene? Coming closer to home, we (speaking now of us as a society) do not know what to think about homosexuality, abortion, or euthanasia. There are problematic situations here where there is conflict and confusion within our society and sometimes within ourselves as

57

individuals. What to do is, at least socially speaking, clearly in doubt. Faced with such situations, we should proceed in ways that are not fundamentally different from the ways a scientist would proceed in seeking a cure for AIDS or for cancer or seeking to date a newly found skull. We seek to clarify and to isolate just what the problem is or the cluster of problems are. What, we should ask, are the various beliefs about the problem, including the various convictions involved, and how plausible or reasonable they are? Among the ones we deem plausible or reasonable, and particularly where there is actual conflict concerning the ones we deem plausible or reasonable, we should proceed as follows. We should try to get a tolerably clear conception of how the various pieces fit together. And, after careful reflection and examination, including the drawing of the consequences (logical and causal) of accepting them and a gaining of some conception of how they fit together, we should try to get as clear a picture as we can of what it is that we do not know and what it is that we really need to know concerning the problem at hand. For example, in considering euthanasia we need to consider (of course, among other things) the likely effects of a policy of legalizing euthanasia on the family of the person opting for euthanasia. We may start by thinking that it is *just* a matter up for individual decision, the effects on others being of a decidedly secondary importance. After all, it is the individual's own life and what he wishes to do with it that is essentially in question. That still may be right. But it also seems evident enough that it would be important to ascertain, if we can, what the likely effects would be on others close to the person contemplating euthanasia. After all, we do not live alone; we all plainly owe things to others.[1] If bringing an end to his life is very likely to be devastating and would continue to be devastating for the people involved even after the problem was carefully thought through by them, and taken to heart, then perhaps we should put in question a policy of making euthanasia available simply on carefully considered demand by the person wishing to end his life. That is, it should make us look again at what attitude we should take toward euthanasia. I am not, even for a moment, suggesting a resolution here to the problem. I am merely saying that these are the sorts of things we need to get clear about in considering what is to be done in that problematic situation.

More generally, for whatever the problem is first we need to delineate clearly the problem, consider various proposed resolutions, and consider their relative plausibility and reasonableness. When the problem is practical—a problem about what to do or how to try to be—we need to consider what resolutions are likely to be favored and accepted when they are presented clearly and with their rationale up front. And sometimes we should make suggestions about what is to be done or as to how we should view and respond to what is done. In doing these things, we need also to consider as well what are the considered convictions of the people involved. We need to consider whether there is a consensus or whether there is the likelihood of a consensus after the matter has been clarified and duly reflected on. If there is not, then we are very often in deep trouble, for we will be without the background conditions necessary, but, of course, not sufficient, for a rational resolution of the problem. What we need to do is to deliberate carefully and to take our deliberations to heart and see whether on due reflection we should either modify the recalcitrant considered convictions or even abandon some, carrying out these alterations until we get a cluster of convictions and beliefs that do consistently hang together and, in doing so, square with facts that are readily available to us. We should try to get a coherent package here.

We should go for the best approximation we can get to maximal coherence of considered convictions, beliefs about what is the case, and observations about what is the case. We should seek a consistent and otherwise coherent cluster of all that we care about, know, reflectively think, and can reasonably be expected to come to know. It is rational generally to seek to maximize the coherence of our beliefs and convictions, remembering that we justify beliefs and convictions principally by establishing a consistent and coherent fit.

However, in doing this it is important also to go with the Peircean-Deweyan insistence that we only seek to achieve sufficient coherence to resolve the problem or problems at hand, rendering the problematic situation into an unproblematic one. We should not seek timeless solutions to problems arising in determinate problematic situations. With diligence and luck we may attain a reflective equilibrium for a relatively determinate time and place, but this will at most be around a cluster of problems and, as the world changes and as we, as small parts of that world, change too, the reflective equilibrium will be upset and it will become necessary to achieve a new reflective equilibrium. Our web of belief and conviction is that of a changing, open-system; a timeless, changeless reflective equilibrium is both impossible and undesirable. And there is no such a thing as getting a *complete* reflective equilibrium.[2] What we should seek to achieve instead is a, for a time, resolution of our problems at hand, problems emerging from partially indeterminate situations where, even when we reflect, and particularly when we reflect, we have real live doubts about what is to be done or believed. That kind of resolution is all we should ask for or reasonably expect, but it is sufficient. We should not go on a quest for certainty and totality seeking some total system with a maximum coherence. Neither, after the fashion of a Cartesian or Leibnizian foundationalism, should we seek certainty in rational intuitions nor, with the foundationalism of the classical empiricists, seek certainty in what have sometimes been taken to be primitive sense certainties. Similarly we should not go for the total system of a Hegelian-style Absolute idealism.[3] Rather, we are always faced with a bootstrapping operation where we are always weaving and unweaving the threads of our patterns of belief, seeking to get a pattern of sufficient coherence to resolve for the day the problem, or cluster of problems, at hand. Searching for indubitable foundations from which timeless resolutions of our problems can be derived will prove fruitless and will, if resolutely persisted in, very likely generate a needless and utterly unrealistic skepticism. We can and should be fallibilists without being skeptics.

So far I have followed a roughly pragmatist method of both approaching and specifying problems for philosophical treatment. Particular problems—problems generated by real doubts about what to believe or do—well up from the stream of life. In using our brains and sensibilities in resolving them, we render the specific problematic situation unproblematic, or at least less problematic, thereby taking away, or at least lessening, the particular irritation of doubt. Perhaps it is the case that this is the best that we can do. Indeed, it may even be all that we can do. Certainly that is what I have been giving to understand above. But most philosophers, and many other persons as well, have wanted something more than that. Moreover, the pragmatists themselves have wanted something more. Philosophers, as I remarked in the last chapter, generally have wanted to see how things hang together. They have wanted to know who we are, were, and whom we might reasonably aspire to become. They have wanted to gain some conception of what a just society would be like and to gain, as well, some idea of how we could approximate it. They have also wanted to gain, if anything like this could be had, some tolerably coherent conception of what a good life for human beings would be. They have wanted to see if we can gain some understanding of what life would be like in such a circumstance. They have wanted to see how their (that is, our) various beliefs, desires, hopes, conceptions, and convictions fit together. Can we—maximizing coherence—place them together into a coherent whole and in doing so can we make sense of our lives? Such a wish is as old as philosophy is. Perhaps we can never get such a perspicuous and truthful rendering of our lives, perhaps the very idea of a "truthful rendering of our lives" does not make sense, but it is certainly natural enough to wish for such a thing, opaque as it is, and to proceed to try to get it, until it can be shown, if indeed it can be shown, that this is a senseless or hopeless endeavor.

II

Wilfrid Sellars characterized that philosophical enterprise as "the attempt to see how things in the broadest possible sense of the term, hang together in the broadest sense of the term."[4] This could be taken as speculative metaphysicians (particularly Absolute Idealists) have taken it as the attempt to show how all things hang together in a consistent and comprehensive total system of ultimate reality.[5] All relations in such a system are said to be internal. We are said to have a system in which everything is logically linked to everything else such that they all exist in this tight web, all necessarily hanging together into a total system of logically interlocked ultimate reality. This probably makes no sense at all. But many people (including many philosophers) have taken to heart Sellars's conception of philosophy without giving it anything like that extravagant Absolute Idealist reading. They have rather taken it in something like the modest way I have characterized it in the previous paragraph. In an attempt in that broad sense to see how things hang together, they seek to give a perspicuous representation of our fundamental categorial concepts (goodness, truth, cause existence, truth, warrantability, etc.) as well as other concepts that are important to us. They seek to forge a consistent pattern of our desires, beliefs, convictions, conceptions that will yield a coherent conception of ourselves and of our world.[6]

That is still a tall order and perhaps should be cut down to a still more modest size. Perhaps we should content ourselves with the attempt to order our beliefs and convictions into a coherent pattern with a stress on those beliefs and convictions which are important in making sense of our lives. But even the more ambitious conception is still a long way from metaphysical conceptions of an interlocking system of *total ultimate reality*, yielding a final theory which will show us what the universe is really like and indeed must be like. Both of these more modest attempts to achieve coherence eschew all such metaphysical thinking. They make no claims about ultimate reality, final theory, ultimate truth, or to have an *a priori* grasp of what The Truth is let alone must be. Such conceptions are met with either positivist scorn or with bemused indifference or with Kierkegaardian irony. But that does not keep such a pragmatic nonfoundationalist naturalist, with her coherentist conceptions, from, in a modest way, trying to see how things hang together in a way that makes no appeal to any metaphysical or otherwise transcendental conceptions.

However, this goes beyond the problems-orientation that I gave to the pragmatist a few pages back. But it is perfectly compatible with it. We always have background beliefs that wittingly or unwittingly are assumed when we attempt to resolve particular problems of life in determinate problematic situations. Many of these beliefs are utterly unproblematic. There is no real doubt concerning whether they are to be plausibly regarded as being true: plausibly taken for true. But there are also not a few others, sometimes just assumed as background beliefs, that are supposedly to "go without saying," that, as we engage ourselves in the world, as we struggle with actual problems of life, become in various degrees problematic. Some we might, on reflection and after investigation, want or need to jettison. Faced with these actual irritations of doubt, we want to see if we can get a coherent package of beliefs that will help us in our struggles in life, and in our reflecting about those struggles, to make sense of what we are doing and thinking.

It is also important to recognize that that cluster of beliefs that are part of our actual cultural pattern do not form a closed system. Many of them, however, are unproblematic background beliefs, the great mass of which we must rely on in engaging in any problems-oriented philosophical inquiry.[7] They, in most circumstances at least, stand fast for us, though the possibility is always there that some circumstance could arise in which we would come to have a specific reason to doubt one or even several of them together. But while we could in some specific situation doubt some specific belief or beliefs we could not intelligibly doubt all our beliefs together. To even be able to doubt, something must stand fast which may in turn very well be one of the factors occasioning the doubt or instead could be part of what is appealed to in resolving the doubt. But, if it is a factor occasioning the doubt, then something else must stand fast for us to have that doubt at all. So, while in some problematic situations, we could come to doubt any one of our beliefs or several of them, it is not possible to doubt them *all* together. *Universal doubt is unintelligible.* If I doubt that someone will keep his appointment, I can do that only if I do not doubt that there is someone who made the appointment and that there is something which could be done which would constitute the keeping of the appointment; that there are such things as a time, place, people, and the like. If I try to doubt everything at once, I will no longer have any sense of what I am doubting.

In coming to grips with any particular problem of life or with any scientific problem, we will be operating with, routinely and unproblematically, certain background beliefs, many of which are so deeply embedded and so basic that we are hardly aware of holding them or of having them, though once they are mentioned we usually recognize immediately that we hold these beliefs, that they are part of our repertoire of commonly accepted beliefs that we have no reason at all to doubt. I have in mind such things as our belief that people have desires, hopes, expectations; that they need food, air, and the like. How many such beliefs I have I cannot say. To speak of coming to know and to state the total set of such beliefs is nonsense. But we do know that we do have an indefinitely large number of them. Typically, though not invariably, they are beliefs that, in most circumstances at least, are quite unproblematic, indeed they are less problematic than the *philosophical* beliefs that would try to put them in question. Put otherwise, a philosophical theory which would attempt to reject them holus-bolus, or so put them all in doubt, or even most of them in doubt, would be less plausible than the beliefs themselves. We usually fail in doing philosophy, or just in thinking about our thinking, to recognize the mass of unproblematic background beliefs that we actually have; *we fail to realize the extent of our groundless believing that is actually unprob-*

lematically there. And, if we tried by a thought experiment to remove these beliefs, to put them in doubt, we would hardly know what it would be like to think, to doubt, to carry out the thought experiment, and the like. We would be at a complete loss here. They are beliefs we have, as Hume had it (*pace* Descartes), involuntarily, but actually still beliefs that for the most part we have no reason at all to doubt or to attempt to critically review. It is important, in being a reflective human being, to know when to ask questions and make inquiries, but it is equally important to understand when not to and, as well, to further understand when the very idea of making inquiries is just so much nonsense.

Still, for at least most of our beliefs—perhaps even for all of them—they, taken individually, or in some determinate cluster, could in the appropriate circumstances be doubted. But what is necessary for such doubting to be reasonable is that, in some actual circumstance emerging from the living of our lives, there is some specific reason for doubting them or some reasonable situation-oriented simulation of this and that this not be an attempt at "universal doubt." There may very well be no indubitable beliefs; not even our most deeply embedded considered convictions may be such. But it is also the case that universal doubt is impossible, for all of our beliefs cannot be doubted at once. Only if the vast majority of our beliefs are not in doubt, can, in a problematic situation, some specific belief or cluster of our beliefs be intelligibly doubted. There is no possibility of universal doubt, methodological or otherwise. Cartesianism is incoherent and there is not even room for Hume's skeptic.

I want in doing philosophy to go in a Deweyan fashion. I want, that is, to grapple with central and urgent particular problems of life—problems such as abortion, euthanasia, pornography, market socialism—problems for us, standing where we are now, concerning work and the quality of work and the deep alienation of people with or without work. But in taking this Deweyan turn, we also, in the very wrestling with these problems, will come to have some conception of who we are and of how we should live our lives and with what priorities. If we intelligently engage in campaigns over particular issues of injustice, we can hardly help coming to see things a little more in perspective, seeing a little better how our society works. We can hardly have much of an understanding of what a good life for human beings would be or how we should live our lives without also having some understanding of how things hang together. To know how to live, we need to have some understanding of what life is like and of what it could be like in changed circumstances. This remains so even if we do not believe that we can deduce fundamental values from facts.[8] Similarly, in making up our mind about what to think about abortion, euthanasia, or pornography, we will come to have a sense of what we think about what is valuable in life and of how we think human beings should regard themselves and what a good life for human beings would be.

We will also need to gain some grasp of what life as a matter of fact is really like, what our condition of life is, and what it can be.[9] Here again we need, among other things, to come to see how things hang together; we need, that is, to come to have some view of the world and our lives in it. This requires the Sellarsian thing. And we have, as well, the coherentism and contextualism discussed in the previous chapter. Conceived as centrally concerned with the problems of human beings and in doing so as resolutely setting aside, as idle, metaphysical inquiries or foundationalist epistemological inquiries, philosophy, so conceived, is distinct from philosophy conceived as an attempt to see how things hang together. Still, these two conceptions of the proper office of philosophy fit well together, given the modest nonmetaphysical readings I have given to the Sellarsian thing.

III

In concerning itself with what Dewey called the problems of men and in trying to see a little more adequately how things hang together, my contextualist, historicist, antifoundationalist, coherentist naturalism without foundations, unlike the neopragmatism of Richard Rorty and Stanley Fish, is *not* a naturalism without method. I use what I have called the *method of reflective equilibrium* (more accurately, though more pedantically, the method of an appeal to considered judgments in wide reflective equilibrium). But I also utilize what Peirce and Dewey call the scientific method (alternatively the pragmatic method, the experimental method, the method of intelligence). As used by me, this problem-solving, self-correcting, scientific method—this core method of my naturalism—should include what has been called the *method of an appeal to considered judgments in wide (broad) reflective equilibrium.* It has been used in moral and political contexts by John Rawls, Norman Daniels, Richard Rorty, and myself.[10] Where it is linked with scientific method, 'scientific method' is construed very broadly and is to be utilized in our inquiries and theory construction in all domains of life. Indeed, it seems to me that scientific method *so construed* and the method of wide reflective equilibrium come to much the same thing. But I will not try to insist on that point. I utilize them both in philosophizing as I do. *To repeat, my naturalism is without foundations, but not without method.*

The method of wide reflective equilibrium has been used, as I remarked in the preface, in broader philosophical contexts explicitly by Nelson Goodman and Hilary Putnam and in effect by W. V. O. Quine and Donald Davidson.[11] It is a coherentist method that avoids a foundationalist claim to have a linear mode of justification, but justifies beliefs and actions by showing how they form a consistent and coherent system of beliefs and actions. We should pursue a strategy, as far as it is feasible, of maximizing the coherence of our beliefs and actions: of seeking to get the most coherent cluster of beliefs, with their related policies of action, that we can obtain. We justify, for example, a conception of justice, and its attendant principles, by showing how they fit together with our other beliefs and actions into a consistent set. The principles of justice that are acceptable are consistent with our firmest considered judgments that in turn are the considered judgments that are mutually consistent. A proposed conception of justice, replete with its proposed principles of justice, should be rejected if it does not square with a critical mass of our considered judgments.

A recalcitrant considered judgment which does not square with a critical mass of considered judgments will also rightly be rejected. When two considered judgments conflict—when both of them are very firm considered judgments and one, but not the other, also conflicts with a principle of justice (perhaps itself a more abstract considered judgment) which in turn squares well with and explains many considered judgments, including explaining why that considered judgment is incompatible with it and with, as well, many other considered judgments—then the conflicting particular judgment should be either modified so that it is no longer in conflict with the rest or, if that is not possible, it should be rejected. The thing to do is to achieve a consistent pattern of such moral conceptions, but not only of such moral conceptions (moral considered judgments), but as well with other beliefs, namely with ordinary well-warranted empirical beliefs relevant to the considered moral judgments, well-founded empirically based theories about the function of morality, as well as with well-warranted psychological, economic, and sociological theories and their specific claims of general import where they are in turn warranted. It is also important that there be an extensive consensus among the people in a position to be knowledgeable about these matters, concerning what in these various specific domains is well warranted. *Controversial* psychological, sociological, or economic theories should not be appealed to in establishing such a wide reflective equilibrium in moral and political domains. But, where they are noncontroversial, and where they are, as well, relevant to the moral and political questions at hand, it is essential that they be appealed to. Similar things should be said about biological theory and physical theory, though perhaps they are not so frequently and immediately relevant. The thing to do is to try to get the mass of those of our beliefs that we need to take notice of, cutting and pruning for consistency and coherence, into a coherent and consistent whole that we can on reflection accept. For a belief to be firmly justified, it must fit into such a coherent pattern, fit, that is, into a wide reflective equilibrium.

Here things are subject to change, for what is a reflective equilibrium at one time may very well not be at another. Still, it is possible for some beliefs—say, crucial beliefs about justice—to form, for a time, a coherent pattern and to be in such an equilibrium. It is in this way that we can justify beliefs about justice, about morality more generally, as well as about art, religion, politics, and science. Even more ambitiously—and far more subject to failure—would be to so justify the way in all domains we see how things hang together, yielding a fallibilistic worldview. Philosophy, taken in the Sellarsian way, would in doing this use the method of wide reflective equilibrium. Philosophy, that is, would be done within the limits of wide reflective equilibrium alone. It is itself the attempt to see how things, in the widest sense of the term, hang together in the widest sense of the term. But the sensible way to try to do that is to resolutely use the method of wide reflective equilibrium. Good philosophy should just come to trying to achieve wide reflective equilibrium in one domain after another, and perhaps sometimes, where a worldview is our aim, synoptically in all domains together. This is the way we should try to do philosophy. This coherentist methodology should be a key element in a naturalism without foundations.[12]

IV

There is a standard objection to all coherentist models of justification that such a naturalist should face. Could we not have several consistent systems of beliefs all of which were false? Could not many, or even all, of the beliefs in a consistent set of beliefs be false? Consistency and coherence, the objection could continue, is one thing; truth and justifiability or well warrantedness is another. The beliefs of Christian Science could perhaps form a consistent set, but consistent or not, given their content, are they not absurdly false and indeed do we not know them to be so? Consistency is necessary but not sufficient for warrantability. The same thing holds for coherence, if it really is distinct from consistency. The beliefs of Christian Science might marvelously cohere together, but still be absurdly false. That they are the considered convictions of Christian Scientists does not help one bit.

Moreover, two or more distinct systems of belief and action could both be consistent, but still logically incompatible with each other. And to say that all these mutually incompatible systems are true, since they are all consistent, seems, to put it minimally, absurd. Moreover, scope does not settle things, for we can have a consistent system, even a big system (Christian Science, for example), which still is absurdly false.[13] A coherentist method cannot yield a complete system of justification; the justification of a belief, it could plausibly be argued, cannot just consist in showing that it is consistently and coherently related to other beliefs which are similarly so "justified."

However, the appeal to considered judgments in wide reflective equilibrium is not *just* a coherentist model, for it appeals to considered judgments, some of them very particular ones. And these considered judgments are taken to have a presumptive *initial* creditability on their own. That the considered judgments are so regarded does not mean that their credibility is taken as a bedrock appeal to certainty as it is in classical foundationalism. Any of these considered judgments could be jettisoned if they do not fit with (are not consistent with) a critical mass of the other propositions in our cluster of beliefs. If that obtains, it is not only that they could be jettisoned, they *should* be jettisoned. Indeed, that is required by the very method of wide reflective equilibrium. But they are still always taken to have at least an *initial* credibility. In some domains, but not all, it is so because we have evidence for them. Suppose, to take an ordinary empirical considered judgment made on a particular occasion, I say, or think, that the wind is blowing very hard. What gives that judgment an initial credibility is things like I hear it, see the trees swaying, see the porch umbrella tip over, and the like. Suppose another considered judgment of mine is that I ought not go sailing when the wind is blowing so hard. Here the support for it is not simply a matter of looking and seeing, but a recognition that to go sailing in such circumstances is very dangerous and that one should not do dangerous things without very good reasons for doing so. These are further considered judgments of mine that are not likely—unless one is just doing philosophy—to be questioned. But if they are queried I can remark that one is likely to be drowned if one goes sailing in such conditions, relying, in saying that, on the very firmly embedded considered judgment that that is a bad thing. In most circumstances that would not at all be in doubt. It is just a commonplace, but still a firm, considered judgment: a platitudinous, but still presumptively correct, considered judgment of ours. Moreover, it is a considered judgment that fits well with other considered judgments of ours over which we have no real doubt at all.

If some of these considered judgments, and judgments like them, do not have initial credibility, then nothing has. And to reply that nothing has is just to engage in a pointless lament. That—that is, with these considered judgments—is where we start and, if the philosophical argument goes in a certain way, then generally we have no reason to doubt them at all. However, if, after some inquiry or reflection, we come for some actual reason to doubt some specific one or specific ones for some determinate reasons, we could do so—could come to have that specific doubt—only if other beliefs, many of which also have initial credibility, hold fast. We have no coherent conception of what it would be like to doubt them all holus-bolus. And, for all of our firmest considered judgments, they come with a *presumption of initial credibility.* Without that we could not, for example, engage in moral deliberation at all. Special circumstances can, of course, arise in which we have some specific reason to doubt one or another of them, but that reason for doubt, as all reasons for doubt, would be specific-situation dependent. Standardly, we have no reason at all to doubt them. Moreover, no sense can be given to saying that nothing has initial credibility. For something to lack credibility, or for the credibility of something to be doubted, or for it to be doubtful, something else must be taken to have credibility. There is no better place to start than with our own firmest considered judgments. In any event, to even start doubting at all we have to take something to have initial credibility.[14]

And so it goes with a number of very deeply embedded considered judgments in many different domains. That—that is, with these considered judgments—is where we start and standardly we have no reason at all to doubt them. If someone unwisely ignores Peirce's methodological dictum and goes Cartesian and asks: "But why care about drowning? Why care about whether you live or die?" I can appropriately respond that we just do. That is one of the things that human beings in most circumstances just do care about. It is one of our firmest considered judgments and it matches well with other things we believe and care about. We have absolutely no reason at all to doubt it. Only an impossible metaphysical urge to try to wipe the slate clean would let us think that we do. Our considered judgments have in that way initial credibility. Reflective equilibrium is not *just* a matter of coherence.

To the reply that we are still seeing things by our own lights, the proper response is: "Whose lights do you want us to see them by?" There is no escaping starting by our own lights. But, with both the scientific method and the method of wide reflective equilibrium, we have a *self-correcting* method. We can and do go bootstrapping along through life. If some of our considered judgments are ethnocentric, as often they will be, in trying to get them into wide reflective equilibrium, which is to get them into a wide coherent pattern, we will unavoidably come to see that they do not fit with many other things (including scientific things) that we also believe, or will come seriously to consider, with the shock of contact with rather different others. In these ways we will come to see that we have very good grounds for rejecting some of our considered judgments or at least for modifying them so that they will fit well with our other beliefs or the beliefs of others that we also, after critical examination, come to make our own. In doing this, our initial considered judgments, if they survive such winnowing, will (when this is completed or is reasonably on the way to completion) no longer be ethnocentric.[15] In this way we can filter out, or at least modify, some of our considered judgments so that they will fit, or fit better, with our other beliefs and in that way overcome the ethnocentrism that may have been there at the beginning. We can in this way filter out our ethnocentric and even (if we can stick with that method) our irrational, but still tenacious, judgments. However, very many of our considered judgments will not have these arbitrary features at all and will well stand the test of coherence.

The Christian Scientist, of course, will have his considered judgments, too, and some of them will not square with ours. But some do, so we are not caught in different incommensurable frameworks with both of us being imprisoned in our own conceptual scheme. Of course, his considered judgments will have an initial credibility for him. That comes close to being a tautology. But he will have a very hard time indeed in getting certain of them into wide reflective equilibrium. Two firmly embedded considered judgments for him are that matter does not exist and that evil is an illusion. But translating into the concrete, he must then say, if he is to be consistent, that there are no rocks or trees and that there is nothing evil about Belsen, rapes in Bosnia, massacres in Rwanda, children dying while being wracked by the pain of cancer, animals in stockyards being kept under intolerable conditions, and the like. He has to say, and bring himself to believe, that all these things are illusions. But that flies in the face of what both he and we know. Similarly, if he stubs his bare toe on a big rock and cries out in pain, his very behavior shows that he knows that at least one rock exists and thus that matter exists and that stubbing his toe against it hurt him and thus that pain is not an illusion. (He grants that if pain exists that that is an evil. But it is part of his belief system to deny that pain is real.) He, like Berkeley, can to some small extent protect himself by creating epicycles. By the coherentist criteria of wide reflective equilibrium, and by appealing to the full range of his considered judgments (criteria that, *ex hypothesis,* he was supposedly using), his account becomes very implausible indeed. Implausible, someone might say, but still *possibly* true. But that does not dispute what the naturalist accepts, namely that fallibilism is where it's at. We neither get, nor can get, absolute certainty and must rest, and easily can rest, content, with a species of plausible reasoning.[16] To ask for more—to go on the traditional philosophical quest for certainty—is to ask for the impossible.

V

There is an objection to such a naturalistic and pragmatic method that is very natural to make. I, like the classical pragmatists, advocate the scientific method—the experimental method for fixing belief—but, in arguing for it, which itself is a characteristic bit of philosophy, as, for example, in the way I have argued in this chapter, I do not use anything even remotely like the experimental method. I simply reason—use what Peirce called and criticized as the *a priori* method, the method of reason: the in reality subjective feeling an individual has that something is "agreeable to reason." The rhetoric, in what Descartes called an appeal to the natural light of reason, is of something objective—the point of view of reason (whatever that is)—but the reality is a subjective matter of feeling. In using this *a priori* method for fixing belief, if

you look at what philosophers actually do, you will see that they simply reflect carefully and, seeking to remain consistent and plausible, try, in addition,
rather systematically and carefully, to reflect on the matter at hand. After such
reflection, they decide or intuit, by "the natural light of reason," what to
think. My method, if that is what it is to be called, in doing philosophy, like
everyone else's, is actually not experimental, but reflective and intuitive, my
proclamations to the contrary notwithstanding.

"Philosophical method," as Ernst Tugendhat puts it, "is reflective" and it
has to do, in being reflective, "with a clarification of concepts."[17] Philosophers, including the pragmatists themselves, characteristically do not state hypotheses, elaborate them, draw consequences from them, and seek empirically
and experimentally to test them. Pragmatists argue that this is what goes on
in science and is something close to what goes on in some departments of
everyday life as well when people are reasoning effectively. Moreover, as
John Dewey argued, this method should be extended to the domain of morals
and politics where, unfortunately, it is not being presently utilized.[18] But this,
the criticism continues, is not what I do in this chapter, or what I do elsewhere
when I do philosophy; moreover, and more importantly, it is not what pragmatists characteristically do or what philosophers generally do when they *philosophize*. Instead, if they are any good at what they are doing, philosophers
engage in careful, somewhat systematized reflection on fundamental conceptual matters. Most typically they concern themselves with the clarification
of our fundamental concepts through dialectical reflection (careful discursive
reasoning). It is a mistake, or at least very misleading, to characterize such reflective activity as using the scientific method.

I think we need a tolerably complicated yes and no here. On the yes side,
it must straight off be admitted that philosophical inquiry or deliberation is
largely, and sometimes exclusively, reflective. Philosophers have no need for,
and indeed cannot use, laboratory equipment or laboratories. But then neither
did Einstein or Keynes. Much of the theoretical side of many sciences (most
particularly physics and economics) is reflective, centrally a matter of the conceptual clarification, elaboration, and inferential extension of a network of
concepts and, as well, the articulation of new concepts designed for distinctive purposes. But, all that notwithstanding, the firm establishment of relativity theory, as any scientific theory, required experimental corroboration.
Still, a good bit of science and scientific method is reflective and a matter of
conceptual elucidation and clarification and systematic perspicuous representation. But it also standardly has an experimental side and very crucially.
Without that, there is no distinguishing it from what is just disciplined speculation. By contrast, the claim goes, it is certainly the case that very little, if
any, philosophy is experimental in any straightforward sense. To say, with any
plausibility, that philosophy utilizes the experimental method, "experimental

method" needs to be identified with scientific method where the latter is taken in a very broad sense which includes, still as being scientific, conceptual elucidation and analysis *sans* experimental or otherwise empirical corroboration. What the classical pragmatists should be taken as saying, and part of what I want to say myself, is that the best way to fix belief over questions of fact, physical and social, is through the use of the experimental method. But pragmatists also claim more, namely that philosophy itself should use the scientific method, and that, for the above stated reasons, is problematic.

However, on the no side to the above familiar criticism of pragmatism, it is important to keep firmly in mind the way I have argued in my first chapter for a transformation of philosophy, as did Dewey before me.[19] So transformed philosophy is no longer *just* a clarification and perspicuous representation of concepts or the "understanding of reflection."[20] It is rather the attempt at the resolution of the problems of human beings, the attempt to articulate and justify a conception of what would be a just social order at least in certain social circumstances, what a good life for human beings would be, whether the best understanding of the world we can get should include a belief in God. More generally, such a transformed philosophy should attempt to see how, in the various departments of our lives, things hang together, yielding a plausible conception of who we are, were, and who we might become. This would involve coming to have a good understanding of our social practices and the workings of our institutions, including the tensions and defects in our social practices and institutions, and including among these defects whatever (if any) incoherencies they might contain. This involves much more than being reflective about our concepts and engaging in a clarification and perspicuous representation of them. Here philosophy is closely linked with the social sciences and has an experimental side, e.g., to know what a just society would be it is necessary, but not sufficient, to know what an efficient society would be like, to know that it is necessary to understand the various ways a society could utilize its productive wealth, and to know that requires, among other things, experimentation.

It is also the case that in fleshing out my conception of scientific method, I developed an account of wide reflective equilibrium. This is, as its name attests, a reflective method, but as a coherentist method it attempts to forge a maximally coherent account of how things hang together. What I have in mind is an account of how the various things that we know, observe, infer from what we observe, and hypothesize and, as well, an account of the things that are a matter of our firmest reflective convictions all hang together. We want here, in forging our outlook on life, to gain the most coherent overall conception that we can get. This, among other things, requires attention to the empirical facts, to logic (seeing what fits together and what does not), and hypothesis construction, i.e., seeing what best explains the facts, enabling us best to predict and retrodict. But it also will require the stating of "clarificatory hypotheses" enabling us best, among the alternative such hypotheses, to understand the meaning (uses) of the network of our words (words expressive of our concepts) and, as well, to state "normative hypotheses" such as Rawls's two principles of justice or the principle of utility or a perfectionist principle. They are principles which both explain our considered convictions and aid us in deciding between our considered convictions when they conflict and also aid us in the coming to form convictions in situations which are genuinely new, where we have no antecedent considered convictions over the matter at hand or where they only weakly impinge on our decisions about what to do in such circumstances. In all these ways, philosophy so practiced is very much a critical social science or at least very like one. It goes beyond, while still crucially utilizing, conceptual clarification and has, as its method, not just 'a method of reflection' but something that, without exaggeration, should be called scientific method.

Still, for that part—that very central part of philosophy—that is conceptual clarification, how is its method to be understood? It has been traditionally claimed that it seeks to gain clear and distinct ideas. In a tradition stemming from Plato, classically expressed by Descartes, and reexpressed paradigmatically by Husserl, clear ideas are said to be those we gain directly through intuition. This is most forcefully claimed for our most fundamental concepts (e.g., truth, cause, existence, identity, goodness). These concepts, like all concepts, are said, on such an account, to be *essences* that must be inwardly perceived or grasped. But, as is now widely recognized, such notions are replete with very fundamental difficulties. As Ernst Tugendhat well put it, first, "no one has succeeded in giving this metaphor of intellectual intuition a concrete sense and showing how such an inward perception supposedly occurs."[21] Moreover, and secondly, "even if there were something like it, it could not be mediated intersubjectively. For philosophy as a communicative undertaking, therefore, the intuitive method would be altogether worthless."[22] This would plainly be so, if what, as Peirce puts it, is "agreeable to reason" "does not mean that which agrees with experience, but that which we find ourselves inclined to believe."[23] What so-called rational intuition yields, after reflection, as both Peirce and Russell argue, is in reality not an intellectual operation, but something very much like an expression of taste. Thinking, or perhaps better feeling, makes things so; put otherwise, what an individual's reflection tells him is "agreeable to reason" is in reality what he, after reflection, is inclined toward or what he wants or is inclined to believe. There is no intersubjective or public test for what is "agreeable to reason," no test against the facts in the case, as discovered by intersubjective observation or experiential or experimental reasoning or demonstration of what is consistent with what. With such an "intuitive method" there is, as again Peirce stressed, no distinguishing an idea merely *seeming* to be clear from its *really being* so.

Descartes and Leibniz and all rationalists utilizing an *a priori* method stressed that our ideas, to be adequate, not only must be clear, but they must be distinct as well. Perhaps they would only really be clear if they could also be shown to be distinct and we could show them to be distinct only by giving them an *abstract definition*. In that way, perhaps, the *a priori* method would go beyond an appeal to intuition. But this is illusory, for, as Peirce argued forcefully, simply relying on an abstract definition, without the addition of an experiential translation into the concrete in an operational definition or specification, would give us little understanding of what we are talking about or what we are referring to. Moreover, to know whether an abstract definition is correct—one that would, that is, give us a "real definition" and not a stipulative or purely conventional one—would require us to be able to, à la Husserl, inwardly grasp essences which, on such a conception, is what concepts really are.[24] That is, we must "inwardly perceive" what is common to and distinctive of everything that is referred to by the term expressive of the concept in question. But this assumes (1) that all meaningful terms have extensions, (2) that there is always something common to and distinctive of the objects they refer to, and (3) that individuals can inwardly grasp essences (grasp the intension or connotation of terms). These very claims are at best false; or, at least, put more cautiously, and alternatively, we have been given no good reason to believe they are so. Suppose we define *human being* as "rational animal" rather than "laughing animal." To know whether this definition is true— that it yields a "real definition"—we must go beyond just giving abstract characterizations and, translating into the concrete, going experiential and operational, we must specify concretely what we mean by "rational animal."

I will worry this out a bit more. Peirce pointed out that Leibniz, in trying to go around the difficulty—"that we may seem to ourselves to have clear apprehensions of ideas which are in truth hazy"—adopted, following Descartes, "the distinction of *clear* and *distinct* notions."[25] But Leibniz described a distinct notion "as the clear apprehension of everything contained in the definition."[26] It is fair enough, for a start, Peirce continues, to make "familiarity with a notion the first step toward clearness of apprehension, and the defining of it a second."[27] But, in the struggle to make our ideas clear, we cannot rest here with definition relying so exclusively on clear apprehension—again the illusive notion of inwardly grasping essences—and thus remaining firmly in the intuitive trap.[28] It does not take us, in Peirce's phrase, to "any higher perspicuity of thought" by which we could make our ideas clear and firmly fix belief. To gain such clarity, we need to go experimental, for without doing that we will not gain the necessary intersubjectivity to properly anchor our thoughts in the world. To gain what Peirce calls "the third grade of clearness of apprehension," we should proceed as follows: "Consider what effects that might conceivably have practical bearings, we conceive the object of our conception to have. Then, our conception of these effects is the whole of our conception of the object."[29]

This third degree of clearness can be illustrated by using one of Peirce's simplest examples. Consider our ascertaining what we mean by calling a thing *hard*.[30] "Evidently," Peirce remarks, in saying that something is hard we mean "that it will not be scratched by many other substances."[31] We see that a diamond is hard in the way sandstone is not, by seeing that diamonds will not be scratched by many other substances, while sandstone will, including, of course, being scratched by diamonds. We, in various contexts and for various substances, can go through similar tests: pudding is cut by a knife but few things (certainly not pudding) will scratch a knife, so we say the pudding is softer than the knife. In comparison with the pudding, the knife is hard. Similarly, we may develop a notion of one thing being hard or soft relative to another thing (i.e., the one thing being harder than the other) by, for example, noting—experimentally noting—that, while a knife cuts through pudding, the knife is in turn scratched by a diamond, so while the knife is hard relative to the pudding, it is not hard relative to the diamond, but is still hard relative to sandstone, since the knife scratches sandstone when scraped against it, but the sandstone cannot scratch the knife. We look to the experiential effects (intersubjectively experiential effects) to clarify our understanding of the meaning of *hard*. An abstract definition *by itself* will teach us very little. Here, in proceeding as I have above, we have something that is both reflective and experimental, but the experimental side is crucial, for otherwise we are struck with the empty notion of an apprehension of essences or just a telling ourselves, without any kind of check on the truth or warrantability of what we are saying, that something is "agreeable to reason." Where we do that, we are claiming that we have immediate knowledge of something. We are back to Plato, Descartes, and Husserl. And that is to go back into the cave.

Similar, but not identical, things should be said for logical notions and moral ones. We understand *if* and *then* by coming to understand the logical operations they enter into. And to gain such an understanding in any perspicuous way, we have to translate into the concrete by doing some logic and showing how these ideas operate in the appropriate logical practices as well as in our ordinary speech and writing. Similarly, in understanding what we mean by fair and by decent, we need much more than abstract definitions; what we must see is how these terms fit with certain considered judgments and to understand, as well, how they work in various of our social practices. Again, even in the very clarification and elucidation of ideas, and not just for scientific and empirical ideas, we go experimental: we utilize scientific method. Yes, philosophy is a reflective activity, but we should not set "being reflective" in opposition to "being experimental."

NOTES

1. Annette Baier, *Postures of the Mind: Essays on Mind and Morals* (Minneapolis: University of Minnesota Press, 1985); Lorraine Code, "Second Persons," in *Science, Morality and Feminist Theory,* ed. Marsha Hanen and Kai Nielsen (Guelph, Ontario: Canadian Association for Publishing in Philosophy, 1987), 357–82; and Kai Nielsen, "Equality of Condition and Self-Ownership," in *Ethics and Basic Rights,* ed. Guy Lafrance (Ottawa, Ontario: University of Ottawa, Press, 1989), 81–99.

2. John Rawls, *Political Liberalism* (New York: Columbia University Press, 1993), 96–97. See also John Rawls, "Reply to Habermas," *Journal of Philosophy* 92, no. 3 (March 1995): 141–42.

3. Kai Nielsen, "Jolting the Career of Reason: Absolute Idealism and Other Rationalisms Reconsidered," *Journal of Speculative Philosophy* 7, no. 2 (1994): 113–40.

4. Wilfrid Sellars, *Science, Perception and Reality* (London: Routledge and Kegan Paul, 1967), 160.

5. Brand Blanshard, "The Philosophic Enterprise," in *The Owl of Minerva: Philosophers on Philosophy,* ed. Charles J. Bontempo and S. Jack Odell (New York: McGraw Hill, 1975), 163–77; and my "Jolting the Career of Reason."

6. Stuart Hampshire, "Identification and Existence," in *Contemporary British Philosophy,* ed. H. D. Lewis (London: Allen and Unwin, 1956), 191–200; Stuart Hampshire, *Thought and Action* (London: Chatto and Windus Ltd., 1959); P. F. Strawson, "Analysis, Science and Metaphysics," in *The Linguistic Turn,* ed. Richard Rorty (Chicago: University of Chicago Press, 1967), 312–30; P. F. Strawson, *Individuals: An Essay in Descriptive Metaphysics* (London: Methuen and Co., 1959); and P. F. Strawson, *Analysis and Metaphysics* (Oxford, England: Oxford University Press, 1992).

7. Donald Davidson, *Inquiries into Truth and Interpretation* (Oxford, England: Clarendon Press, 1984), 183–94; and his "The Myth of the Subjective," in *Relativism: Interpretation and Confrontation,* ed. Michael Krausz (Notre Dame, Ind.: University of Notre Dame Press, 1989), 159–72; Kai Nielsen, *After the Demise of the Tradition* (Boulder, Colo.: Westview Press, 1991), 57–90; and Stan Stein, "Wittgenstein, Davidson and the Myth of Incommensurability," in *Méta-Philosophie: Reconstructing Philosophy?* ed. Jocelyne Couture and Kai Nielsen (Calgary, Alberta: University of Calgary Press, 1993), 181–221.

8. Kai Nielsen, *Why Be Moral?* (Amherst, N.Y.: Prometheus Books, 1989), 13–38.

9. Here the social sciences and literature are of much greater value than philosophy.

10. John Rawls, *A Theory of Justice* (Cambridge, Mass.: Harvard University Press, 1971), 19–21, 48–51, 577–87; John Rawls, "The Independence of Moral Theory," *Proceedings and Addresses of the American Philosophical Association* 47 (1974/75): 7–10; John Rawls, *Political Liberalism* (New York: Columbia University Press, 1993), 8, 28, 45, 72, 96–97; Norman Daniels, "Reflective Equilibrium and Theory Acceptance in Ethics," *Journal of Philosophy* 76 (1979); Norman Daniels, "Some Methods in Ethics and Linguistics," *Philosophical Studies* 37 (1980); Norman Daniels, "Reflective Equilibrium and Archimedian Points," *Canadian Journal of Philosophy* 10 (March 1980); Norman Daniels, "Two Approaches to Theory Acceptance in Ethics," in *Morality, Reason and Truth,* ed. David Copp and David Zimmerman (Totowa, N.J.: Rowman and Allanheld, 1985), 120–40; Richard Rorty, *Objectivity, Relativism and Truth* (Cambridge, England: Cambridge University Press, 1991), 175–96; Kai Nielsen, *After the Demise of the Tradition,* 195–246; Kai Nielsen, "Philosophy Within the Limits of Wide Reflective Equilibrium Alone," *Iyyun* 43 (January 1994): 3–41; and Kai Nielsen, "Methods of Ethics: Wide

Reflective Equilibrium and a Kind of Consequentialism," *Windsor Yearbook of Access to Justice* 13 (1993): 200–16.

11. Nelson Goodman, *Fact, Fiction and Forecast* (Cambridge, Mass.: Harvard University Press, 1955), 65–68; Hilary Putnam, *Renewing Philosophy* (Cambridge, Mass.: Harvard University Press, 1992), 130.

12. Andrew Lugg has remarked that he is not so enamored as I am and as Rorty is with Sellars's conception of philosophy as an attempt to see how things hang together. When philosophers try to do things like that, Lugg remarks, they end up making things even worse by creating more fog, leading us into all sorts of conceptual confusion and, indeed, often into ideological confusion as well. (Ideological confusions are often conceptual confusions, but then they are conceptual confusions with certain determinate effects on the class interests of people.) The sole path, Lugg has it, should be the *critical path* and in that endeavor what we primarily need is a critique of ideology. Moreover, even if we could get a Sellarsian overview, what, he asks, good would it do? All the real problems of life would remain. Half of me wants to go along with Lugg here. I think, and have frequently so argued, that critique of ideology is a crucial thing that philosophers should engage in and that philosophical construction tends to be love's labor lost. Still, if we are to show that a certain belief, practice, or way of looking at things is ideological, we will need ourselves to have some conceptions which get some of the relevant things roughly right. If everything is ideological, then nothing is. If we can gain a little better conception of how certain relevant things hang together, then we will be in a somewhat better position to critique ideology and to escape (partially escape) being caught in ideological entanglements ourselves. And that would be a very considerable good indeed. The real problems—the socially demanding problems—would still remain, but to see clearly what to do, or at least have a reasonable idea of what to do, to resolve them is something that we, as struggling agents in the world, should very much want. Marx famously, and rightly, said that "the philosophers have only *interpreted* the world, in various ways; the point, however, is to *change* it." But he would never have thought for a moment that we could sensibly and desirably change it without understanding it, including in that understanding a coming to some understanding of the mechanisms that turn the world, or at least one's part of the world, and, as well, a coming to understand something of how best we can use these mechanisms in the cause of human emancipation. This is what Marx's *Capital* is about. For something of the import of the critical way vis-à-vis philosophy, see my "Anti-Philosophy philosophy: Some Programmatic Remarks," *Diàlogos* 64 (1994): 149–58. On ideology, see my "The Concept of Ideology: Some Marxist and Non-Marxist Conceptualizations," *Rethinking Marxism* 2, no. 4 (Winter 1989): 145–73.

13. This could be challenged. A determined coherentist could respond that if the coherent system were inclusive enough we could not have a coherent system with beliefs which are known to be false. The Christian Scientist's beliefs are not placed in a wide enough pattern; they do not, by a long shot, take into consideration everything that we know. If they did, then we would not get a system with beliefs which were coherent, *but still known to be false.* The most basic *tests* for truth or for warrantability always remain that of consistency and coherence.

14. It is here, and more generally concerning my arguments against the coherence of ubiquitous doubting, that the import of the work of Peirce, Wittgenstein, and Davidson, as different as their work is in certain respects, comes together.

15. See Rajeev Bhargava on how social science, while remaining contextual, can be critical social science and overcome ethnocentrism. Rajeev Bhargava, *Individualism in Social Science* (Oxford, England: Clarendon Press, 1992), 233–49.

16. J. J. C. Smart, "Philosophy and Scientific Plausibility," in *Mind, Matter and Method: Essays in Philosophy and Science in Honor of Herbert Feigl,* ed. Paul Feyerabend and Grover Maxwell (Minneapolis: University of Minnesota Press, 1966), 377–90.

17. Ernest Tugendhat, "Reflections on Philosophical Method from an Analytical Point of View," in *Philosophical Interventions in the Unfinished Project of Enlightenment* (Cambridge, Mass.: MIT Press, 1992), 113–24.

18. John Dewey, "Logical Conditions of a Scientific Treatment of Morality," in his *Problems of Men* (New York: Philosophical Library, 1946), 211–49.

19. John Dewey, *Problems of Men,* 8–20; and John Dewey, *Reconstruction in Philosophy,* enlarged edition (Boston: Beacon Press, 1957), original edition, 1920.

20. Tugenhadt, "Reflections on Philosophical Method," 116.

21. Ibid., 117.

22. Ibid.

23. Charles Sanders Peirce, *Collected Papers,* vol. 5 (Cambridge, Mass.: Harvard University Press, 1934), 238–39. When Peirce (and Dewey as well) speak of experience, they do not speak of it after the fashion of British empiricism, but as something which in its very nature is intersubjective and public.

24. Richard Robinson, *Definition* (Oxford, England: Oxford University Press, 1954).

25. Peirce, *Collected Papers,* vol. 5, 250.

26. Ibid., 251.

27. Ibid.

28. Ibid.

29. Ibid. I think Peirce overstates his point when he says it is the *whole* of our conception of the object. To make his essential pragmatic and operational point, he need not make such a strong claim.

30. Ibid., 259.

31. Ibid.

Chapter Three

How Reasonable Is Religious Belief?: Wide Reflective Equilibrium and Religion

I

How does religious belief fare when we use as our justificatory method the method of wide reflective equilibrium? More specifically, and more to my immediate purposes, how does belief in supernatural entities fare if we utilize such a method of fixing belief? The sister religions Judaism, Christianity, and Islam share a belief in a transcendent supernatural God who is said by the adherents to these religions to be the Father of us all and they share as well a belief in an immortality in which, after our "bodily death," we will live again in heaven, if we have lived a certain kind of life, under the loving providential care of our heavenly Father and creator.[1] How does this "standard theism," as Alvin Plantinga calls it, fare if we apply reflectively and intelligently the method of wide reflective equilibrium?[2] Given what we know and what we reasonably can believe, would our deepest considered convictions have among their number, and indeed in a very central place, the religious beliefs of standard theism? Would we have those religious beliefs where we resolutely seek to maximize the coherence of the full range of our beliefs? Would they be beliefs which we could get into wide reflective equilibrium and in this way show that they are justified?

In one way, a not unimportant way, this is plainly impossible. To see that that is so we have to add something to our characterization of wide reflective equilibrium that we have not yet emphasized. We spoke of getting our considered judgments into wide reflective equilibrium. Who is the "our" and the "we" here? We are clearly appealing to some kind of consensus. We want to say that there is a rational or reasonable consensus when we get our considered judgments into wide reflective equilibrium. That, I am claiming, is the highest grade consensus that we can get. But, again, let me ask, who are the "we" and "our" here? It will, inescapably, be people of our time and place. That is—running the risk of ethnocentrism or provincialism—at least the people in Western cultures and people of other cultures who have been well educated in the manner in which people are well educated in Western cultures. (I do not suggest for a moment that all or even most people in Western cultures are so educated.) In short, I have in mind people whom Hume, using the term both in certain respects more widely and in others more narrowly than we would today, called "men of letters." That is to say, the "we" refers to what in our time would be people who are lucky enough to in one way or another get a relatively good education and, in particular, besides general culture, including a good dipping in literature, have, from that general culture, come to learn something of science and philosophy. In discussing religion, if we ever can get the considered judgments of such people into wide reflective equilibrium, then we would have attained the desideratum of wide reflective equilibrium in the domain that I am seeking in discussing religion. And we would, if we attained that, have thereby shown, for whatever came to be believed there concerning religion, that these beliefs were justified in societies such as ours and for the present.

This sounds both elitist and ethnocentric, but it is not. I am not, for a moment, suggesting that there is anything which is at all intrinsically superior about those persons, that they are better or superior persons or anything of the sort. Indeed, in certain respects completely untutored people may have better moral and political insight than Hume's men of letters. We certainly have to face that possibility in gaining the relevant wide reflective equilibrium. We also have to allow for class, race, and gender bias. We must get firmly into the "our" women, people of color, proletarians, and lumpen-proletarians. Some of this is very difficult to attain for they must also have what Freud called a sober education. Because of their oppression and their various disadvantaged positions in society, they are not likely to have had such an education, though their tough education in life, as Berthold Brecht liked to stress, gives them some offsetting advantages. (That, of course, is small comfort for the lives they have had to live.)

To overcome various pernicious forms of ethnocentrism and to gain the wide reflective equilibrium desired, such variously disadvantaged people should cease to be disadvantaged and stand on an equal educational footing with people educated in a scientific, philosophical, and humanistic tradition of letters. However, Gilbert Ryle (if indeed he really ever said it) is mistaken, and ethnocentrically so, to have quipped that the only light that comes from the East is the sun. There are long traditions of Indian and Chinese philosophy and literature, and people with a sophisticated and subtle understanding of them. Ideally speaking, they need to be a part of that consensus as well and with an equal standing (the consensus of a fully wide reflective equilibrium). Similar things need to be said of many other cultures—the Arabs of North Africa, for example. The hope is that someday the "our" can be so widened. Still, it is true that science and philosophy, as an argument-based activity, is pretty much, though not entirely, a Western invention and a Western or Western-influenced practice.[3]

Still, all that notwithstanding, a central difficulty for us is to overcome the cultural bias of my initial appeal. I spoke of a consensus of those with a good Western education or its equivalent. Such a consensus is surely likely to be in some respects badly skewed. This makes things very difficult indeed and makes our operation inevitably both to some extent *parti pris* and, as well, a bootstrapping operation. For practical purposes, and without any cultural arrogance at all, we have to start by trying to gain a consensus—a wide reflective equilibrium for our time concerning religion—principally in our Western world among soberly educated men of letters in Hume's sense of the term:[4] that is to say, among humanistically educated people with such a broad understanding of science, philosophy, and literature. People with the good luck to have such an education are in a better position than most others to understand the various considerations that need to be appealed to in gaining something approaching wide reflective equilibrium. Still, in seeking to forge such a wide reflective equilibrium, it is vital to take careful note of the considered judgments, most particularly the rather specific considered judgments, of those who have not been so fortunate. They may reflect very great insight indeed. *The "we," whose considered judgments are taken into account and the "we" who judge of the reflective equilibrium will not always be the same. Indeed, they will typically not be the same.* It is critical intellectuals, as specified above, who principally do the forging of a reflective equilibrium, but, for the considered moral convictions initially appealed to in starting out on that forging, their considered moral convictions (among the moral beliefs culled) have no pride of place. It is vital that this distinction and this claim be firmly kept in mind.

Let us now return to my claim that in a certain sense in our world, as distinct from the medieval world or even Locke's and Hume's world, there is not much of a chance of getting religious beliefs into such a wide reflective equilibrium. This is so, for the very simple sociological reason that we have (perhaps Islamic societies aside) a deeply secularized culture among the educated elites in our societies. The disenchantment of the world is pervasive. Still, it by no means has completely won the day. There is also a sizeable minority among our elites, and deeply entrenched institutionally, that is composed of various species of religious believers. Among philosophers, for example, they include such different philosophers as Alasdair MacIntyre, Norman Malcolm, Bas Van Fraassen, Saul Kripke, and Charles Taylor. Indeed, there has emerged in the last little while in a very secularized philosophical culture something called the Society for Christian Philosophers. Given these entrenched differences, there is little chance, as things stand, of getting the necessary consensus. There is, that is, little chance that we will be able to *so* justify religious beliefs, or for that matter, *so* justify antireligious beliefs or an utterly secular attitude toward the world. There is perhaps not even any very good reason to believe, as things are likely to go in the future, that chances of a consensus will significantly increase, though this, from a secularizing perspective, may be too pessimistic a picture. Our world is very different from Hume's world or Feuerbach's or even, still later, Peirce's. Weberian disenchantment of the world seems at least to roll relentlessly on. Yet perhaps this last remark is overstated? Perhaps it is more Enlightenment wishful thinking than an accurate description of social reality and of social trends? Guesses about what the future will bring may be better as a kind of Rorschach test for the guesser than as sober predictions of what our future will be like. The secularizing of intellectuals may not be so firm and irreversible as I would like to think it is. Rudolf Carnap and Hans Reichenbach were, while remaining rather distant from such concerns, atheistic and through and through secularizers. Moving along a generation, by the time we get to Hilary Putnam and Stanley Cavell, we get very thoughtful and very deep philosophers entangled in complex and, indeed, in rather obscure ways, with religion. With them, in this respect, the spirit of Wittgenstein (intertwined with that of Kierkegaard) has triumphed and not that of Bertrand Russell and George Elliot.

However, and be that as it may, in so appealing to wide reflective equilibrium is there something patently unfair to religious believers? I do not believe so. Suppose a religious believer has read Quine, Goodman, Putnam, Rawls, and Daniels and has become convinced that wide reflective equilibrium is the proper method of justification for beliefs of any kind. Does that, by itself, push him in the direction of secularism? Does that stand in the way of his reasonably attempting to justify his religious beliefs by such a method? Not at all.

Let me show why I say this by first bringing out a parallel between the way that Hume may be plausibly understood as having stood toward his culture and reasoned in that culture with the ways contemporary religious intellectuals stand in our intellectual culture now and how they could legitimately proceed to reason in it. Hume, a powerful, though still a subtle and prudent secularizer, while seeing clearly that there was no such consensus cutting in a secular direction during his time, or even much of a prospect of one coming into being, utilized, what in effect, was a method very much like the method of wide reflective equilibrium to very cautiously and prudently provide reasons for his society to consider the possibility of a *new* wide reflective equilibrium that jettisoned some of the old considered judgments—considered judgments which were, pervasively for his time, deeply embedded beliefs. We were, as he saw it, to jettison them because they could not be gotten into a position which was, for the time, a position of maximum coherence with other, even more extensive and essential, equally deeply embedded beliefs. To gain the fullest coherence possible, these religious beliefs should, he thought, be rejected and a new wide reflective equilibrium established with a new consensus.

To show that it was so justified, Hume's argument would actually have to achieve that pattern of coherence. To achieve that would be to provide an account of things which yielded a more extensive coherence, than the dominant one of his time, of the considered judgments of his time and place, as well as having in this package the most reliable factual account of things that was reasonably available at that time, including the best scientific and philosophical accounts similarly so available and similarly so judged. Hume's account to be so justified would actually have had to achieve that and, further, it would have had to gain a consensus that it had achieved that among his relevant peers. There was, as he clearly recognized, little likelihood of his succeeding in this latter endeavor. And Hume's account to be *so* justified would actually have had to achieve that. It would have had, that is, to gain a consensus among his relevant peers that it in fact had achieved that. But to accept that is not to rule out the reasonability of Hume arguing that it is in this secularizing way that we could achieve the widest reflective equilibrium possible, given *the full range* of considered judgments of his peers. (Reflective equilibrium *pace* R. M. Hare is not an appeal to received opinion.) Hume would have had to argue that in spite of their contrary expectations their religious beliefs were actually anomalous, in conflict with many other deeply embedded considered judgments of theirs, such that their beliefs could not be made to fit together consistently or at least be made to be the more maximally coherent pattern of beliefs. This being so (if it in fact is so), wide reflective equilibrium could be best approximated only by jettisoning the religious beliefs.

Hume might be right or he might be wrong about this, but the claim for his being either would have to rely on at least three things, namely (1) who actually had the more coherent pattern, (2) a consensus about that, and (3) a reflective consensus among his peers concerning the soundness of the reasoning I am attributing, somewhat high-handedly, to Hume. He might be mistaken in thinking that there would, under such ideal circumstances, be a consensus, and he might, as well, be mistaken in believing that there was such pattern of coherence. But at any moment in asking if such claims to coherence were justified, we would have to rely on such appeal to consensus. Not to do so is pure arrogant counterassertion.

What I am saying, to come to my parallel, is that in our time a religious intellectual could legitimately use exactly the same pattern of reasoning as I attributed to Hume. Suppose Christian philosophers such as Alasdair MacIntyre, Alvin Plantinga, or Richard Swinburne (undergoing a methodological but not a religious conversion) became convinced that the right way of fixing belief was by the method of wide reflective equilibrium with its appeal to considered judgments. Being so convinced, they came to utilize that method of reasoning in philosophical argumentation. They could, I shall now argue, legitimately argue, *methodologically speaking* just as Hume did, though from a very different cultural and historical context. Realizing full well that among their peers (other intellectuals in their and similar societies) the secularization of thought was so entrenched and pervasive that there was no consensus concerning religious belief, or even any present likelihood of one coming into being, they still could legitimately argue, in a manner *methodologically* parallel to that of Hume, that, given the other things that we know or at least reasonably believe (things that would generally be agreed upon in the society), the dropping of naturalistic beliefs and assumptions and replacing them with certain religious ones would result in a more coherent cluster of beliefs than the ones we have with our naturalistic worldview. That, they could argue, by taking a religious turn, and using the method of wide reflective equilibrium, we would, by doing so, if we utilize it intelligently, attain something closer to the maximum congruence of considered judgments attainable in our situation than if we stick with our old naturalistic ways. The secularizing of thought has by now, they agree, the very great pervasiveness that Max Weber attributed to it, but, such a defender of religion could counterargue, the secularizers are mistaken in thinking that in that way lays the greater coherence of belief and practice.

Such a religious believer, or his defender, in an attempt to show that this is so, throws out, for consideration, an alternative candidate for maximum coherence of considered judgments in wide reflective equilibrium. He hypothesizes that by so viewing things religiously we will get a new and more adequate wide reflective equilibrium than the one attained by viewing things purely secularly. That view, he predicts, will yield more coherence (including, of course, a greater coherence of our considered judgments) than a resolutely secular view of the world. This, as far as I can see, is a legitimate *methodological* move for the believer or his defender. It is, that is, as legitimate for a religious believer as the parallel move is for Hume. *They both can, and I believe they should, use exactly the same method of reasoning.* It is the method of appealing to considered judgments in wide reflective equilibrium that I have recommended for the naturalist. (I would include Hume among the naturalists.[5]) We cannot legitimately rule out *on methodological grounds alone* that in our time religious beliefs can be gotten into a wide reflective equilibrium. The argument, rather, must be substantive; it must consider the various actual beliefs themselves and their fit and consider, as well, which account actually yields the greater coherence and thus is the best candidate for actually articulating a wide reflective equilibrium such that if our beliefs were so ordered they would be in, or at least approximate being in, wide reflective equilibrium.

II

I want now to consider this *substantive* issue. I want to consider whether, standing where we are now in history and culture, we can plausibly get belief in God—standard Jewish, Christian, and Islamic belief, or at least the beliefs of one of these religions—into wide reflective equilibrium. It is vital to keep firmly in mind that the "us," "we," "our" are as characterized in the previous section. They are intellectuals (taken as a collective body) with a reasonable understanding of science, philosophy, and literature.[6] And the religious belief system in question is what we have noted that Plantinga has called "standard theism." As robust and unyielding a Calvinist philosopher as Alvin Plantinga and as equally robust and unyielding an atheist humanist as Antony Flew agree that this is the conception of religion that should be at the center of our attention.[7] If—or so I would argue—we were in a Confucian, Buddhist, or Hindu culture, that would not be so. I can see no reason why, generally speaking, any of the sister religions, committed, in their most orthodox conceptualizations, to standard theism, should have pride of place among the religions of the world. But we are in a particular context, namely a context in which, for the vast majority of us, at best one of these sister religions is a live option for a religious orientation for us. So for these perfectly contingent historical and cultural reasons, *but for no others,* we should center our attention on standard theism.

Both Flew and Plantinga are aware, of course, that not a few religious believers, particularly those who are also intellectuals, depart, sometimes rather extensively, from standard theism. And Flew, in effect following Hume here, well reminds us that we should not just start by taking the "several characteristics," taken to be the defining characteristics of the God of standard theism, as something we already know to characterize a single, unitary, existent Being, as such theists just generally assume, and hence also assume that what "might be good evidence for the existence of something with some of these defining characteristics must be equally good evidence for the existence of a Being having them all."[8] He goes on to remark, perceptively, I think, that "the various characteristics customarily attributed to the Christian God do not all mutually entail one another, and some are such as no one would *a priori* expect to be attributes of a Being characterized by others."[9] Still, it is this conception of God that has, whether in Judaism, Christianity, or Islam, been the object of faith for vast numbers of believers who are really deeply committed Jews, Christians, or Muslims as well as for many who conventionally, and often complacently, go along with whatever religion, with its constitutive set of beliefs, that they just happen to have been socialized into.

We need to characterize standard theism somewhat more fully to see if these religions with such a belief structure, including most deeply, a belief in the God of Abraham, Isaac, and Jacob—a concept God common to the three sisters of religion—can be seen to be in wide reflective equilibrium or to be somehow gotten into wide reflective equilibrium. Standard theism has a conception of God as "an immaterial person who is all-knowing, all-powerful, perfectly good, the creator and sustainer of the world."[10] Or, as in the first article of the Thirty-Nine articles of Religion—the articles of faith of the Anglican church—there occurs the proclamation of the "one living true God, everlasting, without body, parts, or passions, infinite in power, wisdom, and goodness, the Maker and Preserver of all things both visible and invisible." Put more pedantically, but somewhat more fully, by Richard Swinburne, a major competitor, along with Plantinga and William Alston, for top contemporary Christian philosopher, this central conception of God is stated thus: God is a "person without a body (i.e., a spirit), present everywhere, the creator and sustainer of the universe, able to do everything (i.e., omnipotent), knowing all things, perfectly good, a source of moral obligation, immutable, eternal, a necessary being, and worthy of worship."[11] So this God of standard theism is thought to have the following characteristics.

1. He is a person and thus has aims, intentions, purposes and acts to achieve these aims with an awareness of what He is doing.
2. He is an immaterial person; that is, a person without a body.
3. He is an infinite person (individual) transcendent to the world.
4. He is an eternal utterly unchanging person; He is a person whose being is timeless.
5. He is all knowing (omniscient); that is, He knows everything that can be known. (He, of course, cannot know what it is logically impossible to know. But that is no limitation.)
6. He is all-powerful (omnipotent); that is, He can do anything that it is logically possible to do.
7. He is wholly good and benevolently disposed to humankind and indeed to all His creation.
8. He is the ground of morality, including moral obligation; He is the ultimate source of all goodness.
9. He created the universe out of nothing and sustains the universe under His providential care.
10. He is the object of ultimate commitment for believers and is taken by them to be supremely worthy of worship.

11. He has revealed Himself, and with this the truth of religion and the truth of life and of the world, through the Holy Scriptures and sometimes, as well, by allowing direct encounters or a direct awareness by human beings of His Divine reality and something of His purposes. This knowledge is noninferential, completely infallible, and certain. It is impossible that it, even in any part, should be false or incoherent.

12. This revealed knowledge must be accepted on authority as infallibly true. Any beliefs which even seem to contradict it cannot be accepted as beliefs which are actually taken to contradict it. Nothing will be taken as contradicting a genuine revelation. The faithful must accept these articles of faith as infallibly true and as articles of faith unquestioningly to be followed and to be acted in accordance with. If reason (our human ratiocination) can show us how they are true or that some of them are true, so much the better, but, whether this can be done or not, the faithful must accept this Revealed Truth humbly on God's authority. He who does not, some standard versions of Christianity assert, let him be anathema.

13. God can and does perform miracles for the good of humankind and in order to make more manifest and tangible the truth of the faith: a truth which reveals to us both ultimate reality and what is needed for our salvation.[12]

III

This is the conception of God of standard theism and, for some considerable amount of it, the conception of God of some less standard theisms as well. It is true, particularly among intellectuals who are also religious believers, that there are revisionist tendencies.[13] But moderate revisionists have still kept from standard theism such conceptions as that of God as the creator and sustainer of the world to whom human beings owe their allegiance and obedience, who is the object of their love and trust and who in turn relates to them with infinite love. But it is these beliefs, common to standard theism and to moderate revisionist theism alike, to say nothing of the whole barrage of beliefs distinctive of standard theism, which, as I see it, and as I shall argue, are resistant to going into the sort of reflective equilibrium of which I have been speaking. But this is the full-fledged conception of God of our Western religions. As such it should be the God of our reflective concern here and not some pared-down conception of God of some theologians or philosophers: a conception which is very likely to be a halfway house on the road to atheism. We want to see if, after all, this full-fledged conception can be part of the requisite wide reflective equilibrium. More generally, we want to see if we are justified in having such beliefs. So, if we are to engage in this exercise at all, we should follow Plantinga and Flew and consider the God, not of some theologians and of the philosophers, but the God of our fathers: the God and associated conceptions of mainstream religious thought and traditional religion. Extreme revisionisms, as exemplified by such Wittgensteinian fideists as Ilham Dilman and D. Z. Phillips and by such empiricist philosophers as Richard Braithwaite and R. M. Hare, are not even theisms.[14] With them we do not even have Christian belief at all, but rather conceptions which are substantially atheisms with a Christian rhetoric. (With Phillips the rhetoric is more flamboyant than with Braithwaite.) I shall follow the Calvinist philosopher Plantinga and the atheist philosopher Flew in ignoring such conceptualizations of religion here.[15] I shall be concerned instead with a God who is said to be an infinite bodiless person who has created the universe out of nothing and sustains the universe with His providential care.

These thirteen propositions summarize the core of standard theism. One cannot be a Jew, a Christian, or a Muslim in any reasonably orthodox sense without accepting these propositions. This, of course, scandal to the intellect or not, involves the acceptance of the last three propositions (along, of course, with the others) of the thirteen propositions listed above. Conveniently for him, Plantinga leaves these last three propositions out in his characterization of standard theism.[16] But that cannot be legitimately done, philosophical embarrassment or not, for standard theism is not free-floating or freestanding, but is always, where it is serious, housed in some religion, and particularly substantially, housed in Judaism, Christianity, and Islam, all three of which have, and inexciseably, these last three features.[17] For these religions there is no alternative to accepting them, though different believers will give them *somewhat* different readings. But they cannot be so deeply demythologized that they lose their core sense. I shall argue that these beliefs cannot be put into wide reflective equilibrium, or in any other way justified, if indeed there is any other reliable way.

The claim that there is or even can be a revealed truth that just must be accepted as infallibly true is plainly incompatible with the coherentism and fallibilism of reflective equilibrium. Beliefs, some of which, as we have seen in the last chapter, have an *initial* credibility, on such an account, get their fuller justification from other beliefs: from fitting into a coherent pattern of beliefs. But no belief, however deeply embedded, can just be accepted independently of how it fares with respect to other beliefs. Though it may have an initial credibility, if it does not cohere with a critical mass of the other beliefs in the culture, then it must be rejected, however important it may be to the person who is trying to get her beliefs in reflective equilibrium. Remember wide reflective equilibrium is a social matter. A given belief may have some initial credibility, but, if it fails this test of fitness with other beliefs, it must be rejected. Moreover, even if it does square with the other beliefs, it still cannot escape the *possibility* of being rejected, for if further examination shows that it does not cohere as well as some alternative and incompatible belief does with a critical mass of the other beliefs in the culture, then the belief, even if it is a revealed belief, must be rejected. Beliefs get their justification or warrant principally by such coherence with other beliefs. On such an account, no belief can be immune to the possibility of rejection, for it is always possible that it might fail such a test of coherence. But revealed beliefs—"revealed truth"—claim precisely this immunity. Some beliefs may *in fact* always stand fast—their initial credibility may always be sustained—but this can never be more than a contingent standing fast, for if they do not fit, or fit less well, with the other beliefs than some alternative, then the belief in question must be rejected. That just is what it is for us to be fallibilists. But that is completely incompatible with appealing to revelation. Perhaps we should junk reflective equilibrium and stick, where religion is concerned, with claims to divine revelation? But that is a different matter. What is at issue here is whether acceptance in one's system of belief of claims to divine revelation is compatible with fixing belief by means of wide reflective equilibrium. It is not.

Similar things should be said about statement twelve, namely the appeal to authority. In reasoning in accordance with wide reflective equilibrium, it is reasonable to make some appeals to authority. Indeed, I do not see how such an appeal could be plausibly avoided. But it is a very different kind of appeal to authority to what we have in the religious case, as expressed in statement twelve. In, for example, trying to fix our beliefs about what old age is like, we would, among other things, seek certain information about life expectancy and here we might utilize, without trying to check that data ourselves, what some medical authorities have written on that. Similarly, we might utilize certain statistics about conditions in old-age homes and the like. Sometimes about many factual matters there are fairly standard sources of information that it is reasonable to rely on and take as authoritative. (However, without taking any of this back, we should take Michel Foucault's cautionary remarks to heart about such appeals.[18]) But, unlike the religious case, the claim to authority over such factual matters is never ultimate. If what is being claimed on authority in these nonreligious cases seems somehow problematic to us, does not square with other things we think we know or at least we suspect might be the case, we can go to other workers in the field or to related disciplines. In the extreme case we can do the work ourselves to master the techniques and the field of knowledge in the relevant discipline and make our own investigation, though we could never do this in any wholesale manner. Many things we must in fact simply take on trust. Still, in specific cases where the irritation of doubt is great enough, we sometimes can make our own investigations. (We always "in principle" can, but sometimes, no doubt typically, where what is at issue is very distant from anything we have any expertise in, the "in principle" is pretty formal.) Still, though in practice we can hardly avoid taking a lot of things on trust, we do not have to just take these things on someone's authority or on the authority of some text. In the case of science and our common life, such as in matters moral or political, there is no doctrinal demand that we just accept something on authority. There is nothing in such areas of our lives that we must just accept because some authority tells us to on pain of being judged irrational or made anathema. But the appeal to authority in religion tells us that there are certain doctrines that we must just accept and act in accordance with no matter whether they seem plausible to us or not, no matter what else we may know or think we know. Again that is incompatible with the fallibilism and coherentism of wide reflective equilibrium. No belief, on such a methodology, can stand in such an authoritative position. (It is also probably incompatible with a respect for the autonomy of human beings—with the very idea of respect for persons—but that is another matter.)

There is also the problem of the multitude of diverse, not infrequently conflicting, *putative* revelations. There are the different religions that are conventionally called the great world religions. They all have their sacred texts and their claims to revelation and authority. And these claims frequently fundamentally conflict. Not all the world religions are even theisms, let alone standard theisms. Confucianism and Hinduism are not such theisms, and a classical form of Buddhism has neither a god nor worship.[19] Yet these religions, as much as Christianity, are long established religions with complex and developing traditions and many adherents over a long time. Even within the standard theisms, Judaism, Christianity, and Islam have revelations which conflict at key points. "Christ is part of the Godhead" could not be accepted by Judaism or Islam. Their central doctrines—revealed in their sacred texts—are not open to even the possibility that a man could become God or God a man, but that belief—that putatively revealed truth—is absolutely central for all even remotely orthodox forms of Christianity.

There is, moreover, a further factual matter to take into consideration. We have only talked, speaking ethnocentrically, of "the great world religions." But anthropologists bring to our attention that when we consider all the cultures there are, or until relatively recently were, there are a multitude of religions with a multitude of putative revelations. Why appeal only to the claimed revelation of one of "the great world religions"? That societies with these religions have a literary, scientific, or philosophical culture in the way nonliterate societies do not does not show that their putative revelation is superior for such revealed truth was suppose to come from the claimed revelation infallibly without appeal to science, philosophy, and the like. Moreover, that a culture is more developed in one area, say, in science or philosophy, does not entail or show that it must be more developed in other areas as well. We have seen cases where primitive art is very sophisticated indeed. In short, we have many candidates for revelation with no nonquestion-begging, nondogmatic, and nonethnocentric way of claiming that one putative revelation or one set of putative revelations of any religion gives us the true revealed word: the truth about our nature and destiny and about what ultimate reality is like and how we must order our lives. Christians tell us that Christ is The Truth and The Way. But we have no good reasons for accepting the putative revelation that supposedly guarantees that claim, and no other religion fares any better in trying to make such appeals. There is no getting appeals to revelation into wide reflective equilibrium and, that aside for a second, it is unreasonable simply to try to ground one's faith on what one takes to be the revealed word of God or whatever is the supposed source of the alleged revelation.

IV

Some theoreticians for some religions—moving away, perhaps not very consistently, from the starkness of an appeal to revelation—do not try to take revelation neat, but seek to show that an alleged revelation is indeed a genuine one by showing that the authenticity of the revelation can be established by an appeal to one or more miracles which show that the revelation actually took place and was genuine.[20] Such a move has been particularly prominent in some forms of Christianity. I will now argue that neither the very notion of a miracle nor the claim that miracles actually have occurred can be gotten into wide reflective equilibrium.

A miracle is standardly said to be a kind of naturally impossible event. Some theologians want to add that it has to be both a religiously significant and a naturally impossible event. I do not wish to contest that theological addition, though I think that it makes the case for miracles that much harder. In any event, I shall simplify things and just speak of a miracle as a kind of naturally impossible event. What I want to say critically concerning miracles is this: It seems to me that the very concept of a miracle is incoherent. Distinguishing between logical impossibility and physical impossibility, to go on to say that, though a miracle is not logically impossible it is *physically impossible*, we are thereby giving to understand that it cannot happen, for, if it is really physically impossible, then by definition it cannot have happened, for physical impossibilities are things that do not, and indeed cannot, occur. But *perhaps* this sounds a bit too much like ordinary language philosophy of a particularly unsubtle and perhaps even sophistical kind. We cannot, perhaps legitimately cannot, take such a high *a priori* road. That notwithstanding, I am still inclined to reposite, "But what exactly is wrong with what I have just argued?"[21]

Still putting that short way with dissenters aside and following David
Hume and Antony Flew, who basically supplements Hume's classic on the
subject, I shall argue not that the concept of miracle is incoherent or that there
can be no miracles, but that it is always more reasonable for us to believe that
the alleged miracle did not occur, than to believe that it did occur.[22]

Consider an alleged miracle that Christians are very centrally concerned
with, to wit the miracle of the resurrection of Jesus Christ. In the Apostles'
Creed we are told that a Christian is one who believes "in God the Father
Almighty, Maker of heaven and earth: and in Jesus Christ his only Son our
Lord, who was conceived by the Holy Ghost, born of the Virgin Mary, suffered under Pontius Pilate, was crucified, died, and buried" and who on "the
third day . . . rose again from the dead." The resurrection of Jesus is a physically impossible event and thus a miracle. It is a crucial miracle—indeed, *the*
crucial miracle—for Christians. Paul put it famously when he remarked, "If
Christ be not risen then is our preaching vain, your faith is also vain." Is it reasonable to believe in this miracle? Is it reasonable to believe in the resurrection of Jesus? Hume, and Flew following him, argued no.[23] Why? Why reject
this core belief of Christianity? This is an event, Hume points out, that happened, *if* indeed it happened at all, in the distant past. If it is a miracle, it is
also supposed to be a factual claim: a claim that something so remarkable as
to be a physical impossibility actually happened. But, as Hume points out, in
this case it is a factual claim about what happened a very long time ago. It is
not supposed to be a myth or just a story, some consoling narrative, but a factual truth about something momentous that happened in the very distant past.
But how do historians, Hume asks, actually assess claims about what happened a very long time ago? (Remember Hume was both a historian and a
philosopher.) Flew interprets Hume's response to this as running thus: "the
criteria by which we must assess historical testimony and the general presumption that alone makes it possible for us to construe the detritus of the past
as historical evidence, must inevitably rule out any possibility of establishing,
upon purely historical grounds, that some genuine miraculous event has indeed occurred."[24] Why so? Why think this? In trying to do history and to assess impartially what is likely to have occurred for any event in the distant
past, we need, whoever we are, to operate with our present criteria for what
we can know or think we can know or what we think is probable and improbable or possible and impossible. We cannot but see things here, as elsewhere, by our own lights. Moreover, relics of the past cannot be interpreted
as historical evidence at all unless we assume the same fundamental regularities obtain in the past as obtain now. Flew then asks: did what Christians call
the resurrection actually occur? Given our understanding of what the fundamental regularities of nature are, given our understanding of what is probable and improbable, physically necessary and physically impossible, we can-

not reasonably conclude that the miracle occurred. This would also be so for any other alleged miracle—a claimed violation of the laws of nature—that was supposed to have happened in the distant past and for the same reasons. That seems decisive enough for a claimed event in the distant past such as the resurrection of Jesus.

However, what if the alleged miracle was something that was supposed to have happened today? Let me, to illustrate this, give a fanciful but somewhat gruesome scenario. Suppose without the use of force, but purely by the power of persuasion, secular humanists began to conquer the world. Everywhere religion is on the decline. Yet also suppose there remained a sizeable Christian minority that understandably felt threatened and that from their ranks a new charismatic hero arose who took it as his evangelical task to save Christianity from the atheistic menace. He launched a holy civil war—a Christian *jihad*—against a liberal but secularizing government. Suppose further that this liberalizing secular government was not so liberal or so enlightened as to have abolished the death penalty and still used the method of the guillotine. Suppose the charismatic hero is captured, tried for treason, found guilty, and sentenced to death by guillotining. Suppose I am the doctor in charge of observing the guillotining. I see the hero, now candidate for martyr, guillotined. His head is cut off, blood spurting from the hole where his head had been, and I feel his heart stop beating. Suppose a few minutes later I, and a number of other people around me, see, or think we see, quite vividly, a new head emerge from the neck, the man stir, get up, and begin to walk away, all the while talking to us. This looks like a contemporary miracle, the happening of a physical impossibility. Should I, standing there with others cold sober in the midst of these goings on, believe that a miracle has occurred? Not to believe that a miracle had occurred, or so it would seem, would be to run against the testimony of my senses and what I take to be the senses of others. Remember that there are several people with me. Still a Humean would argue, and I believe rightly, that we should not—I should not, even given my privileged position—believe that a miracle has occurred. We should think rather that we, where we take ourselves to have been on the scene, suffered from some mass hallucination or some elaborate fraud or at least that something we do not understand has happened. But not that this something is a miracle. If it is a miracle then it is a physical impossibility and physical impossibilities cannot happen. Moreover, talk of physical impossibilities aside, we know that things like that do not happen. It is more reasonable to continue to think that, than to think that the event actually occurred. It is more reasonable to believe that either there was a cognitive malfunctioning on our part or that there was some very clever deception or something of the sort. Such an alleged happening just too fundamentally conflicts with too many things we know to be admissible.

Suppose, however, it starts to be the case that very frequently people will after guillotining in a few minutes grow new heads, wake up, and walk away. If that began to happen, and under carefully controlled conditions where many people observed it to happen—in a nonfrenzied state observed it to happen—then we would have found, to our very great surprise, a new law-like regularity. What we said we know does not happen and cannot actually happen, after all, does start to happen with considerable intersubjectively observed regularity. But then, with such regularities firmly confirmed, we would come to have established that what we had thought was a physical impossibility really wasn't. Things like that, we say with amazement, after all really do happen and we should recognize that what some claimed was a miracle really occurred. But, as an instantiation of a newly established lawlike regularity, it was not, after all, *a miracle.*

The defender of miracles could at this point make two rejoinders. First, he might respond, that if you really, especially in the company of others, saw the guillotined man on the spot grow a new head and get up and go off it would be just dogmatic of you to insist that somehow you must be hallucinating or that some elaborate deception had taken place. You would reasonably, even in such a bizarre circumstance, trust your own and other's senses, or that is at least what you should do. I am not at all convinced that that is so and that that would be the reasonable course of action. But, to continue the discussion and not to repeat what I have just argued, let me, simply for the nonce, grant that point. But then it is important to make two rejoinders. First, that things like that do not *in fact* happen, so we are talking about an altogether hypothetical case. This plain bit of common sense should not be overlooked. Secondly, it would still not at all undermine Hume's arguments about allegedly miraculous events—such as the resurrection of Jesus—that took place in the distant past. Hume's arguments about how we assess *historical* evidence still stand. In such circumstances it would not be reasonable to believe that a miracle had taken place. The present-day hypothetical examples at best show that a miracle could have taken place, that the very notion of a miracle is not incoherent. They give us no reason to believe that it ever has been reasonable to believe that a miracle actually has occurred.

Suppose, alternatively, to move to a second way a defender of miracles might argue: the defender of the faith drops his claim—given these surprising regularities—that what allegedly happened was physically impossible. But then he also drops his claim that, on Hume's own conception of a miracle as a violation of a law of nature, it was a miracle.[25] So again we have no reason to think a miracle has occurred. If, by way of response, it is argued that modern science has no use for the concept of causality and that all its laws are statistical laws, and not laws in the strong sense in which we were talking of physical possibilities and impossibilities, then it should in turn first be replied that this is at best only true of particle physics and is certainly not true of the natural sciences generally. Still, it could in turn be responded, good Humeans should not believe in physical necessities and physical impossibilities; there are only observed regularities, *de facto* constant conjunctions of events. The only kind of necessity that there is, the claim goes, is *logical* necessity. But, even more to the point, and secondly, if the above account of science is right and all its laws are statistical laws and science has no use for the concept of causality, and there is no such a thing as physical necessity, then the very notion of a miracle drops out too, for a miracle (by definition) is an event that is physically impossible, an event contravening natural laws. But if there are no such natural laws (laws of nature), then there is nothing for the supposedly miraculous event to contravene. We have, instead, only some statistical probabilities and improbabilities. *But the very idea of a miracle hangs on the presumption that there are natural laws.* Miracles, if there are any, are not just marvellous happenings, ridiculously unexpected happenings, very improbable happenings, or for a time or perhaps forever *de facto* inexplicable happenings, but events which, though physically impossible, still actually happen. (This continues to incline me to think that the very idea of a miracle is incoherent. Perhaps, after all, we should take a short way with dissenters?)

Christians believe that Jesus' resurrection was physically impossible, yet they also claim it actually occurred, but, if it really is physically impossible, then we have very good reasons for believing that it did not occur and indeed could not have occurred. But, if the marvelous event is not physically impossible, then it is not, and cannot be, a miracle. It is just, if it indeed actually happened, a very unusual happening. So we can see that it is never reasonable to believe that a miracle has occurred and perhaps it is even reasonable to believe that the very concept of a miracle is incoherent. Given that, a belief in miracles (a) cannot be in, or be placed in, wide reflective equilibrium, and (b) cannot be used to authenticate claims to revealed truth.[26]

V

I turn now to a consideration of both belief in God and immortality and to consider whether they square with what, using the method of reflective equilibrium, it would be most reasonable for us to believe concerning these matters. Again, unsurprisingly, I shall argue that these beliefs cannot be made to square with our considered judgments in wide reflective equilibrium. I shall initially, for reasons which will become apparent in a moment, treat belief in God and belief in immortality together.

Belief in God, for standard theism, is a belief in a bodiless person. So, if God existed, He would be a person without a body, but—or so I shall argue—

there can be no persons without bodies, for the very idea of a bodiless person is incoherent. God could perhaps, as Mormons and pantheists believe, be the world's body or perhaps, à la Spinoza, the world looked at in a certain way. But that would be, to understate it, a radical departure from standard theism as embedded in the belief systems of our historic religions. In that belief system, as we have seen, we have the belief in the God of our fathers, but, as well, Jews, Christians, and Muslims also have the belief that we have immortal souls. Deeply, but not invariably, embedded in those traditions, is a belief in a Platonic-Cartesian self. We are, according to such accounts, composed of two realities, mind and body, and these two realities are radically distinct substances. Normally the mental side of us—our self, our soul—is housed in a body, but, as it is an immaterial, indestructible substance, it also can, and sometimes does, exist apart from and completely independent of our bodies. So we, after the death of our bodies, are completely bodiless, purely spiritual persons. But, the reply goes, this is impossible for the very idea of a bodiless person or an immaterial self is incoherent.

So, for the idea of God to be viable, the idea of a bodiless person must be viable. If talk of bodiless persons is incoherent, or in some other way mistaken, then talk of God is as well, though it could be the case that talk of bodiless existence made sense while talk of God did not. I shall argue that neither conception makes sense. Belief in immortal souls and belief in God are both incoherent. God is, of course, very different from us, for He is an infinite individual, somehow out of time, omniscient, omnipotent, and perfectly good. But He is like us in being a person who exists without a body just as we—or so the claim goes—can exist without a body. But, if the notion of a bodiless person is incoherent, then God cannot exist and we cannot have immortal souls. We, if that is so, cannot exist as the Platonic-Cartesian scheme conceives of us as existing.

However, is it just a dogma of naturalism to believe that it is impossible for there to be a person without a body? Our actual experience in life is such that the persons we know are plainly creatures of flesh and blood. We have never encountered a bodiless person. All the people we know or know about have died or, we are confident, will die. No one in the past has lived forever, and this has included all the human beings there have been: a very large sample indeed. "All men are mortal" may not be analytic or true by definition, but it is a plainly true generalization. There is no good reason at all to think that it may turn out to be false, for we have never known anyone to live forever and we have no experience of resurrected persons. If we try to imagine a bodiless person, we have no idea of how to identify one so that we could know that we had met or encountered or somehow had "seen" a person without a body. We have some faint idea what it would be like to encounter or see a person with an astral body: a kind of blithe spirit with a kind of thin smoky, cloudlike body. We are familiar with this from the movies or from certain ghost stories that we read, or were read to us, when we were children. But this astral body, that it is sometimes imagined that people may come to have, is still a body—a physical object, though a peculiarly diaphanous one. To the extent that the astral body gets too amorphous, then we begin to lose the sense we have of such a body when we have the ghostlike, cloudlike thing we are shown in the film *Blithe Spirit.* Where the astral body is sufficiently ghostlike to count as a body—as kind of cloudy bodylike something—it remains an empirical claim that a certain strange kind of bodily person exists. Still, the claim here is that the person has a physical body, *recherché* though it be. Here we have something intelligible, but plainly false. We have no good reasons at all for believing there are such persons. Where, by contrast, the astral body gets completely invisible we have no reason to regard it as a body, any kind of body, astral or otherwise. We have, with such an alleged person, with such an alleged body, all the problems of identification and reidentification that we have with a person conceived as a Platonic-Cartesian soul or self: an utterly bodiless person accidentally and temporarily housed in a body, but essentially completely incorporeal, invisible, intangible, and imperishable.

We can identify and reidentify persons of flesh and blood, the only kind of persons we have any actual acquaintance with, but we have no idea how to identify, let alone reidentify, a bodiless person so *utterly negatively* described. We have no idea at all of what we would have to see or encounter or fail to see or encounter to identify or fail to identify a bodiless person; we do not understand what the phrase "bodiless person" refers to.

Suppose, to try at an illustration, we are standing around in a group discussing politics (remember Italy and people standing in a piazza talking together). Suppose, suddenly, just like that, someone in the group says that there is a bodiless person among us and then adds that it is Jones who died last week, a man who had intense interest in the political issues we are discussing. Suppose someone else says, "Nonsense, when you are dead you are dead. There is no bodiless person here and/or anywhere else." Suppose you, with a fine empiricist, skeptical temperament, want to be open-minded. How are you going to go about ascertaining whether there is among us a completely incorporeal, invisible, intangible person? You and we have no way of knowing how to proceed here to ascertain who was most likely telling it like it is. Evidentialist arguments do not work here for we have no understanding of what it would be like to have evidence for or against such a claim. It has the look of an empirical claim, but, when we think about it for a moment, we recognize it isn't one. We have no idea of what counts as identifying a bodiless person, so that we could say, "Yes, there is such a person among us or there very well may be such a person among us." We literally do not know what we are talking about here such that we could have any idea at all of whether there was some such person in our midst. If we were quite confident that we did not see the flesh-and-blood Jones there, but that we heard a voice that sounded just like Jones's voice speaking softly but distinctly, as if from among the group, but we could not, even after careful examination, locate it as coming from the mouth of any flesh-and-blood person standing there, we would be very startled and puzzled indeed. We would assume, perhaps, that it was in some subtle way piped in or that there was a very clever ventriloquist among us or something of that nature. Or, if all of these hypotheses were judged to be very unlikely, we would still not assume, or at least need not assume, that it was a bodiless Jones there talking to us, for we have no idea of how a bodiless person could talk or how to identify him. At worst we would be utterly baffled as to where the voice came from. We could not plausibly, or perhaps even intelligibly, take it as evidence for the existence of a bodiless person.

What it is to be a bodiless person has, it is crucial to note, only had an utterly negative characterization, i.e., an intangible, incorporeal, invisible person. With the troubles characteristic of the *via negativa,* we can only say what such a person is not, but then it is also impossible to say what he is, for to do this we must be able to give some positive characterization of what we are talking about. But we cannot. Put bluntly, we have no idea of what "bodiless person" refers to so that we could recognize one when we encountered one or, even more radically, understand what it is for there to be such a reality.

For us to have some understanding of whether there is or even could be such a reality, we would have to have at least some minimal understanding of what it would be like for there to be such a reality so that we could know what we are talking about or thinking about here. What we cannot conceive of we cannot conceive of and, in such a circumstance, there can be no intelligible speculation as to whether there is or is not such a bodiless person, for we do not understand what we are talking about or trying to conceive. We cannot even coherently speculate about whether there even could be such a reality, for we have no understanding of *what* it is we are talking about. Indeed, we can make nothing determinate of our talk here. "Bodiless person" is intended as a referring expression, but we have no grasp of what its supposed referent is. "A person" refers to a determinate flesh-and-blood reality or supposed reality, except in secondary uses such as "corporate person" where it still refers to a tangible, physically specifiable reality. But we cannot identify at all the referent (supposed referent) of "bodiless person." It seems to work something like "temperatureless heat." Hobbes seems at least to be on the mark with his harsh remark: "If a man talks to me of 'a round quadrangle' or 'accidents of bread and cheese' or 'immaterial substances' I should not say that he was in error, but that his words were without meaning: that is to say, absurd."[27]

It has been responded that, even with its ancestory in Hobbes, this is in reality still little better than the evocation of a logical empiricist or logical positivist dogma, and even crudely put at that, for, if we start from the *first person perspective*, we can all imagine witnessing our own funerals. This being so, we can, after all, give empirical sense (meaning) to being bodiless persons, immaterial beings. We can, that is, find a context for its significant use. We can do this because we are immediately aware of the person, namely us, who does the witnessing of his own funeral. Thus I, for example, can imagine looking down at my body there in the coffin dressed in my best suit and cleanly shaven. We can all imagine things like that, so, it is said, we all have an understanding—a first person understanding—of what it would be like to be immaterial beings.[28] Indeed, we can all imagine looking down at a body looking exactly like, or at least very like, our own body, indeed being everything but numerically identical to our own body. It is like our sitting in a Ford suspended in air, and in this way hanging above another Ford looking exactly like the Ford we are sitting in, as we look at the other identical-looking Ford. But what we have no idea of is for *us*—that is, for us as individuals—to so observe our *own* bodies, as if we understood what it would be like to survive whole body amputation or even to observe our whole body as distinct from looking down at our arm (one part of the body observing another part). The image actually is of our being so observed as a body. That is perfectly intelligible. We can, of course, well imagine *someone else doing* it, but we cannot intelligibly imagine doing it *ourselves*. We cannot intelligibly imagine our whole body being amputated from our self and our observing this whole body amputation. We cannot imagine this or even understand such talk. The "I" here, that is supposed to do the observing, has been given no sense. It has no use in our language. We do not understand what it is for a person to look down at that very person's whole body, which is his body, and to observe it as a corpse, though we, of course, do understand, to our horror, what it would be like for us to observe a severed part of our body (say, a hand). What sometimes tricks us here is that we can readily imagine ourselves looking down at a body exactly like ours (except numerically) that others could falsely, but still intelligibly, say is my dead body. This, of course, is perfectly intelligible. But what is not intelligible is for a person to witness that very person's own funeral. That makes no more sense than it makes sense to speak of Flew's sleeping faster than Plantinga or Alston's being a prime number. Language in such circumstances, in Wittgenstein's famous phrase, has gone on a holiday.

VI

I have assumed that the central criterion for personal identity, that is, the criterion for being the same person over time, is bodily identity. That assumption is essentially involved in asking what it is to be the same person at time two as she was at time one.

Why not, instead, use memory beliefs—true memory beliefs—rather than bodily criteria? Suppose our friend Jones dies, that is, his body ceases to function, he is pronounced dead, and he is cremated. This is all firmly and quite unequivocally established. Jones so dies and is cremated in Cleveland. But suppose an hour after Jones's funeral in Cleveland another person suddenly pops onto the scene in Chicago in a way that cannot be accounted for and says, though not looking a bit like Jones, that he is Jones. But suppose it also transpires that this person, whoever he is, has all the memories, including the most intimate and private memories, of Jones. Would we have now to say that, surprising as it is, this person really is Jones and that the fundamental criteria for personal identity is not bodily identity but thorough continuity of memory? Or at least that it is another perfectly reliable criterion that is sometimes—so the claim goes—even more fundamental than bodily identity. That is, that on certain occasions it overrides bodily identity in determining personal identity. And, if such a thing transpired as I have just described, would that not be a plausible thing to believe? And if such a thing happened, would it not also be a reasonable assumption to make that Jones had an immaterial self that is essential to his personhood? Some think that we should believe, given that sequence of events, that Jones has an immaterial soul or self that once was housed in one body, for a time (perhaps very short) was housed in no body at all, and then it came to be housed in another body. Given the strange sequence of events, the argument goes, this seems to be the most plausible thing to say. And thus, after all, we have shown that it makes sense to talk of immaterial existence. Personal identity does not have to be established by bodily identity and continuity, but can be established by true memory beliefs. True, such things do not happen, but it is conceivable that they could and we have given an empirical description of what it would be like for such a thing to have happened; we have attached sense to "bodiless existence" and "bodiless personhood."

We should be very careful about what conclusions we draw from such puzzle cases. Ordinary language may breakdown in extraordinary circumstances and we may not know what to say. It may very well be the case in such circumstances that there is nothing we *must* say. In such circumstances, if indeed they ever happen, we are very likely to be at a loss as to what to say and think; what we should realize is that there is nothing we *must* say or think there. The person claiming to be Jones could be said instead to be someone with powerful telepathic powers or someone with a very intimate knowledge of Jones and all the details of his life. These alternative accounts do not sound very plausible, but neither does the account which says it just must be Jones, since he has, as far as we can ascertain, the same true memory beliefs. The point is that we just would not know what to say or think in such cases. (Cases that do not occur anyway, to return to something similar to what we said about miracles.) There is nothing in such puzzle cases to break, or even put in question, the firmness our reliance in real-life contexts of the establishing of personal identity by bodily continuity. Puzzle cases should be discounted for there our language bears no firm sense and we would, if such things really happened (though they do not), have to make new stipulations concerning our use of language. But they would be *stipulations* and they would not show that we had an understanding of what it was to talk of a bodiless person.

What should be recognized is that we do not know what to say or think in a host of such imaginary puzzle cases. Consider, for example, the following: suppose you see me get into bed and you see perfectly clearly that there is no one else in the bed when I get in and you watch me continuously while I sleep through the night completely covered with blankets and you also observe that no other person comes in during the night and crawls under the blankets. The alarm clock rings at 7 A.M. and simultaneously two identically pajamaed persons get up, one from the right-hand side of the bed and the other from the left, both looking exactly like the Kai Nielsen that went to bed that night and both, as it was subsequently discovered, with identical memory beliefs. Should we say that some weird parthogenesis had taken place and that Kai Nielsen had somehow, we do not understand at all how, divided like an amoeba and now there are two Kai Nielsens, or should we say that neither is Kai Nielsen or that one of them is Kai Nielsen and the other not or what should we say? And what would be the point of saying any of these things? Could any of these things that we could say be established as being true or more even plausible or, for that matter, false or more implausible than the others? It at least does not appear to be so. We could say any of those things; there is no way of determining, even with some mild probability, who Kai Nielsen is in such a circumstance. Our language was not tailored for *such* counterfactual situations and we do not know how to extend it to cover such cases.

Consider our friend Jones again. Suppose he is lecturing to his class. Slowly, right before the class, his physiognomy begins to change and with it his voice. He gets more and more features that are froglike until finally, right there before the class, he has lost his human voice and power of speech altogether and croaks like a frog and has the body and the bodily organs of a giant frog. Is that froglike thing that hops about before the class still Jones? Again, we would not know what to say here and indeed, there is nothing we *must* say here to be speaking intelligibly and correctly: to be saying what is most likely, though surely we should, and probably would, treat that froglike creature rather specially. But someone who persisted in saying that it was really Jones would have no warrant or justification for his claim. But exactly the same would obtain for the person who said that this froglike thing was not Jones. Our language and thought are not tailored to respond to such situations.

Let us take one final example. Frank is standing lecturing before his large class of some two hundred students. Suddenly his body disappears into thin air. One second he is clearly seen leaning on his lectern lecturing, the next second no Frank is seen. It is also the case that the lighting is very clear and the floor solid with no trap doors. But still a voice identical to Frank's keeps right on lecturing (making, if you will, the sounds of a lecture) without a break in sense or sound. If that happened, should we not say that Frank continued on as an immaterial person, for it is surely Frank talking to us? But again we would not know what to say. We could say it is Frank, we could say it was a trick with Frank's voice artfully recorded so that it seemed as if it were coming from the lectern, or we could say that the class was massively hallucinating. Most likely we would have to frankly confess that we did not know what to say or to think. Again our language and our thought are not fitted for such use. If things like this really happened, we would very likely have to rework our criteria for personal identity as well as some other very fundamental and pervasive ways we talk and conceive of things.

An important thing to keep in mind here is that things like that do not happen, and in the real world of our familiar experiences bodily continuity serves as our criterion for personal identity. Consider, for example, a police lineup or a law court. If I can identify one of the persons in the line as the person whom I saw rob the bank, I do it by bodily identity. I see that he has the same body as the person I saw point the revolver at the teller. If I and others in good position to see the robber report the same thing, that settles the matter. That he underwent a complete personality change in the night in his cell and now has no sense of whom he previously was does not effect the point that it was he who did it, though it may effect the sentence he will, or at least should, receive. Similarly, the long time of confinement between the time the person who committed a murder and the time he is tried may bring about a deep change in the person who committed the crime, and this again should affect the attitude we have toward him, but not our beliefs about the identity of the person who committed the crime. That is established by bodily criteria. When we say, as we sometimes do, that a person has become a quite different person from the person who did the deed, the sense of "quite different person" is a secondary sense of "person." The other two occurrences of "person" in the previous sentence are primary senses, a sense presupposed by the secondary sense. Flew put the matter nicely when he remarked that the "secondary presupposes the primary sense: no one would say their son was quite a different person since he passed through Marine Corps boot camp if they were not sure that he was, in the primary sense, the same."[29]

Bodily criteria, to sum up what we have been saying, are essential for determining personal identity. Our understanding of a person requires our understanding of what it is for her or him to be a live flesh-and-blood human being acting and reacting in the world. Our understanding of a person requires at its most basic level our understanding of an embodied being endowed with distinctively personal characteristics. But we have no understanding of either the concept or the conception of an incorporeal or purely spiritual self or person—a bodiless person—let alone how such a person could possess such personal characteristics. Such talk is absurd and incoherent. But God, in standard theism, is said to be a bodiless person. But then the very concept of God, at least of such standard theism and its city cousins, is incoherent. In fine, the very concept of a bodiless person, and thus of God as well, seems at least to be self-contradictory. It is the absurdity that Hobbes said it was and that Flew following him reaffirms. Again such a conception—to understate its difficulties —is not something we could get into wide reflective equilibrium.

VII

However, now, let us assume, so as to continue the argument, that we have been mistaken and that "bodiless person" makes sense. There are, however, further difficulties that beset the very concept of God. Standard theism not only takes God to be a person without a body, it takes this person to be present everywhere, to be infinite, to be both "in the world" and "transcendent to the world." God is said to be a person who created the world from nothing and sustains the world from moment to moment such that the world could not exist without His sustaining power; He is able to do everything (that is, He is omniscient), all-knowing, perfectly good, the source of moral obligation, immutable, eternal, a necessary being, holy, and supremely worthy of worship.

There are a host of difficulties with this standard conception of God that the last two hundred years of atheological argument have brought out, to say nothing of the careful reasoning, always, at least ostensibly, in defense of the faith, that took place during the Middle Ages. I shall concentrate on only a few very central difficulties. On the above perfectly orthodox conception of God, God is taken to be a person. Suppose there is nothing awry (we are now assuming) with the notion of being a purely spiritual person, but, as a person, God is also said to be an individual and a very peculiar individual at that, for He is also said to be an *infinite* individual transcendent to the world though still somehow in the world. But the very notion of an "infinite individual," and thus of an "infinite person," is self-contradictory. If something is a person she must be a determinate, bounded being distinguishable from other determinate beings, but if we try to say a person is everywhere and is infinite we in effect are denying she is a person, for our only understanding of a person is that of someone who is determinate, distinctive through having a distinct identity, rather than just being all-pervasive and everywhere.[30] Something with those features cannot be an individual by the very meaning of what an "individual" is. In short, "infinite individual," like "round quadrangle," as we have seen Hobbes putting it, is a use of "words without meaning: that is to say, absurd."[31]

Moreover, we also have trouble with the notion of an individual, a person, being "transcendent to the world." What is it to be transcendent to the world? How can we find or assign a use for those terms? What are we saying when we use them? Someone says, "There is a person transcendent to the universe"; another denies it; a third says she does not understand what is being said. How are we to decide who is right here and what other than a *purely verbal* difference is there between them? What would give us the slightest reason to think that we had gained something of a handle on "There is a person transcendent to the universe" so that we might have some evidence for its truth or falsity or some other kind of reason to believe it is either true or false and, if so, which it is? It certainly appears that anything that could conceivably happen—anything which could possibly be experienced—would be equally compatible with its assertion or its denial. (Here our discussions of Peirce in the previous chapter with his conception of how we are to make our ideas clear are worth reflecting on again.)

Some will immediately and routinely respond that this is just verificationism raising its ugly head again, when, after all, we all know now, and indeed for a long time, that it is mistaken. But what, if anything, is wrong with verificationism *in this context*? And, verificationism aside, how do we understand the notion of person being transcendent to the world? How is it anything but an empty phrase? Perhaps, unlike "infinite individual," it is not self-contradictory, but we nonetheless have no understanding of it. We seem at least to have a mere empty string of words here without meaning.[32] We, that is, do not know what we are talking about when we utter them. Or is this too strongly assertive? Even so, given their strangeness, it is up to the person who uses such utterances to explain: give a sense to what it is he means when he says that a person is transcendent to the world or show what sense it has *if* it has a sense. We add insult to injury, as *Christian* theists do, when they say that God is not only wholly other—utterly transcendent to the world—but is also pervasively in the world as well. It makes no sense to say that something is utterly transcendent to the world and is in the world at the same time. A transcendent reality is not part of the universe, but God is still said to be eternally everywhere. He is also said, while still being everywhere, to be a being acting in the universe at specific times. Again we have a cluster of words which do not actually coherently fit together and in that way are without meaning.

It is only because we have grown up in a Christian culture where we have so often heard such talk that many of us, rather understandably, have been lulled, by its very familiarity, into thinking such utterances make sense. When anthropologists report some very strange religious beliefs of very different cultures, we frequently at least have no difficulty in recognizing their incoherence.[33] They seem to us plainly absurd. If we could take the disinterested stance of an alien anthropologist studying our culture, we would similarly, I believe, react to much of the religious talk of standard theism, including, of course, the central bits I have just been discussing. It is only our own socialization into such talk, including, not infrequently, a deep emotional involvement with our religion, that keeps us from seeing things with anthropological eyes and thus from seeing them, as the incorrigible Hobbes did, as utter absurdities. (I do not intend here to deny that they all the same can have powerful social and psychological functions. But these can, and I shall argue in part 4 should, be viewed in utterly naturalistic terms.)

Some have said that we must move away from the literal-mindedness and simplicity of standard theism and give up talk of God being a person, an individual, an infinite individual, acting in the world with aims and designs and the like. We should say instead, where we are speaking literally and not metaphorically, that God is a necessary being and, because God is the necessary being that God is, that the universe is personal and ultimately good. All that talk of God as a person or God being a pure spirit or an individual is just metaphoric talk to give people something of an initial grip on what they are speaking of when they speak of or to God. (If my argument has been near to the mark we actually have not been helped here, but mystified. But, for the nonce, let that go.) Our literal talk of God is of God as a necessary being: an eternal being, who could not not exist. Indeed, the argument continues, it might even be more accurate to speak of God as the ultimate ground of the universe, the ground of being and meaning, but not itself being a being or even being but the very *ground* of all being.[34]

For a moment, set talk of a necessary being aside, but, for the rest at least, language has again gone on a holiday. We have no idea at all about what we are talking about when we speak of the ground of the universe or the ground of all being and meaning. Such phrases have no use in any established discourse. However, in theological talk, such as Paul Tillich's, we have such talk and other equally incoherent phrases. But we have here no established discourse embedded in a cluster of social practices. Yet sometimes, with his talk of ultimate commitment (what we finally put our trust in), his verbose talk gets tied to the world. But where that happens and we get something that makes sense, we have only utterly secular talk about our commitments, trust, our concerns and how all of us, whether we recognize it or not, have our ultimate commitments and concerns. *Perhaps* this is true, and perhaps important, but it gives us nothing that is not utterly secular, not something that a through-and-through atheist could not accept. *If* this is all religious belief comes to, atheists could be led gently into belief. Such talk and such conceptions give us no understanding of what it is for something to be the ground of the universe. However, with talk of the ground of the universe and the like, we are just utterly in the swamp.

The same thing is true of "The universe is personal." It is something that we have no understanding of unless we treat it, in effect, reductively by saying that it is just an obscure theological way of saying that things, appearances sometimes to the contrary notwithstanding, will not go so badly for human beings or at least ultimately will not go so badly (whatever that means) for human beings. We really do care for one another and that caring is often effective. We are saying this or something of the sort in saying "The universe is personal." We then have something here that is intelligible enough, but, taken nonhyperbolically in its most straightforward way, it is not very likely to be true. But taken less straighforwardly, it is more like remarks such as "People are always alone" and "People are never alone." We understand why both of them are said; hardly taking them to be utterances which are either literally true or literally false or even utterances which are incompatible, some of us, at least, think it is important and even, in some obscure sense, right to say such things in some circumstances.[35] But, that aside, what is of moment here is that we have talk which is utterly secular; talk which could be in place in a thoroughly naturalistic world. The same thing is true with reductive construals of "The universe is personal," which in turn are thought by some religious persons to be the literal meaning of the analogical-metaphorical sentence "God is a person." If we take such thoroughly reductive turns, then all nonbelievers can be turned into believers or at least into persons who will accept the intelligibility of religious belief *so construed*. But such reductive belief is not religious belief at all, but just atheism in obscurantist and religiose dress. But, if we do not so reductively read "The universe is personal," we again have something like "God is the ground of being and meaning" which is without coherent sense.

Some will say that this is not true of talk of God as a necessary being or even as necessary being (being that could not not exist). Indeed, it will be said that whatever sense "God is the ground of being and meaning" has, it is picked up by talk of necessary being which is coherent and literal. After all, someone with severe Platonizing tendencies might say, natural numbers are necessary beings so we can hardly say that the very idea of a necessary being is incoherent. Aside from the fact that it is rather extravagant and unnecessary to describe natural numbers as necessary beings or as eternal objects or anything of the sort, the necessary being that God is must be significantly different than that of the necessary being of natural numbers. God is a necessary being who is somehow an individual who is said to have created the universe out of nothing and to sustain it and to give providential care for all the creatures in it. God is also said to be, and necessarily so, an utterly unique being; unlike a natural number, He is not a member of a species of beings. But this makes His very beingness and necessity very strange indeed. What is this necessary being which is neither a genus nor a species? Moreover, in saying God is a necessary being or is necessary being, we need to ask is God a logical necessary being or a physically necessary being or what? In saying, that is, that God could not not exist, are we saying His existence is logically necessary so that it is self-contradictory to say that there is no God or is God a reality or reality that just in fact is necessary, that never in fact will not exist, is a being that could never have started to exist and as a matter of fact never will cease to exist?

If we say that God's existence is *logically* necessary, to take the first possibility first, we are saying something that is at best false. It could not be false that bachelors are unmarried men for that proposition is analytic (if any propositions are), but that does not establish that there are any bachelors. It only establishes that *if* there are any bachelors that they are unmarried. That there are some bachelors can be denied without self-contradiction. Similarly, "God is eternal" is analytic (if any propositions can be said to be properly analytic), but it does not follow that there are any eternal beings or that there is a God. What does follow from that analyticity is that if God exists He could not have come to exist or to sometime cease to exist, for then He would not be an eternal being. But God by definition is an eternal being. But such a definition does not establish, or give us any reason at all to believe, that there actually are any eternal beings. It could be true that there are no eternal beings; eternally it could be true that there are no eternal beings.

It has been said, again going analytic, and definitional, that God is that than which no greater can be conceived. From this definition Saint Anselm tried to conclude that God must exist, for if He did not exist, then He would not be that than which no greater being can be conceived, for a really existing God is a greater being than a being which is only conceivable, but does not actually exist. So God, given our definition of Him, must exist. God is a logically necessary reality. The atheist, when she says there is no God, contradicts herself. But, the traditional response goes, existence is not a predicate characterizing God or anything else. And, it is not, to put much the same point nonlinguistically, a characteristic characterizing God or anything else either. It is, rather, a way of saying that there is something of whatever kind is being spoken of. When we speak of God's existing, it is not like speaking of Him as loving, good, powerful, all-knowing, and the like. Nothing is added to our *conception* of God by saying that He exists as there is by saying He is loving and the like. So we do not contradict ourselves when we assert that there is no God.

To this, it has in turn been responded, that Anselm was not asserting that God just happens to exist, but that He *necessarily* exists. A being than which no greater can be conceived could not just begin to exist or go out of existence or just happen to exist, but must exist necessarily. "Necessary existence," unlike "existence," is a predicate, a real attribute of things. But this will not help Anselm, for, if this is so, then, "There is a necessary existence" like "There is eternal being" could be denied without self-contradiction. It is not a proposition or a sentence like "Bachelors are unmarried," "God is eternal," or "What exists exists" that is logically necessary. Moreover, it makes no sense to speak of being, beings, or existences as being logically necessary. Only propositions or sentences can be logically necessary. A logically necessary being is a contradiction in terms or at least an incoherence.

Suppose, alternatively, we contend that in saying that God is a necessary being we are speaking of a *de facto* necessary being. It is logically possible for God not to exist, but God just always does exist and will never, as a matter of fact, cease to exist. But this will not do at all, for having even the clearest conception of such a factually necessary being does nothing at all to establish that there are any such necessary beings. We could clearly conceive of them as existing when in fact they do not exist. That is just what is involved in saying that they are *de facto* necessary beings. Moreover, and independently, in speaking of *de facto* necessary beings or existence, we could just as well say that of the universe or of nature or of the top quark or the Higgs particle or subatomic particles generally. There are lots of candidates for being a necessary being *in that sense.* How do we know that it is God and not the fundamental particles of physics which has or have such *de facto* necessary existence, if indeed anything has necessary existence?

Some might say that physical cosmology gives us, with the big bang theory, good grounds for believing that the universe could not have *de facto* necessary existence, for we now have excellent natural scientific reasons for believing that the universe did have an explosive beginning. Three things should be said here. First, that this does not show that it was God who brought the universe about: who caused the big bang. Second, and more fundamentally, even if the big bang theory is true, it does not show that the fundamental particles were brought into explosive existence by the big bang. The Higgs particle need not be thought to have so come into existence, or to have come into existence at all, and it still stands as a candidate for a necessary being and a more plausible one than God. With God we have to try to postulate a necessary being that is not a physical reality, and that, along with the principle that we should not multiply entities beyond need, makes the Higgs particle the more plausible candidate of the two. Third, and perhaps most fundamentally, we should not build very much on physical cosmology, for it is very speculative and subject to rapid changes. The seemingly best account now is that the universe did in fact have an explosive beginning. But that was not what was thought twenty years ago and it is not very evident that that is what will be thought in ten years, let alone in fifty years. Scientific theories *of this sort* are very speculative, subject to repeated changes, and have many interpretations. We have no good reason to go from physical cosmology to the conclusion that God or some nonphysical reality is our best candidate for a *de facto* necessary being or being.

Finally, if God is said to be neither a logically necessary being nor a *de facto* empirically necessary being, but a *metaphysically* necessary being, then we have a complete nonstarter, for we do not understand what kind of necessity, if any kind of necessity, that is or whether there is anything coherent that could count as metaphysical reality or as a metaphysically necessary being.[36]

I have in this chapter looked at traditional arguments in favor of standard theism, arguments which appear at least to be essential for the defense of Judaism, Christianity, and Islam, and I have argued that they are all wanting. If that is so, then continued allegiance to these belief systems becomes, or so at least it would seem, problematic. And it would seem, as well, as a kind of corollary, that, if my critique is on the mark, being a Jew, Christian, or Muslim or any kind of theist would also become problematic. It is anything but clear, if we would be reasonable and take these matters to heart, that being any of those things is anything that we should be. These religious beliefs cannot be placed in wide reflective equilibrium or be otherwise justified. It looks like, for people placed as we are in the world, that some broadly secular humanist orientation is the more reasonable and humanly desirable option.

NOTES

1. "Bodily death" goes in scare quotes because I think it should be pleonastic. But that, of course, requires arguments and argument we shall have in this chapter.
2. Alvin Plantinga, "Belief in God," in *Perspectives in Philosophy,* ed. Michael Boylan (Fort Worth, Tex.: Harcourt Brace and Javanovich, 1993), 389–90. See also the essays in *Faith and Rationality: Reason and Belief in God,* ed. Alvin Plantinga and Nicholas Wolterstorff (Notre Dame, Ind.: University of Notre Dame Press, 1980).
3. Kwasi Wiredu has gently but persuasively argued that in his *Philosophy and an African Culture* (Cambridge, England: Cambridge University Press, 1980).
4. There is here in that very way of putting things a problem of sexism. "Men of letters" should be read as "persons of letters" as awkward as that sounds.
5. Norman Kemp Smith, "The Naturalism of Hume," *Mind,* n.s., no. 54 (1905): 149–53, 335–47; Norman Kemp Smith, *The Philosophy of David Hume* (London: Macmillan, 1941); and David Pears, "The Naturalism of Book 1 of Hume's *Treatise of Human Nature,*" in *Rationalism, Empiricism and Idealism,* ed. Anthony Kenny (Oxford, England: Clarendon Press, 1986), 104–23.
6. A philosopher, who knows a lot more science, history of science, and philosophy of science than I do, has cautioned: "I am suspicious of intellectuals with 'a reasonable understanding of science, philosophy and literature.' I think the best that we can have is a very superficial grasp of these subjects." There is a lot of truth in that, but it is a mat-

ter of degree and the degree is important. Charles Peirce, Max Weber, Hans Reichenbach, Ernest Nagel, Paul Feyerabend, Stephen Toulmin, Sidney Morgenbesser, and Hilary Putnam all have a pretty good grasp of these matters and have put their knowledge to good use. Others, less knowledgeable about these matters, have had science in school and in university, including sometimes courses in the history of science, and can learn from people like Peirce and Feyerabend. This need not, and typically does not, carry with it depth, but reflective people can, I think it is plausible to believe, have some reasonable understanding of what is going on here. Wittgenstein's attitude was too elitist here. In spite of the vast professionalization of knowledge, there is still cultural space for critical intellectuals, though they should be very modest about scientific claims concerning which they only have secondhand knowledge and they should look on popularizations of science with suspicion, particularly when they smack of the extravagant.

7. Antony Flew, *Atheistic Humanism* (Amherst, N.Y.: Prometheus Books, 1993), 23–28.

8. Ibid., 23–24.

9. Ibid., 24.

10. Plantinga, "Belief in God," 389.

11. Richard Swinburne, *The Coherence of Theism* (Oxford, England: Clarendon Press, 1977), 2.

12. As I read over these thirteen propositions, it seems to me that they only need to be stated for us to realize how incredible they are, what a scandal to the intellect they are, how they for us are really beyond reasonable belief. My reaction is akin to William James's comment (who was not tone deaf to religion) that the Bible only needs to be tolerably carefully read to be disbelieved. I remember acutely feeling this Jamesian way when I was a freshman instructor and had to teach the Bible as literature in a humanities course at Amherst College.

13. Shabbir Akhtar has well characterized and criticized this *revisionist* tendency. Shabbir Akhtar, *Reason and the Radical Crisis of Faith* (New York: Peter Lang, 1987), 134–206; and in his *The Light in the Enlightenment* (London: Grey Seal Books, 1990).

14. D. Z. Phillips, *Faith and Philosophical Enquiry* (London: Routledge and Kegan Paul, 1970); D. Z. Phillips, *Religion Without Explanation* (Oxford, England: Basil Blackwell, 1976); Ilham Dilman, "Wisdom's Philosophy of Religion," *Canadian Journal of Philosophy* 4 (1975): 473–524; Ilham Dilman, "Wittgenstein on the Soul," in *Understanding Wittgenstein,* ed. G. Vesey (London: Macmillan, 1974); Richard B. Braithwaite, "An Empiricist's View of the Nature of Religious Belief," in Malcolm L. Diamond and Thomas V. Litzenburg, Jr., *The Logic of God: Theology and Verification* (Indianapolis, Ind.: Bobbs-Merrill Co.,1975), 127–48; and R. M. Hare, "The Simple Believer," in *Religion and Morality,* ed. Gene Outka and John Reeder, Jr. (Garden City, N.Y.: Anchor Books, 1973), 393–427.

15. For criticisms of the views listed in the previous note, see my *God, Skepticism and Modernity* (Ottawa, Ontario: University of Ottawa Press, 1989), 94–189.

16. Andrew Lugg remarks that even if most ordinary believers accept these last three propositions, many, perhaps most, religious intellectuals would be willing to drop them fairly quickly. "Certainly I can imagine," he remarks, "such folk being satisfied if the remaining propositions could be brought into wide reflective equilibrium." I think this is true of religious intellectuals who are religious intellectuals with *strong revisionist* tendencies, but many religious intellectuals (including some distinguished ones)—think of someone like Karl Barth or Emil Brunner, to say nothing of Plantinga, Alston, and Wolterstorff—would realize that those last three propositions remain central to the Christian faith

and cannot be dropped or be radically demythologized if we are to persist in it. There is no room for a tolerably orthodox Christian to give here.

17. This is clearly recognized by Hume.

18. Michel Foucault, *Power/Knowledge* (New York: Pantheon Books, 1980); and *The Foucault Reader,* ed. Paul Rabinow (New York: Pantheon Books, 1984), part 2.

19. Ninian Smart, *A Dialogue of Religions* (London: SCM Press, 1960); Ninian Smart, *Reasons and Faiths* (London: Routledge and Kegan Paul, 1958); and Ninian Smart, "Truth and Religions," in *Contemporary Philosophy of Religion,* ed. Steven M. Cahn and David Shatz (New York: Oxford University Press, 1982), 291–300. Smart remarks that "Modern Hindu ideology, if one may so dub it, consists in a neo-Sankaran theology in which all religions, albeit existing at different levels, ultimately point to the one truth" (294). Christ and Krishna, on this account, "are different manifestations of the one God" (294). All religions are true, for they, in different ways, point to the same truth. Their differences are in their symbolization of *that one ultimate reality.* God in the main Christian tradition (the standard theism of Plantinga) is symbolized in a more personal way than is the neo-Advaitin Brahma, but, according to neo-Sankaran theology, these are superficial differences in symbolism while in fact they are talking, in their different halting ways, about the same ineffable ultimate reality: the ground of all being and meaning. They are, that is, all talking, in their different (though in all instances inadequate) ways, about the same "ineffable ultimate truth." Moreover, the Hindu claim is that all religions are true, but some attain a "higher truth" than others. "The best religion . . . is one which is explicitly synthesizing, all-embracing (this being the merit of Hinduism)" (294). Christians of a reasonably orthodox sort (say, Catholics, Lutherans, or Calvinists) cannot accept this and, for similar reasons, reasonably orthodox Muslims and Jews cannot either. For such Christians, for example, there is the basic belief that "Christ is uniquely son of God: there are no other incarnations" and, as well, the belief, also basic, that "Christ alone is to be worshiped." Even if we go in a more revisionist direction than would Plantinga or Wolterstorff and, more tolerantly, like John Hick or Ninian Smart himself, make no such exclusivist claims for Christianity, or for any other religion, there is still the difficulty, for such a Hindu claim, that Smart has powerfully pressed home, namely that where we go descriptive about the religious experience of the various religions, we do not get "a basic common core of religious experience" which could perhaps be used to warrant the claim that these different religions are talking about, albeit it in different ways, the same ultimate reality. "There is," as Smart puts it, "incompatibility (at present) between religious truth-claims" and there is, as well, "divergence in practice-claims" (294). In his *Reasons and Faiths*, Smart—going descriptive about religions—has fully documented that *there is no common core to religious experience*, "but rather that there are different sorts of religious experience which recur in different traditions, though not universally. From a phenomenological point of view it is not possible to base the judgment that all religions point to the same truth upon religious experience. Nor is it reasonable to think that there is sufficient conceptual resemblance between God and nirvana (as conceived in Theravada Buddhism) to aver that the Theravadin and the Christian are worshipping the same God (for one thing, the Theravadin is not basically worshipping)" (299). This is like a breath of fresh air after the stultifying rigid dogmatism of Plantinga and Wolterstorff. All the quotations from Smart in this note are from his "Truth and Religions."

20. The standard, and historically important, discussion of miracles is in David Hume. For Hume on miracles, see David Hume, *Writings on Religion,* ed. Antony Flew (La Salle, Ill.: Open Court, 1992), 63–88. See, for a sympathetic discussion of Hume on miracles, Antony Flew, *Atheistic Humanism,* 69–87; and Flew's "Hume's Philosophy of

Religion," in *Philosophers Ancient and Modern,* ed. G. Vesey (Cambridge: Cambridge University Press, 1986), 129–46. Alasdair MacIntyre, giving Hume his account of miracles (at least on some cleaned up form) in the natural theological role which it has played and which Hume was attacking, tries to find a different role for the notion of a miracle in a context where theism is generally accepted. Miracles, on his account, are not used to *ground* theism, but are something we could expect God, upon occasion, to perform, given that we have *independent* grounds for believing that God exists and has the nature Christians believe Him to have. This altered conception of a role for miracles can take a different conception of miracle than the one Hume was attacking and perhaps showing to be incoherent. Miracles are no longer conceived as violations of laws of nature, but, following Aquinas, "as something not occurring in the accustomed natural course of things, which therefore requires a cause exceeding the power (*facultas*) of nature." Alasdair MacIntyre, "Hume, Miracles, Nature, and Jansenism," in *Faith, Skepticism and Personal Identity,* ed. J. J. MacIntosh and H. A. Meynell (Calgary, Alberta: University of Calgary Press, 1994), 91. Thomas Aquinas, *Summa Theologiae* 1a q. 105, a.7. But Aquinas's conception of a miracle is too problematical to have any theological or apologetic force. Miracles become unexpected, remarkable happenings which somehow *require* the postulation of a cause exceeding the power of nature. But we can make no more sense of "a cause exceeding the power of nature" than we can of "a violation of a law of nature." To say that we can make sense of Aquinas's notion, is, to put it minimally, to make a very problematical claim.

    21. Flew, *Atheistic Humanism,* 74.

    22. Ibid.

    23. Ibid.

    24. Ibid.

    25. Ibid., 78–79.

    26. Ibid., 79. Note that while MacIntyre would disagree with much that Flew claims, he does agree with Flew about this essential point. MacIntyre, "Hume, Miracles, Nature, and Jansenism," 89. However, given what I have argued above, some might say that, though the resurrection should no longer be called a miracle, given our, and Hume's, definition of a "miracle," it should be called instead a "marvelous event" and its possibility admitted. Yes, so construed, its *possibility* should be admitted, but we still have intact Hume's argument (perhaps the core of his case) about how historians assess, and reasonably assess, historical evidence. It will remain, even on the revised classification of the supposed event, more reasonable to believe that such a marvelous event did not occur, than to believe that it did occur, given what we know or can reasonably believe. And, after all, that is all we have, or can have, to go on. Again, and incidentally to the argument just made, we can see confirmed our general claim, as argued in the previous chapter, that nothing of much substance turns on definitions or on what can be achieved by *just* engaging in conceptual analysis. "Oxford science" never takes us very far.

    27. Thomas Hobbes, *Leviathan,* chapter 5.

    28. Note the fundamental assumption working here uncritically, the assumption so resolutely attacked by Wittgenstein, that intention can fix meaning.

    29. Flew, *Atheistic Humanism,* 102.

    30. Axel Hägerström, *Philosophy and Religion,* trans. Robert T. Sandin (London: George Allen and Unwin Ltd., 1964), 175–308.

    31. Hobbes, *Leviathan,* chapter 5.

    32. Hägerström, *Philosophy and Religion,* 182–84, 196, 209–10, 221, 234–41, 252.

    33. Hume, long before the rise of anthropology, recognized something like that.

34. Paul Tillich, *Systematic Theology* (Chicago: University of Chicago Press, 1951). Paul Edwards, "Some Notes on Anthropomorphic Theology," 241–50; Kai Nielsen, "Is God So Powerful That He Doesn't Even Have to Exist?" 270–81; and Sidney Hook, "The Atheism of Paul Tillich," 59–64, all in *Religious Experience and Truth,* ed. Sidney Hook (New York: New York University Press, 1961).

35. John Wisdom, *Philosophy and Psychoanalysis* (Oxford, England: Basil Blackwell, 1953), 140–68; and John Wisdom, *Paradox and Discovery* (Oxford, England: Basil Blackwell, 1965), 1–22, 43–56. Ronald Hepburn, "Review of *Paradox and Discovery,*" *Scottish Journal of Theology* 19 (1966): 471–73; Ilham Dilman, "Wisdom's Philosophy of Religion," *Canadian Journal of Philosophy* 4 (1975): 473–524; and D. A. T. Gasking, "The Philosophy of John Wisdom," in *Wisdom: Twelve Essays,* ed. Renford Bambrough (Oxford, England: Blackwell's, 1974), 1–41.

36. I think, in this respect at least, Father F. J. Copelston's debates with both Bertrand Russell and A. J. Ayer are very revealing. He seems, along with his talk of a "transcendent cause" (whatever, if anything, that means), to be stuck with something like a *metaphysically* necessary being and some strange conception of "ultimate" metaphysical explanations. But the debates are well worth studying, for they bring out starkly the differing underlying presuppositions, on the one hand, of two clearheaded empiricists and, on the other, of a clearheaded Thomist. They also show clearly the extremes to which such a classical metaphysician can be driven to defend his position. These debates have been reprinted in the following places: Bertrand Russell, *Why I Am Not a Christian* (London: George Allen and Unwin Ltd., 1957), 144–68; and A. J. Ayer, *The Meaning of Life* (New York: Charles Scribner's Sons, 1990), 18–52. The debates originally occurred on the "Third Programme" of the BBC. See as well my discussion of Copletson in my *Reason and Practice* (New York: Harper and Row, 1971), 488–89.

Chapter Four

Can Religious Beliefs Be Both Groundless and Reasonable?: The Basic Belief Apologetic

I

I believe the cluster of arguments given in the previous chapter, or at least some more developed and more carefully nuanced version of them, to be sound. In various books over the years I have extensively articulated and defended them.[1] Moreover, I not only think the arguments given in the previous chapter (or at least some more careful statement of them) are sound, I think (risking *hubris* here) they should be persuasive and compelling for anyone standing where we stand now in our cultural history who also has a good philosophical and scientific education. I think such people should find them compelling, particularly when they are taken to be a part of a *cumulative* argument that has been developing over the last two hundred years about religion. But I am also keenly aware that a number of philosophers, able analytic philosophers among them, do not think such arguments embedded in such narratives are sound or compelling. They argue, sometimes vehemently, that we should not be persuaded by arguments of this sort. Very often the claim is that these atheological arguments presuppose a discredited positivism.[2] I have been at pains to respond that they do not. To the extent that they reflect positivistic assumptions, I have argued, they only reflect a residue that has passed into the mainstream of our thinking that has a very considerable merit. Indeed, their merit is such that the burden of proof rests with these critics to show how such "positivistic" arguments are mistaken. It is not enough to make a general blast against positivism.

A better response to my arguments, and those like mine, is, I think, to argue that any arguments which rest on contentions concerning what it makes sense to say, positivist or otherwise, are very precarious indeed.[3] For one thing, the development of analytic philosophy in the last two decades has made it evident that no one has constructed a good *theory* of meaning. Philosophy of language, with a proffered theory of meaning, has no legitimate claim (*pace* Michael Dummett) to the role of First Philosophy or any streamlined replacement of it.[4] There is no consensus about theory of meaning, no consensus about whether it is even reasonable to expect that one can be constructed which could come to command a rational consensus or whether we even need one, if one could be constructed. My naturalism without foundations is a form of naturalism that argues that a *theory* of meaning is something we can very well do without. But then how do I get off, it is natural to respond, with putting such weight on considerations about what it makes sense to say, or what is intelligible, what is coherent, what is absurd, and the like? Without a *theory* of meaning, can we plausibly make any such claims at all as I have made about the intelligibility of religious and theological utterances? I assume that we have some litmus test for what it makes sense to say. But without a theory of meaning, it is natural to respond, we can have no such test.

It is just this counterclaim that I think is mistaken. Wittgenstein, in his post-*Tractatus* work, has powerfully argued that without a *theory* of meaning we have such a litmus test.[5] A word, expression, or sentence is intelligible if it has an established use in a public discourse: our use of language embedded in its social practices. Where a mark or string of marks has in such a practice a use such that we know how to go about employing it or them to make assertions, ask questions, utter commands, express wishes, evince hesitations, and the like, then the mark or string of marks is intelligible and makes sense. It is not like "An infinite individual, bodiless and transcendent, acting in the world." That string of marks taken together has no established use in our public discourse, though the individual marks taken individually do. "The universe is personal," "God is pure act," "God is a metaphysically necessary being," "God is the ground of being and meaning" all lack such a context of significant use and cannot be acceptably paraphrased into sentences which have such a use. (The reductive paraphrases, as we saw in the previous chapter, are never adequate.)

However, it will in turn be responded, if having such a use in an established discourse is your criterion for what is meaningful, then at least some metaphysically unencumbered religious discourse fits the bill. Forget about this talk of necessary being, the ground of the universe, and the like, that, no doubt, is pure fluff. Stick instead with the plain words of the first sentence of the Thirty-nine Articles of Religion of the Anglican church which says that God is the "one living and true God, everlasting, without body, parts, or passions; of infinite power, wisdom, and goodness, the Maker, and Preserver of all things both visible and invisible." That is at least relatively plain English and has been uttered over and over again by many native speakers of English quite innocent of metaphysics or natural theology. Moreover, it is embedded in their social practices. It plainly has an established use in the language and thus, on your own view of things, is unequivocally intelligible.

It is perhaps in someway intelligible, though, given the trouble that many people have in understanding such utterances—and not just when they are doing philosophy—it is not clear that it has a clear context of established use. But even granting that it is *somehow* intelligible, still, when the users of such language go on to make further statements at least seemingly entailed by it, they end up uttering other sentences which they and we do not understand and which have no firm use in our language. They are sentences such as "God is a person without a body," "God is the maker of the world out of nothing," "God is an individual yet infinite," and the like. "God, everlasting without body" is something close to ordinary English all right, but when we try to understand its use—its sense—we are led naturally to such metaphysical whoppers. Indeed, it is a metaphysical whopper itself. Even looking at the plain English religious sentence embedded in its language-game, we are still baffled by it and not just by what would be, its proper *analysis*. We are at a loss in trying to understand what sense, if any, it has. We are, that is, back in the swamp.

It is in trying to find a way out that has led philosopher-theologians to utter the metaphysical monstrosities that we have seen are quite without a use in any established language. A small band of metaphysicians and theologians try to employ them, but to no avail. They lack any footing in our public discourse and are certainly not something we have some overlapping consensus about such that they could be expressive of our considered judgments, judgments that we might get into reflective equilibrium. And the same thing is true of the religious utterances made in plainer English.

So I continue to go with Wittgenstein here. We can and do have a litmus test—roughly having a use in a language—for what is intelligible and what is not. Minimally this is a necessary condition for something being intelligible and we have this test without having, or even desiring, any *theory* of language or a *theory* of meaning at all. What we need to do instead is to carefully attend to how our language actually works, where it is troubling us, to see if what we are trying to say or think really has a use or whether some philosopher or theologian or someone else, trying to make some grandiose claim, has used expressions in such a way that they actually have a use (a way of functioning) in our language. We need to see if we can use them to make assertions, convey information, express our emotions, ask questions, carry out deliberations, and the like. We need not construct a theory of meaning here, but we need to attend carefully to the actual functioning of our words and sentences in their actual living contexts in our linguistic/social practices.

Still, this very Wittgensteinian therapeutic turn is very much in dispute.

There plainly is no overlapping consensus about that among philosophers, to say nothing of a wider public. So I stand on precarious ground in appealing to it. Again, like the return of the repressed, comes the criticism that appeals concerning what it makes sense to say are very fragile appeals in philosophy. We should not, the claim is reiterated, put the weight on them that I have.[6]

I would agree that it is too strong taken *alone* as an atheological argument concerning religion, but it is not taken alone. It is in reality part of a *cumulative* argument for atheism, or at least for skepticism concerning the claims of religion, that has been building up over the last two hundred years. Hume and Kant (or at least some rational reconstruction of their arguments such as J. L. Mackie's) have shown that none of the attempted demonstrations of the existence of God are sound.[7] Appeal to religious experience or to straightforward inductive evidence for the existence of God designed to replace the failed demonstrations have also not worked. Appeal to miracles to establish the truth of a religion have been discredited and the diverse and often conflicting putative revelations have made the appeal to revelation (a straightforward appeal to faith) very suspect. Some of this I have argued in the previous chapter and it has been very extensively argued in our century and in the previous century, to say nothing of Hume's, Bayle's, and Kant's arguments which proceeded them.

Arguments that we must base our morality on belief in God, if our morality is to have any objectivity or viability, have also been discredited—a discreditation that goes at least as far back as Hume—as well as the related claim that we need belief in God to make sense of our lives or to avoid social disintegration.[8] Similarly, the claim is groundless that only with Christianity, or alternatively with Judaism or Islam, will we find the deepest, most adequate form of morality. (I return in the final chapter of this book to an extended argument for the claims made in this paragraph.)

I will flesh out a bit more some of what I have said above. Two historically important, at least putative, discreditations of religious apologetic have been the discreditations (alleged discreditations?) of (1) attempts by natural theology to demonstrate the existence of God and (2) of later appeals to religious experience or to inductive considerations to establish that God exists. Terence Penelhum has well argued that "classic natural theologians were not just arguing for the rationality of believing in the existence of God or the providential governance of the world. They were trying to show that it was irrational not to believe in these things. That is what we mean when we say they were trying to prove them."[9] Yet, as Penelhum would be one of the first to say, all these attempts at proof have failed and we have no good reasons to think that a new one may be just around the corner which will do the trick, where the classical ontological, cosmological, and teleological arguments have not.[10] There are, to be sure, a few holdouts here who still think that God's existence can be proved. Hugo Meynell and Richard Swinburne, as I mentioned in the previous chapter, are two such distinguished holdouts.[11] But they are very much in the minority, except among Catholic philosophers, who are under the *authoritarian* constraint that they must believe, *as a religious dogma, an article of the Catholic faith*, that God's existence can be proved in some sense or other: that there is a natural knowledge of God, which is available to all normal adult human beings unless they are corrupted by sin. But even here there is by now a not inconsiderable waffling. But plainly that there is such a natural knowledge of God, if indeed there is, or that God's existence can be proved, if it can, is not something that can be established by dogmatic *proclamation* or any kind of proclamation. Here we must, to even get anything that would count as a proof, be free to use our reason, our powers of ratiocination, and to accept what that delivers. That just is the name of the game when it comes to proving something. Where philosophers or theologians or any of the people who carefully think about these things are under no such institutional constraints and are free to use their own brains in discoursing with others, there is a considerable, though still not complete, consensus that God's existence cannot be demonstrated or otherwise proved. Even the Calvinist philosopher Alvin Plantinga, who perhaps more than anyone else in recent times has stressed the importance and the strength of the ontological argument for the existence of God, agrees that we have no conclusive or coercive argument for the existence of God. Taken as demonstrations, he avers, they all, including the ontological argument, fail. They do not provide natural theology with what it needs. They do not, that is, help it to achieve what we have seen, following Penelhum, is the aim of natural theology, to wit to show that it is irrational *not* to believe in God. They do not show, as Plantinga put it, "that any rational person who is intellectually honest will believe the premises and will see that these premises do indeed entail the intended conclusions."[12] None of them seem to be, to put it cautiously, "real demonstrations" like "say, the Pythagorean Theorem or Kurt Gödel's demonstration of the incompleteness of arithmetic."[13]

Plantinga, as usual very confident, is not, as we shall see in a moment, in the slightest troubled by this. But what is to the point here is that Plantinga is here asserting something over which there is a wide consensus among reasonably philosophically sophisticated believers and skeptics alike, namely that the grand hope to make such proofs to establish such a natural knowledge of God—a hope once shared by natural theologians, a very considerable majority of philosophers, and many others following in their wake—is no longer a hope of very many. Such hopes have not survived Hume's and Kant's at least putative undermining of the key arguments of natural theology. Natural theology is a nonstarter today. There is no good reason to expect that God's existence is going to be demonstrated and very powerful reasons for thinking it will not be demonstrated. With this, as rather common knowledge, or at least as a common perception of things, interest in such purported demonstrations has waned. The announcement of a new demonstration of God's existence is almost on a par with an announcement of a new demonstration of a perpetual motion machine. A return to a consideration of the new argument, or to such arguments in general, will produce, for most skeptics and believers alike, a yawn and a kind of weariness. If they are philosophers or theologians, it may be their professional business to examine such matters; they have to go through what may be, if the argument is at all subtle, the complicated process of spotting the error in the reasoning. But, given the state of the discussion here, there is no reasonable expectation that this time, after all our well-explained failures in the past, it will come to something. My arguments about the coherence of God-talk were made against the background of these considerations and the cumulative argument that gives the rationale for such a shift in the *Weltgeist*.

II

In the nineteenth century and early twentieth century, after the Humean-Kantian destruction, to substitute evidential proof for the failed demonstrations would be to attend to religious experience. This would yield, some claimed, certain knowledge of the existence of God or, others claimed, at least a probabilistic or less than certain knowledge, but still a genuine knowledge of God's existence, with something like an inductive argument or alternatively with what I shall in a moment characterize as a seeing-as argument. But these arguments also fail.[14] Anything that could be literally seen or otherwise empirically noted or encountered or met with could not be God. We can have religious experience all right, but we cannot legitimately, or perhaps even intelligibly, claim that it is God we experience, for God is a nonmaterial, nonphysical infinite individual transcendent to the universe. It is just the kind of reality that cannot be seen or observed or otherwise directly empirically detected or even intuited (assuming we understand what that means), for anything that could be so detected would not be God. Some religious people do indeed speak of encountering God or say that at least mystics do so during moments of mystical illumination. More commonly they speak of standing in the presence of God or of experiencing God in their own lives, but that talk must, given God's transcendence, His infiniteness, and His invisibility, be an attempt at metaphorical or symbolic talk. But they are metaphors (attempted metaphors) or symbols which cannot be cashed in or, put less crudely, since we cannot give them a nonmetaphorical or nonsymbolic paraphrase, we cannot say what they are metaphors or symbols of and thus we do not even know that they are metaphors or symbols. Moreover, only a nonmetaphorical, nonsymbolic rendering of "seeing God," "experiencing God," "standing in the presence of God," "encountering God," and the like could have noetic value: could give us even an inkling of a knowledge of God, certain or uncertain.

Inductive arguments will also not do. Suppose it is said that God is not *directly* experienced, seen, or encountered, but is encountered *indirectly* through His works and in His providential care of His creation. We do not directly verify God's existence by seeing Him or otherwise directly detecting Him, but we indirectly verify His existence by making inductive inferences from His works.[15] But it is a *logical* impossibility, the above argument has claimed, directly to experience God (to see Him or to talk to Him, for example) so a direct verification of His existence is *logically* impossible, but then an indirect verification is *logically* impossible as well, for, if we do not know what it is we are directly verifying, if direct verification here *makes no sense,* than neither does indirect verification. There cannot be one without at least *the logical possibility* of the other; if the direct verification of something is *logically* precluded, then so is indirect verification.

If walking in the foothills of the St. Victoire I see smoke in the distance, I can legitimately infer that there is a fire there, using the platitudinous generalization that where there is smoke there is fire. But that induction, and the associated inductive generalization, is only justified because I know what it is directly to observe fire and because many people have many times directly observed fires after they have observed smoke. Many times, of course, what is directly observed, or is directly observable, is more illusive than fires. Sometimes we will have, *as a matter of fact,* to be satisfied with indirect observation and indirect verification. But where we do not have any understanding at all of what it would be like directly to verify the existence of the alleged reality, then the very idea of indirect verification also becomes problematical. But the idea becomes thoroughly questionable, or even worse, where the very idea of direct observation is self-contradictory, as is the case with God. In that case, there can be no indirectly observing Him or verifying His existence either. Inductive arguments for God's existence are all plainly nonstarters.

Suppose it is responded that this talk of seeing God or observing God or inductively verifying His existence is all too *scientistic.* What people who talk of religious experience should have been talking about is not of seeing but of *seeing-as* phenomena. We can get a handle on the notion of "seeing-as" by bringing to mind Jastrow's duck-rabbit drawings—his ambiguous figures, figures which can be seen-as, looked at in one way, a rabbit, or looked at in another way, a duck.[16] There is no seeing or looking or argumentation or inferring that is going to establish that it really is a drawing of a duck or that instead it really is a drawing of a rabbit that is being seen. Some *at first look-*

ing at it will see it as a duck and others will see it as a rabbit. After a little talk, and repeated viewing, both will see that it can be seen in either way: that is, as a duck or as a rabbit. There is, between the two, no one way of seeing it that is the right way. We cannot rightly say that it is a drawing of a duck or a drawing of a rabbit, but it is a drawing of an ambiguous figure —a duck-rabbit— that can be seen as either a duck or as a rabbit with no way of intelligibly saying that the correct way of seeing it is one way rather than the other.

We are in the same boat, it has been argued, with God. The believer looks at the world (invariably a part of the world) and sees it as the creation of God and as something reflecting His providential care. The atheist looking at the world (indeed, the same part of the world) sees it as just the product of natural forces and processes. In this way, the claim goes, the world is ambiguous like the ambiguous duck-rabbit figures. Believer and nonbeliever see the same thing as, in a parallel way for their phenomena, do people looking at Jastrow's figure. One sees it as one thing and the other sees it as another in both cases.[17] Again, in the religious case, as in the Jastrow's figure case, there is no possibility of one being right and the other being wrong. So, while there can be no literal experience of God, still, the believer can experience the world as the creation of God. There is no seeing God, but there is a seeing the world as under God's providential care: a seeing the world as being under God's governance.

As suggestive as it is, that analogy will not work and the argument relying on it does not succeed. We can see Jastrow's ambiguous duck-rabbit figure as a duck and as a rabbit just because we know what it is to see a rabbit and what it is too see a duck or at least sometimes to see unambiguous pictures or at least less ambiguous pictures of rabbits and sometimes to see unambiguous pictures of ducks or at least less ambiguous pictures of ducks. But we do not know what it is to see God or to otherwise observe God and thus we do not understand what it is to see something as God or experience something as God or to see the world as God's creation or as under God's governance and the like. *Only where it is possible to literally see something is it possible for us to see something as that thing.* It may be nonscientistic, but the seeing-as argument or claim is also as much a nonstarter as the argument or claim about directly experiencing or encountering God or inferring His existence from what we observe in the world.

Even if my assertion that these various defenses of theism have been discredited is too strong, still reflective dialectical examination has certainly made religious beliefs very problematic. They are (*pace* Plantinga) certainly not claims that the defender of religion can make with any rational confidence. They are certainly not judgments that are our—where the "our" ranges over people society-wide—considered judgments that could be set in wide reflective equilibrium such that we could say that they are beliefs which are for us rationally justified. Alasdair MacIntyre would probably say that this just reflects the sickness and radical inadequacy of our secular and liberal culture, including its intellectuals. We need to go back, he believes, in certain very fundamental respects, to the worldview of the Middle Ages.[18] But he also very well understands that we cannot go back in any full sense to the Middle Ages. There is, of course, no escaping for us the seeing of things by our own lights. We, whoever we are, cannot but start from there. We should then work from there with the method or methods of justification that are available to us given our starting place. We (*speaking now of the intellectuals in our society as a group*) do not, when we so reason, accept such religious beliefs and metaphysical beliefs as being just *unproblematically* true. Indeed, some of us can find no adequate grounds at all for accepting them or in some cases even making sense of them. We have no consensus here, so we have not been able to place our beliefs about religion in wide reflective equilibrium and so we have no grounds for saying such beliefs are justified or warranted.[19]

III

So both arguments of natural theology and their experiential replacements break down. It very much seems at least that there is no justification or warrant for believing in God. It looks like, if we are clearheaded and stand in a cultural context in which something like the above arguments have become widely available—most centrally the cumulative argument against belief in God that has slowly become widely available in the years of discussion since the Enlightenment—belief in God becomes very problematical and very difficult indeed. Such a skepticism has gradually become a part of our intellectual cultural heritage. Where we continue to believe in God our believing tends to be a fideistic groundless believing rooted in the heart. To believe, if we are clearheaded, we must just be knights of faith. The argument then becomes whether that groundless believing is a reasonable option for persons aware of, or who readily can become aware of, the cumulative atheological arguments and who also have a good knowledge of philosophy and science. Is Christian, Jewish, or Islamic belief now still a live option for a reasonable and well-informed person? Certainly she could not justify her beliefs by showing them to be among our considered judgments in wide reflective equilibrium: the holistic pattern of justification that we have been explicating and arguing for, a pattern of justification that in practice, though not, of course, in articulation, is deeply implanted in a least cultures such as our own. But perhaps she could show, not that they were so justified, but instead that such a method could show that they are nonrational, but still not irrational, options that could reasonably be accepted even by intellectually articulate and informed people in our modernist cultures. Perhaps she could show that standard theism is such an option for reasonable, well-informed, intellectually so-phisticated people in our culture, such that there is nothing irrational, unrea-sonable, intellectual irresponsible, or even mistaken about their having such theistic beliefs.

It is just such a conception that is argued for by some fideists and in a somewhat similar fashion by analytical Calvinist Christian philosophers such as Alvin Plantinga and Nicholas Wolterstorff. I now turn to an examination of their arguments.

Both groups (the Kierkegaardian-Wittgensteinian fideists and the ana-lytical Calvinists) argue that the rational status of theistic beliefs—their rea-sonability or intellectual acceptability—does not depend "upon whether there are good theistic arguments available" for those beliefs.[20] Plantinga thinks with his usual confidence—displaying what he takes to be the virtue of Chris-tian self-confidence—that there are plenty of good arguments for theistic be-lief, though, as we have noted him saying, none of them amount to demons-trations or have sufficient force or warrant such that any rational and reasonably informed person must, on pain of some failure or diminishment of her rationality, assent to them. But, that notwithstanding, he agrees with Wolterstorff in believing that a believer in God can "be perfectly rational even if he doesn't believe on the basis of arguments, even if in fact there aren't any good theistic arguments."[21] We have asked, and this has been the traditional way of considering religion by philosophers in the past few hundred years, whether belief in God—belief that there is such a person as God—"is ratio-nal, or reasonable, or intellectually up to snuff."[22] The ruling assumption seems "to be that if the arguments for theism are stronger than those for athe-ism, then belief in God is rational; but if the arguments for atheism are stronger, then atheism, or at any rate agnosticism, is the more reasonable at-titude."[23] But Plantinga and Wolterstorff think, as do the Kierkegaardian-Wittgensteinian fideists as well, that this traditional philosophical attitude, or at least the traditional philosophical attitude in modern societies, is through and through mistaken.

We should, they argue, start by querying this traditional attitude. Why ac-cept it? Plantinga and Wolterstorff call the belief, or the assumption underly-ing it, *evidentialism,* which they take to be little more than a dogma of some philosophers. Moreover, they argue, these philosophers are not consistent here or at least they are not evenhanded. They offer evidentialist objections against religious belief, but they do not offer evidentialist objections against belief in other minds, the material world, or the reality of the past. The latter beliefs are just steadfastly and, they agree with evidentialists, reasonably *groundlessly* believed. But when we come to religious belief, no groundless believing is taken to be acceptable by evidentialists. The religious case is treated by evidentialists as being just plainly different. Their governing assumption seems, at least, to be that the reasonability of theistic beliefs depends on whether there are good theist arguments or good evidence available for them. If there are they are reasonable, if not, not. Many modern philosophers (Bertrand Russell and J. L. Mackie are paradigmatic here) have believed that there is no, or least no adequate, evidence for theistic belief and that therefore, they have concluded, it is irrational to believe in God.[24] This is so because it is irrational to believe in God or in anything else unless there is adequate evidence for the belief in question.

Plantinga and Wolterstorff counter that it is absurd to hold the Cliffordian belief—a belief which is a fundamental underlying assumption of these evidentialists—that it is always wrong to accept a belief for which you do not have adequate evidence or a good argument. We would, for example, be very unreasonable to take that attitude toward belief in other minds, the external world or the reality of the past. Plantinga cites Russell's famous example that it is logically possible to believe that the world is only a few minutes old, having come into existence just five minutes ago complete with all its apparent traces of the past, all the apparent memories, dusty books, faded pictures, crumbling mountains, massive oaks trees, and the like. But surely, this logical possibility notwithstanding (if indeed it is a logical possibility), it is rational, justified, and reasonable to continue to believe in a substantial past. Indeed, it would be crazy, paradigmatically insane, to believe otherwise. And Hume has shown that similar considerations obtain for our belief in the external world and in other minds. But Russell's five-minute-old world is, as far as the evidence is concerned, equally compatible with the evidence as is a belief in a substantial past. Similar arguments can be deployed concerning our belief in the external world or other minds. The denial that there is an external world or other minds is as compatible with the evidence as are the assertions that there is an external world and that there are other minds.

Both Hume and Russell realized that there was something outrageously absurd about such skeptical doubts and Hume, like Santayana in our century, appealing to our natural beliefs, our natural dispositions to believe, argued for the reasonability of setting aside these skeptical doubts. Indeed, Hume regarded these natural beliefs as inescapable and as plainly desirably so. But this looks like an appeal to a kind of animal faith, a complete abandonment of evidentialism concerning our acceptance of such basic beliefs. But, if this is so, why not accept *parity*, Plantinga and Wolterstorff argue, and similarly accept fundamental or basic theistic beliefs even if we cannot establish them or justify them evidentially or produce good arguments for them? Why the asymmetry here? It looks like the evidentialist is just prejudiced against religious beliefs and cannot sustain an attitude of judicious impartiality here. To accept this parity argument is to accept what Terence Penelhum has called *the basic belief apologetic*.[25]

IV

One bad argument by way of response, an argument frequently used by skeptical philosophers, is to treat theistic beliefs as hypotheses, analogous to scientific hypotheses and thus open to experiential or experimental testing. However, fundamental religious beliefs such as a belief that there is such a person as God or the belief that He providentially cares for His creation or the belief that He is omnipotent do not function in living religious discourse as empirical hypotheses or even significantly like hypotheses.[26] For believers they are rather, in a nontechnical way, basic beliefs, beliefs which stand unshakably, or at least that is the way they are taken by genuine believers, even if they are not believed on the basis of evidence or argument. In this way, the claim goes, they function more like our belief in the past, other minds, or our belief in the external world: beliefs which are surely not empirical hypotheses or indeed hypotheses of any kind. Even if we do not have evidence or noncircular arguments for commonsense realism, even if we cannot show phenomenalism to be false or incoherent, it would not follow that philosophers, who had taken epistemological skepticism seriously, must think that because of this that the belief that there are physical objects (e.g., rocks and trees) ought to be discouraged or taken as irrational or as being intellectually out of order.[27] To think so would be utterly mad. But then Plantinga asks:

> . . . why, then, should we think it follows in the case of theism? Suppose these beliefs are no more probable than their denials with respect to the body of beliefs shared by theists and nontheists alike, why should we conclude that they are not rationally defensible? Perhaps it is perfectly rational to take belief in God and related key theistic beliefs in the way we ordinarily take belief in other minds, material objects, the past, and the like. Why isn't it perfectly sensible to start with belief in God? Why does belief in God have to be probable with respect to some other body of evidence in order to be rationally defensible? [28]

If that was the only problem about belief in God, then perhaps belief in God would not have to be so grounded on evidence or reasons or direct experience to be reasonably accepted and lived in accordance with. But there is the problem that there is a great diversity of very fundamental beliefs about religion, while, by contrast, and disanalogously, there is no such diversity of belief concerning the external world or other minds. Anthropologists have not unearthed a culture somewhere that does not believe in the external world or in other minds. The idea of even looking for one or expecting one to turn up is just a very dumb joke. As Plantinga recognizes, there are some reasonable people, including some religious believers, e.g., some Buddhists, who do not believe in God, and there are, of course, some that do. There are no reasonable people who do not believe in other minds, the external world, or the reality of the past.

Epistemological skeptics take their "doubts" concerning such matters to be intellectual teasers; they are not, for them, or for us, as their and our behavior reveals, real doubts. Hume recognized this as fully as did Peirce. Skeptics believe these things like the rest of us, though for them it is, at least supposedly, on the basis of animal faith. Or at least so they think. But concerning religion there are real-live doubts and diverse and conflicting sets of belief and this against the background of a realization that a demonstration of God's existence cannot be given or any claim to just know experientially or immediately that God exists justified. Our societies, over matters of religion, are awash with live crucial doubt—good Peircean doubts, not Cartesian paper doubts. This generates intellectual and sometimes spiritual discontents. Religious beliefs cannot (*pace* Plantinga) be properly basic in the way, or even in a very similar way, to the way that some of our memory beliefs, our belief in other minds, our belief in the reality of the past and of the external world may be said to be properly basic. The basic belief apologetic is fatally wounded by this and similar disanalogies.[29]

In saying for the sake of this discussion that such beliefs (belief in the external world, other minds, the reality of the past) are basic, I am not in effect abandoning my holistic contextualism and implicitly adopting foundationalism or assuming a foundationalist conception, either strong or modest.[30] I am not appealing to the atomism of a Russell, Ayer, or Schlick. I am not going atomist or molecularist at all. I am simply saying that these beliefs are inescapable. All peoples at all times and at all places have such beliefs. No one, except when he is doing philosophy or has gone very plainly insane, ever tries to question them. And it is anything but clear whether we can even coherently question them. It is true that epistemological skeptics try to question them and foundationalist philosophers try to answer their attempted questioning, taking such skeptics very seriously. Classical foundationalists—what Plantinga calls strong foundationalists—try to show that such beliefs are absolutely certain and incorrigible. Surely, the foundationalist and epistemological skeptic agree, we have a philosophical problem about showing how these inescapable beliefs are absolutely certain, yielding certain knowledge, and thus, they say, there is a problem about how we can know them. But we know a lot of things that we do not know for certain and we reasonably believe a lot of things that might not be items of knowledge. "Certain knowledge" is not pleonastic.[31] The skeptic in effect shows that, given the foundationalist's conception of absolute certainty, we do indeed have good reasons for believing that they are not absolutely certain. But this only comes to showing either that "There is an external world" or "Some memory beliefs are reliable" or "There are other minds" are not, like "There is an infinite number of natural numbers" or "There are no three-sided squares," either *a priori* true or *a priori* false or that these beliefs are not like "I have a headache" or "I seem to see a red patch," in some way sense certainties. Not being either, there is a problem about how we can know *for certain* that they are true. But if we do *not* try to require *certain* knowledge here, there is no problem about how we can know them and know that they are true. They are, as W. V. O. Quine might put it, such deeply embedded beliefs because they are implicit, as background assumptions, in everything we know or warrantably believe. They are so deeply embedded that we have no idea of how we could give them up and go on making sense of our world. They could in no way be problematic unless everything is and, if everything is, then nothing is. To doubt, as was argued in chapter 2, we must have something which, for the time at least, stands fast which enables us to frame our doubt and to consider what it would be like to resolve our doubt. This familiar pragmatist and Wittgensteinian point is, I think, perfectly well-taken, but if to some of you it seems too dialectical to be philosophically very reliable, then consider, that argument aside, the most fundamental claim against Plantinga's and Wolterstorffs's claim for *parity* between certain key religious beliefs and these inescapable beliefs (Hume's natural beliefs), to wit, that the religious beliefs, even the most fundamental ones, are not similarly inescapable. Some people in our culture have them and some do not. Outside our culture there are whole cultures of people, with long-established religions, Confucian culture or Theravada Buddhist culture, to take key examples, which do not have them. These various religious beliefs, as well as antireligious beliefs opposed to them, unlike these inescapable beliefs (belief in the reality of the past, for example), are the subject of real-live doubts and assertions and counterassertions and arguments and counterarguments. Moreover, as we have seen, there are serious questions about the very intelligibility or coherence of such religious beliefs.

Given these differences, it is not reasonable to say, as Plantinga and Wolterstorff do, that we are justified (where we are, as they are themselves, the sort of intellectuals I have described) in taking, or are even being reasonable in taking, these religious beliefs as basic beliefs, or any other kind of acceptable belief, where we have no evidence for them or other grounds for believing them, to say nothing of claiming to know that they are true. Plantinga claims that he has *immediate knowledge* that there is such a person as God, but we have no reason at all to believe him. He, like his mentor Calvin, who says the same thing, is just proclaiming. But saying it firmly with Christian self-confidence will not at all help.

However, matters cannot be let to rest here, for Plantinga does not just take this fideist turn, but argues, as Plantinga puts it, at least seemingly taking us back into the jungle again, that it is dubious that "there is no evidence, or at least no sufficient evidence, for theistic belief. . . . There are many good theistic arguments, and putting them together results is an impressive case indeed."[32] Here we see Plantinga, again confidently proclaiming, and that, of course, is very distant from the sensitive fideistic spirit of Pascal, Hamann, or Kierkegaard. But before we conclude that much turns on Plantinga's bold claims, we should note the very weak sense Plantinga has in mind when he speaks of good arguments. "A good argument," Plantinga remarks "would be one that started from premises many people rationally accept (or are inclined to accept) and proceeds via steps many people reasonably endorse to . . . (a) . . . conclusion."[33] He thinks that in that way we can have good arguments, and plenty, for the belief that there is such a person as God.[34] That is to say, Plantinga has it, that, though we cannot *demonstrate* that there is such a person as God, we can have a considerable variety of good arguments for believing that there really is such a person.

We can have, he avers, filling out his meaning here, good arguments, in the weak sense of "good argument," in which we also can have good arguments for particular resolutions of the various classical problems of philosophy (e.g., free will versus determinism). There we have "good arguments" for many various and at least ostensibly conflicting philosophical positions, while knowing full well, Plantinga stresses, that there are many reasonable, informed, and intellectually sophisticated people who will not accept the proffered argument. Over such "good arguments" we never get anything more than a local and temporary consensus (much caught up in some passing philosophical fashion) concerning which of our many "good arguments" are the better arguments, let alone a consensus concerning which are the best arguments or which are really sound arguments. There is no getting right here. In discussions over religion, like those in rather purer philosophy, we never get, as Plantinga pugilistically puts it, arguments which are knock-down-drag-out demonstrations, but we do sometimes, all the same, get good arguments *in the very weak sense* he has specified. If we can do it for the standard philosophical arguments, he rhetorically asks, why not for the at least ostensibly conflicting theses concerning the existence of God? Again he is asking, in what looks like a fair-minded manner, for parity.

His dragging in the perennial problems of philosophy very much weakens rather than strengthens his case. The whirligig of philosophical fashions and the persistent irresolvability of such classical philosophical problems, and even often a sense of not knowing how to proceed to even gain a plausible resolution, has led pragmatists, positivists, ordinary language philosophers, and Wittgensteinians to turn away from attempts to either solve or resolve those classical problems of philosophy. They went in importantly different ways, but they all came to believe that it was a mistake to try to provide good arguments to support, by taking a position, and with that sometimes claiming a solution, based on one of these "good arguments," for one or another of these classical problems of philosophy. They took it to be a mistake to proceed in this traditional way attempting to establish traditional theses in philosophy. Pragmatists sought to change the subject by transforming philosophy into a consideration of the problems of human beings and to benignly neglect the problems of the philosophers. Wittgensteinians sought to dissolve these classical problems through conceptual therapy and in doing so to show their unreality. Ordinary language philosophers tried to show that they rested on category mistakes and positivists tried to show that they were pseudoproblems. Philosophers, as distant from any of these tendencies, as were Henry Sidgwick and C.D. Broad, noted the depth and persistence of irreconcilable disagreements in philosophy and the lack of anything like a consensus in philosophy.[35] They also noted here its distance from science and from many of the beliefs of common life. Where we have, as we surely have, such endemic disagreements—disagreements going on over centuries—to think, as Plantinga does, of having good arguments aplenty is very dubious indeed. Rationalists have had too strong criteria for what counts as "a good argument," but Plantinga's way goes to the opposite extreme by radically relativizing "good argument."

This is illustrated in Plantinga's very practice. After making the remarks we have characterized above about what he takes to be a good argument, he goes on to give us a bunch of rather slap-dash arguments in favor of the existence of God and then a cluster of good arguments (good by the same weak criteria), some of them also rather slap-dash, against believing that God exists. He also stops to criticize those good arguments against theistic belief, but he neglects to criticize the theistic arguments.[36] But he is fully aware, though he neglects in this context to advert to it, that, just as it is the case for any "serious philosophic conclusion," telling criticisms could be made against the theistic arguments as well. That is just the nature of the game of giving good arguments in the weak sense that he specifies. Many people will rationally accept or be inclined to accept atheistic or religiously skeptical premises and will proceed via steps many people reasonably endorse to the conclusion that there is no such person as God or (alternatively) that we have no sufficient reason to believe that there is such a person. Just as for arguments about freedom and determinism, for physicalism versus phenomenalism, and for dualism versus epiphenomenalism, we will, concerning the existence of God, have all sorts of arguments differently reacted to and variously accepted or rejected or set aside, often by manifestly reasonable people, but with no good non-question-begging reason for thinking that one argument or cluster of arguments takes us closer to the truth or to a more reliable way of fixing belief than another.[37]

With such a conception of a "good argument," we could just as well say that there are many good antitheistic arguments and that putting them all together results is an impressive case indeed for atheism. This is exactly parallel to Plantinga's claim previously quoted that "there are many good theistic arguments, and putting them all together results in an impressive case indeed."[38] Atheists can reasonably assert what they assert and theists assert what they assert and there are no non-question-begging grounds to choose between them *given Plantinga's conception of things.*

It is roughly such considerations that led Penelhum to argue that parity is not enough.[39] I have argued that we neither have parity nor would it be enough if we did have it. It was in an attempt to give good arguments, in a stronger, more objective sense, of "good argument," that lead both defenders and articulators of natural theology (philosophers proceeding after the fashion of Aquinas, Scotus, or Paley or, in our time, Richard Swinburne), on the one hand, and natural atheological evidentialists such as Bertrand Russell, Sidney Hook, Ernest Nagel, Paul Kurtz, J. L. Mackie, Russell Norwood Hanson, Ingemar Hedenius, Michael Martin, and Michael Scriven, on the other, to try to ascertain whether the theist or the atheist or the agnostic has the better argument.[40] They tried, as well, to articulate, in sufficiently objective terms, a conception of "better argument" that they could use in arguing for theism, atheism, or agnosticism. In seeking an answer here, defenders of natural theology have tried to argue that for a properly informed person it is irrational not to believe in God. There is, the claim went, objective knowledge of God that is available to any adult person of normal intelligence. The atheist's denials and the agnostic's doubts, the claim goes, can be shown to be irrational. This, as Penelhum stresses, was the agenda of natural theology. Resisting this, philosophers skeptical of religion (atheists or agnostics) have argued that religious beliefs lack justification; we have, they think, good reasons to believe them to be without either justification or warrant. Some atheists have put the matter even more strongly by claiming not only do they lack justification, or warrant, but that they are so plainly implausible, as well as being unnecessary to make sense of our lives or to yield moral stability, that it is irrational to believe in them. Other atheists, among whom I include myself, limit that last claim to philosophically and scientifically sophisticated people in modern societies and people like them living during the last couple of centuries. It was reasonable for Aquinas or Maimonides to believe in God, but it is not for Plantinga or Kripke, though it does not follow from this that Plantinga or Kripke are unreasonable persons, for it is plain that reasonable people can, and usually do, have some irrational or unreasonable beliefs, particularly when those beliefs are close to their hearts. Indeed, we are all vulnerable here.

VI

Sometimes what we seek is something weaker, though not so weak as what Plantinga and Wolterstorff in effect content themselves with. Philosophers thinking about religion—skeptics and believers alike—want to see if it could be ascertained whether is is more reasonable or better (everything considered) to believe in God than not to believe in him. Plantinga and Wolterstorff offer us no help on this humanly fundamental question. They do not want to be fideists, but they in effect leave us with just a fideist plumping for faith. We can have no reason to believe that we can know, or believe with justification or warrant, that God exists without believing that on the basis of argument, experiential evidence, or direct experience.[41] But they do not meet our needs here. Pascalian or Kierkegaardian fideism (the former being a key object of Hume's antitheistic arguments) is much more compelling than are Plantinga's and Wolterstorff's claims that belief in God is a properly basic belief and that, this being so, it is rational to accept that religious belief, even if there is no direct experience of God or no evidence or good arguments for such a theistic belief. Unlike Pascal's or Kierkegaard's Christian, their Christian will, of course, suppose that belief in God is entirely proper and rational even if it is not grounded on argument or based on evidence or on experience. There is no room for the anguished knight of faith, faced with sickness unto death, believing in what he knows to be absurd. There is no room with such Calvinist rationalism for stark existential choices and existential pathos.

There is a further argument that Plantinga and Wolterstorff could press that turns on considerations about what rationality or reasonableness comes to. I talk, they might contend, as if we could talk of rationality or reasonableness *überhaupt* and, in doing so, I completely forget my contextualism and historicism. Rationality, properly conceived, "is in good measure period specify and situation specific."[42] What it is rational for children to believe, for example, is often rather different than what it is rational for adults to believe. For "a person reared in a traditional tribal society who never came into contact with another society or culture, there will be things rational to believe which for members of modern Western intelligentsia, would not be rational to believe."[43] Some of the things it was rational for Aristotle to believe would not be rational for Marx to believe. Some of what was rational for Augustine to believe would not be rational for Hume to believe, and so on. Wolterstorff generalizes as follows: what it is rational to believe can only be determined in context—historical and social contexts and, even more narrowly, personal contexts. It has long been the habit of philosophers to ask in an abstract, nonspecific fashion whether it is rational to believe that God exists, whether it is rational to believe that there is an external world, whether it is rational to believe that there are other persons, and so on. Mountains of confusion have resulted. "The proper question is always and only," Wolterstorff maintains, "whether it is rational for this or that particular person in this or that situation, or for a person of this or that particular type in this or that type of situation, to believe so-and-so. Rationality is always situated rationality."[44]

I agree that rationality is always, or nearly always, situated rationality and the same thing even more obviously goes for reasonability. I further agree that it is a mistake to ask, as philosophers not infrequently do, in some abstract, nonspecific fashion, whether it is rational to believe that God exists. The same is true for many things, though I do not think, for the reasons I have already given, that it was ever rational for anyone to really wonder if there is an external world or other persons. But the rationality of almost all beliefs is situation specific. But Wolterstorff is far too *individualistic* here. It is not true that the proper question is always and only whether it is rational for this or that particular person or type of person to believe so and so in this or that situation. Sometimes we want to ask, and should ask, a *socially specific* question about what it is reasonable to believe or do. Thus we might want to ask whether it is rational or reasonable for a typical member of the Western intelligentsia, typically situated for such intelligentsia, to believe in God. We are not concerned here with whether it is rational or reasonable for Peter or Elizabeth to believe in God. They might be members of the intelligentsia, but their particular circumstances of life might be unusual; they might have some particular hang-ups. For that reason, they might not, and reasonably so, believe what Western intelligentsia normally reasonably believe. However, sometimes we want to ask a *socially specific,* socially and historically context-dependent, question, about what it is reasonable for a typical member of a group, typically situated, to believe.[45] That is my naturalistic question about the *reasonability* of religious belief. It would be a good thing if we could ascertain what it is reasonable for typical members of the Western intelligentsia—that is us—living in typical situations to believe in this respect. This would give us a handle on the socially specific question of whether belief in God is reasonable for people in a position to have the best grip possible, for that time and place, on how things are.

Wolterstorff's and Plantinga's conception of an individualizing situated rationality takes the rationality of belief in God to be *person* specific and, in doing this, illicitly conceptually blocks the question of whether it is more or less rational or reasonable for people (representative individuals) typically placed in a determinate situation to believe in God. Often what we want to ask is a question about what it is rational or reasonable for a certain type of person placed in a certain type of circumstance to believe about so and so. All our questions are not about individual psychology or about what might excuse or explain why a given individual had a certain belief without our attributing irrationality or even 'epistemological irresponsibility' to him or her. We ask, for example, what it is reasonable for a teenager living in a ghetto in New York in 1994 to believe about AIDS or what it was reasonable for the German intelligentsia living in Germany in 1944 to believe about Nazi genocide.

Such questions are sometimes important—indeed, normatively important—to ask. And given the importance of belief/nonbelief—a religious commitment versus a purely secular one—in our lives, it is important to see, if only we can, what it would be more reasonable for properly informed people, but still people caring about their lives and the lives of others, now living in relative security in the rich capitalist democracies, to believe about God and not to have that question shuffled aside by sticking with Wolterstorff's purely person-specific conception of rationality. Moreover, as individuals thinking about our own lives and about what we are to believe concerning such matters, we would not infrequently want to know, if that knowledge could be had, what it is reasonable, and, everything considered, the right thing to believe for well-informed reflective people situated as we (most readers of books like this) are situated now. Perhaps there is no one right thing to believe, but that is something we would also very much want to know. We would, that is, want to know if that indeed is so. William James remarked that these are momentous options in our lives. We want, if only we can, to come to appreciate what it is we should believe here. In struggling with this, or in trying correctly to picture the struggle, we are not forced to choose between speaking of rationality *überhaupt* and speaking of a purely person-specific rationality. To see that we are not so stuck is of very considerable importance to us in making these momentous life choices.

VII

There is another turning that might be taken in trying to see if sufficient sense can be made of belief in God and the attendant theistic beliefs to get such beliefs into wide reflective equilibrium, or at least to make them in some other way acceptable. (Not everything that is accepted is acceptable, anymore than that everything that is desired is desirable.) Consider a broadly Pascalian-Hammannian-Kierkegaardian-Barthian fideism that would set aside both natural theology and Calvinist rationalism (if that is the proper phrase for it). It could also take the form of a Wittgensteinian fideism such as has been articulated by D. Z. Phillips and Ilham Dilman.[46] What I shall say here applies to both forms of fideism. The mistake, fideists would argue, is to try to justify religious belief by showing that religious beliefs are true or reasonable. Even if we cannot show anything of the sort, we are all the same being reasonable in believing in God as we are being reasonable in believing in the reality of the past even if such a belief cannot be evidentially or experientially grounded and even if there is no direct knowledge (awareness) of the presence of God. Belief in God and his providential care is neither rational nor irrational, but nonrational, and the believer's only real option is to believe nonrationally. As both Hume and Wittgenstein saw as well as anyone else, it can, in certain circumstances, be rational or reasonable to believe what can only be believed nonrationally. But, unlike Hume, fideists will maintain that to make sense of our lives, or at least to make the fullest sense of our lives, we must opt for a nonrational religious faith. Even where there can be no grounds or reasons for believing something to be true or probable or argumentatively established or warranted, it still sometimes can be rational or reasonable to have faith (if only we can have it) to make sense of our lives. We must, it is further and now nonhypothetically claimed, opt for a nonrational faith to make sense of our lives or at least for our lives to have the fullest sense attainable. We should become knights of faith and put all philosophizing aside, except to utilize it negatively and therapeutically to get rid of philosophizing about religion either in defense of religion or faith or in criticism of religion or faith. We should give up on both natural theology and natural atheology as well as such rationalistic Calvinist turnings as we have seen Plantinga and Wolterstorff engaging in.

It is often a good idea to follow Locke in trying to get our belief-forming mechanisms oriented toward getting in touch with reality (coming to have a good idea of what the facts of the matter are in the actual world we live in).[47] This, note in passing, is quite different from getting all excited about something as arcane and probably as pointless as possible worlds "theory." But such a Lockean orientation is plainly not the only goal we should have in life and it is not, to put it minimally, evident that it should always be our overriding goal. It has been a deeply embedded presupposition from Socrates and Plato to Russell and Freud that "nothing could take priority in belief governing over our obligation to expand our hold on truth and to avoid or to eliminate falsehood in our beliefs."[48] But that, the argument goes, is just a prejudice of philosophers and other persons inclined to be rationalistic.[49]

How, if we think it is not such a prejudice, we should ask, could we, if indeed we could, justify such a strong rationalist presupposition? It is hardly controversial to say that it is usually a good idea to try to have, where we can conveniently get them, reasonably well-warranted beliefs and to avoid having false or unwarranted ones. We will often get unnecessarily hurt, as Peirce well argued, if we do not. But that is a much weaker claim than a claim giving *absolute priority* to truth seeking and error avoiding. We may be justified in having a belief that is not rationally founded. To say we are justified in holding that belief is to say that we are permitted (reasonably permitted) to hold it and not, of course, that we have good grounds for the belief and that *in that familiar sense* it is justified. Justifying the belief in this sense in that case is precisely what we have *not* done and perhaps cannot do. But sometimes it may be necessary, to make our lives tolerable, to set aside giving priority to the search for truth and to attend instead to coming to grips with what Kierkegaard called sickness unto death. We need to come to sense fully, and to take to heart, our fragility and the tenuousness of life. We can hardly avoid feeling the force, as Katherine Mansfield put it, of its sadness, something we feel often in her writings and even more forcefully, as well as more pervasively, in the writings of Anton Chekhov. When we are nonevasive about our situation, we will see, the claim goes, that we very much need to have faith, if we can, with its commitment to God. We must believe in God groundlessly and non-rationally, but, all the same, we rightly do so, for without belief in God nothing really matters. We need to have a passionate commitment to God. If there is no God, then our life is just one damn thing after another until we die and rot. The establishment of truth and the avoidance of error through a relentless taking of the critical attitude is not something that *should* always be center stage in the living of our lives.

Such fideism has had a powerful articulation in Pascal and Kierkegaard. But still it relies on a false assumption, namely, that if God is dead nothing matters, that life is without meaning without God, that, if there is no God, morality is feckless and pointless and, indeed, withers. It never really faces Hume's powerful counterargument against such a Pascalian reaction. *The false assumption is that life is senseless in a Godless world.* Being in what these fideists regard as that terrible situation, the unjustified Pascalian claim goes, we are compelled to believe in God to make our lives tolerable. The implausibility of our belief in God to the contrary not withstanding, we must, if only we can, believe in God to give our lives meaning.[50] But *au contraire* there are plenty of things we can do and ways that we can be and purposes that we can have in a Godless world and we can think them carefully through, take them to heart, and weave them together into a morality that answers to our needs and to our caring about ourselves and others.[51] We similarly can give meaning to our lives. The Dostoyevskian conception that if God is dead nothing matters says more about the projections of some believers than it does about the human condition.

VIII

Some fideists will say both theology and atheology and standard work in the philosophy of religion give too much importance to religion as a *belief system*. It is, they acknowledge, a belief system all right, but we should not give so much importance to that as is standardly done in the philosophy of religion business. Faith is essentially having trust and the hope it inspires. Jewish, Christian, and Islamic fideists just stumblingly articulate a sense of trust in which the trust does not significantly depend on its articulations.[52] If a given articulation leads us into falsity, incoherence, or unreasonableness, we will, or at least should, such fideists say, abandon the articulation while keeping the trust and the hope and seek another more adequate articulation of our trust, our faith. This is something we can nonevasively, reflectively, and creatively do. Moreover, trust and hope can be expressed in many different ways. They all are our stumbling, only partially articulate, efforts to articulate our sense of trust. We should not attach too much importance to those belief systems which are the provisional vehicles for expression of the essential things, which are trust and hope. We should rather, with this trust and hope, fasten on the *existential* functions of religion, functions which have to do with religion helping people to face the problems of life and to overcome, or at least come to terms with, the despair in their hearts. It is not beliefs which are essential here, but the attitudes that religion can inspire in the face of these existentially very human issues. *It is trust and commitment that is at the heart of religion, not the belief system with its set of doctrines.* Commitment to truth should not *always* be the primary thing. Again, reason isn't always the primary thing; sometimes considerations about how to hold together one's life can and should take precedent, though the idea that these two things (i.e., the holding on to one's life and the acknowledgement of a belief system) will very often conflict is romantic exaggeration. In most circumstances, taking nonevasive thought is very important in taking hold of one's life or finding a sense in one's life and making one's own life and the lives around us at least a little more decent, if not more flourishing. But again, reason isn't everything. Human feelings and the attempt to cultivate them and to give an articulate expression to our feelings are central to a really human life. And *sometimes* it is very much the wrong question to ask if doing so and so or developing such and such sensibilities is the rational or even the reasonable thing to do. Again, we should remind ourselves that what is nonrational may not be at all irrational. We have many nonrational desires and aims which are not thereby irrational and indeed there is nothing unreasonable about having them. In some instances it would even be unreasonable not to have them.

The parts about belief systems and trust and articulation of trust are tricky. Religion, or at least Western religions, are systems or at least comprehensive conceptions of salvation. And we have a sense of what that comes to and what makes a system a system of salvation. (Having this understanding is fully compatible with believing that such systems of salvation never deliver the goods.) Similarly, we need to understand what makes trust a "religious trust," what makes faith a religious faith, for *not* every trust, every hope, or even every faith is religious. But to have a grip on that, so that the very trust can work, a religious person, or a person who wants to be a religious person, must give some careful attention to the belief system of the religion in question.

She or he can, and I think should, agree with the fideist that religion's language (in stories, myths, poetry, songs) expresses a hope which plays for religious persons a crucial role vis-à-vis the existential problems of their lives. But then she should also recognize that that role is not so much dependent on true beliefs as on the *attitudes* religion can inspire in the face of the existential surds that are a part of our lives. Still, the belief systems remain there as an essential part of the background that makes these attitudes possible or at least intelligible. The believer can seek, and indeed give, new articulations of his faith, but he cannot just change belief systems as he changes his clothes or be through and through pragmatic about them. If he does any of these things or things like them, he may take himself out of religion and religious faith altogether, as D. Z. Phillips and Richard Braithwaite have in effect done, where for them the "religious belief system" becomes morality touched with emotion in an embedded narrative which we at least entertain, but where belief in what we entertain is *optional*. It is true that trust and hope are very essential, but it is also true that the belief system *cannot* be treated simply as a convenient device or a pragmatic instrument. But with the recognition of the indispensability of the belief system, we have come full circle and are back to the difficulties with religion that have already been discussed.

IX

I have looked both in this chapter and the previous one at some of the tangle of considerations that are at work concerning the choice between taking a religious stance or taking a thoroughly secular stance toward the world. And I have argued that taking a religious stance is so very problematic that it would seem that the better thing to do would be to take a secular stance. The claim I am making is in large measure a philosophical claim and it is, for the most part, rooted in philosophical argumentation. As a philosophical claim, it is, in the very nature of the case, controversial, perhaps even essentially contestable. Philosophy is not the sort of enterprise where we can list the theorems proved or list its established experimental results such that we could record in a newspaper or some bulletin its established results. The confident expectations of some analytic philosophers to the contrary notwithstanding, we will not assert, if we are reasonable, reflective, and philosophically knowlegable, that now at long last we have got it right. Dispute and disagreement, as we have already noted, is endemic and intractable in philosophy.[53] The most that can reasonably be hoped for is that for a time, and for a rather local community (for philosophers and other intellectuals at a given time and place), certain philosophical claims can be made more plausible than others such that for a time such people, when they have carefully considered the argument in question, or a cluster of arguments set in a narrative, will come, on careful reflection, to accept it or them. But such arguments and claims should, and usually will, be challenged and there will be intelligent dissent. (There will, of course, unfortunately, be unintelligent dissent as well.)

The most that I can hope for from the above cluster of arguments about religion is that they may win the reflective assent of my peers. Plantinga is right (but hardly original) in remarking that we do not get demonstrations in philosophy. We have arguments and persistent and sometimes careful argument, but they always leave room for doubt and disagreement. Fallibilism, as I remark earlier, is pervasive in all domains of our cultural life and is particularly evident in science. But philosophical doubts run deeper, and are more intractable, than ordinary fallibilistic ones such as we characteristically have in science. Consensus in philosophy is more local and more transient and disagreement deeper and more endemic. We hardly have anything in philosophy like science's establish results. Plantinga puts it well when he remarks, "Take your favorite argument for any serious philosophical conclusion; there will be plenty of people who don't accept the argument and are not thereby shown to be dishonest."[54] He should have added, and I believe he would be inclined to, "or unreasonable or thick or bloody minded." Being dishonest is the least of our problems concerning such issues. If all that was required was some minimal approximation to purity of heart such that we do not lie or try to deceive here, we would long ago have been well enough home and free. But contestable conceptions of how to think about philosophical disputes, how to conceptualize them, how to judge what is fruitful or plausible or worth doing in philosophy or what is coherently conceivable run very deep and they are very pervasive and persistent. There is no reasonable hope of a nontemporary and nonlocal consensus here. The typical self-conceptions of philosophers and the realty of their practices are very different.

If this is so, then does it not mean that I must be accepting for my own argument, if I am to be consistent, the conception—the very weak conception—that we have seen Plantinga give, for a good argument in philosophy and in like matters, for example, argument concerning whether there is such a person as God? Recall, that for Plantinga, a "good argument would be one that started from premises many people rationally accept (or are inclined to accept) and proceeds via steps many people reasonably endorse" to a determinate conclusion.[55] For me, in the above cluster of putatively good arguments that I have proffered, the "many people" are philosophers and other intellectuals of our time in the rich capitalist democracies and any other societies similarly developed. (They could, of course, be socialist societies.) They are the people in the best position to critically appreciate and appraise the critical force of such arguments. But this does situate rationality and good arguments in the way Plantinga does and thus, as I argued in discussion of his views, I must be making the very weak claims as to what constitutes a good argument that he does. In the next paragraph I will qualify that, but I do substantially agree with him about what a good argument could come to *for a traditional philosophical belief* and, if we are right here, this, in part, explains why there is so little progress in philosophy and why philosophical dispute, unlike much scientific dispute, is so intractably contested and indecisive. Indeed, it is this very feature of philosophy that, along with other considerations, generates metaphilosophical skepticism about philosophy.[56]

However, this should not be as troubling for a naturalist (particularly a historicist pragmatic naturalist) as it should be for a Christian philosopher. This is so because a naturalist *could be*—I did not say *should* be—a historicist *skeptic*.[57] *Taking Plantinga's conception of a good argument,* he could say, and indeed should say, that many reasonable Confucianists rationally accept or make good arguments for Confucianist conclusions and the same is true for Zen Buddhists for their conclusions and for Muslims, atheists, agnostics, Freudians, Marxists, and the like for their conclusions. But since rationality is person-specific *and* situation-specific, there is no way, or at least no non-question-begging way, of assessing the comparative adequacy of these various good arguments. The Christian can rationally believe one thing, the Muslim another, the Confucian still another, the Buddhist still another, and agnostics and atheists, again appropriately, believe still different things. They can all do this, such a historicist skeptic avers, reasonably. Moreover, these things are not only different things, they are frequently conflicting things all buttressed, upon occasion, by good arguments. It looks like, on such a conception, that *Alles ist relativ.* But, for the Christian, in a way that is not the case for the historicist skeptic, this poses a problem, for Christians, even Christian fideists, accept believingly the biblical proposition that Christ is The Truth and The Way. But, given Plantinga's conception of a good argument, this claim loses its force. It comes to no more than for a Christian Christ is The Truth and The Way, but for a Nazi Hitler is The Truth and The Way, and there is no saying what The Truth and The Way is *überhaupt.*

Rational, reflective people have wanted something somewhat less relative than that. If that cannot reasonably be had, they would want, if they care about being accurate, to stop talking about anything being The Truth and The Way and the like. But Jewish, Christian, and Islamic belief presupposes an Absolutism that is hardly compatible with fallibilism, to say nothing of being compatible with historicism or relativism.

I do not think that I am in the same pickle as Plantinga and Wolterstorff for the following reasons. First, as we have already seen, while I agree that rationality is in large measure situation-specific, I do not think it is completely so.[58] I think there are general principles of rationality that are not situation-specific, e.g., rational persons *ceteris paribus* will take the most efficient means to achieve their ends; rational persons *ceteris paribus* will seek to make their judgments impartially; rational persons *ceteris paribus*, will attend, where it is relevant, to the results of a well-conducted experiment; rational persons *ceteris paribus* will not ignore disconfirming evidence. These general principles always need contextual application and always have what in effect are *ceteris paribus* clauses, but they still have a partially situation-nonspecific content. (Even in primitive societies, as Bronislaw Malinowski showed, there are in everyday life rough equivalents to experiment.)

Secondly, the arguments critical of religious belief, the arguments I made for maintaining that, for philosophically and scientifically educated people situated as we are situated, it is not reasonable to believe in God and that belief in God is not rationally justified, were not *purely* philosophical arguments, turning on the metaphysical and epistemological considerations that Plantinga takes to be definitive of philosophical arguments. Indeed, I did make conceptual and logical arguments—traditional philosophical claims—and these, of course, have the vulnerability of all traditional philosophical claims. But I also appealed to historical and anthropological considerations and to empirical considerations from the history of the world's religions. Crucial here were empirical considerations about the diversity and often conflicting diversity of religious faiths: of claimed revelations. This is not a matter of philosophical argument, but a matter of getting the anthropological and historical facts right, though a consideration of them led us, not to a further empirical claim, but to an interpretative one that appeals to our sense of fairness and reasonability, e.g., how, we were led to ask, with these diverse and conflicting putative revelations, some with as long and distinguished traditions as that of Christianity, can we rightly appeal to the putative revelation of Christianity or any other faith as *authoritative*? We have *a right,* if we choose to exercise it, to accept them on authority, but, as we have seen, many things we have a right to do we do not rightly do and sometimes they are not even reasonable things to do, let alone things we ought to do.[59] There are also things from psychology and sociology about religious belief formation and the stable sustaining of religious belief that are vitally important empirical matters relevant to the critique of religion. In short, we do not have in my argument a purely philosophical (conceptual, metaphysical, epistemological, normative ethical) argument concerning religious belief and so, while general fallibilism applies to my argument, the peculiar and distinctive difficulties of all *purely* philosophical argumentation has here a limited force.

What I have tried to do here briefly, and elsewhere at considerable length, is to give a cumulative cluster of arguments in the tradition of the Enlightenment, and as a part of an Enlightenment narrative, where many considerations other than purely traditional philosophical considerations are brought to bear. This cumulative cluster of considerations—something that has been going on for the last two hundred years—is not so vulnerable as are purely philosophical arguments.

Thirdly, and lastly, the claim about the intractable contestability and the lack of progress in philosophy that I stress above, and that Plantinga in effect appeals to, with its relativization of the conceptualization of a good argument, is overstated. Plainly there is a lot of disagreement in philosophy and very intractable and deep-seated philosophical differences and there is much that is fashion-prone, but, though less extreme, there are similar differences in science as well. And, the above not withstanding, there is some progress and development in philosophy, though it is very modest.[60] While it is perhaps plausible to portray Aristotle, and perhaps even Plato, or at least Aristotelians, as being in there arguing it out with Rawls and Davidson, it is completely implausible to put Plotinus and Paracelsus in that role. *Some philosophical ends are just dead ends, some philosophical traditions are just dead traditions.* Moreover, as Alastair MacIntyre and Charles Taylor have stressed, philosophical traditions, and intellectual traditions more generally, are not infrequently growing and developing traditions and late in the day they can become self-conscious about themselves as traditions and in doing so they sometimes become self-critical and amenable to taking on elements of other traditions in the refashioning and refinement and expansion of their own traditions.[61] MacIntyre, for example, thinks of himself as a Thomist, but unlike Thomas himself, he writes with an acute awareness that his articulation and the placing of himself in that tradition is also to place himself in a tradition that needs elaboration and development in relation to a world that has turned and to subsequent traditions, including the Humean tradition and more generally (as much as he dislikes it) the liberal tradition. So in MacIntyre, we get a more nuanced and developed philosophical account than we get in Thomas himself or in Augustine or Aristotle. Similarly, Martha Nussbaum's development of Aristotle's ethics is certainly a more satisfactory account of Aristotelian ethics than Aristotle's own or Aquinas's, though she is clearly, and self-consciously, standing on Aristotle's shoulders.[62]

It is not only scientists, but sometimes philosophers as well, who stand on each others shoulders, though the slippage is much greater than with scientists. But what we said of MacIntyre vis-à-vis Augustine and Aquinas could at least as accurately be said of John Rawls vis-à-vis Locke, Rousseau, and Kant and Donald Davidson vis-à-vis the logical positivists. (Some would say Quine as well, but that, to understate it, would be very controversial.) It needs even to be said in relation to our above discussion of belief in God. Since the writings of Hume and Kant on the attempted demonstrations of the existence of God, it is no longer plausible for a Thomist or anyone else to go back to Thomas and Anselm vis-à-vis these arguments as if Hume and Kant had never written. Good modern attempts to prove the existence of God (e.g.,

Swinburne's and Meynell's) carefully consider the arguments of Hume and Kant and make self-consciously improved arguments, or at least attempts at improved arguments, for the existence of God in the light of their critiques. Similarly the verificationist arguments I deploy and the rather different ones Dummett deploys could not be reasonably made without an awareness of critiques made of logical positivism. So it is too extreme to say that there is no progress *at all* in philosophy and that in philosophical argument we are simply stuck with various tradition-dependent and culture-dependent or sometimes perhaps even persons-dependent conceptions of rationality. Things are not that simple, or quite that bleak. So, for all the reasons articulated above, I do not think that we secularists are in the relativistic morass into which Plantinga's and Wolterstorff's ways of conceptualizing things seem at least to land us.

Given the great diversity of beliefs concerning religion, argument (*pace* Plantinga and Wolterstorff) is required for belief in God to be viable for people circumstanced as we are. Moreover, for the belief to be viable, it must be rooted in argument or considerations that can be articulated in a tolerably objective and non-question-begging manner. The relativization of what counts as a good argument is not as deep as they seem, at least, to presume. Moreover, one does not have to be an Enlightenment *rationalist* to believe that. That is open, as well, to a historicist pragmatist to argue. Historicist pragmatism is one thing, historicist skepticism or relativism are quite different things.

X

My naturalism, as I remarked initially, is a contextualist holism that utilizes, in articulating its holism, an appeal to considered judgments in wide reflective equilibrium. Its place in my thought is similar to the place of scientific method in the thought of Peirce, Dewey, Hook, and Nagel. Indeed, I take the two methods as having close affinities, though mine arguably has a more general application. (To have such a general application was surely something the classical pragmatists sought.) In arguing, as I have above, against theism, and thus against Judaism, Christianity, and Islam, I did not, for the most part, appeal to this method or seek to explicitly articulate my thought here in accordance with it, but argued, for the most part, discursively and dialectically, in the familiar manner of the more informalist strand of analytic Anglo-American philosophy, eclectically taking whatever method came conveniently to hand.[63] Though in doing so, I hope I have always proceeded logically with attention to relevant distinctions and with attention to providing sound arguments placed in a hopefully persuasive, if not compelling, narrative.

However, I also said in an earlier chapter that my naturalism without foundations, like Dewey's naturalism, sets out to transform philosophy from a consideration of the perennial problems of philosophy (the grand metaphysical and epistemological problems) to a consideration of the live problems of human beings. Religion straddles this distinction. It both makes grand metaphysical claims *and* is a system of salvation. As such it is a very gripping and entangling option for many people. So to make the case for my naturalism, or indeed for any naturalism, I must provide good grounds for rejecting supernaturalism. That I have sought to do in this and the proceeding chapter. In part 4 I shall discuss religion as a human problem; discuss religion, that is, in its existential role. Indeed, I wish for the day in which that would be the only way we would seriously discuss religion, naturalism having become so embedded in our thought and in our very ways of responding to the world, that religion as a metaphysical construction (a belief system) would no longer be a live option, for we would have come to live comfortably in a postmetaphysical age.[64] But that is not yet our time and perhaps such a time never will be. (It seems to me that Hume, some considerable time ago, was wishing for much the same thing, though the Calvinist culture he was living in made it prudent for him to put the matter more guardedly.) Too many people speak loosely and irresponsibly, and without much in the way of intellectual discipline, of our already living in a postmodern, postmetaphysical age. But in fact many people, including reflective, intelligent, well-educated people, in a certain sense, inhabit a premodern belief system, though still a system that is also touched by modernity and even in some rare cases by postmodernity. So it remains, if we would philosophize in the public sphere, necessary to discuss religion traditionally and that is what I have done here.

However, my philosophically transformative naturalism also takes the method of wide reflective equilibrium to be its fundamental method of justification. Whatever is true of my above arguments about the rationality of religious belief (eclectic as they are in method), it is true that what Plantinga called standard theism, or even any more sophisticated supernaturalisms, will not for us (reasonably educated people living in the rich capitalist democracies) be something that will match with our considered judgments in wide reflective equilibrium and this, for at least, two reasons. First, we will not get the needed overlapping consensus concerning religion in our intractably pluralistic societies, where, as Clifford Geertz put it, "we are living more and more in the midst of an enormous collage" where our world "at each of its local points" is coming to "look more like a Kuwaiti bazaar than like an English gentlemen's club."[65] The Kuwaiti bazaar bit is one of Geertz's characteristic exaggerations, but behind the exaggeration (perhaps it was only a hyperbole) there is a solid kernel of truth. The Kuwaiti bazaar phenomena is becoming more and more a part of our social reality: we are such different peoples—indeed, we are often so very different—that there just is no consensus, or practical possibility of a consensus, in our considered judgments over *such matters*. But, if that is so, we cannot *so* justify our beliefs concerning religion to such a mélange of people. We are a society of believers and nonbelievers, some (among both groups) militant, some others more or less indifferentists riding along with whatever is standardly believed in their particular subculture, and others remain somewhere in between. Among believers there are all kinds of sometimes very different believers in our Kuwaiti bazaar. Not only is there the traditional (for many of us) divisions between Jews, Christians, and Muslims, but, as well, divisions between Hindus, Shintoists, Buddhists, Confucians, Taoists, believers in native religions, and various cultists. Whatever may be the prospect for an overlapping consensus concerning some judgments and convictions about what is just in our societies, there is no possibility at all that there will be such a consensus concerning belief in God and related matters. And the dissensus here will, for a time, possibly grow as our world with its Kuwaiti bazaar becomes more and more a global village. (The two metaphors only apparently conflict.)

This lack of consensus by itself is sufficient to show that in our present circumstance religious convictions, as well as areligious or antireligious convictions, cannot be justified on the holistic basis of wide reflective equilibrium *where we try to appeal to society-wide considered judgments* in our intractably pluralistic societies. However, where the appeal to wide reflective equilibrium (including their considered judgments) is to what Hume called "men of letters" in societies such as ours, a strong case can be made for secularism.

Secondly, even if by some magnificent social transformation of such a society a wide social consensus came into being, something which short of a very considerable and sustained coercion, and probably not even then, could not happen, still we could not get standard theism or any theism or supernaturalism into wide reflective equilibrium. We need to gain wide reflective equilibrium, to get the ensemble of our beliefs into the best possible fit, the most coherent, economical, and perspicuous arrangement that we can, for a given time, muster. But our religious beliefs, with their supernaturalistic metaphysical claims, fit badly with the physical system that constitutes our physics. Similar things obtain with our biology and our psychology-cum-physiology. The assumptions made and the way of proceeding and viewing things in these domains are very different than those that are part of supernaturalistic belief systems.

Modern Thomistic-Aristotelians, such as Frederick Copleston and Alasdair MacIntyre, wish (in broad terms) to take Aristotle's metaphysics, ethics, and politics while setting aside his physics and biology. But this is difficult, if not impossible, to do. They are closely tied together in Aristotle's thought. It is, they realize, difficult (perhaps impossible) to take one of them without taking the others as well. They seem, at least in Aristotle's systematic thought, to come as a package. The metaphysics comes with the physics and the ethics with the biology. But a teleological-oriented universe replete with final causes fits badly not only with modern philosophical thinking, but also with modern science. There isn't the tight, neat, economical fit between the religious beliefs of theism and the scientific beliefs of our society that wide reflective equilibrium seems to require or at least seeks. Modern Thomistic balkanization works badly. Perhaps the various beliefs, from different domains, cannot be squared with each other or can only be squared by constructing artificial and arbitrary epicycles (deus ex machina), utilizing arcane conceptions, whose only purpose is to achieve the fit. Shotgun marriages (to switch the metaphor) might be the appropriate metaphor. But, when these beliefs are viewed more straightforwardly, there is no fit; the plain most economical thing would place secular beliefs in place of religious ones, thereby gaining a tighter and more economical fit.[66]

For at least these two reasons religious beliefs do not, and for modern societies cannot, stand in wide reflective equilibrium with our other beliefs. I have mentioned scientific ones, but, as well, many other beliefs and ways of thinking of our common life, including our morality, fit badly with them. If to justify our beliefs is to get them into wide reflective equilibrium, then our religious beliefs are not and cannot be justified. If it is responded that the failure in the religious case is good evidence that the method of wide reflective equilibrium should *not* have the fundamental role that I and others have given it, then to this it should in turn be responded that (a) in arguing philosophically more conventionally (perhaps *sans* method), as I have in the above discussion of religion, I have at least arguably made a strong case for antisupernaturalism, and (b) that something like wide reflective equilibrium seems at least to be how we do reason in domain after domain (including many commonsense domains of our common life) and that to reject wide reflective equilibrium because it does not produce the results, in reflecting about religion, that theists and other religious people want, is suspect, given the antecedent, and independently established, problematicity of religious beliefs and the pervasiveness and at least seeming good sense of such holistic reasoning.[67]

NOTES

1. Kai Nielsen, *Contemporary Critiques of Religion* (London: Macmillan Press, 1971); Nielsen, *Reason and Practice* (New York: Harper and Row, 1971), 138–257, Nielsen, *Skepticism* (London: Macmillan Press, 1973); Nielsen, *Philosophy and Atheism: In Defense of Atheism* (Amherst, N.Y.: Prometheus Books, 1985); Nielsen, *An Introduction to the Philosophy of Religion* (London: Macmillan Press, 1982); and Nielsen, *God Skepticism and Modernity* (Ottawa, Ontario: University of Ottawa Press, 1989).

2. Alvin Plantinga in a series of straw man arguments attempts to refute the verificationism of logical positivism. Plantinga, "Analytic Philosophy and Christianity," *Christianity Today* (October, 25, 1963): 75–78; Plantinga, "Advice to Christian Philosophers," *Faith and Philosophy* 1, no. 3 (July 1984), 256–58; and Plantinga, "Verificationism," in *The Logic of God: Theology and Verification*, ed. Malcolm L. Diamond and Thomas V. Litzenburg, Jr., (Indianapolis, Ind.: Bobbs-Merrill Co., 1975), 446–55. See my response to Plantinga's arguments in my *Contemporary Critiques of Religion*, 55–71.

3. Rodger Beehler's criticisms of my account of religion should be noted here. Rodger Beehler, "Religion v. Militant Atheism," 131–42 and his "Hounding Heaven," 159–66. See my response in "God and the Crisis of Modernity," 143–58. All the above articles are in *Studies in Religion* 23, no. 2 (1994). For a further response to Beehler, particularly to his "Hounding Heaven," and for a clearing of the decks concerning how atheism is to be understood, see my chapter "Atheism without Anger or Tears" in part 4 of this volume.

4. Michael Dummett tries to use *theory* of meaning to reconstruct a First Philosophy, in other words a return to The Tradition via a 'scientifically' articulated philosophy of language. Michael Dummett, *Truth and other Enigmas* (Cambridge, Mass.: Harvard University Press, 1978), 437–58. This is very distant from my own thinking and from the thinking of Wittgenstein or such Wittgensteinians as Peter Winch or Cora Diamond or that of Hilary Putnam in his latest work. These philosophers all deny both the need for a *theory* of meaning in philosophy and would not, like Dummett, regard the philosophy of language, or anything else, as a kind of scientific First Philosophy or as foundational for philosophy. See the references in the next note. It is also very distant from Quine's scientistic naturalism.

5. Ludwig Wittgenstein, *Philosophical Investigations* (Oxford, England: Blackwell, 1953); Wittgenstein, *Remarks on the Foundations of Mathematics* (Oxford, England: Blackwell, 1956). Peter Winch, *Trying to Make Sense* (Oxford, England: Blackwell, 1987), 18–80; Cora Diamond, *The Realistic Spirit* (Cambridge, Mass.: MIT Press, 1991), 1–72, 179–266; and Hilary Putnam, *Words and Life* (Cambridge, Mass.: Harvard University Press, 1994), 245–375. See also, in a similar vein, though a little more laid back about it, Richard Rorty, *Objectivity, Relativism and Truth* (Cambridge, England: Cambridge University Press, 1991).

6. Beehler, "Religion v Militant Atheism," 131–42 and "Hounding Heaven," 159–66. Wittgenstein often speaks of philosophers going wrong when they are dominated by a picture. Perhaps someone would argue, in spite of what I have said above, that I am still here dominated by a positivistic or scientistic picture and, dominated as I am, I just cannot see how religious talk works. Dominated by a picture, I do not see the language's actual use in our religious life; I am blocked from coming to command a clear view of our use of language here. But Wittgenstein also stresses that while some pictures so block us other pictures can facilitate our commanding a clear view of our language; pictures can be crucial in gaining a perspicuous representation of our language, including our religious discourse. So there are good and bad pictures. Bad pictures keep us from seeing the actual use of our language; good pictures facilitate our understanding of that use. Well, *if* my picture, as Beehler believes, is a bad positivist picture distorting our understanding of how religious discourse actually works, what then is a good picture? We get, as we have seen, reductive ones such as Braithwaite's and D. Z. Phillips's, but they altogether fail to capture the nonsecular, *transcendent-aspiring* thrust of religious discourse. Accounts with pictures that are not so reductive do not turn religious talk into purely secular talk, but then, as we have seen, we get incoherent metaphysical talk (not ordinary language based)

which does not give us a coherent picture of the use of religious discourse. But what is a good picture then? Religious discourse itself is baffling and fits badly with other bits of our talk, other social practices. Philosophers and theologians, trying to capture the illusive sense of this talk, are not infrequently driven to talking about (trying to talk about) the ineffable or of religious discourse as being inherently mysterious: beyond our understanding. Surely religion, and rightly so, is wrapped in mystery; to ask for it not to be mysterious is to ask for it to cease being religious. But, if it is *so* mysterious as to be really ineffable, beyond our understanding, then trivially there is nothing to understand. It must have a use to be intelligible and, if it has a use, it is, at least in some minimal sense, intelligible. But we seem, at least, not to be able to specify a use *that would meet the religious expectations* of believers. We seem, as well, not to be able to find a picture which makes sense of that talk without turning it into either superstition or into something incoherent: into a "picture" that fails to picture. And it is an *a priori* dogma to say that religious uses of language *must* be capable of being so pictured so that the picture would perspicuously represent it in a way that would meet religious believers' expectations; the job, *the dogma* has it, just is to find that right picture. It just *must* be there to be discovered by a sufficiently reflective and creative thinker. But why believe we have any such *must* there? It is perfectly true that there are religious uses of language and we can see that there are deviant and nondeviant uses of religious talk. "God's eyes are blue" is deviant, but "God's eye is always upon us" is not. Someone who asked what color God's eyes are would show a very considerable noncomprehension of religion and religious discourse. A necessary condition for coherence is to have a use in the language. *First-order religious discourse* often, perhaps always, has a use, though much of the meta-twaddle about it does not. But that first-order use is not sufficient for coherency. Talk can be meaningful—have a use in a language-game, in a cluster of social practices—and still be incoherent for all of that. There are both deviant and nondeviant utterances that go with astrology, alchemy, and magical practices and still the practices themselves are incoherent. Among other things, they do not fit with other social practices which are quite unproblematic; they conflict in a glaring way with things that we know to be the case; and, they make central claims of which we can make nothing. It is at least possible that religious uses of language and the social practices in which they are embedded are like astrological practices in being incoherent. That cannot reasonably be ruled out *ab initio*. It is not sufficient to establish coherence to say, and say truly, this language-game is played. People can play language-games that are incoherent or have social practices that do not make sense and cannot withstand critical reflection. For how a practice-oriented, contextualist, social theory can still be critical, see Rajeev Bhargava, *Individualism in Social Science* (Oxford, England: Clarendon Press, 1992), 213–52. For perceptive remarks about use and pictures, see Hilary Putnam, *Words and Life*, 276–77 and see, as well, James Connant's perceptive introduction to Putnam's book, xlvii–lviii. See here, as well, my discussion of D. Z. Phillips's Wittgensteinian account of religion in *Philosophy and the Grammar of Religious Belief*, ed. Timothy Tessin and Mario von der Ruhr (London: Macmillan, 1995).

7. J. L. Mackie, *The Miracle of Theism* (Oxford, England: Clarendon Press, 1982); Antony Flew, "The Burden of Proof," in *Knowing Religiously*, ed. Leroy S. Rouner (Notre Dame, Ind.: University of Notre Dame Press, 1985), 103–15. See also Alvin Plantinga's discussion of Mackie in his "Is Theism Really a Miracle?" *Faith and Philosophy* 3, no. 2 (April 1986): 109–34. For a more evenhanded discussion of Mackie than we find in Plantinga, see Bernard Williams, "Is He or Isn't He?" *Times Literary Supplement*, March 11, 1983, 231.

8. Kai Nielsen, *Ethics Without God* (Amherst, N.Y.: Prometheus Books, 1990) and

Nielsen, *Philosophy and Atheism*, 159–85. But see, for contrast, Terence Penelhum, "Ethics with God and Ethics Without," in *On the Track of Reason*, ed. Rodger Beehler et al. (Boulder, Colo.: Westview Press, 1992), 217–18. See, as well in this context, Alasdair MacIntyre, *After Virtue* (Notre Dame, Ind.: University of Notre Dame Press, 1981).

9. Terence Penelhum, "Parity is Not Enough," in *Faith, Reason, and Skepticism*, ed. Marcus Hester (Philadelphia: Temple University Press, 1992), 98–120.

10. Terence Penelhum, *Religion and Rationality* (New York: Random House, 1971), 11–87, 365–80.

11. H. A. Meynell, "The Intelligibility of the Universe," in *Reason and Religion*, ed. Stuart C. Brown (Ithaca, N.Y.: Cornell University Press, 1977), 23–43; and Meynell, "Criticisms of a Cosmological Argument," in *Faith, Skepticism and Personal Identity*, ed. J. J. MacIntosh and H. A. Meynell (Calgary, Alberta: University of Calgary Press, 1994), 43–60. Richard Swinburne, *The Existence of God* (Oxford, England: Clarendon Press, 1979).

12. Alvin Plantinga, "Belief in God," in *Perspectives in Philosophy*, ed. Michael Boylan (Fort Worth, Tex.: Harcourt Brace Jovanovich, 1993), 302.

13. Ibid.

14. Indeed, in his classical discussion of the argument to design (the argument to design being an inductive argument), Hume undermines inductive arguments for the existence of God. See the edition of Hume's *Dialogues Concerning Natural Religion* with a masterful introduction by Norman Kemp Smith (Edinburgh, Scotland: Nelson, 2d ed., 1947). See also Kemp Smith's "The Naturalism of Hume," *Mind*, n.s., no. 54 (1905), 149–53, 335–47; and Kemp Smith's *The Philosophy of David Hume* (London: Macmillan, 1948). See also Terence Penelhum, *David Hume* (West Lafayette, Ind.: Purdue University Press, 1992), 160–92; J. C. A. Gaskin, *Hume's Philosophy of Religion*, 2d ed. (New York: Macmillan, 1988) and his "Hume on Religion," in *The Cambridge Companion to Hume*, ed. David Fate Norton (Cambridge, England: Cambridge University Press, 1993), 313–44. See also the convenient collection of Hume's writing on religion edited by Antony Flew, *David Hume Writings on Religion* (La Salle, Ill.: Open Court, 1992). For judicious remarks on Hume and atheism, see Penelhum, *David Hume*, 187.

15. This still runs up against Hume's powerful criticism of inductive arguments for the existence of God. But here even a deeper question about intelligibility arises. There can be no proof or evidence for x if x is unintelligible or incoherent and there can, if this is the case, be no direct knowledge of x such as Plantinga speaks of either. *If* the concept of God is unintelligible or incoherent, then Calvin's and Plantinga's bold claims about a direct knowledge of God that is certain beyond dispute can come to nothing.

16. Wittgenstein deploys the Jastrow duck-rabbit figure in his *Philosophical Investigations*, 194–206.

17. See the reference in note 35 of chapter 3.

18. MacIntyre, *After Virtue*.

19. I use these notions interchangeably. If, as Plantinga believes, they should be distinguished, still nothing changes as far as my argument is concerned, for religious beliefs are neither justified nor warranted. Alvin Plantinga, "Justification in the 20th Century," *Philosophy and Phenomenological Research* vol. 50 Supplement (Fall 1990): 45–71.

20. Plantinga, "Belief in God," 402.

21. Ibid., 405. For Plantinga on Christian self-confidence, see his "Advice to Christian Philosophers," 254–56.

22. Plantinga, "Belief in God," 405. "What I really want to discuss is whether it is rational to believe that God exists—that there is such a person as God." Plantinga, "Is Be-

lief in God Rational?" in *Rationality and Religious Belief*, ed. C.F. Delaney (Notre Dame, Ind.: University of Notre Dame Press, 1979), 7.

23. Plantinga, "Belief in God," 405.

24. Ibid. and Plantinga, "Is Theism Really a Miracle?" 109–34.

25. Terence Penelhum, "Comments and Responses," in *Faith, Skepticism and Personal Identity*, 235–37. See also his "Parity is Not Enough," 98–120 and his *God and Skepticism: A Study in Skepticism and Fideism* (Dordrecht, Holland: Reidel, 1983).

26. Plantinga, "Is Theism Really a Miracle?" 151–53.

27. Plantinga, "Belief in God," 405.

28. Ibid.

29. Penelhum, unlike me, thinks the basic belief apologetic is all right as a way of warding off criticisms that belief in God is irrational, but not enough for the needs of natural theology, for it does not show that it is irrational *not* to believe in God. Plantinga could respond that natural theology and natural atheology take in each other's dirty linen. They are both trying to do something that is impossible. No such grand claims can be made about either what is irrational or what is rational. I argue, in turn, in this chapter, that we are not so fettered. There is a firm sense in which we can justifiably say that belief in God is irrational. But what is relevant at the above point of the argument in the text is that I am assuming at that point, *simply for the sake of the discussion,* that it is all right to speak of some beliefs as being basic. Actually that, in my view, smacks too much of *foundationalism.* It would be better if we would go much more holistic and drop such conceptualizations. This is not to deny that there are ordinary nonphilosophical contexts where we can in a thoroughly contextual and holistic way (as does Quine, for example) speak, and rightly, of certain beliefs as being basic. But this ordinary use does not add up at all to foundationalism or to anything even remotely like it.

30. Plantinga is just off the mark in identifying what he calls evidentialism with foundationalism. Descartes and many other rationalists were foundationalists without being evidentialists. Plantinga, "Is Belief in God Rational?" 7–27.

31. This goes way back to Rudolph Carnap, "Truth and Confirmation," in *Readings in Philosophical Analysis,* ed. Herbert Feigl and Wilfrid Sellars (New York: Appleton-Century-Crofts, Inc., 1949), 119–27. This is actually a translation of an article written in German by Carnap in 1936.

32. Plantinga, "Belief in God," 43. See also his "Is Belief in God Rational?" 17–24.

33. Plantinga, "Belief in God," 393.

34. Ibid., 393 and 403.

35. Henry Sidgwick, *Philosophy: Its Scope and Relations* (London: Macmillan and Co., 1902); C. D. Broad, "Critical and Speculative Philosophy," in *Contemporary Philosophy,* ed. J. H. Muirhead (London: Allen and Unwin, 1924), 17–99; C. D. Broad, "Philosophy I & II," *Inquiry* 1 (1958): 99–129. See also Kai Nielsen, "What is Philosophy?" *History of Philosophy Quarterly* 10, no. 4 (October 1993): 389–404.

36. Plantinga roundly criticizes atheologists for not being evenhanded, but in his discussion of religion he is himself remarkably partisan.

37. Plantinga, "Belief in God," 393–402.

38. Ibid., 403.

39. Penelhum, "Parity is Not Enough," 98–120.

40. The following are distinguished examples of what Plantinga calls "natural atheology." Bertrand Russell, *Why I Am Not a Christian* (London: George Allen and Unwin Ltd., 1957); Sidney Hook, *The Quest For Being* (New York: St. Martins Press, 1961); Ernest Nagel, *Logic Without Metaphysics* (Glencoe, Ill.: Free Press, 1956); Paul Kurtz,

Philosophical Essays in Pragmatic Naturalism (Amherst, N.Y.: Prometheus Books, 1994); J. L. Mackie, *The Miracle of Theism* (Oxford, England: Clarendon Press, 1982); Wallace Matson, *The Existence of God* (Ithaca, N.Y.: Cornell University Press, 1965); R. N. Hanson, *What I Do Not Believe and Other Essays* (Dordrecht, Holland: D. Reidel, 1972); Michael Scriven, *Primary Philosophy* (New York: McGraw Hill, 1966); Michael Martin, *Atheism: A Philosophical Justification* (Philadelphia: Temple University Press, 1990); and Richard Robinson, *An Atheist's Values* (Oxford: Basil Blackwell, 1964). Peter Angeles has made a useful collection of contemporary atheological writings. Peter Angeles, ed., *Critiques of God* (Amherst, N.Y.: Prometheus Books, 1976).

41. It is important to keep in mind our previous remarks about Plantinga's weak conception of "good argument." This very relaxed sense of "good argument" may be relevantly related to the very uncritical way in which he takes it that Christian believers have a direct experiential knowledge of God: a direct awareness of God. Beliefs such as "'God is speaking to me" or "God disapproves of what I have done" are for him vertibale *paradigms* of religious beliefs that are properly basic—beliefs, he claims, that are just directly known to be true by believers and beliefs which need not be grounded on argument or based on evidence from other propositions. Moreover, Plantinga believes, if these beliefs are not properly basic religious beliefs, then none are (12–14, 16). We must work from below, he reasonably claims, by working with examples and these he claims are examples (15–16). We can, at least if we are Christians, in suitable situations, just be directly aware of their truth. They are, on his view, like "I see a tree" or "I had breakfast more than an hour ago," something we can just directly know without their being based on evidence or on argument. Under the right conditions, both types of belief (relatively specific and concrete beliefs) can just be directly known to be true without supporting evidence or argument. It is fair enough to go on to say, as Plantinga does, that even *so* there are, for such perceptual beliefs and memory beliefs, "justifying conditions . . . or conditions that confer justification on the one who accepts them as basic" (14). He thinks, amazingly, that the same can and should be said for "God is speaking to me" or "God disapproves of what I have done." They are, he has it, parallel to such perceptual beliefs or memory beliefs. But that is absurd. There is no such ubiquitous consensus about such religious beliefs. There is no general acceptance that they are properly basic beliefs, or even an acceptance of them period, even among the Christian community, to say nothing of a wider community, as there is a very wide acceptance of such perceptual beliefs or memory beliefs. Indeed, there is no consensus at all, revealing an acceptance of these religious beliefs, except among a few fundamentalistically inclined Christians. Even many religious believers of a fairly orthodox sort (e.g., some Catholics or Anglicans) would not take them as literal statements that might be taken to be literally true and to be immediately known to be true. Does God speak Chinese, too, as Rilke quipped? They are rather, these less fundamentalistically inclined Christians believe, religiously important metaphors or symbolic remarks, but not literal religious truth-claims (if such there be) or even putatively literal religious truth-claims. We can only take them, as Plantinga must, for them to be candidates for proper basicality and as something directly known to be true, by having a "standard theism" that is *grossly anthropomorphic, so anthropomorphic as to be idolatrous.* God is not the sort of being that can be seen or who literally speaks. (As it is conceptually out of order to ask about the color of God's eyes or ask if he has eyebrows, so it is also conceptually out of order to ask how loud God speaks or what his voice is like or whether he speaks with an accent.) To so treat religion is to turn it into a superstition. This is something that Plantinga, for all his *philosophical* sophistication, seems to be doing. Faced with these difficulties, it is way off the mark to say, as Plantinga does, that these

religious beliefs are "not groundless or gratuitous" (14). It is understandable that some people in thinking about the basic belief apologetic began to speak of analogies with belief in the Great Pumpkin. The Kierkegaardian or Wittgensteinian path of self-conscious groundless believing is not superstitious, but Plantinga's extreme anthropomorphism is. It is the kind of religious belief of which Wittgenstein, and I believe rightly, so disapproved. See here Plantinga's "On Taking Belief in God as Basic" in *Religious Experience and Religious Belief,* ed. Joseph Runzo and Craig K. Ihara (Lanham, Md.: University Presses of America, 1986), 1–17. Quotations and citations in this note are from this article with its pagination. It has also been published in *Faith and Rationality,* ed. Plantinga and Wolterstorff.

42. Nicholas Wolterstorff, "Can Belief in God Be Rational If It Has No Foundations?" in *Perspectives in Philosophy,* ed. Michael Boylan, 444.

43. Ibid.

44. Ibid.

45. A kind of skeptical worry here is that in the very posing of that question we are going away from anything like a *normative* turn in philosophy and asking a question which seems at least to be *merely* a question of sociological fact. I do not think that matters are that straightforward. But there is a good bit of sorting out that needs to be done here. *Some* of it is done in the text that follows the above note.

46. D. Z. Phillips, *Faith and Philosophical Enquiry* (London: Routledge and Kegan Paul, 1970); D. Z. Phillips, *Belief, Change and Forms of Life* (Atlantic Highlands, N.J.: Humanities Press, 1986); and Ilham Dilman, "Wisdom's Philosophy of Religion," *Canadian Journal of Philosophy* 4 (1975): 423–524.

47. Nicholas Wolterstorff, "Tradition, Insight and Constraint," *Proceedings and Addresses of the American Philosophical Association* 66, no. 3 (1992): 43–57.

48. Wolterstorff, "Can Belief in God Be Rational If It Has No Foundations?" 445.

49. For an acute assessment of such rationalism in philosophy, see Barry Allen, *Truth in Philosophy* (Cambridge, Mass.: Harvard University Press, 1993). See also, for both amusing and keen criticisms of rationalism and its city cousins, Paul Feyerabend, *Against Method,* 3d ed. (London: Verso Press, 1993).

50. For a compelling portrayal of a person who very much wants to believe but cannot, see Fyodor Dostoyevsky, *The Devils.*

51. Kai Nielsen, "Linguistic Philosophy and 'The Meaning of Life'" in *The Meaning of Life,* ed. E. D. Klemke (New York: Oxford University Press, 1981), 177–204. See also A. J. Ayer, *The Meaning of Life* (New York: Charles Scriber's Sons, 1990), 1–17, 178–97.

52. Hendrik Hart in a personal communication has made this point.

53. For remarks about the intractability of philosophical problems, see Fredrich Waismann, *How I See Philosophy* (New York: St. Martin's Press, 1968), 1–38; and Kai Nielsen, "Can There Be Justified Philosophical Beliefs?" *Iyyun* 40 (July 1991): 235–70.

54. Plantinga, "Belief in God," 393.

55. Ibid.

56. Nielsen, *After the Demise of the Tradition: Rorty, Critical Theory and the Fate of Philosophy* (Boulder, Colo.: Westview Press, 1991); Kai Nielsen, *Transforming Philosophy: A Metaphilosophical Inquiry* (Boulder, Colo.: Westview Press, 1995); and *Méta-Philosophie: Reconstructing Philosophy?* ed. Jocelyne Couture and Kai Nielsen (Calgary, Alberta: University of Calgary Press, 1994).

57. A historicist skeptic is only a certain kind of historicist. A historicist need not be a skeptic, though, of course, she could be. I am, for example, a historicist, but not a relativist or a skeptic. But these different things can get mixed up as they do in Richard Rorty's

"Dewey between Hegel and Darwin," in *Modernist Impulses in the Human Sciences,* ed. Dorothy Ross (Baltimore, Md.: Johns Hopkins University Press, 1994), 56–58.

58. Kai Nielsen, "Principles of Rationality," *Philosophical Papers* 3 (October 1974), 55–89; Nielsen, "Distrusting Reason," *Ethics* 87 (October 1976), 49–60; and Nielsen, "The Embeddedness of Conceptual Relativism," *Diálogos* 11 (November 1977), 85–111.

59. H. L. A. Hart, "Legal and Moral Obligation," in *Essays in Moral Philosophy*, ed. A. I. Melden (Seattle, Wash.: University of Washington Press, 1958), 82–107.

60. I overstated the "no progress theme" in my "Can There be Justified Philosophical Beliefs?" C. B. Martin in conversation has been very persuasive on this point.

61. Alasdair MacIntyre, *Whose Justice? Which Rationality?* (Notre Dame, Ind.: University of Notre Dame Press, 1988); Alasdair MacIntyre, *Three Rival Versions of Moral Enquiry* (Notre Dame, Ind.: University of Notre Dame Press, 1990); and Charles Taylor, *Sources of the Self* (Cambridge, Mass.: Harvard University Press, 1969).

62. Martha Nussbaum, "Virtue Revived," *Times Literary Supplement,* July 3, 1992, 9–11; and Nussbaum, "Non-Relative Virtues: An Aristotelian Approach," in *The Quality of Life,* ed. Martha Nussbaum and Amartya Sen (Oxford, England: Clarendon Press, 1993), 242–69.

63. Kai Nielsen, "Formalists and Informalists: Some Methodological Turnings," *Critica* 25, no. 73 (April 1993): 62–71.

64. I did not say of religion that it is *"only* a metaphysical construction." Religion has never been just that and I have always stressed that, though sometimes my critics have forgotten that.

65. Clifford Geertz, "The Uses of Diversity," *The Tanner Lectures on Human Values,* vol. 7, ed. Sterling M. McMurrin (1986), 273. See Richard Rorty's response in his *Objectivity, Relativism and Truth* (Cambridge, England: Cambridge University Press, 1991), 203–10.

66. I want to say something about Plantinga's manner of argumentation. It is plain enough that Plantinga is very bright, very well informed *philosophically*, and intensely partisan about religion. This combination has, I believe, an unfortunate *effect*. The effect—I do not speak of his intentions, for I have not the remotest idea of what they are—is that of sophistry. (I hope here that this is not the pot calling the kettle black.) In his philosophical arguments concerning religion, his usual manner is to make very heavy weather indeed with matters not favored by what he calls his prephilosophical opinions and to treat those favored by his prephilosophical opinions, e.g., belief in God, very uncritically. For things not favored by his prephilosophical opinions, he immediately finds a host of difficulties, a lot of unexamined presuppositions. As a Cartesian doubter, rather than a Peircean doubter, he finds almost nothing clear and distinct among the things he has a prephilosophical inclination to reject. He finds in them no sound or even good arguments, *even in his weak sense of "good argument."* (Given his own characterization of "good argument," there should be plenty of them for the various firmly entrenched sides of all deeply contested philosophical issues. His procedure here seems at least to lack consistency.) But his vigorous nay-saying—his fierce critique of atheology—standardly, but not invariably, comes to little more than in effect pointing out that we do not, over these matters, get self-evidence and incorrigibility. We do not, as he likes to put it, get knock-down, drag-out demonstrations or arguments. But that is a trivial and uncontroversial point for by now fallibilism is a truism (but true for all of that). Nothing substantive is going to be established about anything, if self-evidence, certainty and incorrigibility (or any one of them) are going to be our standard(s) of success. But "certain knowledge" is neither a pleonasm nor something that has much of an application. Atheologists (going way back

to Hume) are not on the quest for certainty and their arguments do not require that. More-over, people who are on such a quest will establish nothing substantial one way or the other. Plantinga, who, I would surmise, knows this very well, still, rationally inexplica-bly, argues as he does anyway. For these reasons I say that his manner of arguing is not infrequently sophistical. For an example of what I have in mind see his discussion of J. L. Mackie's views in his "Is Theism Really a Miracle?" *Faith and Philosophy* 3, no. 2 (April 1986): 109–34. See, for another illustration, his "Belief in God," 390–402. It is in-structive to contrast his attitude toward philosophy, as well as that of his atheistic coun-terpart, Antony Flew, on the one hand, with the very different attitudes of such philoso-phers as Hilary Putnam, Stanley Cavell, Robert Nozick, and Arthur Danto, on the other. To get something of the flavor of how their attitudes contrast with those of Plantinga and Flew, note their openness, self-doubt over matters philosophical, and their *explorative* way of thinking in their remarks about philosophy. These things emerge forcefully in their con-versations with Giovanna Borradori. Borradori records these conversations in her *The American Philosopher* (Chicago: University of Chicago Press, 1994). For Putnam's putting those attitudes to work philosophically, see his *Words and Life*. Here we are in a different philosophical world than the one Plantinga and Flew inhabit.

67. Plantinga would not accept the method of wide reflective equilibrium, at least as I deploy it, as a method of justification for theistic beliefs and probably not even more gen-erally. In particular, in arguing, say, for Christian beliefs, the "we" concerning whose con-sidered judgments a consensus must be gained, and then set in reflective equilibrium, would not for him be those of the critical intellectuals (Hume's "men of letters") of our time or even just the philosophers, but, by contrast, *Christian* philosophers and (perhaps) other *Christian* intellectuals or even the *Christian* community (suitably Orthodox) at large. Plantinga regards philosophy as a communal enterprise, but, consensus or no con-sensus, Christian philosophers are perfectly in their rights, says Plantinga, in taking be-lief in God to be *properly basic* and in just starting there in philosophizing: that is, in "sys-tematizing, developing, and deepening" this religious belief—"this prephilosophical opinion"—in relation to other prephilosophical opinions without at all trying to show, to nontheists, that this belief is reasonable, let alone warranted (271). But, *pace* Plantinga, the issue is not what they have *a right* (even an "epistemic right") to do or to believe, but what it is *reasonable* for them to do and to believe. People have a right, at least in many circumstances, to neglect their health by overeating, by drinking too much and by not ex-ercising; but their having that right is one thing, their being reasonable in so acting is an-other as is, as well, whether their so acting is a good thing to do or the right thing for them to do. (We have *a right* to do some things that even we may recognize are not *the right* things to do.) Similarly, no one is challenging the Christian's *right* to believe (even his 'epistemic right') as he does, but what is at issue is the reasonability of believing as he does, particularly when he is placed as intellectuals are placed in our societies, in our time. To simply just stick with the Christian, or even with the theistic community, is for us, as it was *not* for Aquinas or for Calvin, evasive and not very reasonable. Plantinga and Wolterstorff are not in Aquinas's or Calvin's cultural position. What is reasonable for the latter need not be for the former. Plantinga urges on Christians, and amply displays it in his own manner, Christian self-confidence, but it actually comes out more like Christian bullheadedness in his case. Like his mentor John Calvin, he takes it that ". . . there is within the human mind, and indeed by natural instinct, an awareness of divinity. *This we take to be beyond controversy.*" He takes, with his basic belief apologetic, such an aware-ness-based belief, to be like belief in the external world and in other minds. It is some-thing, according to him, we can reasonably have without being able to justify it, without

having grounds or good reasons for it. It is rooted in an awareness yielding a truth concerning religion that he takes to be *beyond controversy*. It is not just that we (or some of us, some supposedly favored some of us) have this sense that is beyond controversy, but that it is a *genuine awareness* of a reality is also something that is supposed to be beyond controversy. But it is clearly not so inescapable as these other beliefs: the beliefs that Hume adverts to that Norman Kemp Smith has called natural beliefs. Many people do not have this religious awareness, including some genuinely religious people, e.g., Zen Buddhists, and, since its being a genuine awareness is extensively controverted by reflective and informed people, among others, it is *not beyond controversy*. Unless one simply wants to stick one's head in the sand and dogmatically fix one's belief by *the method of authority*, one must go to the intellectual community at large and not merely to the community of Christian philosophers or Christian believers more generally. Alvin Plantinga, "Advice to Christian Philosophers," *Faith and Philosophy* 1, no. 3 (July 1984): 253–71. The reference to John Calvin is from his *Institutes of the Christian Religion*, tr. Ford Lewis Battles (Philadelphia: Westminster Press, 1960), Bk. 1, chapter 3, 43–44. For a discussion of Hume's natural beliefs, see Kemp Smith, "The Naturalism of Hume," *Mind*, n.s., no. 54 (1905): 149–53, 335–47.

Part Two

Social Philosophy within the Limits of Reflective Equilibrium Alone

INTRODUCTION

My contextual, historicized naturalism without foundations, given its Deweyan emphasis, puts questions of social, political, and moral philosophy center stage. It is with these questions, and the methodology of their proper treatment, that I shall be principally concerned in part 2 of this book. But there is some important unfinished business about the appeal to considered judgments in wide reflective equilibrium that should first be cleared up. I shall devote most of this introduction to it.

The "we" and the "our" has, as we have already had some occasion to see, remained a persistent problem for such an account. The charge of relativism, provincialism, and ethnocentrism has repeatedly been made. What has not generally been realized, and what I have not realized in the past, is that sometimes—and most particularly in talking about morality and politics—the "we" and "our" both in the initial appeal to considered judgments and in a similar appeal to considered judgments where they serve as checking points of a theory (its data, so to say) are not the same as the "we" and "our" who are articulating the reflective equilibrium and who are trying to decide if it has been achieved or whether it is the sort of thing that should be achieved. It is vital that we keep this firmly in mind.

What is involved here is in some respects analogous to the relationship between language and linguistics. Whether we can or cannot say so-and-so in English is determined by what native speakers of English say or would say in certain determinate circumstances. Linguistic theory or what linguists say cannot gainsay that. While the linguist's generalizations and theorizing about language cannot gainsay that (must, where relevant, actually be in accordance with it), still there are theoretical claims linguists make that the native speaker, if he is himself not a linguist or someone who understands linguistics very well, can have no responsible opinion about. Similarly, when the philosopher or some other theoretician seeks to collect together the considered moral judgments which will serve as the crucial content in the reflective equilibrium he seeks to articulate or forge, the considered judgments collected are what are so regarded, and firmly so regarded (taken to be firm considered judgments), very generally in at least the rich modern societies, e.g., England, Sweden, Holland, France, Canada, and the like. Whether racism is evil, suffering bad, promises are to be kept, torture is evil, oppression is wrong actually are our considered judgments is determined by what people pervasively in such societies sincerely believe, and will continue to believe on reflection in a cool hour. They are also the judgments that many moral philosophers— I think all should—seek to put together into a consistent and coherent whole that fits together with the rest of what we know or at least reasonably believe. These considered judgments must be taken at least initially as given. In this way they are to the moral philosopher significantly like what the linguistic data are for the linguist.[1] The theories that moral philosophers and other similar theoreticians develop, they develop to explain these considered judgments and to justify those of them that go together into a coherent whole that also squares with the other things we know or reasonably believe. *But these theories themselves are not established to be true or to be the most reasonable of the available theories or, except at the extreme, to be mistaken by what those plain people think*, though—to bring out what is intended by "at the extreme"—if a theory ends up by counterintuitively saying it can see nothing bad about pain or wrong about suffering and the like, it can, and with good reason, just be summarily set aside. It cannot, if it is sound, so fundamentally conflict with such firm considered judgments.

In that way the considered convictions, or rather those that can consistently be held together, come in as checks on the claims of moral philosophers. But that is only the beginning (a kind of minimal thing to be done in such an assessment); there are a host of accounts which are in accordance with those considered judgments and thus appealing to those considered judgments cannot help us to decide between these accounts or even incline us in one way rather than another. But, if the theories do conflict with such firm considered judgments, or more accurately massively so conflict, then the plain person can rightly conclude that, whatever else the theory in question has going for it, it is to that very considerable extent mistaken. If it is a consequence of the theory that there is nothing wrong with pain or with people being indifferent to whether they tell the truth or not, then, if those things are really an implication of the theory (are its repugnant conclusions), then the theoretician in question needs to go back to the drawing board at least until he has been able to free his theory from those implications, those repugnant consequences. But normally moral theories will not have *such* counterintuitive implications, normally they will not conflict with such deeply entrenched considered judgments. Where the moral theorist discovers to her dismay that her theory suprisingly actually does have such untoward and counterintuitive implications, she will revise her theory until they are no longer implications of her theory or, failing in that, abandon her theory. To generalize, where it can be shown that moral theories really do have such counterintuitive implications, then the theoretician in question should, and probably will, take that as a *reductio* of her theory and will alter her theory to escape that repugnant consequence or, if she cannot, she will abandon, if she is reasonable, her theory or at least that part of her theory which has that consequence. She seeks, among other things, a consistent set of considered moral judgments which also matches with her beliefs and her knowledge about the world.

A consensus among such moral theorists is sought both concerning whether such a reflective equilibrium has been achieved and over whether it is the case that such a reflective equilibrium is a *desideratum* in theorizing about morality or society. The "we" here is a different group than the "we" who must be taken into consideration in gaining the data for theorizing: the considered judgments or convictions we appeal to and theorize about and try to get in reflective equilibrium. (This last "we" is the "we" of the theoretician.) That, for example, a Rawlsian account is closer to achieving a reflective equilibrium than utilitarianism, that it has achieved a greater coherence of our various considered convictions, factual knowledge, theories about society, and the like, than utilitarianism or Rossian pluralistic deontology or a perfectionist account, is something for such *theoreticians* to ascertain. What a plain, theoretically uninformed person will think here is something that normally will carry little weight. When we speak of our considered judgments being in reflective equilibrium or not being in reflective equilibrium, the judgment about whether they are really *ours* gives *all the weight to the plain person*, but whether they are in *reflective equilibrium* is to be determined principally by the *theoretician*. So the "our" and the "we," depending on what we are talking about, have quite different referents.

In some other domains we do not have this difference. Sometimes the referent is the same. In particle physics, microeconomics, mathematics, or geology, for example, consensus and considered judgments will sometimes play a role, too, and there will be attempts to achieve a reflective equilibrium. But the consensus sought about which are the considered judgments, what they are about, and whether they have been gotten into reflective equilibrium will appeal to what the experts in the field think, or can be brought to think, after careful examination and discussion, and not by what is generally thought in society (if anything is thought about it at all) or by other intellectuals (including philosophers) and the like. This will be most plainly true when the science, or area of the science, is a hard science firmly established. At the most, what is thought by some experts in some closely related field might also be appealed to in establishing what the relevant considered judgments in question are and whether they are in reflective equilibrium.

The crucial point to keep in mind is that in such domains there is only one "we" that is a player, namely the "we" constituting the relevant experts. But this is not true when the subject is morality or politics. The "our" in "our considered convictions" refers to the people living in what is conventionally called the developed world and people in similar intellectual situations. They will include, of course, moral philosophers and political theorists, but only as a small fraction of the people appealed to and *as people who have no special expertise in determining what are our considered convictions*. What is appealed to are the considered moral convictions that the overwhelming majority of people in such societies have. But these theoreticians are the key players in determining which accounts, if any, have been able to place these considered convictions in a wide reflective equilibrium and whether this conception is the appropriate method in explaining and justifying moral and normative political theories and accounts.

The discipline of biblical studies is more like the hard sciences with respect to the "we" and the "our" relevently appealed to. The age, the ordering, the language used, whether there are many priestly redactions in certain of the books or not is determined by the scientific experts in the field in ways similar to the ways in which things are determined in archaeology, geography, and geology. The considered judgments appealed to, and, as well, the claims to reflective equilibrium or the lack thereof, are those of the relevant scholars. What the plain person thinks is of little or no relevance here. But, as we saw in the last chapter, arguments about religion, as distinct from arguments in biblical studies, are different. In some respects they are close to what is the case in morality and politics, but, as we gestured at in the last chapter but did not spell out, in some other respects they are also importantly different. They are like those of morality in that religion like morality is a form of life that everyone (or, at least, almost everyone) *in some sense* is socialized into in our culture. (In Hume's time the socialization was much fuller, more uniform, and even more pervasive.) Physics, mathematics, geology, economics, anthropology, and biblical studies are not forms of life everyone gets socialized into, but disciplines with a set of practices that everyone is not privy to and where only the considered judgments of experts in the discipline in question normally count in appealing to considered judgments concerning such matters. This is not so with morality, politics, and religion. There, at least initially, everyone's considered judgments, as far as more fundamental convictions are concerned, count and count equally if they are adults or near adults and are not mentally enfeebled or insane.

However, that notwithstanding, morality and politics, on the one hand, and religion, on the other, differ in our cultures in the following crucial way. In our contemporary societies, unlike what was the case in the Middle Ages or even in the sixteenth and seventeenth centuries, among the diverse peoples in these present-day societies—societies, as was remarked in the last chapter, becoming more like a Kuwaiti bazaar—there is no consensus about a core of *religious* notions. People do not agree on a core of considered judgments here while, at least arguably, along the lines that John Rawls has argued, there is consensus concerning some core moral and related political notions such that we can speak intelligibly and correctly of *our* considered judgments here. There is no such consensus concerning religion and there is no reason to expect that we soon, if ever, are going to achieve one. We have, that is, concerning religion no such considered judgments and convictions to start from and to guide our deliberations. The Christian coalition and secular humanists are worlds apart. But Jews, Christians, and Muslims also differ very fundamentally on certain, to them, not unimportant matters. And between fundamentalism, on the one hand, and Anglicanism and Catholicism, on the other, there are also deep differences. Moreover, in our societies there are Hindus, Confucionists, and Buddhists with very fundamental differences in belief from Jews, Christians, and Muslims, as well as from each other. That their numbers are fewer is hardly relevant. Individuals and sects, of course, have characteristic determinate considered convictions, and often hold them very intensely, but there is no *society-wide consensus* concerning them. We can not find an overlapping consensus concerning such beliefs.

It may be true, as Alvin Plantinga claims, that "some two-thirds of the world's population of approximately five billion people profess belief in God—the God of Abraham, Isaac, and Jacob."[2] But (a) it is also the case that within almost all of these cultures there are acute differences in religious belief and resulting deep conflicts in considered judgments and (b) there are in these cultures skeptics and indeed sometimes not merely nonreligious people but antireligious people as well. Moreover, the skeptics very typically come from the better educated strata of the society. (This is not, of course, to say that all, or even most, of the better educated are skeptics, but there are a goodly proportion of skeptics from that strata.) In the societies where modernization is most developed and where there is economic and political security and high levels of education, the number of secularizers and secularized grows and the number of religious believers diminishes. The Scandinavian countries and Holland are good cases in point. Where there is reasonable wealth, somewhat reasonably distributed and high levels of education again fairly generally distributed in the society, Weberian disenchantment of the world can be expected to go on rolling along. The key thing to see is that while there are very many religious believers, or at least nominal religious believers, in modern societies, and particularly in the United States and Canada, there is no consensus about religious belief, unless, for countries like the United States, which in any event is in these and similar matters the odd man out, we want to let mere numbers count, something which was never appealed to by philosophers such as Rawls, Daniels, and myself when we appealed in some moral matters to our considered judgments. As C. D. Broad once said somewhere: "Moral issues are not vote issues"; and it is equally true that we do not establish a consensus by majority vote. The same obviously applies in considering the viability of the various religious beliefs and practices. Plantinga's big battalions are of scant justificatory relevance, though they plainly have the *power* to deeply influence the politics of the United States such that Rawls's envisioned liberal world of a reasonable pluralism or Rorty's conception of a social democracy are far from being realized in the

United States. Both can come to seem, particularly given the current (1995) severe swing to the far right, like very utopian ideals.

The above depressing considerations to the contrary notwithstanding, in our intractably pluralistic modern societies, I do appeal, following Rawls here, in arguing for a conception of political justice and related matters, to a *society-wide* consensus in considered judgments in such societies.[3] We need that overlapping consensus in such considered judgments to ground our conceptions of political justice for constitutional democracies. If we do not have such a consensus, or cannot get one, we will not be able to forge the relevant reflective equilibrium. We may, of course, have, or come to obtain, that overlapping consensus and still not be able to forge a reflective equilibrium. But that is another matter. Having such an overlapping consensus in considered judgments is a *necessary* but not *sufficient* condition for achieving the relevant reflective equilibrium concerning matters of political justice in our pluralistic societies.

However, in the case of the examination of religion, I argue, as we have seen in the last two chapters, for a *projected* agreement in considered judgments in wide reflective equilibrium among the *intelligentsia* of such societies: Hume's "men of letters." I say "projected agreement" because even with the considered judgments about religion among the intelligentsia, to say nothing of their beliefs about what it is or is not for them in wide reflective equilibrium, there is now nothing even resembling a consensus or even an acknowledgment that we need anything like such a consensus. What I have done is lay out an argument about how I get, or think I get, *my* beliefs and considered judgments into wide reflective equilibrium in this domain and then ask people to consider whether this naturalistic account of religion has yielded an account which is in the ballpark of being in wide reflective equilibrium and thus, at least by those lights, justified. We should, if we are to get our beliefs in this area into wide reflective equilibrium, go naturalistic and atheist. Or so I hypothesize. I throw it out, that is, for the reflective consideration of intellectuals in our society. Do not such arguments, I ask, embedded in such narratives, tell it like it is? Following my arguments and my narrative, and similar arguments and narratives in our intellectual culture, isn't this what we should conclude, if they are sound, or could be made sound with some inessential amendments? And indeed, are they not sound or nearly so? Isn't what I see as an equilibrium something that should be taken to be a genuinely social equilibrium? I suggest, risking *hubris*, that the considered convictions I think I have in wide reflective equilibrium would be also the considered convictions concerning religion for other intellectuals as well, if they would get their considered convictions into wide reflective equilibrium. I could, of course, be very, very mistaken here. But what I claim is intersubjectively testable and should be so tested. It is not a *parti pris* untestable dogma of mine.

An important test for whether I am on the road to being right in my atheism is whether, in societies fortunate enough to have reasonable wealth broadly distributed, high levels of education widely diffused throughout the population, and considerable security over a reasonable period of time, such secularizing arguments and beliefs and attitudes toward the world become stably dominant at least among the intelligentsia in a world where more and more people are in a condition like that of the intelligentsia (becoming intelligentsia, if you will). If that comes to obtain, something which is not beyond the range of feasible possibility for the richer parts of the world, then my account will be justified. I will have shown, that is, how such an atheistic account is in wide reflective equilibrium and squares with the relevant considered judgments of the people in such societies fortunate enough to have had a reasonable scientific, humanistic, and philosophical education. My hunch is that this is what would happen in such circumstances. Moreover, and distinctly, my belief is that this would be a good thing.

In part 2, I turn, as I initially remarked, to moral and political philosophy. It is there where the method of wide reflective equilibrium is most paradigmatically at home. In chapter 5, I argue for a *political* conception of justice rather after the fashion of John Rawls. Given a Deweyan transformation of philosophy into, most crucially, a moral, political, and social philosophy oriented to coming to grips with the problems of life that emerge in such problematic situations, I argue that such a transformation of philosophy should be a philosophy within the limits of wide reflective equilibrium alone. I explicate it and defend it against some critiques that are both familiar and at least *prima facie* plausible. I also argue there, following the Rawls of *Political Liberalism*, that arguments for political justice, articulated for a conception of justice for the basic institutions of our societies, should be constrained by seeking an overlapping consensus of people in our society who are parts of a reasonable pluralism. We have a reasonable pluralism where, to be part of such a pluralism, standardly people who are members of the differing groups and life orientations that are a part of such a pluralism are committed to democracy, nonfanatical, prepared to be self-critical, reason and deliberate in generally accepted, publicly accessible ways, are attentive to readily available facts, and are willing to accept the results of such reasoning and such deliberations, where they are intersubjectively validated, and where people, by and large, who are part of the groups in such a reasonable pluralism, generally act in accordance with such results.

In our arguments about political justice for such societies—arguments essentially concerned with the *institutional* principles of political justice for such societies—we are concerned with the structural design of such societies. Our arguments will seek to get the considered moral and political judgments of such people, so socially located, into wide reflective equilibrium. Such an account will only be concerned to articulate a *conception* of political justice with its associated *principles* of political justice for such societies. It will not even attempt to articulate a conception of justice for the institutional design of *all* societies in conditions of moderate scarcity and limited altruism. *It* is only a conception of political justice for constitutional democracies in conditions of reasonable abundance and stability where a reasonable pluralism prevails.

Thinking of the Christian coalition again makes us see how far people are in the United States from circumstances in which a reasonable pluralism exists. But all constitutional democracies are not in such bad shape, e.g., Sweden and Iceland, and we still have what is arguably a feasible *model* for constitutional democracies in the circumstances I have described. In any event we have a model for something that could obtain in the rich capitalist democracies. (If some were to come into existence, it could obtain as well in rich socialist democracies.) It is not, of course, a conception of justice to be applied to the institutional design of *all* societies under all historical conditions and it certainly is not a conception of individual justice: some attempt to ascertain what in particular circumstances is an individual's due. It is rather a conception of justice for institutions in constitutional democracies, though, where such a conception actually guides practice, it will, of course, deeply affect the lives of individuals in ways, that, if it is a sound conception of justice, are morally toward and answer to human interests.

In chapter 6, I argue for a conception of social justice not limited to constitutional democracies, but for any developed society in conditions of relative abundance with some scarcities and with limited altruism. The conception of justice deployed there is importantly similar to Rawls's in being strongly egalitarian. Justice, on my conception, requires a kind of *impartiality* where there must be an equal consideration of interests.[4] What this comes to is carefully characterized. However, I also argue in chapters 7 and 9 that sometimes in some horrible circumstances not everyone's interests can be protected and, distressing and morally unsettling as it is, some must be sacrificed, though still their interests must have at least an initial equal consideration. Moreover, the sacrifices required of people must be sacrifices that can be justified on principled lines. They are not just arbitrarily imposed on people. Still, sometimes, in these terrible situations (triage situations, for example), some people sometimes turn out, after such an initial equal consideration, to be, through no fault of their own, expendable. Indeed, they are not only expendable, they must in such desperate situations be expended. Consider, for example, a group of wounded comrades abandoned on a beach during a frantically hurried and desperate evacuation after defeat in a battle. They are still not treated as means *only*. If there is anyway to evacuate them without the very overwhelming likelihood that all the other troops will be captured and most almost certainly killed, or that related things of similar magnitude are very likely to happen, then these wounded comrades must be evacuated as well. And it is *generalizable* features about their condition which are relevant in determining what is to be done. There is also the usual test of role reversal here. Still, all that to the contrary notwithstanding, in such desperate circumstances, their legitimate interests are on that occasion legitimately overridden. In such circumstances, and in some others as well, an appeal to consequences is necessary. Indeed, the need for a consideration of consequences is always at least in the background when we deliberate morally or act morally. This will be extensively argued in chapters 7 and 9.

We should not, to anticipate what I shall argue there, treat considerations of justice as having *absolute* weight over other moral considerations. Characteristically justice outweighs considerations of utility, but not in all circumstances and not always. This leads me to articulate and defend a conception of *nonutilitarian* consequentialism, but still a consequentialism (unlike most utilitarianism) that is justified by an appeal to our considered judgments in wide reflective equilibrium. Rawls and I use basically the same methodology, but draw partially differing substantive conclusions from its use. Political morality sometimes requires hard choices; we must not, I argue, Michael Kohlhaas fashion, do justice though the heavens fall. To illustrate that I consider in chapter 9 the problem of dirty hands: a problem that some have mistakenly thought leads us into irresolvable moral dilemmas where to do what is right we must do what is wrong.

NOTES

1. There is, of course, this difference between considered judgments and judgments concerning what can and cannot be said in a given language. "Promises are prime numbers" cannot be said because it is unintelligible while "Promises need not be kept" is perfectly intelligible, but is something that goes against our considered judgments. We understand it perfectly well, but cannot accept it, while we do not understand "Promises are prime numbers." See here Thomas Nagel, "Rawls on Justice," in *Reading Rawls*, ed. Norman Daniels (New York: Basic Books, 1974).

2. Alvin Plantinga, "Belief in God," in *Perspectives in Philosophy,* ed. Michael Boylan (Fort Worth, Tex.: Harcourt, Brace Jovanovich, 1993), 389.

3. To the extent that we do not have it, to the extent there is really not a society-wide consensus that religious intolerance or racial discrimination are wrong, then our account is an idealization, though still a feasible idealization, of what our societies could be like.

4. It bears in broad outline, though not in all details, a family resemblance to my *Equality and Liberty: A Defense of Radical Egalitarianism* (Totowa, N.J.: Rowman and Allanheld, 1985).

Chapter Five

How to Proceed in Social Philosophy: Contextualist Justice and Wide Reflective Equilibrium

> Most Anglo-American academic books and articles on moral philosophy have a fairy-tale quality, because the realities of politics, both contemporary and past politics, are absent from them.
>
> —Stuart Hampshire

I

I articulate and defend a contextualist and historicist conception of social philosophy that deliberately eschews foundationalist speculations: that is, epistemological, metaphysical, and "grand moral" theories. It sees, instead, questions of justification as practical and pragmatic questions. In so proceeding I build on some conceptions of John Rawls, and, in the course of this building, I defend his conception of wide reflective equilibrium from criticisms that not a few have come to regard as effectively undermining his account and indeed of any similar account. I practice and theorize a practice which is a form of social philosophy (including moral, legal, and political philosophy) that travels metaphysically and epistemologically light. Conceptions of justice and conceptions of the good life (and the relations between them) are central in social philosophy as are questions concerning their practical rationalization and justification. This method for the contextual and pragmatic justification of principles of justice and of social practices is defended from claims that it is too status quo-oriented or too relativistic or is blandly, or at least unwittingly, ethnocentric. However, unlike Rawls, and more like Richard Rorty, this conception of appealing to considered judgments in wide reflec-

169

tive equilibrium is aligned with a metaphilosophical conception that is Wittgensteinian and Deweyan. I shall briefly explain that in the next paragraph and in the first endnote.

What is involved with the above gesture at Wittgenstein is a form of Anti-philosophy *philosophy* building creatively on Wittgenstein's therapeutic conception of philosophy.[1] Anti-philosophy *philosophy* affords a powerful rationale for setting aside the ontotheological tradition of philosophy, the grand old tradition of philosophy, very much the dominant tradition from Plato to Hegel and the neo-Kantians right down to its contemporary reincarnations in, their subversive intentions to the contrary notwithstanding, much of the actual work of the logical positivists and explicitly, and absent subversive intentions, in the work of analytical metaphysicians. (In its late formulations, understandably, it becomes more self-conscious and nervously defensive.) There is in all of these philosophers a hankering after the gaining of some necessary truths that would solve rather than dissolve the great ontotheological problems of philosophy. Wittgenstein, Richard Rorty, and Hilary Putnam, by contrast, show us how we can legitimately set those great problems of the tradition aside.[2] Wittgenstein contents himself with nay-saying, while Rorty and Putnam go on, with some yea-saying as well, to an articulation, though more in the *idiom* of a kind of laid-back linguistic philosophy, of a Deweyan-like pragmatism, thoroughly historicized, in which the problems of human beings, the problems of our epoch, become the central subject matter of philosophy and this puts moral, political, and social philosophy center-stage, though now done in a thoroughly antifoundationalist way. Where philosophy is so focused, the work of John Rawls and, though in a very different way, the work of Michel Foucault become central. This is no place to state the detail of their work, let alone analyze it, but I shall, taking Rawls as a paradigm, show something of how philosophy looks, and what its essential tasks are, when it is so construed. We will then look a bit at whether this does yield a new (given our present history) and legitimate thing for philosophy, particularly social philosophy, to be.

In "Kantian Constructivism in Moral Theory," most programmatically in "Justice as Fairness: Political not Metaphysical," in a series of subsequent articles, and then most comprehensively in his *Political Liberalism*, Rawls argues, to cite from the first mentioned article, that "the justification of a conception of justice is a practical social task rather than an epistemological or metaphysical problem."[3] He deliberately travels philosophically light, avoiding making claims, for example, about "universal truth" or "about the essential nature and identity of persons."[4] He doesn't say, positivist style, that these are pseudoproblems, or even problems without interest or significance, but that, for the purposes of arguing for a normative political philosophy for modern constitutional democracies, such questions must be set aside.[5]

In "Justice as Fairness: Political not Metaphysical," Rawls starts by explaining why his conception of justice does not rest on controversial philosophical claims and why this is a good thing, given what he takes it that the aims of political philosophy should be in societies such as ours, and what he takes a political conception of justice to be for such societies. Our constitutional democracies are deeply, and ineradicably in our present situation, and for the foreseeable future, pluralistic (indeed, they will probably grow more so). In such a world, Rawls argues, "the public conception of justice should be, so far as possible, independent of controversial philosophical and religious doctrines. Thus, to formulate such a conception, we apply the principle of toleration *to philosophy itself:* the public conception of justice is to be political, not metaphysical" (R 145, italics added).*

It is important to see that the work in political philosophy here, the articulation, clarification, and defense of a political conception of justice, is not the second-order activity characteristic of analytical philosophy.[6] It is resolutely first-order discourse, normative, descriptive, interpretative, and explanatory, as well as a discourse articulating a method of moral reasoning (reflective-equilibrium) or at least of moral reasoning in certain domains. It is not metaethical or metapolitical. It does not analyze the concept of justice or any other normative concept. It articulates certain conceptions of justice showing their rationale, how they balance off the demands of liberty and equality, and what a well-ordered society would be like. Rawls doesn't, as I remarked, analyze the concept of justice, but takes "justice" to be a primitive we understand well enough to engage in reasonable political deliberation, discussion, and theorizing. He does not, except incidentally, talk about our talk about politics, morality, law, and society. Most positivists thought that the only thing in the domains of morals and politics a philosopher, *qua philosopher*, could do would be metaethical or metapolitical, i.e., discussions of the logic of such discourse. Rawls, and most of the political and moral philosophers coming after him, resolutely violate that constraint.

On the firm terrain of first-order moral and political discourse, Rawls remarks that, while "a political conception of justice is, of course, a moral conception, it is a moral conception worked out for a specific kind of subject, namely, *for political, social, and economic institutions*" (R 146, italics added). His political conception of justice, but this could apply to the political conceptions of justice of others as well, *is meant to apply to the basic structure of modern constitutional democracies where he means by "basic structure" a "society's main political, social, and economic institutions, and how they fit together into one unified system of social cooperation"* (R 146, italics added).

---

*References to John Rawls "Justice as Fairness: Political not Metaphysical" will be given in the text. See note 4 of this chapter for the extended references.

It is important that we keep the scope of Rawls's inquiry firmly in mind. Unlike the principle of utility or perfectionist principles, "justice as fairness is not intended as the application of a general moral conception to the basic structure of society"(R 146). The reason for this restriction may have theoretical grounds, but it has, as well, and imperatively, practical ones. In pluralistic societies such as our own, "as a practical political matter no general moral conception can provide a publicly recognized basis for a conception of justice in a modern democratic state" (R 146). Constitutional democracies emerged after the wars of religion between Protestants and Catholics. These wars resulted in a stalemate and in the exhaustion of the contending sides. This in turn led to a grudging *modus vivendi*. Both sides realized they could not win and that to continue to struggle would just lead to ever more destruction, chaos, and misery. So reluctantly, and grudgingly, they agreed to tolerate each other. Slowly, what was first accepted bitterly as having instrumental value only came to be accepted as something which has intrinsic value as well. A principle of toleration came into play as an indispensable condition and *desideratum* for the constitutional democracies that came into existence in formerly contending societies and societies like them. Under adverse circumstances the principle was often overridden or only given lip service. Indeed, in a Marxian sense, it often functioned ideologically, but, where the constitutional democracies worked well, where conditions were stable, and there was some reasonable social wealth, a principle of toleration became deeply entrenched allowing for "the plurality of conflicting, and indeed incommensurable conceptions of the good affirmed by members of existing democratic societies" (R 146). By now such a pluralism has become a practically unquestionable background assumption for a political conception of justice for a constitutional democracy. It is part of the very conditions of life for such societies.

Rawls's political conception of justice works, and is meant to work, within the confines of that tradition and does not try to show what in some ahistorical sense for any human being at any time and place just social structures would look like. In this contextualist justification of a political conception of justice, justification is viewed as a practical and social task. Here a necessary condition for justifying such a conception of justice is the achieving of an overlapping consensus about it within such societies. This consensus, about a political conception of justice and on practices of justice, "includes all the opposing philosophical and religious doctrines likely to persist and to gain adherents in a more or less just constitutional democratic society" (R 147).

The first task of his political conception of justice—justice as fairness— is to, in "a reasonably systematic and practicable" way, "provide a more secure and acceptable basis for constitutional principles and basic rights than utilitarianism seems to allow" (R 147). Utilizing, what Rawls calls a "method of avoidance," and, with that, "applying the principle of toleration to philosophy itself," he does not seek to articulate "a conception of justice that is true, but one that can serve as a basis of informed and willing political agreement between citizens viewed as free and equal persons" (R 151). Deep and persistent questions about the nature of human nature, the nature of the good, how moral and other normative principles can be established to be true (if indeed they can), questions about the nature of practical rationality, the logical status of moral utterances, "the controversy between realism and subjectivism about the status of moral and political values," are all difficult and demanding questions that Rawls seeks to avoid in his articulation of a political conception of justice and in his articulation of a political philosophy. These philosophical questions about morality are, as noted, not regarded with indifference by Rawls or thought to be unimportant. Indeed, our *particular* conceptions of the good may very well be of very great importance to us in our private lives as individuals. Surely they will be of such importance to us if we have much in the way of moral sensitivity. Moreover, our respect for persons will require, where other people's often rather different conceptions of the good do not conflict with our political conception of justice, that we will respect them and hope that the persons in question can realize them. But we also recognize, if we have an ounce of realism about our world, that there is, short of the autocratic use of state power to enforce a particular conception of the good, no way to achieve consensus about *such a distinctive* conception of the good. This will be doubly true of philosophical articulations of comprehensive conceptions of the good. There just is no chance at all of obtaining an overlapping consensus on the acceptance of one of them as the one true account of the good (R 150). What we must recognize is that, "just as on questions of religious and moral doctrine, public agreement on the basic questions of philosophy cannot be obtained without the state's infringement of basic liberties. But this is far too high a price to pay for philosophical agreement" (R 150). Indeed, it is not even the kind of agreement philosophy seeks. It has many of the paradoxes and drawbacks of forcing faith or trying to force faith. People in societies such as ours—modern constitutional democracies—will not, if they are committed democrats, on reflection, accept such a way of attaining agreement. Where they are clear that no unforced agreement can be attained, they will, if they reflect carefully, and stick with their deepest considered convictions, opt for the method of avoidance, setting aside, in their political deliberations concerning justice, such philosophical questions. They will seek instead a workable conception of political justice "so that social cooperation on the basis of mutual respect can be maintained" (R 151). Rawls concludes that "philosophy as the search for truth about an independent metaphysical and moral order cannot . . . provide a workable and shared basis for a political conception of justice in a democratic society" (R 150).

What would provide such a basis for social cooperation, what would resolve or at least ameliorate our sharp, politically relevant, moral conflicts—those we cannot relegate just to our private lives—would be a stable overlapping consensus concerning principles of justice for political and social guidance for the institutional design of constitutional democracies that was also a consensus that could be sustained when the people in question get their beliefs in wide reflective equilibrium. We would look, that is, for agreement that would even obtain when we made a sustained use of the method of wide reflective equilibrium: the method that Simon Blackburn's nay-sayer, and *perhaps* Blackburn himself, thinks is such a nonstarter.[7] Looking, as Rawls puts it,

> to our public political culture itself, including its main institutions and the historical traditions of their interpretation, as the shared fund of implicitly recognized basic ideas and principles . . . [we] hope . . . that these ideas and principles can be formulated clearly enough to be combined into a conception of political justice congenial to our most firmly held convictions, at all levels of generality, on due reflection (or in what I have called "reflective equilibrium"). (R 149)

There have in the last few centuries been deep and persistent controversies over "the way basic institutions of a constitutional democracy should be arranged if they are to specify and secure the basic rights and liberties of citizens and answer to the claims of democratic equality when citizens are conceived as free and equal persons . . ." (R 147). It is part of the shared convictions of all involved (part of an overlapping consensus) that citizens, indeed all people, should be taken as free and equal persons. It is a further such conviction that equality, *in some form*, is a good thing and that it is important to secure the basic rights and liberties of everyone alike. There is no Nietzschean, Stalinist, or de Maistrean rejection of such things. They are not part of the "we" we seek an overlapping consensus with; they are not people committed to democracy. It is only to people so committed to whom justification is being addressed on Rawls's conception. But between democrats themselves there are "deep disagreements as to how the values of liberty and equality are best realized in the basic structure of society" (R 147). What are the respective weights to be given to certain basic rights of the person and of property as over against political liberties and the values of political life? All of these separate conceptions are, in a very considerable part at least, rooted in our considered convictions. We care, and care very deeply, about self-ownership, freedom of thought, and conscience and we care as well about having political control over our own lives. (Deep cynicism about it attests to how much we do care about it.) What justice as fairness tries to do is to articulate principles of political justice—e.g., Rawls's famous two principles of justice—which seek to adjudicate between the Lockean democratic tradition with its giving greater weight to individual liberties and to the Rousseauian tradition with its giving greater weight to political liberties and the values of political life. The two principles of justice proposed are "to serve as guidelines for how basic institutions are to realize the values of liberty and equality, and second by specifying a point of view from which these principles can be seen as more appropriate than other familiar principles of justice to the nature of democratic citizens viewed as free and equal persons" (R 148). Other philosophers, in articulating alternative conceptions of political justice, or, using the same conception or similar conceptions, articulating different principles of political justice for constitutional democracies, should be concerned to show "that a certain arrangement of the basic structure, certain institutional forms, are more appropriate for realizing the values of liberty and equality" in such societies and that their principles of justice more adequately articulate this than does Rawls's principles.

Finding a shared basis here for settling such a central political and moral question "as that of the most appropriate institutional forms for liberty and equality" is done by collecting together our deepest most firmly embedded shared considered convictions, such as our belief in the necessity of religious toleration and the rejection of slavery, and taking them, together with our well-established relevant factual beliefs, to "organize the basic ideas and principles implicit in these convictions into a coherent conception of justice" (R 149). We start with these considered convictions, regarding them as "provisional fixed points which any conception of justice must account for if it is to be reasonable to us"(R 149). We, that is, use the method of reflective equilibrium to gain a consistently held together, perspicuously displayed, collection of such considered judgments and related factual beliefs. To justify a political conception of justice is to do just that: *reflective equilibrium is enough*. In practical deliberations, such as trying to work out just practices, we always start in an embedded context, giving initial weight to our considered judgments, but trying, as well, to justify them in relation to other beliefs by gaining, and clearly articulating, a coherent pattern of beliefs. There is, moreover, no breaking out of the circle of beliefs. Similarly, with Rawls, no attempt is made to "get behind" these considered convictions and to show that they represent some antecedently recognizable moral reality. Applying the method of avoidance, all such philosophical questions are left, for the purpose of articulating and justifying a conception of political justice, with its matching principles of justice, to benign neglect.

The key question for the political philosopher should be: have we succeeded in collecting together such beliefs and settled convictions into a consistent package, perspicuously displayed, which yields a coherent conception of justice to guide us in determining how our basic institutions are to realize the values of liberty and equality? What we need to articulate, in doing political philosophy, is "a new way of organizing familiar ideas and principles into a conception of political justice so that the claims in conflict, as previously understood, are seen in another light" (R 149). A conception of justice can achieve its aim only "if it provides a reasonable way of shaping into one coherent view the deeper bases of agreement embedded in the public political culture of a constitutional regime and acceptable to its most firmly held considered convictions" (R 149). The doing of this is crucial, for, if it can be done, "this conception provides a publicly recognized point of view from which all citizens can examine before one another whether or not their political and social institutions are just" (R 149–50). It "enables them to do this by citing what are recognized among them as valid and sufficient reasons singled out by that conception itself " (R 150). This, of course, without taking political or legal philosophy onto ontotheological grounds, or even to epistemological grounds, would give it a scope far greater than that sanctioned by the positivist's limitation of political or legal philosophy to a logical or conceptual analysis of the language of politics or the language of law. We would have got beyond the sterile formalism typical of most analytical philosophy. Philosophy, without going either second-order or back to the grand metaphysical tradition or to a foundationalist epistemological tradition, would have a new lease on life.

II

This distinctive, and indeed powerful, conception of political philosophy, and hence of philosophy, has been strenuously resisted even by some generally sympathetic to Rawls's contractarianism and to his conception of justice as fairness. Some have thought this conception of the task of political philosophy for constitutional democracies is fundamentally wrongheaded. It is an account which, if accepted, would destroy the fundamental Socratic ideal of doing philosophy, including political philosophy. I shall argue that *au contraire* it does not reject the Socratic ideal but shows how in a disenchanted, intractably pluralistic world it might reasonably be realized.

It is said against Rawls's method of avoidance that we neither can, nor, even if we could, should, avoid meeting head-on, in articulating a substantive normative political philosophy, the examination of controversial philosophical views and the providing of a defense of those views we have good reason to believe are the more adequate.[8] In doing normative political philosophy in a way that is faithful to the Socratic ideal, that is, in a way that is genuinely critical, we cannot avoid (the claim goes) taking positions in the epistemology of morals, in metaethics, on the ontology of value, and we cannot avoid the articulation and defense of controversial moral principles, including principles which state a conception of the fundamental good for human beings.[9] In attempting to travel light philosophically, to, with the method of avoidance, set aside controversial philosophical issues, Rawls will not be able to confront, the claim goes, the critical moral and political problems of our time. We will get rather an analytical and systematized sanctioning of the *status quo*. His very method, it has been claimed, makes a critical political or moral philosophy, and even a reflectively critical public moral-political stance, impossible.

Moreover, considerations about the *status quo* aside, we would get a stable constitutional democracy, where such a political consensus would work, only if there were a sufficiently extensive overlapping consensus in the society such that there was no substantial minority in the society advocating intolerance toward the beliefs of some others. Critics of Rawls, such as Jean Hampton (temperately) and John Gray (intemperately), claim that Rawls's world is not the real world of our democracies.[10] Our societies are pluralist all right, but there are not in them the conditions of tolerance—the reasonable pluralism—necessary for Rawls's political conception of justice to have an application. Rawls, Gray claims, is living in a liberal's dreamworld. There is, for example, the extensive phenomena of religious fundamentalism. Religious fundamentalists, and not they alone, accept a principle of tolerance not as a moral principle to be adopted and cherished, but merely as a matter of expediency in the circumstances in which they find themselves.

Those empirical and pragmatic considerations for the moment aside, not a few moral and normative political philosophers think that both political and moral philosophy must concern itself with *the pursuit of truth and not, except perhaps incidentally, with achieving overlapping consensus.*[11] The central task is to find out what is the truth about moral and political matters. It is a secondary matter, not at the heart of political philosophy, to rationalize our considered convictions so as to form a consistently and perspicuously characterized representation of these considered convictions sustainable in an overlapping consensus. The philosopher's job is to ascertain, if she can, consensus or no consensus, true moral and political norms and to get as close as she can to the truth about such things.

Jean Hampton, in a typical response to Rawls's program, remarks, "Socrates, the founder of our discipline, characterized philosophy as the pursuit of truth."[12] This Socratic ideal is part of the very vocation of what it is to be a philosopher, but Rawls abandons it, Hampton has it, when in political philosophy "noncoerced social agreement is to be our goal" rather than truth.[13] What really bothers her, and bothers some other philosophers as well, is Rawls's "eschewing of attempts at philosophical proof through argumentation that involves the appeal to and defense of controversial philosophical premises."[14] It is an important part of philosophy, Socratically conceived, to

resist True Believers, that is, people who put their cause over any consideration of truth. Philosophers wish to "examine the theoretical foundations of society as much to overturn what is unjustifiable as to find shared bases for
agreement" and this means steadfastly to maintain a search for truth whether
the principles discovered are controversial or not.[15] In doing political philosophy, in a way that is true to the vocation of philosophy, "there can be no
avoiding an activity that is based upon substantive philosophical beliefs about
the nature of human beings."[16] We must not, even in doing political philosophy with a properly critical intent for societies such as our own, use Rawls's
method of avoidance and set aside all controversial philosophical beliefs and
questions. Hampton is claiming that we, to remain true to our vocation as
philosophers, cannot do that even for the purposes of doing political philosophy in defense of constitutional democracy. To use the method of avoidance,
even in this circumscribed context, is in effect to be antiphilosophical, implicitly denying what it is to be a philosopher, for a philosopher must, to be
a philosopher, be prepared to follow the argument where it will go. That, in
Max Weber's sense of "vocation," is just an essential part of his vocation as
a philosopher.

However (*pace* Hampton), to characterize Rawls's method of doing political philosophy as concerned solely with persuasion and consensus building and not with trying to ascertain what is warrantedly assertible is just a
plain error about what Rawls is up to. To be sure his judgments are context-
dependent, but they are all the same judgments concerning what is reasonable,
in the circumstances in which we find ourselves, to believe about what a just
society would be and how people would, and should, act in such a society.
Moreover, he is saying that such and such is what it is to be a well-ordered
constitutional democracy worthy of our allegiance. Rawls, early and late, is
centrally concerned with justification. He wants to make sense of our dis-
parate moral and political beliefs, to show how many of them can at least reasonably be seen to fit together into a coherent web of belief and conviction,
and to articulate underlying moral-cum-political claims, such as justice as
fairness, which will reveal their rationale and show how this rationale is reasonable, indeed more than reasonable, powerfully attractive, perhaps even
compelling, to people situated as we are. This is not (*pace* Hampton) failing
to follow the argument wherever it will go, for Rawls is after the justification
of certain very fundamental moral and political beliefs. He seeks to show
which ones are the most reasonable to hold in the circumstances in which we
find ourselves and in changed circumstances that are feasibly possibilities:
that is, circumstances that could be brought about by resolute, but still morally
acceptable, action. Rawls wants to show how certain of them (ones central to
constitutional democracies) can be justified. He wants to show which principles of justice for the structure of a society are the more reasonable to accept

in such a circumstance for human beings, constituted as we are, or as we could feasibly become if we became somewhat more informed and reflective.

Rawls's argument is a justificatory argument that is both context-sensitive and empirical-fact sensitive. It is analogous to asking, and proffering an answer, to the question of how we should live given the inescapability of death. Rawls is asking, and proffering an answer to the question, what political conception of justice should we hold given (a) that we are in constitutional democracies that are intractably pluralist, (b) that in such societies no controversial philosophical premiss will gain acceptance in a justificatory argument that is meant to gain society-wide acceptance, and (c) that "ought" implies "can." What in such a situation should be taken as the most adequate political conception of justice with its associated principles of justice? (He is, of course, concerned to articulate a conception of justice that would actually guide conduct.) In the broad sense of a Socratic ideal, you can (without distortion) call this the search for truth. It is the attempt to find out what conception of justice under the circumstances is the best justified, the best warranted, and that comes to saying that it, as what is best warranted, is what is most plausibly thought to be true or taken to be true or as true.[17] But this does not entail a belief in a speculative philosophical doctrine that a noncognitivist or error-theorist would reject, namely, that there is something called moral truth or a claim that moral utterances are bivalent (are either true or false) or anything of the sort. It does, however, involve the belief that some moral beliefs are warranted. Where the argument is about how we are to justify our moral and political beliefs here and now, we will proceed by using wide reflective equilibrium. This is the way in such a context to follow the argument where it will go. Rawls does not think that the traditional Socratic ideal (the ideal articulated by Hampton) can yield a rationally justified political conception of justice in the circumstances in which we find ourselves. Hampton's conditions cannot be met. Instead, we should proceed, more internally and holistically, to realize a very similar ideal, adjusting here and there the web of beliefs and norms, until we get the most coherent account we can, for the time being, attain, which is also, of the alternatives, the most reflectively attractive to people such as ourselves situated as we are situated.

It could be objected—going again at another round of putative self-referential contradictions—that Rawls's method of wide reflective equilibrium is itself a controversial philosophical conception and thus, given Rawls's own method of avoidance, should be avoided. Rawls should in turn respond that while this method starts as a controversial philosophical thesis, that it, on examination, commends itself to reflective common sense and is a systematization of a way of proceeding we pervasively apply commensensically in inquiry and in the justification of belief and action. The method of wide reflective equilibrium, I would contend, is enlightened common sense rooted in our considered judgments and our use of public reason. Adequately reflected on, it should not remain controversial as one philosophical framework set against another, but, like much of John Dewey's work, it should be seen as a method squaring with, and in effect explicating, a part of our reflective common sense. It is a way of conceptualizing what we do when we are being reflective and careful and are not being carried away by some religious, philosophical, or ideological extravagance or other. We are claiming that for Rawls to avoid pragmatic self-contradiction the method of wide reflective equilibrium must be so defensible.

Rawls (again *pace* Hampton) is not just after the acceptance of some principles of justice but after their *rational* acceptance. Moreover, it is also important to remember that, for Rawls, as for Jürgen Habermas, for the acceptance to count as a rational acceptance, it "must be informed and uncoerced and reached by citizens in ways consistent with their being viewed as free and equal persons" (R 229–30). The consensus achieved will, of course, be a particular consensus, gained for a time and place. This may seem to imply some kind of relativism. But, while there is clearly an inescapable contextualism and historicism, there need be no relativism. Rawls, like communitarians, takes very seriously indeed the shared values, beliefs, and traditions of our society. Moreover, there is no *ahistorical Archimedean* point in accordance with which we can gain a critical purchase on them. But wide reflective equilibrium gives us an *internal* way of gaining a critical purchase on them and this enables us to evade relativism or being stuck with some traditional morality. After all, wide reflective equilibrium, though giving initial weight to our considered judgments, is also a holistic coherentism. It gains a critical purchase on traditional morality because the beliefs of traditional morality must, to be reflectively sustainable, yield a consistent cluster compatible with what we know or justifiably believe about people, society, and nature. And further, it must, as well, be compatible with our general moral principles (principles which also may be our considered judgments), conceptions of morality, and morality's underlying rationale where they, in turn, are compatible with our public shared political conception of justice and its attendant political principles of justice. These are principles and conceptions that we devise and, reflecting on that devising, find reflectively attractive or perhaps even compelling. We must, to rationalize our morality and politics, get all of this into a consistent and coherent package. For them to so stand to each other sometimes even comes to modifying or even abandoning a more general moral principle. In this adjusting here, to gain consistency and coherence (if they do not come to the same thing) there no doubt will be quite a winnowing of the considered convictions coming from the tradition or from the life-world. This yields a historicist, but nonrelativist, critical morality. The source of moral legitimation is not simply society or the community. We start with the norms and values of our tradition, but they, though not all at once, get critically assessed in various concrete situations.

Socrates characterized philosophy as the pursuit of truth, but there is not much to the pursuit of truth without a pursuit of the *knowledge* of the truth and that in practice, in what we can achieve, can be nothing more than a pursuit of what we are best justified in believing at a given time and place and that in turn comes to what is the most reasonable thing for us to believe at a given time and place. This is a demythologized sense of the Socratic conception of philosophy. In the pursuit of what it is most reasonable for us to believe are the most just social structures for constitutional democracies, either here and now, or as those democracies might reasonably be expected to be transformed during our epoch, I should, as does Rawls, take the "us" quite literally as the people living in these constitutional democracies *and* committed to them. The "us" or the "we" are also taken to be in favorable circumstances (circumstances such as described in his early "An Outline of a Decision Procedure for Ethics") and reasoning in a certain way, namely, the way described in the method of wide reflective equilibrium or some reasonable approximation to it. With such an application of this demythologized conception of the Socratic conception of philosophy to political philosophy, Rawls shows how we can fallibilistically argue for certain social structures being the most just social structures possible in such societies, while eschewing attempts at philosophical proof through argumentation that involves the utilization of controversial philosophical premisses: premisses we would never get a reflective consensus about in our pluralistic societies.

III

We need to return to the factual claim, made by Hampton and Gray, among others, that there is not in fact in our societies the overlapping consensus that Rawls finds necessary for the carrying on of political philosophy as he conceives it. The principle of toleration, which is at the heart of the self-conception of a liberal society, is, they claim, only accepted as *a mere modus vivendi* by religious fundamentalists, Stalinists, and very right-wing conservatives. If they had sufficient power, they, depending on who they are specifically, would not be tolerant at all of the beliefs of communists, socialists, atheists, agnostics or liberal theologians or more generally of liberals. Religious fundamentalists and right-wing conservatives would, in circumstances of secure power, not be tolerant of any of the above mentioned people. And Russian communists were not tolerant of liberals or religious believers and were not even tolerant of dissident communists.

It is also the case, and relatedly, that there are sharply divisive moral beliefs with clear political implications in our society. Moreover, these are beliefs that many of us are very attached to indeed. Concerning them there is no foreseeable possibility that we would achieve consensus, even after some extensive reasonable discussion of them (assuming—which is surely to assume a lot—that we could ever get something even approximating that). Moreover, we should keep firmly in mind that for some of these beliefs, at least, there is little toleration of dissent. We cannot in fact gain a consensus concerning them, but still many people (including some sincere democrats) in such contexts, *over such matters*, are not willing to be tolerant: to agree to disagree and to let everyone, in these respects, live and act as they will. Yet they are beliefs which require a political solution. Differences about the morality of abortion or pornography are such issues. As a matter of sociological fact, people in our actual constitutional democracies sometimes have very different and, indeed, conflicting considered convictions about them. Moreover, there are a not inconsiderable number of people in our societies who are vociferously intolerant of the views, and sometimes even of the persons, with which or with whom they so fundamentally disagree.

There are a number of responses that could plausibly be made here. I will restrict myself to one line of argument. Rawls's justificatory arguments were made not to all and sundry but to people committed to constitutional democracy. That fascists, Stalinists, and religious and racial fanatics (e.g., the Aryan Nation, the Jewish Defense League, and the KKK) cannot be brought into the consensus is beside the point. They do not start, except instrumentally and manipulatively, by accepting constitutional democracy. Rawls sought to justify a conception of political justice for a constitutional democracy and to people committed to such a democracy, but who are sharply divided over issues like positive and negative liberty; the respective weights of liberty and equality; the role, weight, and the scope of rights, and the like. (That will include people who will dispute over whether there are any collective rights.)

However, this response is not sufficient to meet all the objections discussed above. Sincere democrats can, and sometimes do, differ in the way described above over issues such as abortion and pornography. But, as I noted, many, perhaps most, people who have deep-seated convictions about abortion or pornography are not prepared to be tolerant about it or to those they oppose. Indeed, when they lack the power to do anything about it, they grudgingly tolerate those they deeply oppose, though surely not in the spirit of tolerance. They would make their views over such matters prevail if they could, but, since they cannot, they will, though with hostility, accept the presence of those people with their, to them, utterly abhorrent views. Doctors in Canada who practice abortion frequently get harassed, but nobody tries to kill them or drive them from the country. (Here, when I first drafted this, I was too sanguine. Shortly after I wrote this a doctor who works in an abortion clinic in

Vancouver was seriously wounded by a sniper and, in the United States, a doctor who performs abortions was murdered by a fanatical antiabortionist.) Still, these True Believers, including people who engage in such harassment (particularly when they are also sincere democrats), will also have many other beliefs, including central moral and political beliefs, that are within the overlapping consensus of constitutional democracies. And at least some of these beliefs will conflict with their beliefs which are not in an overlapping consensus, e.g., their beliefs concerning abortion, homophobia, or pornography and, most importantly, with their belief that they are justified in using violence against some of those with opposing convictions who act on those convictions. Moreover, they will want, unless they are utterly irrational (something it would be rather *parti pris* to ascribe to them), to have their own beliefs form a consistent cluster. There is, of course, extensive room for rationalization (in the bad sense) here, and being captive to an ideology, but it is not inevitable that such things will obtain and, in struggling against the rationalization when it occurs, there remains room for argument and argument in accordance with Rawls's model. Similar things obtain for the grip of an ideology. Moreover, even where rationalization occurs, that is something that can be noted and again argument can continue, only there it will be more difficult. But being difficult should not be translated into being impossible.

It is a deep underlying belief of modern democrats (including True Believers) that all persons, the greatest and the smallest, are to be respected—indeed, they are deserving of equal respect. Hampton, and presumably Gray as well, believe, on the contrary, that "there is no consensus on the idea that all humans deserve equal respect." The plain facts are, Hampton points out, that sexism, racism, and exploitation are a pervasive and enduring part of our world, including our modern democracies. This certainly is true, but it is also true that everywhere in such constitutional democracies they are on the defensive. Moreover, in such societies it is only from culturally speaking marginal figures that such beliefs get *explicit* and *self-conscious* defense. Exploitation goes on, but apologetically so, and its defenses are indirect. It is said, by its defenders, to be an inescapable evil, or a necessary evil, tolerated only so as to avoid still worse evils. Still, it is acknowledged that in itself it is a bad thing to be gotten rid of, if we can and if the costs are not too great. It is not something simply to be viewed with equanimity or indifference. Its defenders, however, argue that we could only get rid of it by creating still worse evils. There is plainly room for argument here. It is also true that racist and sexist attitudes remain, but they are usually not defended as such. Everywhere, except with a few marginalized people, racism and sexism are taken to be evils. Now, as distinct from times in the not too distant past, their expression characteristically comes out in indirect ways that could not be consciously defended and, when brought to the light by critical analysis, explicitly racist and sexist views will usually be rejected. Often there will be a lot of resistance (in the psychoanalytic sense) to recognizing them as racist or sexist but that is a different matter. The relevant fact is that they cannot be consciously accepted. However, I certainly do not wish to sound complacent about these culturally marginalized forces. Thirty black churches put to the torch in the United States in 1995–96 and the continued and pervasive molestation of women speak eloquently enough for themselves. There is a good bit of racism and sexism that is alive and well.

Still, political philosophers from right to left believe in rights, the good of self-respect, the equality of persons, equality of opportunity, and moral equality (the life of everyone matters and matters equally). As modernization goes on, these beliefs, ever more extensively, trickle down to the nonintelligentsia in our societies. However badly people violate it in practice, people in such societies, very extensively, give conscious assent to the belief that all human beings deserve equal respect. There are, of course, hold-outs, but they grow fewer as modernization runs its inexorable course and where political conditions are secure. (Contrast Israel here with Norway.) So, where there are people with sexist, racist, and exploitation-justifying beliefs, it is reasonable to believe, or at least to hope, that they (or their children or grandchildren) can over time be relevantly and rationally argued out of them using what is in effect the nonmetaphysical apparatus of wide reflective equilibrium. Some of them will just be socialized out of them, but remember that even so that socialization will have the argumentative background conditions captured by wide reflective equilibrium. (Remember, also, that reflective equilibrium is little more than a philosophical, and perhaps pedantic, articulation of reflective commonsense reasoning in social contexts.)

Still, that this can be said about beliefs about abortion, pornography, and homosexuality is less clear. *Some* moral disputes *may* remain intractable. There is no *principle of sufficient reason in morals*. This does not show that reflective equilibrium does not work, but only that not all beliefs, at a given time, or perhaps ever, can be gotten into reflective equilibrium. Reflective equilibrium will always be incomplete. It is not a kind of unacknowledged rationalism about morality. But even here, it is not evident, even over such seemingly morally intractable issues, that socially speaking (that is, at the level of society) in the long run wide reflective equilibrium could not, or even would not, be effective, bit by bit, case by case, in gaining a resolution. Sometimes what is intractable in one epoch is not in the next. Racism, though still extensive, is on the defensive today; in a decade or so, given struggle, general affluence, security, and education, it is reasonable to expect that homophobia will be similarly on the run. Already there are signs of it. The moral world does not stand still. Moreover, even concerning, for a time at least, such intractable issues, what is to be believed here could still be the subject of rational argumentation. To illustrate: someone who rejects a ban on hard pornography on the grounds that banning it would violate our rights to freedom of speech would have to face, if he would use wide reflective equilibrium arguments, carefully attending to what free speech comes to, to seriously consider whether freedom of speech is really at issue here at all and, even if it were, to consider in comparison the weight of other considered convictions held by him concerning the wrongs of exploitation and degradation (particularly of children), conceptions of respect for persons and the wrongness of the coarsening and brutalization of people and the like. It is not reasonable to just take the undoubted value of free speech just by itself as some kind of "absolute value" without considering how it also squares with other things we deeply care about and with, as well, what it is sensible to believe, e.g., does a ban on pornography really violate our free speech rights?

It still may be felt that my above account of democratic consensus in the rich capitalist democracies is too optimistic. It remains, some believe, a liberal's myth, distant from social reality. This issue is, of course, empirical and cannot be settled in a philosopher's or academic lawyer's armchair. Certainly there is a lot of racism, sexism, exploitation, and homophobia around. That is all too evident. Moreover, while an overt and conscious defense of racism and sexism is limited to a few marginalized groups, this certainly is not true of homophobia. On the contrary, it is entrenched in a broad social majority in many, perhaps most, of the liberal democracies. It has, for example, had an articulate elaboration and defense by the Supreme Court of the United States (*Bowers* v. *Hardwick*) and by the Roman Catholic church. Similar reactions have come from many parliamentarians in the liberal constitutional states. There is no overlapping consensus here any more than there is over pornography and abortion. But I did not claim, or give to understand, that there is an overlapping consensus on all major social issues. Far from it. But what I did claim is that there is a not inconsiderable overlapping consensus on many social issues as well as on many other normative and factual matters and that this affords us a toehold to use in deliberations aimed at widening the consensus. Indeed tolerant, to say nothing about egalitarian, views about sexuality (including attitudes about homosexuality) are pretty much limited to a liberal cultural elite and to those institutions where such opinions are influential. But a few decades ago this was also true of sexism and racism. It is, however, indeed true that racism and sexism, though on the run, are still very much with us. But, that notwithstanding, we have now, rather across the board, at least at the level of the media and medialike expressions of belief, and in the expressed attitudes that tend to follow along with them, a kind of vague "official egalitarianism" directed against racism and sexism and paying at least lip service to the belief that the life of everyone matters and matters equally. In such a modernizing society everyone, at the level of ideology, at the level of public conception, has equal moral standing. But this, as a recognition of these sociological and anthropological facts trickle down into the society, has put racism and sexism on the defensive and it is reasonable to expect that in the next few decades—and, indeed, there are already signs of it commencing—the same thing will happen about homophobia, though, probably, for Freudian reasons, resistance will be more entrenched.

Some might continue to resist my account. They could still claim that it is too optimistic, though the reason that it is so, they claim, is not what was discussed above. What I crucially fail to note, the claim could go, is that while the citizenry of the liberal democracies do indeed pay lip service to antiracism and antisexism and a very large majority of these citizens sincerely believe they are not racists or sexists, they do so in the context of a considerable lack of consensus about what practices are in reality racist or sexist. I shall illustrate this with respect to sexism only. But similar things can be said about racism. Some say that pornography is sexist, others deny it; some say that failure to include unpaid household labor as productive labor is sexist, others deny it; some say that affirmative action programs for women are sexist, others deny it. Behind a general consensus about the wrongness of sexism there stands deep disagreements about what it is to be sexist and about what practices are actually sexist. So my optimism is not warranted.[18]

I certainly do not deny, and indeed I would wish to stress, that there is a lot of sexism, racism, homophobia, exploitation, severe class and caste divisions and stratification, and the like in the world along with powerful currents of blind fanaticism, including, as I write (1994), the rise of neo-Fascist parties in Europe, the occurrence of "ethnic cleansing," and the growing power of ethnocentric and antiliberal forms of nationalism. Such things make our world a very bleak (to understate it) place, concerning which it is hard to generate much optimism. Issues like fascism that we thought were settled come again on the agenda.

However, if we take the long view, look at things over the last few hundred years, it is the case that there is more equality in the world now than there was at the turn of the century, to say nothing of the seventeenth and eighteenth centuries. If our world can attain something approaching the economic wealth of the richer capitalist states and, as well, reasonable security widely dispersed, it is reasonable to expect that there will be an increasing movement in the direction of social equality and with that a withering away of homophobia and the remaining hidden forms of racism and sexism, including the forms that show themselves in some concrete understandings of what racism or sexism really come to. But the world may not turn that way. We may not be able to generate that much wealth, our educational systems may remain impoverished, and it is a fact, even in the wealthy capitalist democracies, that economic insecurity is on the rise. If these things are not overcome, racism, sexism, and the other ills I have just described will not be overcome and may even be exacerbated. But it is not impossible to believe that we may muster sufficient economic and moral reasonableness to solve these problems. It is not evident that we cannot construct and sustain a socioeconomic order that is both efficient and egalitarian.

IV

Using wide reflective equilibrium looks like just a fancy way of talking about being reasonable and commonsensical. It is far from evident (*pace* Hampton and Gray) that Rawls's metaphysics-free method would not suffice for argumentation and deliberation about the proper institutional design for a just society. Even when we are imaginatively disputing with the great figures of the past, this remains so (*pace* both Rawls and Rorty). It isn't that figures such as de Maistre, Nietzsche, Loyola, or the people depicted in the Icelandic sagas have systems of belief which are incommensurable with ours. We cannot, at a minimum, rule out *a priori* that somewhere in the web of our and their beliefs and convictions we could find some toehold in our and their beliefs and considered convictions which would allow us, if we could (counterfactually could) actually be together, to deliberate together, fragile though our deliberations would be. Considerations about what is necessary for communication to obtain would make it seem very unlikely, perhaps even impossible, that we could be so totally distant from each other such that no argument and resolution, or at least narrowing of differences, would be possible. For people even to conflict, there will have to be some understanding of each other and with some understanding there are some grounds for reasoning together and there are grounds for believing that sometimes people reasoning together will change some of their beliefs. Sometimes the change in moral or political beliefs would be on one side only, but sometimes (perhaps even more characteristically) the adjustment and change would be one in which both sides altered to some extent some of their beliefs as a result of honestly deliberating together. They would, in such a circumstance, come to a mutual accommodation that was not just, or perhaps even at all, a *modus vivendi*. This, of course, is an idealized picture, for often people just throw insults or slogans at each other or even fight. Indeed, as we know too well, genocide is not infrequently the result of such being together. But sometimes people do deliberate together reasonably or the force of circumstances can bring them to deliberate reasonably. That always remains an open possibility. And, in some places in the world this has its approximations. It is not a liberal's myth. We, in short, have available here a social instantiation, or at least the possibility of an approximation, of the holist's conception of reflective equilibrium such that we would be justified in saying with the holist that "reflective equilibrium is all we need to try for," there being "no natural order of justification of beliefs, no predetermined outline for argument to trace."[19] And this does not entail or justify relativism. It is not even clear that it is even compatible with any of its several forms.[20]

V

Reflective equilibrium, whether narrow (partial) or wide, is, as we have noted, principally a coherence conception of justification. When wide reflective equilibrium is used, which is what I am defending, the intent in the justification of moral principles is "to make sure support for the moral principles is brought from as wide a justificatory circle as possible."[21]

I will briefly characterize what this coherence method of moral justification is, starting with a characterization of narrow (partial) reflective equilibrium, and then I will contrast wide (broad) reflective equilibrium with it. Narrow (partial) reflective equilibrium is an inadequate method typically used by contemporary intuitionists. It is sometimes just taken to be *the* appeal to considered judgments in reflective equilibrium by its less perceptive critics. It consists in getting a match between our considered particular moral convictions (judgments) and a moral principle or cluster of moral principles (which may themselves be more general considered convictions) that systematize the more particular considered convictions so that we can see how they all could be derived from that principle or those principles, or at least come to recognize that they are in accordance with that principle or those principles, and are explained and rationalized by them, so that, together with the more particular moral convictions and more generalized moral principles, they form a consistent whole perspicuously displayed. Moral principles that do not so match with the great mass of our specific considered judgments will rightly be rejected. Also to be rejected are specific considered judgments in conflict with the mass of specific considered judgments and, as well, specific considered judgments different from (but not in conflict with) the mass of specific considered judgments but in conflict with moral principles widely and reflectively held. Furthermore, when two specific considered judgments conflict and one is in conflict with, or simply not covered by (if that is possible), a moral principle widely and reflectively held, and the other specific considered judgment is in accordance with it, then the latter specific considered judgment is to continue to have our acceptance and the former is to be rejected or modified until it is no longer in conflict with the other considered judgment and the relevant moral principle or principles.

Wide (broad) reflective equilibrium retains the features characterized by narrow reflective equilibrium, though subject to further constraints that I will specify. Wide reflective equilibrium, as its name connotes, casts a wider net than narrow reflective equilibrium. Many more considerations become relevant in giving a coherence account of moral and normative political justification. It seeks to produce, and perspicuously display, coherence among (a) our considered moral convictions, (b) a consistent cluster of moral principles, (c) a consistent cluster of background theories (including moral theories) about our social world and how we function in it, (d) an empirically based, broadly scientific, conception and account of human nature, and (e) accurate social description. The aim is to seek to show which moral judgments, including which political conception of justice and its allied principles, coheres best with these various elements. Those that do so are the judgments and principles we should accept (take to be justified) for as long as that equilibrium holds and is not replaced by another equilibrium which is wider and/or even better cohering (fitting) together than the previous equilibrium. But coherence is given pride of place throughout. The intent is to get a consistent package, giving our moral principles and conceptions, such as the conception of justice as fairness, the widest consistent justificatory circle possible. The method is unreservedly holistic. We want a moral and political theory, more broadly a social theory, which we are also taking to be a philosophical theory. It is crucial, however, to recognize that here I am taking "philosophical theory," as a pragmatist would, as a theory which seeks to help us understand how things hang together and to see how some of the ways in which things could (in an empirically feasible sense of "could") hang together answer more adequately to human needs and are more liberating of human powers than others. (See here my first endnote.)

VI

Simon Blackburn, or at least Simon Blackburn's nay-sayer, thinks all that talk of reflective equilibrium is a very considerable mistake.[22] Indeed, there is in such an account, he believes, a kind of unwitting rationalism that the development of philosophy should have taught us to set aside. As Blackburn puts it, there "is an implicit *rationalism* in the pursuit of theory, as if the common intelligence of mankind (in place of God) must have dictated a hidden order in the various deposits, whose nature and whose unfolding the initiate is privileged to uncover" (B 92).* He comments: "But there is no reason to believe this in the case of intellectual and moral deposits from the shifting seas of cultural necessity and history" (B 92). I do not think that there is any such

---

*References to Simon Blackburn's "Can Philosophy Exist?" will be given in the text. See note 7 of this chapter for the extended reference.

implicit and unwitting rationalism in such thoroughly historicist defenders of reflective equilibrium as Rawls, Daniels, or Rorty. They are all constructivists in normative political or moral theorizing and are not looking, as do moral realists or rational intuitionists, for the hidden underlying structure to be revealed by moral or normative deliberation. They are not trying to discover some hidden moral structure of the world or even of the social or moral world. What is done instead, as Rawls puts it, is that we "collect such settled convictions as the belief in religious toleration and the rejection of slavery and. try to organize the basic ideas and principles implicit in these convictions into a coherent conception of justice" (R 148). The idea is to try out a conception of justice, in a way analogous to how a scientist would try out a hypothesis (something she invents and does not find) to see how well it rationalizes (makes sense of) our considered convictions at all levels of generality where our considered convictions themselves are not taken to have the status of rational intuitions. (Here Rawls's procedure is very like John Dewey's.) If it so rationalizes our considered convictions and does it better than any of the extant alternative conceptions, then it is, for the nonce, a justified conception of justice. For such a "conception of justice, to be acceptable, [it] must be in accordance with our considered convictions, *at all levels of generality*, on due reflection" (R 148, italics added). But this is not the uncovering of hidden structures, but the forging, inventing, constructing of a consistent package of beliefs, norms, theories, and the like. Shuttling back and forth between an extensive range of considerations—not infrequently conflicting considerations—by pruning here, deleting there, by rejecting or reformulating elsewhere, and, sometimes as well, by bringing in view new conceptions, or by articulating new norms, we seek to forge a consistent pattern of beliefs, coherently organized.

As Blackburn stresses himself, we cannot avoid starting with our beliefs (our considered convictions) but that is compatible with jettisoning or modifying many of them as we go along. (The often cited metaphor of rebuilding the ship at sea is apposite here.) We seek in doing these things a reflective equilibrium, taking this to be a philosophical and rational task, but there is no implicit rationalism there, either with a belief in an underlying moral structure there to be discovered or with the assumption of some principle of sufficient reason in ethics. There is no rationalistic belief that if we just try hard enough for a very long time, we will achieve reflective equilibrium and discover some underlying structure revealing what the truth about morality really is. There is no belief at all—even as heuristic ideal—that if we apply this procedure long enough, diligently enough, intelligently enough, we will finally have some approximation of "the one true morality." That is no more possible, or perhaps even intelligible, than is the idea of there being a uniquely true description of the world: a one true description of the world. We may or may not gain a temporary, and invariably incomplete, reflective equilibrium (as any reflective equilibrium must be) in a world in which that is as much as it is reasonable to expect: that is, in a world which has taken to heart the lessons of fallibilism. But the achieving of such a reflective equilibrium remains a crucial *desideratum* of moral and political thinking. But it need not be, and is not thought to be, by Rawls or by Daniels or by myself, to be the discovery of some underlying structure that our moral notions, or at least some of them, must answer to.

A difficulty with coming to grips with Blackburn's attack on reflective equilibrium is that he creates a straw man. He does not argue against any of the extant accounts of reflective equilibrium such as Rawls's or Daniels's. And what he takes to be reflective equilibrium does not mesh well with their conceptions: conceptions of reflective equilibrium of which they, along with Nelson Goodman, are the creators. After all, "reflective equilibrium" is a term of art. It is difficult to ascertain whether the difficulties which Blackburn finds in what he calls "reflective equilibrium"—difficulties which, in the view of his naysayer, would make ethical theory impossible—reflect difficulties in *reflective equilibrium*.

All that to the contrary notwithstanding, my guess is that Blackburn's account will be thought to be persuasive by many and, moreover, the errors he isolates in his straw man are errors that should not be made by articulators of reflective equilibrium or anyone else. So I shall examine his arguments. Blackburn starts by remarking:

> Let us suppose that an ethical or political theory would aspire to do two things. It would simplify and explain the apparent complexity of everyday ethical or political judgment. And it would *thereby* gain didactic authority, dictating or at least certifying verdicts in new and disputed cases. (B 90)

Reflective equilibria accounts, such as Rawls's and Daniels's, do indeed both seek to explain (using an approach which is analytic and explicative) and to give a coherence-type justificatory account of certain moral and political conceptions. What is so justified would have (though this is not their language) some didactic-authority. But there is no suggestion that it would *dictate* anything. There is nothing even remotely like a totalitarian or authoritarian streak in Rawls or in Rawlsians. What reflective equilibrium would rather aspire to is to fallibilistically justify some ethical or normative political principles. But it sees the explicative (explanatory) and the justificatory tasks as distinct. The former Daniels refers to as the *modest* role for reflective equilibrium and the latter the *daring* role.[23] They are, of course, related but from the first we cannot claim that anything thereby follows for the second, though what is ascertained of the first is relevant to the second.

Blackburn maintains (though without citation) "that the best descriptions of what ethics is and how it is actually conducted suggest very strongly that there is no serious place for any such theory" (B 90). Reflective equilibrium yields, he has it, nothing like a stable balance of the competing considerations. Rather, the conflicting and competing considerations lock, leading to bafflement. What we get by way of resolution is in reality a plumping for one or another alternative rather than anything approaching a reasoned resolution. Blackburn doesn't cite or articulate who or what establishes this or even who makes this claim. But, while, as we have seen, there remains lots of disagreement about justice, about its relation to equality and liberty, and about issues concerning entitlements and distribution, there has also been a gradual refinement of the accounts and *some* agreement about some not unimportant things. (It should be kept in mind that a similar state of affairs obtains both in science and in the philosophy of science.) If one looks at recent analytical accounts of justice, it will become evident that there are important areas of agreement as well as disagreement and it is not unreasonable to think some progress has been made and will continue to be made. Whether the method of wide reflective equilibrium is subscribed to or not, in practice, at least, it, or something rather like it, appears at least to be in operation here and as affording a way of characterizing this progress. Such philosophers, social theorists, and legal theorists dispute and, even though they continue to dispute, it is clear enough that their views undergo modification in terms of each other. Moreover, it would hardly be accurate to say that they end up, when push comes to shove (as it never does), just plumping for one account rather than another: just cheerleading for equality or autonomy or an entitlement account or a distributive account. They highlight different things on the moral and political map and they make mistakes, and some turnings may be simply wrong turnings, but through the conflict—the point counterpoint of their accounts—we gain an increasingly more adequate drawing of the moral and political map. It is clear, after reading Susan Okin, for example, that Rawls, Nozick, and MacIntyre have not found an adequate place for the family in their discussions of justice.[24] But in the case of Rawls, it can be seen how Okin's arguments show how a theory of a basically Rawlsian type would be strengthened by taking on board something like her account of the family.

Settled intuitions, Blackburn claims, can have no didactic authority. He remarks that the "settled intuitions are the unreflective convictions of a particular kind of animal with a (very) particular experience, history, and cultural background. Such a background will largely include infection by the attitudes, emotions, and beliefs of other imperfect parents, mentors, and peers operating in circumstances in which some ways of life worked and others did not, and in which some attitudes were fashionable and others too expensive to be functional" (B 91). For starters, in responding to this, the "settled intuitions" are precisely not the "*unreflective* convictions" but the "*considered* convictions" held by people who have reflected in a certain way, roughly in the way the ideal observer theory specifies. This restriction on appeal to convictions and judgments is very clear in all the writers who use the method of reflective equilibrium. In Rawls, for example, it was stressed from his early "An Outline of a Decision Procedure in Ethics" on.[25] Moreover, with the stress by Rawls, Daniels, and Rorty on appealing to an overlapping consensus in constitutional democracies, the convictions being appealed to are plainly not those of the very particular experience of someone with a very limited history and cultural background.[26] In those considered convictions there is the input of a complex, varied, extensive, and long Western tradition. To be sure, the Western tradition is not everything, but it is very *parti pris* and inaccurate to describe these as very particular local, rather accidental, attachments. It is also again *parti pris* and distorting to describe the considered convictions in the overlapping consensus as a "jumble of attitudes" that theory (i.e., wide reflective equilibrium) systematizes for a very ethnocentric point.

Blackburn tells us that "it is a delusion to expect there to emerge one theory that best justifies present intuitions, and guides for future cases. We came to those intuitions not by a synchronic exercise of selection and weighing, but by a historical evolution: the theories whereby earlier participants in that history might have justified their intuitions to themselves are very probably virtually unintelligible to us, and there is no reason to imagine just one synthesis covering all the heterogeneous deposits" (B 91–92). Surely that would be a reason to expect, as Rawls in fact does, many competing reflective equilibria. They compete, and usefully so, but in seeking *wide* reflective equilibria, we seek equilibria which would, among other things, appeal to general social theory, theory of moral development, theory of the role of morality in society, and theory of human nature, as well as to a wide range of factual considerations. With such varied things being appealed to, we have ways of coherently discussing, being through and through holistic, the comparative adequacy of different reflective equilibria. Some, after such discussion, might come to be seen, for a time, to yield a more comprehensive, more coherently articulated equilibrium than others. But, of course, there will be no claim that that one, or any other, yields the "true comprehensive account for all time." Such an account is at best unattainable and at worst (and more probably) incoherent. And even if we drop "for all time," things are not much improved.

To say we didn't come by those intuitions by "a synchronic exercise of selection and weighing" is both true and false. It is true that they result *non*rationally from enculteration, but it is also true that with poets, dramatists, philosophers, essayists, critical journalists, theologians, legal and political theorists, historians, among a host of others, there is a long tradition of critical reflection on these intuitions (refining them, pruning them, interpreting them, reinterpreting, or reconceptualizing them, reflecting on how they fit together, making strenuous efforts to forge a better fit, and the like) and this, if we do not mind sounding scientific and pedantic, could very well, at a given time, be described as "a synchronic exercise of selection and weighing." Moreover, such weighing and historical evolution do not exclude each other; both factors are at work and it is not clear which influence has the greater causal import.

However, let us suppose, perhaps not implausibly, that it has been historical evolution. But it is also reasonable, on analogy with natural selection, to believe that those intuitions which have remained and become so culturally ubiquitous so as to be a part of an overlapping consensus were those which had the greatest importance to human beings or at least the greatest survival value. Blackburn objects to this by saying we are just arbitrarily handing ourselves "a Burkelike confidence in the inherited wisdom of the ages" (B 92). There is, he adds, no reason to believe such a Burkelike story for what "has evolved is unlikely to be a masterly capacity for thinking through life's problems in a coherent and principled way, but a series of 'kludges' or *ad hoc* and partial responses to pressures that have at best stood our genes in good stead in some local circumstances" (B 92).

Again, this is a very partisan and problematic way to describe things; there is no reason to accept that rather than to accept a more Rawlsian one. Indeed, there is very good reason for accepting the Rawlsian one instead, on a principle of interpretative charity, namely, a methodological principle that says that, if without other costs, we can make sense of the phenomena in question, by all means characterize it in a way that enables us to make sense of it. Again, what has survived over the centuries of cultural and historical winnowing, facing challenges, skepticism, and the pressure of human living is hardly likely to be such ad hoc responses as Blackburn alleges. (One doesn't have to be a Burkean conservative, or any kind of conservative, to recognize that.) Moreover, the alternatives proffered by Blackburn are by no means exhaustive alternatives. We do not have to choose between extensive Socratic capacities and "kludges." It is not that individuals—indeed, any individual at all—should have such masterful Socratic capacities. What is being claimed is that through reflection, debate, argument, and cooperative efforts over the centuries, we human beings, viewing ourselves collectively, have come to have such an understanding of such issues, have, in our theories of morality and politics, been able to make some sense of our social life and to have articulated some norms which are reliable but fallible guides to action and social policy. The most that is being claimed for individuals is that some philosophers or other all-purpose intellectuals have developed something of a capacity to think about life's problems in a coherent and principled way. Socrates, Montaigne, Pascal, Spinoza, Hume, Mill, Nietzsche, Arnold, Emerson, James, and Dewey have developed this capacity in some rather refined ways. Similar things could be said about (among our contemporaries) Rawls, Berlin, Dworkin, Rorty, Foucault, Walzer, and Habermas. This is a rare ability, an ability that no one has completely, but there are some rudiments of it in some of us. But the crucial thing to see here is that in our deliberations together we—"we" as a collectivity—have slowly over time developed some understanding of morality and have articulated something like critical and reflective moral beliefs and attitudes and have a rather commonsensical way of doing this. It is the way society has of deliberating and reasoning—thinking out in a tolerably disciplined way—our social problems. Thus, we have good reasons for being skeptical of the conclusion of Blackburn's naysayer (roughly the tradition of noncognitivism) that there will be no ethical or political theory but only practical advocacy and cheerleading for various social orders and ways of life. Such a view has not been sustained.

VII

Moral, social, and political philosophy should travel metaphysically and epistemologically light for both Rawlsian and Rortyan reasons: reasons which are different but do not conflict. Rorty accepts Rawls's reasons, but has some reasons of a very different type of his own.[27] Rawls, however, would not accept, or would, at least for the purposes of political philosophy, remain agnostic about the Rortyan ones. The Rawlsian ones, as we have seen, are *not* rooted in metaphilosophical, metaphysical, or epistemological considerations, but in (1) a distinctive liberal moral belief, i.e., the principle of tolerance, and (2) what he takes to be, it seems to me rightly, a pervasive and intractable fact about modern societies, i.e., their pluralism. There are different, indeed, often conflicting, conceptions of the good, including comprehensive conceptions; there are differing, and not infrequently conflicting, conceptions of how to live our lives and of what is really worth having and doing. Moreover, there is no even remotely realistic possibility that this plurality of views, often rooted even in the same person, will end and we will attain some consensus about the good life or human flourishing. This could only be achieved, if it could be achieved at all, by authoritarian state force. Rawls's distinctively liberal moral belief, a belief that would be widely shared, is that such forced consensus is too high a price to pay for agreement about the good life or for the common acceptance of any comprehensive moral or social doctrine. Yet we plainly need some public agreement on a political conception of justice with its derivative rights, freedoms, and duties. We need a way of adjudicating in a fair way conflicts of interest in a world of moderate scarcity and limited altruism. (What we should do when we consider the world at large, where it is a lie to speak of moderate scarcity, is a very different matter.) However, because of the intractable facts of pluralism and the moral unacceptability of authoritarian state enforcement of any comprehensive conception of the good, we cannot ground our political conceptions of justice in a comprehensive conception of the good. So if we are to ground it at all, it must be in a way that travels philosophically light, using what Rawls calls the method of avoidance.

Rawls argues that his conception of justice as fairness, with its linked contractarian and wide reflective equilibrium methodology, does just that. It makes no controversial philosophical assumptions: neither having nor unwittingly assuming any controversial metaphysical or epistemological doctrines. Philosophical avoidance in Rawls's case is rooted in moral, political, and factual considerations and not in any metaphilosophical argument that such philosophical conceptions are all moonshine. Rawls could be resisted, as Michael Sandel and Charles Taylor resist him, on the grounds that his own account unwittingly makes just the epistemological and metaphysical assumptions he would avoid.[28] But he could also be resisted, as Blackburn and Gray do, on the grounds that the method of wide reflective equilibrium can neither produce nor articulate a reasonable consensus. I have in turn resisted the second critique of Rawls here and the first has been adequately resisted by Rawls himself.[29]

Rorty, with a social democratic liberalism similar to Rawls's, would, as I have already remarked, accept Rawls's factual-moral-political rationale for setting aside epistemology and metaphysics and the like (in short, the baggage of the grand tradition), but he also has another reason for doing so, namely, that they are all moonshine. There can be no ahistorical God's-eye view of the world, an "absolute conception" of the world, either moral or physical. Such philosophical foundations are impossible. We need, he maintains, Davidson's nay-saying against the coherence of global skepticism or conceptual relativism (Davidson's nay-saying itself not being a metaphysical doctrine) and we need Rawlsian wide reflective equilibrium.[30] We should see them as being both a part of a holism that should be seen as being resolutely commonsensical and antimetaphysical.

Rawlsian justice as fairness can, as did Dewey's work, articulate more clearly and perspicuously liberal social democratic values, showing how they fit together into a coherent view. But it cannot provide a philosophical grounding for them for, Rorty has it, no such philosophical grounding is possible. But it is also important to see that no such grounding is necessary and not to be spooked by the specters of postmodernist nihilism, or be caught in a premodern nostalgia for the Absolute. Wide reflective equilibrium is enough. The rest is more spinning our wheels in mud.

VIII

Moral philosophy, even politically relevant moral philosophy, does not stop at the coastline of a contractarian problematic. In Anglo-American philosophy, most prominently in the last thirty years, conceptions of justice and the dialectic between various forms of Kantianism, Hobbesianism, and utilitarianism have been center stage. Much of this—though not all—has been foundationalist in a way I think is fundamentally mistaken. (Moral philosophy typically tags along behind the cutting edge of philosophical development.) But, as we have seen in the recent work of Rawls, there are accounts of justice which have broken free of foundationalism and traditional philosophical preoccupations classically captured in moral theory in the work of Kant and Sidgwick. But there also has very recently been a return to the ancients in the form of "virtue ethics."[31] Much of it, as in the work of MacIntyre, Allan Bloom, and Leo Strauss, is, though *sometimes* expressed in an updated idiom, in reality a throwback to premodernity and is thoroughly entangled in the grand old problems of philosophy, though with MacIntyre there is also an acute sensitivity to the philosophical problems involved in such a turning to a premodern tradition. Here the wheels are really spinning in mud. But there are others—Stuart Hampshire, Martha Nussbaum, and Charles Taylor—for which this is not true.[32] Their "Aristotelianism" is not at all caught in an anti-Enlightenment traditionalism of a deeply conservative nature. They do indeed defend particularity and recognize the importance of our historicity. But they do this while still fully accepting the Enlightenment-rooted values of universality, impartiality, and equality. They criticize what they regard as certain excesses of Enlightenment *rationalism*, but they do not set themselves in opposition to the Enlightenment. Moreover, Martha Nussbaum gives us an Aristotelian ethics which, no more than Rawls or Rorty, becomes entangled in epistemological or metaphysical issues or any kind of foundationalist issue. Yet, for all these Aristotelians, it is vital that we work out a *comprehensive theory of the good*: that we ascertain, if we can, what is the good life for human beings. There is, for them, no ascertaining what justice is, even what political justice is, and then either stopping there or going on, as a separate matter, to ascertain what the good life for human beings is or vice versa. These inquiries are so linked that in determining what the good for human beings is we will also have automatically determined what justice is and in determining what just institutions and social practices are, what entitlements human beings have, and what fair distributions are, we will also have to determine at least something of what the good life for human beings is. There is, they believe, no resolving the problems of a just society without working out a comprehensive theory of the good.[33]

This runs square into and, as far as I can see, indeed it flounders on, Rawls's political objection, to wit, that then, by requiring such a comprehensive view, in intractably pluralist societies such as our own, we will never get an account of justice that can also function as an effective practical guide in our societies for the structure of just institutions. This is so because in our societies it is *de facto* impossible that there will in the foreseeable future ever be agreement on, given their pluralism, the good for human beings. I do not see any way around Rawls's point here. One might try to respond, weakly it seems to me, that practically, as a matter of political expediency, we can perhaps, along Rawls's line, come to agree on some approximation to justice, some political conception of justice, that we can live with in our pluralistic societies, while acknowledging that we will only *really* know what justice is when we know what the good for human beings is and we will only know that when we know what justice really and truly is. The two moral notions, though conceptually distinct, go together like equilateral triangle and equiangular triangle, or, like hand and glove, to switch the analogy, and along with it, something of its conceptual force. Moreover (*pace* Rawls), and more powerfully, we can make a philosophical inquiry into the good, throwing it out as an idea to be *entertained* in our society, without ever attempting to give it, to use Blackburn's phrase, didactic authority. That seems fair enough, and will not violate the respect for persons and the principles of toleration that are so central to liberalism, but it will mean, as Rawls stresses, that such a norm can never be, in pluralistic societies, an effective norm governing, or even just guiding, the conduct of our social life. Practically speaking, we will have to live with what the Aristotelian regards as an approximation to justice.

However, the Aristotelians (Nussbaum is particularly effective here) are right in stressing, as both Habermas and Foucault do as well, how questions of self-understanding (who we were, are, who we might become, what is the best sort of life for us to live) are central ethical questions for us, which only a pervasive skepticism and despair would let us set aside.[34] They are questions which we face individually and collectively when we think about our lives.

According to Aristotelian theories, the "goal of human choice . . . is eudaemonia or 'human flourishing', the good (complete) life for a human being."[35] Nussbaum makes very clear how complex such a conception is and its very great distance from a hedonistic utilitarianism. What makes Aristotelianism attractive is that it takes as the subject matter of ethics "not simply a narrow domain of specifically moral duties and obligations, but the whole conduct of life. Its starting point is the question, How should one live? It considers the whole living of a life. . . ."[36] It, unlike many foundationalist inquiries, stresses, what Marx, de Beauvoir, and Sartre stressed as well, that "good lives have material and institutional necessary conditions" and that serious ethical inquiry (*pace* Sidgwick and Moore) cannot ignore these necessary conditions.[37] It is a central task of moral philosophy, Nussbaum asserts in good Aristotelian fashion, to enumerate the most important functions of human life and to inquire into how well people in societies such as ours are enabled to perform them and how society can be and should be altered so human flourishing would be as widespread and as full as possible.

To find out what human flourishing comes to, it is still vital to identify, and to come to have a clear understanding of, the most important functions of human life. *One* important function of human life—Dewey rightly stresses it is only one—is to become reflective and to achieve something by way of self-understanding and, as well, an understanding of others and of the society and epoch in which one lives.[38] To exercise and cultivate one's capacity to be reflective is vital here. This reflectiveness about life, about the human good, and what general human possibilities there are, will force, both Hampshire and Nussbaum argue, such moral agents out of any kind of uncritical acceptance of local habits toward the commonly human. Our very reflective capacity, if exercised carefully and without evasion, will drive a moral philosopher into "telling an outline story about the form of life of a rational being in a world of nature."[39]

Nussbaum recognizes that "neither in science nor in ethics can judgments be justified by an appeal to an altogether extrahistorical reality."[40] But she also stresses, and not incompatibly with that, that there can and should be universalizing reflection about human goods, human flourishing, general human possibilities, and the functions of human life. Virtues are the modes of characteristic human flourishing. A central task of moral philosophy is to specify what they are and to see, as Nussbaum puts it, how they are "answers to questions about how best to deal with a variety of problems faced by more or less all human lives."[41] Moral philosophers need to ask, as they have characteristically not, What are the most common problems of human life and what is a good way to face them? So, against Hobbesian, duty-based, and rights-based traditions, questions about what a good life would be become central for these neo-Aristotelians. Also against the antitheory conceptions of Foucault, Rorty, or Walzer, they would stress the desirability of a systematic ethical theory yielding a universal theory of the human good.

This seems, at least on the face of it, to take us back into the philosophical swamp with the specter of more wheels spinning in the mud. But, while such an account is compatible with foundationalism and a return to epistemology and metaphysics, it plainly does not require these problematic things. Dewey, as much as Aristotle, considered what are the most common problems of human life and what is a good way to face them and Putnam has recently gestured at the importance of philosophers returning to that task.[42] But they both do this without taking us back into the ontotheological swamp. There is, moreover, nothing in what Nussbaum has set out that requires us, or justifies us, or should urge us, to go back into the ontotheological swamp. For Plato, Aristotle, and the Stoics, their talk of the good and of the functions of human life was embedded in a metaphysical theory. But Nussbaum, in vivid contrast with MacIntyre, does a very good job of bringing out the ethical and political import of their theories without getting entangled in such contestable, perhaps even incoherent, philosophical disputes or doctrines. In enumerating the most important functions of human life, epistemology and metaphysics—pure philosophy of the grand tradition—have very little to say, but literature, history, psychology, and the social sciences have, in their different ways, a lot to say. Moral inquiry, given Nussbaum's aims and the aims of other such non-Thomistic Aristotelians, like critical theorists or Rorty's conception of philosophy, after the end of philosophy, should be something that is integrated into the human sciences and into literature. It has lost, and blessedly so, its distinctive *fach*.

That seems to me to be all to the good. We can, and perhaps should, have a comprehensive account of the good without philosophical foundations. In articulating it we will use, as we did in articulating a political conception of justice, wide reflective equilibrium. Utilizing the empirical, but not simply being either an empirical inquiry or a formal one, we have an inquiry which could yield a critical morality and a critical politics: a morality and a politics which could be of some use in guiding conduct and in our coming to have a knowledgeable and reflective grip on our lives.[43] Whether it should attempt to articulate a comprehensive account of the good, as Nussbaum and Taylor believe, or, whether it should limit itself to a political conception of justice, as Rawls believes, or be, still giving priority to justice, more general, as Dworkin believes, is a vital internal dispute within a common conception of what moral theory could be, and how it could flourish, even after the demise of the tradition.[44] In other words, even if, as I have argued, metaphysics, epistemology, and foundationalist ethics should come to an end—and perhaps are slowly coming to an end—these contemporary philosophers, as did Dewey before them, have set out a not unimportant something for philosophy to be: a something which is common to them, notwithstanding their anything but trivial differences.[45]

NOTES

1. See my *After the Demise of the Tradition* (Boulder, Colo.: Westview Press, 1991); my "On There Being Philosophical Knowledge," *Theoria* 56, part 3 (1990): 193–225; my "Can There Be Justified Philosophical Beliefs?" *Iyyun* 40 (July 1991): 235–70; and my "Anti-Philosophy Philosophy: Some Programmatic Remarks," *Diálogos,* 64 (1994): 149–58. Anti-Philosophy *philosophy* is not antiphilosophy *simpliciter*. It is not Aristophanes lampooning Socrates or, in our time, some academics (to say nothing of

some nonacademics) dismissing philosophy as bull, as either being rhetorical hot air or nit-picking "logic chopping" to no point. Some anti-Philosophy philosophers will acknowledge that there is sometimes more in such scoffing dismissals than many philosophers are willing to acknowledge. (The usual defense mechanisms are at work here.) But anti-Philosophy philosophers also realize, and acknowledge, that there are deep intellectual as well as other pressures that drive some people into thinking philosophically. Philosophy has a long history in our Western tradition and cannot, and should not, be just shrugged off. Anti-Philosophy philosophers do not just engage in ridicule and such shrugging off, but, with all the problems of pragmatic self-contradiction, argue *philosophically* for the end of philosophy as it has been traditionally conceived (conceived of either in the grand metaphysical-epistemological tradition or in systematic analytic philosophy). Both Ludwig Wittgenstein's and Richard Rorty's work are crucially paradigmatic here. I suspect, however, that neither Wittgenstein nor Rorty would welcome the term *anti-Philosophy philosophy*. (To say that of Wittgenstein is a radical understatement.) Rorty rightly argues that there is no sensible talk of "the end of philosophy" *sans phrase*. (Richard Rorty, "Habermas, Derrida and the Function of Philosophy," *Revue Internationale de Philosophie* 4 (1995): 437–59.) But all the same both Wittgenstein and Rorty perfectly and brilliantly exemplify what I have called anti-Philosophy *philosophy*. Rorty is the more explicit of the two. He distinguishes in a way that is very germane to this chapter, and indeed to this volume as a whole, between *philosophy* and *Philosophy*. The former is something he takes to be quite unproblematic and as something that is not about to come to an end. It is—Rorty adopts the phrase from Wilfred Sellars—"an attempt to see how things, in the broadest sense of the term, hang together, in the broadest sense of the term" (xiv). He goes on to add that in "this sense, Blake is as much a philosopher as Fichte, Henry Adams more a philosopher than Frege. No one would be dubious about philosophy taken in this sense"(xv). But besides *philosophy*—a desirable and, he believes, an unproblematic activity—there is *Philosophy*, something which is much more specialized, and, he believers, very dubious indeed. It is *Philosophy*—either in the grand metaphysical and epistemological traditions or in the naturalistic and scientistic form of Quine and Armstrong—that Rorty opposes and rejects. He agrees with the pragmatist, indeed, he is himself a pragmatist, in believing "that one can be a philosopher precisely by being anti-Philosophical, that the best way to see how things hang together, or to forge a bit of their hanging together, is to step back from the issues between Platonists and positivists, and thereby give up the presuppositions of Philosophy"(xvii). Key programmatic statements by Rorty occur in his *Consequences of Pragmatism* (Minneapolis, Minn.: University of Minnesota Press, 1982), xiii–xlvii, 211–30. It is from this text that I have been quoting in this note. Given Rorty's distinction between *philosophy* and *Philosophy*, to call someone an anti-*Philosophy* philosopher, the anti-Philosophy part is with a capital *P*. Wittgenstein, however, might plausibly be thought to be an anti-philosophy philosopher in both of Rorty's senses of "philosophy." See here Michael Williams, "The Elimination of Metaphysics" in *Fact, Science and Morality,* ed. Graham Macdonald and Crispin Wright (Oxford, England: Basil Blackwell, 1986), 20–24. Joseph F. McDonald, in an unpublished doctoral dissertation, *Wittgenstein's Therapeutic Conception of Philosophy* (University of Ottawa, 1993) sets out a convincing textual and argumentative case for claiming that, from his early *Notebooks*, through the *Tractatus*, the *Philosophical Investigations*, and on to, and through, *On Certainty*, Wittgenstein retained a thoroughly therapeutic conception of philosophy.

    2. Ludwig Wittgenstein: *Remarks on the Foundations of Mathematics* (Oxford, England: Basil Blackwell, 1956); *Philosophical Investigations*, trans. G. E. M. Anscombe

(Oxford, England: Basil Blackwell, 1953); and *On Certainty*, trans. Denis Paul and G. E. M. Anscombe (Oxford, England: Basil Blackwell, 1969). Richard Rorty: *Consequences of Pragmatism: Contingency, Irony and Solidarity* (Cambridge, England: Cambridge University Press, 1989); *Objectivity, Relativism and Truth* (Cambridge, England: Cambridge University Press, 1991); *Essays on Heidegger and Others* (Cambridge, England: Cambridge University Press, 1991); and "Feminism and Pragmatism," *Radical Philosophy* 59 (Autumn 1991): 3–14. Hilary Putnam, *Renewing Philosophy* (Cambridge, Mass.: Harvard University Press, 1992).

3. John Rawls, "Kantian Constructivism in Moral Theory," *Journal of Philosophy* 77 (1980): 518. See also Rawls: "Justice as Fairness: Political not Metaphysical," *Philosophy and Public Affairs* 14, no. 3 (1985): 223–35; "The Idea of an Overlapping Consensus," *Oxford University Journal of Legal Studies* 7 (1982): 1–25; and "The Domain of the Political and Overlapping Consensus," *New York University Law Review* 64, no. 2 (1989): 233–55. See also John Rawls, *Political Liberalism* (New York: Columbia University Press, 1993). The above essays, along with some others, have been conveniently collected and perspicuously arranged in French translation. See John Rawls, *Justice et Democratie* (Paris: Editions du Seuil, 1993).

4. John Rawls, "Justice as Fairness: Political not Metaphysical," reprinted in J. Angelo Corlett, ed., *Equality and Liberty: Analyzing Rawls and Nozick* (London: Macmillan, 1991), 145. Subsequent references to this article will be given in the text and from the above reprinting.

5. "Must be" is *perhaps* too strong. And "are much better" might seem to be preferable. But, given the intractability of pluralism and the irrealism of a belief that any comprehensive doctrine could gain society-wide acceptance, "must be" seems the more appropriate.

6. It is tempting to say, instead of "*characteristic* of analytic philosophy," "*definitive* of analytical philosophy," but that is overly strong, for, since Quine's attack on the significance of the analytic/synthetic distinction, analytic philosophy has taken many turnings and divided in many ways. Indeed, probably so many of both that, apart from a concern for clear articulation and careful argument (certainly valuable things), there is not much left that is distinctive about it. Yet, if we are going to speak of analytic philosophers at all, Rawls would certainly count among the analytic philosophers.

7. Simon Blackburn, "Can Philosophy Exist?" in *Méta-Philosophie: Reconstructing Philosophy?* ed. Jocelyne Couture and Kai Nielsen (Calgary, Alberta: University of Calgary Press, 1993), 83–105.

8. Jean Hampton, "Should Political Philosophy Be Done without Metaphysics?" *Ethics* 99, no. 4 (1989): 791–614. In critical response, see my "Rawls and the Socratic Ideal," *Analyse and Kritik* 13 (July 1991): 67–93. Some philosophers of a more antique kind than Hampton make broadly similar charges against Rawls. See Allan Bloom, *Giants and Dwarfs* (New York: Simon and Schuster, 1990), 322.

9. John Gray, "Against the New Liberalism: Rawls, Dworkin and the Emptying of Political Life," *Times Literary Supplement*, July 3, 1992, 13–15.

10. Jean Hampton, "Should Political Philosophy Be Done Without Metaphysics?" and John Gray, "Against the New Liberalism."

11. Hampton, "Should Political Philosophy Be Done Without Metaphysics?"

12. Ibid., 807.

13. Ibid., 808.

14. Ibid.

15. Ibid., 813.

16. Ibid., 814.

17. It might seem that I am unsaying what I just said. If moral utterances need not, or perhaps even properly cannot, be said to be bivalent (true or false), then how can a conception of justice or any other moral conception be taken as true? The answer is that *"taken as true"* in such a context need not be understood as being anything more than a firm way in which it is said, and thought, to be very strongly warranted, having as much warrant as we reasonably believe such a claim can have in the most propitious circumstances feasibly possible for such a claim. This is what "thought to be true" or "taken as true" comes to in such contexts.

18. I am indebted for the above cluster of observations both to a referee and to Jocelyne Couture.

19. Richard Rorty, "The Priority of Democracy to Philosophy," in *Virginia Statute for Religious Freedom,* ed. M. D. Peterson and R. C. Vaughan (Cambridge, England: Cambridge University Press, 1988), 271. This essay is reprinted in Rorty's *Objectivity, Relativism and Truth,* 175–96.

20. Kai Nielsen, "Relativism and Wide Reflective Equilibrium" *Monist* 76, no. 3 (January 1993): 316–32.

21. Norman Daniels, "Reflective Equilibrium and Archimedean Points," in J. Angelo Corlett, ed., *Equality and Liberty: Analyzing Rawls and Nozick,* 105.

22. Simon Blackburn, "Can Philosophy Exist?" I speak of Blackburn's naysayer for Blackburn first develops a case against philosophy, and analytic philosophy specifically, and then briefly responds to it. The case against, I call the "nay-saying" part. But much of that is something Blackburn articulates only to reject. His remarks about reflective equilibrium occur in that nay-saying part. But the trouble is that it is not clear how much of that nay-saying Blackburn, after giving it a run for its money, is repudiating. Further references to Blackburn are given in the text.

23. Daniels, "Reflective Equilibrium and Archimedean Points."

24. Susan Moller Okin, *Justice, Gender and the Family* (New York: Basic Books, 1989); and her "Political Liberalism, Justice, and Gender," *Ethics* 105, no. 1 (October 1994): 23–43.

25. John Rawls, "Outline of a Decision Procedure for Ethics," *Philosophical Review* 60 (1951): 177–97.

26. Rorty, "Priority of Democracy to Philosophy."

27. Rorty, "Priority of Democracy to Philosophy" and *Consequences of Pragmatism,* 191–210. See also his perceptive "Paroxysms and Politics," *Salmagundi* 97 (Winter 1993): 61–68.

28. Michael J. Sandel, *Liberalism and the Limits of Justice* (Cambridge: Cambridge University Press, 1982); Charles Taylor, *Philosophy and the Human Sciences* (Cambridge: Cambridge University Press, 1985), 289–317; Charles Taylor, "Cross-Purposes: The Liberal-Communitarian Debate," in *Liberalism and the Moral Life,* ed. Nancy Rosenblum (Cambridge, Mass.: Harvard University Press, 1988).

29. See Rawls, "Justice as Fairness: Political not Metaphysical." See also Rorty, "Priority of Democracy to Philosophy."

30. Donald Davidson, *Inquiries into Truth and Interpretation* (Oxford: Clarendon Press, 1984), 181–242; and Davidson, "The Myth of the Subjective" in *Relativism,* ed. Michael Krauz (Notre Dame, Ind.: University of Notre Dame Press, 1982), 159–81. Rorty, *Objectivity, Relativism and Truth,* 1–17, 163–96; and Rorty, "Pragmatism as Anti-Representationalism," in John P. Murphy, *Pragmatism from Peirce to Davidson* (Boulder, Colo.: Westview Press, 1990), 1–6. Nielsen, *After the Demise of the Tradition,* 57–90, 195–248. Kai Nielsen, "Perspectivism and the Absolute Conception of the World," *Crit-*

ica 25, no. 74 (August 1993): 105–16; and Nielsen, *Transforming Philosophy: A Metaphilosophical Inquiry* (Boulder, Colo.: Westview Press, 1995).

31. For a brilliant brief overview, see Martha Nussbaum, "Virtue Revived: Habit, Passion, Reflection in the Aristotelian Tradition," *Times Literary Supplement,* July 3, 1992, 9–11. See also for traditionalist articulations of such views Allan Bloom, *The Closing of the American Mind* (New York: Simon and Schuster, 1987); Leo Strauss, *Natural Right and History* (Chicago: Chicago University Press, 1950); Alasdair MacIntyre, *After Virtue* (Notre Dame, Ind.: University of Notre Dame Press, 1984); and Alasdair MacIntyre, *Whose Justice? Which Rationality?* (Notre Dame, Ind.: University of Notre Dame Press, 1988).

32. Martha Nussbaum, *The Fragility of Goodness* (Cambridge: Cambridge University Press, 1986); Nussbaum, *Love's Knowledge: Essays on Philosophy and Literature* (Oxford: Oxford University Press, 1990); and Nussbaum, *The Therapy of Desire: Theory and Practice in Hellenistic Ethics* (Princeton, N.J.: Princeton University Press, 1993). Stuart Hampshire, *Morality and Conflict* (Cambridge, Mass.: Harvard University Press, 1983); and Hampshire, *Innocence and Experience* (Cambridge, Mass.: Harvard University Press, 1989). Charles Taylor, *Sources of the Self* (Cambridge, Mass.: Harvard University Press, 1989); and Taylor, *The Ethics of Authenticity* (Cambridge, Mass.: Harvard University Press, 1992).

33. Nussbaum expresses this view succinctly in her "Virtue Revived," 9–11.

34. Jürgen Habermas, *Autonomy and Solidarity* (London: Verso, 1992), 245–71; and Habermas, *Moral Consciousness and Communicative Action* (Cambridge, Mass.: MIT Press, 1990); and Michel Foucault, *Foucault Reader*, Paul Rabionow, ed., 333–90; and James Bernauer and David Rasmussen, eds., *Foucault: The Final Foucault* (Cambridge, Mass.: MIT Press, 1988), 1–20.

35. Nussbaum, "Virtue Revised," 10.

36. Ibid.

37. Ibid

38. John Dewey, *Reconstruction in Philosophy* (Boston: Beacon Press, 1957); and John Dewey, *Theory of the Moral Life* (New York: Holt, Rinehart and Winston, 1960). For Dewey updated and powerfully developed, see Isaac Levi, "Conflict and Inquiry," *Ethics* 102 (July 1992): 814–34.

39. Nussbaum, "Virtue Revised," 11.

40. Nussbaum, "Virtue Revised," Rorty, *Consequences of Pragmatism*, 191–210. Hilary Putnam, *Renewing Philosophy,* and Putnam, *Realism with a Human Face* (Cambridge, Mass.: Harvard University Press), 120–200. Habermas, *Autonomy and Solidarity*, 187–210, 235–71.

41. Nussbaum, "Virtue Revised."

42. Putnam, *Renewing Philosophy*.

43. Hampshire, *Innocence and Experience*.

44. I say something about what I mean about the demise of the tradition in my *After the Demise of the Tradition* and in my "Philosophy as Critical Theory," *Proceedings and Addresses of the American Philosophical Association*, Supplement to vol. 61, no. 1 (September 1987): 89–108.

45. It still might be objected that wide reflective equilibrium is "larger than life." In aiming at it, we, as we have seen, appeal to general social theory, theory of moral development, theory of the role of morality in society, to conceptions of human nature, and to a wide range of more purely factual considerations. This, taken together, is, to put it minimally, a lot. Is it at all plausible to believe that such an equilibrium will emerge or even receive a reasonable approximation? I am not, of course, saying that individuals can

master that range of material. But the method of wide reflective equilibrium is appealed to as a *social* conception. It is, as a way of going about things, something (though very likely not explicitly so conceptualized) that requires wide social acceptance to be effectively and collectively utilized on a social level (the level for which it was conceptualized) and to, as well, be embedded in the procedures of institutions. Moreover, it would need, to be effective, to be extensively practiced. It is envisioned as a way that a society should explicitly and consistently come to fix its beliefs and plans for action and as the method to be used in devising its social policies. At least, if such a method obtains, this is how it would have to obtain to be thoroughly effective. But it is also thought that not infrequently something like this, though not self-consciously, is approximated in some of our common sense and in our scientific practices. Is it so implausible, or even implausible at all, to believe that at the level of institutions and institutional practices such an array of considerations can be handled to good effect? Of course our equilibrium will always be incomplete. Fallibilism, to repeat what I said earlier, is the name of the game. However, it is not unreasonable to believe, or at least to hope, that in societies in fortunate circumstances (reasonable economic abundance and security and with high levels of education), we can gradually achieve an approximation of such an equilibrium, an equilibrium which will change again and again as our knowledge and our circumstances change. For an argument that this does not imply relativism, see my "Relativism and Wide Reflective Equilibrium," *Monist* 76, no. 3 (January 1993): 316–32. For remarks about wide reflective equilibrium repeatedly changing and always being incomplete, see Rawls, *Political Liberalism,* 96–97.

Chapter Six

Justice as a Kind of Impartiality

I

"Is justice impartiality or mutual advantage?" may not be a well-formed question. It may be neither or both. It may instead be fair reciprocity, what would be agreed to in an ideal bargaining situation, how conflicts of interest are adjudicated under conditions of undistorted discourse or something significantly different. The fact of the matter is that justice cannot be reduced to any of these or indeed to anything else for familiar Butlerian-Moorean reasons. But such antireductionism does not preclude a central component of justice being one or another of these things. I shall argue that justice is properly viewed as a kind of impartiality, namely, that justice requires the equal consideration of the legitimate interests of everyone alike. And, it could be equally said, as the previous sentence reveals, that justice is a kind of equality.

Justice as mutual advantage, by contrast, is not a different conception of justice yielding different principles of justice but something—or so I shall argue—that could not be justice at all, and justice as fair reciprocity suffers, though less clearly so, a similar fate, for where it is not so indeterminate as to be problematical it reduces to justice as mutual advantage. Appeals to mutual advantage will not show what justice is or what the principles of justice should be, but can at best provide a rational amoralist with a motive for reasoning and acting in accordance with the dictates of justice. Even here rational self-interested people might not be persons of moral principle. Rationality *permits* justice but does not *require* it. Solving the problem of compliance does not show what justice is or what its principles should be. Indeed, it should not have the position of importance it now often has in discussions of justice, but should be relegated to a problem of little theoretical normative interest about how children are to be socialized. Properly understood, as W. D. Falk put it years ago, it is a problem of *goading,* not of *guiding.*[1] An individual can be rational through and through and still, for all of that, not be a person of moral principle though, without Gyges ring, as Kant agreed with Hobbes in stressing, he will, as things can be expected to stand, have to be, if he is sensible, a man of good morals, though, particularly where he is in a situation of very considerable and stable power, this will give him lots of *lebensraum.* So much so that he may take himself out of morality altogether, except as something to manipulatively use to serve his own interests or the interests of his class or clan.

II

Enough of grand proclaiming and the uttering of dark sayings, I shall now turn to the business of providing arguments placed in something of a narrative. For theories mainly concerned with justice as a property of basic social institutions, there have been two quite different stresses. One stress, as in John Rawls and Brian Barry, to cite its major contemporary representatives, is that the function of justice is to provide a reasonable basis for agreement among people who seek to take due account of *the interests of all*; the other stress, as in neo-Hobbesians such as David Gauthier and James Buchanan, sees the function of justice as the construction of social devices which enable people who are essentially egoists to get along better with one another while doing the best they can for themselves.[2] The first conceives of justice as *impartiality*, the second as *mutual advantage*. Both accounts in their most powerful contemporary formulations are in some sense constructivist accounts not relying on moral realist beliefs of either an intuitionist or naturalist sort in which moral truths are discovered as articulating some antecedent reality not dependent on human construction. Constructivist accounts, as with Gauthier, reject such meta-ethical claims or, as with Rawls, do not rely on such claims (meta-ethical claims rejecting other sorts of meta-ethical claims), but proceed in a contractarian manner by selecting criteria for the correct principles of justice, or for just social practices, that would be agreed on in some suitable hypothetical situation or, to be more Hobbesian than Rawlsian, what would actually be agreed on when reasoning under certain constraints and in conditions of undistorted discourse.[3] Both accounts are contractarian and both constructivist. (A contractarian constructivist is not a redundancy.) What Gauthier rejects Rawls more prudently sets aside as unnecessary for the articulation of a theory of justice. He travels, as he puts it himself and as we saw in the previous chapter, metaphysically, and, indeed philosophically, light. (This seems to me, as it has not seemed to some others, a not inconsiderable virtue.[4])

Historically speaking, the tradition, conceiving of justice as impartiality, has a broadly Kantian source, and that of conceiving of justice as mutual advantage has a Hobbesian source. Brian Barry, Will Kymlicka, and Allen Buchanan have recently powerfully argued that these two traditions are in conflict and are in a conflict of such a sort that they cannot be reconciled.[5] Barry and Kymlicka, but not Allen Buchanan, further argue that in much contemporary theorizing about justice, including most importantly that of John Rawls, these two at least seemingly incompatible traditions are mixed together in ways that will not withstand critical scrutiny. We cannot, they argue, have it both ways as Rawls, and Hume as well, in effect believe. These conceptions and traditions are in conflict and they cannot be so juggled as to be coherently combined. The correct move, Barry, Kymlicka, and Allen Buchanan all agree, is to reject the Hobbesian mutual advantage tradition. The way to go is to accept and clarify the tradition stressing that justice is the impartial consideration of all the interests of everyone. Here they have as an ally Jeffrey Reiman, though he puts the matter somewhat differently.[6]

Influential formulations of both accounts, as is seen paradigmatically in the work of Rawls and Gauthier, share the belief, a belief also held by Habermas and Reiman, that justice is what everyone could in principle reach a rational agreement on. This, of course, is standardly taken as being partially definitive of social contract theories: whether bargaining-theory contractarianism à la Gauthier or moral contractarianism à la Rawls, Barry, and Reiman. However, the justice as impartiality view and the mutual advantage view have, of course, a different conception of why people are trying to reach agreement. Indeed, when we see what these conceptions are, with their differing rationales, we will recognize that they are set in very different theories. The mutual advantage view says that the motive for justice is the pursuit of individual advantage. People in societies such as ours pursue justice, neo-Hobbesians claim, for mutual advantage. More generally, they will do so in what Hume and Rawls call the circumstances of justice, namely, circumstances of limited material resources, confined generosity, and conflicting interests or goals. In the circumstances of justice, which are the actual conditions of human life or at least most human life, people, the claim goes, can expect to advance their interests most efficiently through cooperating with other members of society, rather than living with them in conditions of conflict. Rational people on such a view will agree on certain constraints—say, the ones Gauthier specifies—as the minimum price that has to be paid in order to obtain the cooperation of others.

By contrast the motive for behaving justly on the justice as impartiality view is not reducible to even a sophisticated and indirect self-interest. Rather, the correct motive for behaving justly, on that view, is the belief that what happens to other people matters in and of itself. This being so, people should not look at things from their own point of view *alone,* but should seek to find a basis for agreement that is acceptable from all points of view.[7] People, as Rawls puts it in a Kantian vein, are all self-originating sources of valid claims. We accept their claims because we think their interests are as important as our own and, indeed, that their interests, whoever they are, are all equally important. The life of everyone, no matter how mentally enfeebled, matters and matters equally. We do not just, or perhaps even at all, take their interests into account because we are trying to promote or at least protect our own interests. For the impartiality approach, at least on some of its formulations, justice would be the content of an agreement that would be reached under conditions that *do not allow for bargaining power to be translated into advantage.* By contrast, on the mutual advantage theory, justice can obtain even when people make agreements that are obtained by bargaining under conditions where the bargainers stand in differential power relations and have differential bargaining power. Indeed, where people are so differentially situated, any agreement they come to *for mutual advantage must reflect that fact.* Such an approach is inescapable if appeal to self-interest is the motive for behaving justly. "If," as Barry puts it in characterizing that position, "the terms of agreement failed to reflect differential bargaining power, those whose power was disproportionate to their share under the agreement would have an incentive to seek to upset it."[8] They would have no sufficient reason, on that account, for sticking with the agreement. By contrast, the impartiality approach uncouples justice from bargaining power, since it does not require that everyone find it in her advantage to be just. They can have good reasons for being just even when being just is neither in their short run nor their long run advantage. That the powerful have an incentive to upset agreements they would enter into in such circumstances with the weak is a morally irrelevant reason for their not sticking with their agreements. From the moral point of view it cannot even be considered. (How we can *get* them to *comply* [*goad* them into complying] with what morality requires is another matter entirely.)

Given this difference in orientation, the kind of agreements that could even count as just agreements for the impartialist do not allow bargaining power to be translated into advantage. Indeed, they specifically prohibit it. Barry, Kymlicka, and Allen Buchanan all argue that the mutual advantage approach does not even count as a theory of *justice.* While the mutual advantage approach may generate some basic principles of social cooperation and coordination, these will not always yield just agreements, since they allow as "just agreements" agreements obtained in situations where the power people have is very different, undeserved, and differently exercised, and yet these very considerations are deemed, on such an account, to be morally relevant.

The resulting system of cooperation with its resulting system of rights and duties lacks one of the basic properties of a moral system, namely, the property of giving equal weight to the interests of all the parties to the agreement. So while it articulates a system of social cooperation, it is not a moral theory and thus it is not a theory or an account of justice.

On the mutual advantage account some persons can fall outside the system of rights, at least as normally understood, altogether. In contrast with the Kantian impartiality approach, those without bargaining power will fall beyond the pale of morality. Not every individual will have an inherent moral standing, let alone an equal moral standing. Some, on such an account, can be treated as a means only. This would be true of young children, of the severely retarded, of the utterly powerless, and it would be true of future generations (if they are to be spoken of as persons at all). All these people lack bargaining power for they have no way of retaliating against those people who harm them or fail to take into consideration their well-being. They thus on such an account lack moral standing; they can have no rights and we have no duties or obligations to them, though we can rightly treat them kindly *if we so choose.*

Those are the extreme cases, but sometimes at least the powerful in our class-divided and stratified societies can with impunity treat the weak without moral concern. They can exploit them and push them against the wall. Where the dominant class is very secure, as for a time it sometimes is, it can rationally proceed in this way knowing that the dominated class has no effective means of fighting back. If, indeed, some gain an irresistible, effectively unchallengeable power, then they have with such power, on Hobbes's account, as well as for contemporary Hobbesians, something which "justifieth all actions really and properly in whomsoever it is found."[9] But in a world so ordered, the constraints of justice would have no place. We could have perhaps (given the circumstances) a rational system of cooperation and coordination. But we would not have a morality. There is no reasoning here in accordance with the moral point of view. Where the strong can and do enslave or exploit the weak to the advantage of the strong, we have something which is paradigmatically unjust. Barry puts the point thus:

> This gives us the defining characteristic of the second approach [the impartiality approach], namely, that justice should be the content of an agreement that would be reached by rational people under conditions that do not allow for bargaining power to be translated into advantage.[10]

Mutual advantage theory perhaps provides a good analysis of what genuinely rational, purely self-interested people would do if they were well informed and in good control of themselves. If we are going to intelligently engage in amoral *realpolitik*, this is perhaps how we should proceed, but it does not provide us with anything that even looks like a method of *moral* justification. A cluster of practices that could be correctly characterized as just practices could not be a set of practices which would sustain or even allow those with greater bargaining power to turn it into such an advantageous outcome for them that the weak could be killed, come (where this could be avoided) to die of starvation, or live in intolerable conditions of life when that could be avoided. Such practices are paradigmatically unjust practices. If they are not unjust, then nothing is.

A mutual advantage theorist might respond that his theory could never allow those things to obtain, for no matter how severe the power differentials, such driving of a hard bargain (as a matter of fact) would never be to the mutual advantage of the parties (neither the weak nor the strong). But to so respond is clearly to rely on a rather chancy empirical claim.[11] Faced, under steep and relatively secure power differentials, with the possibility of starvation, the weak might rationally settle for subsistence wages. Faced with a very marginal subsistence living, families might find it to their advantage (including the children's advantage) to opt for child labor under harsh conditions. With one's back against the wall, one might even find it to one's advantage to sell oneself into slavery or to agree to play a kind of Russian roulette where one might be killed. It is itself a rather chancy empirical claim to say that such uses of power would never be in the advantage of people in positions of power because the likelihood of relying on the weak sticking with such harshly driven bargains would be too risky. That this would be so in all, or perhaps even in most, realistic conditions is far from evident. We can hardly be very confident that positions of power might not for a considerable time be so secure that it would not be to the advantage of the powerful to drive such hard bargains. But whatever is in fact the case here about mutual advantage, we can know, impartiality theorists claim, that such bargains are unjust. Even if they do turn out to be mutually advantageous, given the circumstances people are in, they remain *morally* unacceptable. To summarize, if they are not mutually advantageous, they are wrong on both accounts. If they turn out, after all, to be mutually advantageous, they are still wrong, mutual advantage theory to the contrary not withstanding. It allows, as we have seen, as an open moral option, if consistently applied, at least the possibility of things obtaining which are grossly immoral if anything is.

III

Let us now consider impartiality theories. They take several forms, but whether or not they require the postulation of an original position or a state of nature or anything of that sort, such theories view moral reasoning not as a form of bargaining but as a deliberation concerning what is to be done between agents who share a commitment to impartiality, to the giving of *equal* weight to the interests and needs of all. Put differently, moral agents are people who are deliberating about which principles should be acceptable to all points of view. That, Barry has it, is the basic idea of impartiality. Impartiality theorists such as Rawls, Hare, Nagel, Reiman, Barry, Scanlon, and Dworkin disagree over which principles of social justice are to be adopted, but they all are egalitarians and argue (*pace* F. H. Hayek) that justice as impartiality requires (where possible) the elimination of or neutralization of morally arbitrary inequalities, namely those inequalities arising from differences in social circumstances or natural talents. How fundamentally such an approach differs from the mutual advantage approach can be seen from the fact that an underlying rationale for appealing to impartial agreement is that it substitutes a *moral equality* for a *physical inequality*. As Kymlicka well puts it, the two views are, morally speaking, a world apart. "From the point of view of everyday morality, mutual advantage is an alternative to justice, not an alternative account of justice."[12]

However, appealing here to everyday morality, and not to something more abstract such as the moral point of view, begs the question with mutual advantage theorists, for they are willing to jettison much of everyday morality for a streamlined morality they regard (correctly or incorrectly) as more rational. There are on Hobbesian accounts no natural duties to others and no real moral difference between right and wrong which all persons must respect. There is, as well, no moral equality underlying our physical inequality. All these notions are illusions generating what they regard as bits of moral ideology. To the liberal appeal to moral equality (the life of everyone matters and matters equally) the Hobbesian can ask (as James Buchanan does), "Why care about moral equality?"[13] (I think, as I shall argue in the last section, this comes to asking "Why care about morality?")

Hobbesians, to continue the mutual advantage theorist's counter to impartiality theory, will argue that impartialists do not push questions of justification to a deep enough level. They do not realize that a person only has a reason to do something if the action the person contemplates doing satisfies some desire of that person or answers to her interests, so that if something's being just is to count as a good reason for doing it, justice must be shown to be in the interest of the agent.[14] Keeping this in mind we frame the Hobbesian question: Why should people possessing unequal power or intelligence refrain from using it in their own interests?

To this the impartialist can in turn respond in good Kantian fashion that morality needs no external justification. Morality itself provides a sufficient and original source of determination within us that is no more and no less artificial than the Hobbesian self-interested motivation. People can be motivated to act morally simply by coming to appreciate the moral reasons for doing so.

Hobbesians with their instrumentalist conception of rationality will find this impartialist acceptance here artificial and perhaps even evasive. Indeed, they may even regard it as irrational. But they in turn must face Barry's claim that to equate rationality with the efficient pursuit of self-interest is a view which rests on pure assertion. This is not to say, or to give to understand, that rational egoism is an inconsistent view, for it is not. There is (*pace* Alan Gewirth) no showing that to be consistent one must be an impartialist. But there is also no good reason to believe that the very meaning of "rational" is such that if one is rational one must be an egoist or a constrained maximizer. The acceptance of the formal criterion of universalizability together with a recognition that others are fundamentally like us in having needs and goals and, indeed, in having, generally speaking, some of the same needs and goals, gives us powerful, though not utterly decisive, reasons for accepting the claims of an impartial morality.[15] A person is not being inconsistent if he does not care about the needs and goals of others; he does not violate the criterion of universalizability, but, as Barry puts it, "the virtually unanimous concurrence of the human race in caring about the defensibility of actions in a way that does not simply appeal to power" suggests that this appeal to impartiality and to moral equality are very deeply embedded considered convictions to some extent held across cultures and over time.[16] They also can be put into wide reflective equilibrium. To say that such persons act irrationally if so acting is not in their individual self-interest is to utilize what is in effect an arbitrary *persuasive* definition of what it is to be rational.

Gauthier *au contraire* assumes that the "prudent pursuit of one's own ends is obviously rational, concern for the impartial justifiability of one's actions is not."[17] But how, if at all, is Gauthier's belief to be established? Some reflective and well-informed persons (Henry Sidgwick among others) think both concerns are rational. How is Gauthier to show that they are mistaken? How can Gauthier, or anyone else, show that *only* a prudent pursuit of one's own ends is rational or even that it is a rational motive for action that always overrides for a rational person other motives for action? Gauthier's view appears at least, as I quoted Barry remarking, to rest on pure assertion. But, given that is all that Gauthier's claim about what is rational and irrational has going for it, it "can therefore fitly be opposed by a counterassertion, namely, that it is equally rational to care about what can be defended impartially."[18] Barry then goes on to add, though, "I do not know how to prove that the term 'rationality' is appropriately employed in this way; I think that the virtual unanimous concurrence of the human race in caring about the defensibility of actions in a way that does not appeal to power is a highly relevant supporting consideration."[19] Perhaps almost all the human race is irrational in believing that, and only a few Hobbesians, identifying rationality with a prudent pursuit of self-interest, have a sane view on such matters, "but until somebody produces more than an argument by definitional fiat for the equation of rationality and self-interest we can safely continue to deny it."[20]

We, in fine, have no sound argument to justify believing that it is *inconsistent with reason not* to put, in either the short term or the long term, one's informed self-interest first.[21] A person who puts her own interests first can be acting rationally, but so can the person who acts on principles that can withstand impartial appraisal when the interests of all people affected (including herself) are given equal weight.[22] Reason does not *require* that we act according to principles that all can reasonably accept, but in so acting a person's actions are as much in *accord* with reason as those of a person who acts out of self-interest. A person in acting either way need make no deductive or inductive mistake, need not be conceptually confused, lack a firm grasp of the facts, or not have the ability to hold firmly in mind the relevant considerations, including the relevant arguments. The Hobbesian who claims that it is either irrational, or even less than fully rational, to be an impartialist is just arm-waving.

IV

All constructivist *contractarian* theories of justice, and of morality more generally, whether mutual advantage theories or impartiality theories, construe justice as those principles and that set of practices on which everyone at least in principle could reach agreement.[23] Barry and Reiman as much as Rawls construe justice as impartiality in terms of agreement. But there are those, myself included, who are justice-as-impartiality advocates but reject construing justice in terms of agreement. Barry gives us a sense of what the stress on agreement would come to.

> [T]he function of justice is to provide a rational basis for agreement among people who do not simply look at things from the point of view of their own interests but seek to take due account of the interests of all. Justice, on this conception, is what can be justified to everyone. . . . It is inherent in this conception that there is a distinctively moral motive, namely, the desire to behave in accordance with principles that can be defended to oneself and others in an impartial way.[24]

Following Thomas Scanlon, Barry takes the underlying moral motive to be "the desire to be able to justify one's actions to others on grounds they could not reasonably reject."[25] Conceptions of this sort are widely held, but Kymlicka among others thinks that they are, that notwithstanding, fundamentally mistaken.[26] Perhaps such a conception would work if we were only considering moral relations between competent adults. But there are, as well, moral relations between competent adults and children, mental defectives, and other sentient creatures as well. It is senseless to talk about impartial agreement with infants or mental defectives, to say nothing of animals; it is senseless to speak of giving them grounds they could not reasonably reject. Considerations of justice are very stringent between us (assuming we are competent adults) and the severely mentally retarded, but there is no room for talk of justice coming to what they and we could come to an agreement about.

> If someone is incapable of being a party to an agreement with us, that certainly does not mean we lack any moral motive for attending to his or her interests. The emphasis on agreement within impartiality seems to create some of the same problems that the emphasis on bargaining power creates within mutual advantage theories: some people will fall beyond the pale of morality, including those who are most in need of moral protection.[27]

It is a mistake to claim, as Scanlon does, that morality only applies to a being if the notion of justification to a being of that kind makes sense."[28]

Scanlon maintains in defense of his thesis that a being that can feel pain shows that that being has a center of consciousness and, because of this, that the notion of justification to such a being makes sense. It is because of this, Scanlon claims, that pain is so often taken as a relevant criterion for moral status. But it is false that if a being can feel pain, justification can be addressed to that being and that we can in principle at least attain agreement with him. Agreement requires the being not just be able to feel pain, and to be a center of consciousness, but of comprehension as well, and while infants, severe mental defectives, and many animals can feel pain they cannot comprehend things so that they could enter into agreements with us such that the notion of justification could even make sense to them. Yet surely they have moral status. That we cannot address justification to a baby does not mean the baby lacks moral status. We give moral status to an infant or to a dog not because we can address justification to it or to its moral trustee. We give moral status to it because it can suffer or flourish, because the lives of such beings "can go better or worse, and because we think their well-being is of intrinsic importance."[29] Some beings we can address justification to and some we cannot, but what "makes them all moral beings is the fact that they have a good, and their well-being matters intrinsically."[30] But to so argue is to break altogether with the contractarian tradition, including its impartialist versions. But that would seem at least to be required of an adequate account of morality.

Kymlicka argues that we should construe justice as impartiality not in the manner of the contractarian as based on some kind of agreement but that we should simply take impartiality as a criterion that, with or without agreement, gives all interests equal weight. Our *moral* motivation is not in reaching agreement but in responding to legitimate interests. We simply come to recognize, if we are moral beings, that others have legitimate claims to have their interests taken into account. The thing is to try to find or articulate principles of justice that give equal weight to everyone's interests. Agreement, Kymlicka claims, drops out *at the most basic level.*

We have clear obligations to those who are powerless to defend or to represent or sometimes even to understand their own interests. In this vein, and abstracting a little, our clearest obligations are, Kymlicka claims, not to try to reach agreement, but will involve taking people's interests into account and to the giving of equal weight to the interests of all human beings. *This is the clear and central claim of justice as impartiality.* Our principles of justice are justified when they do that. If they do not give such equal weight to the interests of all, whether we agree about these principles or not, any agreement we might come to will not justify them. This commits us to the substantively egalitarian view that the interests of all human beings matter and matter equally. Where that is not our guiding conception, we do not, at least on modern conceptions of justice, have justice. Agreement is, of course, Kymlicka acknowledges, of vital *epistemological* and *political* import. But at the foundational level, Kymlicka has it, it does not apply; that is to say, it does not apply where we are saying what justice is and what the foundations of a just society are.[31] "At the deepest level," Kymlicka continues, "justice is about equal consideration of our legitimate interests, and the many virtues of agreement are assessed by reference to that underlying idea, not vice versa."[32]

V

There is plainly something right about Kymlicka's argument here, but there may be something wrong as well which, in some diminished way, gives morals by agreement another inning. What justice as impartiality substantively comes to is the giving the interests of all equal weight such that everyone's interests matter and everyone's interests matter equally. Proper names or positions of prestige or power are not relevant in determining whose interests have pride of place when people have conflicting interests and both interests cannot be met. Still, in such a situation we must depart from *simple* equality and it is there where the careful articulation of principles of social justice such as we find in Rawls, Scanlon, Reiman, and Barry becomes vital. But in making such a differential weighting, such as to proceed by benefiting the worst off maximally in ways that are compatible with retaining autonomy (including equal liberty for all) and fair equality of opportunity for all, we should start from a position where we give equal consideration to the interests of all and where we start by giving an initial equal weighting to all interests. It is, as Barry puts it, this baseline of equality from which we must start when we reason morally. However, when we recognize that we are in a circumstance where not all interests can be satisfied equally, we look for impartial and fair ways of departing from simple equality. But these considerations do not gainsay the point that justice is about the equal consideration of our legitimate interests. This obtains whether or not there is anything that everyone competent to make such judgments and bent on being reasonable would agree on. So far things seem at least to continue to cut against contractarians.

However, let us now ask how do we—or do we—know that this is what justice is and that this is what justice requires such that we must act in this way if we would be just and that for there to be just social institutions our social practices must be so structured? It is here where agreement may come in by the back door.

Kymlicka writes as if we could just somehow intuit or directly recognize that this is what justice is: that we could just "see" that these claims are true. But if there are any accounts which are by now widely recognized to be non-starters, it is intuitionism (what Rawls calls rational intuitionism) and natural law theories where we in some mysterious way must just have direct access to the truth—indeed, even on some accounts, the certain truth—of some moral propositions. How then does Kymlicka know, and how can we know, that his fundamental substantive moral claims, claims not subject to agreement, are true or justified? Perhaps they are—though Kymlicka does not claim that for them—*conceptual* claims such that we can know that they are true by having a grasp of the concept of justice, where to have a grasp of the concept of justice is to know how to use "justice" or cognate terms correctly. Perhaps the following conceptual chain holds: to be just is to be fair, to be fair is to be impartial, and to be impartial is to give equal consideration to the interests of all human beings. If this is so, we could know the truth of Kymlicka's claims by coming to have a good understanding of the use of "justice." We would have what Simon Blackburn somewhat ironically calls Oxford Science.[33] But even then there would have to be some agreement to even justifiably make that conceptual claim, for there would have to be agreement that that is how we use "justice," that that is how we play such language-games.[34] But even so, even with such agreement, that may not at all give us a way of meeting mutual advantage theories. Gauthier, for example, perfectly well understands the ordinary use of "just" and "justice" and what it commits us to, if we would stick with it, but he will for his theoretical purposes modify that use until it is compatible with a set of principles which are—or so he believes—rationally sustainable when we reason carefully. We cannot go very far in sustaining substantive claims and substantive principles of justice through being clear about the use of "just" and allied terms. Such considerations may undermine certain absurd claims but they leave many competitors for what is just in the field.

It may, that is, give us something like the first word but it will not carry us very far beyond that. But then how does Kymlicka know that his substantive claims about justice are justified? He leaves this mysterious. Rawls, Daniels, and I, as well, explicitly, and others implicitly, have in such contexts appealed to considered judgments or convictions in wide reflective equilibrium.[35] It has been mistakenly thought that this is a thinly disguised form of intuitionism with all its difficulties plus even more evident worries about ethnocentrism. However, these charges are mistaken given the kind of coherentism involved in the appeal to considered judgments in wide reflective equilibrium. It starts from our firmest considered convictions such as to enslave people is wrong, racial prejudice is evil, religious intolerance is unacceptable, and it tries to set out a consistent cluster of such beliefs. But it also seeks to show how such specific considered convictions can be derived from, are explainable by, or at least are in accordance with more general moral principles, some of which themselves may be considered judgments. "The interests of all human beings are of equal importance" is one such principle which is also such an abstract considered judgment in societies such as ours. We seek, as was argued in the previous chapter, by a reciprocal adjusting of many elements, sometimes modifying or abandoning a specific considered judgment or sometimes modifying or even abandoning a more general principle or sometimes by coming to articulate a new one with a powerfully rationalizing power, until we get what we can recognize to be a consistent and coherent cluster of beliefs. We do this by sometimes trimming, sometimes expanding, our cluster of considered judgments and principles, but always adjusting this mélange of convictions and beliefs. We do this, repeatedly seeking to maximize coherence, until we have something which we have good reasons to believe form a consistent and coherent cluster. So far we have nothing more than what an ethical intuitionist, though not only an ethical intuitionist, could affirm, though there need be, and indeed should be, no claim to a bizarre epistemic status or to a truth capturing or tracking power for the moral beliefs and principles. Indeed, as I argued in the previous chapter, we can, and I believe should, following Rawls, avoid making any claim about the logical, epistemic, or metaphysical status of our considered judgments, our principles of justice, or our other various moral claims. We should, to repeat, travel philosophically light.[36]

Where wide reflective equilibrium clearly goes beyond ethical intuitionism, which only utilizes a *narrow* reflective equilibrium, is in its stress that other things besides specific moral beliefs and moral principles must be appealed to in gaining the coherent web of belief and conviction that would constitute a wide reflective equilibrium. The consistent set we seek is not only of specific moral convictions and more general principles but of whole theories of morality, conceptions of the function of morality in society, factual beliefs about the structure of society and about human nature, beliefs about social change (including beliefs about how societies will develop or can be made to develop), as well as specific historical and sociological beliefs about what our situation is. The equilibrium we seek is one in which all these elements are put into a coherent whole where the aim remains to maximize coherence. In narrow reflective equilibrium a specific considered conviction might be abandoned because it conflicted with many equally weighty specific considered convictions or with a more general moral principle that has considerable appeal. But in wide reflective equilibrium such a conviction might be rejected as well, or alternatively, because it was incompatible with some well-established empirical facts about society or human beings or about our particular situation or because it made demands which, given what we know about the world, could not be realized or were beliefs which had moral alternatives which made much more sense in light of some carefully elaborated social or moral theories or theories about the function of morality in society. There are here a considerable range of considerations, including empirical considerations, that are relevant to our decisions about what to do or how to live. We normally start with relatively specific considered convictions, but they are correctable by a whole range of empirical and theoretical convictions as well as by moral principles or moral theories, though sometimes, in the case of moral principles and theories, it will go the other way around and the principles or theories will be correctable by the specific considered judgments where just noting certain empirical facts may not be enough to undermine certain moral principles or theories. There is, in such a circumstance, the further consideration whether these nonmoral facts (if that isn't pleonastic) are unalterable givens in our situation. There is the question of whether in this respect the world can be changed and whether, if it can, it should be changed. We need also to consider, in the widest sense of "cost," the cost of such a change. Maximizing coherence by means of such considerations yields a *critical* morality that does not have the dogmatism and, as Bertrand Russell noted, what in effect, though not in intention, is the conventionalism and subjectivism of ethical intuitionism. (Dogmatism and subjectivism combined is a really unappealing repast.) Moreover, that critical morality also functions as a guard against ethnocentrism. Some of the specific judgments we start with may be ethnocentric, but by the time we have got them into wide reflective equilibrium the ethnocentrism will be winnowed out. This is itself plainly a form of objectivity, as a kind of intersubjectivity, and all the objectivity, at least in such domains, we need or are likely to be able to get.

So, if Kymlicka would avail himself of such a procedure, he at least arguably would have a method for arguing for his fundamental claims of justice and he need not just assert them, somehow taking them to be natural laws or basic intuitions recoverable on reflection. The method of wide reflective equilibrium could, of course, be used, as well, to argue against an account like Kymlicka's. Its advantage, whichever way it is used, is that we do not with it need to just assert or to rely on intuitions, but can appeal to a method that is very like methods used in science and in other domains. Moreover, it does not wildly depart from how we very often proceed in commonsense contexts when we have our feet planted firmly on the ground.

However, in doing this Kymlicka would be implicitly appealing to some agreement, to some consensus, for it is *our* considered convictions that we seek to get into wide reflective equilibrium. This means we are in effect appealing to the convictions of a spectrum of related specific peoples living in specific and related communities with their traditions situated in a determinate cultural space and time, though these traditions will also be various subspecies of the wider and long-lived tradition we call the Western tradition. In our specific case, the circumstances would be those of the constitutional democracies under conditions of modernity. We rely on a consensus in such communities though the shared considered convictions need not be, and typically will not be, *only* the shared convictions—the considered judgments—of those communities. They *might* in some instances be quite pan-human. But for them to be *our* considered judgments they must rest on a rough consensus in our family of communities (groups with different conceptions, sometimes different comprehensive conceptions, of good or the good) of constitutional democracies and this, of course, implies some rough agreement at least in those communities. This agreement (consensus) is not *an* agreement, a contract, the sort of thing contractarians talk about. Unanimity is not even expected, let alone required. It is just the kind of agreement that goes with—is, I suspect, the same thing as—a rough consensus. Moreover, this is not to assume with Barry that principles of justice are the objects of a collective choice or contract. It steps out, as much as Kymlicka does, of the contractarian tradition entirely. But it does require for moral reasoning even to proceed some rough consensus. As Peirce argued against Descartes, and Wittgenstein could have, if we have no place to start as social creatures with a battery of beliefs, we cannot even start. Put alternatively, we must see things by our own lights—irreducibly social lights—but we can, and indeed should, if we are reasonable, repair the ship at sea. *For starters*, there are no other lights we could see things by. But this does not conceptually imprison us, for we can reflect and think and question our beliefs, and indeed should where there is the real irritation of doubt. Moreover, our repairing the ship at sea will not be holus-bolus but a plank here and a plank there, bit by bit and almost constantly, repairing what will again and again be in need of repair. As Peirce and Dewey saw, it is not in Cartesian doubting, but it is in such circumstances, with such repairing and bootstrapping, where critical intelligence is displayed. Thus (*pace* Kymlicka) agreement (consensus) enters in at a very fundamental level indeed. To show that his impartiality account of justice is justified, he must show that its principles and claims can, relying on considered judgments, be placed in wide reflective equilibrium. But still they must be *our* considered judgments and thus there must be a rough consensus. But this need not mean that it appeals to *an* agreement (a contract) or to the agreement of everyone to whom it is addressed. There is no reason to believe that we can get such an agreement, that we can get such an Archimedean point, but there is also good reason to think that we can avoid both ethnocentrism and authoritarianism here with such a rough consensus and without an Archimedean point. We avoid ethnocentrism by our means of correcting our intuitions; we avoid authoritarianism by the democracy of consensus rooted in impartial and informed collective deliberation.

Some philosophers appealing to wide reflective equilibrium and in doing so relying very fundamentally on considered convictions—Rawls most prominently—are also constructivists and contractarians and take the method of wide reflective equilibrium and contractarianism to form a coherent mutually reinforcing whole. For Rawls, for example, in deciding on how thick the veil of ignorance is to be or how the original position is to be characterized, we at crucial junctures rely on considered convictions as we do in deciding on what it is reasonable to accept. But, in turn, in deciding on whether we have *for a time* achieved a wide reflective equilibrium—there is never anything like a timeless wide reflective equilibrium—we would need a conception of justice which would be acceptable to the parties under certain idealized conditions. So again at a very fundamental justificatory level agreement is appealed to. But, I shall say again, it is not *an* agreement, the contract, hypothetical or otherwise, of a contractarian, Rawls to the contrary notwithstanding, but a rough consensus. It isn't that the substantive principles and claims of social justice are not what Kymlicka says they are—that they don't have that content and scope—or that justice is what we can agree on in certain idealized situations, but that, if we are to show that Kymlicka's or anyone else's substantive claims of justice are justified, we must show that there is such agreement (such a rough consensus) about what they are and how they stand together. But this (*pace* Rawls and Barry) does not require or even need contractarianism. And we do not mean by "justice" what we would agree on in such situations and, in addition, this is not what justice is. But we can only be confident that our claims about what justice is are *justified* if they are rooted in such a consensus.

We should note in this context that justice is significantly like truth. Truth is not what researchers investigating under ideal conditions and over a considerable time would agree is the case. But that may be the best *test* for truth. Similarly, justice is not what would be agreed to or on in the original position, but that *may* be the best *test* for what is just. We have carefully to distinguish what truth and justice mean and what they are from how we ascertain what is true or just.

VI

I want now to consider a way, though a rather partial way, in which the impartiality approach to justice and the mutual advantage approach *might* be shown to be compatible, while not being competing, compatible, or even congruently partial *conceptions of justice*. The impartiality approaches show us what justice is, how we have to be to be just persons of moral principle, what just institutions would look like, and what principles of justice people, reasoning carefully from the moral point of view, would find during some epoch, and for some determinate culture or cluster of cultures, to be most justified and why. We are asking for moral reasons here which only *per accidens* may sometimes also be reasons of self-interest. Assuming there is something called the moral point of view (one element of which is the impartial consideration of the interests of all), people of moral principle will reason in accordance with it. They will hope, and reasonably expect, that most of the time their interests will not be hurt by doing so, but they will not think they are justified in doing so *only* when doing so answers (directly or indirectly) to their own interests or at least does not go against their interests. Their motive for pursuing justice is not the pursuit of individual advantage or even mutual advantage. What happens to other people matters in and of itself whatever the upshot for mutual advantage. But we can still ask, and they can ask, *Why be just*? This question cannot be asked from inside the moral point of view; if we are to be persons of moral principle, and not merely persons of good morals, we have no alternative but to try to be just. Suppose, however, someone does not *aspire* to be a person of moral principle, does not *care* about rendering justice simply because of what it is. Such an amoralist can still perfectly intelligibly ask *if justice pays*, if he ought (prudentially ought) to do what just people do in order to improve his prospects or at least to protect his interests? In that way, as a good prudential question, he can ask, stepping out of morality, so to speak, why be just?

Can we give good reasons of a broadly prudential sort which will show why, or even that, a purely self-interested person, if through and through rational, and clear about the facts, will do, though out of self-interest, what a just person will do? Kant, as we have seen, distinguished between a man of good morals (something an egoist could be) and a morally good man (someone genuinely committed to the moral point of view). Can we show that rational, purely self-interested people would, if they were through and through rational, do what just people do, or even do roughly what just people do, though not, of course, for the same reasons? We should recognize in pressing that question, that Why ought we to be just? Why be fair? Why ought we to do what is right? or Why should we be moral? are questions that we could not coherently ask from a moral point of view. To so ask them from *that point of view* is like asking, Why ought we do what we ought to do?[37]

However, as the extended discussion of Why be moral? has brought out, we can intelligibly ask: *Why take the moral point of view at all?*[38] From the moral point of view, moral reasons by definition override nonmoral reasons, but why take that point of view at all? From the point of view of individual self-interest, from purely class interests or from the point of view of a group of constrained maximizers bent solely on cooperation for mutual advantage, moral reasons are at most only *contingently* overriding.[39] From the moral point of view they are *necessarily* overriding, but not from these points of view. But why take the moral point of view? Justice, fairness, and morality indeed require it. But so what?

Hobbesian theory can be taken as a powerful attempt to show that we (where "we" is taken collectively) have very strong prudential reasons for being, as the world is and will continue to be, *men of good morals*. We have in terms of long-term self-interest the best of reasons to support the continued existence of some moral constraints, including some just practices. (We could not—logically could not—have moral institutions, at least where the circumstances of justice obtain, that did not include just social practices.) Rational persons, the claim goes, may not be morally good men, but they will be men of good morals.

The impartialist arguments, such as we have seen Barry, Kymlicka, and Allen Buchanan articulating, show, I believe, that Hobbesians (pure mutual advantage theorists) cannot get justice out of purely self-interested reasoning, including constrained maximization, which in the end is itself purely self-interested reasoning.[40] Indeed, it is true, as some modern Hobbesians have powerfully argued, that people can expect to advance their interests most effectively by cooperating and in doing this by agreeing to accept certain constraints on their direct individual utility maximization. By moderating their demands and by cooperating with others they will, as the world goes, in the long run do better. David Gauthier makes a powerful case for that. But these forms of cooperation will not give us morality, will not give us a system of justice, where the interests of all count equally, where what happens to other people, no matter how they are placed or how enfeebled, matters in and of itself, and where the reasons for action must not just be acceptable from the point of view of the agent doing the reasoning but from all points of view. For a social practice to be just, it must not only answer to the interests of some individual or some class or some elite, but it must answer to the interests of all, including those incapable of entering into relations of mutual advantage or of any kind of reciprocal relations. But, as we have seen, there can be all kinds of situations (class differentials, gender differences, caste systems, hierarchical strata, adults and children, mental competents and mental defectives, developed cultures and nonliterate ones) where there are differential power structures and where by pursuing mutual advantage intelligently in certain circumstances the powerful would exploit the weak and not for all of that be acting *unintelligently*. It could, as we have seen, very well in some of these circumstances be in the mutual advantage of everyone involved. But so acting would be unjust all the same. *Justice cannot allow differential bargaining power to be translated into advantage.* People in such circumstances, given their weakness, have reason to cooperate with the strong for otherwise they will be still worse off. And in societies as we know them these circumstances are not infrequent. So, given the differential power situation and the determination of the powerful to do the best they can for themselves, the weak have prudential reasons to cooperate even though they are exploited, indeed, even severely exploited. But they are not in such a circumstance being treated justly: the resulting system of cooperation though rational is unjust. Indeed, such treatment of people is immoral. We do not get to morality from Hobbesian premises and thus we do not get to justice. The impartialist does not ask why be just, but shows what justice is; the Hobbesian asks why be just and tries to show that we should, prudentially speaking, be just because justice pays. What has been shown is (a) that paying does not make something just and (b) that it is not true that *justice always pays*. Some form of social cooperation always pays, but the form of social cooperation people engage in, including mutually advantageous social cooperation, may be very different from justice. We may have a society or, at the extreme, a world, where there is mutually advantageous social cooperation which is still a society or even a world which is grossly unjust. The impartialist has not shown that an enlightened egoist or an intelligent and informed constrained maximizer must, to be through and through rational, be just. And the Hobbesian has not shown that we can get justice out of enlightened egoism in the circumstances of justice.

To this the Hobbesian might reply that a good bit of morality is irrational. (Here we return, but now from a different angle, to something we considered earlier.) He may say, as David Gauthier does, that "traditional morality as such may be no more than a ragbag of views lacking any single, coherent rationale."[41] The moral point of view requires the equal consideration of interests, but, the Hobbesian would claim, it is irrational for an individual or a group to do so when it isn't in their own interests. What is rational to do is determined by the interests of the *individual* who is acting. Where parts of morality do not so answer to individual interests they should, the Hobbesian can claim, be jettisoned, and what is kept as a system of social cooperation, though considerably less than morality as it has been traditionally conceived, is *the critical rational core* of morality. That is all we should keep of the moral point of view.

This purely instrumentalist conception of rationality, as we saw Barry arguing, rests on pure assertion. That it is just this that rationality comes to is not established through an examination of the use of 'rationality'. To give equal weight to the interests of all, as I argued, is not irrational. But to say that it is a rational thing to do is no more or no less rooted in the use of 'rational' than is the claim that to be rational is always to give self-interested reasons pride of place.[42] We can try to appeal to theoretical considerations to support such a Hobbesian instrumentalist conception of rationality and its linked reduced form of morality: what in reality is more likely a streamlined *replacement* of morality. But there are other conceptions of rationality answering to different theoretical purposes. Given Hobbesian purposes we can use that Hobbesian conception of rationality, but, given Habermasian or Aristotelian purposes or the purposes of impartialism, we can use instead these quite different conceptions of rationality. There *may* be no good reasons, external to these particular purposes and systems of the organization of things, to accept one of these purposes rather than another. Rather it may be the purposes themselves, and the problem-solving activity that goes with their achievement, that determines, and displays, respectively, what is rational to do. There may be no Oxford Science telling us what rationality is. But to say that the Hobbesian ones are *the really rational* ones is plainly question begging. Moreover, the Hobbesian conception is subject to *reductio* arguments. *If* it fits the interests of one class to enslave another class and work them to the edge of starvation that would, on such a Hobbesian account, not only be what reason *permits*, it would, *for them*, be what both reason and justice *require*. But a theory of rationality which had that implication would not only be morally repugnant, it would be groundless and thoroughly implausible.

NOTES

1. W. D. Falk, *Ought, Reasons, and Morality* (Ithaca, N.Y.: Cornell University Press, 1986), 42–66.

2. John Rawls, *A Theory of Justice* (Cambridge, Mass.: Harvard University Press, 1971); "Kantian Constructivism in Moral Theory," *Journal of Philosophy* 77, no. 9 (September 1980): 515–72; "The Basic Liberties and Their Priority," in *Liberty, Equality and Law*, ed. Sterling M. McMurrin (Cambridge: Cambridge University Press, 1987), 3–87; and "Social Unity and Primary Goods" in *Utilitarianism and Beyond*, ed. Amartya Sen and Bernard Williams (Cambridge: Cambridge University Press, 1982), 159–86. Brian Barry, *Theories of Justice: A Treatise on Social Justice*, vol. 1 (Berkeley, Calif.: University of California Press, 1989). David Gauthier, *Morals by Agreement* (Oxford: Clarendon Press, 1986); *Moral Dealing* (Ithaca, N.Y.: Cornell University Press, 1990). James Buchanan, *The Limits of Liberty: Between Anarchy and Leviathan* (Chicago: University of Chicago Press, 1975).

3. The phrase "undistorted discourse" is, of course, from Jürgen Habermas. Rawls, with his veil of ignorance and original position, restricts discourse while Habermas's model of undistorted discourse requires full information. But Rawls's account in normative domains aims as well, though in a way quite different from Habermas, at undistorted discourse by eliminating, with the veil of ignorance, morally irrelevant factors that would impede impartial assessment.

4. See centrally here John Rawls, "Justice as Fairness: Political not Metaphysical," *Philosophy and Public Affairs* 14, no. 3 (Summer 1985): 223–51. But also see relatedly his "The Idea of an Overlapping Consensus," *Oxford Journal of Legal Studies* 7, no. 1 (1987): 1–23; his "The Domain of the Political and Overlapping Consensus," *New York University Law Review* 64, no. 2 (May 1989): 233–55; and his "The Priority of Right and Ideas of Good," *Philosophy and Public Affairs* 17, no. 4 (Fall 1988): 251–75. Rawls's fundamental approach in these essays is challenged by Jean Hampton, "Should Political Philosophy Be Done Without Metaphysics?" *Ethics* 99, no. 4 (1989): 791–814; Joseph Raz, "Facing Diversity: The Case of Epistemic Abstinence," *Philosophy and Public Affairs* 19, no. 1 (1990): 3–46; and defended by Kai Nielsen, "Rawls and the Socratic Ideal," *Analyse and Kritik* 13, no. 1 (1991): 69–73.

5. Barry, *Theories of Justice*; Will Kymlicka, "Two Theories of Justice," *Inquiry* 33 (1990): 99–119; and Allen Buchanan, "Justice as Reciprocity versus Subject-Centered Justice," *Philosophy and Public Affairs* 19, no. 3 (Summer 1990): 227–52.

6. Jeffrey Reiman, *Justice and Modern Moral Philosophy* (New Haven, Conn.: Yale University Press, 1990).

7. Kymlicka, "Two Theories of Justice," 100.

8. Barry, *Theories of Justice*, 250.

9. Thomas Hobbes as quoted in Patrick Riley, *Will and Political Legitimacy: A Critical Exposition of Social Contract Theories in Hobbes, Locke, Rousseau and Hegel* (Cambridge, Mass.: Harvard University Press, 1982), 39.

10. Barry, *Theories of Justice*, 302.

11. This is reminiscent of utilitarian arguments to ward off *reductio* arguments against utilitarianism.

12. Kymlicka, "Two Theories of Justice," 103.

13. James Buchanan, *The Limits of Liberty: Between Anarchy and Leviathan*, 54. See also David Gauthier, *Morals by Agreement*, 55–58.

14. Barry, *Theories of Justice*, 363.

15. Ibid., 273, 285. To say that something is universalizable is to say that if x is good for y or is something y ought to do, it is something that is good for anyone else or something anyone else ought to do if that someone is relevantly like y and is relevantly similarly situated. "Relevantly" here needs to be cashed in contextually. Kai Nielsen, "Justice, Equality and Needs," *Dalhousie Review* 69, no. 2 (Summer 1989): 211–27. See also Kai Nielsen, "Universalizability and the Commitment to Impartiality," in *Morality and Universality*, ed. Nelson T. Patter and Mark Timmons (Dordrecht, Holland: D. Reidel Publishing Co., 1985), 91–102.

16. Barry, *Theories of Justice*, 261.

17. Ibid., 285.

18. Ibid.

19. Ibid.

20. Ibid.

21. Ibid., 303.

22. Will Kymlicka, *Liberalism, Community and Culture* (Oxford: Clarendon Press, 1989); and "Two Theories of Justice."

23. Barry, *Theories of Justice*, 272.

24. Ibid.

25. Ibid., 284.

26. Kymlicka, "Two Theories of Justice," 110–12.

27. Ibid., 110.

28. Thomas Scanlon, "Contractualism and Utilitarianism," in Sen and Williams, eds., *Utilitarianism and Beyond*, 113–14. Indeed, it is much the same mistake as mutual advantage theorists such as Gauthier make.

29. Kymlicka, "Two Theories of Justice," 111.

30. Ibid.

31. Ibid., 113.

32. Ibid., 112.

33. Simon Blackburn, "Can Philosophy Exist?" in *Méta-Philosophie: Reconstructing Philosophy,* ed. Jocelyne Couture and Kai Nielsen (Calgary, Alberta: University of Calgary Press, 1994), 25–26, 94–95, 105.

34. Kai Nielsen, "On There Being Philosophical Knowledge," *Theoria* 56 (1990): 193–225.

35. For discussions of reflective equilibrium see John Rawls, *A Theory of Justice*, 19–21, 48–51, 577–87; John Rawls, "The Independence of Moral Theory," *Proceedings and Addresses of the American Philosophical Association* 47 (1974/75): 7–10; Norman Daniels, "Wide Reflective Equilibrium and Theory Acceptance in Ethics," *Journal of Philosophy* 76 (1979); Kai Nielsen, "Searching for an Emancipatory Perspective: Wide Reflective Equilibrium and the Hermeneutical Circle" in *Anti-foundationalism and Practical Reasoning,* ed. Evan Simpson (Edmonton, Alberta: Academic Printing and Publishing, 1987); and Kai Nielsen, "In Defense of Wide Reflective Equilibrium," in *Ethics and Justification,* ed. Douglas Odegard (Edmonton, Alberta: Academic Printing and Publishing, 1988), 19–38; and Kai Nielsen, "Philosophy Within the Limits of Wide Reflective Equilibrium Alone," *Iyyun* 43 (January 1994). See also the previous chapter.

36. John Rawls, "Justice as Fairness: Political not Metaphysical," 223–51.

37. Kai Nielsen, *Why Be Moral?* (Amherst, N.Y.: Prometheus Books, 1989).

38. Kurt Baier, *The Moral Point of View* (Ithaca, N.Y.: Cornell University Press, 1958); William Frankena, *Thinking about Morality* (Ann Arbor, Mich.: University of Michigan Press, 1980); Kai Nielsen, *Why Be Moral?*; and David Gauthier, ed., *Morality and Rational Self-Interest* (Englewood Cliffs, N.J.: Prentice-Hall, 1970).

39. Allen W. Wood, "Marx's Immoralism," in *Marx en Perspective,* ed. Bernard Chavance (Paris: Editions de l'Ecole des Hautes Etudes en Sciences Sociales, 1985), 681–98; and "Justice and Class Interests," *Philosophica* 3, no. 1 (1984): 9–32. See my discussion in Kai Nielsen, *Marxism and the Moral Point of View* (Boulder, Colo.: Westview Press, 1989).

40. Gauthier remarks: ". . . my discussion assumes rational, utility-maximizing individuals who are not mistaken about the nature of morality or, more generally, who recognize that *the sole rationale* for constraint must be ultimately a utility-maximizing one." David Gauthier, "Morality, Rational Choice and Semantic Representation," *Social Philosophy and Policy* 5, issue 2 (Spring 1988): 182.

41. Gauthier, *Moral Dealing*, 270.

42. Kai Nielsen, "Can There Be Justified Philosophical Beliefs?" *Iyyun* 40 (July 1991): 235–70.

Chapter Seven

Rights and Consequences: It All Depends

We can imagine extreme cases where killing an innocent person may save a whole nation. In such cases it seems fanatical to maintain the absoluteness of the judgments to do right even if the heavens will in fact fall.

—Charles Fried

The question of whether these side constraints are absolute, or whether they may be violated in order to avoid catastrophic moral horror, and if the latter, what the resulting structure might look like, is one I hope largely to avoid.

—Robert Nozick

I

Are there any moral rights that must be respected come what may: that must, to disambiguate a bit, never be overridden no matter what the circumstances or consequences? In speaking of moral rights (if, indeed, there are any) I am speaking of rights which are not merely legal. Our grounds for them, if we have any, are moral. They do not cease to be rights if they are not embedded in some legal system. In that way we have them on moral, not legal, grounds. I principally have in mind here those moral rights that were in earlier centuries called *natural rights* and in the twentieth century came to be called *human rights*, i.e., rights possessed by human beings simply in virtue of being human beings.[1] "The idea of a human right," as Peter Jones puts it, "remains that of a right which is 'natural' in that it is conceived as a

229

moral entitlement which human beings possess in their natural capacity as humans, and not in virtue of any special arrangement into which they have entered or any particular system of law under whose jurisdiction they fall."[2]

It is possible, of course, on epistemological grounds or logical grounds, to be skeptical about or even dismissive of the very idea of moral rights, either human rights or more particular moral rights rooted in specific context-dependent entitlements. Jeremy Bentham thought the only real rights that there were were legal rights, remarking that "right is the child of law; from real laws come real rights, but from imaginary laws, from 'laws of nature', come imaginary rights. . . . Natural rights is simple nonsense."[3] There is plainly a fact of the matter that establishes the truth or the falsity of "A has a legal right to x" but there is no fact of the matter that establishes the moral claim that "A has a human right to x." The mistake that the natural law tradition and the natural rights tradition of Locke make is that of believing that natural rights or natural moral laws are as much a fact of the matter as the existence of legal rights. Matters are not improved if we say, with John Locke and Thomas Aquinas, that God's natural law establishes that no one ought to harm another in her life, health, liberty, or possessions and that God's law could be said to give everyone a natural right to their life, liberty, and property and a natural duty to respect the lives, liberties, and properties of others. The traditional thinking goes as if the existence of God and the existence of His natural moral law were additional facts that we could just come to know. However, these, if they are even *possible* facts, are very arcane facts indeed. They are not conceptually unproblematic facts, if facts at all, that we can plausibly say we can just know as we can know that there are amendments to the American Constitution or what the rule of recognition is in the legal system of the United Kingdom.

The central skeptical claim about such natural laws and natural rights is that we have no reason at all to believe that there are any facts of the matter which would either constitute or establish such rights. Moreover, if we go nonnaturalist and assert that these natural rights are self-evident synthetic *a priori* truths concerning some mysterious nonnatural and noumenal realm of which we are just directly and intuitively aware, we say something that is at the very least equally obscure. Indeed, what we do is pile obscurity on obscurity. We have (to put it minimally) no clear sense of what it is for there to be such a nonnatural realm or for a norm to be true, or, even waiving that, we have no agreed on criteria for establishing the truth of such a claim. We do not even understand how to proceed to gain criteria for establishing the truth or the falsity of such putative truth claims.

This skeptical challenge was pushed even more deeply by the Scandinavian legal realists and metaethical noncognitivists, Axel Hägerström, Karl Olivercrona, Ingemar Hedenius, and Alf Ross.[4] Their account not only set aside natural rights, but legal rights as well construed as Hans Kelsen and Wesley Hohfeld construed them, as a world of legal relations—another noumenal realm—to be contrasted with a world of natural relations such that we Platonistically could conceive of a world of moral relations, legal relations, and natural relations existing side by side.

The Scandinavian legal realists, as thoroughgoing positivists, denied the existence of such a metaphysical world contending, mixing an error theory with noncognitivism, that rights and duties (both moral and legal) are purely. fictitious or imaginary powers or bonds existing only in the minds of human beings. We can have true or false beliefs (beliefs of a sociological sort) about whether people hold such beliefs in rights, but their "beliefs" (if that is the right word for them) themselves are neither true nor false and cannot be warrantedly asserted. I think both that such skeptical claims concerning the ontology of norms and noncognitivist or error theorist readings of their logical status are much harder to refute than has usually been thought since the demise of positivism. (People have used the demise of positivism as an excuse for slackness over such matters.) I have argued for that elsewhere,[5] but I shall set aside such considerations here for I think some rights-based theories avoid such problems by being *constructivist* accounts. While being constructivist accounts, they also take rights seriously. John Rawls's, Ronald Dworkin's, and Thomas Scanlon's accounts are such accounts. They have given plausible articulations of rights which rightly, I believe, take no position at all on such ontological and metaethical issues. Following what Rawls calls the method of avoidance, such accounts avoid such controversial issues.[6] Instead, traveling light philosophically, they stay with considered judgments about first-order moral rights-claims without ever taking any controversial philosophical stance, including taking any position at all about whether moral beliefs could be either true or false. Without taking any such controversial and perplexing philosophical positions at all, we can know what moral rights we have and how they differ from merely legal rights, from goals, from goods, from obligations, from virtues, from mere preferences, and how what we have a right to do is not necessarily something that is the right thing to do. (*Rights* and *right* should not be confused.) We can very well know these and related things, including knowing that the overriding of a right takes very special justification and that rights can be overridden without being forfeited, without knowing or even having a view about what is the correct *analysis* of rights or the most perspicuous conception of rights, just as we can know what a chair is or what power is and, as well, know a good deal about chairs and the way power is exercised without having any views at all about the correct or incorrect analysis of what it is for something to be a chair or to be an exercise of power.[7] The same goes for rights.

I shall, like Rawls, use the method of avoidance, and eschew (if I plausibly can) in considering my question taking any stance at all on such onto-logical, epistemological and metaethical issues.[8] I shall also avoid, if I can, taking a position on the various contending theories of rights or conceptions of our at least supposedly common concept of rights. The main contenders for theories of rights include the *Benefit Theory*, where to have a right is to be the intended beneficiary of someone else's duty, where—or so this theory has it—the relation between rights and duties is expressed in the idea of correlativ-ity: A's right to some good is just another way of talking about B's duty to pro-vide that good for A. To be contrasted with the Benefit Theory is the once very popular *Choice Theory* of rights where A may be said to have a right only if B's duty is owed to A in the sense that A has the power to waive it if she wishes or chooses to. The third contender is the *Interest Theory* of rights which contends that a person (an individual) is correctly said to have a right whenever an interest of hers is regarded as sufficiently important to justify holding others (including the State) to be under a duty to promote or at least protect that interest in some way. The claim is not, absurdly, that every inter-est is the subject of a right, but that only when that interest is a sufficiently important interest and that interest can be so protected is that interest a right. Rights are such protected interests and they *generate* duties.

All of these accounts have well-known difficulties, but they all in their nuanced forms, and over certain considerations relevant to taking rights se-riously, also have at least some initial appeal. If I were in the business of opt-ing for a theory of rights, I would be inclined to go the route of some form of the Interest Theory. But it is my hunch and working hypothesis that we can reasonably resolve many (perhaps all) substantive moral and political prob-lems about the justification of rights and their proper role in morals and pol-itics without any such theory choice at all.

II

Let us see if this is so of my initial question stated at the beginning of this chapter and let us further see if we can, so traveling light philosophically, plausibly answer it in a reasonably decisive manner. My question was: Are there any human rights that must be respected and whose claims can never be overridden in any circumstance and no matter what the consequences? (Re-member a right may be overridden without being forfeited.[9])

In morality, as by now familiar and widely accepted criticisms of Kant and Kantianism, Utilitarianism and Perfectionism have made evident, it is very questionable indeed whether there are any tolerably specific norms or values which are actually unconditionally or absolutely justified in all con-ceivable circumstances. That this holds for rights along with other norms should not be surprising. But it is also the case that we (reflective moral agents in societies such as ours) are prone to feel and sometimes to believe that there are certain things we have a right to expect or a right to do or to have, and that others (including the State) must not interfere with us here and in some instances must actively protect our rights in such circumstances. There are situations, we (or at least some of us) are inclined to believe, where this holds unconditionally.

Skeptics about human rights will argue either or both (a) there is no appeal to fact and/or rational principles or rationality that, independently of what just happens to be the considered convictions of a given people, will establish or show that there is anything that any person in any circumstance and anywhere has a right to do or to be protected from having happen to her or—and I think more interestingly—(b) that there are no such rights to do certain things or to be protected from having certain things happen to one that are not rightly over-rideable in some particular circumstance. Moreover, the claim goes, their overrideability in those circumstances will be acknowledged by reflective moral agents with the typical considered convictions of moral agents in societies such as ours when the agents are adequately informed, not conceptually confused, and in other appropriate ways have their considered judgments in wide reflective equilibrium.[10] My question is whether either (a) or (b) is so.

I will argue that it is at least in principle (theoretically) possible that any substantive human rights claim might rightly (justifiably) be overridden in certain circumstances. I will also argue that sometimes we cannot reasonably avoid in considering what are at least putatively conflicting rights-claims an appeal to consequences and to human interests and needs. I think this supports some weak form of consequentialism against the Absolutism of the currently fashionable rights-based, duty-based, and virtue-based normative ethical theories and normative theories of politics. (What this *weak* consequentialism comes to will be explicated in the last section of this chapter.) For now, following David Lyons and Brian Barry, I want to make it clear that this *weak* consequentialism is not what in contemporary times has been called utilitarianism (e.g., by Bernard Williams and Charles Fried among others) and is widely believed to be utilitarianism and even defended as utilitarianism by J.J.C. Smart and Peter Singer, among others. It, however, as Lyons and Barry show, is not the classical utilitarianism of Bentham and the Millses.[11] Those classical views are closer to what I call *weak* consequentialism.

III

In looking for a right that can never justifiably be overridden, let us start with the rights that have characteristically been thought to be human rights and, as at least rhetoric has it, are in some sense, not infrequently, thought to be inalienable, imprescriptable, indefeasible, and unforfeitable. John Locke summarized some of them as the right to life, liberty, and property. Some later human rights advocates would balk at property, but perhaps not at (to make a reasonable reduction) personal property (as distinct from private ownership of the means of production) and certainly not at the right to self-ownership. The right to liberty must at the very least be the right to do what there was no rule or moral reason against doing. The right to liberty or to freedom was typically taken to devolve into the right to freedom of thought and expression, the right to freedom of association, the right to freedom of movement including the right to emigrate, and the right not to be subject to arbitrary arrest and imprisonment.

There are, however, circumstances where the consequences are of a certain sort such that all of those very fundamental, and generally acknowledged human rights—acknowledged to be human rights if anything is—could—or so I shall argue—rightly be overridden. A. I. Melden and Joel Feinberg are right, however, in saying that though they are rightly overridden, they are not forfeited.[12] If, to translate into the concrete, my right not to have my mail read without my permission is overridden, as it was during the Second World War, due to censorship restrictions designed to protect a nation at war, my right not to have my mail censored or read remains there in place when the emergency is at an end. I do not lose my right because it is on occasion overridden. It remains there fully in force in the standard situations. But it is widely believed by many, even in Western constitutional democracies, that this right can in certain circumstances be rightly overridden as (for example) in wartime circumstances because of the grave threat to security it poses. But, if it becomes routinely overrideable, it is not a right at all. People so reasoning recognize that, while freedom of expression and privacy are very important to them, they all the same believe in the justifiability of censorship in such a circumstance. They recognize that it is one of their considered judgments and indeed a judgment that would remain a considered judgment even when they get their judgments into wide reflective equilibrium. They do not, that is, believe it to be a considered judgment that would be extinguished by such a winnowing. Perhaps they are mistaken about this, but that they are is anything but evident. This being so, we are hardly on safe ground in claiming that freedom of expression is a right that can never be rightly overridden.

Freedom of thought, more in control of one's will and more private, is harder to control, and the justifiability of its control (where it can be had) is even more questionable, but if a man thinks he should kill his quite innocent neighbors because they irritate him, and might very well do it, and there is a pill that we could give him to erase that particular thought, it is anything but clear that the pill should not be smuggled into his food. Similar considerations, even more obviously, apply to right of freedom of association, movement, and emigration. Normally the right to emigrate should not be challenged, but if a person is a general or a weapons systems expert in country A on the verge of going to war with country B, where country B is a dangerously aggressive and expansionist nation and A is not, it is again anything but clear that the general or the weapons systems expert should be allowed, in those circumstances, to emigrate to country B. What is plainly an unforfeitable human right is rightly overrideable in those circumstances.

Admittedly these are extreme circumstances and normally there can be no legitimate question of overriding these rights. But an examination of such extreme situations does show that whether such rights—really fundamental and paradigmatic human rights—can rightly be overridden depends at least in part on the consequences of overriding them. Trading on an ambiguity in "respected" and even more evidently in "unconditional," it is not sufficient to respond that, though in some extreme situations they are rightly overrideable, they are still not forfeited, or perhaps even forfeitable, and that that shows, the claim continues, that these human rights are still being respected and thus remain unconditionally in force. I shall comment on the latter ambiguity only, for it is crucial for my case. There is a respect for rights in that they are not forfeited and can only in the gravest of circumstances rightly be overridden. In that weak sense human rights are unconditionally held—meaning that such a right is not something that we can ever rightly disregard; however, in a still plainer sense of "unconditional," it is, in being rightly overridden, not unconditionally held, for allowing the exercise of that right, no matter what the circumstances or what the consequences, is not something that is always and quite categorically and unconditionally to be done. Moreover, it is not generally thought that this is anything that *should* be unconditional, let alone *must* be unconditional. Thus in that very plain and important sense those human rights are not unconditional.

Let us consider another cluster of paradigmatic or (in some instances) arguably paradigmatic human rights: the right to protection by one's government (or by the society in which one lives, so as to cover Stateless societies), the right to a fair trial, the right to due process, the right to protection of the law, the right to be free from arbitrary arrest, the right to personal property, and the right to self-ownership. Consider the last two first. If in the town in which I live there is a devastating earthquake and my house is one of the few houses remaining intact, I may rightly be required by the city officials, my wishes to the contrary notwithstanding, to billet people during the emergency. My right to the exclusive use of my personal property is rightly overridden in such circumstances as it is, less dramatically, in situations where there is a pressing need to construct a highway that runs through my property. The right of *eminent domain* is a well-established legal right that is, in some of its applications, morally unproblematic.

The right of self-ownership lies even deeper than the right to own personal property, but even there my right (my right to self-ownership) may in extreme circumstances rightly be overridden. Suppose I do not want to give blood transfusions, but I have a very rare blood type and I live in a very isolated community where only I and one other person is known to have that blood type. Let us also stipulate that I do not have religious convictions that go against blood transfusions. I just do not want to give blood. The other person, through no fault of his own, is involved in an accident and will die without an immediate blood transfusion and I am alone able to give it to him. I may rightly in such a circumstance be required (strapped down and forced, if necessary) to give my blood. Libertarians will say that that does not respect the independence of persons to which nonlibertarians should reply that not being required to give blood there does not respect the interdependence of persons and how much each person owes to others for what he is and what he can do. Moreover, it is the latter attitude and not the former which most clearly shows respect for persons.

Let us now turn to the right not to be subject to arbitrary arrest, the right to the protection of the law, the right to due process, the right to a fair trial. We have to be careful here that some of these rights-claims are not so read (so understood) that they fail to be substantive: that they become what in the bad old days would be called analytic, like "Murder is wrong" where "murder" means "wrong killing" so that "Murder is wrong" is understood to be equivalent to "Wrong killing is wrong." (This is a vacuity not dissimilar in its emptiness to Aquinas's first principle of the natural moral law: "Good is to be done and evil is to be avoided.") If "arbitrary arrest" means "everything considered *unjustified* arrest" or "through and through *wrongful* arrest," we get something equally vacuous and we can protest by noting that and then adding that that is not the only way these sentences can be understood. They can be read substantively and they naturally would take substantive readings and, with these substantive readings, or so I shall argue, they all have exceptions: they all could be rightly overridden in certain circumstances. Again, to see that this is so, we must go to extreme situations. Let us suppose a country A (a country that in no way was aggressive, expansionist, or even exploitative) was seriously threatened by another country B. One way B did this was by, for a long time before B's intentions were well known, systematically infiltrating agents into A to, when the time was ripe, engage in all sorts of acts of sabotage, assassination, and mayhem, but that it is also the case that there was a not inconsiderable amount of perfectly legitimate and innocent emigration from B to A: emigrants with no evil intentions toward A and very glad to be out of B. A, now gravely threatened by B, let us postulate, is often not able to make even a good guess at who are the innocent immigrants and who are not. This situation could very well provide sound grounds—morally justifiable grounds—for preventive detention. But this preventive detention remains in a way a form of arbitrary arrest. (If we deny that this in any way counts as "arbitrary arrest," we are on the way to making the rights-claim nonsubstantive.)

Similar things should be said for the right to a fair trial, the right to due process, the right to the protection of the law, the right to security of person. I shall treat them all under the following case. Suppose a fragment of an army, devastated and nearly defeated, is trying desperately to escape from behind enemy lines, where the enemy in question is a brutal enemy that is known to take no prisoners. Suppose the retreating soldiers come upon a civilian of the enemy country. There is, let us further suppose, absolutely no feasible way of taking the man with them and it is very likely that if, even bound and gagged, they leave him there, he will alert the enemy army, when it arrives in hot pursuit, and the retreating soldiers will all be killed. With a trial it might be ascertained that he did not come into that region for that purpose and anyway would do nothing of the kind. He might, though there is no way of ascertaining this, even sympathize with the retreating soldiers and hope their country would defeat his own. But there is no time for a trial for the army must speedily retreat. The army commander will be justified, if that plainly is really the circumstance, in overriding all of the above rights-claims and ordering the man killed, though as painlessly and humanely as possible.

The cases I have considered involve the standard and paradigmatic human rights-claims. Less standard, less clearly paradigmatic human rights-claims, such as a right to education, a right to work, a right to health care, a right to social security, a right to a decent standard of living, are even more plainly claims that are sometimes overrideable *if* only for the reason that in some circumstances (e.g., in very poor countries) they cannot be met. It can hardly be intelligibly said of a government that it *must* do what it *cannot* do. (We also need to be confident that it really cannot do it, that there is no reasonable redirection of resources possible to meet the more pressing need.) Such "rights," where at a given time they cannot be met, are better thought of as desirable goals, though not the less important for all of that, though where the situation becomes one in which they can reasonably be met, they may become rights, perhaps they even *must* become rights.

Perhaps more specific human rights are unconditional and are never rightly overrideable. Consider here Maurice Cranston's two examples, which he apparently at least believes to be unconditional and in no conceivable circumstance overrideable. He takes them as things which "should never be done," "freedoms which should never be invaded."[13]

A black student in South Africa is awarded a scholarship to Oxford, and then refused a passport by the South African government *simply because he is black*. We feel this is a clear invasion of the human right to freedom of movement. Jews are annihilated by the Nazi government *simply because they are Jews*. We feel this is a manifest abuse (an atrocious abuse) of the human right to life.[14]

These are clear violations of rights (if anything is) and they are plainly inexcusable. These are evil things if anything is and plainly some things are evil. We do not need philosophical or any other kind of theory to tell us that. Indeed, any theory which gave to understand that this was not so would itself be, at least in that respect, a mistaken theory, a mistaken account of morality.[15] (This is an application, out of its Moorean home in metaphysics and epistemology, of G. E. Moore's defense of common sense against philosophical extravagance. Here Moore, the defender of common sense in matters metaphysical and epistemological, was far better than G. E. Moore the moral philosopher.)

Nonetheless, Cranston's cases are not exceptions to my contextualist consequentialism: my *weak* consequentialism. First, note the phrases in the above passage from Cranston that are italized. To do what is done to him "simply because he is black" or to them "simply because they are Jews" gives to understand that what is done is plainly done for no good reason, indeed, is done arbitrarily and, given the grave harm (the plain evil) of what is done, to do such things arbitrarily is equally plainly to do them unjustifiably. (Indeed, "unjustifiability" is too weak a word here.) Thus there can be no justification for an override here. But then the rights-claims are in reality nonsubstantive claims. Again, they are like "Wrong killing is wrong." They say, "The issue of a passport should not be restricted *arbitrarily*" and "The freedom of movement should not be restricted *arbitrarily*." Being so nonsubstantive, they are, of course, exceptionless in the way "Good is to be done and evil is to be avoided" is. (Where we get something that is exceptionless, we get something empty. That is the price we pay for certainty.)

If we give it substance by changing it to say "If a black is allowed on campus at Oxford there will be race rioting with extensive plunder, killing, and general mayhem in Oxford," then it is not so clear (if this will clearly be so) that the refusal to give the passport, and with it the consequent restriction of movement, is not justified under the circumstances. Even more desert-islandish and fanciful, and indeed offensively so, is the following case. Suppose the Jews were a very small minority (try Gypsies instead in a gesture, though still offensively fanciful, toward reality) living among a much larger population of non-Jews. Further suppose the Jews, and only the Jews, had an incurable but strongly contagious disease which would eventually kill them all and would, if they were not themselves killed with some quick dispatch, eventually, through infecting them, though, of course, unintentionally, kill the whole population as well. (We have to assume, to pile implausibility on implausibility, that none of the non-Jews were already infected.) It is not so clear that under these stringent circumstances that their right to live or (by *universalizability*) anyone's right to live so situated should not be so overridden. Given the vileness of the Holocaust and the gross brutality of the Nazis, I hesitate to use this desert-island example, though Cranston's case calls for it and in responding I would be evasive if I did not use some such case. Still, I can't help but feel that the very articulating of it is something like an insult to the memory of all those who were so murdered. All the same, offensive though it may be, it is true that *if* the circumstances (the wildly counterfactual circumstances) were as I described them, then such killing (though not in the way the Nazis did it) would be justified unless we are justified (as we are not) in taking the Hebrew-Christian turn of saying that we must never do evil that good may come. But in the above case we are doing a very great evil to avoid a still greater evil. Moreover, the stern Hebrew-Christian injunction admittedly only makes sense if we can bring ourselves to believe that there is such a sovereign and providential God as is conceptualized in those traditions. But that takes a bit of believing, perhaps even a crucifixion of the intellect. Atheists who think they need to so crucify their intellects to make sense of the moral life should think again.

Considering all the above examples of human rights-claims taken together, it should be noted that to find circumstances in which it is plausible to claim that any of these rights-claims could be overridden, we need to go to extreme situations (typically catastrophic or near catastrophic situations) and in a few instances to desert-island situations as well. Where the cases are desert-islandish we can be assured, given that desperate expedient, that in our actual moral life we can rely on the moral claims or practices for guidance. The theoretical appeal of such desert-island cases in our context is to show against deontological Absolutism that these rights-claims were not really free of consequentialist considerations.[16] If certain consequences were to obtain, these allegedly *unconditional* Absolutes would be shown to be non-Absolute and (trivially as a consequent of that) mistaken when taken as unconditional claims. Pointing out that these consequences will not in fact obtain obscures the fact that the viability of the moral claims is dependent, in part at least, on what the consequences actually are. If the consequences were very different from what in fact they are, what we should say and believe would very likely be different as well.

English-language moral and social philosophy, and social and political philosophy out of the analytic tradition even more specifically, with its greater fastitidiousness and penchant for understatement, has tended not to concentrate much on how morality should go in extreme situations. Deontological Absolutists such as Robert Nozick and Charles Fried have, rather as asides, admitted that in catastrophic situations their strong rights-claims do not hold, but they have not integrated that into their theories. Moreover, it is not clear how they could integrate such considerations without extensively recasting their theories. Their admissions (note the quotations with which this chapter starts) are rather like the black sheep in a family. They are better kept out of sight. It has been left to Continental philosophers such as Jean-Paul Sartre and Maurice Merleau-Ponty, and (as well) their liberal critics, Raymond Aron and Leszek Kolakowski, to respond to such situations. But while their accounts have frequently been insightful, there has not been a lot of argumentative development here. What I think I have shown, against rights-based moral theories of an Absolutist sort, is that we cannot avoid appealing, in trying to ascertain what must be done, to circumstances and consequences.

IV

I have canvassed a thorough sampling of actual rights-claims, indeed, typically paradigmatic rights-claims, and I have argued against rights-based or deontological Absolutism that circumstances can arise in which any of them could rightly be overridden. In that vital sense none of them is unconditional. However, I have left aside philosophical articulations of rights-claims: general principles that have been articulated by philosophers and other theorists as *the* ultimate or at least *an* ultimate grounding of rights, where, unlike the fundamental principles of utilitarianism or perfectionism, these principles are themselves very general rights-claims. They are meant to rationalize and justify (typically only partially justify) the more particular rights-claims as well as concrete appeals made in the courts and elsewhere to rights.

I shall conveniently but somewhat inaccurately call them *meta-rights-claims* or *meta-rights*.[17] They might be thought (mistakenly I shall argue) to be exceptionless and claims, general though they be, that can never rightly or justifiably be overridden. The following are key examples.

1. All people have a right to be treated as equals, not because they happen to be equal in some particular respect or other but simply because they are human.

2. All people are of equal worth, and have a right to be so treated however unequal they may be in merit, abilities, or even in moral sensitivity.

3. All people have a right to be treated as ends (as something of intrinsic worth) and never merely as means.

4. All human beings, capable of such choices, have an equal right to choose how they shall live.

5. All human beings have a right to an equality of concern and respect, a right they possess not in virtue of birth, characteristic, merit, or ex-

cellence, but simply as human beings with the capacity to make plans and give justice.

These meta-rights are all quite similar and each has been taken as the fundamental rights-claim by some natural rights theorist or proponent of a rights-based ethical theory. Ronald Dworkin defends number 5, J. L. Mackie number 4, Kant number 3, Gregory Vlastos number 2, and Maurice Cranston number 1.[18] I have in some detail elsewhere argued that these principles are all subject to plausible skeptical challenge.[19] An iconoclastic moralist such as Nietzsche or Stirner, a defender of aristocratic morality, a consistent Hobbesian, or utilitarian would not accept such claims or, specifically in the case of the utilitarian, if she accepts them at all, she will not accept them as fundamental or basic principles but as derivative principles that can in theory at least be overridden by the principle of *utility*: for the utilitarian the sole fundamental principle of morality.

I further argued that we have no better grounds for believing these meta-rights to be true (or false) than we have for believing the alternatives to be true or false. Setting considerations of truth aside, we also have no good grounds for believing that rationality requires any of these meta-rights principles any more (or any less) than their alternatives or certain clear denials of any of them. *Pace* Plato, Kant, Gewirth, and Gauthier (among others), I argued that *morality is underdetermined with respect to rationality*. There are, that is, no systems of moral principles, beliefs, and attitudes *required* by reason either in or outside a contractual situation, but there are a range of diverse moral principles, beliefs, attitudes, and whole systems of morality that are *compatible* with reason and *perhaps* (if we could figure out more clearly what this means) equally compatible with reason. Reason (rationality) does not require any particular moral system, but it is compatible with a considerable range of such systems: they are, that is, in accordance with reason without being required by reason. I am not saying or suggesting that anything goes and that there are no irrational moral beliefs. They abound in our moral life. To take some random examples: masturbation is wrong for it will stunt your growth; all humans are corrupted by original sin; selfishness is the first virtue of a person of principle; or integrity is the *only* virtue. But I did argue that there remains in the field for a rational critical morality a range of competitors from Nietzschean iconoclasm and Aristotelian elitist perfectionism, to Hobbesianism, justice as fairness à la Rawls, justice as impartiality à la Brian Barry, justice as mutual advantage à la Gauthier, to Sidgwickian classical utilitarianism (if its rationalistic epistemological apparatus is dropped). All these moral theories no doubt have some defects, some more than others, but there can, and have been, and no doubt will continue to be, piecemeal rational reconstructions to rectify the defects. Defects remain but many of the theories do get articulated in increasingly more adequate forms. They remain in the field as competitors with each other. No one theory for very long, and then only locally, wins the day. But the crucial thing to see in this context is that there are no good grounds for believing that reason itself (independently of our considered moral convictions) requires us to be utilitarians, Gauthierian contractarians, Rawlsians, perfectionists (Aristotelian or Nietzschean), or Rossean pluralistic deontologists, though I am not suggesting, as the argument of my last chapter should have made plain enough, that all the bodies are equally healthy. Rationality is under-determined with respect to morality, though such a rationalism (a rationalism that denies this) dies hard, as the history of moral philosophy (including our recent history) shows. It may be more difficult than we usually think for people with philosophical inclinations to live without at least an *Ersatz* God.

I also discussed—developing, and turning to my own purposes, some arguments from John Rawls and Norman Daniels—whether, starting with our considered judgments and using the method of wide reflective equilibrium, we could give grounds, admittedly of an indecisive sort (after all fallibilism is in place as much in science as in morality and politics), for favoring over an elitist perfectionism an egalitarian rights-based account that is something in the rough neighborhood of Dworkin's account or at least an account which develops from taking as basic one or another of the meta-rights principles listed above.[20]

I argued that a modest case could be made for such an account. However, I also raised the "worry" that such a grounding of a human rights approach may only work when the moral agents involved have the specific considered judgments of people who are broadly speaking liberals or Enlightenment-based extensions of liberals such as Bentham or d'Holbach or Marx or Luxemburg or some modern communitarians such as Michael Walzer or Charles Taylor. Where we try to include Stirner, Nietzsche, Loyola, or Aristotle and *perhaps* even Alastair MacIntyre or Jacques Maritain or a very hard-nosed *realpolitik* Hobbesian, we may get very different and *perhaps* even incommensurable reflective equilibria. I do not think that issue is by any means near a resolution yet, but I do not despair of a rational resolution.

Pursuant to that, I think we should share Donald Davidson's and Isaac Levi's skepticism concerning the fashionable claim that fundamental moral principles, beliefs, ways of moral reasoning, or even whole moralities are incommensurable: that there is no way for a Loyola and a Mill to argue with each other, that Rawls and MacIntyre occupy incommensurable moral spaces such that between them there is no room for fruitful exchange or any reasonable way of establishing which view is the more plausible: that there is not even any way of comparing their views with an eye to normative assessment. If these beliefs of mine are justified, then, if what I claim to gain out of a careful application of the method of wide reflective equilibrium is also arguably near to the mark and this gives us *lebensraum* to argue for a Dworkin-like or Rawls-like defense of human rights.[21]

I do not want to step, or even try to step, in the same river twice, so I simply report here on what I have argued in some considerable detail elsewhere. But what I said there and now report is relevant to central claims of this chapter, though I think its main argument will stand even if my above hunches and reported contentions are importantly mistaken. But if they are well taken, we get a rather more valuable package: we will have overrideability of rights, a defense of human rights, and a *weak* consequentialism all in a coherent and plausible package that is not caught up in incommensurabilities or hobbled by being just one reflective equilibrium among others. With this we have the prospect of gaining a greater objectivity than that with an account of morality which is stuck with many reflective equilibria all incommensurable with each other.

What is central to what I argue in this chapter is the correctness of the claim that an appeal to any of the above meta-rights will not justify reversing the judgment that, neither appealing to reason (our rationality) nor to our considered judgments in wide reflective equilibrium, will provide a sound basis for claiming that any of the human rights-claims discussed in the previous section could never rightly, on a particular occasion, be overridden. This, I believe, can be justifiably extended to other first-order rights, claims as well as to the meta-rights listed above. Neither reason nor wide reflective equilibrium provide us with a sound basis for revising our claim that there are no unconditional rights.

We could have Hobbesian *realpolitik* or Nietzschean reasons for denying that all people are of equal worth or somehow deserve or are entitled to equal concern or respect. The Hobbesian and Nietzschean might join hands in thinking that that belief in equal human worth is the merest sentimentality. What parades as Enlightenment reasonability really has, they might say, a Christian stink. There is no reason, they could add, why a thoughtful and informed person should embrace that sentimentality about everyone having equal worth: Einstein and Nixon, for example.

I argued in my *Equality and Liberty* that on utterly secular grounds we could, using the method of wide reflective equilibrium, reasonably argue for such meta-rights principles, though not for unconditional rights. But the case I made there is by no means obviously correct and I am not very confident that I have convinced many people who did not already basically agree with me. This does not, of course, mean that I was mistaken, but only just what I said: that I was not very persuasive.

If one sticks with Hobbesianism, eschewing considered judgments or at least egalitarian considered judgments in any sort of reflective equilibrium, then there is no reason to think human rights-claims cannot on occasion be overridden. That, of course, squares with my central claim in this chapter. But, and more interestingly, even if we appeal to considered judgments of a distinctively liberal sort à la Dworkin, Scanlon, Rawls, or myself, we have, with such approaches, with their family resemblances, no good reasons, accepting as we do some such meta-rights, for believing that first-order rights-claims, such as we discussed in the previous section, cannot rightly, depending on the circumstances and thus on the consequences, sometimes be overridden. Nothing changes this because we accept one or another of these philosophical "backups" for our first-order rights-claims. We still do not get any substantive unconditional rights.

What about the meta-rights principles themselves (numbers 1 through 5)? Can they ever rightly be overridden? Let us look first to their justification or lack thereof and to how trying to justify such principles proceeds. As we have seen, it is not clear what it would be like to prove them. They are hardly self-evident truths clear to the light of reason; they are hardly principles that all rational contractors (in or out of the state of nature), apart from any considered convictions they might just happen to have, must, or even predictably would, unanimously agree on, and it is not even clear that there would be a sufficient consensus (if we get at all cross-cultural, and perhaps even within our Western cultures) concerning what considered judgments crucially to rely on even when they are winnowed by a resolute utilization of the method of wide reflective equilibrium.

Such considerations certainly makes the justification of these meta-rights principles look a bit wobbly. It is certainly not unreasonable to wonder whether we have available a method which would yield sound grounding principles for human rights: the first-order human rights-claims. These meta-rights principles *may* be the articles of faith—the here I stand, I will do no other—of social democratic liberals, nonconfused Marxians (e.g., G. A. Cohen and Andrew Levine), and libertarian socialists (anarchists à la Mikhail Bakunin and Noam Chomsky). Still, we cannot plausibly claim that these meta-rights principles cannot be overridden, meaning by that in this context that a properly informed person must, if she is rational, reason in accordance with them.

In another trivial sense they *may* not be overrideable. To see what is involved here, contrast number 2 with the first-order human rights principle "Each person has a right to his individual assets." A believer in human rights might accept that first-order right and still consistently believe that in certain situations it could be rightly overridden. Where A has plenty and there is extensive starvation, some of A's personal assets may rightly be taken from him. In short, it can be specified, and perhaps even widely agreed on, when the first-order principle applies and when it does not. But it may seem, though I shall argue appearances are deceptive here, that nothing like that obtains for the meta-rights principles. I shall seek to show, using number 2 as an example, that this is a mistake and that, vis-à-vis overriding, the first-order rights and the meta-rights principles are more alike than different. Number 2 says, "All people are of equal worth, and have a right to be so treated however unequal they may be in merit, abilities, or even in moral sensitivity." Unlike the first-order rights principle just discussed, it is rather unclear, or at least indefinite, what number 2 asserts. Sometimes we rightly award A a fellowship and not B. Is this really a denial of the equal worth of A and B? *If* it is, then number 2 can in some even rather routine circumstances be rightly overridden. Presumably those who assert number 2 do not think that so awarding fellowships is incompatible with treating A and B as having equal worth or anything like that. But then perhaps it is not clear what treating people as being of equal worth comes to. What would we have to do or fail to do to *not* treat people as having equal worth? Presumably if we treated a person as a mere instrument, a slave without any rights at all, to do anything we like with whatever their wishes or interests might be, that would *not* be treating them as persons of equal worth to other people who were not so treated. Suppose, so purely instrumentally treating a person, we simply took him off the street and dragged him into a hospital and, against his will, operated on him and took both his good eyes and gave them to a famous scientist whose eyes were failing. If that were done we would plainly not be treating him as a person of equal worth to at least the scientist. So acting would be incompatible with reasoning in accordance with number 2.[22] But could we never *in any possible circumstances* be justified in so acting and thus overriding number 2? Would this be categorically and unconditionally wrong (forbidden) no matter what the possible circumstances, no matter what the consequences?

Again, there are desert-island cases that might persuade us to deny such categorical unconditionalism. Suppose the scientist was a kind of Einstein of cancer research and she was on the verge of a discovery that would finally definitively and for all types of cancer prevent the occurrence of cancer, and that she was going blind and needed good eyes to be able to complete her research and that only by having new eyes could she have the good eyes she sorely needed to complete her research. Suppose, further, that no one could plausibly take over her research and complete it and that there were no fresh cadavers about with useable eyes and none were to be expected and that there were no volunteer donors and that there was no time to set in place a lottery system for who is to be the unlucky person. All these are (to put it minimally) very desert-islandish assumptions indeed, but if these were the circumstances it is at least arguable that number 2 should in those circumstances be overridden. The person's claim to equal worth in that circumstance should be overridden, though not forfeited, and the meta-right turns out to be in that respect very much like the first-order right.

Suppose, implausibly, number 2 is not said not to be overridden even in that circumstance. The two people, even with such different treatment, are still said, and somehow correctly said, to be taken to have equal worth and to be of equal worth. That plainly strains credulity. Still, in its defense, it might be pointed out that there is here no violation of *universalizability* and we could further speak of role reversibility.[23] If the abilities and needs were similarly shifted around, then the eye-loss and eye-gain should also be shifted around. Decisions, hard decisions, are made on relevant differences: *universalizability* and impartiality are kept. Hard cases are indeed hard cases, but we are being morally evasive if we do not bite the bullet here.

It seems to me that this is just a way of pointing to their unequal worth. But if bizarrely this is denied and the two are said to be persons, as are all persons, of equal worth and are being so treated even in that situation, then it is not evident (to understate it) what "equal worth" means in number 2. Does it mean anything other than a claim to some "commitment" to *universalizability*, a completely formal property? If that is so it doesn't come to much.[24] We should ask, concerning the above case, if that is not a case (given its circumstances) where number 2 is rightly being overridden, and people are arguably rightly treated as not being of equal worth, what could count as a case of overriding, and arguably rightly overriding, number 2? If nothing is forthcoming, number 2 is threatened with vacuousness. Such a meta-right seems to be doing no work at all: providing no guidance at all. But it, to repeat, would be very implausible in the above circumstance to maintain, as we just have, that number 2 was not overridden. If all the same someone did maintain that, it would be reasonable to believe he was trying to save a paradoxical philosophical thesis at any cost. That, of course, is not unknown phenomena in philosophy. But that not uncommon philosophical phenomena is surely not a cause for celebration.

I think that very similar things can and should be said about the other meta-rights principles listed above (number 1, number 3, number 4, and number 5). When they are inspected, these "background rights" or allegedly "foundational rights" behave, in respect to overriding, very much like the first-order rights, except that, unlike some first-order rights, the only circumstances in which the meta-principle rights are plausibly rightly overrideable are in ridiculously fanciful desert-islandish circumstances. This shows, I believe, that in real-life situations, as distinct from not so near possible world situations, they would *in fact* never be overridden. If they are acceptable at all (the skeptical challenge again) they are always to be acted in accordance with in the real world. And Rawls will say, and perhaps Dworkin as well, that he constructed his ethical theory for this world and not for all possible worlds.[25] That, I believe, is fair enough—and Rawls for his purposes rightly stresses that—but there still remains a point to such desert-islandish adventures. These examples show, against rights-based and other deontological Absolutisms, *that circumstances and consequences always do count. It is always the case that it all depends.* Because the consequences in real-life circumstances are sometimes predictably of a certain sort—in certain circumstances practically certain to be of a certain sort—certain reasonably definite things must be done or left undone. There is in those practically inevitable circumstances a kind of practical quasi-unconditionality about them. If, however, the consequences were very different, that would not be so. That we are talking about counterfactuals here does not alter, does not diminish, the theoretical force of this point. Circumstances do massively intrude into moral deliberations. For certain general claims, the relevant circumstances are in fact very stable. But if they were to change, what would be the right thing to do or leave undone would very likely change as well. Anscombian and Donaganish Absolutism fails to take proper note of this.[26] But we should no more be spooked by the falsity of Absolutism then we are by the possibility of global epistemological skepticism. They are both philosopher's artificial constructions. For the purposes of practical political and moral argumentation, it is important not to lose sight of the practical quasi-unconditionality of such meta-rights principles. The moral horror of *The Heart of Darkness* is certainly not upon us because of the *logical* possibilities I have canvassed.

There is a further point of importance that follows, if my arguments about the proper overrideability of these meta-rights are well taken. The point is this. Sometimes in moral deliberations justice does not (*pace* Rawls and Dworkin) outweigh all other moral considerations such that to take the moral point of view requires that justice trump not only utility but any other moral consideration. Whether one conceives of justice as the impartial consideration of interests or (mistakenly, I believe) as the mutual advantage of all the persons involved in the situation, sometimes we rightly do what even, everything considered, is unjust. When (as in one of my cases) a person is not given a fair trial and, though possibly innocent, is shot to protect the lives of a retreating army, that person is not being treated justly. Indeed, he is not only being treated unjustly, the moral horror is even greater. Still, there we override, and rightly so, considerations of justice in terms of other moral interests; when a person is forced to give up his eyes, as in my above example, it is *perhaps* a dreadful travesty to speak of an impartial consideration of interests (where each is to count for one and none to count for more than one) or of a respecting of what would be in the *mutual* advantage of the parties. In such a situation, we arguably act unjustly but still rightly. Moreover, we come very close to treating in those circumstances some persons as means only and not as ends in themselves: not as members of a Kantian kingdom of ends. However, while we may override the requirements of justice, we still do what is morally appropriate in the circumstance. Sometimes, while acting unjustly, we still act rightly. You do not have to be a utilitarian to believe that moral agents, faced with the necessity of the choice, should (without engaging in rationalizations about double effect and the like) always do the lesser evil even when doing the lesser evil involves overriding what justice requires. Fixing on your own moral purity here, as Bernard Williams and Charles Fried do, shows a lack of moral seriousness. What gets decked out as moral integrity is either confusion, moral evasion, or a squeamishness which amounts to acting wrongly. Jean-Paul Sartre is right in his paradox: sometimes not to choose is to in effect choose and to choose evasively and wrongly.

V

Someone might follow me so far but counter that it is a confusion to think that any of this refutes anything but the naivest forms of rights-based ethics. Where I point to the consequences as showing that in a certain circumstance a specific rights-claim should be overridden, a sophisticated rights-based account, such as Ronald Dworkin's, would appeal to a conflict of rights and to one rights-claim overriding another rights-claim in that circumstance. Sometimes a liberty right is overridden by a security right and sometimes a security right by a liberty right. The proper dispute should be over whether we just have a plurality of sometimes competing rights-claims all on the same level and, like Rossians, just have to decide or judge or come to appreciate (without any rule to follow) in the particular situation which right makes the more stringent claim or whether instead we have something of a hierarchy of rights, perhaps even in lexical order or at least capable of nonarbitrarily being lexically ordered. Whatever we should say here, what we have, hierarchy or no hierarchy, is, the claim goes, *rights against rights* and not a right against some other value or somehow simply against consequences, showing, against a purely rights-based account, that our well-being or welfare would be diminished (perhaps only somewhat diminished) if we stuck with these rights-claims. That, for Dworkin, would not defeat the rights-claim. Rights, Dworkin has it, always trump utilities or any other evaluative considerations. On his account, we always work in moral deliberation within a system of competing rights-claims together (where this obtains) with their correlative duties and obligations. Rights, Dworkin has it, always trump utilities or any other evaluative considerations. If we reason properly, he has it, we work, in moral deliberation, within a system of competing rights.

Dworkin's own view appeals to a modest hierarchy of rights. When a specific right (typically one of the garden variety of rights) comes into question, he says, we justify it (if we can justify it) by deploying a more basic right.[27] Rights-based theories, as Dworkin puts it, place "the individual at the center, and take his decision or conduct as of fundamental importance."[28] Its "basic idea . . . is that distinct individuals have interests that they are entitled to protect if they so wish."[29] Moreover, Dworkin has it, the rights-based theory "must be a theory that is based on the concepts of rights that are natural, in the sense that they are not the product of any legislation, convention, or hypothetical contract."[30]

However, Dworkin's conception of natural rights (as does J. L. Mackie's), keeping in mind the critique of natural rights of the Scandinavian legal realists, travels metaphysically light; no strange noumenal realm or realm of moral relations is invoked or in any way appealed to. What is done instead is to stress the importance of "the protection of certain individual choices as fundamental, and as not properly subordinate to any goal or duty or combination of these."[31]

In chapter 7 of *Taking Rights Seriously*, Dworkin develops the idea that when a right is rightly overridden, we do not have a right trumped by something else but one right trumping another right. "The claim that citizens have a right to free speech must imply that it would be wrong for the government to stop them from speaking, even when the government believes [and believes correctly] that what they say will cause more harm than good."[32] Dworkin agrees that the State may sometimes be justified in overriding a particular right of an individual when it is necessary to protect the rights of others, perhaps their rights to life or security, or it might, Dworkin allows, override even a deeply entrenched particular right in order to prevent a catastrophe. The first is clearly a case of security-rights winning out in a particular circumstance over the right to free speech. Consider, for example, where to avert an impending catastrophe—say, a situation where there will be looting and rioting in the streets, perhaps the putting of a whole town to the torch—the free-speech rights of a charismatic leader inciting riot are in that circumstance rightly overridden, though not forfeited. But what we appeal to, Dworkin maintains, in justifying such an overriding, are our security rights and the right to life.

So, given this perfectly natural way of characterizing the above situation, we still seem at least, with this conflict of competing rights, to be operating within the parameters of a rights-based theory. We have rights conflicting, or at least competing, with rights. And, consonant with that, but also not in conflict with how I argued, what the government cannot do is, in rightly on certain occasions overriding the right to free speech, to justify such an overriding simply on the grounds, however certainly true that that claim may be, that by so acting it will "produce, overall, a benefit to the community."[33] We justify, Dworkin argues, overriding or limiting some specific right by invoking "the notion of competing rights that would be jeopardized if the right in question were not limited" or (in more extreme cases) overridden.[34] "The law of defamation . . . limits the personal right of any man to say what he thinks, because it requires him to have good grounds for what he says. But this law is justified, even for those who think that it does invade a personal right, by the fact that it protects the rights of others not to have their reputations ruined by a careless statement."[35] Dworkin goes on to remark that the "individual rights that our society acknowledges often conflict in this way."[36] What the government must do, to the best of its ability, is to protect the more important right at the cost of the less important right, always operating, in so adjudicating, within a system of competing rights.

However, we need to ask this question: how do we judge which rights are *the more important?* We need, Dworkin's answer goes, to look at the situation and to the consequences but not simply with an eye to what maximizes or optimizes welfare and minimizes ill-fare. That, Dworkin has it, takes us down an illicit utilitarian path. We could say, alternatively, whichever right meets more adequately the requirements of justice. But for Dworkin that still will not do, for Dworkin, as becomes clear in his discussion of Rawls, believes that we need in doing that (in ascertaining what justice requires) to appeal to a deep underlying rights-principle that is prior to anything that could be contracted, that is, that that would be unanimously agreed on in the original position. It is a principle that Dworkin holds himself and that he believes Rawls implicitly appeals to and it is, as well, the basic right in accordance with which, he has it, we judge the relative importance of conflicting rights. It is the claim that "individuals have a right to equal concern and respect in the design and administration of the political institutions that govern them."[37] (This is closely related to meta-right number 5.[38])

As we have seen in our discussion of meta-rights in the previous section, such meta-rights can rightly be overridden or limited. This being so, such a meta-right cannot be effectively used in the foundationalist way that Dworkin does.[39] Where a state—let us say a social democratic liberal state—is gravely threatened or at war, say, with a Fascist state, there are extreme situations, as we have seen, where some individuals are not treated, and justifiably not treated, in that circumstance with equal concern and respect. Where, as in my earlier example, a perhaps innocent man is simply executed or innocent children are simply killed by intense saturation bombing designed to destroy a munitions factory which must be put out of commission to win the war, individuals, in any straight meaning of the words in question, are not being treated with equal concern and respect. The very design of the liberal institutions allows in extreme circumstances for such eventualities. If we proceed in Dworkin's foundationalist way, we must say, contrary to what he wants to say, that something other than a right sometimes trumps even a basic right. (Recall that there is, at least on Dworkin's account, no more ultimate or basic right to appeal to.) If instead we appeal to a thoroughly coherentist model of rights and say that in that situation security-rights trump the right to life, because they are the more important in that particular context, our test for "the more important" rests on interests and on an appeal to consequences. And the consequences that are appealed to are the grave harms that human beings will suffer. There is no evading such considerations in gauging the more important interest. With either justificatory move, foundationalist or coherentist, we break out of the self-containedness of a rights-based theory. We have no purely rights-based Archimedean point here (or elsewhere).

An alternative foundationalist super-right (putatively foundational meta-rights principle) might be invoked, namely, the equal right of all persons to the most extensive liberty compatible with a like liberty for all. Some might object to this on the grounds that it is too much like utilitarianism in being concerned (among other things) with maximizing, or at least optimizing, liberty and, relatedly, for departing from the core idea behind a rights-based theory, namely, that of protecting individual rights. On such an account, the individual, as we saw Dworkin putting it, should be center stage.

To see what is involved here, consider the following: there is in liberal practice both the right to be left alone by the government and citizenship rights to equal effective participation in government.[40] They are both rights that are highly prized in constitutional democracies, but, with the differential power structures that obtain in these societies, the above super-right in effect favors the right to effective participation over the right of people to be left alone with their own initiatives provided they do not interfere with others. Through the institutions that will emerge or, if they already exist, that will be strengthened, a very considerable increase of liberty in the society will obtain, if the democratic participation is effective. Simply being free from interference, by contrast, is compatible with a less extensive liberty in the society. In short, accepting that super-right forces us to give priority to the citizenship rights of fair cooperation over the right to be left alone by our government. But it is precisely the latter and not citizenship rights that is really taken to be crucial for many people in our societies. (The individual center stage again.) Horatio Alger types abound and they will favor that right to be left alone over the right to political participation and they will not, if they are being at all clearheaded, accept the above super-right with its interest in maximizing liberty. Important, and at least seemingly legitimate interests of theirs, will be harmed or at least threatened by accepting that super-right (meta-right, if you will). We may get social democratic welfarism rather than pure *laissez-faire*. Horatio Alger types will then not be committed to favoring the most extensive liberty compatible with a like liberty for all—the maximizing doctrine—for what they want, as individualists, is to give pride of place instead to the right peacefully to pursue their own endeavors without interference from others. Whether that will lead to a more extensive liberty all around is another matter and is not at the center of their interests.

It looks, at least, as if there is no non-question-begging way of claiming that that super-right should be taken as foundational. Consistent social democratic liberals will go for it; consistent individualistic liberals will not. Moreover, in the early days of capitalism to have taken it as foundational would have so impeded the development of the productive forces that it would very likely have made factually impossible the kind of society of productive wealth in which that super-right could even plausibly have had a feasible application. There was an economic need then for Horatio Alger types. (Again, we see how contextual—this time historically contextual—moral claims can be.) In arguing about priorities here, and more generally in arguing for what is to be done, there are no sound grounds for remaining with a rights-based theory. Any particular rights-claim can in at least certain conceivable circumstances be rightly overridden. In deciding when this is so, and what justifies the overriding, we not infrequently cannot just appeal to conflicting rights and claim, in that situation at least, one right to be overriding. Interests and consequences, including a reckoning of the harm, misery, and pain that predictably would result from certain actions or policies, come importantly to the fore. It all depends.[41]

VI

Another likely response to what I have argued is to claim that it is consequentialist and *thus* utilitarian and by now people, who know anything at all, know that utilitarianism and consequentialism are mistaken.[42] I shall, running against current intellectual fashion (a fashion that has been in the making since about 1970), defend a form of consequentialism, distinguishing it from what in our times has come to be called utilitarianism. I do not dispute that contemporary utilitarianism has grave mistakes. But it is at least as grave a mistake to believe that we can make adequate moral assessments, while ignoring consequences, and by simply noting the intrinsic nature of acts and actions.[43]

To be a consequentialist is to believe that the morality of an action is to be judged by its consequences or in part by its consequences and not just, or perhaps even at all, by the intrinsic nature of the actions. (The two occurrences of "or" here allow for a distinction between *strong* and *weak* consequentialism. My consequentialism, as I remarked initially, is of the latter sort.) It is further the case that the consequences that most consequentialists, including this consequentialist, are interested in are interests and needs (typically human interests and needs). I want to know the bearing that certain actions, practices, and policies have on the interests and needs of people: how they are aided or harmed by them. Here, like a utilitarian, I am plainly concerned with human well-being and with what can undermine it. I am, moreover, interested in the consequences that affect all human beings and to a lesser extent all sentient creatures. I am, that is, a universal consequentialist as distinct from an egoistic or class consequentialist.

The core arguments of this chapter have been made in the service of resisting and refuting Absolutism, namely, the doctrine that actions are right or wrong just according to their nature, though the thrust of my critique of Absolutism was on rights-based rather than on duty-based or virtue-based forms. Similar arguments, however, could, and should, be deployed against duty-based or virtue-based forms. Indeed, I think the case there is rather simpler.

Anticonsequentialism in its purest form (Elizabeth Anscombe and Alan Donagan being prime examples) argues that certain things should be absolutely (unconditionally) prohibited or forbidden simply in virtue of their description as such-and-such identifiable kinds of actions regardless of further consequences.[44] I have been at pains to show that this is not so at least for rights-claims. Consequentialism can, as Barry remarks, be usefully seen as a negative doctrine that "denies that it is possible to specify a list of act-descriptions in terms of their 'nature' such that it would never under any circumstances—whatever the consequences—be right to do an act of a kind that was on the list."[45]

This negative form of consequentialism is *weak*, so weak, as Anscombe realized herself, that even W. D. Ross and C. D. Broad (good rule deontologists) could properly be counted as *weak* consequentialists.[46] Stronger forms of consequentialism, identified as utilitarianism by Kurt Baier and Bernard Williams, and subsequently by a host of others, is the view that each person has a *duty* to act at all times so as to maximize the greatest total amount of good achievable.[47] This view is what J. L. Austin would have called dotty. It would mean that an individual, indeed, all individuals capable of moral agency, would at all times be obligated to work as hard as possible to maximally contribute to so maximizing the good. She would only be justified in resting or doing what she wants to the extent, and just to that extent, that by not so resting or relaxing the achieving of the total maximum good, or total aggregate good, would be likely to be adversely affected. People would be required to drive themselves relentlessly, to the limits of their powers, in the making of an effort (indeed, their best effort) to maximally increase the total amount of good in the universe. The only respite from effort here would be to tool oneself up so that later one could, with better chances of success, make still greater efforts.

It is not a mistake for *strong* consequentialists (utilitarians) to say that *prima facie* everyone's interests are to count equally (each to count for one and none to count for more than one) and that we must start from a baseline in which everyone's interests do count equally and to only depart from that baseline for the gravest of reasons or because it is impossible in a certain circumstance to so proceed. Where such utilitarianism went most obviously wrong is in making it the *duty* of a moral agent to maximize, or try to maximize, the net benefit, to, as G. E. Moore put it, take "I am morally bound to perform this action" to be equivalent to "This action will produce the greatest possible amount of good in the universe."[48] That is a dotty view first because nobody has even the faintest idea of what this greatest possible amount of good in the universe is and secondly, as Barry puts it, by "making it a duty that the agent act to maximize net benefit, it makes acts that would be heroic [and I would add superogatory] into routine duties."[49] It is simply not the case, whatever utilitarians and communitarians may believe, that to find out in some specific circumstance what it is that we must do that we must be able to ascertain what the good is.

Barry nicely articulates the differences and relations between *strong* and *weak* consequentialists as follows:

> Weak consequentialism holds that there is no class of cases, definable in advance, such that the consequences are never relevant to the question of what is the right thing to do. Strong consequentialism holds that there is at all times a duty to act so as to maximize the amount of good—to maximize aggregate happiness if one is a utilitarian, to maximize something else if not. Strong consequentialism entails weak consequentialism and the denial of weak consequentialism entails the denial of strong consequentialism. But it is logically possible to accept weak consequentialism and reject strong consequentialism.[50]

Barry remarks that the classical utilitarians, Bentham and J. S. Mill, were *weak* consequentialists.[51] He could, as well, have added Henry Sidgwick. In fine, and paradoxically, the *classical* utilitarians were not utilitarians *in the contemporary sense*. The appeal to consequences, articulated in this chapter, is that of *weak* consequentialism. *Strong* consequentialism seems to me, for most of the reasons adumbrated in recent analytical literature, a very flawed doctrine and is not needed for the contextualist and consequentialist arguments developed in this chapter and in chapter 9 against Absolutism.[52]

It does seem to me, however, that Sidgwick rightly argued that the kind of classical utilitarianism that is a weak consequentialism needs to add, to do justice to justice, an independent axiom(s) or principle(s) of fairness: perhaps something like Rawls's two principles or the two principles I articulated in my *Equality and Liberty*. An adequate account of morality will not only be concerned with maximizing or optimizing the aggregate satisfaction of interests but will also be concerned with a fair distribution of interests. Sometimes these two considerations conflict as Sidgwick saw. A carefully crafted and nuanced ethical theory may be able to help us to see how such conflicts can reasonably be resolved and perhaps even yield some guidance concerning what is to be done. Here John Rawls's and Thomas Scanlon's work is the best we have to date. Both theories, in spite of their eschewing such labels, are forms of *weak* consequentialism.[53] But so (as we have noted) are W. D. Ross's and C. D. Broad's pluralistic deontology and so, as we have *in effect* seen, is Ronald Dworkin's rights-based theory. Rights for him are protected, extremely important interests. And these interests sometimes conflict. We must try to determine in such circumstances which interest is the more important. Consequences are brought in all along the way here. Where rights conflict Dworkin looks as much to interests and consequences as do I.

However, the reference to W. D. Ross and C. D. Broad shows how weak *weak* consequentialism is (though, as her contemptuous remarks about the Oxford Objectivists—Ross and Pritchard—reveal, it still offends Anscombe's rigid Hebrew-Christian Absolutist sensibilities.[54]) Only that weak consequentialism (so offensive to Anscombe) is required for my case against unconditional rights-claims.

Something that does remain is the task of seeking a more discriminating form of *weak* consequentialism. John Rawls and Ronald Dworkin believe that we are never justified in acting unfairly, in overriding what everything considered is the just thing to do. I, on the other hand, and I think Brian Barry as well, believe that in extreme situations—among them some situations in politics that have been characterized as the problem of dirty hands—considerations of human well-being and, even more evidently and decisively, massive suffering, justify overriding even what everything considered justice requires. We should not, as Kleist's *Michael Kohlhaas* dramatizes, do justice though the heavens fall. We act morally, in those circumstances, while doing things that conflict with the requirements of justice. Rawls and Dworkin and just about everyone else are right in claiming that just a slightly greater utility will not justify overriding considerations of justice, but they are wrong in thinking a very great disutility will not justify overriding justice. Sometimes justice trumps utility and sometimes utility justice. There is no lexical order here and we are not going to find an algorithm to decide which one trumps when. *Sometimes* we may even find, even after careful reflection, no answer at all, for in certain circumstances there may be no answer. We should beware of claiming anything like a principle of sufficient reason in ethics or politics. But a somewhat more robust consequentialism—a not quite so weak *weak* consequentialism—(if we can clearly articulate it) might sometimes give us somewhat more definite guidance than any theory presently yields. It was not part of my task to attempt that here but instead to argue that we have very good reason indeed to believe that there are no unconditional, utterly categorical rights. Such an Absolutism should be seen to be a relic of the Hebrew-

Christian tradition and (*pace* Fried) quite indefensible without that tradition. But since, that tradition itself is not defensible, such Absolutism is not defensible at all (*pace* Anscombe and Donagan).[55]

NOTES

1. Maurice Cranston, *What Are Human Rights?* (London: Bodley Head, 1973). I. Brownlie has assembled some of the basic documents in his *Basic Documents on Human Rights*, 2d ed. (Oxford: Clarendon Press, 1981).

2. Peter Jones, "Human Rights," in *The Blackwell Encyclopedia of Political Thought*, ed. David Miller et al. (Oxford: Basil Blackwell, 1987), 223.

3. Jeremy Bentham, *Anarchical Fallacies*.

4. Axel Hägerström, *Inquiries Into the Nature of Law and Morals*, trans. C. D. Broad (Stockholm: Almquist and Wiksells, 1953); Karl Olivercrona, *Law as Fact* (London: 1939); Ingemar Hedenius, *Om Ratt och Moral* (Stockholm, Almquist and Wiksells, 1941); and Alf Ross, *On Law and Justice* (Berkeley, Calif.: University of California Press, 1959).

5. Kai Nielsen, *Equality and Liberty: A Defense of Radical Egalitarianism* (Totowa, N.J.: Rowman and Allenheld, 1985), chapter 2; and Kai Nielsen, *God and the Grounding of Morality* (Ottawa, Ontario: University of Ottawa Press, 1991), chapters 8 and 9.

6. John Rawls: "Justice as Fairness: Political Not Metaphysical," *Philosophy and Public Affairs* 14, no. 3 (Summer 1985): 223–51; "The Idea of an Overlapping Consensus," *Oxford Journal of Legal Studies* 7 (1987): 1–25; "The Domain of the Political and Overlapping Consensus," *New York University Law Review* 64, no. 2 (May 1989): 233–55. These later views of Rawls, by contrast with his earlier views, have not been very well received. For two trenchant critiques, but I believe all the same largely mistaken critiques, see Jean Hampton, "Should Political Philosophy Be Done Without Metaphysics?" *Ethics* 99, no. 4 (July 1989); and Joseph Raz, "Facing Diversity: The Case of Epistemic Abstinence," *Philosophy and Public Affairs* 19, no. 1 (Winter 1990): 3–46. I, by contrast, think there is a very considerable plausibility and importance in the later work of Rawls. I seek to show this in my "John Rawls's New Methodology: An Interpretive Account," *McGill Law Journal* 30, no. 3 (May 1990): 573–601; "Rawls Revising Himself: A Political Conception of Justice," *Archiv für Rechts und Sozialphilosophie* 76, no. 4 (1990): 1–17; and "Rawls and the Socratic Ideal," *Kritik and Analyze* (Fall 1991). Richard Rorty, in a swashbuckling but very perceptive way, brings out some of the importance of Rawls's later work in his *Objectivity, Relativism, and Truth* (New York: Cambridge University Press, 1991), 175–96.

7. Barrington Moore, Jr., shows this adeptly for power in his "Authority and Inequality under Capitalism and Socialism," in *The Tanner Lectures on Human Values 7*, ed. Sterling McMurrin (Cambridge: Cambridge University Press, 1986), 103–244.

8. I try more generally to show the virtue of such avoidance in my *After the Demise of the Tradition: Rorty, Critical Theory, and the Fate of Philosophy* (Boulder, Colo.: Westview Press, 1991). See also chapter 5 of this volume.

9. A. I. Melden, *Rights and Right Conduct* (Oxford: Basil Blackwell, 1959) and *Rights and Persons* (Oxford: Basil Blackwell, 1977); Joel Feinberg, *Rights, Justice, and the Bounds of Liberty* (Princeton, N.J.: Princeton University Press, 1980), 131–55, and *Social Philosophy* (Englewood Cliffs, N.J.: Prentice-Hall, 1973), 88–94.

10. Kai Nielsen: *Equality and Liberty*, chapter 2; *God and the Grounding of Morality*, chapters 3–9; and "Reason and Sentiment," in *Rationality Today,* ed. T. Geraets (Ottawa, Ontario: University of Ottawa Press, 1979), 249–79. For a forceful criticism of the latter, see E. J. Bond, "Morality and Reason," in *On the Track of Reason,* ed. Rodger Beehler et al. (Boulder, Colo.: Westview Press, 1992), 97–106.

11. David Lyons, "Human Rights and the General Welfare," *Philosophy and Public Affairs* 6, no. 2 (Winter 1977): 113–29; Brian Barry, *Liberty and Justice* (Oxford: Clarendon Press, 1991), 40–77; and Bernard Williams, "A Critique of Utilitarianism," in *Utilitarianism: For and Against,* ed. J. J. C. Smart and Bernard Williams (Cambridge: Cambridge University Press, 1973) and Smart's defense in the same volume. See also J. J. C. Smart, "Distributive Justice and Utilitarianism," in *Justice and Economic Distribution,* 2d ed., ed. J. Arthur and W. Shaw (Englewood Cliffs, N.J.: Prentice-Hall, 1991), 106–17; Charles Fried, *Right and Wrong* (Cambridge, Mass.: Harvard University Press, 1978). For two volumes of essays that bring out something of the range of antiutilitarianism and anticonsequentialist arguments now current see *Utilitarianism and Beyond,* ed. Amartya Sen and Bernard Williams (Cambridge: Cambridge University Press, 1982) and *The Limits of Utilitarianism,* ed. Harlan Miller and William Williams (Minneapolis, Minn.: University of Minnesota Press, 1982). See also *Consequentialism and Its Critics,* ed. Samuel Scheffler (New York: Oxford University Press, 1988).

12. A. I. Melden, *Rights and Right Conduct* and *Rights and Persons*. Joel Feinberg, *Rights, Justice and the Bounds of Liberty* and *Social Philosophy*.

13. Maurice Cranston, "Are There Any Human Rights?" in *Ethics and Basic Rights,* ed. Guy Lafrance (Ottawa, Ontario: University of Ottawa Press, 1989).

14. Ibid., italics mine. There are situations, truly horrendous situations, where, when we describe them in some detail, they can be seen to involve the doing of things which should never be done. But the doing of such things, some place or other in the world, are reported almost daily in our newspapers. I have in mind such things as the gunning down for no reason of a lot of innocent people in a shopping mall. Such killing *in just that situation* is unconditionally wrong. But—and this shows how dependent this whole story is on the circumstances—change the circumstances a little and we get a different story. Suppose Hitler had been in the crowd and this was the gunman's only chance to kill him. Then it would not be so obvious that shooting into the crowd would be wrong. (We are supposing that the only way to kill Hitler also involved the unintended killing of others and that these others were innocent persons.) So we see that even in such horrendous situations it all depends. Consequences are always relevant and actions become justifiable or excusable in accordance with them. Some things should—indeed must—never be done, never allowed, where they can be prevented, just because of their truly horrendous consequences.

15. This utilization of G. E. Moore, and Ludwig Wittgenstein as well, is theoretically articulated in my *After the Demise of the Tradition,* 82–110, and in my *On Transforming Philosophy* (Boulder, Colo.: Westview Press, 1995), 164–67 and chapter 6.

16. Where we are actually trying to ascertain what should be done in some fairly determinate circumstances, we should point to the irrelevance of desert-island cases. Where the context, as in the present chapter, is more theoretical, there are situations where this is exactly what we should appeal to. See for a discussion here of the use of desert-island cases P. H. Nowell-Smith, *Ethics* (Harmondsmith: Pelican, 1954).

17. I say "inaccurately" because they are not actually second-order claims *about* our moral talk—and hence genuine meta-claims—but actually very general, philosophically articulated rights-claims themselves. But the label is useful to briefly have a way of referring to these distinct claims. They are much more theoretical than the standard rights-claims.

18. Maurice Cranston, "Are There Any Human Rights?" in Guy Lafrance, ed. *Ethics and Basic Rights*; Gregory Vlastos, "Justice and Equality" in *Social Justice,* ed. Richard Brandt (Englewood Cliffs, N.J.: Prentice-Hall, 1962), 31–72; J. L. Mackie, *Persons and Values* (Oxford: Clarendon Press, 1955), 105–19; and Ronald Dworkin, *Taking Rights Seriously* (Cambridge, Mass.: Harvard University Press, 1977), 171–77.

19. See references in notes 5 and 10.

20. I shall argue in the final section of this chapter that classical utilitarianism significantly differs from what is now commonly regarded as utilitarianism and that the later version does not represent progress. See also references in note 11. Some excellent essays making clear what classical utilitarianism was about are reprinted in Samuel Gorovitz, ed. *Utilitarianism: John Stuart Mill with Critical Essays* (Indianapolis, Ind.: Bobbs-Merrill, 1971).

21. See my *Equality and Liberty*, chapter 2, and *After the Demise of the Tradition*, part 2.

22. Something very like that in fact happened to an eighteen year old in a New York hotel, though with a kidney taken out rather than his eyes.

23. Kai Nielsen, "Universalizability and the Commitment to Impartiality" in *Morality and Universality,* ed. Nelson Potter and Mark Timmons (Dordrecht, Holland: D. Reidel, 1985), 91–101.

24. Ibid.

25. John Rawls, "The Independence of Moral Theory," *Proceedings and Addresses of the American Philosophical Association* 47 (1974/75): 7–10.

26. Elizabeth Anscombe, "Modern Moral Philosophy," *Philosophy* 33 (1958): 1–19 and Alan Donagan, *The Theory of Morality* (Chicago, Ill.: University of Chicago Press, 1977). Brian Barry ably criticizes the rationalizations around the doctrine of double effect. Brian Barry, *Liberty and Justice*, 40–77. See also Jonathan Bennett, "Morality and Consequences" in *The Tanner Lectures on Human Values 2,* ed. Sterling McMurrin (1981), 47–116.

27. Dworkin, *Taking Rights Seriously*, 170.

28. Ibid., 172.

29. Ibid., 176.

30. Ibid.

31. Ibid., 177.

32. Ibid., 190.

33. Ibid., 192.

34. Ibid., 193.

35. Ibid.

36. Ibid.

37. Ibid., 180.

38. See, for the statement of number 2, ibid., 182.

39. Ibid., 177–79.

40. Richard Miller, *Analyzing Marx* (Princeton, N.J.: Princeton University Press, 1984), 20–36; and Kai Nielsen, *Marxism and the Moral Point of View* (Boulder, Colo.: Westview Press, 1989), 203–15.

41. As I remarked when I introduced them, what I usefully, but inaccurately, called 'meta-rights', are not strictly speaking meta-rights at all, for they are abstract general principles and not statements about the use of 'rights'. But, all the same, it is a felicitous and, in the context, nonmisleading way of speaking of them.

42. Classically John Rawls, *A Theory of Justice* (Cambridge, Mass.: Harvard Uni-

versity Press, 1971). Dworkin, Fried, Williams, Philippa Foot, Scanlon, Jon Elster, and David Gauthier have been the major players here. See note 11 and Samuel Scheffler, *The Rejection of Consequentialism* (Oxford: Oxford University Press, 1982); and Philippa Foot, "Utilitarianism and the Virtues," *Mind* 94 (1985): 196–207. For perceptive but more historically oriented critical reactions to utilitarianism, see Isaiah Berlin, *The Crooked Timber of Humanity* (New York: Alfred A. Knopf, 1991), 1–19, and his *Four Essays on Liberty* (New York: Oxford University Press, 1969). For a succinct statement of what makes utilitarianism initially attractive together with a similarly succinct account of how it is fatally flawed, see Will Kymlicka, *Contemporary Political Philosophy* (Oxford: Clarendon Press, 1990), 9–49.

43. This has been well argued by Barry, *Liberty and Justice*, 40–77.

44. Elizabeth Anscombe, "Modern Moral Philosophy;" and Alan Donagan, *The Theory of Morality*.

45. Barry, *Liberty and Justice*, 73.

46. Anscombe, "Modern Moral Philosophy," 198. See also her "Who Is Wronged?" *Oxford Review* (1967): 16–17. For an earlier critique on my part of such Absolutism and anticonsequentialism, see my *Ethics Without God*, rev. ed. (Amherst, N.Y.: Prometheus Books, 1990), chapter 6, and my "Against Moral Conservatism," *Ethics* 82 (1972): 219–31.

47. Barry, *Liberty and Justice*, 73–74. See Paul Gomberg, "Consequentialism and History," *Canadian Journal of Philosophy* 19, no. 3 (September 1989): 383–404. For a brilliantly conceived short critique of utilitarianism coupled with a defense of consequentialism, see Will Kymlicka, *Contemporary Political Philosophy*, 9–49.

48. G. E. Moore, *Ethics* (London: Oxford University Press, 1912), 140.

49. Barry, *Liberty and Justice*, 74.

50. Ibid., 76.

51. Ibid., 75.

52. Again see the references in notes 11 and 41. I tried very simply to bring out the nonutilitarian side of my consequentialism in chapters 5 and 9 of my *Ethics Without God*.

53. Rawls's work is, of course, familiar. Scanlon's is less so. See his "Contractualism and Utilitarianism," in Sen and Williams, eds., *Utilitarianism and Beyond*, 103–28, and his unfortunately neglected "Rights, Goals and Fairness," in *Public and Private Morality*, ed. Stuart Hampshire (Cambridge: Cambridge University Press, 1978), 93–112.

54. Anscombe, "Modern Moral Philosophy."

55. I have argued the "moral side" of that in my *Ethics Without God* and in my *God and the Grounding of Morality*. For the cognitive, cosmological side—a side Anscombe, Donagan, MacIntyre, and many other traditionalists would take to be vital to really ground the moral side—I argue against that in fairly traditional ways in my *Reason and Practice* (New York: Harper and Row, 1970), 152–275. In less traditional ways, getting more to what I believe is the heart of the matter, I carry forward the argument in my *Skepticism* (New York: St. Martin's Press, 1973), *Contemporary Critiques of Religion* (London: Macmillan, 1973), *An Introduction to the Philosophy of Religion* (London: Macmillan, 1982), *Philosophy and Atheism* (Amherst, N.Y.: Prometheus Books, 1985), and *God, Skepticism and Modernity* (Ottawa, Ontario: University of Ottawa Press, 1989). See also J. L. Mackie, *The Miracle of Theism* (Oxford: Clarendon Press, 1982); and Keith M. Parsons, *God and the Burden of Proof* (Amherst, N.Y.: Prometheus Books, 1989). I also so argue in part 2, chapters 3 and 4 and again in part 4, of the present volume. For a companion piece to this chapter see my "Rights-Based Ethics: A Critique and Replacement," *The Windsor Yearbook of Access to Justice*, 14 (1994): 162–94.

Chapter Eight

On Eschewing Considered Judgments

I

In thinking about morality, including justice, we cannot avoid starting with considered judgments, including those very centrally and pervasively considered as moral. Many (perhaps most) of such judgments are independent of any moral theory we might be trying to articulate and defend. Instead, the theory in question must assume those very judgments as a "given to."[1] If someone does not acknowledge that it is a bad thing for there to be a society of superstitious, ill-fed, mistrustful people living in conditions of squalor, I do not know how to find feet with him. Any reasons I could give for saying those things are bad would be no stronger (no better established) than the judgment itself. If I am a tolerably good philosopher, I might be able to show how this considered judgment could fit into a pattern of coherence that has been called wide reflective equilibrium. I could perhaps show someone who professed to doubt such a considered judgment that given other things he also believes that he could not, if he wants to be consistent, not believe these things are bad. But if someone claims not to believe or accept such deeply embedded considered judgments, or truisms, there is little to be said to him except that he has a rather precarious grasp on what it is for something to be bad.

There is no standing free of considered judgments, including considered moral judgments, while still making sense of morality. If this be intuitionism, make the most of it, but it does not carry with it any of the epistemological and ontological baggage of what John Rawls calls *rational* intuitionism with its commitment to moral realism and a realm of moral truth.[2] Indeed, it is not intuitionism in the sense that has come down to us in the history of moral philosophy. One could be a noncognitivist in metaethics or an error theorist and accept all of what I have just said.

Similarly, if I kill someone simply to gain the few dollars he has in his wallet or beat up someone because I do not like his looks, lie to someone when I want to and think I can get away with it, or break my promises whenever it is convenient, I have done things that are morally wrong and anyone who does not acknowledge this just does not know what moral wrongness is. Again, considered judgments are central. They do not require intuitionism or natural law, though they are compatible with such doctrines when considering, if that is what we choose to do, their relationship to such arcane forms of epistemology and moral metaphysics, e.g., moral realism.

Again, similar things should be said for the distinctive moral wrongs that are injustices. Plain injustices exist where: it is acknowledged that there is no morally relevant difference between blacks and whites but the law still mandates the death penalty for a black murderer and long-term imprisonment for a white murderer; or, where it is acknowledged that there is no morally relevant difference between men and women, yet men are allowed to go to public bars unaccompanied while women are not; or, where there is no morally relevant difference between Jews and Catholics but the former are required to privately finance religious schools while the latter have their schools financed from state funds. Any theory of justice which did not recognize these injustices would itself be mistaken. We have more reason to be confident in accepting and sticking with these considered judgments than of accepting *any* moral theory which purports to show that they are not acceptable, or even that they are problematic, and that there is no injustice if these things are done. Again, we see the centrality, in taking morality seriously, of considered moral judgments.

We can analyze why these morally objectionable things are wrong in an attempt to explicate or articulate their wrongness by finding its underlying rationale as opposed to trying to prove they are wrong, or to justify a belief in their wrongness. As we do this analysis we come, as I argued in chapter 6, most obviously in the injustice cases, to the idea that morality requires impartiality. Justice, that is, requires the equal consideration of the interests and needs of everyone alike. It is this condition that we aspire to when structuring a system of just institutions.

We do not have justice, whether or not we can correctly view society as a cooperative venture or whether the resolutions of conflicts of interest involved in the justice-claim are to the mutual advantage of everyone involved, if the interests of *all* involved are *not* equally and impartially considered in that each person's needs and well-being is given at least *prima facie* equal weight. Even if the resolutions of conflicts of interest are to the mutual advantage of the parties involved, we do not have justice if the interests of all parties to the dispute are not given at least *prima facie* equal consideration. I am not claiming this is how justice has been conceived throughout history, but I am claiming that this is how we construe justice in modern societies such as our own. Such a general consideration itself is one of our considered judgments.

To translate this into the concrete, consider a group of capitalists who have possessed unshakable power for an extended period of time and a group of workers who have grown very, very dependent on them. If the capitalists use their very considerable power to drive home a harsh bargain that the workers will accept—indeed, will rationally accept—because they recognize that it is the best they can get, given their unequal bargaining positions, then the workers are not being treated justly, even though, as things stand, the bargain struck is mutually advantageous, i.e. each gets the best they can get given the unequal baseline from which they start. Agreements based on mutual advantage will be just agreements only if certain background conditions obtain. Perhaps the most important one is that the agents stand in roughly equal conditions of *power*. Here again, considered moral judgments or convictions play a central role in what I have just claimed.

II

Officially, David Gauthier, in contrast with what I have been claiming, eschews any appeal to considered judgments.[3] He develops an intricate, carefully reasoned and philosophically sophisticated form of neo-Hobbesianism where justice is construed as mutual advantage. Brian Barry, utilizing examples, though not only examples, and in effect appealing to considered judgments, thinks he can show that Gauthier's theory is plainly inadequate.[4] He points to the deeply counterintuitive conclusions of Gauthier's account of justice.[5] To highlight this, Barry cites two passages from Gauthier's *Morals by Agreement*. First: "the rich man may feast on caviar and champagne, while the poor woman starves at the gate. And she may not even take the crumbs from his table, if that would deprive him of his pleasure in feeding them to his birds."[6] Second: "Animals, the unborn, the congenitally handicapped, and defective fall beyond the pale of a morality tied to mutuality. The disposition to comply with moral constraints . . . may be rationally defended *only* within the scope of expected benefit."[7] Such vulnerable people have, on that account, no rights—there being no human or natural rights on such an account—and thus they have no moral standing. No rights accrue to people just by virtue of being human; there are no constraints that must be maintained toward them just because they are human beings. Where they are so utterly vulnerable, we can, without doing anything morally untoward, do with them what we will. We wouldn't be very charitable if we let them starve; or nice people if we bronzed them. Still, *on such an account*—on a morality tied to mutuality—we would not, if people capable of mutually advantageous bargaining did not just happen to dislike such behavior, violate the constraints of morality by so acting. This is so because such vulnerable people have no moral standing.[8] A has moral standing only if A is capable of entering into relations of *mutual benefit* with some other person B.

These are not just quirky judgments on Gauthier's part or the result of moral blindness. They are, as Barry shows, conclusions that Gauthier should draw given his *own moral theory*. In drawing them he is simply being consistent and nonevasive. He is being a good Hobbesian. Gauthier, again consistently, will have no truck with appealing to considered judgments, though, his official theory to the contrary notwithstanding, the subterranean pressure of considered judgments on him exerts itself in his remark that he finds such situations—the cases Barry cites and that I have just referred to—distressing.[9] That, however, is common sense mistakenly insinuating itself. *Given his theory*, Gauthier should not find them distressing. *He rationalistically trusts theory over intuition.*

Gauthier begins chapter 9 of his *Morals by Agreement* by quoting John Locke's remark that "a Hobbesist will not easily admit a great many duties of morality."[10] Gauthier, in a very general sense, sees himself as, and indeed is, a Hobbesian and is willing to bite Locke's bullet and to accept the repugnant conclusions of his own theory. He is willing to set aside as irrational those aspects of morality that conflict with his *theory*. They are, not infrequently, central elements of what Locke calls morality full stop; and what Gauthier conveniently rebaptizes "conventional morality." When aspects of what he calls "conventional morality" conflict with his theory, he rejects them. In an extremely important and revealing methodological remark Gauthier says:

> We shall find no simple fit, or lack of fit, between our theory and the supposedly "plain duties" of conventional morality. *Trusting theory rather than intuition*, we should advocate the view of social relationships sketched in this chapter without regard to the intellectual fashions of the moment. If the reader is tempted to object to some part of this view, on the ground that his moral intuitions are violated, then he should ask what weight such an objection can have, if morality is to fit within the domain of rational choice. We should emphasize the radical difference between our approach, in which we ask what view of social relationships should rationally be accepted *ex ante* by individuals concerned to maximize their utilities, from that of moral coherentists and defenders of "reflective equilibrium," who allow initial weight to our considered judgments.[11]

In a footnote linked with this passage, Gauthier cites a passage from Thomas Nagel's *Mortal Questions* as an able articulation of a view flatly contrary to the view underlying *Morals by Agreement*. He says of Nagel's methodological stance, I believe somewhat exaggeratedly, that there is no better account of such a contrary view.[12]

Let us see what this view looks like. Nagel remarks:

> I believe one should trust problems over solutions, intuitions over arguments, and pluralistic discord over systematic harmony. Simplicity and elegance are never reasons to think a philosophical theory is true: on the contrary, they are usually grounds for thinking it false.[13]

As the previous chapters make clear, I am one of those moral coherentists and defenders of reflective equilibrium that Gauthier refers to and aside from the fact that I do not think any *philosophical* theory is likely to even get in the ballpark of being true or for that matter false, I otherwise agree with the thrust of Nagel's passage. I trust intuitions (considered judgments) over theories, *when they clash or even appear to clash*. Elegance and simplicity in moral theory are very good reasons for suspecting the theory. Gauthier's remark, vis-à-vis the passage from Nagel, "Why should philosophy differ from science?" commits the fallacy of the complex question. We should for Kuhnian reasons be a little leery of thinking that science is so different. Still, and that aside, I think a reasonable case could be made for trusting theory in the hard sciences, e.g., chemistry, biology, and the like, but, given the controversy, the lack of progress, the absence of universally accepted paradigms, the culturally dependent parades of shifting fashion, etc., and *perhaps* for deeper conceptual reasons as well, there are good reasons for thinking that philosophy, moral theory, and perhaps even the human sciences are different from science, that is, *hard science*. We should, like Nagel, place more trust in such domains in intuition (reflective deeply embedded considered convictions) than in theory.[14]

However, for coherentists such as John Rawls, Norman Daniels, and myself, reflective equilibrium is not just a replay of commonsense morality. It leaves room, as we have seen, for both social theory and critique. But, *pace* Gauthier, there is no bypassing considered moral convictions or judgments.[15] A moral theory or an account of morality which massively overrides them must be mistaken. A theory which said that people who can make no contribution have no moral standing and that we can do with such people what we will without doing anything wrong must be mistaken. Our judgment that such treatment is evil far outweighs any theory, no matter how elegant and seemingly well argued it may be, which claims or attempts to support the premise that that treatment is not evil. We know, if that is the repugnant conclusion our theory drives us to, that we have to go back to the drawing board and rework our theory. If it entails these repugnant conclusions it cannot be

sound, and must be rejected, unless it can be revised without resorting to repugnant conclusions which deny our firmest considered moral convictions.

III

Gauthier, on Hendrik Hart's, Barry Allen's, and perhaps even Wesley Cragg's
typology, is a rationalist.[16] I am not. My trust in our deepest convictions and
my skepticism about theory should make this plain. Hart remarks: "His
[Nielsen's] favorite appeal to considered judgments strikes me as a willingness to allow other than rational factors into the rational arena for rational consideration, but not a preparedness to submit rational criteria to the constraints
of these considered judgments."[17] But that is exactly what I do. As demonstrated earlier, I put, as does Nagel, the allegedly rational criteria of rational
choice theory or more generally of any ethical theory to the test of being in
accordance with considered judgments. Where a theory is out of sync with a
considerable number of our considered judgments and where these considered
judgments are consistent with each other, then it is the theory which must be
abandoned or at least modified until it is compatible with those judgments.
(Here it is very important that our consistent pattern be in a *wide* reflective
equilibrium.)

For Gauthier, if our considered judgments clash with rational choice theory, then so much the worse for our considered judgments. As we have seen,
Gauthier believes that rational choice theory yields a mutual advantage theory of justice and that in turn entails that persons who cannot at least potentially contribute have no moral standing and thus they have no rights, and
without rights they stand outside the scope of justice and thus we owe them
nothing. If someone is so irredeemably enfeebled that he neither has con-
tributed nor can contribute in any cooperative scheme, we do nothing wrong,
if we have no considered anti-attitudes toward doing so, if we torture him,
bronze him, or let him starve on the streets.[18] Gauthier thinks (whether correctly or incorrectly, I do not pretend to judge) that that is the consequence of
rational choice theory and bites the bullet. Counterintuitive as it is to him, and
to us, we do nothing wrong if we do these things. We should trust our theory,
not our intuitions. That is a clear giving pride of place to reason, if anything
is. It is a clear case of being a rationalist in Hart's sense. And the above also
clearly shows that such rationalism is mistaken.

In contrast to Gauthier, I, like Nagel and Rawls, when faced with such a
circumstance, stick with intuitions (considered convictions). Here it is crucial
to see that what we are adhering to is not just an isolated intuition or cluster
of isolated intuitions but a cluster of deeply embedded intuitions integrally
linked with a critical mass of other intuitions and beliefs. If, in the grip of a

theory, we jettison this as merely "conventional morality," then we reject a lot of what is very central to our morality in order to keep faith with a particular reading of rational choice theory. *If* such a rationalism is the consequence of accepting rational choice theory, then it is plainly time to go back to square one and revise rational choice theory until it is formulated in such a way that it does not have such repugnant conclusions or, reject rational choice theory, *tout court*, if it cannot be so revised in these domains.

I am willing to say, given the deep counterintuitiveness of rational choice theory, that we should go on to look for, or, if necessary, to construct, another theory, perhaps a radically different kind of theory, a theory which in the traditional sense may not even be a *philosophical* theory at all. However, even without a theory we can, and we should, rely on such a critical mass of our considered convictions. We may have reasons, indeed perhaps even good reasons, to trust *both* theory and intuition, but where moral theory extensively conflicts with very firmly embedded intuitions, then the greater trust should go to the intuitions (considered convictions). Nagel's methodological instincts here are more reasonable and more plausible than Gauthier's. Sometimes, at least, it is reasonable not to be a rationalist.

In different contexts I have, again and again, said things bearing some family resemblance to this, though not in the course of discussing Gauthier's method, and this surely shows that I am prepared (*pace* Hart) "to submit rational criteria to the constraints of . . . considered judgments."[19] Gauthier is a rationalist in Hart's sense and so perhaps is Brian Barry, but I plainly am not.[20] I am even less of a rationalist than Thomas Nagel for I am far more skeptical of the truth tracking capacity of philosophy than Nagel is. It seems that my elective affinities here are with Wittgenstein and Rorty and, historically speaking, with Hume—or, at least Hume as Strawson reads him.[21] I am, in this respect, worlds apart from Hobbes, d'Holbach, and the tradition of Enlightenment *rationalism* as I am from contemporary utilitarians such as J. J. C. Smart, R. M. Hare, Peter Singer, and Richard Brandt and rational choice theorists like Gauthier, Jon Elster, and John Roemer. All of them reject considered judgments, coherentism, and the reliance on context and history which I believe are requirements of an adequate articulated understanding of morality.

It is perhaps fair enough to say that one important thing that a moral theory would do, including, of course, a theory of justice, is to give us a model to use in coming to an understanding of morality, but it would have, to be an adequate model of morality, to be a model of something we could *antecedently* recognize to be morality. A model, in certain respects, is like a map. (I say "in certain respects," for in other respects, not relevant to what I argue here, they are importantly different.) A map of (say) Prince Edward Island which did not enable us to recognize where the sea starts and the land ends, denote the bays and rivers, provide distinguishable markings for the differing terrain, and indicate where the cities, towns, and villages are located would be a very inadequate map indeed. Different maps constructed for different purposes would latch on to different features of Prince Edward Island, but a map which failed to delineate any of the salient features of the island, features that were recognizable and identifiable independently, would not be a bad map but no map at all.

Similarly, a model of morality that represented no salient features of morality, independently recognized and identified as such, would not be a bad model of morality, it would be no model of morality at all. Considered judg-ments locate salient features of morality, including the things which are just and the rights we have. To bypass them is simply to bypass morality. A model that does so, whatever else it models, does not model morality. *Pace* Gauthier, it is rational choice theory, not coherentism and the appeal to considered judgments, which is held captive "to the intellectual fashions of the moment."[22] Wide reflective equilibrium sticks with the often messy, thickly textured reality of morality. It tries clearly to display it, and to show how we should proceed in both explaining the rationale and in articulating the justificatory basis of basic moral structures. It seeks to display morality's underlying rationale, as well as its dissonances. By its own use moral structures can be clearly seen: if you will, clearly modeled.

IV

Wide reflective equilibrium is, however, not a defense of conventional morality. This can be seen in the work of Rawls, Scanlon, Daniels, and Barry and in my work, including my "Rights and Consequences: It All Depends."[23] All of these accounts appeal (some more explicitly than others) to a coherentist method, which, at least in effect, more specifically, utilizes what has been called an appeal to considered judgments in wide reflective equilibrium. The consequentialism articulated in my previous chapter utilizes considered judgments as an integral element. This might be thought to be a jarring element in such a picture for most contemporary consequentialists (Hare, Smart, Singer, and Brandt) will have no more truck with considered judgments than does Gauthier. It might, of course, have led me to drop consequentialism, but, in fact it led me to accept it and utilize a version of it.

Absolutism would, I believe, wither away if people would resolutely use the method of appealing to considered judgments in wide reflective equilibrium. We must, of course, start by seeing things by our own lights. We start in moral domains with, among other things, our moral judgments (convictions). Yet we need not, and indeed should not, end there. We are not held captive to any particular considered judgment or limited cluster of considered judgments; none are unquestionable at least in principle and none are foundational. The method of wide reflective equilibrium with its commitment to maximizing coherence is itself self-correcting. In this respect, it is similar to Charles Peirce's and John Dewey's conception of scientific method.[24]

By using this method, as I argued in the previous chapter, we can show that none of the considered convictions should be given an Absolutist reading such that there could be some rights-claims which could never, even in principle, be rightly overridden. Rights, of course, cannot be routinely overridden, or they would not be rights, but in extreme situations, where not overriding them would cause extensive harm, they can be rightly overridden. However, in being overridden, as we have seen in the previous chapter, they are not thereby forfeited and they will remain inalienable, particularly if they are human rights.[25]

There are moral rights (natural rights or human rights) both specific and very general, but they are not unconditional rights. Whether they are to be acted in accordance with in a particular situation depends on what the actual circumstances and the consequences are. The recognition of this does not at all depend, à la Bentham, J. J. C. Smart, or Gauthier, on the setting aside of an appeal to considered judgments, but goes with the very coherentism that Gauthier wrongly identifies with the acceptance of, and the sticking with, conventional morality. However, in my use of wide reflective equilibrium there is no such sticking with conventional morality. The anti-Absolutism and weak consequentialism that I developed goes with the careful employment of the method of wide reflective equilibrium. We start with central elements of our commonsense moral beliefs—if you will, the moral intuitions of our tribe—but, in maximizing coherence until we achieve wide reflective equilibrium, we pass to a *critical* morality that sets aside the Absolutism of *commonsense* morality (*if* indeed that is *commonsense* morality) without embracing relativism.[26] Not one of our considered convictions must be acted on come what may, none have a categorical prescriptivity, but many, for all of that, are reliable norms and, as such, reasonable guides for action. Appeal to considered moral judgments, the coherentism of wide reflective equilibrium, weak consequentialism, and critical morality go together like hand and glove.

NOTES

1. I take the notion of a "given to" from E. W. Hall. It should not be confused with an appeal to "the given," as in C. I. Lewis, Roderick Chisholm, or A. J. Ayer. It is the idea that any philosophical account or philosophical system can never be self-contained and will at some point, as R. Carnap recognized when he spoke of considerations and questions external to the framework, appeal, either explicitly or, more typically, implicitly, to some external ground or basis of judgment for the philosophical account. Russell's appeal

to logic, Moore's appeal to common sense, Malcolm's appeal to ordinary language are cases in point. What is "given to" is what philosophers, in assessing their own accounts, or the accounts of others, finally appeal to or rely on. *Philosophy, in fine, is not self-contained, yielding its own warrant.* E.W. Hall, *Philosophical Systems: A Categorial Analysis* (Chicago, Ill.: University of Chicago Press, 1960), 138–64. See also Kai Nielsen, "On There Being Philosophical Knowledge," *Theoria* 56, part 3 (1990): 193–225. However, even here, someone particularly influenced by a Davidsonian holism with its rejecting of the third dogma of empiricism (the scheme/content dichotomy), will worry about (1) this internal/external division, (2) any talk about what is "finally appealed to" (as if we had any understanding of what it would be like, in any more than a pragmatic sense, to have the last word), and (3) will recognize that it is in the very nature of the philosophical game that any external perspective can be legitimately challenged—there being no premises that just must be accepted in philosophy. Perhaps it should be responded that there is at least a kind of historicized fallibilistic given to: something which is always in principle at least challengeable but often for a time unchallenged. Russell and Carnap accept the authority of logic, Patricia Churchland and Paul Churchland the authority of science, C. S. Peirce and J. Dewey the authority of scientific method, T. Reid and G. E. Moore the authority of common sense, G. Ryle and N. Malcolm the authority of ordinary language. For these authors, as in the practice of other philosophers, philosophical claims which are not in accordance with their particular given to are rejected as mistaken. (Sometimes, to complicate matters, philosophers, particularly when they do not realize they have a given to, have more than one given to and no pecking order between them or specification of different domains where these different given tos apply.) But they all recognize, if they have a reasonably sensitive philosophical understanding, that there is something self-reflexive here, for philosophy allows—and as a matter of philosophy—that there is no permanent and unquestionable Archimedean point or squarification base—a given to—for philosophy. But, all that notwithstanding, there can be, for a time and for a certain culture, certain resting places that are deemed more plausible than others. There is no escaping a thoroughgoing historicism. But historicism is one thing; relativism or an attitude of "anything goes" is another.

2. John Rawls, "Kantian Constructivism in Moral Theory: The Dewey Lectures, 1980," *Journal of Philosophy* 77, no. 9 (September 1980): 554–72; and Kai Nielsen, "John Rawls's New Methodology: An Interpretive Account," *McGill Law Journal* 35, no. 3 (May 1990): 572–600.

3. David Gauthier, *Morals by Agreement* (Oxford: Clarendon Press, 1986), 217–19, 268–70; David Gauthier, *Moral Dealing* (Ithaca, N.Y.: Cornell University Press, 1990), 168–70, 270.

4. Brian Barry, *Theories of Justice: A Treatise on Social Justice*, vol. 1 (Berkeley, Calif.: University of California Press, 1989), 249–54, 295–96, 362–64.

5. See also Allen Buchanan, "Justice as Reciprocity versus Subject-Centered Justice," *Philosophy and Public Affairs* 19, no. 31 (Summer 1990): 227–52. Barry and Buchanan have both argued in a broadly similar fashion.

6. See note 3, *Morals by Agreement*, 218.

7. Ibid., 268 (emphasis added).

8. Gauthier's account is generally and powerfully Hobbesian. Yet, in describing the state of nature and in appealing to the Lockean proviso, Gauthier falls from Hobbesian grace and, more like John Locke and Robert Nozick, gets, in effect, very intuitionistic and distant from his usual tough-minded Hobbesianism. I stick here with the Hobbesian Gauthier rather than the tender-minded Lockean one of the proviso. A good expression of his

Hobbesian attitude is the following: "We are not concerned with reflective equilibrium. Although it would be surprising, did no commonly recognized moral constraints relate to mutually beneficial cooperation, yet traditional morality as such may be no more than a ragbag of views lacking any single coherent rationale. My account of morality does not attempt to refute our ordinary views, but rather to provide constraint with a firm foundation in rational choice." Gauthier, *Moral Dealing*, 270. For a critique of Gauthier's appeal to the Lockean proviso, see Michael Milde, *Gauthier, Rawls and the Social Contract in Contemporary Political Philosophy* (unpublished doctoral dissertation, The University of Calgary, 1992), chapter 4.

    9. Gauthier, *Morals by Agreement*, 218.

    10. Ibid., 268.

    11. Ibid. *(*emphasis mine).

    12. Ibid., 269.

    13. Thomas Nagel, *Mortal Questions* (Cambridge: Cambridge University Press, 1979), x.

    14. For some of the deeper, putatively conceptual reasons, see Peter Winch, *The Idea of a Social Science* (London: Routledge and Kegan Paul, 1958); and Charles Taylor, *Philosophical Papers,* vol. 2 (Cambridge: Cambridge University Press, 1985), 15–151.

    15. John Rawls, *A Theory of Justice* (Cambridge, Mass.: Harvard University Press, 1971), 19–21, 48–51, 577–87; John Rawls, "The Independence of Moral Theory," *Proceedings and Addresses of the American Philosophical Association* 47 (1974/75): 7–10; Norman Daniels, "Wide Reflective Equilibrium and Theory Acceptance in Ethics," *Journal of Philosophy* 76 (1979); Norman Daniels, "Reflective Equilibrium and Archimedean Points," *Canadian Journal of Philosophy* 10 (March 1980); Norman Daniels, "Two Approaches to Theory Acceptance in Ethics" in *Morality, Reason, and Truth*, ed. David Copp and David Zimmerman (Totowa, N.J.: Rowman and Allenheld, 1985); and Kai Nielsen, *After the Demise of the Tradition* (Boulder, Colo.: Westview Press, 1991), chapters 9–11.

    16. Hendrik Hart, "Whither Reason and Religion?" in *Search for Community in a Withering Tradition,* ed. Kai Nielsen and Hendrik Hart (Lanham, N.Y.: University Press of America, 1990), 148–235; Barry Allen, "Atheism, Relativism, and Critical Theory" and Wesley Cragg, "Reflections on *Search for Community in a Withering Tradition,*" both in a symposium of the Canadian Philosophical Association, May 25, 1993, Charlottetown, Prince Edward Island.

    17. Hart, "Whither Reason and Religion?" 159.

    18. Considered pro and con attitudes are the dispositional form of Gauthier's considered preferences. It might be said that there is not such a great distance between considered preferences, on the one hand, and considered judgments or considered convictions on the other. If someone doesn't have certain attitudes, certain preferences, there is in certain contexts no definitive showing him to be mistaken in moral matters, just as (it might be claimed) if someone does not have certain considered convictions, there is no definitive showing him wrong in certain contexts in moral matters. Both Rawls and Gauthier appeal to certain, logically speaking, contingent nonrational but not irrational factors in moral reasoning. Why, then, is it legitimate for Rawls to appeal to considered judgments or convictions but not for Gauthier to appeal to considered preferences? One important difference is that convictions or judgments are not just matters of feeling or dispositions to feel, as are preferences and attitudes. Rawls is not appealing to what people on reflection like or dislike. What we like and dislike may be irrelevant to what is right and wrong. But this *may* be an illusion, as the long tradition of subjectivism and noncognitivism in

ethics has argued. It is, however, not so obvious that what we approve of and disapprove of are in the same boat as what we like or dislike. On attitudes, see P. H. Nowell-Smith, *Ethics* (London: Penguin Books, 1954) and C. L. Stevenson's much misunderstood, undervalued, and often caricatured account of their role, *Ethics and Language* (New Haven, Conn.: Yale University Press, 1944); his "Ethical Fallibility," in *Ethics and Society,* ed. Richard T. De George (Garden City, N.Y.: Anchor Books, 1966), 188–217; and his "The Scientist's Role and the Aims of Education," in *Philosophy and Education,* ed. Israel Scheffler (Boston, Mass.: Allyn and Bacon, 1958), 43–50.

19. See Kai Nielsen: *After the Demise of the Tradition* (Boulder, Colo.: Westview Press, 1991); "On There Being Philosophical Knowledge," *Theoria* 56, part 3 (1990): 193–225; "Can There Be Justified Philosophical Beliefs?" *Iyyun* 40 (July 1991): 235–70; and in Kai Nielsen, *Transforming Philosophy* (Boulder, Colo.: Westview Press, 1995).

20. See how Barry waffles on considered judgments in Barry, *Theories of Justice,* 271–92.

21. P. F. Strawson, *Skepticism and Naturalism* (London: Methuen, 1985), 10–30. See also David Pears, *Hume's System* (Oxford: Oxford University Press, 1990).

22. David Gauthier, *Morals by Agreement,* 269.

23. See Kai Nielsen "Rights and Consequences: It All Depends," *Canadian Journal of Law and Society* 7, no. 1 (1992). See also chapter 7 of this volume.

24. See Kai Nielsen, "Peirce, Pragmatism and the Challenge of Postmodernism," *Transactions of the Peirce Society* 29, no. 4 (Fall, 1993): 513–60. See also chapter 2 of this volume.

25. Joel Feinberg, *Rights, Justice, and the Bounds of Liberty* (Princeton, N.J.: Princeton University Press, 1980), 143–55.

26. See all the following by Kai Nielsen: "John Rawls's New Methodology: An Interpretive Account," *McGill Law Journal* 35, no. 3 (1990): 573–601; "Rawls Revising Himself: A Political Conception of Justice," *Archiv für Rechts und Socialphilosophie* 76 (1990): 439–56; "Rawls and the Socratic Ideal," *Analyse and Kritik* 13, no. 1 (1991): 67–93; and *After the Demise of the Tradition,* 195–248.

Chapter Nine

There Is No Dilemma of Dirty Hands

I

I turn now to the moral and political problem of dirty hands. In doing so, I deploy in my discussion and further characterize the method of ethics, with its appeal to considered judgments, and with its distinctive kind of consequentialism, that I elucidated in previous chapters. Politicians, and others as well, sometimes—or so at least it is often argued—must take horrible (at least normally completely unacceptable) measures to avoid even worse evils. They must, that is, sometimes dirty their hands to do what is right. When, if ever, are they justified in doing that? And in doing that are they guilty of committing moral crimes?

I shall take an austere line about the problem of dirty hands. Treating it principally as a moral problem for political leaders and for other political and moral agents as well, I shall argue that what should be done, in the horrifying circumstances in which problems of dirty hands arise with the greatest urgency, is to, where that is possible, always seek to do the lesser evil. The choice here, where there is a choice, is not between good and evil, right and wrong, but between evil and evil or, if you will, between wrong and wrong. It is a truism, though for all of that true, that we should avoid evil altogether if we can. But often we cannot. Where we cannot, and yet when we still have some *lebensraum* to act, we should choose what we have the best reason to believe is the lesser evil.[1]

Anyone in such a circumstance with an ounce of humanity will feel anguish in so acting and very deep remorse for having so acted or for condoning such acts. It is not that he should just feel saddened over such acts. Tha⁺

is hardly an appropriate response. Indeed someone who did not feel anguish and remorse in such situations would hardly count as a moral agent. But in so acting or in condoning such acts such an agent is not guilty of wrong doing, he has (*pace* Michael Walzer) committed no moral crime, though, psychologically speaking, it is perhaps inevitable that he will feel guilty.[2] But to *feel* guilty is not necessarily *to be* guilty. Plenty of people feel guilty without being guilty and plenty of others are guilty without feeling guilty. The connection is a contingent one. Where our choice is inescapably a choice between evils—where there is no third possibility—we should, as responsible moral and political agents, batten down the hatches and try to do the lesser evil. Jean-Paul Sartre's character Hoederer in his play *Dirty Hands* is exemplary: a paradigm of what a morally committed political agent should be in the world in which he found himself. In dirty-hands situations to Pontius-Pilate-like-wash—try to wash—one's-hands-of-the-whole-affair, to say that it is none of my business, my hands are clean, is impossible, where some choice on our part might make a difference. We do not escape responsibility by so acting, failing to act in such a circumstance being itself an action. We, by so refraining, dirty our hands just as much, and perhaps more, than does a person who resolutely acts to achieve the lesser evil, though in doing so he does horrible things.

It is a conceptual confusion with unfortunate moral residues to describe the problem of dirty hands as Michael Walzer, Bernard Williams, and Thomas Nagel do.[3] They start out on what seems to me to be the right track by contending that even when our political ends are the noblest of ends, it is sometimes true that to succeed in politics, political leaders, and not infrequently others as well, must get their hands dirty. That is, they will have to do things or condone the doing of things which in normal circumstances at least would be utterly morally impermissible. Moreover, it is sometimes right to try to succeed even in those circumstances and thus it must be right in those circumstances to get our hands dirty. To not so act would be irresponsible and immoral, or at least a not inconsiderable moral failing, on the part of those political actors. Walzer et al. get off the track—or so at least I shall argue—when they maintain that we are caught in a paradox here. This very paradox, they take it, is the problem of dirty hands. Walzer puts it thus:

> sometimes it is right to try to succeed, and then it must be right to get one's hands dirty. But one's hands get dirty from doing what it is wrong to do. And how can it be wrong to do what is right? Or, how can we get our hands dirty by doing what we ought to do?[4]

In certain circumstances—Hoederer-like circumstances—political agents, Walzer et al. have it, *must do wrong to do right*. But that, *if* not a contradiction, is at least a paradox. *One cannot—seemingly logically cannot—do what is right by doing what is wrong.*

However, this—or so at least I shall argue—is a mistaken way to conceptualize things. Where, *whatever we do, or fail to do, leads to the occurrence of evil or sustains it, we do not do wrong, everything considered, by doing the lesser evil. Indeed, we do what, everything considered, is the right thing to do; the thing we ought, through and through ought, in this circumstance, to do.* In doing what we ought to do we cannot (*pace* Walzer et al.) do wrong. We do things that in normal circumstances would be horribly wrong, but in these circumstances of dirty hands, they are not *everything considered wrong.* It is difficult enough in such situations to ascertain what the lesser evil is and to steel ourselves, where we are the agents who must so act, to do it, without, by adding insult to injury, making artificially and confusedly, a conceptual and moral dilemma out of it as well.

II

It is a mistake to say that this is just the same old utilitarianism all over again and that, as we all know very well by now, utilitarianism is mistaken: a thoroughly inadequate moral and normative political theory. We can not use that to dismiss the way I am arguing about dirty hands. In the contexts described, the above conception of always doing the lesser evil, is, of course, *compatible* with utilitarianism, but does not *require* it. However, it may require, or at least its clear articulation will be facilitated by what I have, following Brian Barry, characterized as *weak consequentialism.*[5] But this view, as we have seen, is compatible with accepting, as I do and as Barry does as well, a *roughly* Rawlsian conception of justice as fairness, where in addition to Pareto-optimality an independent principle of just distribution is required for the structuring of our institutions, if they are to be morally acceptable institutions. But, unlike Rawls, I am not saying that, morally speaking, considerations of justice always override considerations of utility.[6] Normally they do, but, again, as we have seen in the previous chapter, in certain extreme situations they do not. We should not—morally should not—Michael Kohlhaas-style, do justice though the heavens fall.[7]

However, what I am committed to denying, with such a conception, is that there are any absolute side-constraints that must always, where they apply, determine what we are to do no matter what the consequences. The serious moral and political problem over dirty hands is not over some trumped-up moral dilemma rooted in conceptual confusion, and perhaps even in moral evasiveness as well, but over whether it is the case that moral agents, including sensitive and aware moral agents, acting in the political sphere, who have taken Machiavelli's lessons to heart, should always do, or try to do, the lesser evil in inescapably dirty-hands situations or whether instead they should follow Leszek Kolakowski, and a host of others, in believing that we must always stick with such putatively absolute side-constraints, no matter what.[8] I shall argue, against Kolakowskian Absolutism, that that is not the way to have clean hands. It is rather a way of evasively and irresponsibly dirtying our hands even more than we would by resolutely and intelligently seeking, in such circumstances, to do or assent to the lesser evil.

In many, perhaps most, circumstances, we cannot ascertain what the lesser evil is and, in such circumstances, we should be *morally conservative.* This is particularly evident where it is possible not to act in such a circumstance: where inaction is not itself a form of action. There we should not do things which would in normal circumstances plainly be horrendous. Where doing nothing is possible (and not in effect a taking sides on the issue in question) and where, as well, doing what we only have a hunch is the lesser evil, would be the doing of something that, if it were not the lesser evil, would be horrendous, then we should not do it. In such a circumstance, we should not risk doing something that normally is an unquestionably evil thing to do. In that respect, and in that context, moral conservativism is a good thing.

Similarly, where the foreseen consequences of our proposed actions or policies are opaque, and careful reasoning and investigation will not make them tolerably clear, then we should, in most circumstances, stick with the normal moral verities, i.e., our firmest considered convictions. But the probable consequences are not always that opaque and, moreover, and more crucially, in some circumstances, even where they are so opaque, and it is also evident enough that we do considerable evil, *no matter what we do or fail to do,* then, in such trying circumstances, we should act on our best hunches about where the lesser evil lies, even when our best hunches are not very good. Where so acting is a moral necessity, moral action is traumatic. There is no escaping anxiety and anguish here. This in some circumstances is just what the moral life is like. But to try to do nothing—as understandable as it is—is, in most circumstances of this sort, deeply morally evasive, though there is the phenomena of how much we can expect from human beings, including, of course, ourselves. It is not very reasonable to expect, or to try to require, for the status of moral agency, people to be saints or heroes. But, again, people who can and do so act are morally admirable. Their actions are often so supererogatory that we can hardly say of others that they *ought* to so act, let alone that they *must* so act. That is both morally sanctimonious and unreasonable. But that does not gainsay the fact that each of us, when we reflect on what we as individuals should do in such situations, will, if we are reasonably clearheaded, hold out, as *ideal,* for ourselves, that this is what we should do, if only we can summon up enough courage to so act. Some of Jean-Paul Sartre's and Bertolt Brecht's moral heroes are persons who, though not without anguish and remorse, act resolutely in dirty-hands circumstances. I think, if we will carefully reflect on what morality is, they will be our heroes and our exemplars, too, even where we do not share Sartre's and Brecht's background politics.

III

It might be thought that I am begging questions and sweeping things under the rug with my conception of the lesser evil. I am just implicitly assuming, it might be argued, that the lesser evil is what results in the least harm (the fewer deaths, the lesser misery, pain, undermining of self-respect, autonomy, security, and the like). But, the objection will continue, the "lesser evil" may not be that, but the *not* doing of certain things—e.g., not violating someone's rights, not administering of unjust laws, not taking (let alone the shooting of) hostages, not refusing to take prisoners, not lying, and the like—in short, the not doing of these plain moral evils. Where any of these rights violations that go with the doing of these forbidden things occur, we have a greater evil than if they do not. Suffering and misery are bad, but rights violations are even worse.

It seems to me that this is an implausible response. Sometimes violating someone's rights may avert a catastrophe. And then, it seems to me, their rights should be violated. But there are other sorts of examples that drive home my point as well. Even when under the Nazis it became apparent that he would be required to administer abhorrent (and thoroughly abhorrent to him as well) Nazi racial laws, a German judge, appointed during the Weimar republic, might rightly not resign. He does not resign because he realizes that he might very well in the discriminatory way he applied these vile laws be able to save lives that would not have been saved if he had been replaced by a Nazi hack. And, to move to a still different example, shooting some hostage, and threatening to shoot some others, might prevent the sacking and putting to the sword of a whole village or at least give the villagers time to flee. (Remember here, Bertolt Brecht, as well as Karl Marx, on the Paris Commune.) It seems to me that there is no serious question where the lesser evil lies in such comparisons, e.g., violating someone's rights to prevent a massacre. The violating of a person's rights is there plainly a lesser evil. It is blind rights worship or rule worship not to see that.

IV

The view I take here, as I remarked, is compatible with utilitarianism, but it does not require it, for it is also compatible with a pluralistic deontological view of the familiar and sophisticated sort set forth by W. D. Ross and C. D.

Broad. For them we start with a collection of familiar prima facies duties. But these prima facies duties are just that, namely prima facies duties. They not infrequently conflict with each other and, in such situations, we must just come to appreciate, in the particular situation in question, which of these conflicting prima facies duties is, in that situation, our *actual* duty. There is, for such deontologists, no overriding moral rule or moral principle—no categorical imperative, no lexical ordering of prima facies duties—which will tell us in any situation what we must do. They, no more than utilitarians, appeal to any absolute moral prohibitions that we must always act in accordance with come what may. My account, however, is incompatible with Kant's Absolutism about particular moral principles or Elizabeth Anscombe's and Alan Donagan's Christian Absolutism, which maintains that there are some things —some particular things—that must never be done no matter how much evil results from our not doing them. But in rejecting such Absolutism, I am not saying anything that for us now is at all iconoclastic or even unusual. Williams, Walzer, and Nagel no more accept such an Absolutism than do I. But I am trying to think through such a non-Absolutism consistently, while still starting, as they do, too, with our considered convictions and continuing to take them seriously, realizing that they are a rock-bottom court of appeal, in moral deliberation.

V

In so reasoning, I utilize, as we have seen perhaps ad nauseum, the justificatory method of an appeal to our considered judgments in wide reflective equilibrium (a thoroughly holistic form of coherentism) and I appeal, consistently with that coherentism to consequences.[9] But my consequentialism is, as I remarked, a weak consequentialism that does not commit me to utilitarianism. I shall now, briefly, expanding a bit on what I said in previous chapters, explain my consequentialism.

As we have seen, there are certain things, Absolutism has it, that we must never do no matter what the consequences of not doing these things are. It will forbid certain kinds of actions, even if they will produce lesser overall harm than the other alternatives. Torturing someone, for example, can, on such an account, never be justified. My *weak* consequentialism, by contrast, neither affirms nor denies that sometimes an individual may rightly refrain from doing that which will have, or may be reasonably expected to have, the *best* overall consequences, everything considered. I do not (*pace* G.E. Moore) argue that we have a duty to try to produce or secure the greatest overall good; I do not argue that we have a duty or an obligation to do our best to achieve either the greatest average utility in the world or the greatest total utility. I refrain, as contemporary utilitarians do not, from making such strong claims. Weak consequentialism is most usefully seen as a negative doctrine that denies (*pace* Elizabeth Anscombe and Alan Donagan) that it is possible to specify a list of act-descriptions which in terms of their very description can be recognized in all circumstances to be the wrong thing to do, where the wrong in question is an everything considered wrong. My *weak* consequentialism rejects such Absolutism and asserts, rather, that it all depends. Acts of a kind which we are inclined to believe would always be wrong (wrong everything considered) might very well not be if the circumstances were altered and the consequences were very different than they usually are. *There are no acts, such a consequentialism avows, that we can rightly say never should be done without taking into consideration their circumstances and consequences.* And with such consideration of circumstances and consequences our judgments concerning whether they can rightly be done in some particular circumstances may shift.

"Weak consequentialists," as Brian Barry puts it, "hold that there is no class of cases, definable in advance, such that the consequences are never relevant to the question of what is the right thing to do."[10] By contrast, strong consequentialism holds that there is at all times a duty to act so as to maximize the amount of good in the world. More generally, consequentialism, characterized sufficiently broadly so that it will cover both weak and strong consequentialism, should be conceptualized as follows: the morality of any action is to be judged by its consequences, or in part by its consequences, and not just, or perhaps even at all, by what the action is apart from its consequences. Weak consequentialism takes the two weaker alternatives in the above characterization; strong consequentialism, the stronger alternatives. Both deny that there are any actions, just in virtue of what they are, apart from considering their consequences, their circumstances, and their relations to other actions, that just must be done or avoided *sans phrase*.

Pace Absolutism, there can be no justified *categorical denials of permission to act to avoid the lesser evil*. There are no such *categorical prescriptivities* which are justified. My defense, in dirty-hands situations of doing the lesser evil even when that evil is very considerable indeed, cannot be defeated by arguing that my consequentialism commits me to utilitarianism, as any consequentialism does (or so the claim goes), that is consistent. There can be forms of consistent nonutilitarian consequentialism.[11] We can reject the inflexibility of moral Absolutism without ending up in the straightjacket of utilitarianism. Still, with the type of appeal to consequences that I have defended, we can attend to important factors of context, circumstance, and situation without committing ourselves to utilitarianism. We need not go from one inflexibility to another.

VI

Even where (if ever that obtains) the government truly represents the people, there still may be dirty work for it to do and in such a circumstance the dirty work is ours [12] When, if ever, is it, everything considered, morally justified? My answer is that it is justified where the dirty work cannot be avoided without there remaining or resulting still greater evil, everything considered, than would obtain without the government so acting. In such circumstances its "dirty work" is morally justified and so we have the scare quotes. If that situation does not obtain, then the dirty work is not justified and should not be morally condoned.

This doctrine is generally thought to be both too simple and too morally insensitive to be right. Is smacks, even if not strictly utilitarian, too much, it is often thought, of the spirit of utilitarian calculation. In the gloss I have given it in the previous sections, I have tried to show that it is neither too simple nor morally insensitive nor committed to utilitarianism or to simply relying on utilitarian calculation. In so arguing I am running against a rather persistent orthodoxy over the problem of dirty hands articulated in sophisticated forms in some of the writings of Bernard Williams, Thomas Nagel, and Michael Walzer.[13] Michael Walzer's "Political Action: The Problem of Dirty Hands" is a particularly developed and reflective statement of such a view.[14] I argue in this final part of this chapter that we are not caught in the dilemma that Walzer and others think we are caught in and that he has misconceptualized the problem.

Walzer believes, as does Nagel, that sometimes we must choose between two courses of action both of which it would be wrong for us to undertake. This obtains wherever we must choose between acting in accordance with some important moral principle and avoiding some looming disaster. Here we have the stuff of moral tragedy. Walzer remarks that "a particular act of government . . may be exactly the right thing to do in utilitarian terms and yet leave the man who does it guilty of a moral wrong"(161).* But it becomes clear from what he says later that Walzer, like Nagel, could, and in effect does, drop the above "in utilitarian terms" and claims, more generally, that a particular act or policy of a government could be exactly the right thing for it to do *full stop* and yet leave the people who carry out the act or the government policy guilty of a grave moral wrong. It is this claim I am resisting. For me the dirty-hands *dilemma*, psychological anguish to the contrary not withstanding, is unreal. There are indeed problems about when to take normally unacceptable means, but there is no resulting moral or conceptual dilemma.

---

*See full reference to Walzer in endnote 2. Future references to Walzer will be given in the text.

For Walzer, Nagel, and Williams, the alleged dilemma is thought to be very real. As Walzer puts it, the very "notion of dirty hands derives from an effort to refuse 'absolutism' without denying the reality of the moral dilemma" (162). I want to argue that this position, psychologically attractive as it is, is incoherent. It just does, in Walzer's phrase, "pile confusion upon confusion" (162).

To act politically, particularly if you are a political leader, is to put yourself into a position where you might be required to do terrible things (165). Walzer works carefully with a key example—indeed, a realistic and not a desert-island example—that he believes will strikingly confirm his account of how a morally committed politician can be caught in a moral dilemma in which *he must do wrong to do right.* I think it is a key example, indeed a perfect example, for the discussing of such issues, though I shall argue that his moral dilemma account of it is mistaken and that in his commentary on his example Walzer misdescribes and misconceptualizes what is involved.

I shall first quote his own stating of his sample—his paradigm case—in full, then describe his discussion of it, and then finally try to make good my claim that he misconceptualizes the matter. His case is:

> consider a politician who has seized upon a national crisis—a prolonged colonial war—to reach power. He and his friends win office pledged to decolonization and peace; they are honestly committed to both, though not without some sense of the advantages of the commitment. In any case, they have no responsibility for the war; they have steadfastly opposed it. Immediately the politician goes off to the colonial capital to open negotiations with the rebels. But the capital is in the grip of a terrorist campaign, and the first decision the leader faces is this: he is asked to authorize the torture of a captured rebel leader who knows or probably knows the location of a number of bombs hidden in apartment buildings around the city, set to go off within the next twenty four hours. He orders the man tortured, convinced that he must do so for the sake of the people who might otherwise die in the explosions—even though he believes that torture is wrong, indeed abominable, not just sometimes but always. He had expressed this belief often and angrily during his own campaign; the rest of us took it as a sign of his goodness. How should we regard him now? (How should he regard himself?) (166–77)

Let us assume, as I assume Walzer assumes, that there was no other way of defusing the bombs or otherwise effectively cancelling their effects, that there was no other way of extracting the information from the rebel leader in time or otherwise gaining the relevant information, and that the torture ordered was no more severe or prolonged than necessary to get the information in time and that afterwards the rebel leader was promptly and humanely cared for. Given all this, and the case as described, both Walzer and I believe that the politician should order the torture. But Walzer believes it is a case of, on the politician's part, of his doing wrong, indeed committing a moral crime, in order to do right, while I do not.

Walzer remarks:

> When he ordered the prisoner tortured, he committed a moral crime and he accepted a moral burden. Now he is a guilty man. His willingness to acknowledge and bear (and perhaps repent and do penance for) his guilt is evidence, and it is the only evidence he can offer us, both that he is not too good for politics and that he is good enough. Here is the moral politician: it is by his dirty hands that we know him. If he were a moral man and nothing else, his hands would not be dirty: if he were a politician and nothing else, he would pretend that they were clean. (167–68)

This seems to me the wrong way to think about the case and about the morally committed politician forced by circumstances to do such a terrible thing. Walzer will have it that our conscientious and morally committed politician in ordering torture has committed a moral crime. This politician, if he is morally serious, will know that and "he will not merely feel, he will know that he is guilty (and we will know it too), though he may also believe (and we may agree) that he has good reasons" for so acting (174).

Let me first point out where there are important areas of agreement between Walzer and myself. In doing that I will clear the decks. The belief that torture is wrong and *always* wrong is something we both share. I view that belief as one of our most deeply embedded and firmest considered moral convictions. It is not a conviction we, if we are moral agents, are about to, or even can, abandon. And we also agree that that considered conviction and indeed any considered conviction—any deeply embedded moral principle—can be rightly overridden "to avoid consequences that are both imminent and almost certainly disastrous" (171). The torturing case is a good example of where that condition obtains. In addition, we both believe that, where the rules or principles articulating these considered convictions are overridden, and where they are, as they sometimes are, rightly overridden, that still should be a painful process. When, in the case in question, the conscientious politician, after soul-searching, orders the torture to avoid the loss of many lives, including the plainly innocent lives of children, his decision to do so still will leave "pain behind, and should do so, even after the decision has been made" (174). He will, if he is a decent human being, feel that acutely.

About all these things we agree. Where we disagree is over his claim that the man knows he had done something wrong, that he has committed a moral crime, that he is a guilty man, and that perhaps he should repent and do penance fully acknowledging his guilt. He should, I agree, feel pain, anguish, and remorse. He should, to the person he has caused to be tortured, do what he can (incommensurable as it must be) to compensate for the dreadful harm done to him, show that it is something he did not want to do, and to give, if that is possible, a clear accounting to the person, so that the person who has been tortured could, if he can be clearheaded about it, recognize that, if their roles had been reversed, that is what he should have done as well. If the politician is morally sensitive, his pain over this should be a pain that will be with him the rest of his life. It is not something that he will just set aside as he might set aside a bad dream. But guilty he is not; a moral or any other kind of criminal he is not; a person who has departed from the bounds or morality or failed to reason in accordance with the moral point of view he is not. It is, in fine, a mistake to say, as Walzer does, that he has done something that is wrong. He has rather done something that would be wrong—terribly wrong— in almost all circumstances, but in the circumstances under discussion it was not wrong. It was rather the right thing to do, the tragically right thing to do, in that circumstance. He was not doing something which was both right and wrong; he did something which, *everything considered*, was the right thing to do. So he has done nothing wrong, committed no crime, is not guilty of any- thing, but has done what under the circumstances is the right thing to do, though with a very heavy heart indeed, for in doing it he caused great harm to another person. What he did would in almost all circumstances be an ut- terly impermissible, indeed, a heinous and vile thing to do, but in this cir- cumstance, as Walzer himself acknowledges, it was the right thing to do. So, *contra* Walzer, he could not have done wrong in doing it. The best succinct way of describing the situation is to say that the politician in ordering the tor- ture did something which in almost all circumstances would plainly be a very wrong thing to do indeed, but that in that very extraordinary circum- stance, but still a circumstance which is generalizable (*universalizable*), it was not wrong to do it, but right.[15] (It, of course, is always at least prima facie wrong, but it may not always be *actually* the wrong thing to do. And thus when that obtains, it is not the wrong thing to do full stop.)

Where the only choice is between evil and evil, it can never be wrong, and it always will be right, to choose the lesser evil. The politician in the situation described, if he is clearheaded as well as morally sensitive, will not *excuse* his behavior, either implicitly or explicitly acknowledging guilt, but will be pre- pared to publically *justify* it. Whether it is *politically expedient* to do so at a given time is a *tactical* matter and as such is another thing altogether. But it *can* be *publicly justified* and, at least in the fullness of time, it must be publicly jus- tified. (Remember that if something cannot be publicly justified it cannot be justified period.) Since the choice is such a revolting, morally innervating choice between evils, he will not be proud of his choice, but, if he is clear- headed, he will be be able to accept himself, recognizing that he has soldiered on and has done what, morally speaking, was the best thing to do under the circumstances. Doing it, and the memory of doing it, will not make him happy, not give him a sense of satisfaction, certainly will not make him proud; but he will be able to hold his head up, realizing that he did what he had to do and that others in similar situations should do so as well if they are able to act on the most compelling moral considerations. With such an understanding, he can accept himself, look at his face in the mirror. He did not, in so acting, depart from the moral point of view; quite to the contrary, he steadfastly stuck with it where it is very hard indeed to stick with it.

VII

Walzer is aware that a response something like the above could be made. But he thinks he can set it aside because he takes it to be tied up with the acceptance of utilitarianism. He argues, not implausibly, that utilitarianism has certain evident defects which make it a problematical morality. But we have already seen that the lesser evil argument, while compatible with utilitarianism, is also compatible with a Rossian-type pluralist deontology, with a *weak* consequentialism that makes no commitment to utilitarianism, and with my own largely coherentist account of morality which is similar to the justice-as-fairness conception of Rawls. (The latter conception is also compatible with weak consequentialism and, on my account, they fit together like hand and glove.[16])

It seems to me that any coherent morality will be consequence-sensitive (something I do not think Walzer would deny) and in morality we can in some contexts use utilitarian calculations without being utilitarians. Moreover, we not only sometimes can do it, but sometimes we should.

However, while I think that it is important (perhaps even unavoidable) to appeal to consequences in the way I specified, the core of my account about dirty hands does not even require that, *unless* all moral reasoning requires it in some contexts. But I can here leave that open. In deciding what is the lesser evil, we could perhaps treat rules such as "Torture is wrong," "Suffering is bad," "Life should be protected," "Security should be maintained" as being rules that hold prima facie. Moreover, they are rules which *always* hold, prima facie. But what they specify as being things which, prima facie, should always be done or avoided, should also *actually* be done or actually obtain or be avoided, if on reflection we come to appreciate that that principle or rule, of the various principles or rules holding prima facie and applicable in the situation in question, is the rule or principle which has, in the circumstance in question, the most stringent claim on us.[17] All of them always hold prima facie (not doing them or avoiding them, as the case may be, is always prima facie wrong), but they sometimes conflict and when they do, we on reflection will have to, if we can, just come to "see" (appreciate, apprehend, intuit) which moral rule or principle has, in that situation, the strongest claim on us. There is, on such a Rossian account, no higher rule or principle we can appeal to and there is no lexical ordering of rules; we must just reflect and come to appreciate which claim in that particular situation is the most stringent.

Thus the Rossian deontologist in acknowledging that torture is always wrong does not say that torture is *never* permissible as a necessary evil done to avoid a still greater evil. We have a duty (prima facie) not to torture, but we also have a duty (prima facie) to prevent harm to others. The person saying that torture is not wrong in that situation, *everything considered*, need not be a utilitarian; he could be as thoroughly deontological as Ross and Broad. My account here does not have to choose between utilitarianism and other teleological views, on the one hand, and deontological views on the other. What my account is incompatible with, as I have already remarked, is an Absolutism such as Anscombe's or Donagan's which claims that there are some specific laws or rules such as "Torture is always impermissible" which must be acted in accordance with no matter what the circumstances, no matter what the consequences, no matter what human catastrophes follow from acting in accordance with them. To be consistent, such an Absolutism would have to say, in the case of our politician ordering torture, that he should have never ordered it or condoned it. Let the bombs go off, if they have to, and let many people be killed, if there is no other way to prevent the bombs going off except by recourse to torture. That fierce Absolutism is not Walzer's, Williams's, or Nagel's position any more than it is mine. But it would take the establishment of such an Absolutism to undermine my argument that in the situation described by Walzer—and it is a good paradigm for the dirty-hands problem—that it is a mistake to say that our politician has done something wrong—committed a moral crime—in ordering torture to achieve what is plainly right. On such an Absolutism his ordering torture (as something which, on such an account, is absolutely morally impermissible) is a moral crime. It may even be something that such a moralist will describe as morally monstrous. However, such an Absolutist, to be consistent, must agree with me that there is no moral dilemma of dirty hands, for, unlike Walzer, such an Absolutist will not accept that we can do right by using such an absolutely and categorically forbidden means. The politician, on this view, cannot rightly so act. But on that view, as well as mine, there is nothing for him to be in a *dilemma* about, though he will not infrequently be anguished by the consequences of his Absolutism. Indeed, to the extent that he has much in the way of moral awareness, he will have to be anguished. Such Absolutists are often Christians and, as Kierkegaard stressed, it is not easy to be a Christian. There were very few Christians, as Kierkegaard observed, in what was then Christian Denmark.

IX

Let me return to Walzer's argument from a somewhat different perspective. Whatever may be true for utilitarians, I do not take moral rules or moral principles as mere rules of the thumb or mere guidelines to be used in trying to calculate what we should do. Moral rules are very often, as Walzer observes, prohibitions on our acting which, nonetheless, as we both believe, may in the ways we have discussed be overridden. But, we also both agree that in their being overridden "we do not talk or act as if they had been set aside, canceled, or annulled. They still stand" (160). Still they can, however, in certain circumstances be overridden by another rule or principle which takes precedence over them in that situation or by noting that the consequences of following the rule in that situation would be disastrous.

However, this does not make moral rules *mere guidelines*, and some of the more deeply embedded ones in our moral life, such as prohibitions against killing or torture, are not annulled or canceled even when they are rightly overridden. "Moral life," as Walzer well says,

> is a social phenomenon and it is constituted at least in part by rules, the knowing of which (and perhaps the making of which) we share with our fellows. The experience of coming up against these rules, challenging their prohibitions, and the explaining ourselves to other men and women is so common and so obviously important that no account of moral decision making can possibly fail to come to grips with it. (160)

We have these moral rules; they are social prohibitions which partially constitute our morality. There would be no morality without them. They are, that is, just part of what it is for something to be a morality. Still, there are good reasons not to treat these rules as absolute exceptionless prohibitions. And when we do not, we can also see how, without paradox or inconsistency, they can be rightly overridden and still not be annulled or set aside. When a rule in a certain circumstance is rightly overridden, it is overridden by more morally demanding moral considerations. When this obtains, the moral-political agent does not do wrong to do right. Such paradox mongering is confused. Rather he rightly, and justifiably, does what, but for these special circumstances, would be the wrong, indeed in the cases we have been discussing, a monstrously wrong thing to do. This is not relativism, subjectivism, or even historicism (though it is compatible with the latter), but a thorough contextualism.[18] It all depends on the circumstances, and they will vary. But that is no more relativism, subjectivism, or attitudinalism then we have any of these things when we say that in the Yukon people ought to have very warm clothes, but that there is no good reason for people to have them in the

Amazon. What determines the shift in judgment about what is appropriate or inappropriate or about what is right and wrong in these cases is *the objective situation itself* and not the feelings, attitudes, cultural set, or perspective of the people involved. "It all depends" and *"Alles ist relativ"* are very different things. But the importance of circumstance and context is vital. We are not likely to have very useful general rules for determining what is the lesser evil in any complicated case where there is a live moral issue. Philosophical generalizations are more or less useless here. But careful concrete attention to the situation will sometimes give us a good understanding of what is the lesser evil in particular cases, though at other times we simply have to act in the dark. Sometimes we should take hard means (including means that are normally morally impermissible) to achieve morally imperative ends, but we will have very little in the way of general formula telling us when this is so. The formula "Always do or support the lesser evil, when it is necessary to choose between evils" does not tell us very much. It is important not to lose sight of the maxim "It all depends," while also keeping in mind that there are repetitive patterns in the problems of human life. When we know that there are several evils, not all of which can be avoided, we should always go for the lesser evil, but *what* the lesser evil is can only be determined on the scene and contextually.[19]

X

What, in its most morally demanding form, is the problem of dirty hands? Dirty work aplenty goes on in the world (and not only in politics) and the "foundations of kindliness," to use Brecht's phrase, do not seem to be anywhere in sight. Maybe such a notion is like "pie in the sky by and by." The problem of dirty hands in its most pressing form is this: when, if ever, are we justified in using what would in normal circumstances clearly be a morally impermissible means to achieve a clearly morally demanding end? The answer is that we are justified when (1) evil (e.g., killing, destruction, misery, oppression, suffering, and the like) is inescapable and (2) when we have good grounds for believing that using in such circumstances what are normally morally impermissible means will make for less evil in the world, where, in this calculation, we also include the fact that our *not* taking those means would, as far as can be ascertained, most likely plainly and immediately, lead to a greater evil (e.g., more deaths, destruction, misery, etc.) than would obtain from our taking them. When these conditions obtain (sometimes something which is very difficult to ascertain), we should use the otherwise impermissible means. It is in such circumstances that morality enjoins seizing the day and taking measures that otherwise would be totally unacceptable.

This is not romanticism but moral nonevasiveness. There are no categorical prescriptivities built into nature, including human nature, or substantive ones built into our choosing souls, whether our choices are rational, nonrational, or irrational. In morality, it all depends.

NOTES

1. See chapter 7 and Kai Nielsen, "Rights and Consequences: It All Depends," *Canadian Journal of Law and Society* 1, no.1 (1992).

2. Michael Walzer, "Political Action: The Problem of Dirty Hands," *Philosophy and Public Affairs,* 2, no. 2 (Winter 1973): 160–80.

3. Ibid.; Bernard Williams, "A Critique of Utilitarianism," in J. J. C. Smart and Bernard Williams, *Utilitarianism For and Against* (Cambridge: Cambridge University Press, 1973), 98–100, 108–18; Thomas Nagel, *Mortal Questions* (Cambridge: Cambridge University Press, 1979), 53–90, 128–41.

4. Walzer, "Political Action," 164.

5. Brian Barry, *Liberty and Justice* (Oxford: Clarendon Press, 1991), 40–77.

6. Kai Nielsen, "Rights and Consequences: It All Depends," and *Equality and Liberty: A Defense of Radical Egalitarianism* (Totowa, N.J.: Rowman and Allanheld, 1985).

7. Heinrich Kleist, *Michael Kohlhaas.*

8. I discuss Kolakowski's views on such matters in my "On the Ethics of Revolution," *Radical Philosophy* 6 (Winter 1973): 17–19. See also my "Violence and Terrorism: Its Uses and Abuses," in *Values in Conflict,* ed. Burton M. Leiser (New York: Macmillan Publishing Co., 1981), 435–49.

9. See chapters 5 and 7 and see, as well, my "Philosophy Within the Limits of Wide Reflective Equilibrium Alone," *Iyyun* 43 (January 1994): 3–41; and my "Rights and Consequences: It All Depends."

10. Barry, *Liberty and Justice,* 76.

11. Ibid., 40–77; and Richard Miller, "Marx and Aristotle: A Kind of Consequentialism," in *Marx and Morality,* ed. Kai Nielsen and Steven C. Patten (Guelph, Ontario: Canadian Association for Publishing in Philosophy, 1981), 325–52.

12. Martin Hollis, "Dirty Hands," *British Journal of Political Science* 12 (1982): 385–98.

13. See references in note 3.

14. Walzer, "Political Action," 160–80.

15. On universalizability see my "Universalizability and the Commitment to Impartiality," in *Morality and Universality,* ed. Nelson T. Potter and Mark Timmons (Dordrecht, Holland: D. Reidel Publishing Co., 1985), 91–102; and my "Justice, Equality and Needs," *Dalhousie Review* 69, no. 2 (Summer 1989): 211–27.

16. See chapter 7 and my "Rights and Consequences: It All Depends."

17. W. D. Ross, *The Right and the Good* (Oxford: Clarendon Press, 1930); and W. D. Ross, *Foundations of Ethics* (Oxford: Clarendon Press, 1939).

18. See chapter 1 for an account of contextualism.

19. It might be thought I am caught in a kind of pragmatic self-contradiction here. I deny that there are any unconditional categorical prescriptives, but is not "choose the lesser evil" just such an unconditional prescriptivity? It is not, because it, like "Do good and avoid evil," is an empty formal "principle" that does not, by itself, guide conduct.

Where we give "evil" content, so it can guide conduct, we get something that is neither unconditional nor certain. Unconditionality and certainty are bought at the price of emptiness. I do not say that we can prove this *must* be so, but I do say that when we look at how things go, including how our language-games are played, that is what we find. There is no pragmatic self-contradiction here. I am not taking a transcendental stance to prove that nothing can be transcendental. For an amplification of that see pp. 360–63.

Part Three

Critical Social Theory
and the Fixation of Belief

INTRODUCTION

In part 1, in setting out the core features of my contextualistic historicized naturalism, I argued that in its holistic, antifoundationalist way in fixing belief and justifying claims as to the warrant of particular beliefs or clusters of beliefs, it utilized both the method of wide reflective equilibrium and scientific method in the broad and flexible sense in which Peirce and Dewey conceived of it. I have, as yet, said very little about scientific method and its place in fixing beliefs in the web of our beliefs. I make amends for that in chapter 10 where I discuss Peirce's pragmatism, his conception of scientific method, and its relation to what he calls (aptly I think) "critical commonsensism." There I seek to show that Peirce provides us with an account of these matters—an account taken over and extended by Dewey—which yields what in effect is a powerful counter to postmodernist nihilist and relativist challenges. I try to show how Peirce's conception of scientific method does not suffer from the rigidities of positivist conceptions of scientific method, is not *scientistic,* and does not (as Rorty believes) simply dish up a bunch of platitudes. Yet it remains general enough to cover most of the things that are antecedently recognized to be sciences, is a method that runs tandem with the method of wide reflective equilibrium, and, with it, can be usefully applied in fixing belief, including moral and political beliefs, in social life. But I also argue that, suitably demythologized, there is in the postmodernist challenge something deep and important that challenges, and rightly so, some of our most comforting self-images. I try in that chapter to bring to the fore the dialectic of confrontation here without obscurity or evasion.

I turn in the remaining three chapters of part 3 (chapters 11, 12, and 13) to a discussion of Jürgen Habermas's conception of undistorted discourse and of its role in social analysis and critique. This conception, suitably clarified, also meshes well with the method of wide reflective equilibrium and is a crucial conception in the normative critique of the naturalistic philosophy that I defend. I characterize and deploy this conception in chapter 11 and show how it should be used in arguments about the legitimation of state power. In chapters 12 and 13, with this conception in the background, I discuss the challenges that Foucault, in effect, and Rorty directly, pose to Habermas's Enlightenment *rationalism.* Perhaps I should say "alleged rationalism," for it is doubtful if Habermas would, or even should, accept such an ascription. Be that as it may, I argue that we should become more explicitly contextualist and historicist than Habermas, while still acknowledging the vital importance of his conception of philosophy as critical social theory with an emancipatory intent. These conceptions of Habermas's, freed from what may be their rationalistic residues, are central elements in my own naturalism without foundations.

Chapter Ten

Pragmatism and the Challenge of Postmodernism

I

I shall start with some disclaimers. I am neither a Peirce scholar nor an authority on postmodernism. My interests here are thematic and most fundamentally to examine what philosophy should be and indeed can reasonably be after the undermining of foundationalism, metaphysics, and anything like a First philosophy. I shall assume here what I have argued in my *After the Demise of the Tradition,* namely, that such an undermining has been achieved.[1] I argued for it there, but I also claimed, as others have as well, that it is a key lesson of the development of philosophy in the twentieth century. Moving away from Frege, Russell, and Husserl, there has in contemporary philosophy been from philosophers otherwise very different a thoroughgoing rejection of foundationalism, an espousal of holism along with a rejection of metaphysics and anything like a First philosophy. In short, the grand tradition in philosophy, in all its varied forms, has been set aside. Such a turn was initiated by the classical pragmatists (Peirce, James, and Dewey—most consistently and thoroughly Dewey) and was carried on in different ways by neopragmatism with a linguistic turn in Quine, Davidson, Rorty, and in Putnam in his recent work; in England with Ryle, Wittgenstein, and Austin; and on the Continent with Otto Neurath among the positivists, with Heidegger, Lyotard, Foucault, Baudrillard and Derrida, with the Frankfurt School critical theorists, and with Habermas and Wellmar expanding and developing critical theory. And this has also been true of most feminist philosophy.[2] Dewey and Davidson have done this more thoroughly than Austin and Lyotard, but the tendency is across the board. For good or for ill it pervades the various cutting edges of contemporary philosophy. There is a lot that distances Davidson and Quine from Derrida and Baudrillard, but they all have in common a holism rejecting an atomism or a molecularism and they as well share the other abovementioned nay-sayings. I will here assume what I have argued for in part 1, namely that some version of holistic antifoundationalism is right, i.e., the most plausible stance to take in thinking about philosophy. I shall also assume a naturalism broad enough to qualify Quine, Davidson, Putnam, and Rorty as naturalists, their differences over scientism notwithstanding. What I am interested in here is, given a holistic naturalism without foundations and the above nay-sayings, what should philosophy on the other end of that look like? For Quine, Davidson, and Putnam, at least in programmatic intent, not very much would change. Foundationalist epistemology is out as is First philosophy, but for Quine and Davidson many of the old metaphysical issues remain and Putnam, while rejecting metaphysics, continues, as does Cavell, to genuflect before it. However, with Dewey, with the Frankfurt school critical theorists and their developers, with Rorty, with Heidegger, and with the postmodernists, philosophy gets in different ways radically transformed: indeed, some would say in some instances abandoned. But while they all transform or replace philosophy, they transform it in different ways or replace it with different things. Habermas, for example, and powerfully, transforms/replaces philosophy with a systematic critical theory both empirically oriented and emancipatory and eschewing transcendental arguments. The most paradigmatic postmodernists (e.g., Derrida on some readings) collapse the distinction between philosophy and literature and transform/replace philosophy with a kind of writing much more akin to literature than philosophy has traditionally been. It eschews, in such a transformation, argument, proof, conceptual analysis, and systematization. It even eschews the stating of a philosophical position. People get joshed out of philosophical claims, not argued out of them. What replaces epistemology and metaphysics is not a perspicuous representation of our discourse but an ironist, punning form of literary response more like Kierkegaard and much less like Searle.

Peirce, part of the time, and Dewey all of the time in his mature writings, taking his basic approach from a part of Peirce, also transformed philosophy. But Peirce transformed it in a very different way than the postmodernists. In his hands it becomes a distinctive form of critical theory. Peirce arguably articulated the underlying approach more clearly and more subtly than Dewey while Dewey applied it more extensively and more consistently. Taking what is in common to both and explicating Peirce's articulation of it, I shall see if it can plausibly resist the postmodernist onslaught on such thinking as well as Rorty's alternative neopragmatism without scientific method. (Rorty himself, his disavowals to the contrary notwithstanding, has been thought by some to be a paradigmatic postmodernist.)

I shall proceed as follows: In section 2 I shall set out something of what the postmodernist challenge is. I shall then, in section 3, characterize and elucidate what I shall call pragmatist critical theory, working principally from some canonical texts of Peirce's. Finally, in sections 4 and 5, I shall consider what of pragmatism can and should remain in the face of the postmodernist challenge. This will be, in a rather unpostmodernist spirit, something of an attempt to sort out what is viable and what is not in postmodernism.

II

Postmodernism and *postmodernist* are terms of art. Unlike terms of established ordinary use, they do not have a stable and secure meaning. I shall specify what I am talking about in a way that will square with the way these terms—terms originally at home in talk of architecture—are typically used by the social theorists and philosophers who employ them. In speaking of the challenge of postmodernism I shall set out some contentions characteristic of it that contest the beliefs of the Enlightenment, including the Enlightenment beliefs we find in pragmatism. I shall be concerned to specify the beliefs and attitudes, the stances toward the world, that are characteristic of postmodernism and what has been called the postmodern situation of our allegedly postmodern era. It has had its most extensive expression among a rather heterogenous group of French philosophers, namely, Jean François Lyotard, Jacques Derrida, Michel Foucault, and Jean Baudrillard, all of whom are reacting against structuralism and particularly against Althusserian structuralist Marxism. But it also has been extended to the work of such neopragmatists as Stanley Fish and Richard Rorty.[3]

The label "postmodernist" would not be welcome by some of these philosophers, and important interpreters of their work have denied for one or another of them that they should be called postmodernists or identified with that stream of thought. Jacques Derrida, for example, is often taken to be a paradigmatic postmodernist, but both Christopher Norris and Rodolphe Gasché argue that this involves a serious misreading of Derrida.[4] Similar things are even more obviously applicable to Michel Foucault.[5] It is clear that like Rorty he rejects Enlightenment *rationalism*, but it is anything but evident that he rejects the core values of the Enlightenment. Rather he contextualizes, recontextualizes, deontologizes, and brilliantly reveals their sometimes dark sides. Perhaps the closest to a paradigm case of a postmodernist is Lyotard, but even this understanding requires us to stick with his *Postmodern Condition* (1984) and his work around it and to ignore his later (1988), strangely Kantian *The Differend: Phrases in Dispute*.[6]

I shall not be concerned here with such interpretive matters. I am not trying here to take the measure of any of these philosophers but to try to characterize the core stance of postmodernism and to see if it takes the steam out of that fallibilistic, nonrationalist form of Enlightenment philosophy that is pragmatism, though it should also be noted in passing that all of these French thinkers on occasion at least sound very postmodern and that it is indeed understandable that people should turn to them when they are trying to plumb postmodernism. But I shall stick to a thematic approach.

One feature of postmodernism is political. In contrast with pragmatists such as John Dewey, Sidney Hook, and Ernest Nagel and critical theorists such as Jürgen Habermas, postmodernists believe that we are now witnessing the final exhaustion of the resources of modernity and are moving into a situation where all progressive hopes of an enlightened political order, whether liberal, social democratic, socialist, or communist, have been dashed. Progress and emancipatory hopes are illusory. Only disillusionment remains. Moreover, this hopelessness stems from our very human condition and not just from political and economic facts about capitalist and state-socialist societies, facts which have skewed, as both Habermas and Dewey believe, modernity in a way such that its emancipatory potential is impeded. *Au contraire*, postmodernists believe that a Samuel Beckettish world is just our human lot and is not the result of capitalist or communist social structures. But whatever we say here, there is no doubt that there is in our world a deep and pervasive disillusionment and disenchantment. It is very difficult now to be upbeat about our world. Utopian hopes are very much at a discount. The idea that there could be emancipatory theory, a set of practices or politics that would liberate us from our present ugly situation is, it is pervasively believed, at best laughingly false and at worst incoherent. There can be nothing like an emancipated human condition. This culturally speaking pervasive sense of disillusionment perhaps accounts for the not inconsiderable popularity of postmodernists.

Postmodernism is also deeply distrustful of theory. The very idea of theory seems to them an imposture making claims on which it cannot deliver. The most obvious form this takes is in their suspicion of what Lyotard calls grand metanarratives, large-scale accounts, à la Hegel or Marx or even à la Weber, Gramsci, Durkheim, or Habermas, of the past, present, and future development of humankind or of a nation or community. This distrust is strongest when these narratives not only descriptively and explanatorily narrate but as well perform functions of social integration and political legitimation.[7] But postmodernist distrust of theory does not stop there. As is particularly evident with Baudrillard, there is a pervasive suspicion of all theory: great and small.[8] We are moving, postmodernists believe, into a historical epoch where (a) people are no longer able to believe in their history as an epic of progress or emancipation, (b) where the idea that there is even a need for such a justification no longer has a hold, and (c) where, by contrast to earlier contemporary thinkers, such as Merleau-Ponty, de Beauvoir, Sartre, or Camus, there is not, postmodernists claim and themselves exemplify, among people in what they call the postmodern situation even a nostalgia for such grand theory, all encompassing metanarratives, which would enable us, if such a thing could be pulled off, to see how things hang together, to discover what the truth is and what a just society would look like. These things are no longer believed in or even wished for, the claim goes, by people immersed in the postmodern situation.

It is particularly relevant to pragmatists that postmodernists abandon. without nostalgia or regret some of the most cherished beliefs of pragmatists. Whether the promises are socialist or social democratic, there is a pervasive tendency for people to no longer find it possible or desirable to believe in "promises of prosperity, freedom, and justice associated with the Enlightenment project of scientific control over nature and a rational organization of society."[9] Such things have not only failed to materialize, but our world has become increasingly Orwellian and there is no reason to think such a condition of emancipation will obtain in the future. Such skepticism, many think, should not be scoffed away as a new failure of nerve, but should be recognized to be a tough-minded realism about our condition.

The incredulity toward grand metanarratives, the disbelief in theory (more generally in the efficacy of rational discourse) also leads to a disbelief in truth, the possibility of there being critical standards of a critical rationality or any rational standards at all or any coherent conception of objective validity. This takes its most uncompromising form in the work of Baudrillard. Baudrillard claims that we cannot distinguish truth from falsehood, knowledge from ideology, or progress from reaction. He, of all the postmodernists, most deeply rejects the Enlightenment in any of its forms and with this he goes even further and rejects the very idea of there being genuine truth-claims or anything like enlightened critical thought. What on his view is becoming ever more widely the case—and it is, he also believes, nothing to struggle against or regret—is that the very ideas of truth, right reason, or validity are simply being set aside as myths which are both unbelievable and oppressive social realities. Critical theory, the claim goes, is as bad as the old metaphysics of foundational philosophy for the very idea of critique is incoherent. There is no way validly to distinguish between reason and rhetoric. It is an illusion, claims Baudrillard, to believe that we can fix belief, criticize existing beliefs or past beliefs, from some superior vantage point of truth, reason, or scientific method. Both Marxism and pragmatism, he contends, fall into this error as fully as do the philosophies of the grand metaphysical tradition. Truth is entirely a product of consensus-values and science is simply an honorific label we attach to certain currently prestigious modes of explanation.

The recognition that even truth is a fictive, a rhetorical, or an imaginary construct, another idol of our tribe, and that theory is a discredited enterprise, makes it impossible, postmodernists have it, for us to engage in rational argument or *Ideologiekritik.* We can, if we like, be playful, ironic, even abusive, but, even if we are rather more pedantic and sober, all we can be doing is to tell "just so stories" to ourselves and to others. What we take to be reasoned argument is just chatter according to certain perfectly contingent conventions. Moreover, this is not just old-fashioned skepticism or any kind of skepticism in new dress, for if there is nothing to be believed, there is nothing to be skeptical about either. There is no point in making a big dramatic scene about something that is inescapable.

It is not only that to believe in truth, validity, rationality, and knowledge is to believe in myths, they are, as is the Enlightenment world picture itself, repressive myths as well. Here Baudrillard makes common cause with Lyotard and Foucault. Lyotard, like Paul Feyerabend and Nietzsche before him, claims that these mythical notions of truth, objectivity, knowledge, and rational consensus have a powerful coercive and oppressive side. They enforce a worldview, enforce a unified conception of the world, and undermine the plurality of thought. Rather than let many flowers bloom, they coerce us into believing and acting in certain ways: ways that are said to be normal, reasonable, and sensible. The world of Orwell's *1984* is not far from our own. Conceptions of truth, objectivity, and knowledge are in effect coercive powers. Knowledge and power are inextricably fused. These old normative notions, that is, are in effect authoritarian. Moreover, any conception of a God's-eye view of reality—a perspectiveless, determinate, interest-free view of reality—is both incoherent and in its mystified effects authoritarian. All thought is situated; there is and can be no coherent conception of a transcendent reason that can escape this situatedness with its cultural and historical contingencies.

Postmodernists in direct opposition to classical pragmatists have also, and understandably, given the above, looked askew at the growth of the authority of science in modern cultures. It has become the norm in accordance with which beliefs in our society are taken to be justified. It is by reference either to science, or to scientific method, that we are to fix belief in all domains. Where this cannot be done, modernist thought has it, we get mere emoting in one disguise or other. Postmodernists take this pragmatist stance to be scientistic and imperialistic in the sense that the authority of science or scientific method is being extended into domains where it has no authority. With its stress on the pervasive authority of science, it is in effect a colonization of the life-world. More and more science—or what is claimed to be science—determines what it is held reasonable to believe in politics, the media, popular advice manuals, in conceptions of how we are to live our lives, and into what is taken to be normal, acceptable, reasonable, and the like. This, as Foucault graphically and powerfully contended, is a power trip in the name of the claimed superior knowledge and authority of science.[10] What science cannot tell us, the scientistic claim goes, humankind cannot know.

This scientistic positivistic and pragmatist belief, postmodernists have it, has as a background assumption an incoherent philosophical conception and as well a similarly incoherent conception of the very philosophical enterprise itself. It assumes that a philosopher—and, indeed, anyone engaging in this activity is perforce a philosopher—can construct theories of knowledge, of inquiry, or of meaning which, standing free of any practices, any historically and culturally contingent ways of conceiving and doing things, will yield a litmus test for what it does and does not make sense to say, what in any domain is genuine knowledge and what is not, what is literal and what is merely figurative, what is scientific and thus respectable and what is merely superstition and the like. But no such Archimedean point is available, no such litmus test can nonarbitrarily and non-question beggingly be constructed. Such a belief in the attainability of such an Archimedean point, or indeed of any Archimedean point at all, is incoherent. Such a belief in at least the possibility of an Archimedean point is pervasive in the philosophical tradition and it is part of the self-confidence of modernity. But in reality the very idea of an Archimedean point, an absolute historically noncontingent standard of critical appraisal, is incoherent. Epistemologies and theories of meaning are *ersatz* activities that need to be set aside along with general claims to be able to make ideology-critique or to construct foundational theories of morality or politics, including the now fashionable theories of justice (Dworkin, Nozick, Gauthier). Such accounts try to show what we would be committed to if we were through and through rational or reasonable, had a full grasp of the facts, and would carefully take these matters to heart. But no such a transcending of history and a particular culture is possible. Modern ideals, postmodernists claim, of science, of morality (including justice and conceptions of rights), of art, of cultural criticism are *merely* modern "ideals carrying with them specific political agendas and ultimately unable to legitimize themselves as universals."[11] Neither science nor philosophy nor anything else can be the founding discourse for all discourse or the founding discourse for social criticism. The very idea of such a founding discourse is devoid of coherence and the very idea of social or cultural criticism is as well. The very vocation of an intellectual cannot be what modernity has taken it to be.

The idea of writing an essay "On How to Make Our Ideas Clear" would elicit strong Nietzschean laughter from thoroughgoing postmodernists. The very idea that by careful thought our perplexities can be cleared up and that we could come to see the world rightly is now seen to be a childish myth on a par with believing in God or believing à la Marx and Habermas in some general human emancipation in the course of human development. Philosophy from Socrates to Dewey and Habermas has thought, and, indeed, sometimes even just assumed, that something like this can be achieved, but to believe that is by now pure naiveté. The idea that theory carefully and rigorously practiced could help us even address, let alone redress, the frustrations and dissatisfactions of modern life is a childlike substitute for religious faith. Postmodernists take it as by now ridiculous, as it was not for Descartes and Hobbes or even for Kant, to conceive of people as individual subjects, as isolated minds and wills, whose "vocation is to get clear about the world, to bring it under the control of reason and thus make it available for human projects."[12] Theorists of modernity from Descartes to Habermas think that intellectuals, if they are to be true to their vocation, stand under the imperative of giving a rational account of everything, of interrogating everything. (Foucault has taught us, I remark in passing, to see the dark side of such interrogation.)[13] The era of postmodernity is bringing to an end the essentially Faustian drive, in evidence through the long period of modernity, of questioning endlessly and relentlessly to achieve an ever greater and more comprehensive understanding of our world that would, or so it was believed, or at least hoped, finally yield a harmony and unity in which our fundamental problems, particularly our human problems, would finally be definitively resolved and we would gain a rational mastery of the world, including an emancipatory mastery of ourselves. The era of postmodernity, which is ever more firmly becoming ours, sees such Faustianism as mythical, full of *hubris,* and, indeed, as being more dangerous than desirable: the stuff gulags are made of. We do not know, they claim, what undistorted discourse would look like or what it would be to attain consensus under such conditions. But what we do glimpse through a glass darkly should be enough to make us wary. We should look at these faint inklings not merely cynically, but with trepidation as containing a totalitarian potential, high-sounding though they be. Dissonance, nay-saying, rejection, or even the serious questioning of consensus-views simply get pushed aside, marginalized, as distorted, ideological talk, not to be credited.

Postmodernists do not seek either a Cartesian or Peircean clarity or a Hobbesian or Marxian mastery and control of the world, but, instead, as Jean François Lyotard remarked, they see it as the mission of postmodernist intellectuals to bear witness to the extensive dissonance which is there to be seen as a pervasive feature of our lives.[14] Postmodernists seek "to expose and track the way our modern cognitive machinery operates to deny the intractability of dissonance."[15] The harmony, unity, and clarity promised by this machinery have, postmodernists believe, an inevitable cost. And that cost is borne by those growing but heterogenous groups (the chronically unemployed, gays, lesbians, racial and ethnic minorities) who are engendered by the social system and at the same time "devalued, disciplined, and so on in the infinite search for a more tractable and ordered world."[16]

III

There is a whole range of questions and objections that come trippingly to the tongue concerning postmodernism. On some other occasion I shall pursue them and pursue as well the postmodernist predictable response that the very idea of trying to appraise postmodernism to see if it has made its case, to see if its claims are true and its arguments sound, is a blatant missing of the point for their contention is that there is nothing to be done here. There are no arguments to be made or to be refuted. There is no getting anything right or getting it wrong; there is only conversation and writing in accordance with a heterogenous and not very clearly specified or perhaps even specifiable cluster of historically and culturally various norms and practices. Even affirming the consequent and denying the antecedent on their view are labels for plain and rather typical failures to reason in accordance with *our* norms of correct reasoning. If some other culture did not follow them, there is little we could do to show that they are mistaken that doesn't come simply to an appeal to *our* norms: to what we do and reflectively believe we should do. Many of us continue to think that these are not just cultural mistakes. They are not *simply* mistakes in our culture or mistakes in the Western tradition but mistakes *sans phrase*. But what would it be like to show this? We seem at least to reach rock bottom fairly quickly. Yet if the postmodernists are not saying something they think is at least approximately so, why should we read them and accept what they say any more than accept what those who contend they are mistaken say or accept those who continue on, in the good old tried and true analytical fashion, simply ignoring them, say, or accept the views of anyone else? Why do they write and why do we read them and reflect on what they say if in some way they are not saying something they think is worth saying? It surely seems at least that they are not *just* having fun, but in effect are in some way appealing to some kind of standard or to what they think is the most reasonable thing for them to think and do? Even to say "anything goes" makes a claim and as such is an assertion, and there is no possibility of making an assertion without at least implicitly utilizing a standard. It is incoherent to say that there is nothing to be said about the cogency or lack thereof of what they say. There is no escaping something like assessment, though we need not be hidebound about how this will go.

The above suggests what is a frequent, but I still think a mistaken way of disposing of postmodernism. It is an argument as old as Plato and has been used repeatedly to refute skeptics, relativists, sophists, and the like. Postmodernists deny that there is such a thing as truth. If what they say is true it is false and if what they say is false it is, of course, false. Either way they lose. Their very claim is self-refuting. Similar things could be said for what they say about validity, knowledge, and the like. This refutes the letter of what some incautious postmodernists say (Baudrillard, for example), but the force of what they say could be less incautiously put in a way that escapes this classical objection. Various criteria for truth have been offered over cultural space and historical time, but there is in reality only local and historically fleeting agreement about these criteria. Different people at different times have offered different and sometimes conflicting criteria and we have no reason to think that we can show, or even find non-question-begging grounds for showing, certain of these criteria are not just ours but are the "really right" criteria. We seem at least, the claim continues, to be utterly stuck here. It is not that that remark itself soars above all historical contingency and somehow *must* just be so. It is a remark on the same contingent and fallibilistic footing as the others. But, given what we can see standing where we are now, it seems at least to be the most plausible thing to say. Similar things could be said for knowledge, validity, rationality, reasonability, and the like. We do not have, when we view the matter historically and culturally, a consensus beyond a few truisms which are not sufficient to secure cross-cultural agreement about what the criteria for knowledge, rationality, etc., are. We do not have such a consensus concerning what we know or can know or what it is rational to do or reasonable to believe. Perhaps someday we will get such criteria, but given our track record that is hardly likely. This brings out the force of what Baudrillard was saying in an incautious or hyperbolic way and is not subject to self-referential refutation. Postmodernism does not collapse because if what they say is true then it is false and if what they say is false then it is indeed false. They are not so skewered.

Eschewing such allegedly knockdown refutations, what is to be said when we begin to contrast pragmatism and postmodernism? Does postmodernism in anyway importantly (or indeed at all) undermine pragmatism or, put the other way around, does pragmatism refute or show how deeply flawed postmodernism is, so that it should be set aside as a frivolous, or at least a deeply confused, fashion or alternatively, and at a minimum, that it should be seen to be a very problematic view of things which hardly merits the extensive attention it has received? I shall go at this indirectly by first saying something about Peirce's pragmatism (pragmaticism, if you will) and in doing so show in effect how it should respond to postmodernism. I shall then in the last two sections show explicitly where pragmatism can meet the challenge of postmodernism and where things appear at least to be intractable or at least on contested terrain where there does not appear to be any clear resolution in sight.

I shall take certain parts of Peirce's thought, parts that have come down and have become canonical parts of the pragmatic tradition, and set them against the core claims of postmodernism and—doing a very unpostmodernist thing—see if we can sort out what should be said here. But before I turn to that I want first to note what different "worlds" Peirce and the postmodernists inhabit. For the postmodernists, as we have seen, there is no truth, knowledge, justified belief, validity, rightness, desirability, or reasonability to be established, either critically or acritically; there are no methods to be followed which can yield anything objective; theory should be utterly distrusted as a mélange of grandiose delusions; science rather than being a tool of human emancipation is taken to be an oppressive power resting on nothing more objective than what turns out, among a group of powerful ruling elites of our society, to be the currently most prestigious ways of explaining where explaining really comes to telling stories. What, as Christopher Norris well puts it, all postmodernists have in common is "a deep suspicion of any theory that claims a vantage-point of knowledge or truth, a self-assured position of 'scientific' method from which to criticize the various forms of 'ideological' false-seeming or commonsense perception."[17]

Peirce's world, by contrast, is very different indeed. While as a good fallibilist he believes "nothing can be proved beyond the possibility of doubt,"[18] he thinks science yields knowledge and that indeed with the growth of science we gain, and continue to gain, *plus en plus*, more knowledge more systematically and coherently related, and that, in domain after domain, our truth-claims get more adequately validated and more perspicuously displayed. He speaks perfectly unself-consciously of there being progress in science (V 21).* Indeed we live, he stresses, in an era of a great explosion of knowledge and this knowledge can be reasonably utilized in a way that will answer to the interests of humankind. This presupposes there are genuine human interests and that we can ascertain what they are. Moreover, there can, as Peirce has it, be no reasonable doubt that there are genuine discoveries and that there is scientific knowledge. "A man," he remarks, "must be downright crazy to deny that science has made many true discoveries" (V 106).

Peirce not only thinks that science yields genuine knowledge, but that logic and careful reasoning in everyday life yields knowledge as well. What we need to do, he believes, is strike on the right method of inquiry: the right method of fixing belief. Peirce is justly famous for his assault on Cartesianism and the depth and thoroughness of his anti-Cartesianism.[19] But, that notwithstanding, like Descartes, for Peirce, and for the other classical pragmatists following after him as well, the key to coming to grips with our world, to mastering it through a thorough understanding of it, is to gain, and then correctly apply, the right method of inquiry. On this fundamental point, a point postmodernists would scoff away as methodolatry, Descartes and Peirce are one. Where they differ deeply and profoundly is over what the correct method is.

---

*All references to Peirce given in the text are from his collected papers. For exact reference see endnote 18 of this chapter.

For Peirce, logic plays a key role. He—a world apart from postmodernists—believed that there are such things as normative sciences. Logic, along with aesthetics and ethics, was one of them. (It is clear enough that in speaking of normative sciences he is not at all embarrassed by the idea of objective norms.) As a normative science, logic for Peirce is "the doctrine of what we ought to think" (V 25). Normative sciences, he has it, give us grounds for distinguishing good and bad; logic does this "in regard to representations of truth" (V 26). Indeed, it is for Peirce the master normative science of the three and, like Russell, during the period of his life that was most philosophically influential, logic for Peirce was taken to be the essence of good philosophical method, though—including abduction, induction, and deduction—he construed "logic" more broadly than it is generally construed. Logic, he has it, "will tell you how to proceed to form a plan of experimentation" (VII 44). It is *a* core part of scientific method, and scientific method, essentially the experimental method (the systematically joined use of deduction, induction, and abduction), will enable us to gain secure but fallibilistic knowledge; it will, that is, tell us how things really are. Serious thinking, as we argued in chapter 2, is not "mere rumination, reflection, dialectical inquiry"; what is needed in addition, to yield a reliable method of fixing belief, is "experiment, observation, comparison, active scrutiny of facts" (VII 43). Logic, Peirce believed, is vital here; it will not, of course, "undertake to inform you what kind of experiments you ought to make in order best to determine the acceleration of gravity, or the value of the Ohm, but it will tell you how to proceed to form a plan of experimentation" (VII 44). It is, he remarks, "the art of devising methods of research—the method of methods" (VII 44). And this, Peirce continues, "is the true and worthy idea" of the normative science of logic (VII 44).

All of this he regards, being a through and through modernist, as a great liberating force for humankind. "Modern methods have created modern science; and this century, and especially the last twenty-five years, have done more to create new methods than any former equal period. We live in the very age of methods" (VII 45). To improve the logical powers of human beings and their knowledge and understanding of scientific method will be for them, and more generally for humankind, a great liberating force (VII 45–48). Peirce, in a way that would seem utterly wrongheaded to Feyerabend and Rorty, as well as to postmodernists, claims that in this "age of methods the university which is to be the exponent of the living condition of the human mind must be the university of methods" (VII 45). People with a scientific mentality and schooled in scientific method, working together, will "gradually come to find out truth" (VII 38). Peirce exuberantly talks of such people casting "their whole being into the service of science" and of "storming the stronghold of truth" such that with the "triumph of modern science" we will gain real truth, though the truths we gain will never be a complete list. There will, however, with the relentless use of such rational inquiry, be a steady increase in the number of truths that we know and in their systematic interrelation and perspicuous representation. John Dewey followed him in this, and with them we get a through and through modernist picture of the world, the very picture of the world that postmodernists so thoroughly reject.

So here we have two striking and contrasting clusters of attitudes—the postmodernist ones and Peirce's fully modernist ones with not a trace of what one commentator called postmodernist modernity. Against the spirit of postmodernism, Peirce was an unabashed theoretician. I will depict central elements of his theory and then see how well they stand against postmodernism. Here I shall concentrate on his pragmatism and critical commonsensism and their linkage, his assault on Cartesianism (which for him covered the mainstream of modern philosophy from Descartes through Kant), his conception of how belief should be fixed, how to sort out sense from nonsense, what he took scientific method to be and why he took it to be the method which, if carefully pursued, would give us reliable knowledge, enable us to distinguish what it makes sense to say and what should be set aside as nonsense. This cluster of conceptions and beliefs is the part of Peirce that was taken over by John Dewey and such later classical pragmatists as Ernest Nagel and Sidney Hook. It is this pragmatism or, as Peirce called it, pragmaticism, that I think in its essentials, as I argued in the first two chapters, is very close to the mark. It is a way of thinking which I think can withstand the onslaught of postmodernism and provide a sound defense of modernity and the values of the Enlightenment without what Rorty calls Enlightenment rationalism.[20] This influential part of Peirce's philosophy is by no means the whole of his philosophy. I set aside Peirce's metaphysics, his scholastic realism, his doctrines of Firstness, Secondness and Thirdness, his theory of signs, and even his theory of truth. The texts that convey for me the core of that part of Peirce I wish to defend are papers 3, 4, 5, 6, and 7 of his published papers in volume 5 of his *Collected Papers*; chapters 2 and 3 (papers not published in his lifetime) in book 3 of that same volume; lectures 1, 6, and 7 of his 1903 "Lectures on Pragmatism" also published in volume 5 of his *Collected Papers;* and book 2 on scientific method from volume 7 of his *Collected Papers.*[21] The views articulated there I take to be the core of classical pragmatism.

Like the classical empiricists, Peirce believes that "all our knowledge rests upon perceptual judgments," but these are not the isolated sense impressions or sense-data of classical empiricism, but, as part of a web of judgments, they are robust judgments and are linked to human actions. In short, we have with Peirce, as we have with Quine and Davidson, a thoroughgoing holism.[22] Peirce also contended that there were three kinds of reasoning: abduction, induction, and deduction (V 90). Inquiry must make use of all three, but it is abduction, which is itself a concise expression of pragmatism, which has been neglected in the history of thought and which is vital in the attainment of knowledge, for neither induction nor deduction can "originate any idea whatever" (V 90). Deduction is necessary reasoning, as in mathematics, showing what is entailed by what. It is solely concerned with validity and not with the truth or the probable truth of any other correctness of the premises. Induction, by contrast, is "the experimental testing of a theory" (V 90). At any stage of an inquiry, a conclusion may be more or less erroneous; the repeated application of induction will, if persisted in long enough, correct the error (V 90). But it is also important to realize that "the only thing that induction accomplishes is to determine the value of a quantity. It starts out with a theory and it measures the degree of concordance of that theory with fact. It never can originate any idea whatever" (V 90). Rather, Peirce claims, "all the ideas of science come to it by way of abduction" and, indeed, it becomes clear that for Peirce all critical beliefs come by way of abduction. Where there are genuine doubts (doubts always taking place against a massive background of secure belief), if, in fixing belief, we are to get beyond mere word-pictures or idle ruminations, we must use abduction which "consists in studying the facts and devising a theory to explain them" (V 90). In good pragmatic fashion, Peirce claims that "its only justification is that if we are ever to understand things at all, it must be in that way" (V 90 and V 106). Abduction works this way:

> The surprising fact, C, is observed;
> But if A were true, C would be a matter of course,
> Hence, there is reason to suspect that A is true.
> Thus, A cannot be abductively inferred, or if you prefer the expression, cannot be abductively conjectured until its entire content is already present in the premise, "If A were true, C would be a matter of course." (V 117)

This forming of an explanatory hypothesis "merely suggests that something *may* be." Its only justification is that from its suggestion deduction can draw a prediction which can be tested by induction, and that, if we are ever to learn anything, or to understand phenomena at all, it must be by abduction that this is brought about" (V 106). It is in such a manner that we must proceed if we are ever to distinguish genuine knowledge from its counterfeit, to successfully resolve our doubts—our genuine nonpaper doubts—and to ascertain what it makes sense to say: to separate, as Peirce puts it, "the sheep from the goats" (V 26). Reasoning, where it is not mere piffle disguised as reasoning, must so combine deduction, induction, and abduction. He further remarks that "if you carefully consider the question of pragmatism you will see that it is nothing else than the question of the logic of abduction" (V 121).

To see a little more what abduction is we should see how Peirce distinguishes good abductions from bad ones. Good abductions "must explain the facts" (V 122). In seeing what they are we will also see how abduction succinctly expresses the core of pragmatism. To ascertain what these conditions for good abductions are we should consider what end abduction is to meet (V 122–23). Its end, Peirce tells us, is, through subjection to the test of experiment, to lead to the avoidance of all surprise and to the establishment of a habit of positive expectation that shall not be disappointed (V 123). Hypotheses are admissible, no matter how much they may be the result of fancy, flights of the imagination, remote from practical considerations or observation, *"provided they are capable of experimental verification, and only in so far as [they] are capable of such verification"* (V 123). It is these conditions which must be met for it to be the case that we can have a good abduction. This, Peirce goes on to remark, "is approximately the doctrine of pragmatism" (V 123).

Experimental verification, in turn, "involves the whole logic of induction" (V 123). So reasoning of a disciplined scientific sort involves this mix of deduction, induction, and abduction. This is what scientific method comes to and it fits well with the aim of science which Peirce characterizes as seeking "to find out facts and work out a satisfactory explanation of them" (VII 59). Philosophers, metaphysicians, and the like, who are far from the spirit of experimentalism, imagine that they have a more sublime or deeper form of reasoning. They think they have something of a purely conceptual or dialectical character; but, Peirce contends, in good naturalistic fashion, the more distant it is from scientific reasoning, and the closer it comes to having a *purely* conceptual character, "the nearer it approaches to verbiage" (V 91). (Relate this back to my discussion of Tugendhat's conception of philosophical method in chapter 2.)

In what is perhaps his best-known essay, "The Fixation of Belief," Peirce sets the scientific method of fixing belief against three other methods he discerns in human history: (1) *the method of tenacity* (the holding onto whatever beliefs we as individuals may happen to have and the dismissing of any considerations which might appear to conflict with them), (2) *the method of authority* (where the state or the community does what with the first method isolated individuals do), and (3) *the a priori method* (the method of appealing to what is felt to be agreeable to reason) (V 239). This last method is the method that has been repeatedly utilized in the philosophical tradition (the grand tradition in philosophy) and most extensively in modern philosophy of an essentially Cartesian or Kantian conception. But it is the method of any philosophy which is distinctly metaphysical. Peirce argues against these methods not by arguing, as one might expect, that they are irrational but by showing that they break down in practice. That this is so is tolerably evident for *the method of tenacity* and *the method of authority* and I shall not rehearse Peirce's arguments here (V 234–38). But I shall attend a bit to the *a priori method* for (as I have remarked) it has been the method of the Philosophical Tradition and is, either self-consciously or in effect, used by many philosophers. (Again this discussion should be related back to my discussion in the last sections of chapter 2.)

The basic idea of the *a priori method* is that we should not settle opinions by caprice or authority but by an appeal to what after careful inspection is clear to the light of reason. It will "not only produce an impulse to believe, but shall also decide what proposition it is which is to be believed" (V 230). It does this "by showing us which fundamental propositions are 'agreeable to reason' (V 238, Peirce's scare quotes). Peirce remarks that "the most perfect example of it is to be found in the history of metaphysical philosophy. Systems of this sort have not usually rested upon any observed facts, at least not to any great degree. They have been chiefly adopted because their fundamental propositions seemed 'agreeable to reason'" (V 238). Peirce believes that such talk of reason when looked at coolly will be seen to be mere arm waving. To speak of something being agreeable to reason, he remarks, "does not mean that which agrees with experience" or coincides with facts, but it is "that which we find ourselves inclined to believe" (V 239). For Descartes, for example, self-consciousness was to furnish us with our most fundamental truths and decide what was agreeable to reason. But this was to be done by rumination or by reflection or by, in addition, the providing of abstract definitions. But such activities "never enable us to distinguish between an idea seeming clear and really being so" (V 249). We must, rather, to gain a clear conception of what we are thinking, ascertain the sensible effects of our ideas, the observable circumstances that would count for their being true or for their being false: whether, that is, they coincide with ascertainable facts (V 246, 257–58). When, for example, we claim that diamonds are harder than chunks of granite, we will know this is true if we can observe diamonds being used to scratch granite but not the reverse. Without such experimental testing of what reflection, self-consciousness, and abstraction yield through tracing the sensible effects of the propositions expressive of these thoughts, we will not be able to distinguish between an idea just seeming to be clear— being agreeable to reason—and one really being so. The sense of propositions being agreeable to reason does not discriminate, or even give us a hint at how to discriminate, between a clear idea and one that merely *seems* so.

The use of the *a priori method* common to the philosophical tradition "makes of inquiry something similar to the development of taste" (V 241). But taste, Peirce continues, "is always more or less a matter of fashion," and philosophical doctrines, as is evident in metaphysical disputes, disputes in ethical theory, and in epistemology, have like a pendulum swung back and forth between radically opposing views and have led to no rational consensus, or indeed any other kind of nonlocal consensus, as to what is to be believed.[23]

In this way philosophy—or at least philosophy of the traditional sort—stands in a marked contrast to science where there has been a relatively stable growth of knowledge rooted in a reasonable stable consensus by scientific practitioners from many cultures. Applying inductive reasoning to the *a priori* method, we can disconfirm the hypothesis that utilizing the *a priori* method will deliver our opinions from accidental and capricious elements.

The clash of opinions, theories, beliefs, and conceptions is evident enough to us and causes in the big-brained animals that we are the irritation of doubt. The method of tenacity, authority, and the *a priori* method all fail in their very practice to relieve our doubts. "To satisfy our doubts . . . it is necessary that a method should be found by which our beliefs may be determined by nothing human, but by some external permanency," that is, by our beliefs coinciding with facts (V 242). This does not involve some mysterious correspondence of propositions to facts, but the experimental or experiential testing of our ideas by what is either directly or indirectly observable. Whether or not perceptual judgments are or are not our starting point, they are essential for checking the truth, probable truth, or indeed of even the possible truth of our beliefs. Where no such empirical check is possible, we cannot justifiably claim that any substantive matter-of-fact claim is true or even could be true.

It remains for me to say something about Peirce's critical commonsensism, its relation to pragmatism, to his assault on Cartesianism and to, when he proceeds in this pragmatic spirit, his setting aside of metaphysics. Many critics of pragmatism claim that pragmatists do not push their inquiries far enough, do not really challenge the full range of beliefs or presuppositions of our thought. In that way, the claim goes, pragmatism is really a step backwards from the spirit of Cartesianism. Peirce, in the spirit of the above reaction to pragmatism, puts into the mouth of a hypothetical critic the sarcastic comment, "So passionate a lover of doubt [as the pragmatist] would make a clean sweep of his beliefs" (V 364). But this, Peirce responds, incoherently conceives of the mind as a *tabula rasa*. Such a making of a clean sweep of things is as impossible as it is unnecessary. Like Wittgenstein, particularly in *On Certainty,* Peirce stresses that doubt is only possible where there is belief. We have a vast, hardly specifiable in its entirety, body of background beliefs, many perfectly mundane; it is only against this extensive background of secure interlocked beliefs that we are able to doubt at all or question at all. Belief comes first and the power of doubting long after. "Doubt, usually, perhaps always, takes its rise from surprise, which supposes previous belief; and surprises come with novel environment" (V 364). Real live doubt, which emerges from a concrete problematic situation where inquiry becomes blocked, drives scientific inquiry: the setting out and testing of hypotheses to explain anomalous facts which do not square with other facts, facts which form parts of the web of our belief systems.

Cartesianism, Peirce tells us, "teaches that philosophy must begin with universal doubt," that the ultimate test of truth "is to be found in the individual consciousness," and that "the multiform argumentation of the middle ages is [to be] replaced by a single thread of inference depending often upon inconspicuous premises" (V 156). In this respect, as I have already remarked Peirce remarks, "most modern philosophers have been, in effect, Cartesians" (V 156). And it is this Cartesianism which is deeply mistaken in all the above respects. Peirce remarks we "cannot begin with complete doubt. We must begin with all the prejudices which we actually have when we enter upon the study of philosophy. The prejudices are not to be dispelled by a maxim, for they are things which it does not occur to us *can* be questioned. Hence this initial skepticism will be mere self-deception, and not real doubt; and no one who follows the Cartesian method will ever be satisfied until he has formally recovered all those beliefs which in form he has given up" (V 156–57). But these methodological doubts are mere paper-doubts (V 361).

However, so rejecting the idea of trying to wipe the slate clean by universal doubting does not dispense with the need to have a critical attitude, for in the course of our studies, with the rough bumps inquiry will give us, we will *in specific circumstances* find reasons to doubt what we began by believing (V 157). But with such a nonmethodological doubt we will have a *positive reason for* doubting and we will understand how in principle at least to proceed to resolve our doubts. A person may not always be able to resolve his doubt; indeed, he may frequently fail, but he will know how he is to proceed to resolve his doubt, if he can in fact do so, and will understand what counts as success and failure here.

The scientific method is important here, but so is what Peirce called critical commonsensism. Critical commonsensism is, Peirce has it, "A variety of the Philosophy of Common Sense" going back to the Scots philosopher Thomas Reid (V 292). But Peirce's critical commonsensism has certain features that give it a critical edge lacking in the Scottish philosophy (V 293). Peirce's commonsensism is critical because it sticks with the fallibilism and the experimentalism of pragmatism while, with the commonsensists believing

that there are indubitable beliefs which vary a little and but a little under varying circumstances and in distant ages; that they partake of the nature of instincts, this word being taken in a broad sense; that they concern matters within the purview of the primitive man; that they are very vague indeed (such as that fire burns) without being perfectly so; that while it may be disastrous to science for those who pursue it to think they doubt what they really believe, and still more so really to doubt what they ought to believe, yet, on the whole, neither of these is so unfavorable to science as for men of science to believe what they really doubt; that a philosopher ought not to regard an important proposition as indubitable without a systematic and arduous endeavor to attain to a doubt of it, remembering that genuine doubt cannot be created by a mere effort of will, but must be compassed through experience; that while it is possible that propositions that really are indubitable, for the time being, should nevertheless be false, yet in so far as we do not doubt a proposition we cannot but regard it as perfectly true and perfectly certain; that while holding certain propositions to be each individually perfectly certain, we may and ought to think it likely that some one of them, if not more, is false. (V 347)

This is what Peirce calls the core of critical commonsensism and he believes that a pragmatist to be consistent ought to embrace it (V 347). The first part of his characterization seems to me particularly important. For Peirce there are both acritical propositions and acritical inferences that are indubitable in the sense that we cannot in critical inquiry go behind them and give them a foundation or justification. They are acritical beliefs that we do not think can be doubted and we have (*pace* the Kantian critical philosopher) no understanding at all of what it would be like to find a critical foundation which could support them (V 354–58). They are, though vague, as certain as anything we can conceive of (V 293). They are not something we can fix in the fixation of belief; we cannot justify them by reasoning where by that we mean, as we ought to mean, "the fixation of one belief by another as is reasonable, deliberate, self-controlled" (V 292–93). These commonsense beliefs and the acritical inferences that go with them are instinctual and ahistorical in that all people (or all statistically normal people) everywhere everywhen have these beliefs. They are the same as Wittgenstein's *Vor-Wissen* or Moore's commonsense beliefs. Moreover, as Peirce puts it, "instinct seldom errs, while reason goes wrong nearly half the time, if not more frequently" (V 297).

However, what a critical commonsensism realizes, in the way the Scots philosophers of common sense did not, is that these commonsense beliefs "only remain indubitable in their application to affairs that resemble those of a primitive mode of life" (V 297). But it is also crucial to realize that these acritically indubitable beliefs and inferences are invariably vague, though, Peirce stresses, not perfectly so, and they are none the worse for that (V 298). Indeed, for them to play the role in the stream of life that they do, it is essential for them to be vague. That human beings are often selfish is such a commonsense belief, but that "The ultimate spring for action is self-interest; human beings always and only do what they take to be in their own self-interest" is not. "Pleasure is good and pain is bad" are other bits of "acritically indubitable" common sense while "Pleasure and pleasure alone is intrinsically

good and pain and pain alone is intrinsically evil" are not. These latter supposedly more precise beliefs are just bits of bad metaphysics parading as fundamental principles of ethics or deep claims about fundamental human motivation. The vague but sometimes useful acritical commonsense beliefs are
truisms, but true for all of that. (Truisms, after all, can be true.) They are background beliefs that we reasonably accept without argument in our reasonings
and doubtings where the engine is not idling.

If, however, in the course of some real inquiry, caused by some real
doubt, we actually come to have a *positive* reason for doubting one or another
of them, at least on a certain reading of them, then in that context they would
become dubitable and indeed should be doubted, but before in that *context*
abandoning them we should seek to formulate them more precisely, turning
them from acritical beliefs into critical beliefs. But there are many such acritical beliefs that we will never so doubt nor will they ever stand in need of
being doubted. They, vague though they be, are as secure as any beliefs we
have; they are there and should remain as background beliefs for our other believings, believings that occur in the context of our inquiries. Indeed, we do
not have any idea of what it would be like for us to think, inquire, doubt, or
deliberate without their being in the background.

The critical commonsensist attaches real value to doubt, but it has to be
the real thing and not à la Descartes a counterfeit or paper substitute. It must
be a doubt that arises in the course of actual inquiry where something in our
belief system breaks down or threatens to break down. But this doubting
(*pace* the skeptic) can only take place against the background of a massive but
indeterminate number of beliefs which are not in doubt and many of which
will never be doubted. Actual doubting must be specific and roughly *seriatim*
and not holus-bolus where everything all at once is supposedly open to systematic doubt. In the course of actual inquiry anything could, if there is a positive reason for it, be doubted and, if indeed there really is a positive reason,
should be doubted, but many things will not be doubted and indeed the whole
belief system just like that could not be doubted. The very idea of such a thing
is incoherent. Thus critical commonsensism and fallibilism ride in tandem.
We have a commonsensism without dogmas or a crude metaphysics (or indeed any metaphysics at all), and we have with pragmatism a robust empiricism without dogmas and an antifoundationalist naturalism without subjectivism and skeptical danglers. Critical commonsensism and pragmatism are
one in arguing against Descartes and against Locke, and later Husserl and
Brentano, that we have "no infallible introspective power" to ascertain what
is true and what is false or even what we believe and doubt (V 347). A good
philosopher, as a good scientist, will not doubt a whole mass of acritical beliefs. There will for him be a building on the work of other similar like-
minded people. The pragmatist will not, like the Lone Ranger, always be try-

ing, starting from scratch, or rather trying to start from scratch, to raise unshakable foundations. In cumulative, cooperative work with other scientists and philosophers who also have a scientific attitude, she will operate with critical beliefs already for the nonce established; but in the live contexts of actual inquiry she will not take uncritically, as something just to be accepted as indubitable, *any* important proposition. She will go the way neither of the global skepticism of the philosophical skeptic nor of the *a priori* assurances (at best false) of the rationalist. Pragmatism "will be sure to carry critical commonsensism in its arms" (V 348). I shall in concluding my setting out of Peirce's account, give Peirce himself the last word.

> [N]othing is so unerring as instinct within its proper field, while reason goes wrong about as often as right—perhaps oftener. Now those vague beliefs that appear to be indubitable have the same sort of bases as scientific results have. That is to say, they rest on experience—on the total everyday experience of many generations of multitudinous populations. Such experience is worthless for distinctively scientific purposes, because it does not make the minute distinctions with which science is chiefly concerned; nor does it relate to the recondite subjects of science, although all science, without being aware of it, virtually supposes the truth of the vague results of uncontrolled thought upon such experiences, cannot help doing so, and would have to shut up shop if she should manage to escape accepting them. No "wisdom" could ever have discovered argon; yet within its proper sphere, which embraces objects of universal concern, the instinctive result of human experience ought to have so vastly more weight than any scientific result, that to make laboratory experiments to ascertain, for example, whether there be any uniformity in nature or no, would vie with adding a teaspoonful of saccharine to the ocean in order to sweeten it. (V 365–66)

IV

Postmodernists, as well as neopragmatists without method such as Richard Rorty and Stanley Fish, would take Peirce's account to be an extreme form of methodolatry. But they would be one with him, as would Quine and Davidson as well, in repudiating the Cartesian dream of a foundation for scientific method firmer than science itself. There can be no such First philosophy, no such certainty, no such foundations. But a 'scientific philosophy', even as a handmaiden to science, will not, these postmodernists believe, give us objectivity either. We cannot, as Peirce believes, specify something called the aim of science or a set of interests it answers to. Science, they claim, is and does many things answering to many different interests and what it does and what aims (if any) it has are very much dependent on the particular science in question. There is nothing called the aim of science which an activity must aim at to even count as a science. There is no aim of science which will give us a key, or even a clue, as to what scientific method is or to what sort of explanations are admissible. "The scientific method" is a reification that neither can be determined by finding out what the aim or function of science is nor from making a useful general characterization from the diverse practices that are generally accepted in the various domains as science. Moreover, even if we are justified in making some rational reconstructions or stipulations here, there is not much we can in general say about scientific method. Peirce stresses the importance of setting out explanatory hypotheses capable of empirical test. But pure observation, as Karl Popper has well argued, gives us only negative evidence by being able to falsify the observational categoricals implied by a proposed theory. The very holism that Peirce shares with later philosophers such as Quine, Putnam, Rorty, and Davidson makes it the case that on his account it must always be the case that there are alternative ways of accommodating recalcitrant observations. Experimental testing is hardly ever, if ever, decisive. To add further features in the characterization of scientific method such as simplicity, systematicity, economy, and elegance yield criteria which not infrequently conflict, are very indeterminate (what, for example, counts as need in the maxim not to multiply conceptions beyond need), have no lexical ordering rules, do not all apply to all the sciences, and are rather subjective. We have vague maxims for scientific method, but no rules set in lexical order. Physics, biology, archaeology, clinical psychology, and social anthropology are too different for there to be anything determinate called the scientific method that they all utilize. There is just a bunch of different things that different people with different interests and under different conditions do. These diverse practices have (a) no determinate end that they all share, (b) no distinctive method common to them all, and (c) they are not something that could properly be said to provide an objective view of the world in accordance with the objective facts (facts specifiable independently of theory). There is, as well, and similarly, no way that we could appeal to evidence that is independent of any theory to choose between competing theories. Evidence, like facts, is theory-dependent. What counts as evidence and how it is characterized is determined by the theory that is being accepted.

Many think that this, or something bearing a family resemblance to this, is a cluster of lessons that contemporary philosophy of science or the history of science demonstrates. But on Peirce's behalf this much could be said in response: He, unlike Rudolf Carnap, was not setting rigid rules that all or indeed any sciences must follow. He clearly saw, with his very considerable knowledge of science, how different the various sciences are (VII 55–57). But that notwithstanding, descriptive-interpretive sciences such as social anthropology and clinical psychology in much of what they do may not fit very well with

Peirce's conception of scientific method. Yet his conception of scientific method was meant to be perfectly general. While it may not be perfectly general, given these at least apparent exceptions, it does capture crucial elements in most of science such that anything claiming to be physics, biology, geology, or archaeology, for example, while lacking those features, would be at best very problematical examples of such sciences, elements on its speculative edge and thus on its margins.[24] Abduction is vital for we plainly need hypotheses to try to explain anomalous facts (theory dependent though they be) or occurrences; we need deduction to derive testable propositions to test the hypotheses of the theory or show their various implications and connections; we need inductive procedures to test the truth of the propositions so derived. Though our tests may very well never be decisive and what is claimed may be subject to various alternative accommodations, still confirmation and infirmation can and often do show how one theory or one hypothesis can be more plausible than another. Without any kind of experimental testing there is no distinguishing pure speculation from disciplined empirical inquiry and that is a distinction we plainly need. The distinction is not as sharp as was formerly thought, but still there are differences between pure speculation and science; the very practice of science shows that it is not the case that anything goes. Thinking in the case of science (non-formal science, if you will) does not make something so. We have good reasons for rejecting procedures lacking provision for empirically testable hypothesis. Aside from the valuably vague (but not perfectly so) commonsense beliefs, beliefs we have no positive reason to doubt, where there is no such hypothesis construction and elaboration, we have good grounds for denying that propositions not so constrained yield knowledge of the world (to be pleonastic). Moreover, where there is some positive reason for doubting a specific commonsense belief, it must, for it to remain acceptable, be transformed into a more precise critical belief which is verifiable. (Peirce's account is, as we have seen, a *critical* commonsensism.) And it is not so off the mark to say with Peirce that the aim of science is to seek out facts and explain them. This remains true even though it is not the case that there are any facts which exist independently of a theory. There is nothing anomalous in saying that scientists seek to discover the facts and explain them even if it is not the case that there are facts or evidence just there to be discovered no matter what theory we devise or do not devise.[25] Theory may frame what is discoverable, but within that frame discoveries can be made and there can be no genuine discoveries without verification.

Postmodernists, skeptical about knowledge claims and about the objectivity of science, will also be skeptical of the idea that there just are such facts there to be sought out and explained. Peirce, though no defender of the correspondence theory of truth, still speaks unself-consciously of beliefs resting on observed facts, of beliefs coinciding with ascertainable facts and of the concordance of theory with fact. We can, in favorable circumstances, he believes, perceive the facts. Indeed, as we noted, for Peirce, all knowledge rests on perceptual judgments (V 88). All the ideas of science come to it by the way of abduction which "consists in studying the facts and devising a theory to explain them" (V 90). Facts, for him, are something there to be discovered. But it does not follow from that that facts are just there to be discovered *independently of theory.*

It is by so proceeding and only by so proceeding that we will come to understand things at all. And in this struggle to understand, the hypotheses we form in abducting, to be admissible hypotheses at all, must be, as he puts it, "capable of experimental verification" (V 123). Indeed, they are admissible "only insofar as it is capable of such verification" (V 123). But what exactly does this consist in? There seems, on Peirce's account, to be something like the confrontation of facts with experience, his Kantian inclinations to the contrary notwithstanding. But we have a plethora of uncashed metaphors here. It is anything but clear what we are saying. Facts are not like rocks in being something we could stumble on or collide with or simply confront like a bear on a hiking trail. Postmodernists would take them to be constructions. (But such talk is also very paradoxical and unclear.) To say facts are what true statements state may be true enough, but it doesn't tell us much and certainly does not show that facts are just there to be discovered. Facts, unlike stones or trees or bears, are, as we have remarked, very theory dependent. They do not speak for themselves. They are read in the light of theory. (Still they are read; they are there to be discovered.) Peirce, like Quine and Davidson, conceives of beliefs as being determined by some external permanency (V 242). But we have different vocabularies for talking about those external permanancies and it is not clear how we could decide, if we could decide, which is the right vocabulary or when we have the right vocabulary. It is not even evident that we have a coherent conception of what it is to have the *right* vocabulary. But for all of that, it remains true that for all of these vocabularies, if they are to be such that we understand what we are saying when we use them and can ascertain whether they are making claims which can be true or false, they must contain sentences capable of being used to make statements that can be empirically tested.[26] This gives us a way of sorting out sense from nonsense. We are not left with the merry-go-round of postmodernism.

Let us now turn to critical commonsensism. Postmodernists would surely not find much to applaud in critical commonsensism. They would (a) question its criticalness and (b) say that commonsense cannot be the basis for anything, cannot yield truth or provide knowledge or reasonable belief. But that response to Peirce is absurd for there is no doubt at all that fire burns, that water is wet, that snow is normally white, that cats are different than dogs, that people grow old and die, that people are sometimes selfish, that pain is bad, that pleasure is good, that there is some order in nature, and a host of other things. These truths are vague and in most circumstances their assertion is banal, but they are truths and we are more certain of them than we are of any theory which would deny them or try to provide a foundation for them. Any foundational claims we may proffer will be less certain than they are. As for the *criticalness* of critical commonsensism, it enters in the pragmatic link with commonsensism. We have, for example, the banality, true for all of that, that people are often selfish. Suppose a theoretician comes along and tries to strengthen this by saying that people invariably in the key areas of their lives, in their deepest relations with other persons, including the ones they love, put their own interests first. This is generated from the recognition of the truth of the banality, from reflecting on our lives, from observations of things around us, and from perplexities about what selfishness or putting your own interests first comes to. Moving from the vague commonsense belief we go to a critical belief that tries to capture what someone thinking about the import of the commonsense belief surmises (perhaps mistakenly) is really involved in the commonsense belief. Transformed it becomes a critical belief in need of clarification and then test by way of verification or falsification. There is there, where such a transformation is sought, a problematic situation where there is the live irritation of a real doubt. The truth of the truism will not settle the issue, but Peirce, fully recognizing that, has pointed to a method, a cluster of ways, of proceeding which can resolve that doubt in a way that would plainly have intersubjective validity. This is but an example, but there are hosts of similar cases where real doubts are generated as problematic situations arise and in turn are answered in this way. Postmodernists have given us no reason at all to think there is no reasonable fixing of belief or for thinking that speaking of "reasonable" in such circumstances is mere arm waving. (See here the introduction to part 4.)

Let me now turn to matters where the case is not so one-sided against postmodernism. I have, sticking with what they say (or rather some of what they sometimes flatly claim), represented postmodernists as denying that there is knowledge, truth, justice, a way of distinguishing specious from valid forms of argument or a way of distinguishing rational inquiry and reasonable procedures from irrational or unreasonable ones. I have noted their claim that what we call science is little more than the currently prestigious procedures for settling certain things. Peirce shows, if any of this needs showing, that none of this is so. He shows *au contraire* that we have reliable procedures for fixing beliefs and that while science certainly is not everything, it does make discoveries, resolves, not infrequently in an objective manner, some questions about how things are and sometimes in a cross-cultural way provides us with canons of rational inquiry that actually work in many domains. Moreover, its knowledge is cumulative. Scientists, unlike many other scholars and intellectuals, including philosophers, as the decades and centuries go by, stand on each others' shoulders though nothing like ultimate truth or certainty or a grasp of *the truth* is in this progression even contemplated or indeed even understood. Fallibilism is the name of the game.

However, while postmodernists say the absurd things I have just noted them saying, they also say other things with which pragmatists and indeed many others would extensively agree and which I would surmise is what they really have in mind, or at least should have in mind, when they make the above wild denials I have characterized as absurd. (As should always be the case, a principle of charity of interpretation is operating.) They speak in hyperboles and often achieve a shock effect. But, *sans* the rhetorical exaggeration, they, like Paul Feyerabend, have a deep critique of Enlightenment *rationalism* and of whatever residues there are in modernity which are still held captive to rationalism. But that should not include the whole of the Enlightenment. As it developed, the Enlightenment has transcended Enlightenment rationalism. The classical pragmatists, Max Weber, and Sigmund Freud are paradigmatic modernists and children of the Enlightenment. But they (Freud less clearly than the others) are as free of rationalism as any postmodernist and Weber is as pessimistic and Freud nearly so.

So far I have just continued my nay-saying to postmodernism. But it is here meant to lead up to the following which puts things in a somewhat different light. What is on the mark in postmodernism is their rejection of grand metanarratives purporting to give us "ultimate truth," to tell how history must go, and to reveal what it is finally to gain human emancipation so that all human beings can be so emancipated. Postmodernists claim as well and rightly that there are neither privileged epistemic structures securing "final truth" nor a foundational knowledge more secure than anything achievable by sciences or in everyday life and free from the contingencies of time and place. If to say there is no truth or knowledge is to say that there is no *such* truth or *such* knowledge then such a claim is not absurd but arguably true and perfectly in accord with pragmatism and the modern temper.

Similar things should be said for the postmodernist's denial that there is such a thing as a privileged access to reality, any ultimate or final explanations, any final truth behind appearances, any omniscient or God's-eye perspective, any (*pace* Bernard Williams) Absolute conception, any ultimate sources of justification or legitimation in any domain, any guarantees that reality must be such and such, any possibility of our problems being *finally* solved by a closed set of procedures or indeed by any procedures, and the like.

Postmodernists are right in making all these denials, but they do not herald a new postmodern era but are themselves the very hallmark of modernity: the result of the relentless applying of Enlightenment ways of viewing things. And they are also the claims of pragmatism, logical positivism, existentialism (though existentialism does anguish over the absence of the old guarantees). Indeed, many analytical philosophers and scientists would think these postmodernist denials are commonplaces so plainly true as to hardly deserve notice let alone argument about or dramatizing. Where, the claim might go, we stick with a literal reading of the hyperbole postmodernism is absurd; where we set that aside (demythologize postmodernism) it is true but platitudinous.

V

Is that all there is to be said? Not quite. There are three complicating points I want, in completing this chapter, to attend to.

Some postmodernists (Lyotard, for example) take at certain junctures a kind of Wittgensteinian turn. It is not only the case that no 'ultimate meta-discourse' (no language-game for all language-games) will succeed in situating, characterizing, and appraising all other discourses or even that any systematic and relatively holistic social theories (first-order theories), such as Weber's, Durkheim's, Mead's, or Habermas's, will enable us to ascertain the direction of social change, but we should recognize as well, the claim goes, that science (particular scientific practices and disciplines) has no pride of place among our various practices in ascertaining how things are.[27] The various sciences are just one loose cluster of language-games and social practices among a multitude of diverse language-games and social practices, none of which are more authoritative than any other in making discoveries, ascertaining the facts, predicting what will happen, interpreting events, and the like. But (*pace* Lyotard) if you want to take a trip up the Amazon and want to know what shots to have before you go, how wide the river is at its mouth and how deep, what kind of fish are in its waters, what is safe for you to eat and drink, and the like, it is plainly better to rely on scientific language-games than any other. They may, of course, get some of these things wrong or partially wrong, but still it is better to rely on the relevant scientific practices than on any other practices. Here things are not like they may be in discussing quantum mechanics or scientific cosmology. Where there are plainly facts of the matter at issue that might come into question, scientific language-games better guide us here than any of the other language-games. With the development of science in the last few centuries our ability to predict, control, to explain, and to systematically account for what we have explained has grown explosively. Scientism, as Jürgen Habermas has been particularly effective in showing, is indeed an ill and there is, as Peirce stressed, no scientific undermining, or *perhaps* even understanding, of a lot of common sense (as long as it remains common sense), but it is an impoverished understanding of our history not to see how special science is in the business of understanding, explaining, and gaining knowledge: in coming to know how things are.[28]

The second point I wish to make cuts against the pragmatists and for the postmodernists. Pragmatists as a matter of fact have been much too optimistic about the emancipatory or enabling powers of the sciences and all the good things really scientific thinking will bring us. Enlightenment hopes here have not been realized or at best only sporadically so. Peirce's picture of the universe, and even more so Dewey's, was far too rosy, and this continued on (though somewhat muted) with later pragmatists (Hook and Nagel) who, given the actual course of history, should have known better. (Contrast for a more realistic view of things here such other Enlightenment figures as Max Horkheimer and Theodor Adorno.[29]) Science and scientific intelligence has not freed us from prejudice, impoverishment, degradation, exploitation, and other great social and personal ills. The world we live in is not something to cheer about or rest content with. Baudrillard and Foucault powerfully show us how rotten things are and give us good reason to think a rosy future is not just around the corner. Foucault in particular is a genius in revealing the dark underside of things that at first seem emancipatory and progressive or at least as things making for human welfare rather than illfare. He shows how pervasively and insidiously they harm human beings impeding in all kinds of complicated ways their self-realization. But from this we cannot draw the conclusion (something that Baudrillard in particular leaps to) that we cannot know anything, that everything is irrational, that science is a myth, and the like. This cannot follow from his account of how rotten things are. Indeed, it is even incompatible with it. For only if his description is accurate and his interpretations are reasonable (plausible) can it be the case that we have reason to believe that things are as he says they are. If there is no such thing as accurate description, reasonable interpretation, and rational inquiry, then there is no way of showing that things are rotten or indeed are any other way. There just can be no showing what is the case. Moreover, Noam Chomsky in our time, Bertrand Russell before him, and Max Weber still earlier powerfully conveyed a sense of the rottenness of things while resolutely applying scientific procedures. Weber with very few changes could have been a Peircean with respect to underlying methodology and was with Peirce in his respect for and confidence in the explanatory power of science. Yet his view of the world was, if anything, bleaker than even Baudrillard's or Foucault's. Science shows us, he thought, that we are in the iron cage, not that our future is rosy and that democracy (bringing with it great blessings) will triumph. I am inclined to think that science neither shows us that we are in the iron cage nor that our future is rosy. But that is not to the point here, the present point being rather that pragmatism with its trust in scientific method does not commit us to belief in a world of sweetness and light, where, with the progress of science, societies will become free, human beings emancipated, and the world just. A pragmatist could as consistently have a Weberian or Orwellian vision of the world as a Deweyan one. Confidence in the reliability of scientific method in fixing, and objectively fixing, belief and in the explanatory power of well-formed abductions is one thing; belief in science as a force for the good leading to a world that, with the spread of scientific ways of thinking, will become better and progressively more just is another thing altogether. Postmodernist scoffing at the latter (though still perhaps mistaken) is very much to the point, but it shows nothing at all against science's capacity to explain, interpret, and accurately describe how things are.

Finally (thirdly), I want to turn to a powerful point postmodernists have made about the self-image and role of intellectuals in general and philosophers in particular. In that respect almost all philosophers, whether they are pragmatists, Humeans, Kantians, Davidsonian holists, or Dummettian molecularists, see themselves as getting clear or at least clearer about things. Standardly this is viewed as a lonely endeavor, but even if it, as Peirce sometimes viewed it, is seen as a cooperative endeavor of disciplined logicians and scientist-philosophers, it still is viewed as a matter of getting clear about things—in some cases by some philosophers (though not by pragmatists) as getting finally and completely clear about things. The assumption is that there is the possibility of some such getting clear about things and that with that getting clear or at least clearer a greater enlightenment or emancipation will obtain at least for the successful inquirer herself, but more generally it is thought that it will, by spreading the word a bit, be more generally enlightening, emancipatory, and liberating.

This is an image, a deep self-image, yielding, in a Weberian conception of vocation, a sense of the vocation of philosophers. But it is a conception that postmodernists, along with Wittgenstein, challenge: Foucault with a kind of disguised moral passion and Derrida mockingly, ironically, and playfully. There is, as Wittgenstein argued, no coherent conception of complete clarity; we can assemble reminders for particular purposes and sometimes unblock particular conceptual confusions; moreover, as Peirce and Dewey stressed, where in a specific situation with respect to a determinate problem there is the irritation of doubt, we can sometimes clarify these particular things and with a good abduction, subsequently tested, sometimes resolve that doubt. But that this actually incrementally or by some quantum leap would add up to a clearer picture of the world, rather than, as we muddle along, to the generating of still further problems and so on indefinitely, with the old solutions frequently forgotten, is not evident. The underlying but seldom articulated idea is that we can, if we only work at it very hard and very intelligently (using our "scientific intelligence"), finally really get clear about what rationality is, about how language works, about what the concept of truth is really like, and the like.

We will then with this, proceeding as good scientific and commonsense reasoners—or perhaps as philosophical reasoners—gain the truth or at least get an edge up on the truth and what it is to think and perhaps to live rationally.

This familiar and comforting idea is for postmodernists, as for Feyerabend, the subject not only of considerable suspicion but of some not inconsiderable irony and ridicule as well. Truth, as later pragmatists such as Quine and Rorty have argued, is not very useful as an explanatory concept.[30] We may very well, as Quine and Rorty think, get along perfectly well with disquotation: with, that is, a deflationary conception of truth. Moreover, while we can learn many truths (perfectly objective truths) often easily enough, we haven't the foggiest notion of what *the* truth is. Even the notion of a "true theory" is not very perspicuous and the notion of the true perspective of or on the world, the right picture of the world, or the correct (true) description of the world, for reasons Goodman, Rorty, and Putnam have powerfully brought forth, probably (very probably) is a Holmesless Watson. We do not know what we are talking about when we talk about the one true description of the world or the finally correct vocabulary; and without a God's-eye view or perspective or an Absolute conception of the world or a view from nowhere, nothing like this is even possible. But such conceptions themselves are at best impossible and at worst incoherent, with the best betting going on incoherence.

Davidson and Rorty have shown us that this does not land us in conceptual relativism (the very idea being incoherent), in nihilism, or in subjectivism or any such bad things, but it does leave us without a view from nowhere yielding the one true description of the world.[31] We have no idea of what this would be like. Our discontents here, given our traditional self-image of our vocation, will be exacerbated if beyond this we also think, as there are deep impulses in philosophy prompting us to think, that we need this one true description to help us to come to understand, or at least to gain some understanding of, "the truth about life." Perhaps the big-true-picture-image could be separated from the truth-about-life-image, as in Pascal and Kierkegaard, but both images, though for different reasons, are (to put it minimally) deeply problematic and perhaps, in spite of the wish of some of us to gain some inkling concerning "the truth about life," such conceptions are nonsensical, or at least very problematic, and would be set aside by anyone who was clearheaded and toughminded. (Feminists have made us aware that we ought to query such vocabulary.) Indeed, there may be good Freudian reasons for being suspicious of the soundness of the motives of anyone with a penchant for finding what "the truth about life really is," though we should not forget that Freud had his tale to tell here, too. (After all, didn't he think he was telling us, in a way we were bound to resist, something about the truth about life?)

In any event, it is certainly not unnatural to think that such considerations should be set aside. It is not only that we do not have the foggiest idea about what the one true description of the world is, but we do not have the foggiest idea about what the truth about life is either. But what then does our self-image as attempting to get clear about things come to? It is not, let us now assume, getting clear about the "truth about life" or discovering or articulating what a just and truly humane society really is and how it could be sustained or about the gaining of a greater approximation to the "true description of the world." But then what is it? Is it just to resolve, giving a perspicuous representation, some conceptual puzzles? Just any puzzles? Key puzzles? But, if we say the latter, on what grounds do we say they are key? John Austin thought that if we could show that it is not true that all cans are constitutionally iffy, then that resolution of this puzzle about cans would show us either the falseness or the indeterminacy (determinism being a name for nothing clear) of determinism and that such a showing would in turn aid us in gaining a truer picture of the world. Something like this has repeatedly been an underlying assumption of linguistic philosophers and other philosophers as well. But this seems at least to be implicitly appealing (and requiring that appeal) to the at least seemingly incoherent conception of the one true description of the world or at least something which is itself parasitic—or at least seemingly so—on that, namely, a truer or more adequate description of the world. But postmodernists and philosophers such as Wittgenstein, Rorty, Goodman, and Putnam have powerfully challenged whether we have any coherent conception of that. It seems at least that we have nothing coherent here. But then what happens to our self-image—an image which has fueled philosophy—of getting clear or clearer about things?

We might take a Wittgensteinian turn and say we assemble reminders to break the spell of a particular conceptual confusion that has a grip on us. This might be good therapy. But if there is no correct description of the world, why care about breaking conceptual confusion? Indeed, what can "being unconfused" come to as distinct from "being confused"? What can Wittgenstein's sometimes talk about seeing things rightly come to? What, if we look at it toughmindedly, is the virtue of being unconfused, particularly if ever new confusions lurk around the corner and we do not at least, as one by one we dispel them, crawl toward a greater clarity of understanding: we do not come in time, in any *more* global or holistic sense, to command a clearer view of things? That we can come to command such a clearer view at least looks very problematic, so problematic that it is natural enough to wonder if we have any coherent understanding of what that is. But if that is so, what (if anything) is the end of inquiry?[32] What is it that we are trying to do and why do we try to do it?

Wittgenstein sometimes, though with great ambivalence and skepticism, hoped an occasion-by-occasion clarity concerning particular philosophical obsessions, rooted in particular confusions about the workings of our language, might sometimes help us to see our situation a little better and perhaps even to respond to it more adequately, without giving us (what he thought impossible and perhaps not even coherent) the correct or more nearly correct picture of our world or (what very well might come to the same thing) the correct overall picture of our language. (We see here the very great distance between Wittgenstein and Dummett.) But, as Wittgenstein was perfectly aware, there is at least as much reason for incredulity about so responding—that is, about so straightening the bent twigs of lives which are (as Kant believed) by their very nature prone to be crooked—as there is for being incredulous about gaining the right vocabulary which will finally yield the one true description of the world or the for a time best approximation to it. (If we have no understanding of what it is, we will have no understanding of its approximation either.)

What have we left, then? For scientists, abductions that in turn can be confirmed or infirmed and deductively elaborated. For philosophers, by contrast (where they are not themselves practicing a science or characterizing, as Peirce and Carnap did, its logic), all that seems to be left is the solving of puzzles (how is it possible that Achilles can catch up with the tortoise) with no ulterior purpose or rationale. That, though small potatoes, can be good fun for those who like that sort of thing and so we come to a Derridian playfulness.

Peirce endeavored to ascertain how we can make our ideas clear, as did the logical positivists, in an effort to separate the wheat from the chaff, sense from nonsense, by providing us with a criterion of cognitive or at least factual significance, so that we could somehow gain a more adequate understanding of our world. I, for reasons the preceding paragraphs gesture at, am anything but sure that we understand what we are talking about here or that such an endeavor even makes sense. Yet I remain Peircean in retaining some such *hope*. It goes, I believe, with the vocation and the vocation has a grip (perhaps an unfortunate grip) on how we—that is we philosophers—reflectively think about life. Postmodernists do us a good service in challenging this conception of ourselves as philosophers. It is a challenge that as far as I can see has not been met and perhaps cannot be met. It will not do to knee-jerk react to them as the new irrationalists or obscurantists. That clouds things and perhaps does little more than reveal the anxieties of people who so react. What I hope for, to end on a more upbeat note, is that, while for Rortyish-Putnamish reasons we should reject all talk about the one true or correct description of the world, we could, that notwithstanding, perhaps gain some reasonable understanding of the idea of coming to know how things are without identifying the latter with the former. I am ambivalently inclined to think that Peirce did something toward that without having any very clear understanding of what I am saying. I throw it out to you as a vague abduction that might, just might, be precised into something which has something more than a suggestive, and perhaps only a mythical, import.

NOTES

1. Kai Nielsen, *After the Demise of the Tradition* (Boulder, Colo.: Westview Press, 1991).

2. Linda J. Nicholson, ed., *Feminism/Postmodernism* (New York: Routledge, Chapman and Hall, 1990); Nancy Fraser, *Unruly Practices* (Minneapolis, Minn.: University of Minnesota Press, 1989); Seyla Benhabib and Drucilla Cornell, eds., *Feminism as Critique* (Cambridge: Polity Press, 1987).

3. Stanley Fish, *Doing What Comes Naturally* (Durham, N.C.: Duke University Press, 1990); Richard Rorty, *Consequences of Pragmatism* (Minneapolis, Minn.: University of Minnesota Press, 1982); Richard Rorty, *Objectivity, Relativity, and Truth* (Cambridge: Cambridge University Press, 1991); and Richard Rorty, "Feminism and Pragmatism," *Radical Philosophy* 59 (Autumn 1991): 3–14. See also C. G. Prado, *The Limits of Pragmatism* (Atlantic Highlands, N.J.: Humanities Press, 1987).

4. Christopher Norris, *What's Wrong with Postmodernism?* (Baltimore, Md.: Johns Hopkins University Press, 1990), 134–65; Christopher Norris, *Derrida* (Cambridge, Mass.: Harvard University Press, 1978); and Rodolphe Gasché, *The Tain of the Mirror* (Cambridge, Mass.: Harvard University Press, 1986).

5. Michel Foucault, *The Foucault Reader* (New York: Pantheon Books, 1984), 32–120; David Couzens Hoy, ed., *Foucault: A Critical Reader* (Oxford: Basil Blackwell, 1986), 1–40, 109–47; and Hubert L. Dreyfus and Paul Rabinow, *Michel Foucault: Beyond Structuralism and Hermeneutics* (Chicago, Ill.: University of Chicago Press, 1982).

6. Jean-François Lyotard, *The Postmodern Condition: A Report on Knowledge* (Minneapolis, Minn.: University of Minnesota Press, 1979) and *The Differend: Phrases in Dispute* (Minneapolis, Minn.: University of Minnesota Press, 1988).

7. Lyotard, *The Postmodern Condition*; and Frederick Crews, *Skeptical Engagements* (New York: Oxford University Press, 1986), 159–78.

8. Jean Baudrillard, *Oublier Foucault* (Paris: Editions Galilée, 1977); *Les Strategies Fatales* (Paris: Bernard Grasset, 1983); and Mark Poster, ed., *Jean Baudrillard: Selected Writings* (Cambridge: Polity Press, 1988). For critical comment see Christopher Norris, *What's Wrong with Postmodernism*, 164–93. See also W. J. T. Mitchell, ed., *Against Theory: Literary Theory and the New Pragmatism* (Chicago, Ill.: University of Chicago Press, 1985).

9. Peter Dews, *Logics of Disintegration: Post-Structuralist Thought and the Claims of Critical Theory* (London: Verso, 1987), 6. See also his very perceptive introduction to Jürgen Habermas's *Autonomy and Solidarity* (London: Verso, 1986), 1–34.

10. Michel Foucault, *Power/Knowledge* (New York: Pantheon, 1980) and *Foucault Reader*, 239–89.

11. Nancy Fraser and Linda J. Nicholson, "Social Criticism Without Philosophy: An Encounter Between Feminism and Postmodernism," in Linda J. Nicholson, ed., *Feminism/Postmodernism*, 19–38.

12. Stephen K. White, *Political Theory and Postmodernism* (New York: Cambridge University Press, 1991), 3.

13. See references in note 10.

14. Lyotard, *The Differend: Phrases in Dispute*, xiii, 140–42.

15. White, *Political Theory and Postmodernism*, 20.

16. Ibid.

17. Norris, *What's Wrong With Postmodernism?* 28.

18. Charles Hartshorne and Paul Weiss, eds., *Charles Sanders Peirce: Collected Pa-*

pers, vol. 5 (Cambridge, Mass.: Harvard University Press, 1934); and Arthur W. Burks, ed., *Charles Sanders Peirce: Collected Papers,* vol. 7 (Cambridge, Mass.: Harvard University Press, 1958). References to Peirce will be from these texts and will be given in the text with the volume indicated by the volume number.

19. This feature of Peirce's thought is well articulated by W. B. Gallie, *Peirce and Pragmatism* (Middlesex, England: Penguin Books, 1952), 59–138.

20. Richard Rorty, *Essays on Heidegger and Others* (Cambridge: Cambridge University Press, 1991), 164–76.

21. See references in note 18.

22. John P. Murphy brings out these links well in his *Pragmatism from Peirce to Davidson* (Boulder, Colo.: Westview Press, 1990).

23. Kai Nielsen, "Can There Be Justified Philosophical Beliefs?" *Iyyun* 40 (July 1991): 235–70.

24. The "thus" there might be challenged. It is surely elliptical. I think, however, that the ellipses can be filled in. But I would not deny that here I am skating on what may be thin ice.

25. See Ernest Nagel, *Teleology Revisited and Other Essays in the Philosophy and History of Science* (New York: Columbia University Press, 1979), 1–48, 64–94.

26. The holism here leaves the door open for there being individual sentences used to make truth-claims which are not themselves verifiable. It is just that they must be part of a cluster of sentences at least some of which are verifiable. But verification is not the only way of warding off mischief.

27. Nagel in the collection of essays cited in note 25 sought to resist that last claim. I did as well, particularly in chapter 8 of my *After the Demise of the Tradition,* 163–94. But it is not, as I claimed there, that there is a general difference between scientific language-games and other language-games in the way words and things are related. Barry Allen's critique of me there is well taken, but the practices of experimental testing embedded in scientific practices, and thus in scientific language-games, give us a more reliable way of fixing belief concerning matters of fact than we have in other domains. There is, I am claiming, something of central importance about scientific method in the ascertainment of factual truth. Other conversations are not as good at tracking such truths.

28. See the references to Nagel cited above. For Habermas on scientism see Jürgen Habermas, *Toward a Rational Society* (Boston, Mass.: Beacon Press, 1970), 62–122.

29. Max Horkheimer and Theodor Adorno, *The Dialectics of Enlightenment* (New York: Herder and Herder, 1972).

30. See John P. Murphy, *Pragmatism From Peirce to Davidson*; Richard Rorty, *Objectivity, Relativism, and Truth,* 126–61; W. V. Quine, *Pursuit of Truth* (Cambridge, Mass.: Harvard University Press, 1990).

31. Richard Rorty, *Consequences of Pragmatism*; Richard Rorty, *Objectivity, Relativism, and Truth;* and Donald Davidson, *Inquiries into Truth and Interpretation* (Oxford: Clarendon Press, 1984) and his "A Coherence Theory of Truth and Knowledge," in *Reading Rorty,* ed. Alan Malachowski (Oxford: Basil Blackwell, 1990), 120–38.

32. Richard Rorty, "Life at the End of Inquiry," *London Review of Books* (August 2–September 6, 1984).

Chapter Eleven

Legitimation in Complex Societies: Some Habermasian Themes

I

Max Weber's worry about the iron cage is well known. He was keenly aware of the increasing bureaucratization of the state and with that the expansion of the role of bureaucracy in our daily lives and how our very efforts to contain state bureaucracy, or indeed any other kind of bureaucracy, tend to have the effect of increasing it. In the modern world the triumph of science, capitalism, and bureaucratic organization is so extensive that we, even when we can think of alternative ways of organizing our lives together, come, not unnaturally, to feel that we have no ground on which to stand that would make socially effective any critical stance we could take against such an organization of social life. If they have such an inexorable bureaucratic organization, how can those societies have legitimate authority?

We must not only ask, as do Max Weber and Seymour Lipset, how the state generates belief in its own legitimacy, we must, as well, ask about the truth or falsity or justifiedness or unjustifiedness of those beliefs themselves.[1] This is a question that Jürgen Habermas, by contrast with Weber and Lipset, asks. Weber thinks that to ask whether a belief in legitimacy is a true belief puts an impossible demand on any social system. Habermas, by contrast, thinks that, given both our cognitive and moral interests, we cannot, if we attend to them, but put such a demand on the system. Indeed, such a demand is built into the very way we conceptualize ourselves, for if we do not do that, if we do not make such a demand concerning legitimacy, that comes to in effect conceding to ourselves that every so-called legitimate order is in reality grounded in mystification, ideology, and manipulation.[2] That, Habermas maintains, is

329

something that we as self-conscious, caring, reflective agents cannot accept. The very reflective putting it to ourselves causes us to reject it.

What a critical theory of society is designed to do is to elucidate and justify a set of rational standards—universally acceptable rational standards—against which beliefs in legitimacy or illegitimacy can be assessed. But how is this to be done? Or, indeed, can it be done? There are all sorts of ideological distortions around and the unmaskers sometimes are themselves the unwitting wearers of masks. We not only want to know whether people believe in the legitimacy or for that matter the illegitimacy of their social arrangements; we want to know as well when, if ever, people, rational agents, reasonable persons, living under conditions of undistorted discourse (if such conditions can be had), would be justified in believing in the legitimacy of the social order in which they live. Habermas does not, of course, say that people are through and through rational or reasonable or are living under conditions of undistorted discourse, but, like John Rawls, he thinks we are generally sufficiently rational and reasonable to be capable of conceiving of what those conditions would look like were they to obtain. We can conceive of a world in which our moral and other normative beliefs, as well as our factual beliefs and logical conceptions, are formed under conditions of absolutely free and unlimited discussion, reflective deliberation, and debate. The practices and institutions that we should set up or, where they are already in place, should continue to give our allegiance to, if indeed there are any such practices and institutions, are those practices or institutions which best square with beliefs that would survive such a winnowing. They will be the practices and institutions we would freely consent to establish under such ideal conditions where the only constraint on their establishment would be the distinctive force of the better argument or better deliberation. (It is important that it is the peculiar force of the better argument or better deliberation under conditions of undistorted communication.)

Political and quasi-political institutions or practices are at least potentially repressive. They can use force and typically have considerable power. Given this feature of such institutions or practices, they can only have genuine legitimacy (*de jure* legitimacy) if they are practices or institutions which would be established and sustained under conditions of freedom and equality and would be accepted by the unforced consent of all those subsequently liable to be affected by their behavior, and whose acceptance or rejection was only constrained, as I have just remarked, by the peculiar force of the better argument or better deliberation.[3] When people so reason and so act and such conditions obtain these people are rational people reasoning and living under conditions of undistorted discourse. Where we have norms of legitimate authority so formed we have logically and morally valid norms of legitimacy. This, for good or for ill, is a clear articulation of the intellectual and moral stance of modernity firmly reflecting the ideas of the Enlightenment.

Habermas is a powerful spokesman for and interpreter of modernity. Michel Foucault, by contrast, as a paradigmatic postmodernist thinker, believes that such a would-be universalistic communicative ethic is a pure mystification or self-deception which fails to recognize the depth and pervasiveness of the will to power. Indeed, Foucault is often taken, mistakenly, I believe, as I shall argue in the next chapter, to be making the even stronger claim that with Habermas, as well as rather more generally, there is a failure to understand that for modern thought no morality is possible. Modernists, the claim goes, fail to recognize that the deepest norms and standards of modernity are arbitrary constructions. However, he does make the weaker claim that it is a myth to believe, as modernists such as Habermas, Rawls, and Ronald Dworkin do, that we can construct universal rational standards of morality out of historically specific and culturally determinate moral and political conceptions rooted in specific ways of life. No such perspective can be articulated to say nothing of its being sustained. What we need to recognize, Foucault claims, is what Nietzsche recognized, namely, that *power is the basis of order*.[4] There is no rational ground for a positive theory of legitimacy. All we can do, by a kind of negative dialectical attention, is closely, and with a good understanding of their historical development, note how things actually are in our societies and, in particular, take note of their various not-so-nice hidden rationales and agendas and then, in those specific situations, develop strategies of resistance.

II

Rather than directly turning to such substantive matters, let me first make some familiar but still, for the context of our discussion, useful conceptual distinctions. There is a distinction between *de jure* authority (the right to command and to be obeyed) and *de facto* authority (the ability to get one's authority claims accepted by those against whom they are asserted). There is a closely related and parallel distinction between *de jure* legitimation and *de facto* legitimation.[5] *De jure* legitimation would be a legitimation that actually showed that a state, a socioeconomic system, a church, a legal system, and the like rightly deserved acceptance and loyalty. A *de facto* legitimation would be a rationale or procedure which succeeded in convincing people, whether rightly or not, that a state, a socioeconomic system, a church, a legal system, and the like actually rightly deserved acceptance and loyalty. A procedure— it could be an elaborate and carefully orchestrated ideology widely disseminated by a consciousness industry—could convince people that some socioeconomic system rightly deserved our acceptance and loyalty when in reality it did not. In fact, as I read him, that is exactly what Habermas is saying about at least the extant capitalist democracies. Moreover, since we can, and some of us do, draw this distinction, and there is a point in drawing the distinction, we have—or so at least it seems natural to believe—a real distinction between *de jure* legitimation and *de facto* legitimation. It *may* very well be that a *political* legitimation to be a *de jure* legitimation must also be a *de facto* legitimation, but a legitimation can be merely a *de facto* legitimation without being *de jure*.

I take it that Habermas, who does not use this terminology, is, all the same, concerned with the obtaining of *de jure* legitimation. In speaking of the distorted discourse we use in our ideologically befuddled state and contrasting it with the ideal speech situation where we would attain enlightenment and emancipation, Habermas is in effect characterizing a situation where, if it were to obtain, a socioeconomic system which would gain acceptance under those conditions would indeed be a system which deserves our acceptance and loyalty. Were this situation to obtain, we would have not only *de facto* legitimacy but *de jure* legitimacy as well and so we would actually have a social order to which we should be loyal.

However, in his "Legitimation Problems in Late Capitalism" and in his book *Legitimation Crisis*, Habermas is principally talking about what I have called *de facto* legitimation.[6] There he is attempting to show how the system secures belief in its own legitimacy in late capitalist societies, where, through the adroit use of the consciousness industry, ideological befuddlement is very deep and pervasive. He shows, that is, how it secures *de facto*, though not *de jure*, legitimation. However, he also shows, given the way the system works and is likely to continue to work, what possible crises of a systemic nature might arise in the capitalist system which might break up the ideological hegemony afforded by this *de facto* legitimacy. In other words, he is inquiring into what might lead masses of people to cease to believe in the legitimacy of the system and thereby make really fundamental social change possible.

What Habermas takes to be the basic "contradiction" of the capitalist order is in the conflict inherent in the very idea of the *private* appropriation of *public* wealth: a public wealth which, in the *ideology* of the capitalist system, is treated as private wealth. Wealth in the society is produced socially yet it is treated as the private property of certain individuals who are taken to be the owners of productive property. This is a central organizing principle of capitalist society. It is not a principle that a capitalist society could abandon while remaining a capitalist society. Political and social decisions which are made in accordance with that organizational principle cannot, Habermas contends, attain *de jure* authority and legitimacy because they are not principles concerning which there could be a rational or reasonable consensus. That is they would not be accepted in an ideal speech situation. As Thomas McCarthy well puts it in expounding Habermas's position:

They could not be justified in a general and unrestricted discussion of what, in the light of present and possible circumstances, is in the best interests of all affected by them. Hence the stability of the capitalist social formation depends on the continued effectiveness of legitimations that could not withstand discursive examination.[7]

Capitalism is stuck with what appears at least to be the circle squaring enterprise of fairly—and thus legitimately—distributing what is socially produced inequitably. It cannot, while remaining a capitalist system, distribute it equitably, but that means the capitalist system cannot distribute it legitimately. The productive-distributive system under capitalism will have, at best, *de facto* legitimacy. It will never have *de jure* legitimacy. A task for ideology will be to make the worse seem to be the better course and to give the appearance—the veneer—of legitimacy to that which lacks, and necessarily so, any genuine legitimacy.

This is essentially a moral critique, yet Habermas in developing his critical theory does not, at this point and in the course of articulating his account of the legitimation crisis, develop a moral theory. He is not out here, or elsewhere, given his proceduralism, to develop anything like a moral philosophy, after the fashion of Kant, Mill, Sidgwick, Rawls, Gauthier, or Parfit.

Thomas McCarthy, in this connection, aptly points out the different sort of thing that is going on here and shows, in doing it, both an important way in which Habermas's account is linked to the Marxist tradition and differs from orthodox Marxism. McCarthy remarks:

Habermas's critique appears to be essentially moral; social reality is measured against an abstract standard of reason and found wanting. However if we recall his views on the nature of critical social theory—from the 'empirical philosophy of history with a practical intent' to the 'reconstruction of historical materialism'—we might expect that he would not leave off with a moral condemnation. And in fact the burden of his argument in *Legitimation Crisis* is to the effect that the basic contradiction of contemporary capitalism issues in crisis tendencies that can be empirically ascertained. The critique as a whole, then, assumes a Marxist form: what is morally required is being empirically prepared: the seeds of the new society are being formed in the womb of the old. But it is a Marxist critique with important differences. In the first place, the crisis tendencies pregnant with the future are no longer located immediately in the economic sphere but in the sociocultural sphere. They do not directly concern the reproduction of the material conditions of life but the reproduction of reliable structures of intersubjectivity. Habermas thus attempts to make a case for the likelihood of a legitimation crisis, not an economic crisis.[8]

To see and then to critically assess what is involved here I shall first depict how Habermas characterizes and assesses crisis tendencies in advanced capitalism (organized capitalism) in his "What Does Legitimation Crisis Mean Today? Legitimation Problems in Late Capitalism."[9]

III

Jürgen Habermas asks: "is late capitalism following the same or a similar self-destructive pattern of development as classical—i.e., competitive—capitalism? Or has the organizing principle of late capitalism changed so greatly that the accumulation process no longer generates any problems jeopardizing its existence?"[10] In coming to grips with this problem, he first gives "a rough descriptive model of the most important structural features of late capitalist societies."[11] We need to remember, Habermas tells us, that capitalist society sees itself "as an instrumental group that accumulates social wealth only by way of private wealth. . . ."[12] That is to say, bourgeois society "guarantees economic growth and general welfare through competition between strategically acting private persons."[13] The firm move away from competitive capitalism to state or corporate capitalism—a move, that is, to a highly organized form of capitalism with extensive and complex state intervention and steering mechanisms—is a move that makes it increasingly difficult, Habermas maintains, to sell capitalism as a legitimate way of organizing social life.

Habermas, in giving his rough descriptive-explanatory model of organized capitalist societies, distinguishes four possible crisis tendencies in such capitalism. They are tendencies rooted (1) in how the economy functions, (2) in how administration of the society functions, (3) in needs for *de facto* legitimation, and (4) in what he calls motivational needs. It is Habermas's argument that any of these tendencies could—empirically speaking could—erupt into an actual crisis. It is even more likely that the combined force of these tendencies might give rise to an actual crisis that will trigger the breakdown of capitalism. But to say that it *could* occur—that there *could* be a crisis—is not to say that it *will* occur, let alone that it *must* occur. Habermas thinks, rightly it seems to me, that we can have no guarantees here. He is plainly not a believer in historical inevitability. But he is saying that it is not unreasonable to hope for, to struggle to bring about, and indeed to expect such a crisis and he is further saying, as a moral comment, as we have seen, that no genuine *de jure* legitimation can be achieved under capitalism. But he does not commit himself to an unqualified yes to the question "Can a crisis of advanced capitalism be systematically predicted today?" What he does say is that if certain tendencies continue and countervailing conditions do not obtain, then it is not unreasonable to expect a crisis in legitimacy that will trigger the downfall of capitalism and the beginning of the transition to social-ism. Habermas claims nothing more than that it is not unreasonable to believe that there will actually be a legitimation crisis. We get crisis tendencies when the "'organizational principle' of a society does not permit the resolution of problems that are critical for its continued existence."[14] As society is directed by its administrative units—or at least there is the serious attempt at such di-rection—steering problems arise that endanger social integration.

IV

Present capitalist societies are, as we remarked, organized or state regulated forms of capitalism.[15] We should come to understand this in terms of how the accumulation process works in such societies. We now have gigantic na-tional or multinational corporations, some of which are in many ways far more powerful than even middle-sized capitalist states. With this economic concentration, and the globalization that goes with it, we get "the organiza-tion of markets for goods, capital, and labor."[16] Along with this, the inter-ventionist capitalist state keeps filling the increasingly functional gaps in the market. Still, even with the extension of this, "the steering mechanism of the market will continue to function as long as investments are determined by company profits."[17] We do not in the major industries have a freely compet-itive capitalism anymore, but we still have market mechanisms working in capitalism. The interventionist state will restrict the freedom of business ac-tivities of individual capitalists, but there will still in such organized capital-ist societies be no "political planning to allocate scarce resources as long as the overall societal priorities develop naturally."[18] (By "developing natu-rally" here Habermas means "developing as an indirect result of the strategies of private enterprise.")

Habermas then proceeds to characterize (1) the economic system, (2) the administrative system, and (3) the legitimation system of advanced capitalist societies. The economic system is characterized in terms of a "three-sector model based on the distinction between the private and public areas."[19] In the economic system there are two distinct areas: (1) a competitive area dominated by labor-intensive industries such as the clothing industry where labor is not extensively organized and where salaries are low and (2) monopolistic indus-tries that still operate by market mechanisms and allow a competitive fringe. They are large industries and they are capital-intensive. Labor in those indus-tries is generally unionized and paid at a higher level with more benefits than in the competitive sector. In addition to private production there is a "public area" where the investment decisions of the industry operate independently of the market. I refer to such industries as the armament industries and the space-travel industries. These industries are either directly controlled by the government or they are private firms living off government contracts. They, like the monopolies, are also capital-intensive industries with reasonably well-paid workers with generally strong unions.

In addition to the economic system in the state, the state apparatus also has an *administrative system*. This administrative system seeks to improve the conditions for utilizing capital. More generally it "regulates the overall economic cycle by means of global planning."[20] However, in contrast with how it operates in a state socialist system, this global planning in capitalist societies will be constrained by a systemic prohibition against restricting the investment decisions of private enterprises. It will regulate them to a certain extent in crisis management, but it will not decide what investment strategies are to be followed. What global planning, by contrast, is generally concerned with is with crisis management within the capitalist system. It is concerned to have a stable capitalist system wherever that system retains hegemony. There are various imperatives of the capitalist system such as steady growth and monetary stability. In crisis management to meet those imperatives, the administrative system develops certain avoidance strategies sensitive to the standard preference structures of the capitalist class. In so reacting the administrative system takes (a) "fiscal and financial measures to regulate cycles" and (b) "individual measures to regulate investments and overall demand."[21] By (b) Habermas means things like subsidies, price guarantees, government contracts based on business-cycle policies, and the like. The administrative system must, as we have noted, do all this without interfering with investment decisions of capitalist enterprises. Instead, it manipulates the marginal conditions that go along with private enterprise "in order to correct the market mechanism by neutralizing dysfunctional side effects."[22] It does this by creating or improving conditions for utilizing excess accumulated capital.

Such an interventionist capitalist state needs to get into the legitimation business. It intervenes in the production process in such a way that the traditional and basic bourgeois ideology of fair exchange tends to get undermined or at least damaged. The capitalist state and capitalist society must—particularly in the face of that—legitimate itself and it needs, what Habermas calls, a *legitimation system* to do so. The *ideology* of a competitive capitalism, pinnacling, as I have just remarked, in the ideology of fair exchange, has collapsed. But, prior to its collapse, it in turn effectively undermined key traditions of precapitalist societies. Bourgeois ideology undermined the remnants of traditionalism inherited from the feudal order and in turn is undermined by a new ideology rising out of changed socioeconomic conditions.

There is, Habermas argues, no turning back here. Bourgeois ideology has created a universalistic value system with a doctrine of universal human rights, including civil rights such as universal suffrage. These conceptions are thoroughly stamped into the populations of these societies. Advanced capitalist societies are by now human rights cultures. They are, moreover, not the sort of things that people in such societies would readily give up. And, only in rare circumstances can legitimation be obtained without them and then only temporarily. There is no stable legitimation—remember here we are speaking of *de facto* legitimation—in such societies without at least formal democracy. "The thousand-year Reich" did not last very long.

To keep—try to keep—such societies from crises, the legitimation system must so function that the administrative system stands at a certain distance from the shaping of a legitimating will. That is to say the state apparatus must not control the media and the like and there must be voting mechanisms in the society. If that doesn't obtain, the society becomes suspect and its stability is uncertain. However, if the more or less invisible administrative hand does not function very well and in such a circumstance we in some way manage to go from formal democracy to genuine democracy to a situation, that is, where there is "wide participation by the citizens in the process of shaping political will," that would have for capitalism the destabilizing effect of exposing the tension between administratively socialized production and a private form of acquiring the control and value of that socialized production. In productive activity, where that situation is clearly seen, where industrial democracy comes to be seen as a plain requirement of the very idea of democracy, it will be very difficult to convince people of the legitimacy of such private appropriation. What the legitimation system needs to further and sustain its defense of the capitalist system is a belief system which "elicits mass loyalty but avoids participation."[23] Contemporary capitalism needs a citizenry who are passive privatized persons with little political awareness. It does not want what J. S. Mill, John Dewey, and Habermas all take to be essential to democracy, namely a vitalized public sphere.

V

After characterizing these three elements of the capitalist system—the economic system, the administrative system, and the legitimation system—Habermas remarks:

> The structures of late capitalism can be regarded as a kind of reaction formation. To stave off the system crisis, late-capitalist societies focus all socially integrative strength on the conflict that is structurally most probable. They do so in order all the more effectively to keep that conflict latent.[24]

Here keeping class conflict latent is for the capitalist state and its administrators an essential measure. It is, where there is an awareness of conflict at all, vital from the point of view of capitalism to sell the citizenry on some conception of a tolerably equitable class compromise about wages and conditions of work and life where these are causally related to "the bargain" between labor and capital.[25] This, Habermas tells us, has been obtained with considerable success particularly in the vital monopolistic and public sectors. There is a "political price" for the commodity labor. Labor and management can in such circumstances "find a broad zone of compromise, since increased labor costs can be passed on in prices, and the middle range demands made by both sides against the government tend to converge."[26]

However, the defusing of this area of potential conflict in turn generates new areas of at least potential conflict. Such a situation gives rise to very different wages between workers in the competitive sectors, on the one hand, and those in the monopolistic and public sectors, on the other, to the not inconsiderable disadvantage of the workers in the competitive sector. This could in turn trigger social conflict. It is also the case that there is the potentially unsettling factor of permanent inflation which, particularly among unorganized labor, undercuts—indeed more than undercuts—any redistributive advantages they may have temporarily gained. Moreover, the political wage compromise, with its passing off of costs to government, gives rise to "a permanent crisis in government finances, coupled with public poverty"—i.e., "pauperization of public transportation, education, housing, and health. . . ."[27]

Habermas concludes this section of his "What Does Legitimation Crisis Mean Today?" by indicating how, in facing such problems, the capitalist system has been making do.

> Since World War II, the most advanced capitalist countries have kept the class conflict latent in its essential areas. They have extended the business cycle, transforming the periodic pressures of capital devaluation into a permanent inflationary crisis with milder cyclical fluctuations. And they have filtered down the dysfunctional side effects of the intercepted economic crisis and scattered them over quasi-groups (such as consumers, school children and their parents, transportation users, the sick, the elderly) or divided groups difficult to organize. This process breaks down the social identity of the classes and fragments class consciousness. In the class compromise now part of the structure of late capitalism, nearly everyone both participates and is affected as an individual—although, with the clear and sometimes growing unequal distribution of monetary values and power, one can well distinguish between those belonging more to the one or to the other category.[28]

VI

Faced with capitalism's coping up to now, i.e., its successful adjustments to defuse impending crises, Habermas zeroes in on what he takes to be possible crises points in the future. He first considers crises points which are not specific to capitalist societies. Here Habermas refers to ecological crises, some motivational crises in large-scale societies, crises caused by the arms race and particularly the "danger of destroying the world system with thermonuclear war."[29] These crises problems are for the most part both evident enough and horrendous enough, but they are not specific to the capitalism and I shall accordingly pass them over.[30]

Disturbances which are specific to the capitalist system are divided, as we have seen, into economic crises and legitimation crises of which certain motivational crises are a subspecies. Habermas characterizes and critically examines a thesis widespread among rather orthodox Marxists, though defended in different forms, namely the thesis "that the basic capitalist structures continue unaltered and create economic crises in altered manifestations. In late capitalism, the state pursues the politics of capital with other means."[31] Habermas argues that this classical thesis, though plausible, has not been sufficiently sustained to be decisive. However, *in conjunction with legitimation crises*, it might in certain circumstances give us good grounds for predicting a capitalist collapse.[32] Again, I shall not consider Habermas's arguments here. Marxists have been predicting capitalist breakdown for a long time with no notable success. The capitalism that Marx talked about has been modified radically and the capitalist order has repeatedly been advantaged—its capacity to sustain and reproduce itself enhanced—by being made aware of Marxist predictions of breakdown and, with that awareness, it has been able to take avoidance measures to keep the prediction from becoming true. This may well not continue in the future, but this is by now an old story and a story which is better examined by political economists than by philosophers, political theorists, or sociologists.

I shall turn instead to examining the crises Habermas considers rather more fully. They are the things concerning which he has the most distinctive things to say and which he regards as crises that are the most likely to be flash points for present-day capitalism. In examining the legitimation problems in question, Habermas starts by remarking that "legitimate power"—presumably he means *de facto* legitimate power—"has to be available for administrative planning."[33] If order is to be kept intact, "vastly expanded activities of the capitalist state must be justified."[34] To achieve this, the state, Habermas argues, cannot afford to ignore the more generalizable interests of the population for, if the state serves capitalist interests too overtly and too exclusively, it will not be able to "retain mass loyalty and prevent a conflict-ridden withdrawal of legitimation."[35] The state, Habermas continues, has to gauge these interest areas in order to find a compromise for competing demands. What he calls a theorem of crisis has to explain not only why the "state encounters difficulties but also why certain problems remain unsolved in the long run."[36]

One way for the state apparatus to maintain a separation of the administrative system from legitimating will is for it to use various manipulation techniques, various forms of bread and circuses. What it needs to do by the use of the consciousness industry and other similar means is to steer the attention of the population away from uncomfortable themes so that they are hardly at the threshold of their attention. It must engage in the classical practice of distraction—a practice repeatedly used by states in manipulating populations. There are, in doing this, various kinds of propaganda techniques—techniques like advertising techniques—that will distract attention away from explosive issues. The issues, to take some examples, can be personalized, legal incantations can be given, expressive symbols appealed to, prejudices played on, emotional appeals can be used which will trigger the desired responses or at least play on unconscious motives. The techniques here are myriad and varied, and what techniques or combination of techniques will be used in particular situations will be context dependent. However, Habermas points out, what can be done here is more narrowly delimited than Brave New Worldists recognize. Cultural systems, he remarks, remain "peculiarly resistant to administrative control. There is no administrative creation of meaning, there is at best an ideological erosion of cultural values."[37] Once it is seen that the legitimation claims are being manufactured by the state apparatus, the whole thing self-destructs. "Thus there is a systematic limit for attempts at making up for legitimation deficits by means of well-aimed manipulation."[38]

VII

The capitalist state, as it intervenes more and more into our lives, comes to more and more undermine or at least weaken traditional values and in doing this comes to have an even greater need for legitimation. Once tradition came to be challenged, as it was with the emergence of the Enlightenment, then whatever legitimation, if any, that is attained, with the demise of traditional authority, can only be stabilized by way of discourse.[39]

> Thus, the forcible shift of things that have been culturally taken for granted further politicizes areas of life that previously could be assigned to the private domain. However, this spells danger for bourgeois privatism, which is informally assured by the structures of the public domain. I see signs of this danger in strivings for participation and in models for alternatives, such as

have developed particularly, in secondary and primary schools, in the press, the church, theatres, publishing, etc.[40]

Commenting on these considerations, Habermas remarks, that "these arguments support the contention that later capitalist societies are affected with serious problems of legitimation."[41] But, he contends, they are not sufficient to show that the capitalist order might not very well develop techniques to solve these crises problems—solving them, of course, in an ideological way and not in a way that generally, and in a maximally equitable way, answers to the interests of everyone alike. It may, that is, provide us with a social order which has *de facto* legitimate authority, but not with a social order which also has *de jure* legitimate authority.

We must, however, remember here, in asking whether we can safely predict a crisis in legitimation, all that is at issue is *de facto* legitimation. The crucial question is "Will capitalist states in the major industrial societies be able stably to sustain that belief in the mass of the populace?" One way—as can be seen from the Yuppie phenomenon—is that the state apparatus in steering the society may make up for missing traditional legitimations "by social rewards such as money, time, and security."[42] However, where capitalism takes that road, we get a crisis of legitimation when the aspirations for such rewards grow too rapidly or become so widespread that they cannot, given the economic resources of the system, be met. However, as long as the state can maintain within the population a "widespread technocratic consciousness" and an extensive "civil privatism, legitimation emergencies will not turn into crises."[43] An emergency need not lead to a crisis-ridden breakdown.

VIII

The capitalist state apparatus, Habermas believes, cannot, except temporarily and in conditions of desperation, junk mass democracy and run a tight ship by transforming itself into either a conservative authoritarian welfare state or into a fascist authoritarian state. Once a sense of democracy has become as deeply socialized into the cultural consciousness as it has in Western societies it cannot be knocked out of the aspirations of a people. A population can be cowed, as was the case briefly in Argentina and Chile, or even for a longer time as was the case in Spain and Portugal, but it remains in the aspirations of people so socialized. It very much looks as if that socialization cannot, the beliefs of Orwell and Rorty to the contrary notwithstanding, be reversed. Such aspirations have great staying power in societies once so socialized where democracy has subsequently been squashed. The aspirations remain and democracy reasserts itself where the conditions make that possible. This tendency toward democracy just goes with capitalism and modernization. The fascist regimes in Germany, Italy, and Spain may seem to be disconfirming instances, but in world conflict they all turned out to be unstable regimes which did not persist. They carried the bourgeois order through certain crises, but after that their reign came to an end. Neither a conservative authoritarian welfare state nor a fascist authoritarian state, Habermas claims, would in normal circumstances—that is in circumstances where the capitalist order is not threatened—fit as well as a bourgeois democracy with the capitalist order. It is indeed true that state forms that go with capitalism, as Marx showed in *The Eighteenth Brumaire of Louis Bonaparte*, can and will vary extensively to fit changed circumstances. Hitler for a while bailed out capitalism in a certain part of the world. Still, constitutional in its various forms, democracy is the characteristic form of the capitalist state. That very constitutional democracy that has characteristically gone with capitalism creates a sociocultural system which in turn "creates demands that cannot be satisfied in authoritarian systems."[44] However, with a formally democratic form of legitimation in capitalism, it still might become the case that in welfare states expenses will grow to such an extent that they can not be met within the parameters of a capitalist system. The various political parties, competing for acceptance by the citizenry, might end up making such extensive promises in a capitalist welfare state that they would, so to speak, break the bank. Present-day (1996) attempts to reduce the deficit are attempts to avoid that consequence.

These considerations lead Habermas to what he calls *a thesis*, to wit, the thesis that only a rigid sociocultural system incapable of flexibly adapting would lead to a legitimation crisis. This leads Habermas to say, rather obscurely, that we would only get a legitimation crisis if we get a motivation crisis. A motivation crisis is described by Habermas as "a discrepancy between the need for motives that the state and the occupational system announced and the supply of motivation offered by the sociocultural system."[45] Our sociocultural system with its traditions supply us with motives as does the state. Where the motives provided by the state are felt to be in conflict with the motives provided by the life-world, we have a motivational crisis.

In late capitalist societies the most important motivation provided by its sociocultural system (its life-world) "consists in syndromes of civil and family vocational privatism."[46] Where there is such privatism, there are strong interests in the administration's output and minor participation in, or interest in participation in, the process of political will formation. With civil privatism widely defused, we get a depoliticized, passive public. "Family and vocational privatism complements civil privatism. It consists of a family orientation with consumer and leisure interests. . . ."[47] With this goes a competitive career orientation matching what Daniel Bell calls a credentials society with meritocratic preconceptions.[48] Such privatistic conceptions and orientations are essential for maintaining the stability of late capitalist society and are a vital part of its ideology.

Will these motivations be sufficient to keep capitalism straight on the tracks in a stable reliable fashion? Habermas first asks how well they square with what he calls the *performance ideology* of capitalism, namely, the deeply engrained belief that social rewards should be distributed on the basis of individual achievement.[49] A basic condition for this is for there to be "equal opportunity to participate in a competition which is regulated in such a way that external influences can be neutralized."[50] But in spite of various moves toward greater equality of educational opportunity, it is becoming increasingly difficult credibly to maintain that in our class-divided, gender-divided, and stratified societies that anything even reasonably approximating equal opportunity can be attained. Rawls rightly stresses—beyond more formal equality of opportunity—the importance of attaining *fair* equality of opportunity, but nowhere do we find it socially instantiated. It is becoming clear that belief in it is a myth—a bit of bourgeois ideology. But then to the extent that civil privatism is linked to meritocracy, civil privatism will be threatened, for there can be no coherent belief in meritocracy and a credentials society unless there is a belief in equality of opportunity. But this belief in contemporary circumstances in class-divided societies is very difficult to sustain. Belief in it takes a not inconsiderable crucifixion of the intellect. Such factors do not contribute to the stabilization of the legitimation of late capitalism. It requires a very hefty and effective ideological input.

To this it should be added that it is becoming less and less true that educational achievement will produce occupational achievement. Instead, the extrafunctional elements of occupational roles are becoming more and more important for conferring occupational status. But that also undermines a belief in the performance ideology. Where this is seen to be the case—and it is increasingly difficult to disguise it—the belief cannot be maintained that in capitalist society it is usually the case that social rewards are given on the basis of individual achievement. But then this plainly runs against a very central legitimating belief of the society. If that belief is abandoned, a continued belief in the legitimacy of bourgeois society would be difficult to maintain. But how under contemporary conditions is it possible to sustain it?

It is also the case—and this is a linked difficulty here—that we are getting more and more fragmented and monotonous work for more and more people in late capitalist societies. With such work, one cannot find meaning in work; a sense of personal identity and self-fulfillment will not come through the worker's occupational role. There is in such work little intrinsic motivation for work performance. A thoroughly instrumentalist attitude, in such a circumstance, is developing toward work in wider and wider areas.

There are countervailing forces working as well, but this situation still raises motivational problems that may be a part of what might become motivational crises that might trigger legitimation crises.

The scientistic orientation of modernizing societies, an orientation which is pervasive in bourgeois societies as well as in state socialist societies, and which is valuable in supporting the *status quo* in those societies, also has side effects which could be elements in the delegitimization of these societies. It works this way: "the rise of modern science established a demand for discursive justification and traditionalistic attitudes cannot hold out against that demand."[51] Scientism (the belief that what science cannot tell us humankind cannot know) can, it is true, reinforce privatism through its regarding of all normative beliefs as ideological beliefs, or at least subjective matters of attitude: beliefs or attitudes which could be neither true nor false nor justified nor unjustified. But it can also be a challenge to the legitimating beliefs of a society through its critical attitude, just as contemporary art, though very easily cooptable, can also be a subversive counterculture.

The moral system extant in capitalist society is even more troublesome for capitalist legitimation than modern art or modern science. Traditional moral notions are being replaced by notions with a more clearly universalist intent. The morality of bourgeois private persons is a morality "raised to the level of universal principles."[52] This 'principled morality', setting itself against traditionalism and tribalism, is "sanctioned only by the purely inward authority of the conscience."[53] But this claim to universal morality not infrequently conflicts with the positive public morality of the society in question for that morality, as any actual morality, is a morality which is still bound to a concrete subject matter which is culturally determinate and reflects, among other things, the biases of that society. "This is the conflict between the cosmopolitanism of the human being and the loyalties of the citizen."[54] It is a conflict that has been generated in Western societies with the rise of capitalism. The internal logic of capitalism's development pushes against local attachments. Yet local attachments, coming down to us from traditional society, are very powerful indeed and the having of them may, in some way, be necessary, as Johann Gottfried Herder argued, for a flourishing, or perhaps even the very existence, of our self-conceptions and self-identity.

There are, however, developments in late bourgeois society—among them its increasing rationalization of life and demand for a discursive justification—that may erode the dichotomy between inner and outer morality. If those developments go on and our rationality becomes such that we—that is more and more of us—come to think in such a way, to believe, that is, that the validity of all norms has to be tied to discursive formation of the will of the people potentially affected, then the legitimacy of our capitalist order may come under question. If something like that obtained, there would be a built-in societal drive that would push us in the direction of a universalist morality that would hardly be compatible with capitalist legitimation.

Habermas gives us what in effect is a historical materialist account showing how the development of a certain mode of production with distinctive relations of production gives rise to a certain moral system and then how that moral system itself comes, as the forces of production develop, into conflict with the developing forces and relation of production of that society.

> Competitive capitalism for the first time gave a binding force to strictly universalistic value systems. This occurred because the system of exchange had to be regulated universalistically and because the exchange of equivalents offered a basic ideology effective in the bourgeois class. In organized capitalism, the bottom drops out of this legitimation model. At the same time, new and increased demands for legitimation arise. However, the system of science cannot intentionally fall behind an attained stage of cumulative knowledge. Similarly, the moral system, once practical discourse has been admitted, cannot simply make us forget the collectively attained stage of moral consciousness.[55]

This indicates that late capitalism is *endangered by a collapse of motivation*. We can, however, hardly reliably predict such a collapse, but it is not unreasonable to expect one or to work to help bring it about. Perhaps—giving a hopeful sign to those who wish to preserve the capitalist system—the cultural system can be uncoupled from a set of universal moral beliefs; perhaps it can live with some kind of sophisticated relativistic, nihilistic, or tribal base (the latter *may* be what communitarianism really comes to), but the very dissatisfactions and revolts from various sectors in the society give one some reason to believe that that uncoupling is not taking place. Yet there are counter indicators as well in the attempt, spearheaded by some communitarians and hermeneuticists, to recapture traditionalism or, among others, in an uncaring amoralism or in what in effect is nihilism. The indicators either way here are I think at present weak and indecisive. There are, as I have just remarked, and as we have seen in the previous chapter, postmodernist trends of either a nihilistic sort or the sort that says that we can never get a genuine universalist morality and that what we must cultivate instead is loyalty to our tribe in a world which has taught us that there can be no justification for sticking with a universalist moral point of view.[56]

I do not want to hazard any predictions on such a large scale. Moreover, it is not clear that we have any social science with sufficient predictive power to do so. Be that as it may, that is not something I shall take on. What I want to do instead is first to show in the next two sections (IX–X) that we do have a viable *model* for what a *de jure* legitimate state and society would look like.

I shall show how Habermas's conception of undistorted discourse provides a model here. In establishing this I shall have to show that certain familiar criticisms of his account are mistaken. Armed with this Habermasian conception of a *de jure* legitimacy, I shall then argue in section XI that our Western capitalist democracies do not and cannot attain more than *de facto* legitimacy. Similar arguments could be deployed against the states of what was the Soviet bloc or against the People's Republic of China. This leaves us, if my arguments are near to the mark, with a coherent conception of *de jure* legitimacy, but with no state satisfying that conception. That is to say, we have no exemplification of a *de jure* legitimate state, though surely we can correctly say that some states are less illegitimate than others. I argue in the closing sections of this essay that a genuinely democratic socialism, if it were to come into existence, could satisfy that conception. But democratic socialism, unfortunately, still remains a model, though, I hope, a feasible one. (It started to have an exemplification in Allende's Chile before it was crushed with blood and steel.) What must be shown is that something could come into existence in our social world and be sustained which would count as an instantiation of that model. That capitalism is so triumphant at present does not mean that it will last forever or that it will not be replaced by a market socialism.

In the beginning of my essay I contrast the modernist Habermas with the postmodernist Foucault. I read Foucault as giving to understand that a universalistic ethic either Habermasian or Rawlsian rests on a mistake and that *de jure* legitimation is an impossibility. The Habermasian account developed in sections IX–X, with a few borrowings from Rawls, is intended to give the lie to that. Here, what most centrally is at issue is whether my arguments in section X are sound or could be made so by some inessential fiddling.

IX

Let us now see, following Habermas and in the teeth of postmodernism, if we can plausibly articulate what *de jure* legitimate state authority would look like. What, given the large-scale, highly industrialized societies that are, for good or for ill, our lot, would our states have to be like to have such legitimacy, if they can have it all? The postmodernists are right in recognizing that to see, if that is at all possible, what paradise regained would be like, we would need to have a good understanding of paradise lost. We must see first what is wrong with our societies; we must see the depth of the illness and the needless frustration of needs and human aspirations and potentialities that seem at least to be endemic to our societies to see how far they are from being *de jure* legitimate societies and to be aware of the distance and direction they must travel to gain such legitimacy.

I want, in trying to articulate what a legitimate social order with a legitimate state would look like, to rather extensively take some cues from Jürgen Habermas, whose characterization of the difference between distorted discourse and undistorted discourse in the ideal speech situation excised of its needless pedantry and overelaboration provides us with the abstract characterization of the type of situation in which, if state power were exercised under such conditions and restraints, it would be exercised legitimately.[57] (Hereafter, unless otherwise specified, where I use something like "used legitimately" or "legitimate state authority," I mean *de jure* legitimate state authority.)

Habermas, in portraying the difference between paradise lost and paradise regained, starts, following roughly Herbert Marcuse, by depicting the needless human irrationalities of our complex societies. Habermas observes that in important respects in modern industrial societies, both capitalist and state socialist, we are living an unfree, one-dimensional existence. There is in our societies an undermining of perfectly realizable human possibilities for emancipation. Important needs are quite unnecessarily going unmet and there is a not inconsiderable amount of unnecessary, identifiable suffering. Here, with that stress, Habermas is a loyal follower of the Frankfurt School.

Habermas, moving away from a stress more typical of Marxism, contends that the restrictions we suffer are not primarily imposed on us by external forces. Rather, they are restrictions we, as a people, under conditions of an extensive imposed consciousness, impose on ourselves.[58] Our ideological bafflement is such, Habermas claims, that we do not understand the prevailing mechanisms and relationships of power and control in our society and how they, often in rather subtle ways, manage to retain an ascendency over us. He thinks this malaise has cut so deep that in various ways it is causing such alienation that we have in advanced capitalist societies, again in diverse ways, as we saw earlier, problems of what he calls a legitimation crisis.

We have in the fabric of our social life, embedded in our life-world, a cluster of distorted legitimating beliefs. Taken in clusters, they provide us with legitimating myths. These false beliefs and their associated mistaken attitudes are in some considerable measure the norms and attitudes that go to make up our world-picture and our social consciousness and they prompt us to commend as legitimate, or at least to accept as necessary, a network of institutions and practices of a highly repressive character, including political attitudes and the acceptance of an authoritarian work discipline. These are very central ideologically distorted beliefs that underwrite our repressive social system of coercion.

It is because of the pervasiveness and subterranean power of these legitimating beliefs—in a normative sense these ersatz legitimating beliefs—that a critique of ideology is so important and in doing this it is incumbent on us, so that the unmaskers can be seen not to be donning a few masks themselves, that we come to have the ability to understand and to state with reasonable clarity what it would be like to have a set of nonideological legitimating beliefs. We need to know what would really make for our well-being; what are our distinctive human needs, the scheduling of their importance (what comparative weight we would give to them), and what social conditions would have stably to be in place to sustain and indeed increase that need satisfaction. Seeing the world in some reasonable sense rightly—though this surely cannot come to "the one true description of the world"—is something which is vital to us here. (The postmodernist challenge characterized and discussed in the previous chapter gave us a sense of how problematical that is.) We need, that is, to understand the nature and conditions of human flourishing—and what would make for an equitable achievement of that in what would come to be, if these conditions obtained, a world of just institutions. People who had a good grasp of these things would be people who had escaped the beguilements of ideology. They would not be people who are led to uphold and to participate in a gratuitously restrictive set of social arrangements mistakenly believing that they were indispensable for human well-being. They would not be imprisoned by a false consciousness that would help stabilize them into leading frustrated lives where they are deprived—indeed, in a way self-deprived—of many important human potentialities. But what is this "true consciousness" that gives us a true account of society, where, against postmodernist irony and a pervasive skepticism, we would have a correct picture of our human needs and their proper scheduling and an ideologically cleared up self-understanding, enabling us in this important way to see the world rightly? (To have a feel for the magnitude—perhaps the unmanageable magnitude—of this question, consider what it would be like to give a "true account of society" or even to have a good feel for what we would have to know or reasonably believe to have some understanding that we were on the threshold of gaining such an account. But again, as depressingly daunting as all this is, we are not justified in being confident that we can, if we would push rational inquiry unsparingly, have no reasonable approximations here.)

It is in clarifying the distinction between an ideological understanding of one's situation and a nonideological one that Habermas, borrowing and adapting extensively for his own distinct purposes from Stephen Toulmin, John Austin, and John Searle, deploys his theory of universal pragmatics and communicative action and adumbrates his conception of the ideal speech situation. What he seeks to do with those devices is to characterize a set of circumstances which, if they were to obtain, the beliefs we would hold in those circumstances would be nonideological beliefs, a subset of which would be legitimating beliefs which not only would have *de facto* authority but would have *de jure* authority as well. States that governed in accordance with those beliefs would have a genuinely legitimate authority, i.e., a *de jure* authority.

What are these circumstances—the counterfactual states of affairs—of the ideal speech situation which would give us a correct picture of undistorted discourse? What is this situation in which, if it were to obtain, we would be in a situation in which our speech and thought would be undistorted, in which our communication with each other and our self-understanding would be without ideological distortion? Habermas, like a good liberal in the Millian tradition, but also in a way that a Marxist should not disavow, argues that for there to be an ideal speech situation, the situation must be one in which our legitimating beliefs (including, of course, our central normative beliefs) must be formed in conditions of absolutely free and unlimited debate in which all parties to the institutions and practices being set up must be capable of recognizing that they are freely consenting to their establishment under conditions in which the only constraints on their acceptance derive from the force of the better argument. In communication, simply in virtue of what communication is, we seek to reach *understanding*, indeed a mutual understanding. In an ideal speech situation the speaker and hearer aim not only at consensus but at a *rational* consensus in which the only motive for discoursing which is accepted is that of a cooperative search for truth. What will be taken as a rational consensus is that consensus which is rooted in whatever has the force of the better argument or, I would add, to make it less rationalistic, the better deliberation.

This, in ways which are in certain respects similar to Rawls's way of proceeding, is an updating, in a rather different vocabulary, of the claims of the classical social contract theorists.[59] Habermas's account does indeed get a rather considerable embellishment by its utilization of the speech act theories of John Austin and John Searle, but it is unclear that the embellishment adds much to the basic idea beyond a certain technocratese, something which such an acute critic of scientism as Habermas should have been more wary about. Indeed, I think it is reasonable to maintain that a lot of that technical embellishment is like a free-spinning wheel that turns no machinery and what is essential can be stated quite simply without all that technocratese.[60] The ideal speech situation (to boil down what is involved to its essentials) tries to do something similar to what the state of nature does for Locke and Rousseau and what the original position does for Rawls. Quentin Skinner, who has made a similar point, puts the matter very well and very simply when he observes that Habermas is claiming, like Rawls, that "if potentially repressive institutions are rightly to be regarded as legitimate, it must be possible to imagine their creation under conditions of freedom and equality and their acceptance by the unforced consent of all those subsequently liable to be affected by their behavior."[61] A state which succeeds in supporting, nurturing, and protecting such institutions is a state that has legitimate authority. And where we get consensus under such conditions we get rational consensus and where there is no actual rational consent or even consent period, we can reasonably and nonauthoritarianly impute a rational consent where what we are speaking of is what would be so consented to by reasonable people under such ideal circumstances. Whatever it is that is so consented to or would be so consented to under those circumstances has legitimate authority. If and when we get such consent, then we will have rational consent. (It will be important to see—so that it will be clear that no ideological trick is being played with "reasonable" here—how "reasonable" is elucidated in the introduction to part 4.)

We have a model here for what undistorted discourse would be like so that we can distinguish ideology from nonideology, where (if such a society ever comes to be) we would have a society where ideology does not reign, where we would not have the despotism of imposed consciousness. Moreover, where such ideal speech conditions reign, if indeed they ever reign, the state, in such a social order, though it would still, in order to be a state, have a monopoly on the *de facto* legitimate use of force in its territory, would also have *de jure* legitimate authority as well as *de facto* power.

X

There are a number of objections that can and have been made to such an ideal speech conception of undistorted discourse: (1) It has been thought to be far too utopian and unrealistic. People will never get within a country mile of achieving a consensus rooted in the force of the better argument or better deliberation. Particularly where what is to be done is at stake, it will seldom, if ever, be the case that the sole or even the decisive motive for discoursing will be the cooperative search for truth. Our *consensus* will be rooted in many other things than what has the force of the better argument or better deliberation. We will not be equal partners in an absolutely free and unlimited debate. The institutions we shall create in the future, like the institutions created in the past, will not be created under conditions of freedom and open and unlimited debate; they will not be created under conditions of freedom and equality. We are not now and never will be such autonomous and ideally rational or reasonable persons. We are just not wired that way. (2) It has also been thought that such a conception suffers from defects analogous to Kantian formalism. In speaking of what beliefs would be the outcome of absolutely free and unlimited debate and in taking those beliefs, whatever they are, to be genuinely legitimating beliefs, we have beliefs with too little content to give us anything with much substance. What is legitimate is what comes from following certain procedures no matter what their content is. However, we need something more robust which would tell us which beliefs are ideological beliefs and which are not. The Habermasian conception is just liberal formalism all over again in a teutonic guise. (3) Even more fundamentally, it could be maintained, such a conception, when carefully inspected, turns out to be incoherent or at least so problematic as to be without determinable sense. (4) Finally, even assuming that people could so consent, or come to approximate such consent, why *should* people, particularly if they are members of the dominant class in a securely situated class society, so consent or accept that conception of rationality rather than to accept a purely instrumental rationality where they reason as utility maximizers or perhaps as what David Gauthier calls constrained utility maximizers.[62]

The criticism that ideal speech theory is too utopian does not have much force. Habermas repeatedly talks about counterfactuals here. The thing is not that people act that way or even that they will be expected to act that way, but that we have a model for—a benchmark for—how people are to act such that if they did act that way we would have undistorted discourse. Even if the construction turns out to be a mere heuristic device, it would still be of a not inconsiderable value in showing us what we would have to approximate to have the kind of societal understanding that would be required for us to be free of ideological fetters. Moreover, there is no compelling reason to think that human nature is so firmly fixed that we cannot move in the direction of this heuristic ideal and that the closer we come to it the closer we come to a morally attractive social order with a state to which we clearheadedly can give allegiance. Of course, if we could not move anywhere at all in that direction, if we were incapable of becoming more enlightened and more autonomous, if we were utterly unable to create greater equality and a further understanding of our situation, and if a concern for a cooperative and impartial search for truth would have no weight with us at all, then we could hardly treat the model of undistorted discourse as even a heuristic device and indeed we would be in something that was even worse than the postmodernist swamp, but that is not something that a hard, nonevasive look at the situation justifies. Indeed, such postmodernist skepticism may in reality be a convenient and helpful ideological myth in the struggle to secure late capitalism. A deep skepticism making Hamlets of us all has its power in quieting down intellectuals so that they will willingly accept the *status quo*.

The second criticism has more force. As Rawls realized at the outset, if we just rely on procedures without any antecedent substantive moral beliefs at all, in any way, being appealed to, then we will never, with a *purely* communicative ethic, be able to make, even under conditions of freedom and equality, any choices at all. We will indeed ask ourselves what we would choose if we were free agents reasoning together cooperatively with full knowledge of our situation. But if there was nothing at all, antecedent to that deliberation that we wanted, that we thought answered to our interests, that we thought we needed, that we believed to be good, we would not, when we deliberated together in ideal situations, know what to choose. Indeed, we would not be able to choose. We would have no even tentative basis for plonking one way or the other. Indeed, there is no way of determining what would be a fair procedure without making a judgment about what a fair outcome would be. Hence Rawls's primary social and natural goods or (to take a somewhat different conception) what I have elsewhere called our moral truisms, e.g., the belief that health is good, that autonomy is good, that the institution of promise keeping is vital to our lives, that human consideration and concern for each other are good, that suffering is bad, that isolation and alienation are bad, that domination of and torturing of others are evil, or (to take a still somewhat different conception) that we have some tolerably objective conception of human needs and that our firm and reasonable belief in the desirability of the satisfaction of these needs is warranted. We need some such conception, or perhaps a combination of such conceptions, to give some content to what otherwise would be too formalistic and too procedural an approach. But there is no good reason to believe that this could not be added to a basically Habermasian conception without causing an undermining of its basic structure.[63]

However, we also need the Habermasian procedural thing to winnow out in a critical way what otherwise would be a motley of goods. (Something like wide reflective equilibrium could be put to work here.) We need an index of the primary social and natural goods; we need as well a much more nuanced statement of what I have called moral truisms, nuanced in such ways that they will cease to be mere truisms and become critical moral beliefs—they would move from being what Peirce called acritical beliefs to what he called critical beliefs—and we need some way of weighing them when they conflict in a way similar to our needing a scheduling of needs when they cannot all be satisfied. Here the procedures mandated by the ways we should reason in ideal speech situations are indispensable, though probably in themselves not sufficient, to the gaining of these things.

The third criticism, to wit the criticism that the conception of undistorted discourse as specified by the ideal speech situation is itself incoherent, or at least utterly problematic, seems to me to be itself problematic. Just why, if indeed at all, is it *incoherent* or at least through and through *problematic* to speak of beliefs, indeed of legitimating beliefs, formed in conditions of absolutely free and unlimited debate? It is not at all evident to me that it is. Perhaps it will be said that when we try to imagine or conceive in concrete detail of a consensus being forged under freedom and equality we will come to see that very idea is incoherent. It, as we have already discussed, is, of course, unrealistic, but it doesn't follow from that that it is incoherent or even *conceptually* problematic. It is unrealistic for you now, to believe that you will live to be 150, but that belief is not at all incoherent or conceptually problematic. We know perfectly well what it would be like for it to be true, and in future years, for good or for ill, it may well come to pass that people will routinely, or at least not infrequently, live to that age. Conceptually speaking, beliefs being forged under conditions of freedom and equality are roughly parallel. There is no more reason to believe they are incoherent or conceptually problematic than to believe that about the above belief about life expectancy.

The fourth objection seems to me the most powerful. Consider those people who are members of the *haute bourgeoisie* and their well-paid facilitators. Why should they (at least where the "should" is a prudential should) seek a consensus rooted in undistorted discourse? At least for the *haute bourgeoisie*, and probably for many of their highly placed facilitators as well, it is in their interests to have a working class and a *lumpen proletariat* who are manipulated by ruling class ideology. They are hardly being irrational in the straightforward sense of instrumental rationality if they do not seek such a consensus based on undistorted discourse. They might also say, as Bertrand Russell did, that an instrumental conception of rationality is the only coherent sense of rationality there is, but even if in good Habermasian fashion they claimed there is a richer sense of rationality linked with an interest in achieving truth and that an optimal search for truth requires the commitment to cooperative communication that goes with seeking to achieve and sustain undistorted discourse so that it is after all evident enough that there is an interest in truth, interest in truth is still only one strategic and central interest among others. A member of the *haute bourgeoisie*, given his power and domination with its manifest advantages, might very well find that such a passionate concern to gain an optimal achievement of truth is not, everything considered, in his best interests and the best interests of his class. It is not at all evident that he could not clearheadedly, and that his class as a whole could not clearheadedly, have no commitment to the reign of an order of undistorted discourse, though for reasons of moral *ideology* it is not something he or they could publicly defend. And this would even more evidently be so when he and his class peers stick together as they very well might. They need moral *ideology* and "class morality" (they need to stick together), but not morality here. Strong social bonding is sometimes very ethnocentric: limiting itself to one's own kind.

However, this indicates what on other grounds is manifestly true, namely that the *haute bourgeoisie* could not but, *morally speaking*, accept it. ("Class morality" went in scare quotes. It is not really morality and they know it.) Impartiality and fairness requires undistorted discourse, where it is attainable; and morality, just in virtue of what morality is, requires a commitment to impartiality and fairness. To this it could be replied that the ways of ideology are protean. *The haute bourgeoisie*, though not as matters of *public* pronouncement, should, if they reason strictly in accordance with their own enlightened interests, including their class interests, when they are firmly and stably in control, should (prudently speaking "should") become *classist amoralists*—people of good morals but not morally good people—using ideology, as I hinted at above, to make it appear that they are committed to an impartial concern for the interests of everyone alike and that they as well favor conditions of clarity in social relations, while in reality, though necessarily in a surreptitious way, they support their own class position with the obfuscations that that support requires. There is nothing irrational about the *haute bourgeoisie* and their well-placed and well-rewarded facilitators supporting classist amoralism when the modes of production are such that capitalist domination is secure. For it to be secure entails, among other things, that the consciousness industry is firmly in their hands. In such a secure situation, there appears at least to be nothing irrational about the *haute bourgeoisie* and their well-placed facilitators being classist amoralists—a position which is immoral yes, but irrational, no. (Again, we can see the impossibility of getting morality out of pure rationality.)

The beginning of a response should start like this: once, with the rise of bourgeois democracies, democratic ideas get firmly entrenched (as they are by now in rich industrial capitalist societies), this will give rise, inescapably and persistently, to Habermasian and Rawlsian claims about autonomy for all, equality, conditions of undistorted discourse, and the like. The very general thrust of these ideas, as distinct from the details of particular conceptions of them (as in some philosopher or other), cannot be morally, and thus publicly, resisted. This being so they will in a democratic ethos become ever more firmly the accepted norms. There is a certain sociological irreversibility here. Because of this, it will become increasingly difficult for a class bent on preserving its privileges to do so. More and more complicated obfuscation will have to be engaged in—the tides of ideology will have to run even higher—but in the long run such obfuscation will fail. Or so it is reasonable to hope.

We have seen that the *haute bourgeoisie* cannot publicly avow classist amoralism. They will have to commit themselves, as even such conservative theorists as Hayek and Nozick do, to what Thomas Nagel calls *moral equality*, to wit, to the belief that the life of everyone matters and matters equally. One cannot, and get away with it, in anything even remotely like normal circumstances, *publicly* reject morality.[64] But, in present conditions, in the rich capitalist democracies, a clearheaded commitment to morality leads to something which bears some reasonable similarity to this Habermasian commitment to undistorted discourse as well as to moral equality. And it is not unreasonable to hope that conditions of life, given the way the productive forces will predictably develop, cannot in the long run undermine this increasingly clearheaded grasp of the situation. Obfuscation for privilege is, it is reasonable to believe, sociologically and historically speaking, on the losing side.

Things may not take this happy turn, the continued development of the

productive forces may not require such a democratic ethos. Or, given our ecological situations, the forces of production may not continue to develop.
However, in interacting with people, not being committed to reasoning from
positions of equality and equal autonomy and *not* being motivated to freely
accept only what is made out by the force of the better argument or better deliberation, puts one at odds with morality or at the very least with a modern
understanding or morality. But a social order at odds with morality could not
have *de jure* legitimacy and a state, monopolizing force for that social order,
could *only* have *de facto* authority, i.e., effective power; it could not as well
have *de jure* legitimate authority. A social order in which undistorted discourse obtains is not a conceptually incoherent possibility and where it comes
into being (if indeed it ever comes into being), with a matching state, that state
will have *de jure* legitimate authority as well as *de facto* authority. To the extent that societies approximate those conditions, if indeed any of them ever
do, their states will approach being states with *de jure* legitimate authority.

XI

I turn now to an examination and defense of my perhaps *parti pris* sounding
claim that no state in a capitalist society under modern conditions can have
de jure authority. One short way to argue for that is to point out that a capitalist society inescapably is a class-divided society with extensive class domination of one class over another, where a capitalist class owns and controls
the means of production and where a working class must sell its labor power
as a commodity. Moreover, it is a society in which the working class owns and
controls no significant means of production, if indeed it owns or controls any
means of production at all. (That in some of the old sweatshops in the clothing industry, to get a job a worker had to own his own sewing machine, and
thus he had to own some means of production, does not make him a capitalist or any the less a wage slave. It shows, if anything, that his domination by
the capitalist class is even more complete.) Such a society cannot, while remaining capitalist, avoid relations of domination and control by one class over
another and this state of affairs is plainly incompatible with the conditions of
freedom and equality necessary for legitimacy.

This argument I believe to be a sound argument, but it will probably be
thought in some quarters at least to be too short a way to take with dissenters.
So I will seek to marshal a number of other considerations which should, I believe, when taken together, if not in isolation, be persuasive.

First the democracy of such capitalist societies, whatever we may say of
the democracy or lack of it elsewhere, is at best sadly defective and at worst
a farce. I do not, of course, want to knock majority rule as something in ac-

cordance with which state power in a society *must* legitimate itself. Majority rule is, as the discussion in the previous section should have made clear, a necessary but not a sufficient condition for a state to have legitimacy. Naively we take, or at least tend to take, universalistic majority rule as something which has almost self-evident adequacy. But, while granting its indispensability in modern societies at the level of electoral decisions for parliamentary elections and votes, and for referenda for secession, it still, left unsupplemented, will not provide legitimacy for a modern state. There are several reasons for this. First, as Max Weber and Robert Michels pointed out, and many have confirmed and amplified since, mass parties are organized in bourgeois democracies in such a way that individual voters are reduced to passive consumers, having, in a rather plebiscitary manner, a very limited range of political options.[65] Indeed, they involve little more than judgments which a typical citizen of a capitalist democracy principally makes when, on infrequent occasions, he votes, for or against, a limited number of candidates presented to him by these parties who in turn (when we consider the whole array of candidates) have been selected by the various party elites where the differences between their parties are not very considerable. These party elites—elites in all the nonmarginal parties—are, judged by their social-structural composition, a thoroughly unrepresentative ruling strata.[66] Yet these ruling strata in the various parties have thorough control over the personnel proferred for election and built up by a mass media. We need also to keep firmly in mind here that it is a media which is sometimes almost entirely capitalist owned and controlled and always deeply and decisively influenced by that class where it is not so owned and controlled. The BBC and the CBC have somewhat more autonomy than the capitalist-owned news media in the USA. But still the differences here are not considerable. The electorate, to understate it, plays a very inactive political role in the society and indeed has been socialized into accepting this state of affairs as natural, inevitable, and even as democratic. This is just, sadly and ironically, what they take democracy to be.

There is a second problem for democracy and more specifically for majority rule that emerged out of nineteenth-century liberal thought, but was neither resolved by that thought nor has it since been resolved.[67] There are a range of concerns requiring some rational decision about what to do where the majority principle and the protection of freedom—some private sphere where the state may not intervene—come into conflict. There are situations, sometimes elusive and hard to define, where the minority, even a minority with thorough democratic commitments, will not be prepared to accept majority decisions. (Trampling on the rights of a minority is no more justified if a majority goes for it than if another minority does.) There will in certain circumstances be no such acquiescence on their part. What this private sphere is deemed to be will vary from person to person and group to group and from society to society. What is centrally up for decision here is what may or may not be decided by majority rule. Differences here seem at least to be intractable. There just is no rational consensus over just where the state can rightly intervene in our lives. Democratic theory offers us no acceptable guidelines here or at least there is no stable consensus about what they are. Yet these are areas crucial to our lives.

A third criticism of simply resting content with having legitimation through majority rule comes from the way majorities have of making themselves permanent such that minorities become structural minorities with little say in the direction of the society and few effective ways of protecting, let alone furthering, their interests. Racial and ethnic minorities are frequently good examples of such minorities; people (atheists or communists, for example) with political or social views out of the mainstream are another. Gays and lesbians are still another. The old parties have what in effect is a monopoly on the political market and new parties with radically different alternatives find it very difficult, indeed, in many bourgeois societies well nigh impossible, to make it into the political market. They simply do not get heard or do not get heard in anything like a remotely adequate way. Most of the electorate in many capitalist democracies, when they see the names of marginal parties on the ballot box, do not even know who they are or what they represent. This is distant from the kind of open democratic society of which J.S. Mill and John Dewey dreamed. Such a situation is hardly something that confers legitimacy on the political system.

This self-consolidation of majorities, as we have argued above, is not just the power of the established parties. To simply look to the parties is to take a superficial view of the matter. We must remember that the mass parties are controlled by political elites. Such political elites share, for the most part, the interests of the dominant class (sometimes it overlaps with the dominant class), which in capitalist democracies are the *haute bourgeoisie*. This, though sometimes in a rather indirect fashion, gives political control of such societies to the capitalist class. It is very difficult, given such control, to believe that here—ideology aside—we have anything like the legitimating force of popular sovereignty. Moreover, as Claus Offe has argued, it looks like any substantial redistribution of political power is hopeless through the ordinary mechanisms of voting and the like.[68]

Mill and Tocqueville in their classical defenses of representative democracy argued that representative democracy would produce a polity with autonomy, responsibility, and, as well, and connectedly, a polity with citizens with the independent ability to judge about political affairs affecting their lives. This adult autonomy, they thought, would be the inevitable result of democratic participation. Such participation by citizens in public decisions would both improve the quality of these decisions and be a key instrument in their intellectual and moral development; in fine, it would be an instrument in their emancipation. But this has not in fact happened. In most capitalist democracies there is nothing even like a remote approximation of it. This is not the way the capitalist democracies have in fact developed. In our class-divided and complexly stratified societies, where a political-economic elite, which is arguably also a ruling class, runs the show politically as well as economically, average citizens, as we have seen, are reduced to being passive consumers of politics.[69] Their political activity consists largely in responding to mass media images and, at infrequent intervals, spending a few minutes in a ballot box where they make a consumer's choice between political products which, as far as the real choices are concerned, are seldom more than marginally different. People unaccustomed actively to participating in political life, and in various other ways deprived, lack the decision-making competencies of their masters, the ruling elites. With their effective control of the society way down to the sometimes subtle and sometimes not so subtle production of ideology through its control of the consciousness industry, these political elites place themselves in positions of enormous advantage politically. In this way we have class domination and not a pluralism where the various classes and strata achieve a consensus on how social life is to be ordered. Rawls is right in saying we have a pluralistic society in the sense that we have several groups with differing comprehensive conceptions of the good, but we do not have plural groups consensually sharing power. Rather, we have class domination and control by the capitalist class. Far from having brought into being the society that Mill and Dewey dreamed of, we have produced a society where there is, as Claus Offe puts it, "a strong class-and-strata-based *inequality* in the distribution of decision-making competence" and this, as he goes on to say, "is undermining of democracy."[70] The democratic legitimating power of majority rule presupposes, for it to be normatively speaking genuine, a roughly equal distribution of competencies to decide on political and social issues. But to believe that anything like this obtains or can reasonably be expected to come to obtain in our mass capitalist democracies, with their class divisions and sharp stratification, with its consequent not inconsiderable advantages to the upper strata, is to believe in what is patently a myth.

Our mass democracies in capitalist societies have political elites which, within certain fairly circumscribed limits, compete with each other to gain a ratification of their policies by the voters. They vie with each other, that is, to gain the assent of the majority. But this militates against their parties working out comprehensive and consistent long-term objectives. They rather go for the quick fix that will enable them to be successful in the next election. But these governmental decisions motivated by short-term considerations can all the same have long-term, sometimes irreversible, side effects on life conditions. (That they are typically unintended does not make them any the less unfortunate.) Offe comments that like market transactions electoral decisions and votes on the basis of the majority principle, tend to discount the future, that is, to bracket from the calculus of rulers and ruled foreseeable long-term effects and delayed consequences of decisions. As the majority principle makes the creation of a majority the highest condition of political success for the political elite—and a majority which must be created *today* —the result is the opportunistic 'platform party' oriented to the political market place.[71]

Again, capitalist democracy does not get good legitimating marks.

Capitalist democracies stress legitimation through majority rule. I have been concerned here, while keeping majority rule as a *necessary* condition for legitimation, to argue that it is not a *sufficient* condition. In arguing this point, I have been concerned to stress how very far from democratic rule we are if we, in the usual manner, just rest content with majority rule and some platitudinous talk about protecting individual rights. Our societies are hardly societies where there is anything like popular sovereignty or the rule of the people or much in the way of respect for persons. (Forty thousand homeless people in New York City is good evidence for the latter.) It is a bad joke to speak of "we, the people." Indeed, in modern capitalist democracies not a few theorists would sneer at the very idea of the rule of the people, though usually not very loudly for they do not take it as a matter for wide public consumption. It, politically speaking, is a good thing to keep up the *illusion* of popular sovereignty. However, a *de jure* legitimate state authority must not only have popular sovereignty; it must also be the protector of a society committed to equality of condition, autonomy for everyone alike and for a world where the interests and rights of everyone alike are equally the object of societal concern. And, as Rawls has stressed, it must be a society where in some genuine sense the people are sovereign. But in capitalist societies, even in a state welfare capitalist society such as Sweden, such equality, autonomy, justice, and sovereignty do not and cannot obtain.

Let us start with equality first. Even modernizing conservatives, as distinct from their aristocratic predecessors, believe in at least some forms of equality of opportunity. While capitalist societies can, and most of them do, provide formal equalities, such as legal and political equalities (one person, one vote), capitalism cannot provide, for what Rawls calls, *fair* equality of opportunity for there cannot in capitalist societies but be radically different life chances between the different classes and strata and, since this is so, there is no way (for example) that the average child of a young black or Metis, uneducated, unemployed single mother can have even a remotely equal start at the starting gate for job opportunities or educational opportunities to that of the average child of a member of the capitalist class or for that matter the upper or middle stratum of professionals in society. (By now, 1996, one in six persons in Canada, living below the official poverty line, are in circumstances not unlike that.) There just is no possibility of fair equality of opportunity here. The social structures of capitalist society simply do not admit of it. This is a rather extreme example used to dramatize the great differences in life chances between representative people in class societies, but there are also very considerable differences in life chances between representative members of the working class and the capitalist class.[72] The children of someone working on the assembly line for General Motors (for example) do not stand in a condition which is even remotely that of a fair equality of opportunity with representative children of major owners of General Motors, people who could rightly, without evasion or obfuscation, be called members of the capitalist class. They do not start with even nearly equal powers at the starting gate of life. Yet, at least with respect to the children's case, the one group could not coherently be said to be more deserving than the other.

Capitalism with a human face—a thorough welfare state capitalism on the model of Sweden—could, and would, do something to narrow the gap between workers and capitalists, between *lumpen-proletariat* and professionals, but it could not close such gaps. Fair equality of opportunity could not obtain where there are extensive differences in social condition: differences rooted most essentially in their different class positions. Such differences inevitably advantage some over others in the various desirable competitions into which they enter. Where some own and control the means of production and others must sell their labor as a commodity, power differentials and influence differentials will remain sufficient such that representative members of each class cannot fairly compete. There must be a greater equality of condition than capitalism could possibly accommodate for there to be fair equality of opportunity.[73]

Defenders of capitalism will reply that even rough equality of condition will undermine an even more fundamental value in our societies than equality, namely autonomy. Letting, for the sake of this discussion, that comparative ranking stand, it needs to be asked why does—or does—equality of condition undermine autonomy? The standard answer is that, given normal interactions such as people trading things or making gifts or bestowing things, there would have to be to sustain equality of condition a constant interference—presumably state interference—with people's lives to keep anything like even a rough equality of condition in existence. But such repeated interference would undermine autonomy, namely people's being able to control their own lives, their being able to be self-directed.

However, the kind of interference in the lives of people that the prohibition of capitalist acts licenses has to do with is the freedom to buy and sell, to invest, to bestow *productive* property, and the like. Prohibiting such acts cannot realistically be thought to keep people's lives from being self-directed or from their having control over their own lives. A world in which people are so interfered with need not be a world in which people are not self-directed or lack self-ownership. Not all kinds of interference with doing what you want to do weakens your autonomy or your self-directedness. It is only the prohibiting of *certain things* I want to do that keeps my life from being self-directed. If I must wear a seatbelt, it does not follow that my life cannot be self-directed. Indeed, it does not even tend to make it less self-directed, yet it may genuinely interfere with my acting as I wish. If I cannot quit a job or leave the country or write what I believe, then my ability to control my own life, to act autonomously, is seriously affected. But if I cannot hire someone to work in my pin factory, or if I cannot own by myself a pin factory, my capacity to live a self-directed life is not undermined, my being an autonomous being has not been adversely affected. I do not lose my ability to set my own ends. To be sure, one end of mine is interfered with, namely that of owning a pin factory and hiring someone to work in it. But being so constrained does not deprive me of the ability or the opportunity generally to set my own ends, anymore than does my not being able to go to the cinema when I am under quarantine because I have scarlet fever. I may indeed want very much to buy and sell and feel badly done by when I cannot, but my self-directedness or my ability and opportunity to be self-directed is not affected as it would be if I were someone's slave, must engage in political activities that I do not approve of, am denied even the right to fairly compete for a higher education, and the like. These things, unlike the freedom to buy and sell, do affect our living self-directed lives and the extent to which we can be autonomous persons.

Even if I am mistaken in the above argument and such interference does limit somewhat people's autonomy, it can and should be pointed out that any society whatsoever, in virtue of having norms, will in some way interfere with some things that people do or want to do (this may or may not affect their autonomy but it certainly does affect their negative liberty). There being some interference of some kind is simply the price of having a society, any society at all.[74] The real question is whether the interference is justified and whether it affects their autonomy. Granting for the sake of continuing the discussion, what I have not granted in fact, namely that there is some limitation on people's autonomy by a prohibition of capitalist acts, it should be said in reply that, if it is an interfering in such a way that affects the autonomy of some, it is a justified interference for by that limitation of autonomy a more extensive autonomy, more widely distributed, is protected or made possible. By prohibiting capitalism we prohibit an autonomy-undermining form of wage labor and with the adopting of socialism we bring in industrial democracy. Such a shift in the way human beings relate to each other will bring considerably more autonomy into the world then can exist under capitalism. (I refer here to a model of a society where the workers would really own and control the means of production and not to the statism of what once were the Soviet bloc countries and of China.) It will more equitably distribute the *conditions* favorable to autonomy. Even if, by prohibiting the selling of labor power and the private ownership of the means to life (productive property), we do adversely affect the autonomy of a few, this is more than compensated for by the vast increase in autonomy in the society at large that such a limitation would bring about. Where the choice is between a lesser liberty and a greater liberty of the same type, but more fairly distributed, morality requires that we go for the greater liberty. If the life of everyone matters and matters equally, this is the fairer way to arrange things. However, even contemporary conservatives commit themselves to this moral equality, but then it is surely difficult for them to maintain an amoralist defense of privilege, for to will the end requires them to will as well the necessary means to the end and that in turn requires going for the greater and more extensive liberty.

So far I have argued that a democratic socialism comes out better than capitalism in supporting moral equality, though in arguing that I also in effect argued that it does better as well with respect to autonomy. I want now in bringing this chapter to an end to amplify that and develop this contention in some distinct directions. I will start by talking about autonomy, work, and democracy. In capitalism there cannot be an industrial democracy; social ownership and control of the means of production would violate the very essential prerogatives of capitalism. So to any great extent the workers under capitalism do not, and indeed cannot, no matter how benign the capitalism, cooperatively own the means of life. They do not, except perhaps for little bits, own or control the means of life. Rather, they must sell their labor to a capitalist, if they can. Whether they work, on what they work, in what ways they work, and what is done with what they produce is not determined by them. Sometimes they have some partial control here, but finally these things are determinated by capitalists either directly or, more typically, through their managers. But still the final say so here rests with the capitalist owners. Under such conditions work cannot but be alienating. It is not, and cannot be, an autonomous life activity. Under a democratic socialism, by contrast, we have a public ownership and control of the workplace and that means just what it says: ownership and control of the workplace by the public. Where we have that in any genuine form we have industrial democracy and this would take the form of the workers in their different workplaces having a very considerable control over their particular workplaces. (They would not have complete control for the public at large is also involved.)

What we would have, in a world where every able-bodied person is, was, or will be (in a broad sense) a worker, is people deciding democratically on what work is to be done, what is to be produced, how it is to be produced, what is to be done with what is produced, the conditions under which it is to be produced, the working hours, and the like. This would give workers a far greater control over the conditions of their lives, a far greater self-direction in their work, than is possible under capitalism. They would also in a socialist society have a *right* to the means of life, in the way they could not have under capitalism, for there is in a socialist society public ownership of the means of production and this, of course, would mean that they have a right to work as well as its being the case that they, collectively, would have a control over their work in the way they do not have and cannot have under capitalism. In this very vital way their lives would have more autonomy than they could have in even the best capitalist societies.

In addition to being an industrial democracy, a democratic socialism would be a political democracy as well. It would keep in place, and in all likelihood enhance, the autonomy that goes with political democracy: majority vote, protection of individual rights, civil liberties, and the like. All the basic liberties—those, for example, that John Rawls speaks of—possible under capitalism would also be at least as available under democratic socialism. And, as Rosa Luxemburg argued, these rights, as they so often are under capitalism, would no longer be merely formal rights. Democratic socialism would provide the conditions for their being a concrete reality.[75] Furthermore, its commitment to equality, including a rough equality of condition, would make not only for autonomy but for *conditions* making possible equal autonomy. (That people would actually be equally autonomous is another thing again. That, while remaining a heuristic ideal, is not to be expected. But what can be expected is to provide them with the *social* conditions for equal autonomy.) A society which was *both* more autonomous and more egalitarian could not fail to be a better society and indeed a more just society than a society which was not as autonomous and as egalitarian. But democratic socialism comes out better than capitalism (any capitalism you like) in exactly this way. We cannot remain neutral between these two conflicting socioeconomic formations, as Rawls wishes to, if we are to give an account of a just well-ordered society under contemporary conditions. To advocate standing in the way, given this, of the move to democratic socialism from capitalism is not morally justifiable. Thus, where socialism is a feasible possibility, as it, economically speaking, but not ideologically speaking, now is, a capitalist state and a capitalist society (any capitalist society) standing in such a relation to socialism could not have *de jure* legitimate authority.[76]

NOTES

1. Max Weber, *From Max Weber: Essays in Sociology* (New York: Oxford University Press, 1958), 45–46, 77–83, 130–35, 196–201, 253–64. Seymour Martin Lipset, *Political Man: The Social Basis of Politics* (Baltimore, Md.: Johns Hopkins University Press, 1981).

2. Jürgen Habermas, *Legitimation Crisis*, trans. by Thomas McCarthy (Boston, Mass.: Beacon Press, 1975); Jürgen Habermas, *Communication and the Evolution of Society*, trans. Thomas McCarthy (Boston, Mass.: Beacon Press, 1979), 178–205; and Jürgen Habermas, "What Does a Legitimation Crisis Mean Today? Legitimation Problems in Late Capitalism," in *Legitimacy and the State*, ed. William Connolly (Oxford, England: Basil Blackwell, 1984), 134–55. See also my "Legitimation and Ideology," *Ratio* 29 (December 1987): 111–21.

3. In speaking of "genuine legitimacy" here, I speak of *de jure* legitimate authority as distinct from merely *de facto* authority or power which gets accepted, no matter how unjustifiably, as legitimate. It gives certain people, under certain determinate circumstances, the right to command and to be obeyed. A central worry is over whether such a conception is mythological.

4. Michel Foucault, *Order of Things* (New York: Vintage Books, 1973), 328.

5. Robert Paul Wolff, "Violence and the Law," in *The Rule of Law,* ed. Robert Pau Wolff (New York: Simon and Schuster, 1971), 54–72.

6. Jürgen Habermas, *Legitimation Crisis*. However, it is clear that he sees the importance of the distinction between *de jure* and *de facto* authority. See Habermas, *Communication and the Evolution of Society*, 178–80.

7. Thomas McCarthy, "Legitimation Problems in Advanced Capitalism," in William Connolly, ed., *Legitimacy and the State*, 156.

8. Ibid.

9. Habermas, "What Does Legitimation Crisis Mean Today?" 134–55.

10. Ibid., 135.

11. Ibid.

12. Ibid., 150.

13. Ibid.

14. McCarthy, 159.

15. Habermas, "What Does Legitimation Crisis Mean Today? Legitimation Problems in Advanced Capitalism," 135.

16. Ibid., 136.

17. Ibid.

18. Ibid.

19. Ibid.

20. Ibid., 137.

21. Ibid.

22. Ibid.

23. Ibid., 139.

24. Ibid., 138.

25. Charles Taylor, *Philosophy and the Human Sciences* (Cambridge, England: Cambridge University Press, 1985), 248–88.

26. Habermas, "What Does a Legitimation Crisis Mean Today?" 139.

27. Ibid.

28. Ibid.

29. Ibid., 142.

30. Ibid., 140–42.

31. Ibid., 142.

32. Ibid., 142–45.

33. Ibid., 145.

34. Ibid.

35. Ibid.

36. Ibid.

37. Ibid., 146.

38. Ibid.

39. Ibid., 147. See for more detail here his *The Philosophical Discourse of Modernity*, trans. Frederik Lawrence (Oxford, England: Polity Press, 1987).

40. Habermas, "What Does a Legitimation Crisis Mean Today?" 147.

41. Ibid.

42. Ibid., 148.

43. Ibid.

44. Ibid.

45. Ibid.

46. Ibid., 148–49.

47. Ibid., 149.

48. Daniel Bell, "The 'New' Egalitarianism," in *The New Egalitarianism,* ed. D. L. Schaefer (Port Washington, N.Y.: Kennikat Press, 1979), 21–52.

49. Habermas, "What Does a Legitimation Crisis Mean Today?" 149.

50. Ibid.

51. Ibid., 152.

52. Ibid., 154.

53. Ibid.

54. Ibid.

55. Ibid.

56. Richard Rorty, "Postmodern Bourgeois Liberalism," *Journal of Philosophy* 80 (1983): 583–89; and Richard Rorty, "Solidarity and Objectivity," in *Post-Analytic Philosophy,* ed. J. Rajchman and C. West (New York: Columbia University Press, 1985), 3–19.

57. Jürgen Habermas, *Communication and the Evolution of Society* (Boston: Beacon Press, 1979), 1–68; and Thomas McCarthy, *The Critical Theory of Jürgen Habermas* (Cambridge, Mass.: MIT Press, 1978), 162–92, 272–357.

58. It might be thought that there is in Habermas's thought a contradiction or something very like a contradiction here. If consciousness is imposed it is an external force. If the restrictions we impose on ourselves result from our being in a situation where ideology is so thick that there is imposed consciousness, then there plainly are external factors working on us. However, the charitable and reasonable construal to put on what Habermas is saying is that it is our psychologies, whether ideologically deflected or not, which are the major constraints on our being able to emancipate ourselves, and not nonpsychological factors. This *may* be false or an exaggerated claim to make, but I do not think it is inconsistent.

59. There are, however, important differences as Seyla Benhabib shows. See Seyla Benhabib, "The Utopian Dimension in Communicative Ethics," *New German Critique* 35 (Spring/Summer 1985): 83–96. See also the exchange between Habermas and Rawls in *Journal of Philosophy* 92, no. 3 (March 1995).

60. Robert X. Ware probes some of the ambiguities in Habermas's account. Robert X. Ware, "Habermas's Evolutions," *Canadian Journal of Philosophy* 12, no. 3 (September 1982): 591–620.

61. Quentin Skinner, "Jürgen Habermas," *The New York Review of Books* (1983): 36.

62. David Gauthier, *Morals By Agreement* (Oxford, England: Clarendon Press, 1986), 169–70.

63. Habermas's conception of interests (objective interests) should lead him to see

this as a friendly amendment. Raymond Geuss is masterful in the discussion of interests. Raymond Geuss, *The Idea of a Critical Theory* (Cambridge, England: Cambridge University Press, 1981), chapter 2.

64. Thomas Nagel, *Mortal Questions* (Cambridge, England: Cambridge University Press, 1979), 106–27.

65. Max Weber, *From Max Weber: Essays in Sociology*, 154–244; Gaetano Mosca, *The Ruling Class* (New York: McGraw Hill, 1939); Robert Michels, *First Lectures in Political Sociology* (Minneapolis, Minn.: University of Minnesota Press, 1949).

66. Claus Offe, *Disorganized Capitalism* (Cambridge, Mass.: MIT Press, 1985), 259–99.

67. Andrew Levine, *Liberal Democracy: A Critique of Its Theory* (New York: Columbia University Press, 1982).

68. Offe, *Disorganized Capitalism*, 273–74. Even if it is false that these political elites also call the shots economically my general point still holds.

69. Richard Miller makes a strong methodological case for speaking of a ruling class in his *Analyzing Marx* (Princeton, N.J.: Princeton University Press, 1984), 101–67.

70. Offe, *Disorganized Capitalism*, 275.

71. Ibid., 279.

72. Kai Nielsen, *Equality and Liberty: A Defense of Egalitarianism* (Totowa, N.J.: Rowman and Allenheld, 1985), 45–102.

73. Ibid., 132–90.

74. Rolf Dahrendorf, *Essays in the Theory of Society* (Stanford, Calif.: Stanford University Press, 1968), 151–78; and G. H. Cohen, "The Structure of Proletarian Unfreedom," *Philosophy and Public Affairs* 12, no. 1 (Winter 1983): 3–33.

75. See Andrew Levine on the definition of 'socialism' in his *Arguing for Socialism* (London, England: Routledge and Kegan Paul, 1984), 1–12; and his "On Arguing for Socialism: Theoretical Considerations," *Socialism and Democracy* 2 (Spring/Summer 1986): 19–27.

76. On the feasibility of socialism—here a market socialism—under contemporary conditions, see John E. Roemer, *A Future for Socialism* (Cambridge, Mass.: Harvard University Press, 1994); and Andrew Levine, *The General Will: Rousseau, Marx, Communism* (Cambridge, England: Cambridge University Press, 1993).

Chapter Twelve

Habermas and Foucault: How to Carry Out the Enlightenment Project

I

Michel Foucault would challenge Jürgen Habermas's way of carrying out the Enlightenment project. Habermas, as we saw in the previous chapter, believes he has a way of finding an objective basis for the critique of ideology which would, by utilizing a certain sort of ideal speech theory, enable us to sort out distorted discourse from undistorted discourse, thereby giving us a way distinguishing what is ideological from what is not.[1]

However, as different as they are in other respects, Foucault and Habermas would both challenge post-Enlightenment and postmodernist thinkers who would question the very values of seriousness and integrity and who would reject the role of the critical intellectual who takes the achievement of maturity defused throughout the society to be a key ideal.[2] Moreover, they both take that ideal to involve, among other things, and very centrally, the belief that the taking of responsibility for the use of one's critical rationality consists in the classical Enlightenment ideal of engaging without reserve in the unflinching critical examination of our most cherished and comforting assumptions. That much Habermas and Foucault agree about. But they part ways in articulating more specifically what that critical use of reason comes to and what it means concretely for our understanding of society and modernity.

Habermas's approach is intellectual and abstract. He seeks to provide, as we saw in the previous chapter, an analysis of what universal social conditions are necessary for the undistorted use of discourse. His aim is to seek a depiction in some general way of the conditions for validating truth-claims. With the achievement of this we will have both unified critical reasons and social concerns—and indeed have a conception of the unity of reason—and this will yield an analysis of undistorted discourse. And with that we will have articulated "procedural normative criteria by which one can evaluate social organizations."[3]

Habermas, like Foucault, takes it that Kant "is attempting to preserve the normative role of reason in the face of the collapse of metaphysics."[4] They both regard it as established that we have lost, and irretrievably, the *metaphysical* ground of our substantive beliefs.[5] In that way they are as thoroughly antimetaphysical as the positivists, the pragmatists, and neopragmatists such as Richard Rorty and Stanley Fish. There can be for us, if we would be nonevasive, no cosmological comfort. There is no more turning back here than there is turning back to traditional authority. On a thoroughly naturalistic and nonmetaphysical basis, Habermas seeks to carry out the Kantian project of making reason critical by establishing the limits of and the legitimate use of reason.[6] He seeks to do this by showing what is necessarily presupposed in communication and without which communication would be impossible.

Foucault, in contrast to Habermas, takes a far more historicist and contextualist approach. One's thinking arises out of and is an attempt to respond to one's historical situation. One is no longer, on Foucault's conception of the proper use of critical reason, concerned with trying to make universal, ahistorical, moral judgments about what our society should be like. Rather we should make, as Foucault puts it, an "historical analysis of the limits that are imposed on us and experiment with the possibility of going beyond them."[7] Unlike Habermas, Foucault does not look for any universal structure of human existence. This is not something with which he has any concern. Moreover, it is not, on his view of things, something the lack of which should be a matter of deep regret. In that way, as much as Jacques Derrida, he is thoroughly postmodern.

Many have thought that Foucault was being a kind of nihilist in rejecting such a universalistic perspective and in rejecting all talk of universal moral principles or even of a universal procedural reason. Hubert Dreyfus and Paul Rabinow, two sympathetic interpreters of Foucault, take this to be a misreading, though they recognize it is common enough and that there are passages in Foucault that lend themselves to that reading. Still, they claim, it is not a reading that stands up to a careful study of the texts. Rather, Foucault in his contextualist and historicist way "seeks to be responsive to what is intolerable in his current situation so as to frame both a general problem and to embody a style of action which allows us to see, through a test of limits, that there are meaningful differences in the kinds of society we can have and there are ways of being human worth opposing and others worth strengthening."[8]

Foucault would surely follow Nelson Goodman, Richard Rorty, and Hilary Putnam in the belief that there neither is nor can there be a neutral description of the world or some conception of reason which would give us some ahistorical Archimedean point—a God's-eye view—for social assessments, for using language to represent reality or to so use language as a vehicle for undistorted communication.[9] Their belief is that this is a way of bringing the old philosophical jungle back in in disguise. Foucault, unlike the universalists (principally *metaphysical* realists) Goodman, Rorty, and Putnam oppose, is trying to understand our own particular historically specific situation in a way that is, for that situation, perspicuous and will, as well, under certain appropriate circumstances, move us to action. He is not trying to say what undistorted discourse or a clear perception of things in general would look like. He is not concerned to say anything *general*. He is not in the business of making such philosophical claims. Dreyfus and Rabinow, in this vein, remark concerning what Foucault is up to.

> Foucault is not trying to construct a general theory, nor deconstruct the possibility of any metanarrative; rather, he is offering us an interpretive analytic of our current situation. . . . The practitioner of interpretive analytics realizes that he himself is produced by what he is studying; consequently he can never stand outside it. . . . [He] sees that cultural practices are more basic than any theory and that the seriousness of theory can only be understood as part of a society's ongoing history. The archaeological step back that Foucault takes in order to see the strangeness of our society's practices does not mean that he considers these practices meaningless. Since we share cultural practices with others, and since these practices have made us what we are, we have, perforce, some common footing from which to proceed, to understand, to act. But that foothold is no longer one which is universal, guaranteed verified, or grounded.[10]

Foucault does not set out or defend a moral theory. Yet, as Habermas stresses, his work has a moral thrust. Unlike Habermas and John Rawls, and like the philosopher Richard Rorty or the sociologist Robert Bellah, Foucault has *"abandoned the attempt to legitimate social organization by means of philosophical grounding."*[11] Indeed, he "goes even further and refuses to articulate normative principles."[12] Rather than be, à la Habermas or Kant, so intellectualist about things, Foucault, with his interpretive analytics, just seeks to identify concretely and perspicuously our current situation, then to describe in a detached way how the situation arose and, at the same time, utilizing his rhetorical skills, to make us see and feel considerable uneasiness about the danger inherent in the situation. In this way, he engages in critique, though in a way that is very different from critique as practiced and conceived by Habermas and the Frankfurt school.

Foucault in doing this, and as an illustration of his way of proceeding, pinpoints for us in a brilliant way the disguised forms of power and domination in our lives. He shows us how very often knowledge is power, how pervasive power is in its many disguises, how deeply it cuts into our lives, and how it not infrequently undermines truth-claims. Most fundamentally he reveals the ubiquitousness of power relations: how these relations obtain even where people would not expect them and indeed many would deny they obtain. But, all that to the contrary notwithstanding, Foucault does not make the nihilistic and probably incoherent claim that all truth-claims are undermined because of such matters.[13] And he does not recklessly attack every form of power or claim that truth is just the will to power. He should not be understood as making such grand philosophical claims, though he has not infrequently been taken in this manner. Instead, he sees the job of the intellectual as one of identifying the specific forms and specific interrelationships which truth and power have taken in our history. His aim has never been to denounce power *per se* nor to propound an account of truth, but to use his concrete analyses to "shed light on specific dangers that each specific type of power/knowledge produces."[14]

II

Foucault speaks of power/knowledge in a way that may be initially puzzling.[15] In his book on madness he shows us, among other things, how pervasive nonrational forces are in the world and how they can be undermining of some of our images or rationality. He shows us how shifting the boundary is between reason and unreason, between health and disease, and between science and nonscience. Demarcation lines cannot be firmed up here except arbitrarily and ineffectively.

Typically Foucault writes of these things with a detached and often ironic stance. It has led some commentators to speak of his "happy positivism." That notwithstanding, it is also the case that from the perspective of very particular social concerns Foucault also sometimes writes with passion. He, like Max Weber, though he would certainly not put it so grandly, has a conception of the vocation of an intellectual. An intellectual should, as Foucault sees it, be an ironic social critic who, without heavy-handed seriousness, reveals the distinctive dangers that each type of power/knowledge produces. Knowledge, and increasingly so, is very often a form of power. In our societies, power/knowledge frequently takes the form of what Foucault calls "biopower." He is speaking here of the way in which our current social practices work so as to bring about a social order in which we are healthy, secure and productive. Those all, of course, sound like good things and certainly they plainly are, but Foucault, with his ironic interpretive-descriptions, his reconceptualizations, shows that—given what they come to in our societies—they have their downsides and dark sides as well. We are so disciplined and so socialized in our disciplinary society that we become self-disciplined in ways that take a terrible psychic toll on us. In his *To Discipline and Punish* and in his later *The History of Sexuality*, he shows in concrete ways how this works.

Sigmund Freud and Weber, and following them Habermas, urge us to face our modernity-crisis—a crisis in which a taken-for-granted traditional understanding of reality ceases to function as a shared background in terms of which people can orient their lives and justify how they should live. In a modernity-crisis such background beliefs come in for sustained critical assault. In such a situation people with a modern consciousness are thrown back on their own resources. We need, as some modernists put it moralistically, stoically and heroically to face up to our own situation and not to stick our head in the sand and try to return, as Alasdair MacIntyre and Charles Taylor do, to the traditional patterns of authority of premodernity. The attaining of maturity and emancipation, defenders of modernity claim, is just the attaining of such a resolutely modernist outlook.

Foucault is just as resolutely set against a return to the premodern as are they. But he sees the heroic and stoic stance, as exemplified in the work of Albert Camus or Jean-Paul Sartre, as romanticism. (Bertrand Russell and A.J. Ayer would do here nearly as well, for Foucault's purposes, as different as they are in other respects from Camus and Sartre.) Maturity consists not only in lucidly and unflinchingly facing up to our situation and seeing it in its absurdity, but to, as well, taking an ironic and detached stance toward it. We should not, to put it in a very un-French way, make such a big deal about it. We should learn to do without histrionics. It is evident enough anyway that this is our situation. What we need to do, while maintaining this spirit of ironic detachment, is to preserve an "active engagement in the concerns of the present."[16] It will often take the form of seeking in the present those practices which offer the possibility of new, somewhat more liberating ways of acting and living, though it is not at all like Heidegger's search for "a new God" or Habermas's search, in an ideal speech situation, for a model of undistorted discourse which could give us a new model for assessing societies or whole ways of life. Foucault does not believe that we can have or indeed that we even need such an Archimedean point. Such conceptions may be the residues of the old search for the Absolute or *the* truth, as if we had any coherent conception of what these things could come to. But the point is we neither can have them nor do we need them.

Indeed, like Habermas, Foucault wants to change our world, but not through trying to provide us with a grand theory linked to a conception of *praxis* or a new meta-narrative. Instead, he seeks to give us a perspicuous diagnosis of our present dangers together with a better understanding of what a specifically modern ethic concretely articulated and elaborated would look like. This is very different from constructing a critical theory of society or a grand ethical theory following some Kantian or utilitarian or perfectionist or pluralistic deontological or Rawlsian morality of principles or Nozickian or Cohenian doctrine of natural rights. This attention to an ethic (in a very non-traditionalist conception of an ethic), though not to an ethical *theory*, was something Foucault was looking at toward the end of his life.[17]

We must not misunderstand Foucault here. He does not try to articulate any normative account of what would constitute an ideal society. Indeed, he would not only be skeptical about its very possibility, but, as well, be ironically dismissive of the whole endeavor, though this would not be from a lack of passionate moral concern.[18] For him maturity and emancipation would come to facing the possibility that action cannot be grounded in universal, ahistorical theories of the moral agent or in a moral theory somehow rooted in a universal reason or empathetic understanding. (That is to say, we should be neither Kantian nor Humean.) There is, Habermas to the contrary notwithstanding, no duty to conform to a universal imperative implicit in all speech acts. We need neither a morality devoted to the normalizing of populations nor a Kantian morality of universal rules. Rather, we should start, Foucault would have it, by going back to the Greeks, though, it should be quickly noted, his is a very distinctive way of going back to the Greeks. We do not need, Foucault claims, prescriptive moral codes, but we do need careful deliberations about what kind of person to aspire to be. This is what the Greeks were essentially concerned with, Foucault maintains, in thinking about ethics and, Foucault adds, they were justified in so circumscribing the subject. We need closely and skeptically to inspect the kind of life, given our socialization, we are incited to lead and the special moral status we are asked to attain, as in the denial of the self and the lusts of the flesh in traditional Christianity. We need to think very hard and long about what sort of persons we should aspire to be. We need to think nonevasively about how to constitute the self. We need to face up to our own self-images and to our evasiveness and forgetfulness concerning such matters. We need to take the lessons of Pascal and Kierkegaard to heart without at all absorbing their religious environment.

Foucault, of course, does not deny, what is evident enough anyway, that there exists in our moral lives problems about our code, its principles and the application of those principles, as well as ethical problems about how to turn oneself into the right sort of person. Facing that context, Foucault, as one of his commentators well puts it, proposes

> to analyze such ethical problems and their transformations in terms of a scheme in which there is an image of the right sort of person or life of the soul, then the authority which incites, and the practical means provided, to become such a kind of person, and finally, the sort of description under which one's experience becomes relevant for such a self-transformation.

> Thus 'ethics' can be analyzed in terms of practices to constitute people as moral beings, or as 'practices of the self'.[19]

Ethics, as the Greeks realized, should be very much concerned about our lack of self-mastery. Our central problem in ethics should be the problem of becoming the right sort of person. But in doing this we should not, Foucault believes, take a Kantian, utilitarian, or perfectionist turn and seek to work out philosophically universalizing positions. This, he believes, will simply get in the way of a search for our being the right sort of persons. In his last interview, Foucault flatly asserted, "the search for a form of morality acceptable by everyone in the sense that everyone would have to submit to it, seems catastrophic to me."[20] (Here we can see the very considerable distance between Foucault and contractarians.)

Foucault believes that Habermas's position is too intellectualistic and that in that way Habermas is a too *uncritical* child of the Enlightenment. He misses, Foucault believes, among other things, crucial insights that we can learn from Thomas Kuhn on paradigms. Habermas, of course, is fully aware that rational discussion takes place against the "background of a shared understanding"—a preanalytic understanding—"of what is important, what makes sense, what is in the true/false language-games, what counts as a reason, etc."[21] Habermas does not back away from the recognition, a recognition also stressed by pragmatists, Wittgenstein and hermeneuticists, that to be able to understand at all we must start with a whole shared set of cultural understandings.[22] Still, Foucault maintains, Habermas's position is too intellectualistic. This is shown in Habermas's claim that to escape ideology, to rise above distorted discourse, it must be the case "that our shared background understanding is in fact being made more and more explicit in late Western capitalist culture, and that, wherever there is a problem, the background can be made sufficiently explicit so as to allow rational evaluation."[23] In short, Habermas believes not only in the progressive disenchantment of the world, but as well in our increasing capacity to not only control the world through our understanding of it, but to gain greater understanding of ourselves and with that understanding greater self-mastery. In short, Habermas believes in progress. Foucault, by contrast, does not, but believes instead that we constantly in various new ways reenchant the world, remystify ourselves, and, in general, gain neither greater self-understanding nor greater self-mastery as we human beings move through history. We do sometimes have victories here but they are temporary and local. There seems, on Foucault's part, to be no conception of a total defeat of the disciplinary society and the replacement of it, as we have envisioned in Marx, by a truly human society. That notwithstanding, Foucault also believes that there are from human beings with all their warts repeated local flashpoints of resistance and, as I have just remarked, occasional local and temporary victories. Even in a proficient disciplinary society we never become completely disciplined individuals or utter cultural dupes. *Brave New World* or *1984* is never completely victorious. But we cannot claim anything more than that. There is, for Foucault, no general human emancipation in a New Jerusalem. There is no general progress over epochs to greater self-mastery and Enlightenment. Between Marx and Foucault there is here a gulf, and Habermas, child of the Enlightenment that he is, is here closer to Marx and the classical tradition of the Enlightenment than to Foucault.

Between Habermas and Foucault, we have stated starkly (perhaps overstarkly) the contrast between a modern and a postmodern thinker. Let me now run a bit more with this contrast. Even with that great flagship of the Enlightenment, natural science, we cannot, Foucault will have it, gain such an intellectualistic understanding. In the actual practices of the scientific disciplines, paradigms and styles of reasoning (as Ian Hacking has well argued) play an essential role. As Thomas Kuhn puts it, in the cluster of actual scientific procedures that scientists actually standardly engage in, we have practices in which scientists argue by reference to shared exemplars. It is essential, if science is to work, that, along with scientific conflict, there be a massive background of agreement among scientists. Agreement must be the norm and disagreement the exception. This may, as Donald Davidson sees it, be even more broadly true.[24] Against a too intellectualistic way of conceptualizing things in science, we need to recognize that stably to secure that agreement no attempt should be made, *as a condition for that agreement*, to rationalize and clarify these paradigms into a set of clearly articulated assumptions or principles. That is to ask too much. To proceed reasonably and effectively (*pace* Habermas and the whole intellectualistic tradition) we must turn away from a preoccupation with rational procedures—a concern to find the correct deep underlying method—and stick instead with the shared paradigms and the distinctive practices. We need to appeal to them if we are to have a grip on things. To say that "to really understand" we must "get behind" these practices and see clearly their rationale—to see, for example, the deep underlying aim of science—is to ask that the very background we require for understanding be itself first rationalized if we are to be able to understand those very conditions. But it is to those very conditions to which we must appeal to be able to understand at all.[25] We need to stay in contextual saddle here, Foucaultians would say, if there is to be rational communication about content. Habermas seeks to pursue the Enlightenment project by identifying critical reason with the possibility of a universal objective grounding. For Foucault, by contrast, the project cannot be pursued on such a grand scale. Critical reason *pace* Habermas must eschew such a search for a universal grounding. Instead, foxlike and with detachment, while working from within, it should critically and reflexively inspect in the concrete our actual social practices.

III

It is at least plausible to believe that Foucault has a coherent method of cultural analysis that has usefully been called *interpretive analytics*. Repeatedly from all sorts of angles throughout the various shifts in his work, Foucault investigates how we constitute ourselves as subjects and treat others as objects. Repeatedly in doing this he shows how social practices condition cognitive discourse. In the course of spelling this out, Foucault resists the idea that there is a determinate human nature.[26] Rather, he claims, somewhat paradoxically and indeed exaggeratedly, that human beings are beings whose nature is produced historically from their social world. (Here he needs the Aristotelian corrective of a Martha Nussbaum.) Still, behind the exaggeration, there is the important truth that human beings are very differently formed in different cultures and in different historical epochs. Moreover, and distinctly, much of the discursive knowledge that we have is something that is produced in the service of expanding power. And this is a power that increasingly penetrates our institutions: our factories, schools, prisons, police, and our armies. So we should recognize that in some specific ways we are conceptually and culturally imprisoned. The background of our social practices is something that can never at least in practice be completely articulated. (To think that it can, Foucault believes, is Habermas's rationalistic error.) Since this is so, Foucault maintains, we can never get a grand theory or a total theory that will explain all of social reality in some holistic fashion.

Foucault seeks, even as an engaged social critic, to avoid the Whiggish assumption that later theories, and most particularly our own, are necessarily superior to earlier theories. Foucault, once he abandoned his earlier archaeological historical phase and did a genealogical critical history of the present, readily admits that his account cannot be holistic or totalizing and that no one can archaeologically stand outside our social practices and neutrally analyze them. Rather, all analysis and criticism must work from within these social practices and that, if as genealogists we are to do critical history, we should recognize and acknowledge right from the start our polemical interests motivating our investigation and critique of the emergence of contemporary social power. We should not seek to disguise from ourselves the fact that we are political animals in the midst of political struggles. Our intent as political animals is to rectify the malignancies in our social practices. To do that effectively we must clearly understand them in a genealogical manner. But in doing this it is vital that we write *concrete and detailed genealogical histo-*

ries which in effect tell their own story in a way that will reveal in a concrete way the changing history of these social practices. To pull this off they must be studied diachronically and not just synchronically. The genealogy will chart the emergence and the direction of growth of social institutions and it will examine, in studying this, as well, the regimes of discipline and social scientific techniques that reinforce specific social practices. Foucault seeks both to describe social practices, to explain the malignancies in them, and in doing so critique them normatively. His accounts are at one and the same time descriptive, interpretive, and critical.

Habermas criticizes Foucault for being, as he puts it, "crypto-normativist" because Foucault cannot explain the very standards that Habermas at least believes Foucault must presuppose in any condemnation of the present.[27] Foucault, he believes, cannot show us why domination ought to be resisted or why struggle is preferable to submission. Foucault clearly is for struggle and against domination, but he can give us no reasons for so plonking. Such commitments at least seem on his account to be merely arbitrary groundless commitments, Foucault, Habermas believes, needs some kind of moral theory, procedural or otherwise, to defend himself here. He needs this, Habermas claims, to tell us what is wrong with our modern power/knowledge regimes and why we ought to oppose them. In giving us no grounds here and in refusing to see the need for grounds, Foucault shows, Habermas claims, that, his intentions to the contrary notwithstanding, he really is an irrationalist and a nihilist.[28]

Some commentators have come to Foucault's defense here.[29] Dreyfus and Rabinow, for example, think that while Foucault does indeed reject the idea of progress and with it any Whiggish conception of history, that, all that to the contrary notwithstanding, it is a mistake to see Foucault as in opposition to everything in the Enlightenment tradition and that in particular it is a mistake to read him as an irrationalist and a nihilist. Foucault does think, and not unreasonably, that we can make intelligible normative critiques and that we can exhibit one by one the malignancies in our social practices. We will, however, never, he believes, get an *overall picture*, let alone a holistic critical account, of the situation. Our understanding is always, and inescapably, concretely and historically situated. To think otherwise is a rationalistic illusion. Still such situated knowledge can be genuine knowledge with a for the nonce emancipatory potential.

Richard Rorty, going even further than Dreyfus and Rabinow, moves to a counterattack by arguing that Foucault's own critical histories subvert the quasi-metaphysical or cosmological seeking for comfort that is implicit in Habermas's belief in the convergence in the long run on rational standards of an "ideal speech community."[30] That such a convergence will obtain, Rorty has it, is simply presupposed by Habermas. No argument is thought to be necessary for it. Indeed, it might be taken, if we have a touch of cynicism or cultural pessimism, as a touching article of faith in progress, something we well might, if we are tough-minded, be very skeptical of indeed. The persistence of such a need for comfort is something which hardly seems compatible with the skeptical antimetaphysical spirit of modernity.

IV

In addition to the Habermasian criticism that he is a nihilist there are the criticisms of Charles Taylor and Michael Walzer that maintain, though in more concrete detail than does Habermas, the theme that Foucault is a crypto-normativist.[31] Foucault seems at least deliberately to set aside any contrast between the true and the false and he remains silent about any distinction between autonomy and power or what is just and what is not. This fits, they claim, uneasily with his sometimes moral passion. Taylor and Walzer, like Habermas, think that Foucault's social criticism tacitly presupposes the very values he discounts, namely the ideals of truth, justice, and autonomy. In this way he is a crypto-normativist.

Foucault's line of response, a careful interpreter of his work remarks, "has been the indirect one of denying that he either is or needs to be a political *theorist*."[32] He is a critical historian doing interpretive analytics and as such his interests are different than those of a political theorist or philosopher. David Hoy puts this Foucaultian response very well: "As a historian he has been trying to locate cases where their traditional ideals have served only as empty notions blinding humanitarian theorists to the historical reality of the spread of oppressive and conformist tendencies in modern societies."[33] We sing songs in praise of liberty, equality, and democracy while in fact, if Foucault's history of the birth of the prison system and its extension to other carceral systems is near to the mark, we have come to have a social world in which there is a pervasive social molding of people into normal as opposed to abnormal, delinquent or deviant individuals. It leads, Foucault claims, to ever-increasing normalization—that is a homogenizing of people—rather than to a more humane and just social order where people are more autonomous and are more respected as persons, as the distinctive individuals they are.

The Enlightenment, including Marxist forms of the Enlightenment, has not brought the hoped for liberation of human beings. Quite to the contrary, there are deep homogenizing techniques in our disciplinary society, techniques that up to now have grown stronger rather than weaker. Foucault indeed regards them as a social cancer and he is intensely critical of them. He is not content merely, as some believe, to give a detached and ironical description and reconceptualization of such practices. He seeks as well to subvert and disrupt this malignancy. But Habermas, Taylor, and Walzer all respond that such a subversion, such a critical stance, lacks force because "he has no social alternatives to offer, and no moral or political standards on which to base his angry charge that modern society is becoming more and more like a prison, however progressive and benevolent it appears to those who have let themselves be successfully normalized."[34] But, given his setting aside of the ideals of justice, truth, and progress, how, they ask, can he argue that the past was any better or that the future should be different?

Hoy thinks that such criticisms are off-target. He thinks that Foucault's critical history—his genealogical method—can be understood as a "plausible method of immanent social criticism," a form of social criticism, that can "work without presupposing an independent, utopian standpoint."[35] The method works like this: Foucault, like all of us, is a participant in our social practices—he is not like an alien anthropologist viewing them from outside—and he has at least a participant's understanding of them. Subject, like all of us, to the organizing trends of our society, he is still in a position to diagnose them if he can distance himself just a little, as he can, and as we can as well. This is something, disciplinary society or no, we have the ability to do, if we will resolutely try in a reflective way to diagnose them, working from within as it were. Indeed starting there, and so proceeding, may be something there may well be no coherent alternative to. Foucault does not have to have a model of an ideal society to appeal to which will give him a comprehensive frame in which to situate his frustration and resentment. To motivate him to criticize our social arrangements he neither has such a grand basis of appeal nor does he need one. He can, of course, as we can too, have a very concrete sense that things are rotten, some understanding of why specifically they are rotten, a sense of what has to come to an end for this particular rottenness at this particular time and place to be eroded, without having anything beyond an inchoate sense of what a just and truly human society would look like. Unlike Kant, Mill, Rawls, Taylor, or Walzer have, or think they have, we may have no philosophical articulation of this just society at all. We may be quite without anything like a big picture here and remain, for all that, comfortable—and not unreasonably so—in our specific judgments. Being without such a philosophical articulation of a comprehensive, or partially comprehensive, framework does not stand in our way of making reasonably and justifiably concrete judgments about what is just and the like. Moreover, even if we had *some* sense of what such a world would look like, we might very well have no understanding of the mechanisms by which we could bring such a truly human society into existence. We can recognize the plague and resolve to fight the plague even if we do not have much of anything by way of a general conception of a just society and no understanding of what must be done to bring one into existence and to sustain it.

Along with this comes the recognition on Foucault's part that without having any philosophical foundations at all we can still have the resources to recognize and write about carceral techniques and normalizing tendencies and that others in turn can empathetically and reflectively respond to such writings. That we have such capacities shows that we have not been completely normalized, that we have not been inescapably disciplined, that we are not cultural dupes, that we have not been fully coopted.

In writing about society Foucault not infrequently engages in hyperbole. He, as Hoy puts it, "paints the picture of a totally normalized society, not because he believes our present society is one, but because he hopes we will find the picture threatening."[36] If we really were thoroughly socialized into *Brave New World* or *1984*, we would not find it so. Our social criticism must come from within; there is, and can be, no neutral position or superior position "outside of society" (whatever that means) in accordance with which, or by virtue of which, society could be criticized and assessed. Socialized as we are, having the social practices we have, including the pervasive normalizing tendencies of modern society, we will still find them repugnant when they are sharply brought into focus by being described in a certain way. It seems, at least, that our socialization, as a matter of fact, does not run so deep down that we end up in an Orwellian world. Certain descriptions can, imperfectly normalized as we are, be very morally telling and Foucault is a master at giving us these descriptions. Given our feelings, our sensitivities, we set out, if we do not think these practices are utterly inevitable, to resist them and subvert them. This is immanent social critique based on critical history and critical genealogies, rather than on critical *theory*, and it may not be mistaken to believe that it will suffice. This will seem particularly plausible if we are justified in being skeptical about the capacity of philosophers or social theorists to deliver on grand theories.

V

In his last work *The History of Sexuality* and in some very extended interviews given late in his life, Foucault returned, as we have already noted, to a traditional French preoccupation with the self and to a discussion of ethics that is very different from the way that it is usually discussed by moral philosophers.[37] Will this modify and, if so, also advance his method or practice (if 'method' is not a too portentous word here) of immanent social criticism? It is clearly a move beyond the study of power to the doing of a critical history of our ethical self-understandings. Does this advance his critique? It does tend to cut against the rather standard picture of seeing Foucault as a nihilist or relativist.[38] His genealogical studies attempt to show how we form our identities by over time conforming ourselves to tacitly accepted norms and generally accepted practices. In this way we constitute ourselves as human subjects, though this is indeed hardly ever, if ever, something we do in an active, conscious way through deliberation and action. It is done rather through subliminal socialization. As his studies on sexuality or on madness illustrate, Foucault studies features of human beings that we normally take to be fixed—to be just a part of human nature—and he shows them to be more malleable than we would in the normal course of events have thought possible.

He applies this genealogical procedure to the study of sexual ethics in different historical periods. In doing this he focuses on the practices by which individuals train themselves to be certain sorts of persons. His study here is very different from Edward Westermarck's. It is not a history of moral codes. A traditional historical study would concern itself with the sets of moral principles people would explicitly espouse or presuppose. Traditional moral philosophy would inspect more carefully their exact meaning and import and look at what their rationale or justification is, if indeed they have any. Foucault finds very little of interest there. He thinks such notions do not have an interesting history and remarks, in a rather nonrelativist way, that these very general principles are generally stable throughout the different historical periods. He believes, however, that Hegel was right against Kant in stressing that we should attend not so much to abstract moral principles as to the concrete moral life in the societies we study: the 'ethical substance' that keeps the moral code functioning. *Here* Foucault is like a Hegelian or a communitarian, for the moral reality—the ethical substance—from which we must start, if we would understand the morality of a society, including our morality, must include the shared understanding of what it is to belong to a particular community and what it is, in such a community, to aspire to be a good person in that community. The latter gives us our conceptions of the self and that is, Foucault contends, essentially what ethics should study.

He thinks we should return again to the old Greek notion of the care of the self rather than to stick with the Christian goal of self-renunciation. In seeing what this care of the self comes to, it is important to understand the various techniques that people practice in order to make themselves into the persons they want to be. However, this self-understanding that is essential for a proper care of the self is not the same for Foucault as self-consciousness. A genealogy of ethics will, done by a critical historian, move below the level of explicit moral reflection or precepts to factors which are not so easily available to the agent.

Such a genealogist is concerned with practices and patterns of action. In a way very different from that of Ludwig Wittgenstein or Peter Winch, Foucault believes that, while these patterns of action will standardly appear to their practitioners to be "coherent, intelligible, and tolerable, a critical history shows the practices to be not as rational, inevitable, or invariable as they are thought to be."[39] We should study self-understanding objectively, "through a matrix of social and discursive practices. To the extent that these practices turn out to vary historically, self-understanding will vary as well."[40] The things we need to understand are things which can be objectively discerned even though they may never have been articulated self-consciously, though this, of course, does not mean that they are not articulatable. But Foucault, historicist that he is, recognizes that, in all sorts of ways, change is going on all the time. Moral precepts, for example, change slowly. However, not infrequently, the background understanding of these rules changes at a different pace. This can sometimes lead to confusion and indeed to alienation or perhaps even something approximating the social disarray with which Alastair MacIntyre is so obsessed. Because of shifts in the background understanding of the same moral rules, moral agents may understand only very incompletely why they act as they do.

However, meshing with his historicist historian's concern with ethics, Foucault's later position, as well as his earlier one, is still a position that refuses to attempt to assess whole ways of life, whole moral codes, or ethical theories. Foucault resolutely sets aside any attempt to articulate an Archimedean point or to set out the "rational foundation" of ethics or the general canons of social criticism. He is concerned, as a historian and a genealogist, with investigating the different self-understandings which various people at different times and in different conditions have come to have. Self-understanding is an adaptive device we have taken on sometimes as a kind of protective coloring and sometimes with considerable success.

Foucault articulates no standpoint or standard from which we can say one self-understanding is better or worse than another. And *perhaps* he even thinks that no such articulation could be coherently or correctly given. Yet he remains critical of the present and the question remains whether his immanent method of social criticism gives him a sufficient basis for that critical stance. Still, to return to an earlier point, in talking about our various different practices at different times and places—say our sexual practices or our penal practices—do not such genealogies supply in a local way a corrective to the ills in our own practices, do they not make us more aware of the shortcomings in our own self-understandings as we live our lives in these practices? I think the answer should be that they do.

It should also be noted that he is in no way committed to conceptual, epistemological, or metaethical relativism. His interpretive analytics and critical history is simply neutral with respect to such philosophical issues. Foucault does not hesitate to claim that there are truths about how people do understand themselves and about what sort of lives they esteem. But he does not address the further question whether there are certain sorts of lives to which everyone at least in some determinate cultural and historical circumstances ought to aspire. As a historian he is not required to do so. As a philosopher he could give deflationary arguments here and in doing so seek to establish that the question is misguided because it presupposes both an inflated view of what a philosophical theory of morality can establish and an "inadequate moral psychology that ignores the social and historical background supporting the moral code."[41] *Perhaps* some mileage could be gained with this? But again Foucault could remain neutral here, refusing in any of the standard senses to engage in philosophy. However, whether he does or not, it should be plain from the above that Foucault is not making relativistic claims. (He is perhaps not denying them either.) And his close interest in self-formation, the cultural basis of morality, and his hardly morally disengaged interest in politics should deflect the charge of nihilism. Moreover, his account is not a functionalist one in which all aspects of culture are seen as a seamless web. He does not think the various parts of a society are so tied together that no part can change and indeed be improved independently of the others.

Foucault is not (*pace* what Hilary Putnam thinks Foucault is doing) asserting that all social products and every cultural standpoint is irrational, thus hoisting himself by his own petard.[42] He is rather making the more modest claim that careful critical histories will reveal the depth and pervasiveness of irrationality in some of our specific beliefs and practices. And again he is not, like a functionalist, treating culture as a seamless web.

It is a mistake to view Foucault as an antirationalist representative of the counter-Enlightenment or as an enemy the Enlightenment. Foucault saw Kant's essay "What is Enlightenment?" as an essay that was part of the same critical tradition of which he is a part. Foucault, in an essay written late in his life, "What is Enlightenment?" stressed that we "still depend in large part upon the Enlightenment."[43] He, like Adorno and Horkheimer, stands within the tradition of the Enlightenment.[44] What he wishes to do, if you will as a positivist, is to further trim theological and metaphysical residues from it. Central targets for him are its conception of inevitable progress and some of its beliefs about human nature. In the name of the Enlightenment and maturity, he wants to make us see some of its dark underside. He further, and vitally, wants, as did Adorno as well, to historicize the Enlightenment by helping us to see, through his critical genealogies, that rational autonomy is an empty ideal unless we see how in specific historical contexts it can be embodied and situated. Again, we have Hegel against Kant. But surely in Foucault we have no raging against reason or even poking fun at it.

NOTES

1. Jürgen Habermas, *Communication and the Evolution of Society* (Boston: Beacon Press, 1979), 1–69; Jürgen Habermas, "Aspects of the Rationality of Action," in *Rationality Today*, ed. T. F. Geraets (Ottawa: University of Ottawa Press, 1979), 185–212; Jürgen Habermas, *The Philosophical Discourse of Modernity* (Oxford, England: Polity Press, 1987), chapters 11 and 12; Thomas McCarthy, *The Critical Theory of Jürgen Habermas* (Cambridge, Mass.: MIT Press, 1978), 162–92, 272–357; Kai Nielsen, "Legitimation and Ideology," *Ratio* 29, no. 2 (December 1987): 111–21.

2. Hubert L. Dreyfus and Paul Rabinow, "What Is Maturity? Habermas and Foucault on 'What Is Enlightenment?'" in *Foucault: A Critical Reader,* ed. David Couzens Hoy (Oxford, England: Basil Blackwell, 1986), 109–22.

3. Jürgen Habermas, "Taking Aim at the Heart of the Present," in Hoy, *Foucault: A Critical Reader*, 103–108. See also his *The Philosophical Discourse of Modernity*, 238–93.

4. Ibid., 111.

5. Jürgen Habermas, *Autonomy and Solidarity* (London: Verso, 1986), 93–130, 149–216.

6. Jürgen Habermas, *The Theory of Communicative Action*, vols. 1 and 2 (Boston: Beacon Press, 1984).

7. Michel Foucault, *The Foucault Reader*, ed. Paul Rabinow (New York: Pantheon Books, 1984), 50.

8. Dreyfus and Rabinow, "What Is Maturity?" 111–13.

9. Nelson Goodman, *Ways of Worldmaking* (Indianapolis, Ind.: Hackett, 1978); Richard Rorty, *Philosophy and the Mirror of Nature* (Princeton, N.J.: Princeton University Press, 1979); and Hilary Putnam, *Reason, Truth and History* (Cambridge, England: Cambridge University Press, 1981).

10. Dreyfus and Rabinow, "What Is Maturity?" 115.

11. Ibid., 113.

12. Ibid., 115.

13. Charles Taylor gives us good reasons for thinking that such a claim would be incoherent. Charles Taylor, "Foucault on Freedom and Truth," in Hoy, *Foucault: A Critical Reader*, 69–102. But (*pace* Taylor) Foucault does not make such a claim.

14. Dreyfus and Rabinow, "What Is Maturity?" 116.

15. *The Foucault Reader*, 51–75, 239–56.

16. Dreyfus and Rabinow, "What Is Maturity?" 117.

17. *The Foucault Reader*, 333–90. Hubert Dreyfus and Paul Rabinow, *Michel Foucault Beyond Structuralism and Hermeneutics*, 2d ed. (Chicago: University of Chicago Press, 1982), 229–64. Michel Foucault, "The Ethic of Care of the Self as a Practice of Freedom" in *The Final Foucault,* ed. James Behnauer and David Rasmussen (Cambridge, Mass.: MIT Press, 1988), 1–20.

18. See his debate with Noam Chomsky in Noam Chomsky and Michel Foucault, "Human Nature: Justice Versus Power" in *Reflexive Water,* ed. F. Elders (London: Souvenir Press, 1974), 136–89. See also Paul Rabinow's discussion of it in his introduction to *The Foucault Reader*, 3–7.

19. John Rajchman, "Ethics After Foucault," *Social Text* 13/14 (1986): 172.

20. Quoted from Dreyfus and Rabinow, "What Is Maturity?" 119.

21. Ibid. See as well his *Autonomy and Solidarity*.

22. Jürgen Habermas, "A Review of Gadamer's *Truth and Method,*" in *Understanding and Social Inquiry,* ed. Fred Dallmayer and Thomas McCarthy (Notre Dame,

Ind.: University of Notre Dame Press, 1977), 335–63; and Jürgen Habermas, "On Hermeneutics' Claim to Universality," in *The Hermeneutics Reader,* ed. Kurt Muller-Vollmer (New York; Continuum Press, 1988), 293–319.

23. Dreyfus and Rabinow, "What Is Maturity?" 120.

24. Donald Davidson, *Inquiries Into Truth and Interpretation* (Oxford, England: Clarendon Press, 1984), 183–98.

25. Ludwig Wittgenstein, *On Certainty* (Oxford, England: Basil Blackwell, 1969); and *Wittgenstein,* ed. Georg von Wright (Minneapolis: University of Minnesota Press, 1988), 163–82.

26. See his debate with Chomsky. It also brings out how paradoxical this claim is and, I believe, unnecessary. The truth—perhaps the rather banal truth—behind it is that there is a lot more of us that is socially constituted than we are wont to think. See references note 18. For a nonhyperbolic account of what is involved here see Charles Taylor, *Philosophy and the Human Sciences* (Cambridge, England: Cambridge University Press, 1985), 13–57.

27. See reference note 2.

28. Habermas, *The Philosophical Theory of Modernity.* It is bizarre that Habermas should think that justification is in order here. Isn't it as obvious, as obvious can be, that domination ought to be resisted at least where the costs are not too great? Domination is not a good thing and it ought not to obtain. These are banal enough truths. Is a philosophical theory going to improve our justificatory grip here? Only someone held captive to philosophy could think we need a justification for these banal truths. See here, as well, the next chapter and chapter 5. And see also John Rawls, "Reply to Habermas," *Journal of Philosophy* 92, no. 3 (March 1995): 178.

29. See the introduction and, as well, the essay by Hoy, the essay by Martin Jay, and the essay by Dreyfus and Rabinow, all in Hoy, *Foucault: A Critical Reader.*

30. Richard Rorty, "Foucault and Epistemology," in Hoy, *Foucault: A Critical Reader*, 41–49.

31. Charles Taylor, "Foucault on Freedom and Truth," 69–102, and Michael Walzer, "The Politics of Michel Foucault," 51–58, both in Hoy, *Foucault: A Critical Reader.*

32. David Couzens Hoy, "Introduction," *Foucault: A Critical Reader*, 12.

33. Ibid.

34. Ibid., 13

35. Ibid.

36. Ibid., 14

37. Michel Foucault, *The History of Sexuality*, vol. 1 (New York: Pantheon, 1978) and essays referred to in note 17. For a discussion see John Rajchman, "Ethics After Foucault," and Arnold I. Davidson, "Archaeology, Genealogy, Ethics" in Hoy, *Foucault: A Critical Reader*, 221–33.

38. William Connolly, "Introduction" to his *Legitimacy and the State* (Oxford, England: Basil Blackwell, 1984), 15–18.

39. Hoy, "Introduction," *Foucault: A Critical Reader,* 18.

40. Ibid.

41. Ibid., 20.

42. Putnam, *Reason, Truth and History*, 121, 126, 155–62.

43. Foucault, *Foucault Reader*, 32–50.

44. Habermas makes this very clear in discussing Adorno and Horkheimer. See his *The Philosophical Discourse of Modernity*, 106–30. See also his "The Entwinement of Myth and Enlightenment: Re-Reading Dialectic of Enlightenment," *New German Critique* 26 (1982): 13–30.

Chapter Thirteen

Skeptical Remarks on the Scope of Philosophy: Rorty versus Habermas

I

Jürgen Habermas, as firmly as Richard Rorty or any of the French post-modernists, rejects the idea that philosophy can anymore usefully be viewed as an autonomous discipline. Moreover, it cannot be foundationalist, cannot rightly use natural scientific knowledge as the model for all knowledge, cannot usefully do metaphysics or erect some First Philosophy that would tell us what Ultimate Reality is really like. It is also true that philosophy does not have some special way of knowing or understanding that would enable it to serve as the arbiter or judge for the rest of culture. In short, philosophy cannot provide the foundations of anything. (That is what has led me to speak in part 1 of *Naturalism Without Foundations.*) There is no First Philosophy functioning as an ultimate court of appeal as something that could take science, religion, morality, politics, or art up against the bar of reason, sorting out what is sensible and what is sound in these practices or activities or deciding how to alter them or what new ones to adopt or, more generally, to tell us what the good and rational life is. Philosophy is not there to tell us what the life of reason is or even what (if anything) this could come to or sensibly mean.

Yet Habermas also stands firmly against those whom he takes to be bidding farewell and good riddance to philosophy: anti-Philosophy philosophers such as Jacques Derrida, Paul Feyerabend, and Richard Rorty. In spite of what Habermas takes to be the incisiveness of the latter's critique of epistemology and his critique of the Tradition, Rorty is still, he believes, fundamentally mistaken about philosophy. Philosophy is not a genre of literature. Just in virtue of what the practice of philosophy is, philosophical conversation and deliberation cannot but gravitate toward argumentation and justificatory dispute. Moreover it should not acquiesce in Rorty's historicism or any historicism, not even Theodor Adorno's or Michel Foucault's, but should seek to articulate general criticizable claims to validity, should, as Habermas puts it, stick to the claim of reason, stubbornly clinging "to the notion that philosophy is the guardian of reason and to the belief that across the multifarious language-games, practices and forms of life, philosophy can discern some unity to reason, though it may very well be a procedural unity and not, as in the grand metaphysical traditions, and as it was for the early critical theorist Max Horkheimer, a substantive conception of reason."[1] Philosophy should, Habermas remarks, keep a trained eye on the topic of rationality which, he adds, comes to the "inquiring into the conditions of the unconditional."[2] Is such talk on Habermas's part anything more than inflated rhetoric, the residue of the Grand Old Tradition of First Philosophy that Habermas would set aside? I shall return to this, but first I shall remark on Habermas as a yeasayer as well as a naysayer and set out some of the details of his metaphilosophical account.

Habermas is not through and through negative and he is not stuck with vapid generalizations. He does find some roles for philosophy more specific than being the guardian of reason. While philosophy cannot intelligibly set itself up as the judge, arbiter, or the assessor of the rest of culture, it can and should function as placeholder for the sciences by holding open, in a dominantly scientistic culture, such questions of unity and universality that might otherwise be closed or blocked or dropped by empirical or scientific research.[3] He also speaks of philosophy's role as a *placemaker* or *stand-in* for the sciences. For philosophy to have this role it must be in a working relationship with the human sciences and most particularly with the reconstructive sciences. It does this by supplying ideas that are then treated as empirical hypotheses by the sciences which the latter subsequently elaborates, sometimes operationalizes, and finally tests. It is in this way that philosophy can function as a stand-in for empirical theories with strong universalist claims, but it should also be recognized that philosophy and philosophers can no longer do their work single-handedly. Rather, philosophy needs to integrate its own work into that of the human sciences, working as a cooperative partner and not as someone who provides the sciences with foundations or a logic to which it must conform on pain of falling into irrationality. Philosophy as such a cooperative partner is in no way the queen of the sciences. Rather, philosophical modes of analysis and justification are absorbed within the human sciences. In that way—though his meaning is not very clear here—Habermas speaks of the *philosophization* of the human sciences.

Besides being a placeholder and a stand-in for the human sciences, Habermas conceives of philosophy as having a distinctive mediating-interpretive role. What he has in mind here is this: given the extensiveness of compartmentalization in the sciences, the different underlying structures of science, morals, politics, and art, and, more generally, the distance of the lifeworld from the specialized sciences, philosophy can and should function in such a circumstance as an interpreter and mediator between these different domains. It should function as an interpreter and offset the ill effects of such compartmentalization, separation, and not infrequently mutual incomprehension and at least perceived conflict.

Finally, and here Habermas is a faithful follower of the Frankfurt school, philosophy should in a self-conscious and articulate way, and without sacrifice of clarity, develop its capacity for critique so that it, to good effect, can provide a critique of the present age.[4] This sets Habermas at a considerable distance from Rorty and Derrida, but not from the classical pragmatists and, as we have seen, from, Foucault where critique is taken concretely.

II

So Habermas, like Rorty, and a lot of other contemporary philosophers, drops the conception of philosophers as master thinkers as "knowing something about knowing which nobody else knows so well," thinkers who magisterially survey all culture, judging what is justifiably believed and what is not, from an overriding perspective that ushers science, religion, morality, and art into their respective places and tells us what is genuine knowledge and what it not in each domain.

Philosophers, if they wish to be something more than mere mythmakers, must abandon that flattering but utterly illusory self-image. Indeed, it is not only illusory, but, standing where we stand now, it has a kind of *hubris* to it. Along with abandoning such an arrogant self-image, they must "drop the notion that there is something called 'philosophical method' or 'philosophical technique' or 'the philosophical point of view' which enables the professional philosopher *ex officio* to have interesting views about, say, the respectability of psychoanalysis, the legitimacy of certain dubious laws, the resolution of moral dilemmas, the soundness of schools of historiography or literary criticism, and the like."[5] Habermas is quoting Rorty here and quoting him with approval. Rorty, on his view, has produced "compelling metaphilosophical arguments" in support of the view that the traditionally conceived role of philosophy as usher and judge is too big for philosophy's boots.

However, while he agrees with Rorty that philosophy should forswear these roles, he remains, as I have noted, reluctant to accept the view that philosophy must also abandon its role of being the guardian of reason.[6] Habermas thinks that this would be the very undoing of philosophy. For philosophy

to abandon "any claim to reason"—"the very claim that has marked philosophical thought since its inception"—could only mean, no matter how we
sugar it over, the demise of philosophy. Rorty, Habermas has it, unflinchingly
accepts that and further "unflinchingly accepts the end of the belief that ideas
like truth or the unconditional with their transcending power are a necessary
condition of humane forms of collective life."[7] Habermas thinks that here
Rorty has pushed things too far. Philosophy is not such a lost cause as Rorty
supposes. Rorty is mistaken, Habermas has it, in believing that in passing
from modernity to postmodernity we must, if we are to be nonevasive, learn
to live in a postphilosophical culture devoid of universalistic claims to reason.
Habermas plainly does not think we need metaphysics, let alone metaphysical comfort, but he still seems to think that we need something like it for we
need somehow to live under the guidance of a unified conception of reason.

In his important programmatic essay "Philosophy as Stand-in and Interpreter," Habermas gives us a narrative alternative to Rorty's which somewhat
differently places things. It tells, that is, a story that is not so unfavorable to
philosophy as is Rorty's. Habermas admits that by going this narrative route
he cannot settle this controversy about the import of philosophy, but only
"throw light on some of its presuppositions."[8] All the same, he argues, in the
last section of that essay, that while philosophy is "well advised to withdraw
from the problematic roles of usher (*Platzanweiser*) and judge" it "can and
ought to retain its claim to reason, provided it is content to play the more modest roles of stand-in (*Platzhalter*) and interpreter."[9] (Here we can gain just a
glimpse at what he has in mind in speaking of "its claim to reason.") He wants
to provide something of a reasonable rationale for us to remain philosophers
in a stronger sense than Rorty would accept. He wants to persuade us that we
need not say farewell either to philosophy or to reason. To do this we must
transform philosophy in a fruitful way.[10] Again, the skeptical question to ask
is whether he has given us more than philosophical rhetoric linked with a just
so story. (One of the problems about giving philosophical narratives is that
they can very easily come to just that.)

Habermas sees the history of philosophy in our time as evolving or revolting out of critiques of Kant and Hegel, the great master philosophers of
modernity. The reaction to them has been diverse and various philosophers in
reacting have gone in very different directions. Whatever unity reason may
have, philosophy does not have a *de facto* unity, though Habermas aspires to
forge a new unity for our disenchanted world. However, first—and here is
where Habermas's narrative comes in—we must see where we are. The way
philosophers have gone in such different directions can most instructively be
brought out if we consider at least a culturally influential subset of the different ways philosophers have gone into the yellow wood. The contrast to be
made is between two groupings of philosophers (the normals and the antis, so

to say). The normals include philosophers as different as Popper and Lakatos, on the one hand, and Horkheimer and Adorno, on the other: philosophers on both sides of what was once the analytical/Continental divide. Different as these philosophers are, they are at least in putatively important ways united against the antis (the anti-Philosophy philosophers): philosophers, in turn, as different as Derrida, Baudrillard, Feyerabend, and Foucault. The former group (Popper, Lakatos, Horkheimer, and Adorno) try to articulate and defend "a claim to reason, however small in scope, however cautious in formulation." The antis, by contrast, Habermas has it, say farewell to reason. The same divide (reasoning along Habermas's lines) sets Putnam and Davidson apart from Rorty and Wittgenstein.

Pragmatism and hermeneutics, Rorty believes, take us down the garden path to the end of philosophy. We do not, with such accounts, appeal to representational theories of knowledge or a representational conception of how language functions: neither language nor thought can mirror the world. There is no one final correct description of anything which finally yields us nature's own language: tells us just how things are and indeed *must be*. We have, with both pragmatism and hermeneutics, no conception of "the solitary subject that confronts objects and becomes reflective only by turning itself into an object."[11] Without concluding that pragmatism and hermeneutics lead to the end of philosophy, Habermas agrees with much, if not all, of what Rorty says here. Pragmatism and hermeneutics, Habermas agrees, replace that representationalist conception with "an idea of cognition that is mediated by language and linked to action" along with a way of viewing things that emphasizes "the web of everyday life and communication surrounding 'our' cognitive achievements which are viewed as unavoidably intersubjective and cooperative."[12]

Whether the web of everyday life is conceptualized as a cluster of forms of life, the lifeworld, a cluster of social practices, linguistically mediated interaction, language-games, cultural background, or tradition is not essential. At the level at which Habermas is operating in "Philosophy as Stand-in and Interpreter," such smallish differences are mainly stylistic variations for pointing to much the same thing. These notions are for such philosophers the conceptions that replace the basic concepts of epistemology which have been set aside. Pragmatism and hermeneutics, in replacing an epistemological stance, "accord a higher position to acting and speaking than to knowing."[13] These conceptions have no justificatory function of their own "save one: to expose the need for foundational knowledge as unjustified."[14] On such a conception there are in any inquiry or in any deliberation about what is to be done a vast and complex number of background beliefs and assumptions—what Wittgenstein called *foreknowledge*—that cannot be fully enumerated, much less turned into explicit knowledge. And since this web, on such an account, is taken to be holistic and particularistic at the same time, it can never be grasped by an abstract general analysis.[15] We are never able to articulate everything that is in the background. This does not mean that there is some mysterious something that is unarticulatable but simply that there is too much to be articulated and that we have no idea of what it would be like to have finally articulated everything in the background or even everything that is relevant. Things are very open-ended here and it is important, if we are not to deceive ourselves, to recognize that.

Perhaps this way of viewing things has best been explicated and defended by Wittgenstein in his *Philosophical Investigations* and in his *On Certainty*. Habermas asks:

> Do these considerations strengthen Rorty's interpretation of pragmatism and hermeneutics, which argues for the abnegation, by philosophical thought, of any claim to rationality, indeed for the abnegation of philosophy *per se*? Or do they mark the beginning of a new paradigm that, while discarding the mentalistic language-game of the philosophy of consciousness, retains the justificatory modes of that philosophy in the modest, self-critical form in which I have presented them?[16]

Again, Habermas remarks that he cannot "answer this question directly for want of compelling and simple arguments," but he will provide what he takes to be a narrative answer.[17] Habermas's narrative portrays three basic and influential ways in which philosophy itself has said a "dismissive goodbye and good riddance to philosophy," namely, Wittgenstein's therapeutic turn, Heidegger's pathos laden heroic goodbye, and the "salvaging type of farewell to philosophy" given by contemporary neo-Aristotelians where old "philosophical truths," unsalvageable as truths, are refurbished as in some way symbolic "sources of illumination and edification," yielding some nonjustifiable, non-argument-based wisdom of the ages that is somehow supposed to be (is taken to be) essential for our cultural bonding and integration. But, Habermas has it, all of these accounts, paradoxically after their rejection of First Philosophy and foundationalism, still keep on in effect believing, though groundlessly, "in the authority and superiority of philosophical insights, namely their own, over those of science, politics, and everyday life."[18] They continue to claim, after all, that they give the right interpretation of what everyday life is or of what science is and of its scope, its limits, and of the authority of its claims. But this is in effect a turning back to something like the very Kantian conception of philosophy they started out by rejecting. This reveals—though, of course, this is not something they would, or perhaps even could, acknowledge—that they cannot really take their dismissive goodbye and good riddance for real. They cannot really take their dismissal of truth as genuine, for, after all, they are giving to understand that what they say is the truth.

Rorty, Habermas claims, comes closest to avoiding this self-referential refutation or at least paradox with his conception of "edifying philosophers" (Nietzsche, Foucault, Derrida, and Wittgenstein). They are philosophers, of which he is one, who do not articulate theories and do not make philosophical truth-claims. Instead, as debunkers, they use a varied kit bag of conversational gambits to josh us out of philosophy. Rorty's metaphilosophy, which is the most self-conscious form of edifying philosophy we have, combines, Habermas says, "all three types of farewell: therapeutic relief, heroic overcoming, and hermeneutic reawakening. It combines the inconspicuously subversive force of leisure with an elitist notion of creative linguistic imagination and with the wisdom of the ages."[19] It has all of these images, albeit in a rather laidback manner, going for it. But there is, Habermas says, no such thing as truth for Rorty, either in philosophy, science, or in the lifeworld. He cites a striking quote from Rorty: "Edifying philosophers can never end philosophy, but they can help prevent it from attaining the secure path of a science."[20] But, as Habermas gestures at, and Thomas McCarthy has claimed, this still has the air of self-referential paradox about it.[21] This is, after all, or so Rorty believes, the truth about philosophy. Nietzsche, Wittgenstein, Foucault, and Derrida, with a little cleaning up here and there, are, after all, essentially right.[22] Or so the claim goes. But there is there, Habermas maintains, the incoherent appeal to philosophy to end philosophy. If they are right about what they claim then nobody can be right, including themselves. We are back, he maintains, to an old paradox.

Habermas does not rely on such a quick fix to rebut the anti-Philosophy philosophers. It is a type of rebuttal of ancient vintage of which Rorty is very aware indeed and in various ways has sought to deflect.[23] He remarks that he is not trying to prove or demonstrate anything. He is not offering what in effect is a transcendental argument, or even a 'quasi-transcendental argument' (whatever that is), to end all transcendental arguments. He is rather setting out some considerations that, if people reflect on and take to heart, might lead them to stop talking and reasoning in a certain way, concluding that there wasn't, after all, much point in it. Philosophy in the various ways it has come down to us in the tradition turns out to be a rather heterogeneous bunch of bad research programs.

Habermas himself doesn't take much stock in such transcendental turnings, though he does speak obscurely of giving 'quasi-transcendental arguments'. Rather he contents himself, not with any knockdown or even mildly blunting refutation, but with a set of alternative proposals to Rorty's account (if that is the right word for it) which he believes have greater plausibility than Rorty's and fits in just as well with how the state of philosophy, science, and culture have unfolded up till now.

Habermas remarks:

I am partly sympathetic to Rorty's allocation of roles, for I agree that philosophy has no business playing the part of the highest arbiter in matters of science and culture. I find his argument unconvincing all the same. For even after pragmatism and hermeneutics have done their work and curtailed the scope of philosophy, the latter, though reduced to edifying conversation, can never find a niche *beyond* the sciences. Philosophical conversation cannot but gravitate toward argumentation and justificatory dispute. There is no alternative.[24]

He is here reiterating a point made by John Passmore years ago.[25] Argument, of necessity, is at the very heart of philosophy.

Moreover, we should also come to recognize, Habermas stresses, that there is no "exclusive division of labor between philosophy and science."[26]

Ultimately there is only one criterion by which opinions can be judged valid, and that is that they are based on agreement reached by argumentation. This means that *everything* whose validity is at all disputable rests on shaky foundations. It matters little if the ground underfoot shakes a bit less for those who debate problems of physics than for those who debate problems of morals and aesthetics. The difference is a matter of degree only, as the postempiricist philosophy of science has shown.[27]

What has been offensive in this to both traditionalists and end-of-philosophy philosophers such as Wittgenstein, Rorty, and Derrida is the very idea of "research traditions representing a blend of philosophy and science."[28] That is not keeping philosophy pure. Marxism and psychoanalysis are cases in point; they have never found favor with many philosophers. The standard philosophical reaction to them from the positivists to Wittgenstein and most Wittgensteinians has been dismissive. The claim is that they "cannot . . . help being pseudosciences because they straddle normal and abnormal discourse refusing to fall on either side of the dividing line."[29]

Habermas responds that a study of the history of the social sciences and psychology will show that such "hybrid discourses . . . are by no means atypical."[30] Marx and Freud do not stand alone. The same things applies "to all seminal theories in these disciplines, for instance those of Durkheim, Mead, Weber, Piaget, and Chomsky."[31] Indeed, these hybrid discourses "may well stand for a type of approach that marks the beginning of new research traditions."[32]

What is important to see is how the interaction works. Marx, Freud, Durkheim, Mead, Weber, Piaget, and Chomsky "each inserted a genuinely philosophical idea like a detonator into a particular context of research."[33] Habermas's examples are:

Symptom formation through repression; the creation of solidarity through the sacred; the identity-forming function of role taking; modernization as rationalization of society; decentration as an outgrowth of reflective abstraction from action; language acquisition as an activity of hypothesis testing—these key phrases stand for so many paradigms in which a philosophical idea is present in embryo while at the same time empirical, yet universal, questions are being posed.[34]

What we see here is what Habermas calls the *philosophization* of the sciences of man. Given this we can as philosophers working inside the social sciences interject imaginative hypotheses into the scientific discourse in question. Habermas concludes that:

> [P]hilosophy, instead of just dropping the usher role and being left with nothing, ought to exchange it for the part of stand-in (*Platzhalter*). Whose seat would philosophy be keeping, what would it be standing in for? Empirical theories with strong universalistic claims. As I have indicated, fertile minds have surfaced and will continue to surface in nonphilosophical disciplines, who will give such theories a try. The chance for their emergence is greatest in the reconstructive sciences. Starting primarily from the intuitive knowledge of competent subjects—competent in terms of judgment, action, and language—and secondarily from systematic knowledge handed down by culture, the reconstructive sciences explain the presumably universal bases of rational experience and judgment, as well as of action and linguistic communication. Marked down in price, the venerable transcendental and dialectical modes of justification may still come in handy. All they can fairly be expected to furnish, however, is reconstructive hypotheses for use in empirical settings.[35]

He thinks that a good example of a "successful cooperative integration of philosophy and science can be seen in the development of a *theory* of rationality."[36] Fallibilistic philosophers without foundationalist pretensions or illusions have served as suppliers of ideas setting aside claims to certainty or privileged knowledge. With their fallibilism and nonautonomous conception of philosophy, they do not believe that philosophy can construct such hypotheses on its own. They place their trust instead in the hope that "the success that has for so long eluded" philosophy "might come from an auspicious matching of different theoretical fragments."[37] Philosophy should become part of the human sciences or at least work in intimate partnership with them.

He then considers a very natural objection to what he has just said.

> If it is true that philosophy has entered upon a phase of cooperation with the sciences of man, does it not run the risk of losing its identity? There is some

justification in Spaemann's warning "that every philosophy makes a practical and a theoretical claim to totality and that not to make such a twofold claim is to be doing something which does not qualify as philosophy." In defense, one might argue that a philosophy that contributes something important to an analysis of the rational foundations of knowing, acting, and speaking does retain at least a thematic connection with the whole. But is this enough? What becomes of the theory of modernity, what of the window on the totality of culture that Kant and Hegel opened with their foundational and hypostatizing concepts of reason? Down to Husserl's *Crisis of the European Sciences*, philosophy not only usurped the part of supreme judge, it also played a directing role. Again, what happens when it surrenders the role of judge in matters of science as well as culture? Does this mean philosophy's relation to the totality is severed? Does this mean it can no longer be the guardian of rationality?[38]

Habermas responds, consistently with what he has appropriated from Wittgenstein and Rorty, by remarking that the "situation of culture as a whole is no different from the situation of science as a whole. As totalities, neither needs to be grounded or justified or given a place by philosophy."[39] Philosophy is no more a guardian of culture or the lifeworld than it is of science or of art. It cannot tell us what to believe here or do if we would be reasonable and nonevasive. But this sounds very much like the anti-Philosophy philosophy tack.

However, Habermas does not think so. He remarks that modern Western culture has, since "the dawn of modernity in the eighteenth century," generated structures of rationality that can benefit by description, recontextualization, articulation, interpretation, and analysis. These are things that philosophers sometimes are rather good at doing and sometimes there is a point in doing them. But these structures of rationality that have become a part of the cultural life of modern societies themselves neither stand in need nor require some philosophical justification or backup. Indeed, it is anything but clear what it could even mean to claim to so foundationally ground them. Relying heavily on Max Weber, Habermas describes these structures of rationality as follows:

> Reason has split into three moments—modern science; positive law and posttraditional ethics; autonomous art and institutionalized art criticism—but philosophy had precious little to do with this disjunction. Ignorant of sophisticated critiques of reason, the sons and daughters of modernity have progressively learned to differentiate their cultural tradition in terms of these three aspects of rationality such that they deal with issues of truth, justice, and taste discretely, never simultaneously. At a different level, this shift toward differentiation produces the following phenomena: (1) The sciences disgorge more and more elements of religion, thus renouncing their former claim to being able to interpret nature and history as one whole. (2)

Cognitivist moral theories disgorge issues of the good life, focusing instead strictly on deontological, generalizable aspects of ethics, so that all that remains of "the good" is the just. (3) With art it is likewise. Since the turn to autonomy, art has striven mightily to mirror one basic aesthetic experience, which is the increasing decentration of subjectivity. It occurs as the subject leaves the spatio-temporal structures of everyday life behind, freeing itself from the conventions of everyday perception, of purposive behavior, and of the imperatives of work and utility.[40]

These modern structures of rationality with their eminent trends toward compartmentalization constitute the "hallmark of modernity" and "can do very well without *philosophical* justification." However, they do pose problems of mediation. And it is here where the second role for philosophy referred to by Habermas enters, namely, philosophy's role as mediator and interpreter. Habermas remarks, spelling out *ambulando* what he means by mediation:

> First, how can reason, once it has been thus sundered, go on being a unity on the level of culture? And second, how can expert cultures, which are being pushed more and more to the level of rarefied, esoteric forms, be made to stay in touch with everyday communication? To the extent to which philosophy keeps at least one eye trained on the topic of rationality, that is, to the extent to which it keeps inquiring into the conditions of the unconditional, to that extent it will not dodge the demand for these two kinds of efforts at mediation.[41]

But what does this come to? I expect Rorty would again say that this is more scratching where it doesn't itch and, that aside, talk of the "conditions of the unconditional" is not going to help much in mediating and interpreting. Habermas, however, points to what is needed here when he speaks of how the need for mediation emerges from the spheres of science, morals, and art. There are in these domains all sorts of contestable and contesting movements and countermovements and we need, Habermas has it, amidst all the confusion and sometimes conflict, philosophical mediation. There are people, for example, who want an ethics of the good life, an articulating of ultimate ends, while others in the public sphere want to stick exclusively with conceptions of rights and justice. Philosophers say these things but similar things also get mixed into practical debates about public policy. We need, Habermas tells us, philosophical mediation here. There are similar movements in science and art.

These sorts of things, Habermas tells us, "mitigate the rigid compartmentalization of reason, point to reason's unity."[42] Presumably what he has in mind here is how considerations from all sorts of domains are often relevant and that we need to reason with all these considerations in mind. But, after this claim, he adds, in a way that mystifies me, as being something pointing to philosophy's mediating role, that in "this regard, everyday life is a more promising medium for regaining the lost unity of reason than are today's expert cultures or yesterday's classical philosophy of reason."[43]

Habermas goes on to make a remark which I take to be crucial for his account and is something which he was perhaps gesturing at above.

> In everyday communication cognitive interpretations, moral expectations, expressions, and evaluations cannot help overlapping and interpenetrating. Reaching understanding in the lifeworld requires a cultural tradition that ranges across *the whole spectrum*, not just the fruits of science and technology. As far as philosophy is concerned, it might do well to refurbish its link with the totality by taking on the role of interpreter on behalf of the lifeworld. It might then be able to help set in motion the interplay between the cognitive-instrumental, moral-practical, and aesthetic-expressive dimensions that has come to a standstill today, like a tangled mobile.[44]

I understand this as a well-directed arrow against what he calls *scientism*, by which he means "faith in science itself—the conviction that we should no longer apprehend science as one form of possible knowledge but should identify knowledge with science."[45] But the rejection of scientism aside, I do not see how it gives us a link "with the totality" or points to the unity of reason or even helps us understand what we are talking about here. This does not mean that I am not sympathetic to the idea of philosophy coming in, in scientific contexts, and again in ideological disputes, as an interpreter of the lifeworld. We look not just at the fruits of science and technology, but at how things go in our everyday life and how that is influenced by the activities of science and technology. That might very well be a good idea, though we would have to see rather more fully what this comes to. Stated just like that, it is little more than arm waving. For starters, a little translation into the concrete would not hurt. We would also want to come to understand what is particularly philosophical about that activity.

There are these different dimensions or what in his earlier work he called different types of human interests and it is a good thing to try to understand their interplay. Still, what is it for philosophy to play the role of a mediating interpreter here? It is indeed important to see, if we can, how science, morals, and art and "their respective expert cultures" can be "joined to the impoverished traditions of the lifeworld" and how "this can be done (if it can be done) without detriment to their regional rationality."

But the end-of-philosophy philosopher will, as Habermas recognizes, challenge this. Habermas puts this challenge and his response succinctly as follows:

What in the world . . . gives the philosopher the right to offer his services as a translator mediating between the everyday world and cultural modernity with its autonomous sectors, when he is already more than busy trying to carve out a space for ambitious theoretical strategies within the system of the sciences? I think pragmatism and hermeneutics have joined forces to answer this question, by attributing epistemic authority to the community of all who cooperate and speak with one another. Everyday communication makes possible a kind of understanding that is based on claims to validity, thus furnishing the only real alternative to exerting influence on one another, which is always more or less coercive. The validity claims that we raise in conversation—that is, when we say something with conviction—transcend this specific conversational context, pointing to something beyond the spatio-temporal ambit of the occasion. Every agreement, whether produced for the first time or reaffirmed, is based on (controvertible) grounds or reasons. Grounds have a special property: They force us into yes or no positions. Built into the structure of action-oriented-to-reaching-understanding is therefore an element of unconditionality. And it is this unconditional element that makes the validity (*Gültigkeit*) we claim for our views different from the mere *de facto* acceptance (*Geltung*) of habitual practices. From the perspective of first persons, what we consider justified is not a function of life styles but a question of justification or grounding. That is why philosophy is "rooted in the urge to see social practices or justification as more than just such practices."[46]

III

I want now critically to inspect the three putatively legitimate roles that Habermas thinks philosophy still has. I will also in section 5 to say something about philosophy as social critique, another conception of the role of philosophy that Habermas takes to be important.

1. Philosophy, recall, on Habermas's conception, is to be conceived as a placeholder for the sciences. Philosophy's function there is in holding open questions of unity and universality that might be ignored in the course of empirical research or closed off by empirical research or even dropped by researchers. This sounds sufficiently modest and innocuous enough that it could hardly be objected to, but it is also rather hard to see what philosophy, viewed as any kind of discipline or looking back to the tradition in philosophy, has to contribute here. Philosophy in playing the role of placeholder is thought to be the self-reflection of the sciences. Again, translation into the concrete might help. Suppose the dominant social science rejects talk about classes and thinks entirely in terms of social stratification theory and thinks that talk of a ruling class or hegemonic class is pure moonshine. Philosophy could remind

such a reigning sociology (and thus social scientists and their students) that there are alternative accounts of society that talk in a quite determinate way about classes and of a ruling or hegemonic class.[47] It will define these notions as they occur in the theory, clarifying them, if that is needed, and exhibit the role they play in the theory and the characteristic claims the theory makes and what kind of evidence, if any, there is for the theory. Similar things obtain in psychology. Think back to the time when in psychology behaviorism was the reigning orthodoxy. Philosophers doing the work of placeholders in such a circumstance will point to the claims and structure of argument of gestalt psychologies or even of introspective psychologies. They might even go back to old dualist or epiphenomenalist philosophies of mind and show how they might be articulated in the form of a psychological theory. Here it is salutary, perhaps even useful, to remind people of options closed by the actual direction empirical research has taken or of options that have been pushed aside by the dominant theoretical paradigms of a particular science during a particular time. Such forced self-reflection is not infrequently a useful thing and might (though it need not—there is no necessity here) very well result in improved theory in a given discipline. But I fail to see anything that a philosopher *qua* philosopher, operating with a distinctive method (assuming there is such) or with certain substantive philosophical beliefs or using logic or the philosophy of language, has to contribute here. What we need instead is a well-educated scientist, a scientist well trained in the particular discipline in question, but also a person who has a very acute sense of the history of her discipline and, as well, of the history of ideas, including the history of philosophical ideas. Such a person, if anyone, will be someone who will have the good historical sense to be aware of the historical options here. Because she knows so well the state of play in her own scientific discipline, she will have a good idea of how to relate those at least historical options to what is going on in the science in question now. But I do not see how philosophical expertise—extensive analytical or logical capabilities—is of much, if any help here, and I do not see that it is the case that there are any philosophical categories that will be particularly helpful or perhaps even helpful at all in guiding us in how to characterize things here. I see the need in the different domains spewed out by modernity for historically informed intellectuals, in the above circumstances scientific intellectuals, with a very broad understanding of things as well as being people with a good knowledge of their discipline, but I see no role for the philosopher unless by implicit *persuasive* definition the philosopher gets identified with such a historically informed intellectual with a good knowledge of science. Put differently, I can see a role here for the history of science or the history of art, but none for the philosophy of science or aesthetics to say nothing of the sturdy metaphysician or the farseeing epistemologist.

2. I now turn to Habermas's conception of philosophy having a role as placemaker or stand-in for the sciences. It has many of the same difficulties as those I have found in philosophy as placeholder for the sciences. Again the conception, appropriately enough, is to conceive of philosophy in an intimate working relationship with the sciences. Remember, philosophy so conceived is viewed as propounding striking, often rather conceptually revolutionary, empirical hypotheses of a rather general sort for the sciences, particularly for the human sciences. By articulating, ahead, and necessarily so, of thorough testing and theoretical and sometimes operational elaboration, it can, as a stand-in for scientific theories with strong universalist claims, suggest sometimes strikingly valuable ideas that may turn out to be valuable in specific research programs. Here, instructively, all of Habermas's examples—and they are impressive examples—are from sociologists, linguists, or psychologists. There was not a philosopher among the lot. The list was Marx, Freud, Durkheim, Mead, Weber, Piaget, and Chomsky. He said that they "each inserted a genuinely *philosophical* idea into a particular research context. But it was not only that they were not philosophers, their ideas, fascinating theoretical empirical hypotheses, sometimes requiring reconceptualization and recontextualization in the sciences in question, were not in any recognizable sense of the term *philosophical* ideas. Freud showed us how symptom formation works through repression; Chomsky showed us how language acquisition functioned as an activity of hypothesis testing; Durkheim showed how a sense of the sacred was conducive to attaining social solidarity. All of these things were good, fruitful empirical hypotheses to set out for the sciences and it is good to see what the warrants for holding them are and what implications they have and how they aid us, if they do, in understanding our lives. But there is nothing from philosophy here except perhaps, and only perhaps, some rather preliminary and elementary clarification and displaying of logical connections. Sometimes Locke's and Dewey's modest underlaborer conception will yield something, but typically far less than philosophers flatter themselves into believing. Nothing either from the characteristic traditions of philosophy, analytic or Continental, give us any such hypotheses here. Davidson's theory of truth, Dummett's theory of meaning, Kripke's theory of reference, Gauthier's theory of rationality, or Quine's theory of referential opacity do not assert an idea like a detonator, or even more modestly an idea at all, into any particular research program in the social sciences, psychology, or the natural sciences. If they, or some other clearly identifiable philosophical ideas, did so detonate, then Habermas's claim would be attractive. But he makes no such claim and it is entirely unclear how any of these accounts do anything like that. So there seems to be no reason to believe that genuinely philosophical ideas serve as stand-ins in science or that we have any good reason to believe in, let alone applaud, the *philosophization* of the reconstructive

sciences. At most something like Gilbert Ryle's account of mind might, if it were not itself in deep trouble, help behavioristic psychologists to avoid certain crudities. But that underlaborer job is some distance from inserting a new hypothesis like a detonater into a scientific discipline.

Suppose it is responded that such general Freud-through-Weber-through-Chomsky ideas really are, after all, philosophical ideas just as, some philosophers claim, Einstein's ideas about general relativity, Bohr's ideas about quantum mechanics, Arrow's proof of an important theorem, or Gödel's ideas about completeness are philosophical activities or (giving the game away) *really* philosophical activities. But, if that is the line of defense to make the world safe for philosophical detonators, then the response should be that by such a stipulative redefinition of 'philosophy' we are, in effect, closing down the contrast between philosophical and theoretical scientific ideas. Worse still, philosophy thereby cheats by parasitically grasping on to the prestige of science, including formal science, without any justification. Ideas that, though not infrequently only rather indirectly, turn some machinery, get arbitrarily rebaptized as philosophical. It is as if some philosophers, sensing the decline of philosophy, have to grab on to something to justify its continued existence so these philosophers fasten on to some of the great scientific conceptual, though not only conceptual, revolutions.

3. Habermas also sees a role for philosophy, after the demise of the tradition, as that of mediator and interpreter between the sciences; between science and morality, religion, politics, and art; and, more generally, between these "expert cultures," as he calls them and the lifeworld. Does this conception fare any better than the first two? Perhaps, for it is in Habermas's hands a complex conception, much more complex and internal to his own theory than it at first seems. Let us run with it a bit, starting with the simplest considerations.

Slowly with the growth of the Enlightenment and the evolving of modernity, science, law, morality, and art have developed complex structures of rationality that, as Habermas stresses, need no justification, though—and here philosophy enters—they could do with a perspicuous *articulation*. Science, demarcating itself ever more carefully and distinctively from religion, and morality, demarcating itself more and more carefully from both cosmology and religion, are indicative of the way modernity shakes itself out. Philosophy, to repeat, cannot legitimately justify or criticize this trend, but it can articulate it so that it can come to have a more perspicuous representation.

This is fair enough, as far as it goes. Such things have happened and are happening in our culture and some philosophers are rather adept at giving such articulations. But they are by no means unique in this adeptness. But it seems to me that in doing this we need little more, if we have some reasonable acquaintance with our social world, than a careful attention to distinctions rooted in our ordinary uses of words and sentences, a method stressed by ordinary language philosophers of the vintage of Gilbert Ryle, John Wisdom, and J. L. Austin. Whatever its general utility in philosophy, it seems to me a good strategy here. We see, for example, that it is one thing to say that freedom is a good thing (a plain moral truism). It is another thing again—a complicated normatively neutral factual thing—to assert that such and such conditions render freedom more stable and more widespread than in some other conditions. The moral claim is assessed one way, the factual claim another, though this is not to suggest that the ways are completely different. Attention to the way our language works helps us to see that and a little low-level ordinary language philosophy helps us to see how this is so. It is hardly more than what we need in an introductory course in philosophy. It requires no great philosophical expertise. We need, that is, no complicated philosophical reasoning to make the above evident. Still, philosophy judiciously applied can help the common sense of modernity to attain a clearer sense of their beliefs and of how they hang together. But, in doing this we do not need the refined conceptual tools of philosophy (assuming that we even have anything untendentious here).[48] What we have done is to remind ourselves of what language-games we moderns have come to play. Our philosophical interpretations and mediations come to what Wittgenstein, an archproponent of the anti-Philosophy philosophy side, called a perspicuous representation of the workings of our language-games. But these, as he put it, are reminders for *a particular purpose*. They are used to dispel particular philosophical perplexities where we do not command a clear view of the workings of our language and become confused, when we reflect, about how it actually works *in some particular context*. The person with the resulting philosophical hang-up does not, of course, see it that way. She does not think of it as any confusion about language at all, but thinks obscurely that she is faced with some deep metaphysical puzzle that she is struggling to articulate and understand.[49] The philosophical therapy consists in leading the person in perplexity to see that her perplexity is really about the workings of her language and to help her to command a sufficiently clear view at the troubling spot to break that perplexity.[50] She need not have any conception at all of what complete clarity or a knowledge of the totality would come to. Indeed, it may well be, as Wittgenstein believes, that we do not have any such conceptions.[51] We only have, when we get caught up in philosophy, some confused notions which we try unsuccessfully to forge into coherent conceptions.

It seems to me that it is no more than this that Habermas has shown, with his talk of philosophy as mediator and interpreter, of which we stand in need. Plainly he is seeking something more robust. But it is not clear to me what more he could have. How, to push this along a little, does the doing of these things point to "reason's unity"? Well, it shows that we have the brains to sort things out and come to see something of how some of our linguistic practices work and something of how some bits of them hang together. The specific criteria of appropriateness for them varies with the language-games or practices in question and what their point or purpose is. It is not evident, to put it minimally, that there are any super criteria that govern all these diverse linguistic practices, standing over them like some general rule or set of rules, that could rightly be called reason's unity. There seems to be no good reason to speak of either reason's unity or disunity here. But we also do not seem to have come up against anything irrational here or offending against reason. But it also seems to be little more than rhetoric to speak of being up against the bar of reason or sticking with or not sticking with a claim to reason. This all seems at least to be inflated rationalist talk appropriate to another age. We can show against the philosophical skeptic that, generally speaking, the practices of everyday life make sense. But this still remains within the parameters of anti-Philosophy philosophy. The underlying attitude is: "You try to raise a philosophical issue and we will diffuse it."

In a different mood, Habermas speaks of philosophical mediation as giving us such relations to the lifeworld as to afford us a link with the totality. Again, I think this is inflated rhetoric, a holdover from the old philosophies of reason. Rather, the kind of mediation we have been talking about helps us, in the mundane but quite useful way Rorty pointed to, to see a little better how things hang together.[52] It is a matter of reflecting on how things link up and something of the importance or lack thereof of these elements. But literature or careful social description and interpretation can do this just as well if not better than philosophy.[53]

Philosophy conceived as such mediation does not have some distinctive philosophical tools or distinctive philosophical knowledge that it brings to the mediation.[54] It is just that the philosopher as mediator-or-interpreter helps us see, as any reflective all-purpose intellectual could, how things connect. This indeed is not nothing and a culture is well served by having intellectuals who can do this well. But conceived in a way that would link philosophy with a discipline (something we would have graduate schools for and long training), there is nothing in such a conception of philosophy as mediation that roots it in such disciplinary activity or would justify such a disciplinary activity. Moreover, it is not only the case that there is no use for some specialized discipline here, or even a clear conception of such a discipline, it is also the case that the historical tradition of philosophy with its traditional problems makes no such link either. It mainly gets in the way of a good understanding here. There seems to be nothing left for the philosopher to do where what he does is any more specialized than that of the all-purpose critical intellectual. Habermas thinks of a philosopher as an *expert* with a role that is distinct from that of being an *intellectual*. But it is unclear what, if anything, he has to be an expert about.

This Rortyish response may still not do justice to the fullness of Habermas's claims. Habermas persists in believing that philosophy, even philosophy after the demise of the tradition, makes a claim to totality. It is easy to parody this. And perhaps it comes to nothing more than an attempt in a holistic manner to see how things hang together. But Habermas does speak of philosophy contributing "something important to an analysis of the rational foundations of knowing, acting, and speaking."[55] He thinks that a philosophy which does this retains "at least a thematic connection with the whole."[56] This gives us some sense of what talk of totality comes to here. But this raises another difficulty. Habermas rejects foundationalism and First Philosophy along the holistic line of the Quine-Davidson-Rorty tack. But, with such a thorough dismantling of foundationalism and with such a holistic replacement, what does talk of the rational foundations of knowing, acting, and speaking come to? Why the continuation of foundational metaphors after the death of foundationalism? With coherentist accounts of how we justify our beliefs, such as wide reflective equilibrium, nothing is foundational. Justification comes through seeing how things fit together. So why this talk of rational foundations? Isn't this just arm waving on Habermas's part and a verbal holdover from an older, now discredited way of conceiving of justification?[57]

It is perfectly true that our modern expert cultures have compartmentalized things and in precising our inquiries have limited them. Physics does not try to interpret nature as one whole or as totality. Toynbee, and Hegel before him, but not historians, speak of history as a one whole or of a totality. Historical materialism as an empirical theory trying to explain epochal social change does not try to speak of history as one or as a totality.[58] We are now such children of modernity that we are reluctant to speak of the nature and the destiny of humanity anymore, though questions like that still emerge out of the lifeworld. They sometimes come from religion or from literature. But they are at the very least embarrassing for us. How does philosophy mediate or interpret here? Is it supposed to provide philosophical answers where the other expert cultures fail or give mythological answers? Is it supposed to fit us out with a new ideology? Is it supposed to tell us, where physics abdicates, how nature is really one or where history abdicates how history is really one and how the tale adds up to an account of human destiny? But that would not even be to just go back to Kant, but to go back to a pre-Kantian form of traditionalist metaphysics which Habermas, and practically everyone else, thinks has been through and through discredited. That presumably is not Habermas's intent. But then what is his meaning? What does mediation and interpretation come to in such a context?

To see reason as a unity could be to see how various elements in our life are not just a jumble but can be forged into a reflective equilibrium. Things, that is, can be set together into a coherent pattern. This would be a plain, philosophically unproblematic way of specifying reason's unity. But that takes us back to Rorty and the end of Philosophy and to John Rawls's deliberately staying on the surface philosophically and setting aside metaphysical theses.[59] This is also what a sticking to a claim to reason could be demystified into. This may be what it is like to be through and through reasonable and not to be caught out by philosophical extravagance.

However, Habermas seems at least to want more. He speaks of inquiring into the conditions of the unconditional. Can something sensible be made of that? Or is this more scratching where it doesn't itch? The very last page of Habermas's "Philosophy as Stand-in and Interpreter" should be carefully noted in this context. He thinks, as we have already noted, that pragmatism and hermeneutics have joined forces in a way that will help us see our way out of the yellow wood. In place of the old epistemology they have attributed epistemic authority to the community of all who cooperate and speak with one another. The very underlying presupposition of our serious determination to communicate with one another only works with a validity claim to universality and to being unconditional as an inescapable presupposition. The validity claims we make in serious argumentative or deliberative discussion carry assumptions which are not just limited to the particular occasion. In seriously arguing or discussing with each other we look for reasons. We do not just seek to persuade. Moreover, we, in honestly going into that argument, cannot but commit ourselves to stick with what we will, after discussion, take to be the force of the better argument or better deliberation. We have no choice here if we will deliberate with integrity. It is this, or something rather like it, that I think Habermas is referring to when he remarks that built "into the structure of action-oriented-to-reaching understanding is an element of unconditionality."[60] That at any rate is my demythologization of it. Habermas adds, as we have seen, that "it is this unconditional element that makes the validity we claim for our views different from the mere *de facto* acceptance of habitual practices. From the perspective of first persons, what we consider justified is not a function of lifestyles but a question of grounding. That is why philosophy is rooted in the urge to see social practices or justification as more than just practices."[61]

I think Rorty might respond to this in a way similar to the way he responded to Hilary Putnam.[62] That is, he could say that there is here the confused attempt to be both inside and outside our language-games at the same time. It is like trying to make an inquiry and to stand outside of our inquiry at the same time. It is an attempt at the same time both to view things as a field linguist trying to understand the language of an alien culture and to be the language user of that language using that language to assert, question, express emotions, deliberate, and the like. It is like trying to collapse use and mention or at least not keeping them apart.[63]

There *may* be such a confusion in what Habermas is saying there, but I think attention to the very distinction Rorty is making, the distinction between the field linguist's perspective and the agent's perspective (the language user's perspective), when combined with Davidson's rejection of the scheme/content distinction and his resolute holism, will yield, in a less obscure way than Habermas's own, a very similar result to Habermas's. It will be a result which (if you want to talk in that way) will accord epistemic authority to the community of cooperative inquirers without in the slightest transcendentalizing philosophy. So understanding things makes Davidson along with Wittgenstein a powerful edifying philosopher in spite of his traditionalist metatalk.[64] But that is all to the good. We can in this way see Davidson finishing off a task well initiated by Wittgenstein. We can see him gathering up the fugitives as it were. However, it also makes Habermas much more than to his liking an end-of-philosophy philosopher himself, but without the bugbears of relativism, nihilism, or what he takes to be a postmodernist playful irresponsibility.[65] It is, after all, these things which really bother him about end-of-philosophy philosophy. He thinks if you go down that road you get these bad things. But if end-of-philosophy philosophy doesn't have these consequences then he has no reason beyond piety to the tradition to be so resistant.

I will now flesh out and clarify these dark sayings hoping to show that they are more than that. Consider how we proceed when we seriously argue with each other. Say, for example, when we argue about the institutions of marriage and the family as we now have them. Suppose I say, and mean it, that in our society males tend to dominate females and that this domination gets encoded into our institutions of marriage and the family. Suppose you deny it or claim I exaggerate. Using our language with its built-in norms of intelligibility and conceptions of procedures for justification, I am making a claim, to be pleonastic, of putative universal validity and you, if you think I am arguing in good faith, take it as such, though, using the same norms of validity as I do, you think that my claim is not in fact valid, not in fact justified. We are using our language—operating with and not upon our language-games—to make claims and, if we are reasoning in good faith with each other, we must take it that we will acquiesce in the force of what we agree (if we can reach agreement) to be the the better argument. It is that which will bring closure, if anything will bring closure. That we must go with whatever has the force of the better argument is a presupposition of our arguing seriously with one another. Moreover, we have no *a priori* reason to think that nothing will bring closure if we keep the conversation going, if we do not block the road to inquiry. (I do not mean here a closure forever and ever but simply a definite closure for a time in a given problematic situation.) And, as a matter of fact, we often do achieve closure without force or rhetoric carrying the day. What we attain here, when we so honestly deliberate with each other, we do not view as just acquiescing in the operation of our habitual practices or forms of life. We are together reasoning inside our language-games, not standing outside them and observing them as field linguists. That we must stick with what we believe to have the force of the better argument has the force of unconditionality about it. It is just what reasonability and fairmindedness come to here.

That is all well and good, it might be replied, but we can also always, switching perspectives, look at our language-games, look at our practices, as the field linguist looks at the language-games and practices of an alien culture. And there our practices like theirs will be seen as just a tribe's practices or language-games. It just happens that it is our tribe we are examining, or trying to examine, from a perspective external to its framework. The urge to see these practices as something more than a culture's practices *is rooted in our being inside the framework*. But we can always, or so at least it seems, as can the field linguist, step outside the particular framework in question. From that perspective—from a perspective that is outside our practices—they just are the practices of a given tribe at a given time and place in history. To think they can be anything more is a transcendental illusion. Moreover, isn't the field linguist's perspective, after all, *the really objective perspective*? The insider's perspective is subjective (or at least intersubjective) and ethnocentric.

To say just that is, however understandable, an error—perhaps an ubiquitous error of our scientistic culture—but an error all the same. Indeed Davidson, Rorty, and Habermas, in their superficially very different ways, show us that and how this is an error. Just as, depending on our perspective and our interests, we can describe certain of our bodily goings-on either as movements or as actions, without either description with its distinctive perspective being *the* correct one, without either set of interests they answer to being our "true interests," rather than just different interests giving rise to different perspectives, so whether we reason inside our language-games or like a field linguist stand outside them watching their operation and describing, using other language-games, their operation, what we have are just different perspectives answering to different interests. It isn't that one perspective is the perspective "closest to reality," closest to "seeing things as they really are," whatever, if anything, such playing with words means.

This understanding of things should be reinforced if we take to heart the fact that the field linguist, whether he is one of us or somebody from a quite different tribe, will have, in coming to understand the alien language, to use his own language, or some other language he has learned as an insider operating with the language in question. He can't be a field linguist *at one and the same time* for all languages for he must use at least one as an insider to understand, describe, categorize, etc., the alien language or languages he is studying. Moreover, without knowing how to play the language-game of his own tribe, he could have no understanding at all so that he could even be a field linguist. As Quine has remarked, when pushed hard enough we all have to acquiesce in our mother tongue or a natural language that has come for us to function like our mother tongue. (Think here of someone who after many years forgets his mother tongue.) The highest metalanguage will have to be a natural language and indeed for the people engaged in the inquiry the natural language they actually use. There is in this way no escaping the insider's point of view. But using that point of view we can come to understand another's practices and language as they in turn can come to understand ours. We are all in this respect in the same boat. There is no reason at all to think we are imprisoned in incommensurable (untranslateable, noncomparable) conceptual schemes.

Taking this and taking it that Davidson is roughly right about what he calls the scheme/content dogma, we have no reason to think we are inescapably ethnocentric or that the insider's intersubjective point of view is necessarily subjective or ethnocentric.[66] That claim could only stick if it were true that we could gain a God's-eye perspective that would enable us, free of all social practices, forms of life or the norms of a particular language, to see things just as they are and then to so describe them and explain them using nature's own language as Rorty has quipped. But this God's-eye perspective is an incoherent perspective. There can be no such perspective. The field linguist, or for that matter the logician, no more has such a perspective than does the plain person operating with her linguistic practices. This is so because for the field linguist and the logician to understand what they are doing they must themselves use (and here "to use with understanding" is redundant) their own language, operate with their own language-games, reason from the insider's perspective to even be able to do field linguistics or logic.

In trying to contrast the insider's merely intersubjectively valid or intersubjectively objective point of view, with some point of view which is not so intersubjectively valid but objective in some allegedly stronger way, we do not have a nonvacuous contrast, for the supposed alternative, the so-called God's-eye point of view or the view from nowhere, is an incoherent notion. The only kind of validity or objectivity is intersubjective validity or objectivity. (Even Bernard Williams's "absolute conception," *if* such a conception is coherent, would only have intersubjective validity or objectivity. But it would not be humanocentric. Martians and humans could communicate using it.[67] See the Appendix.)

However, doesn't this show (*pace* Habermas) that the talk of unconditional validity is incoherent? All we get, and can get, is intersubjective validity. To think this is so is (a) to still be held captive to the scheme/content dogma and to (b) be unwilling to give a charitable reading to talk of 'unconditional validity'. If Davidson is right, it is not that we humans, separated in different tribes, with different language-games and different linguistic practices, are like people with different geometries, different axiomatic systems, stuck in our perspective, unable to comprehend the perspectives of others. (Indeed, we are not really in that situation even with respect to alternative geometries or axiomatic systems. We are not in some Kantian utterly ubiquitous linguacentric predicament.) There is for starters the social fact that we do communicate, and do communicate across cultures, and that there are no untranslatable or noncomparable languages. Davidson and Habermas can be plausibly viewed as doing much the same thing, namely, attempting to explain how this happens, to explain how, if you will, various field linguists from various tribes studying various other tribes can succeed. (We, of course, know that they do.) For them to do so, we must assume a common human nature in a perfectly unproblematic and mundane conception of human nature. We must assume, that is, that the people from other tribes have, as we do, beliefs, desires, make observations, form intentions, think, question, and the like and that, generally speaking, their beliefs, desires, intentions, questionings are broadly like ours. Sometimes, of course, certain ones are very different, but for us, and for them, to be able even to take note of that they must generally be very much the same. We can't intelligibly attribute *massive* error to them and they cannot do so for us. If that were to obtain we could never, not even in principle, know it nor could they. So we cannot assume we have incommensurable framework beliefs where we stand mute before each other and mutually uncomprehending. Intertribal and intratribal communication does obtain. Only if there is some shared basis of belief could this happen. But it does happen, therefore, there must be some shared basis of belief. Habermas in talking of unconditional validity should be understood as talking of that and so was Davidson when he spoke of beliefs being intrinsically veridical. The phantoms of conceptual relativism disappear like the morning dew. But in exorcising them we have not appealed to any positive philosophical doctrines to mediate anything or to claim some "philosophical truth" or "philosophical knowledge." We have reminded ourselves carefully of how we do think, do proceed, forging what is in effect a reflective equilibrium. So in reality, their images about themselves to the contrary notwithstanding, Habermas and Davidson, like Wittgenstein and Rorty, are edifying philosophers blocking the protean urge to say something philosophical: to announce some esoteric philosophical doctrine.

IV

These remarks, however ill or well taken they may be, have stood at some distance from Habermas's texts and someone might understandably think that I might be imputing to Habermas what is not there. So let me, in partial recti-fication of that, turn to what he has to say about the ideal speech situation.[68] Habermas uses this conception, as we have seen in chapter 11, to articulate a distinction between distorted and undistorted discourse. Like anyone from the Marxian tradition, he stresses how in our societies people live extensively under conditions of distorted discourse. There is plainly extensive domination of one group by another and, through the consciousness industry, working in tandem with capitalists and a largely compliant state, there is an extensive amount of imposed consciousness in our societies. Our ideological bafflement is such, Habermas claims, that we do not understand the prevailing mecha-nisms and relationships of power and control in our societies and how they, often in rather subtle ways, gain ascendency over us. It is a lack of an artic-ulated awareness here that is the weakest spot in the work of Rawls. (This is perfectly compatible, by the way, with Davidson's claims about most of our beliefs being true. It is easy to forget how many perfectly mundane, thor-oughly unproblematic beliefs we have which we have no reason at all to think are ideological. Indeed, if the vast majority of our beliefs were not in fact non-ideological, we would never be in position to even begin to spot those of our beliefs and the beliefs of others which are ideological.) However, given the extent and destructiveness of our ideological beliefs (our patches of distorted discourse), it is, for the purposes of human understanding and social critique, important for us to have a clear conception of what undistorted discourse would look like, what, that is, it is for us to have nonideological beliefs. We can, in this way, without the incoherence of a God's-eye view, come to see the world rightly though still always fallibilistically. Hegel is right about our not being able to leap over history. Still, it is humanly important to escape or at least travel some way toward escaping the beguilements of ideology.

Habermas, borrowing, and adopting extensively for his own distinct pur-poses, from John Austin, John Searle, and Stephen Toulmin, deploys a theory of universal pragmatics and communicative action and using it adumbrates his conception of the ideal speech situation.[69] In accordance with this he gives us his conception of what it would be to have undistorted discourse. I shall put it as simply as I think it plausibly can be articulated. What is this situation in which, if it were to obtain, we would be in a situation in which our speech and thought would be undistorted? It would be a situation where our legitimating beliefs (including, of course, our central normative beliefs) would be formed in conditions of absolutely free and unlimited debate or deliberation in which all parties to the discussion would be capable of recognizing that they are freely consenting to whatever it is they agree on and in which the only con-straints on their acceptance of whatever it is that they accept would derive from the force of what they take on reflection to be the better argument. In communication, simply by virtue of what communication is, we seek to reach understanding, indeed mutual understanding. In an ideal speech situation the speaker and the hearer aim not only at consensus but a rational consensus in which to gain a rational consensus the only motive for discoursing which is accepted is that of a cooperative search for truth. This is not to be understood as a cooperative search for *the truth*. Nobody knows what that means or for the correct *theory* of truth, but a cooperative search for truths: statements that assert things which are so. What will be taken as a rational consensus is that consensus which is rooted in whatever has the force of the better argument. Where we have, if we have, such a consensus, we have rational consensus. This, of course, is a picture of an ideal speech situation and it is counterfactual, a heuristic. Where we get approximations to it we get a consensus which is more or less rational and a speech situation which is more or less undistorted. These things, unlike truth, admit of degrees. When Habermas, following pragmatists and hermeneuticists, attributes epistemic authority to the community of all who cooperate and speak with one another, he is attributing epistemic authority to communities who so reason, to the agreements they reach under conditions that approximate, as far as is feasible under their distinctive conditions, the conditions of undistorted discourse in the ideal speech situation.

We do not now, and perhaps never will, deliberate in anything even very close to conditions of freedom and equality; none of our beliefs, legitimating or otherwise, are formed in conditions of absolutely free and unlimited debate. So none of them could have the unconditional validity of which Habermas speaks. But the very idea of beliefs so formed is not incoherent. Conceptually speaking, beliefs being forged under conditions of freedom and equality is something we can understand. We have an idea of the truth-conditions that would be in place here. Counterfactual assertions are not truth-conditionless. That some toads will turn into mice is counterfactual. But we have *some idea* about its truth-conditions. It is not like "Procrastination drinks melancholy." Habermas's talk about undistorted discourse is not incoherent, or even conceptually problematic, though it does take a different route than Davidson's in escaping the relativism and subjectivism that is so pervasively a part of postmodernist thinking.

V

I shall turn now to what Habermas says about philosophy as social critique.[70] Habermas, though he does not speak about it in his "Philosophy as Stand-in and Interpreter," has stressed that philosophy as critical theory of society has, as a very central component, the role of providing a critique of the societies in which we live and more broadly of the world in which we live with an eye to the possibilities for human emancipation.[71] A very central part of this will be ideology-critique or, if you will, critique of ideology. Here is a side of Habermas and of critical theory which stands at a great distance from Rorty who regards such activities as rather at best bad utopianism and at worst silly self-indulgence, though this is not to suggest that he thinks that in Habermas's hands it is the latter, though he no doubt thinks that Habermas, in looking for alternatives to even welfare state capitalism, and in talking of human emancipation, is being too utopian and failing to be a tough-minded *realpolitik* social democrat à la Sidney Hook or Daniel Bell.[72]

Be that as it may, philosophy as critique, including ideology critique, is an important element in Habermas's work and in the work of the Frankfurt school from which his work springs. Let us look a little bit at what ideology critique comes to. Let me, in starting this, first turn to some remarks of one of Habermas's mentors who was also probably the most original, but also probably the most obscure, writer among the Frankfurt school philosophers. I speak, of course, of Theodor Adorno.[73] Adorno is one of those people, like Collingwood, like Wittgenstein, and like Rorty, who suffers from doubts about the very enterprise of philosophy itself and is led to wonder about its import and point. In doing so, as Wittgenstein saw, they embroil themselves in what is a bit of philosophy itself. Questions about what is philosophy are themselves philosophical questions in the way questions about what is biology or what is ethnography are not biological or ethnographical questions. (It is for this reason that some have not wanted to call metaphilosophy 'metaphilosophy', but by now 'metaphilosophy' has become a term of art to designate philosophical questions about what is philosophy and what, if anything, is its significance and point.)

Adorno, knowing he runs against pervasive elements in the tradition, clearly saw that what philosophers can do, and indeed should do, is itself a key philosophical question. In his *Negative Dialectics*, Adorno takes, among the various possibilities, criticism of ideology to be the heart of philosophy. This is not a claim which will gain much sympathy or even provoke much interest in analytical circles. Yet, overstatement that it is, taking a part for the whole, it still seems to me an important and fruitful claim which needs careful fleshing out and a careful examination.

Adorno in most things is almost everything a positivist is not, but he agrees with positivists in regarding traditional philosophical questions as questions for which there is no solution. However, he believes these "problems" should still be taken quite seriously, for the fact that a society has a need for a given philosophical theory—say, a doctrine of free will or a conception of hard determinism—tells us, he believes, something important about the structure of that society. These very metaphysical theories, Adorno believes, in reality reflect perversions of basic human needs which are not satisfiable in a repressive society. This is reminiscent of Ludwig Feuerbach and Karl

Marx on religion and theology, with for Adorno metaphysics being substituted for theology and religion. These theories or activities, in all three cases, are, of course, not seen as such by the agents involved, for they are themselves the captives of the ideology of the society in which they live. They, too, suffer from false consciousness and their religious beliefs and metaphysical theories give expression to it in a fantastically abstracted and disguised form.

It is against such a background, Adorno claims, that we should see the central task of philosophy. The central task of philosophy, as critical theory, is to refute or reasonably reject these competing metaphysical theories by (a) unmasking them as ideologies and (b) by exhibiting as well what socially imposed frustrations created the need for such ideologies. That is to say, the task is to show in what specific ways these metaphysical theories are socially necessary illusions.

However, as Adorno is quick to stress, it is seldom the case that any metaphysical theory—that is, on his account any ideological theory—is completely false, i.e., that it makes or entails no claims which are true or important. Indeterminism, for example, may be false or even incoherent, yet, even in repressive societies, people within certain limits are sometimes free, that is, able to a certain extent, and in certain domains, to do what they want to do when they want to do it. It is important to show this, as well as the often manifold ways in which the theory in question (in this case, indeterminism) makes false or incoherent claims. However, philosophy, as critical theory, on Adorno's account, does not set out a positive metaphysical alternative to the account it criticizes and unmasks as ideological. It is a *negative* dialectics. In the case of indeterminism, it does not develop another competing theory of human freedom or human bondage, though it may throw out some concrete suggestions concerning how certain institutions may be amended or discarded in such a way that they would no longer be impediments to human freedom. There is, Adorno believes, no need to set out a "positive ideology"—a positive philosophical theory—or any opposing ideology at all, or some general theory of society, though we are, of course, in such a criticism of ideological philosophical theories, being guided by an ideal, indeed a utopian ideal, of a completely nonrepressive society in which there would be no need for ideology. (For Habermas this would be a society in which undistorted discourse reigned.)

There are a host of questions and objections which spring to mind about such an account, not the least of which is in what sense or senses are we using "ideology" and "false consciousness" and whether it is really desirable or even possible to so transcend ideology. And there will also be a host of objections to characterizing philosophy so narrowly. Indeed, philosophy has been many different things and can no doubt continue to usefully and interestingly be many quite different things. (It is not a name, as the slogan goes, for a natural kind.) But it seems to me—difficulties about the proper characterization of "ideology" aside—that Adorno, with what in effect is a persuasive definition of "philosophy," has marked out an important task for philosophy. As Jürgen Habermas has pointed out, ideologies old and new have served "to impede making the foundations of society the object of thought and reflection."[74] If philosophy, as a critique of ideology, unmasks this and destroys this impediment, or at least wins some battles in the continued and perhaps endless struggle against such impediments, it will have performed a crucial emancipatory function and in that role performed what, since Socrates, has been a central part of its historical task.

However, that the unmasking of metaphysical theories should be given the importance it has by Adorno as opposed to other forms of ideological unmasking, e.g., of beliefs about the way the economy works, about the nature of the state, the role of education in society, beliefs about the extent and nature of freedom, equal opportunity, equality, and the like, seems to me a mistaken emphasis. These latter questions are far more central for human beings and far more in need of ideology critique than are metaphysical questions.

With the increasing disenchantment of the world, culturally speaking at least, metaphysics is becoming, as Rorty has stressed and Putnam as well, an increasingly marginal activity.[75] It hardly, as compared to the "good old days," makes any stir outside of philosophy departments. Neo-Aristotelians may lament its passing but its passing hardly receives any large cultural notice. Indeed, as a kind of scientistic inversion of the Middle Ages, where metaphysics is taken seriously at all, it is as some version of physicalism, what Putnam has called metaphysics within the limits of science alone, with the choice being between reductionist versions (say, Paul Churchland or Patricia Churchland) or nonreductionist versions (Peter Strawson or Donald Davidson). The former, for those who like to go in for that sort of thing, might be thought to be exciting, but at best false and more likely incoherent, while the latter are plausible, though bland and rather unexciting, hardly more than dressed up common sense and hardly a metaphysics at all. But, as Putnam remarks, there are simply no serious *metaphysical* alternatives to physicalism today. But physicalism, where it takes a nonreductionist turn, is hardly a metaphysics at all or, if a metaphysics, such a bland one that only someone with either wild reductionist inclinations or someone still fettered to religious illusions would have any desire to contest it.[76] So to take metaphysics as the main object of ideological critique, as Adorno does, is to engage in an atavistic quixotism. Habermas's ideology critique is more in tune with the disenchantment of the world that is common to both modernity and postmodernity. Concern with a non-physicalist metaphysics exhibits not only intellectual error but a nostalgia for the lost world of premodernity: a simpler world in which God is in His heaven and all is right with the world.

An ideology—the object of ideological critique—is a set of beliefs, attitudes, normative orientations, and practices which answer to the interests of a determinate class, usually the dominant class, or to a grouping of allied classes.[77] These beliefs, typically, though not of logical necessity, distort the understanding of those affected by the ideology. They do so in rather different ways, but one crucial way is to help along the bulk of the population to come to believe that what in reality is in the interest of the dominant class is instead impartially in the interests of everyone alike. This is one of the ways in which ideological illusions generate humanly, and politically, unfortunate effects, leading to the continued domination and degradation of human beings. Philosophy as ideology critique can play a genuinely emancipatory role in helping us to become aware of that. It will certainly not replace political action, but it is an important prologemmena to such action and sometimes, as well, a detonator of such action. In that way critical theory can be genuinely critical and genuinely emancipatory. It can play something of the political role its original architects wanted it to play.

Skepticism here parallel to the kind of skepticism I have been raising in other parts of this chapter is not to deny the importance of ideology critique. But it is to ask what is *philosophical* about it. To do ideology critique well we need to (a) know a good bit of social theory, including centrally social science, and (b) know a lot about our societies and connected societies as well, including something of their histories. And a deep reading of at least a certain sort of literature will also help. We need to know these things, to not be rigid, and to have a vivid imagination, also controlled by a good sense concerning what are the feasible possibilities in a given situation. Moreover, we also need to be morally reflective and sensitive, to have developed the habit of reflection and the taking of our reflections to heart, and to have, as well, a certain sort of integrity. This is what is needed to be a good critical theorist. Critical theory will indeed be a social theory using and critically reflecting on social science knowledge and the knowledge we have of the lifeworld, but I (*pace* Habermas and Adorno) see little role here for philosophy. My guess is that beyond a little underlaborer work, *sometimes* not without its point, philosophy for the most part gets in the way.

NOTES

1. Jürgen Habermas, "Philosophy as Stand-in and Interpreter," in *After Philosophy,* ed. Kenneth Baynes et al. (Cambridge, Mass.: MIT Press, 1987), 296–315. This essay was included in a series of essays by Habermas, *Moralbewusstsein und kommunikatives Handeln* (Frankfurt am Main: Surhkamp Verlag, 1983). English translation by Christian Lenhardt and Sherry Weber Nicholsen as *Moral Consciousness and Communicative Action* (Cambridge, Mass.: MIT Press, 1990). See also Richard Rorty, "Habermas and Ly-

otard on Postmodernity" and Habermas's response to both in *Habermas and Modernity,* ed. Richard Bernstein (Cambridge, Mass.: MIT Press, 1985), 161–75 (Rorty), and 191–98 (Habermas). For Max Horkheimer on substantive conceptions of reason, see Horkheimer: *Zur Kritik der Insrumentellen Vernunft* (Frankfurt: Suhrkamp, 1967); *The Eclipse of Reason* (New York: Seabury, 1973); and "The End of Reason" in *The Essential Frankfurt Reader,* ed. A. Arato and E. Gebhardt (New York: Continuum, 1982).

2. Jürgen Habermas, "Philosophy as Stand-in and Interpreter," 296–315.

3. Jürgen Habermas, "The Role of Philosophy in Marxism," *Intransigent Sociologist* 5 (1975): 41–48.

4. Jürgen Habermas: "Does Philosophy Still Have a Purpose?" in his *Philosophical-Political Profiles;* "Why More Philosophy?" *Social Research* 38 (1971): 633–54; "Rückkehr zur Metaphysik," *Merkur* (October 1985): 898–905; and his *Postmetaphysical Thinking* (Cambridge, Mass.: MIT Press, 1992).

5. Jürgen Habermas, "Philosophy as Stand-in and Interpreter," 298. Richard Rorty, *Philosophy and the Mirror of Nature* (Princeton, N.J.: Princeton University Press, 1979), 392.

6. Jürgen Habermas, "Philosophy as Stand-in and Interpreter," 218.

7. Ibid. See also Richard Rorty, "Human Rights, Rationality and Sensibility," in *On Human Rights,* ed. Stephen Shute and Susan Hurley (New York: Basic Books, 1993), 111–34 and his "Something to Steer By," *London Review of Books* 18 (June 20, 1996): 7–8.

8. Ibid., 299.

9. Ibid.

10. Ibid., 303.

11. Ibid., 304.

12. Ibid.

13. Ibid. This is surely not an untendentious claim. This is hardly the way pragmatists would see themselves. They link thought and action, knowledge and action, very closely, but, though they reject spectator accounts of knowing, they do not see acting and speaking as superior to knowledge. They all go together. It is like separating language and forms of life for Wittgenstein.

14. Ibid.

15. Ibid. See Ludwig Wittgenstein, *On Certainty* (Oxford, England: Basil Blackwell, 1969); Georg von Wright, "Wittgenstein on Certainty," in his *Problems in the Theory of Knowledge* (The Hague: Martinus Nijhoff, 1972), 47–60; and Kai Nielsen, *After the Demise of the Tradition* (Boulder, Colo.: Westview Press, 1991), 91–122.

16. Habermas, "Philosophy as Stand-in and Interpreter," 305.

17. Ibid. There will, of course, be those who will say that that gives no answer at all. Only an argument, and a sound one at that, will provide an answer. But that claim itself needs arguing.

18. Ibid., 306.

19. Ibid., 308.

20. Ibid. Richard Rorty, *Philosophy and the Mirror of Nature,* 371.

21. Ibid. Thomas McCarthy, "Private Irony and Public Decency: Richard Rorty's New Pragmatism," *Critical Inquiry* 16 (Winter 1990): 355–70; Richard Rorty, "Truth and Freedom: A Reply to Thomas McCarthy," *Critical Inquiry* 16 (Spring 1990): 633–43; and Thomas McCarthy, "Ironist Theory as a Vocation: A Response to Rorty's Reply," *Critical Inquiry* 16 (Spring 1990): 644–55. See also McCarthy's *Ideals and Illusions: On Reconstruction and Deconstruction in Contemporary Critical Theory* (Cambridge, Mass.: MIT Press, 1991).

22. Richard Rorty, *Essays on Heidegger and Others* (New York: Cambridge University Press, 1991).

23. Richard Rorty: *Consequences of Pragmatism* (Minneapolis, Minn.: University of Minnesota Press, 1982), xiii–xlvii, 90–109; *Objectivity, Relativism and Truth* (New York: Cambridge University Press, 1991).

24. Habermas, "Philosophy as Stand-in and Interpreter," 301.

25. John Passmore, "Philosophy," in *The Encyclopedia of Philosophy,* vol. 6, ed. Paul Edwards (New York: Free Press, 1967).

26. Habermas, "Philosophy as Stand-in and Interpreter," 309.

27. Ibid.

28. Ibid.

29. Ibid.

30. Ibid.

31. Ibid.

32. Ibid.

33. Ibid., 310.

34. Ibid.

35. Ibid.

36. Ibid.

37. Ibid., 311.

38. Ibid. See R. Spaemann, "Der Streit der Philosophen," in *Wozu Philosophie?* ed. H. Lübbe (Berlin, 1978), 96.

39. Habermas, "Philosophy as Stand-in and Interpreter," 311.

40. Ibid., 312.

41. Ibid.

42. Ibid., 313. Still, what is being claimed here is not clear. This is just one of many places where Habermas is not as clear as would be desirable.

43. Ibid.

44. Ibid.

45. Jürgen Habermas, "Does Philosophy Still Have a Purpose?" 15.

46. Habermas, "Philosophy as Stand-in and Interpreter," 314. Again, the quotation is from Rorty.

47. Richard Miller does just this very well in his *Analyzing Marx* (Princeton, N.J.: Princeton University Press, 1984), 101–67. See also Kai Nielsen, "On Putting Marx on the Philosophical Agenda," *Indian Philosophical Quarterly* 15, no. 1 (January 1988): 37–52.

48. Richard Rorty trenchantly challenges the belief that philosophers have any such distinctively conceptual tools or methods in "Philosophy in America Today," in his *Consequences of Pragmatism* (Minneapolis, Minn.: University of Minnesota Press, 1982), 211–30. See also his "Feminism and Pragmatism," *Radical Philosophy* 59 (Autumn 1991): 1–14. Note particularly footnotes 23, 25, 41, 42, and 49. See also Kai Nielsen, "On There Being Philosophical Knowledge," *Theoria* 56, part 3 (1990): 193–226.

49. Alice Ambrose, "Commanding a Clear View of Philosophy," *Proceedings of the American Philosophical Association* 49 (1975–76): 5–21.

50. Ibid.

51. Ludwig Wittgenstein, *Philosophical Investigations* (Oxford: Blackwell, 1953).

52. Rorty, *Consequences of Pragmatism,* xiii–xlvii. Nielsen, *After the Demise of the Tradition,* 3–13.

53. Richard Rorty, *Contingency, Irony and Solidarity* (New York: Cambridge University Press, 1989).

54. Rorty, *Consequences of Pragmatism*, 211–36.

55. Habermas, "Philosophy as Stand-in and Interpreter," 311.

56. Ibid.

57. How justification should be conceived of is well articulated by John Rawls in his *A Theory of Justice* (Cambridge, Mass.: Harvard University Press, 1971), 577–87. See also his "Justice as Fairness: Political Not Metaphysical," *Philosophy and Public Affairs* 14, no. 3 (Summer 1985): 223–51.

58. Or does it? Y. I. Semenov, "The Theory of Socio-Economic Formations and World History," and Ernest Gellner, "A Russian Marxist Philosophy of History," both in *Soviet and Western Anthropology,* ed. E. Gellner (London: Hutchinson, 1980); Kai Nielsen, "On Taking Historical Materialism Seriously," *Dialogue* 22, no. 2 (1983); and William Shaw, "Historical Materialism and the Development Thesis," *Philosophy of the Social Sciences* 16, no. 2 (1986).

59. Rorty, *Consequences of Pragmatism*, xiii–xlvii; and Rawls, "Justice as Fairness: Political Not Metaphysical," 223–51.

60. Habermas, "Philosophy as Stand-in and Interpreter," 113.

61. Ibid., 114.

62. Richard Rorty: "Life at the End of Inquiry," *London Review of Books* (August 2–September 6, 1984): 2–5, and his *Objectivity, Relativism and Truth*, 127–50.

63. Rorty, *Objectivity, Relativism and Truth*, 126–50. See as well references in note 21.

64. Donald Davidson, *Truth and Interpretation* (Oxford: Clarendon Press, 1984), 199–214. See also Kai Nielsen, "Anti-Philosophy Philosophy," *Diálogos* 64 (1994): 49–58.

65. Think here of Jacques Derrida. For Rorty splitting the difference, see Rorty, "Habermas, Derrida and the Functions of Philosophy," *Revue Internationale de Philosophie* 4 (1995): 437–59.

66. Donald Davidson, *Truth and Interpretation*, 183–98. Nielsen, *After the Demise of the Tradition*, 57–80. For a critical probing of it, but still defending it against unrestricted conceptual relativism, see Damon Gitelman, *Conceptual Scheme Differentiation* (Calgary, Alberta: Unpublished Doctoral Dissertation, 1991). However, he believes, in a way that I am less sure of, that problems of restricted conceptual relativism remain.

67. See the Appendix to this chapter. See here also crucially, Rorty, "Pragmatism and Anti-Representationalism," an introduction to John P. Murphy, *Pragmatism From Peirce to Davidson* (Boulder, Colo.: Westview Press, 1990), 1–6.

68. Jürgen Habermas, *Communication and the Evolution of Society* (Boston: Beacon Press, 1979), 1–69; Thomas McCarthy, *The Critical Theory of Jürgen Habermas* (Cambridge, Mass.: MIT Press, 1978), 162–92, 272–357; Kai Nielsen, "Legitimation and Ideology," *Ratio* 29, no. 2 (December 1987): 111–21; and Kai Nielsen, "Legitimation in Complex Societies: Some Habermasian Themes," *Annals of Scholarship* 7, no. 1 (1990): 51–89; and chapter 11 of this volume.

69. Quentin Skinner, "Jürgen Habermas," *New York Review of Books* (1983): 36; and Seyla Benhabib, "The Utopian Dimension in Communicative Ethics," *New German Critique* 35 (Spring/Summer 1985): 83–96.

70. Habermas, "Does Philosophy Still Have a Purpose?" and his *Theory and Practice*, trans. John Viertel (London, 1974).

71. Habermas, *Knowledge and Human Interests*, trans. Jeremy Shapiro (Boston, Mass.: Beacon Press, 1971); Raymond Geuss, *The Idea of a Critical Theory* (Cambridge: Cambridge University Press, 1981); Kai Nielsen, "The Very Idea of a Critical Theory,"

Ratio (1991); and Kai Nielsen, "Emancipatory Social Science and Social Critique," in *Ethics, the Social Sciences and Policy Analyses,* ed. D. Callahan and Bruce Jennings (New York: Plenum Press, 1983), 113–57.

72. Richard Rorty, "Thugs and Theorists," *Political Theory* 15, no. 4 (November 1987); and Richard Rorty, "Habermas, Derrida and the Function of Philosophy."

73. Theodor W. Adorno, *Negative Dialectics*, trans. E. B. Ashton (New York, 1973). See Habermas's discussion of Adorno in his *The Philosophical Discourse of Modernity* (Cambridge, Mass.: MIT Press, 1987).

74. Jürgen Habermas, *Toward a Rational Society*, trans. Jeremy Shapiro (Boston, Mass.: Beacon Press, 1970), 111–12.

75. Hilary Putnam, *Realism with a Human Face* (Cambridge, Mass.: Harvard University Press, 1990), part 1.

76. P. F. Strawson, *Skepticism and Naturalism: Some Varieties* (London: Methuen, 1985).

77. Kai Nielsen, *Marxism and the Moral Point of View* (Boulder, Colo.: Westview Press, 1989), chapter 5; and Kai Nielsen, "The Concept of Ideology: Some Marxist and Non-Marxist Conceptualizations," *Rethinking Marxism* 2, no. 4 (Winter 1989).

APPENDIX

PERSPECTIVISM AND THE
ABSOLUTE CONCEPTION OF THE WORLD
(APROPOS NOTE 67)

Bernard Williams, while rejecting metaphysical realism as thoroughly as Hilary Putnam, Richard Rorty, and Jürgen Habermas, rejects as well what he regards as the localized perspectivism of the former two with its at least alleged relativistic tendencies (tendencies both Rorty and Putnam resist). Williams does this by developing something he has called an "absolute conception" of the world (Williams's scare quotes) which is a conception that abstracts to the maximum degree from the peculiarities of any set of observer (13).* Indeed, it is a conception which seeks to escape perspectivism altogether. Williams notes that descriptions of the world vary in the degree to which they are "local, or perspectival, or anthropocentric" (13). To say of something that it is a forest, that it is a spruce forest, that it is dark, that it is foreboding is to give increasingly more localized and anthropocentric descriptions. Williams's "absolute conception" of the world, which he claims has nothing to do with metaphysical realism ("the view that we can conceive of the world in some way quite independent of our theories and the terms in which we describe it"), is the idea "of an account of the world that would be maximally independent of human peculiarities, the ideal of a description that could be used by any ob-

*Bernard Williams, "Terrestrial Thoughts, Extraterrestrial 'Sciences,'" *London Review of Books* (February 7, 1991): 12–13.

server, even a non-human one, who was capable of investigating the world" (12). This conception, if intelligible, would give us, Williams believes, a view of the world which is not anthropocentrically localized or, in any way, perspectival.

Putnam and Rorty think this conception is incoherent and Williams tries to defend it from their attacks. Williams thinks that Putnam believes it to be incoherent because he thinks it commits one to metaphysical realism. But, Williams claims, it no more so commits one than does Habermas's conception of undistorted discourse. But, by contrast with Habermas, Williams's "absolute conception" is used to try to give sense to the contrast between *"the world as it is in itself"* and *"the world as it seems to us."* Williams believes this is a contrast we need in order to explain the *ambition* of science. Without this contrast we would not capture something that is essential to the self-image of scientists. It might, of course, be retorted that it is *what they do*, not their self-images or their metabeliefs about their activities, that counts. But that point aside for some other occasion, it is certainly at least plausible to think scientists would want to make such a contrast. Most of them think, particularly if they are physicists, chemists, biologists, or geologists, that they are getting at what the world is really like and not at just how it seems to us. Perhaps that is an illusion, perhaps even an incoherency, but it is not implausible to think that that is part of their ambition, one of their deepest hopes that fuels their inquiries. Would they, if they were reasonable, want to go on doing science if they did not think that?

However, and be that as it may, with a rather Putnamish twist, Williams goes on to remark, after claiming that that is the contrast scientists need, that his own aim, by contrast, "was to explain what we might mean by this contrast, not from outside our conceptions, but in terms of reflections we can conduct within human life, the only place (needless to say) in which we can conduct them" (13). A central issue between Putnam and Williams, as it is between Rorty and Habermas, is whether this notion of an absolute conception—or in Habermas's case, on the surface at least, something rather like it—makes sense and whether, even if it does make sense, science really requires it. With respect to whether science needs it, I think the verdict isn't in yet, though I think many philosophers have an ideological proclivity to believe that it *must* be the case that science, or at least scientists, must have such an aim.

Against an absolute conception and on the Putnam-Rorty side, there is the argument Putnam deploys, against both Williams and metaphysical realists, that the world contains no fixed number of objects. Asked whether a grove of trees with ten trees is one object, five, eight, ten, twelve, or whatever, there is, Williams agrees with Putnam, no answer. But this, Williams believes, strangely it seems to me, does not at all count against the "absolute conception" but only reminds us, he remarks, of "the exceedingly well-known point that 'object' is not a concept under which you can count" (13). Still, as in the above example, we can, he continues, correctly say something determinate about the world, namely, that there are ten *trees* in a certain grove. That is not a matter of human *devising*, but of human *discovery*, though what is to count as a tree certainly is a matter of human devising. And there is no making such a discovery without having this conception of a tree which is a matter of human devising. But, by contrast, how many objects there are in the world is not. It is a matter neither of devising nor discovery. To believe that it has an answer, that it asks a genuine question, is to be caught up in an incoherency. Moreover, against the very idea that we could discover that the world is a certain determinate way that *our vocabulary must simply accommodate*, Putnam, along with Donald Davidson, will tell an equally familiar story about the indeterminacy of reference. *The idea that we have representations that simply mirror the world is without sense.* But then it seems as if it cannot make sense to speak of the world as it is in itself apart from any particular way beings, capable of investigating the world, have devised for one cluster of purposes or another, purposes reflecting their interests. No doubt there is some determinate way the world is, but we neither are, nor can become, in any position to say what it is. Kant was right about this.

However this clash between Williams and Putnam will play itself out, it seems to me that both sides need to preserve intact the following two claims: (1) That "we live in a world that exists independently of us and our thoughts," what Williams calls the banal and uncontroversial sense of realism, a thoroughly commonsense realism. Still such a banality is, plainly, incompatible with *all* forms of idealism. But the banality is also plainly true, so idealism is at best false. But this does not undermine all forms of irrealism or antirealism or establish representationalism. (2) The second claim to be preserved is that some descriptions, conceptualizations, and perspectives are more localized than others (sometimes so localized as even to be ethnocentric) and that *sometimes*, in the interests of greater objectivity and getting a better account of things, it is a good idea to go to the less localized, *less* ethnocentric, ways of viewing things. This leaves space for Habermas's conception of undistorted discourse, though not—or so I shall argue—for Williams's absolute conception.

Against what the above *may suggest*, I should add that Habermas's conception of undistorted discourse may not be vulnerable to the worries that beset Williams's absolute conception. Undistorted discourse does not attempt to escape perspectivism and undistorted discourse, as well as distorted discourse, is anthropocentric through and through, but anthropocentricity is one thing, ethnocentricity and parochialism is another. Perspectivism, Williams to the contrary notwithstanding, may be inescapable, but there are, that notwithstanding, wider and narrower perspectives and, what is not at all the same thing, distorted and undistorted perspectives.

We do not understand what it would be like to view things from no perspective or viewpoint at all or to just describe things from no point of view at all, utterly abstracting from all human purposes. Talk of "The View from Nowhere" or of "The Point of View of the Universe" is incoherent or at the very least the burden is on people who would so speak to show how such talk could make sense. (Something like a *via negativia* will not do here. We cannot just say what such a viewpoint *isn't*.) There are, however, plainly wider and narrower perspectives. When, for example, plain people in our societies speak of marriage or of cousins or nephews and the like, they have a rather narrower perspective, have a more limited range of cases and conceptions in mind, than do social anthropologists when they describe marriage, family, and kinship structures. The narrower, more limited perspective will also, in this case, and many like it, be ethnocentric and thereby distorted *if* it takes the only kind of marriage that there can be to be monogamous marriage or takes the very idea of a family to be identical with our conception of a nuclear family. Similar things obtain with religion. In Christian societies many will think that we cannot have a religion without belief in God and when they come to hear about certain forms of Buddhism (forms with neither God, gods, nor worship), they, not infrequently, will deny that such Buddhism is really a religion and will assert that it is simply a way of life or a cluster of moral practices. Students of comparative religion, by contrast, with a wider and more structurally articulated view of what religion is, will see important features in common between Buddhism and Christianity and classify them both as religions. There have been similar ethnocentric characterizations of "the moral point of view."

So perspectives, depending on our purposes and our interests, on how comprehensive we want or need to be, depending on what we know or are in a position to know, can be wider or narrower. But they can also be ethnocentric and distorted, as were the narrower conceptions about what marriage, family, religion, or morality is—"really is"—mentioned above. But narrower perspectives need not be ethnocentric or distorted, as they sometimes are not, when they are invoked for certain clearly articulated, circumscribed, and nonpartisan purposes, as when John Rawls limits his conceptualization of political justice to constitutional democracies, with an overlapping consensus rooted in a reasonable pluralism, under conditions of moderate scarcity. He is concerned to set out a conception of political justice for such societies without at all denying that other types of society could have just political institutions or that it makes sense to speak of global justice. Rawls just narrows his perspective for certain clearly expressed and, at least, arguably defendable purposes. He conceptualizes political justice narrowly, but it does not *follow* from that that his conceptualization is ethnocentric or distorted.

Narrower perspectives are, the above to the contrary notwithstanding, *likely* to be distorted—they are distortion-prone—but, as we have seen, they need not be and wide perspectives can also be distorted. In speaking of a perspective as undistorted, we are giving to understand that it is (a) clearly articulated, (b) does not utilize incoherent conceptions, (c) its premises are good candidates for being true or otherwise warrantable, (d) is free of inductive and deductive errors, and (e) is generated and sustained in a certain way. By (e) I mean that it has been created, and continues to operate, under conditions of freedom and equality and that it would, in such circumstances, gain the unforced acceptance of all normally rational people with the relevant interests and purposes, where the only constraints on their acceptance, their distinctive interests and purposes aside, would be the force of the better argument or the more adequate deliberation. The constraint to relevant interests and purposes is to acknowledge that there is no adopting or seeing a perspective to be more adequate without reference to interests and purposes. *Perspectives do not just stand there, apart from such considerations, as somehow more or less adequate in themselves.* If we want to do social anthropology such and such a conception and characterization of kinship is the more adequate. But the claim itself, though not the interest, must, to be acceptable, be sustained by the force of the better argument or the more adequate deliberation. Moreover, even someone who is not at all interested in social anthropology or kinship classification—it is not a part of her repertoire of purposes—could still come to recognize, examining the soundness of the arguments or the perspicuity of the deliberations involved, that, if she were interested in kinship classification, this for such purposes is the most undistorted perspective available at the time and for the foreseeable future. And to say that is all that we can reasonably claim. Articulators of distinctions between distorted and undistorted discourse should not try for the impossible and to rationalistically attempt to transcend fallibilism or perspectivism. There is no such transcendental perspective. And there is no interest-free determining of what "the correct description of the world" is or what is the everything considered most adequate perspective.[2] Such notions are at best mythical. But, depending on the purposes involved, the undistorted perspective or the less distorted perspective may be either a narrower or a wider perspective, though it is also true that not infrequently, though certainly not invariably, in social and moral deliberations, the wider perspective, if it is also the less distorted perspective, is something devoutly to be sought.

If, as I have argued, an absolute conception of the world is incoherent, then *there is no way of just describing the world as it is in itself or saying what it would be like to give the one uniquely true description of the world, a description which could be utilized by any observer, even a nonhuman one, in describing and, with that description, understanding, what the world is like in itself quite apart from any perspective or any cluster of purposes or inter-*

ests. We are without the possibility of an "absolute conception of the world," instead, we live with it being the case that the very way we describe, and the very terms of our descriptions, are in important ways inescapably dependent on our interests and purposes. Indeed, we can make no sense of this not being the case. And thus, in this important way, there can be no nonanthropocentric descriptions. Thus, since they are all inescapably anthropocentric, and we have no idea of what it would be like for them not to be so, one discourse (*pace* Williams) cannot, *in the relevant sense*, be less, or indeed more, anthropocentric than another. But one discourse can be less localized or less ethnocentric than another, if it is less entrapped in particular, and not infrequently blinkered, culturally peculiar conceptions and interests. By this I have in mind things like some people, forgetting about small-scale societies, claiming that all democracies must be representative democracies or, forgetting about other perhaps feasible possibilities, claiming that all democracies, or (implicity utilizing a *persuasive* definition) all "real democracies," must be capitalist democracies.

Less localized ways of viewing things are ways of viewing things that are less culturally or historically peculiar or less a matter of the distinctive beliefs of a particular historically and culturally situated class, gender, ethnic group, or race. Localized beliefs become ethnocentric when they are not only localized, but, as well, when the localized beliefs are taken by the people who have them to be more than localized ways of construing things. That is to say, though they are local and recognized to be so, they are also, the ethnocentric claim goes, the plainly correct or true way of viewing things for everyone or at least for everyone capable of having superior rationality or insight. It is very likely true that none of us can escape some degree of ethnocentricity, but, that notwithstanding, ethnocentricity plainly admits of degrees, and, moreover, not everyone need believe that his tribal mores, his historically and culturally situated beliefs, are The Truth and The Way. However, we are frequently not that much in the dark about others—Montaigne was wiser here than Descartes— and under fortunate circumstances these others become our conversational partners. *With no absolute conception, there is no such thing as "The Truth and The Way," but in escaping (partially escaping) ethnocentricity, we gain a measure of objectivity* (i.e., intersubjectivity). Being, and inescapably, aboard Otto Neurath's ship, we do not suffer from conceptual imprisonment. We continually rebuild the ship at sea, and sometimes, because of this rebuilding, the ship will become a better ship.

NOTES

1. Bernard Williams, "Terrestrial Thoughts, Extraterrestrial 'Science'," *London Review of Books* (February 7, 1991): 12–13. Further references to Williams will be given in the text.

2. Alan Garfinkel, *Forms of Explanation: Rethinking the Questions in Social Theory* (New Haven, Conn.: Yale University Press, 1981).

Part Four

Toward a Nonscientistic Atheism

INTRODUCTION

I

In these last four chapters I return to a discussion of religion. The first three, in a somewhat different form, originally appeared as separate essays written for different occasions with different ends-in-view and for different audiences. The last chapter of part 4 has been specifically written for this volume and with the rest of the book firmly in mind. I want to make clear there that my atheism, including my atheistic ethics, as it should be to be consistent with my naturalism, is an atheism without foundations: contextualistic, nonscientistic, historicized, and written in the spirit of pragmatism as I see it.

"Perceiving God," the first chapter of part 4, returns to what Terence Penelhum calls "the basic belief apologetic," a way of defending the faith from the wolves of disbelief that I examined in chapter 4 of part 1. The three big guns of the basic belief apologetic are Alvin Plantinga, Nicholas Wolterstorff, and William Alston. I have already critically examined the core arguments, as given by Plantinga and Wolterstorff, for this apologetic. In "Perceiving God" I return to a distinct account by Alston which argues for the *possibility* of a direct *experiential* knowledge of God, an argument which can be used in the service of a basic belief apologetic, but can, I believe, be detached from it and argued for on its own. I agree with Penelhum's assessment of the importance of Alston's work.[1] He, of the three big guns, gives the most persuasive defense of theism. That notwithstanding, I think, for essentially the reasons given by C. B. Martin, Ronald Hepburn, and myself over thirty years ago, experiential approaches to a knowledge of God are utter nonstarters.[2] Still it continues to be attractive to religiously inclined people of a rather empiricist temper who are wary of both metaphysics and the excesses of fideism, but, all the same, are people who want very much to be both reasonable and to be able to believe in God. Alston's work will appeal to them.

Alston writes with a thorough sense of fairness and reasonableness and with an awareness of the standard difficulties in the approach he takes. He seeks, while facing some of them, to make a case for the *possibility* of a perceptual knowledge of God. His argument is, I think, about as strong as such an argument can be. If it is fatally flawed, as I argue that it is, it is very unlikely that that broadly empirical avenue to a knowledge or an awareness of God is open to us.

The next two chapters, "Is Religion the Opium of the People? Marxianism and Religion" and "Atheism without Anger or Tears," though written independently, in fact nicely dovetail and should be read with each other in mind. Both of them, though in different ways, examine the question of whether we can have a viable naturalistic (that is materialist) conception of religion and, with their affirmative answer, they also say something about what it would be like.

I argue, in effect in these two chapters, for a division of labor between Hume and Marx. They are both children of the Enlightenment: Enlightenment figures without being Enlightenment *rationalists* or foundationalists. Hume, more deeply than any of the other figures of his time, provided the grounds for deep skepticism concerning religion. This skepticism is best seen, as Antony Flew and Terence Penelhum see it, as the prudent atheism of a deeply metaphysically skeptical philosopher.[3] My own critiques of religion, as well as those of J. L. Mackie and Antony Flew, should be seen, as I have perhaps overfrequently put it, as mopping-up operations after Hume, though, we write in a cultural climate very different than Hume's, where, for us, there is no need to be even nearly as reticent in statement as Hume felt, and with good reason, he needed to be. Atheists, among intellectuals in our present cultural climate, are as plentiful as blackberries in North Carolina. Moreover, in societies such as our own, in spite of the Religious Right, they do not stand—in contrast with the world Hume lived in—in danger of being ostracized or denied university posts and the like (though, still in our time, such a person would stand no chance at all, and just because of his beliefs about religion, of becoming president of the United States).

Hume's critique shows that God's existence has not been proven or otherwise established, that the very concept of God is at best problematic, and that there is no need at all to make a Pascalian leap of faith to make sense of our lives or for morality to be viable. Indeed, without the enthusiasms and extravagances of religion our lives might very well go better than they now do.

Marx and Engels, as well as Marxists and Marxians generally, simply took those things for granted. They thought that philosophers such as Hume and Holbach had established these things quite definitively and that it was a waste of time, and a distraction from more urgent critical work, to return to such arguments. But, like Freud, they noted that, in spite of the evident unreasonability of religious belief (its evident untenability), religious belief remains pervasive and, very frequently, tenaciously and fervently held. Where there are no *reasons* for a belief, and yet it is still pervasive and persistent, it is well to look for the *causes* of belief: to seek a purely causal explanation, and indeed a causal explanation which is also a functional explanation, of religious belief.

So Marx, and even more so Engels, explored the ideological functions of religious belief. Engels traced Christianity to its origins among destitute, culturally undermined, and utterly dominated people (slaves, impoverished peasants, and destitute freemen). Brutally dominated and abused in the Roman Empire, they lived in what was for them an utterly heartless world and, as well, in a world in which the most fantastic beliefs proliferated among great masses of ill-educated and impoverished people. It was, with such people, in such an environment, that Christianity arose as an *eschatological* hope for "another better world" after bodily death, a purely "spiritual world," in which their aspirations, which could not at all be met in "this world," would finally be fully met. So religion functioned as an *opiate* for such people in such a harsh and heartless world and, at the same time, it functioned as a means of *social control* to be utilized by the ruling classes of the Roman Empire.

Religion, Marx and Engels argue, has again and again served that ideological function in class societies. People learn to accept their lot—their station and its duties—and wait for a better spiritual world, by and by, in which they would be recompensed a thousand times over for all their afflictions. Religion gives people an illusory hope in circumstances that are actually hopeless. In circumstances, which are also the circumstances of many people in our societies today, where things are bad, though often (but not always) not quite as bad as they were for the impoverished in Roman times, religion tends to turn people's attention away from real solutions to real human problems by (a) teaching them to accept their lot, whatever it is, no matter how bad, as what God has ordained for them and (b) to focus on the glorious spiritual life to come after they shuffle off their mortal coils.

These Marxian generalizations are sociological ones and Marxians realized full well that there are exceptions both among religious movements (anti-baptism, for example) and among individual religious believers, but, that notwithstanding, this opiating way is how religion massively and pervasively tends to function and how it indeed answers to the needs of destitute people in desperate situations, as Engels shows, for the slaves in the Roman Empire, the peasants in Germany during Luther's time, and the impoverished and exploited workers in Manchester during Engels's time, and, we could add, now with poor blacks and whites in Mississippi and similar places. (How religion so functions in Mississippi is vividly depicted in Bertrand Tavernier and Robert Parrish's documentary film *Mississippi Blues* [1984]).

Marxians do not ask about the truth of religious beliefs; rather, they, building on Hume, assume that they are not true or even plausible, but seek instead to understand their role in life. I explore their conception in chapter 15 and argue that, while it neglects the existential functions of religion (roughly how we cope with failing powers, human estrangement, and the facing of our own death and the death of those close to us), it correctly catches a central ideological role that religion has pervasively played. I then ask, for various conditions of social life, where there is a *realistic* possibility of people not believing in God, whether their not believing is a *desirable* thing, everything considered. It is in providing a negative answer to this that Hume and Marx are united as are many latter-day Humeans and Marxians.

I pursue these questions, though in somewhat different ways, in both chapters 16 and 17 and argue that a clear answer here is not as easily had as we atheists have been wont to believe. I try to push matters, as far as I can, toward ascertaining what we should think here.

In both my *Ethics Without God* and my *God and the Grounding of Morality*, I argue for a secular, indeed a humanistic, ethics and against both the ethics of divine commands and a natural law ethics. These views of mine have been subjected to searching critique, a critique most forcefully stated by Geoffrey Scott, who, though he does not at all want to return to a religious ethics or to assert that without belief in God morality totters or anything like that, argues that religious alternatives to a secular ethics cannot be refuted in the ways I think that they can and that I am far too foundationalist and rationalistic here, in effect, replacing dogma with dogma.[4] I think that some of Scott's specific arguments are sound and I return in my final chapter, with them in mind, to a consideration of a Godless morality, in an attempt to articulate what is essential here in a way that comports better, than did my earlier views, with my antifoundationalist naturalism.

A related robust critique of my atheism consists in claiming that I, when it comes to religion, in effect, rely on an unacknowledged, unrecognized, and, as well, an utterly unjustified foundationalism (for Rodger Beehler a foundationalist positivism, for Barry Allen a Holbachian Enlightenment rationalism).[5] I face up to this in chapter 16. Such an understanding, if it really is mine, comports badly with my more general antifoundationalism and contextualism. It also functions for me, so Beehler and Allen claim, like an ideology leading me to a *militant* atheism that makes unjustified claims about religious belief, including claims about belief in God being unreasonable. Here, the claims goes, I forget about my contextualism and historicism and make claims that are utterly partisan and unsustainable. I try to show in "Atheism Without Anger or Tears" both that that cluster of criticisms is mistaken and, as well, to show something of the range and diversity of atheisms, establishing, along the way, that (*pace* Allen) 'militant atheism' is not a redundancy and that atheism need not, and should not, rely on a foundationalist philosophy.

More generally, it is my argument—an argument developed most fully in my *Atheism and Philosophy* and in my *God, Skepticism and Modernity* —that for intellectuals in societies such as ours it is unreasonable for them to believe in God and to remain Jews, Christians, or Muslims. This view, which (*pace* Beehler) is not argued on foundationalist grounds, has been thought, by not a few, to be absurdly mistaken and has been taken, as well, by some, to be offensive. I return to those issues in "Atheism Without Anger or Tears." I seek, once again, and with something of a weariness, to make clear (among other things) what I am *not* claiming, namely, that only secularists are reasonable and that religious people are unreasonable or that it is never reasonable for anyone to believe in God. That would indeed be an absurd contention. What I have tried instead to establish is a complicated hypothetical, namely, that if to believe in God is, on the one hand, to have a belief which is false and is reasonably known to be false or very improbable, *or*, on the other hand, to have a belief which is incoherent and reasonably known, or so believed with a very strong warrant, to be incoherent, and if, further, belief in God is not necessary to give meaning to life or to make sense of morality or to secure a more adequate morality than can any secular conception of morality, then, if all these things are readily knowable for people who are in a good position to know these things, then it is unreasonable *for them* to believe in God. I argue that critical intellectuals in our societies and at this time are in a position to know these things and, moreover, that these hypotheticals are true, and not just as hypotheticals, but that those things are actually the case about religion and about the situation of critical intellectuals in our societies at the present time. So I conclude, hardly surprisingly, that religious belief is unreasonable *for such critical intellectuals so situated.*

However, I do *not* conclude that I have shown, or that I know or have good reasons to believe, that someone who disagrees with me concerning these matters is thereby less reasonable than I am. That would be an absurd and arrogant thing for me to say or even to think. Yet this very simple point has been repeatedly missed in discussing my views. Someone who thinks either that belief in God is not incoherent or that it has not been shown to be incoherent or that it has not been shown that God does not exist or that His existence is improbable or even someone who believes that she knows or reasonably believes that God exists need not be an unreasonable person or a less reasonable person than even the most reasonable of secularists. To think, to underscore by repetition, that would be arrogant and *parti pris*, a bit of ridiculous *hubris* on my part. I would be making there a purely dogmatic claim. But I neither claim nor think any such absurd things. I do indeed argue that religious beliefs are incoherent and that it is unreasonable to believe in God for someone in a good position to know that, if that indeed is our situation. But that is an argument of mine that I put forth in an utterly fallibilistic, open-minded spirit, full well knowing that, like any argument of such scope, it may very well be mistaken. This being so, it is surely the case that someone who is not convinced is not thereby shown to be unreasonable. This is not, however, just another example of the philosopher's penchant for first saying it and then taking it back. I am saying that if belief that God exists is at best false, then, for someone in a good position to know that, it is unreasonable for that someone to believe in God. But I am not claiming that someone who believes that it has not been established that the existence of God is at best false must be unreasonable. I am trying to establish that the belief that God exists is at best false. But I certainly am not saying that someone who disagrees with me must be unreasonable or even unreasonable in disagreeing with me.

II

As I have just done, as well as throughout this book, and most particularly in the chapters in part 4, I bandy around the word *reasonable* a lot. It has not infrequently been thought that what is reasonable and what is not is too vague and too context-dependent for it to be a proper term of critical appraisal. It, some have thought, is more like an ideological club to beat down those who disagree with you than it is a critical category to be used in philosophical or any other kind of assessment. Its use is principally emotive or (what is not the same thing) it is an essentially contested concept or, at least, it is so context-dependent, so particular language-game and particular practice dependent, that it could not possibly do the critical work I have assigned to it.

This is a tangled and complex issue that I want to spend the rest of this introduction in some preliminary way addressing. My hope is to afford some plausible reasons for believing that it is, after all, a genuinely critical instrument that can do some critical work.

It is also the case that in part 2, and to a somewhat lesser extent in part 3, I either explicitly or implicitly rely on claims about what it is to be reasonable and on what is reasonable or unreasonable, particularly in discussing political and moral philosophy and, as well, in discussing or in taking political and moral stances. This is even more evidently true of the work of John Rawls who has, as he has so many others, deeply influenced my own work in political theory.[6] We both start by accepting the idea that pluralism is an intractable fact in our societies. But, in the face of that pluralism, for our appeal to an overlapping consensus to have the normative importance that we believe it has, the pluralism must be a *reasonable* pluralism. (That is a necessary condition, but not a sufficient condition for such an appeal to an overlapping consensus to be justified.) *But what is a reasonable pluralism*? When do we have it? Does such a notion have the requisite objectivity to do the work in political theory that Rawls puts it to and that I do as well?

Stuart Hampshire, who is a sympathetic critic of Rawls, and a thoroughgoing, if somewhat pessimistic, nonscientistic naturalist and secularist, thinks that Rawls makes too much of claims about what is reasonable and unreasonable and neglects the deep and ineradicable passions that we have and the differential socialization that yields different conceptions of what is valuable, worth doing and having, differences that give rise to deep and ineradicable conflicts in the life of any society. Rawls's account, Hampshire believes, is a kind of *misplaced rationalism*.[7] To rest such final *authority* in reason, including what Rawls calls public reason, is a bad place for a liberal, a defender of civic humanism, or anyone to occupy because it is a conception, Hampshire claims, that is rooted in a "disastrous illusion descending unashamed to Kant and Rawls from Plato's *Republic*."[8] We, particularly if we are philosophers, tend to be overawed by talk of reason. "We must still feel some awe or fear (*achtung*) before the magnificent words 'reason' and 'unreasonable' brandish in front of us in Kantian style."[9]

Rawls does a lot of such brandishing, particularly in his *Political Liberalism*, and in his response to Jürgen Habermas's critique of his views, and I do as well, not only in political and moral theorizing, but also in discussing religion. Hampshire puts the matter, with his claims about a disastrous illusion, rather, metaphorically, but we can, and should, also proceed prosaically and skeptically, as Allan Gibbard does in queering what he takes to be similar rationalistic presuppositions in the work of Brian Barry, whose account of justice is in *broad* terms like mine and Rawls's.[10] What, Gibbard asks, does the plainly normative term 'reasonable' mean and can it do the theoretical and critically normative work that Barry gives to it and indeed, by extension, Rawls and I do as well? This, Gibbard thinks, needs careful and skeptical examination.

Some day I hope to turn at considerable length to this topic. However, here I will, assembling reminders for my particular purposes, only skirt the surface. I will try to say something of what it is for people in societies such as ours to have reasonable attitudes and beliefs, and I will try, as well, to say something about what it is to be a reasonable person.

It might be said—trying to be very general—that to say that something is reasonable is to say that it makes sense. But that surely is not so on *one* straightforward way of taking "makes sense" where some utterance makes sense if it is intelligible. We can say and believe the most absurd things, indeed totally unreasonable things, and yet, when we give expression to our unreasonable beliefs, what we say is plainly intelligible. Thus, if I say "I am sure that I will live to be two hundred years old," I say something that is intelligible—in *that sense* it makes sense—but it is laughably unreasonable. Indeed, you recognize this to be so because you understand full well what I said.

What instead is plausibly meant in saying that if something is reasonable that then it makes sense is that "makes sense" is taken to mean *not* "is intelligible," but instead "is sensible." That a reasonable view is a sensible view seems, at least, to be a correct thing to say, but, all the same, obviously not a very useful thing to say. For if we are puzzled about "reasonable" we are going to be equally puzzled about "sensible." "A reasonable view is a sensible view" is true (perhaps even analytically true, if there are such things), but hardly enlightening. It is like saying "A true proposition says what is so." That is also true, but utterly unenlightening. *Sometimes* "sensible" and thus "reasonable" means "plausible" where we are speaking of reasonable beliefs, but not of persons, attitudes on actions. "Plausible persons," for example, has no straightforward use.

Only slightly more enlightening is the claim that a reasonable person will be a fair person. A reasonable person, that is, in acting will consider what is fair and she will seek to interact with others on that basis. Again this captures something of what in certain contexts we ordinarily mean by "reasonable" and it usefully points to how "reasonable," unlike "rational," when used in certain contexts, has a plain moral force. But again, like "sensible," until what "fair" means is specified—comes to be thickly spelled out—we have not learned much in saying, however correctly, that a reasonable person will be a fair person. We need in both instances a full translation into the concrete.

I shall in a moment give a list of propositions which together characterize, in its *thick contextuality*, what in modern liberal societies is taken to be reasonable.[11] This will give us plenty of content, but it will also be evident enough that what counts as a reasonable person, a reasonable view, a reasonable belief, a reasonable attitude, a reasonable principle or way of acting will not have all these features at every time and place. Moreover, it is a distinctive liberal conception of reasonability tailor-made for modern persons living in reasonably stable societies such as the rich capitalist democracies and any (if they come to be) similarly stable and similarly rich socialist or communist societies.

However, there is a characterization of reasonableness, with more content than conceptions appealing to bare fairness or to bare being sensible or plausible, that is as old as Socrates and, all the same, has some robust content, yet, while compatible with the still more determinate liberal conception of reasonableness I shall state, is not an expression of it, is perfectly available to non-liberals, and does not catch the fullness of the distinctive liberal conception of being reasonable. Thomas McCarthy puts this robust general conception this way: to be reasonable is to have the central and uncontroversial virtues of reasonableness such as "open-mindedness, avoidance of dogmatism, a willingness to discuss differences, to listen to others, to take their views seriously, and to change our minds, an ability to see things from the perspectives of others (and) to weigh up judiciously the pros and cons of issues."[12]

This characterization of the virtues of reasonableness is indeterminate in certain ways, but not so indeterminate as not to have definite applications in certain plain cases. We all know certain people who in the above uncontroversial sense are reasonable and certain people who are not. We also, if we are at all reflective, will realize that none of us, overall, in all matters, will always be reasonable. Some things will so prickle us so that we cannot see things from another's perspective or judiciously weigh the pros and cons of certain issues. But a few such blind spots does not make us unreasonable persons. Perfectly reasonable people are very rare indeed. Reasonability, unlike truth, is a matter of degree. Still, many people plainly exercise these virtues frequently enough and consistently enough to count as reasonable persons and others so lack these virtues that they are unreasonable persons. Sometimes even very remarkable persons are not reasonable or very reasonable. Erasmus was reasonable, but Luther frequently was not, Rasputin hardly ever was, and Calvin was a borderline case. Wittgenstein, who is arguably the greatest philosopher of our century, was hardly a paradigm of reasonability. To take more humdrum examples: cultists, much (if not all) of the Religious Right, some atheists, some people on the Left, some libertarians—we can all find values for these variables—are so fanatical that they could not correctly be said to be reasonable persons, given the above quite unproblematic characterization of reasonable.

However, this characterization is also in certain respects sufficiently indeterminate to allow for very considerable differences in judgment as to what weighing things judiciously comes to, what open-mindedness, avoidance of dogmatism, taking the views of others seriously, seeing things from another's perspective come to. These notions can and do have different interpretations, different readings, and they are sometimes placed in very different narratives. People will in some cases disagree on what constitutes a genuine application or an exemplification of these notions. Some, for example, will think I am mistaken, indeed so mistaken as to be *parti pris*, in taking quite broadly the Religious Right to be unreasonable (we should be more nuanced and discriminating here) or to think that Calvin might be a borderline case or to regard Luther as often unreasonable. We do—and sometimes heatedly—disagree about who is unreasonable and who is not and about what views, beliefs, actions, and attitudes are unreasonable. But then, again, things are not always so contestable. We have no doubts at all about certain cultists or Rasputin, though again it is salutary to reflect on who the "we" ranges over and how the candidates for unreasonability shrink when we go for cases concerning which there is no reasonable doubt. Still, when cases are more fully described, greater agreement will usually be secured where there is at least rough agreement on the accuracy of the description.

However, the above notwithstanding, there is also, for a given society at a given time, standardly a broad consensus that certain views, beliefs, attitudes, and actions are unreasonable and that certain of them are reasonable and, as in the West for a long time, according to the above criteria. McCarthy is right in saying that these ideas about reasonability are as old as Socrates. There is a similar (though by no means complete) consensus about when people are being unreasonable and about what persons are unreasonable, though we should not turn a blind eye to the fact that these judgments are still, without being completely so, to a considerable degree culture and context-dependent and vary to some extent over time. To take an extreme example, many Germans did not, particularly during the first part of the Nazi period, think that Hitler was unreasonable, though for us, including in the "us" most present-day Germans, he is a paradigm, among other things, of a thoroughly unreasonable person. Still, there is room for people, having the same concept of reasonableness, to sometimes disagree (reasonably disagree) to be a little paradoxical for a moment, about who or what is reasonable, and who or what is not. Moreover, among people sharing the same concept, it will still sometimes be the case that on occasion some of them will be mistaken, and indeed sometimes badly mistaken, in their particular judgments about who is reasonable and who is not.

We should also recognize that what notions like open-mindedness, dogmatism, judiciousness, and the like mean—come to in practice—emerges from what, translating into the concrete, we in some detail specify and what we would take to justify our specifications: e.g., our judgments that some *particular ways* of behaving or thinking show open-mindedness or judiciousness. If we specify extensively, with thick contextuality, what we are talking about, what we mean to be saying when we say, for example, that a particular person is open-minded, we will usually get more determinate judgments and sometimes, if we really tend carefully to the facts, a certain resolution of differences about what open-mindedness really comes to at least in particular types of circumstance. (Here is another, to hark back to chapter 2, application of Peirce's third degree of clarity.)

III

I turn now to my specification of a liberal conception of reasonableness tailored in large measure to our societies (principally the rich capitalist democracies). It is what *we* mean, in some detail, by reasonableness, though I do not mean to give to understand that all of the elements that are said to be part of the liberal conception of reasonability are such that they *only* obtain, when they obtain, in liberal societies. They are common to, and characteristic of, liberal societies, but all of them are not utterly peculiar to liberal societies. But the *ensemble* comes close to being both distinctive of and peculiar to liberal societies.

I shall give two lists of these liberal conceptions of reasonableness. The first list is what I take to be at least relatively uncontroversial elements in a liberal conception of reasonableness and the second I take to be a more controversial list. But I do not mean to take the division here to be rigid or itself uncontroversial. Some might want to shift some items from one list to the other and some might even wish to put many more items than I have in the controversial list. If *some* such shifting takes place, nothing of great moment would obtain for the utilization I wish to make of the concept of the reasonable, though, if very many of the uncontroversial ones get transferred to the controversial list, the conception of reasonability would not have as good a claim to objectivity (a thorough reflective intersubjectivity) as I think it has. (The hunt for a general formula—an algorithm—here, as it almost always is in philosophy, is thoroughly wrongheaded.) Moreover, it is also plainly the case that conceptions and claims can be more or less controversial. But together the two lists specify in some detail a liberal conception of reasonableness, the controversial list revealing a specification of that conception that is more *distinctively* Rawlsian in inspiration and conception than the uncontroversial list in spite of fact that there are more quotations from Rawls in the uncontroversial list. But, for most of the purposes for which I rely on a conception of reasonableness, the conception given by the uncontroversial list will suffice.

It should also be apparent that my characterization, like Rawls's, is a moral (though not a moralistic) characterization from the very start. No attempt is made to set out a nonmoral conception of the reasonable (something which I do not think is intelligible) and then to try to derive morality, or some significant subset of morality, from it. It is not at all, like Hobbes or David Gauthier, trying, with a morally neutral conception of rationality, to derive morality, or a part of morality, from it. The conception of reasonability is a moral conception from the start, though it is not *simply* a moral conception.

The lists (particularly the uncontroversial one) are long and reasonably detailed. We have what Michael Walzer might call a thick rather than a minimal conception of liberal reasonability.[13] I try, with the fullness of these conceptions, to give a conception which will, in its thickness and detail, afford us some ground and means for sorting out a reasonable pluralism from a merely *de facto* pluralism, reasonable from unreasonable persons, views, beliefs, attitudes, practices, principles, plans, comprehensive conceptions of the good and of justice for people in liberal societies. I would also hope that it would, together with the more general conception lifted from McCarthy, enable us to get some grip on questions about the comparative reasonableness of whole societies and ways of life, so that we could intelligibly and usefully, and non-question-beggingly ask, if a liberal social order in the circumstances of modernity (circumstances we live in now) can correctly be said to be more reasonable than a nonliberal one? I want to be able to ask, and hopefully to be in a position to answer, such questions about societies and whole worldviews. My hope is that that specification of a conception of reasonableness will be sufficiently detailed, nonideological, and uncontroversial to yield a critical instrument which will do some of that work. Finally, by way of preliminaries, concerning indeterminacy (partial indeterminacy) of application, what I said about the more general conception of reasonableness should apply to the liberal conception as well.

A LIBERAL CONCEPTION OF REASONABLENESS
UNCONTROVERSIAL LIST

1. The views and beliefs reasonable people hold must be such that they will be prepared to modify them or the actions they take on the basis of them in order to make possible social cooperation on terms of freedom and equality with others who may hold different views and have different beliefs.[14]

2. Reasonable persons "desire for its own sake a social world in which they, as free and equal, can cooperate with others on terms all can accept."[15] Such persons, as a very fundamental desire, will desire to be able to justify their actions to others on grounds they could not sensibly reject.[16]

3. Reasonable people will desire a social world where people stand in relations of freedom and equality and in which reciprocity obtains in such a way that each, from the reciprocity, benefits along with the others.

4. Where people are being reasonable some will seek to articulate the reasons we are to share and publicly recognize before one another as grounding our social relations. And all reasonable persons will welcome and be prepared, where they can see that they are justified, to accept such reasons. They will wish to see worked out, and some will engage in the working out, of the framework for the public social world that it is hoped, and expected, everyone will endorse and act on, provided others can be relied on to do the same.[17]

5. There will be a rejection of all forms of fanaticism.

6. There will be an openness and a tolerance of all those who are similarly tolerant. There will be criticism of the intolerant, and in some instances, resistance to their intolerance, but there may even be tolerance of the intolerant, where (if ever that obtains) their intolerance will do no substantial harm to others. (Intolerant persons, of course, cannot count as reasonable persons.)

7. There will, along with the tolerance mentioned in 6, be a respect for all persons.

8. Reasonable persons will have a sense of fairness, be willing to meet others half way, will be ready to compromise where deep issues of principle are not threatened, will believe in the value of mutual respect and will have a sense of civility.[18]

9. Reasonable persons will be concerned that agreements will be regulated so as to ensure a fair balancing of interests.

10. Agents, if they are reasonable, must be willing "to listen to others"

and display "fair-mindedness in deciding when accommodations to their views should . . . be made."[19] There will, on the part of such persons, be a commitment to public dialogue and public justification.

11. Agreements must—or at least normally must—be obtained through rational dialogue where all taking part are treated as equals with an equal say and an equal consideration of their interests. Agreements must be obtained in this way and not through the employment of rhetorical skill, charismatic influence, physical coercion, or bargaining in which the powerful have a greater say.

12. There will be a commitment to impartiality and fairness and to fair dealing with everyone.

13. There will be a concern to hear, and fairly attend to, all sides of, and all parties to, a dispute before making a judgment concerning any matter at hand or before opting for a certain public policy. And there will always be a willingness to review our judgments or policies in the light of new evidence or newly articulated cogent reasons: our attitudes, manner, and styles of reasoning will be thoroughly fallibilistic.

14. There will be a self-criticalness concerning one's own beliefs, attitudes, and ways of behaving and a critical attitude, as well, though with a valuing of civility, and with a skeptical caution toward the institutions and practices of one's own society and other societies as well.

15. In matters of public concern, there will be a commitment to trying to have beliefs that are at least in accordance with readily available, plainly recognizable facts. And there will be a concern to have a clear awareness of the full range of such facts, or at least as many of the relevant ones as can practically be garnered for the matter at hand, and not to avoid any such facts as may be inconvenient.

16. At least over matters of public concern, there will be a concern (a) to have (where relevant) evidence for one's beliefs, (b) to be consistent and coherent, and (c) to be concerned, where we can, to ascertain the better argument or more adequate deliberation and to accept the force and the practical implications of such an argument or deliberation.

17. There will be a concern to have beliefs and policies which are intelligible and coherent in the light of the circumstances in which reasoning is usually exercised.

18. There will be an acceptance among reasonable people of the view that in a well-ordered and just society none of the contending sides in a dispute can legitimately impose their moral convictions on the society, and thus perforce on others, by forceful domination. What is

needed for ideas to have a society-wide normative force is that they will not be accepted without the recognized procedures of fair discussion and of consistent and rule-governed adjudication being in force which are already established in the society.

19. Even when there is no agreement about certain crucial ends, procedurally correct outcomes will be accepted by reasonable people.

CONTROVERSIAL LIST

1. Among reasonable people there will be a common recognition that it will be unavoidable in our complex modern world that many of our most important judgments will be made "under conditions where it is not to be expected that conscientious persons with full powers of reason, even after free discussion, will arrive at the same conclusion."[20] This fact is to be taken to heart and in such a circumstance, we should seek to avoid imposing any of these contested views or plans on anyone in the society. None of the beliefs that various people have, where there is such a dissensus, are to be taken as *authoritative* social norms that require that in our public life we must act in a certain way.

2. "An understanding of value is fully reasonable just in case its adherents are stably disposed to affirm it as they acquire new information and subject it to careful reflection."[21]

3. Faced with a persistent diversity of equally reasonable, or nearly equally reasonable, comprehensive, or partially comprehensive, conceptions of the good, we should, if we would be reasonable, restrict ourselves, over claims for a just ordering of society, and for similar social norms, to the common ground (if such there be) between such diverse views, acknowledging that reason (careful, reflective reasoning), as far as can be ascertained now, does not mandate a single moral view and because of that, we should refrain from imposing, or trying to impose, our own comprehensive, or partially comprehensive, conception of the good on anyone. Only what is in common to those conceptions—that is, matters over which there is a consensus among reasonable persons—can serve as an *authoritative* ground for the design of a society's institutions or for determining what is required of human beings in the society in question.

4. Reasonable people will recognize that it is plausible to believe that it is a general fact that there will always be people with *unreasonable* views. Indeed, that very well may be an empirical truism. But, they will also recognize, that "the fact that there are some people with un-

reasonable views does not require that we adjust our conception of justice so that it can be supported by an overlapping consensus that will appeal to them."[22] We do not need to accommodate the unreasonable. Indeed, if "we did accommodate the unreasonable in the formulation of fundamental principles, then we would be unacceptably adjusting principles to *de facto* power."[23]

5. Reasonable people will see themselves as "obligated to a public use of reason in publicly discussing fundamental issues of justice."[24]

IV

What I am concerned to ascertain is whether such a liberal conception of reasonability, hopefully giving us a plausible understanding of the concept of reasonability, provides us with a critical instrument to use in criticizing certain beliefs, ways of doing and of viewing things, or whether it is so vague and indeterminate as to be compatible with almost anything we might think or do or, alternatively, whether it is actually an ideological conception giving us, what in effect is, a distorted and prejudiced view of how things should be. Is it just a conception which rationalizes liberal ideology? I think it is the former: that it yields, that is, a critical instrument with a proper contextual and historicized intersubjective objectivity. But it is not more than that. It does not give us some ahistorical objective Archimedian point. Something, as I have argued throughout this book, that we cannot have in any substantive domain.

I have also argued in part 3, employing that liberal conception of reasonability, for a certain conception and account of social justice. I think I have shown it, in the sense of "reasonable" specified above, to be reasonable and indeed more reasonable than some prominent alternative accounts. In doing this the conception of reasonability employed was both procedural and substantive and not just rhetorical and empty, but it also is, as I think the above listing makes clear, something that we—at least if we are liberals and the like—would on reflection wish to see obtain. I have argued, as well, that religious beliefs and religious commitments are unreasonable for intellectuals with a good scientific and philosophical education and situated as we are situated. The crucial arguments for that were in chapters 3 and 4 and I return to that general consideration in the remaining chapters of this book. If my arguments concerning religion are valid, and if I have got my facts roughly right, where I make factual claims, the question still arises whether the liberal conception of reasonableness is adequate to make either such a case or to provide, along, of course, with other considerations, any other cases of sound social critique. Does it yield, as I claim, some substantive normative standards that have a good claim to being objective? When push comes to shove, is it that we just appeal to a liberal conception here such that at best we could show, internal to liberalism, that certain views were more reasonable than others, but we could never show that liberalism itself was more reasonable than nonliberal views without begging the question by just appealing to what liberals in fact accept and no doubt on reflection would continue to accept? Is it the case that all we can say, with any objectivity, is that liberals have their culture and its institutions, but that both historically and actually at present there are about in the world alternative cultures with their distinctive institutions and that's that? Is it the case that we can have no non-question-begging way of claiming that one of these social orders is better—more reasonable—than another? Is our conception of reasonability so *internal* to a given *Weltanschauung* that we can have nothing objective to say here? Is our conception of reasonability in reality little more than a device for cheerleading for liberalism?

The liberal conception of reasonableness I have articulated is indeed a conception of reasonableness for liberal persons. It is, that is, a liberal person's conception of reasonableness. It fits very well with the whole liberal *Weltanschauung*. But, to repeat, does it give us any grounds for believing it to be the most reasonable thing, or even a reasonable thing, where we have a choice in the matter, whether or not to be liberal persons? Perhaps it would be more reasonable, or at least better—though certainly not in the liberal sense of "reasonable"—to become Sunni Muslim *taibaan* or conservative, Orthodox Jews or Pat Robertson-type Christians, in all these instances, by doing so, becoming fundamentalists to the core? Have we been able to show that any person, liberal or not, if she would be clearmindedly maximally reasonable, will try to be a reasonable *liberal* person? Have we at best established only that, if we *want* to be liberal persons—have a *pro-attitude* toward being liberal persons—we will try to be reasonable in the liberal way of conceiving of what it is to be reasonable? But if not, then not; and, given that, that there will be no showing that to be reasonable *sans phrase* we should be liberal persons, reasonable in the liberal's sense of what it is to be reasonable. Indeed, perhaps there is no coherent conception of being reasonable *sans phrase*? Perhaps the question I am trying to ask cannot be coherently put? But then is it just a matter of some people being socialized into being liberals and some not and there is the end of it? The rest is sound and fury signifying nothing? There is no higher perch from which—in accordance with which—we can non-question-beggingly assess things here?

I do not think we are so stuck with a liberal ideology of reasonableness, for we can appeal to bootstrapping arguments here to move from the more general conception of the reasonable—the old-as-Socrates conception—to the liberal conception with the help of some plausible factual beliefs and a few widely shared—widely shared not only in a liberal ethos but beyond it as well—moral truisms, themselves not dependent on the liberal conception of reasonability.

I will now illustrate what I have in mind. *Fundamentalist* views, whether Jewish, Christian, or Muslim, are not reasonable views, even on the more general, more culturally universal, conception of the reasonable—the old-as-Socrates one I initially stated—to say nothing of the liberal conception of reasonableness. (I should add, parenthetically, but I think crucially all the same, that for the arguments I made about religion and reasonableness only the general conception of reasonability, and not the distinctively liberal one, is needed. It is, for the arguments about morality and politics, that the liberal conception is also required. It is there where we need the bootstrapping argument.) Reasonable people, to just stick, for now, with the general conception, are open-minded; they are willing to seriously consider the views of others; they seek to avoid dogmatism, are willing to discuss differences, to see things not only from their own perspective but from the perspectives of others, and they are willing to weigh judiciously the pros and cons of the issues. Fundamentalists will not do any of these things. God has spoken to them and given them the Ultimate Truth about life, about how people are to live, and about how things should be ordered. They claim that they have a Divine Scripture (a Holy Writ) which, unerringly and utterly infallibly, gives them *The Truth*. They further claim that God speaks to them in such a way that there can be no controversy about whether it is God that is speaking, about what God says or about what, concerning such matters, they are to think or what they are to do, and, more generally, about how people are to live. People who doubt these things are deluded and corrupted by sin. Their voices are not to be heard. Indeed, some fundamentalists will even hold that they are anathema. The "ultimate truth of life," fundamentalists believe, has been infallibly revealed to them, as children of God, by God himself.

Such views are unreasonable views. They are unreasonable views, given the very plain meaning of what it is to be reasonable, *both* on the general conception and on the more specific and *perhaps* ideologically skewed liberal conception of reasonable views. Of course, fundamentalists—or at least not characteristically—will not say or think their views are unreasonable. That is perhaps something that no one will seriously say of himself or at least say of himself full stop. But their actions and expressed beliefs show that, given the plain meaning of "reasonable" that we have specified, these views are unreasonable. This is so, even if we, as I do here, so as to not beg any questions, limit ourselves to the general conception.

Such fundamentalists, where they are adults and live in a modern culture, where they can be aware of alternatives, are being unreasonable in having such commitments and their views are unreasonable. They are being unreasonable *sans phrase* or full stop. We, to repeat, are not using "reasonable" in making such an argument according to what may be a liberal ideology, but in the way it is more generally used (the old-as-Socrates view). If we try to stand outside of that, we will lose any understanding of what "reasonable" is, for this is part of what its sense is in the language-games we play with "reasonable." (If it is said that in the above characterization I have made out fundamentalists to be worse than they are, then, *if that is true*, I would say that anyone having the views I ascribed, however mistakenly, to fundamentalists would have unreasonable views. We still have a determinate and unproblematic application of what it is to be unreasonable. Even if, contrary to what I believe, it lacks an exemplification, it very well could have one. And that after all, is what is most crucially involved. Let sociologists dispute, if indeed dispute is called for, whether I have got my characterization of fundamentalism right.)

Starting with this general conception, and thinking through, with some attention to the facts, what it is in some detail and in practice to be open-minded, nonfanatical, weigh the pros and cons, see all sides of the argument or issue, take into consideration the perspectives of other people (sometimes very different people), and the like, we will be led, if we think carefully and take these matters to heart, from the general conception to the liberal conception of reasonableness or at least to something rather like it. That is where, and how, the bootstrapping argument comes in.

I think that one of the reasons that there is a reluctance on our part to say in many circumstances at least that a person is unreasonable or that some of his views are unreasonable is that to do so is to make a very harsh criticism of that person. The very duty of *civility,* that Rawls so much stresses, something which is very important for us as liberals (indeed, I would say for civilized human beings), and, which is tied up, at least if we are liberals, with our own extended conception of what it is to be reasonable, militates against our making such ascriptions or at least it makes us very reluctant to make them. We will, in many instances, worry about whether in doing so we are ourselves failing to be consistently reasonable. We will worry about whether we ourselves, if we make such harsh judgments about other people, are not being in some sense fanatical ourselves. If we are, then we will, of course, have hoisted ourselves by our own petard and will stand convicted, at least in our own eyes, whether anyone else says so or not, of being unreasonable in calling another person or that person's beliefs or point of view unreasonable. So, at the very least, we need to be cautious and charitable here. But that itself has its limits. When someone proclaims that he has *The Truth,* that he does not want to hear what anyone else has to say, for his insight (thinking it is from God) is beyond all controversy, then he is being unreasonable and, in many circumstances, civility or not, it is evasive on our part not to politely, but firmly, say so.

Given the liberal conception of reasonability that I articulated—a conception also held by John Rawls, Brian Barry, and Joshua Cohen—there is no need, as I have remarked, to accommodate the unreasonable. We need not, and indeed should not, adjust our conception of justice or our principles of justice so that they can be supported by an overlapping consensus that will have as a part of that consensus those unreasonable views or any unreasonable views. There is, that is, no need to accommodate our conception of justice or principles of justice to unreasonable views. To alter our conception of justice or social norms to accommodate unreasonable views would be giving in to *power*; it would be wrongly to adjust our principles in the face of unreasoned and unreasoning power. In so resisting unreasonable claims or demands, we are not being ourselves intolerant or fanatical—simply meeting power with power—but are refusing to give into those who fanatically insist on having their way without reason. We remain open to their *arguments,* to hearing their *case* for what they believe should obtain. But they have to make out their case by an appeal to what can reasonably be defended or at least what they believe can reasonably be defended. We should not just give into their demands or to assent to their views just on their, without their even attempting to give reasons, proclaiming and insisting that they just are right and that what they say must be done or adhered to. It is not us who are being fanatical in not budging here in resisting such demands, but they who are being fanatical, and thus unreasonable, in making them and trying to insist on them.

So we can see in the case of fundamentalism and, at least sometimes, the Religious Right as well, where people on the Religious Right differ, if they differ, from fundamentalists, that our conception of reasonableness can serve in a nonideological way as a critical instrument to critique such views and to argue for setting them aside. As we saw in chapter 4, such a critique can be extended, though, of course, in a far more controversial way, to such Calvinist views as those of Alvin Plantinga, when he claims, following John Calvin, to have an awareness of God, the awareness of which is *beyond controversy.*[25] However, the case for using reasonableness as a critical instrument is less clear in other instances.

Let me illustrate that. I, like Rawls and Barry, have argued for an egalitarian conception of social justice. But it is not clear that establishing it can be made out on grounds of reasonableness *alone.* There have been, and still are, illiberal societies with hierarchical and aristocratic theories of justice and with philosophers and other intellectuals articulating conceptions for their defense, which are quite different from liberal conceptions. These intellectuals are sometimes thoroughly reasonable by our *general* conception of reasonable. They can be, and sometimes are, open-minded, unfanatical, undogmatic, open to the examination of evidential claims, willing to discuss differences, to listen to others and to take their views seriously, to change their minds, to be willing, and sometimes even able, to see things from the perspectives of others, and to judiciously weigh the pros and cons of the issues. On this relatively thick, but still unproblematical and uncontroversial conception of reasonableness, they can be thoroughly reasonable and their views can be reasonable. But they are views which firmly support an illiberal society.

Such people believe that, if we can gain a clear and unsentimental view of human nature and the way a stable and well-ordered society works, we will see that all people do not have the same moral and intellectual capacities: we will see that they are not all equally autonomous or equally capable of acting intelligently and reflectively in the ordering of their lives, to say nothing of participating in the ordering of social life. This being so, a really well-ordered and just society, which engenders respect for principles of justice, will allot appropriate privileges and distinctive constitutional powers to a group of superior and discerning persons. These superior people will stand above the great mass of inferior people and determine how the social order is to be structured so that, the various orders of human beings (the people of gold, of silver, and of brass), and indeed for their own good, will have their appropriate stations and duties. There are some things—including some moral, political, and religious things—that the vast majority of people are not even capable of questioning and must just accept on the say so of their betters. This aristocratic conception—very distant from our conceptions of justice—could be argued for or urged in a temperate, tolerant, and soft-spoken manner and with perfect civility, though no doubt rather paternalistically so. Not all conservatives— in spite of what is the usual run—need be shouting moralists.

Given the general conception of reasonableness we have articulated, such conservatives can be, and sometimes are, thoroughly reasonable persons. But not, it is natural to respond, on the thicker liberal conception of reasonableness that we have articulated. To this, it should in turn be responded, that many (but by no means all) of the elements of the liberal conception would apply to them as well, would, that is, be a part of their understanding of reasonableness. Moreover, the parts of the liberal conception which would enable us to say that they are unreasonable are themselves controversial elements where "reasonable" may be, in effect, *persuasively* defined and may very well function as an ideological instrument for liberalism rather than a critical instrument to be used in critiquing society.

Let me give that substance. The liberal conception has it that reasonable people will desire a social world where people will stand in relations of freedom and equality. In ordering our social world, we must, they believe, order it with that in mind. We must, if we are to be reasonable in the liberal sense of "reasonable," take it that all human beings have equal moral standing and that our political arrangements must acknowledge that and effectively support it, if they are to be just. Reasonable persons—that is reasonable liberal persons—will believe in *moral* equality, namely, they will believe that the life of everyone matters and matters equally. Liberals, whether they are libertarians, social democrats, or socialists (the spectrum runs from Robert Nozick and David Gauthier to G.A. Cohen and Jon Elster) will believe that, as will communists as well. But nonliberal aristocrats will not believe that, but will regard those elements of the liberal and communist conception of reasonableness as a moralistic and sentimental intrusion that has nothing to do with reasonableness. It is not their intelligence or open-minded reflectiveness, such conservatives will maintain, that leads such people to desire a social world where all people have equal moral standing: standing in relations of freedom and equality, but their liberal or communist *sentiments* and *sympathies*. It is a cheat—a bit of self-deception—to believe that reasonableness requires that egalitarian commitment. Such egalitarian views, to switch to my own way of looking at things, may be—indeed I think are—*consistent* with reasonableness, but they are not *required* by it.

I think what this shows is that morality, including the claims of social justice, cannot be derived from the general conception of reasonableness *alone*, or even from such reasonableness plus a good knowledge of the nonmoral facts (if that is not pleonastic). *We can no more get morality out of reasonableness, than we can get it out of rationality.* Or, put more accurately (though more pedantically), since reasonability or reasonableness are themselves normative and moral conceptions, from those distinctive moral notions, where it is the general conception of reasonableness that is at issue, we cannot derive what justice requires or what rights we have or how society is to be ordered. Hobbes, and in our time David Gauthier, have made hard-nosed efforts to get a rational kernel of morality out of pure practical rationality. But at best what has been established is that ethical egoism (better *so-called* ethical egoism) is ruled out. But there remains before us the completely open rational choice of a full range (perhaps *the* full range) of moralities and moral views. Moreover, the falsity or incoherence of "ethical egoism" does not show that *personal egoism*—the prudent amoralism of Hobbes's foole—is in all circumstances irrational. Reasonability, as distinct from rationality, already itself in part a moral notion, looks like a better candidate than rationality, for grounding morality. But, as we have seen, hierarchical conceptions of justice and liberal egalitarian ones, while in deep conflict, can both be reasonable. Unless we are already going beyond the general (though still thick) conception of reasonability and are taking the liberal conception of reasonability, already carrying, with that very taking, determinate moral choices, we cannot, just by being reasonable, justify opting for a liberal social order rather than an illiberal hierarchical social order. We cannot justify a commitment to egalitarianism or even a commitment to the weaker notion of *moral* equality (something even Nozick buys into) by an appeal to reasonableness *alone*, unless we widen the conception of reasonableness to include the full, thick liberal conception of reasonableness. But then we have already built that very egalitarian notion into our conception of reasonableness. We have so *persuasively* defined "reasonable" that many plainly reasonable people will no longer be said to be reasonable. But nothing will be established or gained by such word-magic.

I am not trying to set reason and passion in opposition to each other. And I am not trying to collapse the distinction either or to give one precedence or authority over the other. Wide reflective equilibrium appeals to both. Within the holistic, largely coherentist method that is reflective equilibrium, both what it is reasonable to believe and to do and our sympathies (most particularly our considered, reflectively sustainable, sympathies) play an important role. In getting our conception of justice, and of morality more generally, into wide reflective equilibrium, we need to get clear about what is the case (get our views in line with how things are), judiciously weigh the reasons pro and con for claiming things should be ordered in one way rather than another, and to get as clear as we can about how it is that we really *feel* about the various ways that social life may be. We need, as we have seen, to get these, and other matters as well, into a coherent conception. Wide reflective equilibrium is a largely proceduralist form of justification. Whatever considered judgments we can get into a wide reflective equilibrium are the considered judgments for that time that we take to be justified considered judgments. What we shall take to be just, to be good, to be rational or reasonable is what we can get into wide reflective equilibrium, though that will always be a *for-a-time-judgment*, for reflective equilibria will continually be upset and new ones forged. But, in making these judgments, we have in hand, though perhaps not terribly well understood, concepts of justice, reasonability, rationality, goodness, and the like. With them in mind, we seek, in the face of what we now plausibly believe and honestly and nonevasively feel, to forge a coherent conception of things that will articulate for us what we take it to be justified to do and to believe. Considerations of reasonability are central here, but so is the matter of our human sympathies and sensibilities. However, none of these considerations stand alone or have absolute priority over the other considerations. Nothing, neither reason, nor sentiment, nor the facts of the matter, nor "intuitive insight," nor interests, nor needs is "the real foundation" of morality. Morality, without being arbitrary or just conventional, can have no "real foundations." What we have instead is the holistic conception of wide reflective equilibrium, itself filling out, exemplifying, and in a certain way constituting reasonableness. There is nothing—no one sort of thing—that all of morality, or all the nonutterly conventional part of morality, stands on or takes as its basis. We can say, as Stuart Hampshire does, who is as holistic as Rawls or Quine, that "moral philosophy . . . is the inquiry into reasonable foundations for morality. . . ."[26] This, from the philosopher who said Rawls's account contains a misguided rationalism, is his metaphorical and nonpedantic way of saying that moral philosophy seeks, or should seek, to ascertain the rationale of our moral conceptions—to see that and how they are not just a chaos and a jumble—by seeking to perspicuously display how our moral conceptions and convictions fit into a coherent whole with the rest of what we reasonably believe, feel, and know. In seeking to so frame, or to so pattern, things, considerations about what is reasonable, and how one must be to be reasonable, are vital matters and are matters, as I have sought to show in this introduction, which have some determinate content. Appealing to reason is not everything or the rock bottom of everything—there is no "rock bottom of everything"—but it is not a mere expressive-evocative, rhetorical, or ideological flourish either. It is one, and a valuable one, of our critical tools. But, without a Humean or Smithian acknowledgement of the importance of our moral sympathies, that critical tool will not take us as far as most philosophers with their penchant for rationalism are wont to believe.

NOTES

1. Terence Penelhum, "Comments and Responses," in *Faith Skepticism and Personal Identity,* ed. J. A. Meynell and J. J. MacIntosh (Calgary, Alberta: University of Calgary Press, 1994), 235–36.

2. C. B. Martin, *Religious Belief* (Ithaca, N.Y.: Cornell University Press, 1959); Ronald W. Hepburn, *Christianity and Paradox* (London: C. A. Watts and Co. Ltd., 1958); and Kai Nielsen, *Skepticism* (New York: St. Martin's Press, 1973).

3. Antony Flew, "Introduction" to *David Hume: Writings on Religion,* ed. Antony Flew (La Salle, Ill.: Open Court, 1992), vii–xi; and Terence Penelham, *David Hume* (West Lafayette, Ind.: Purdue University Press, 1992), 187.

4. Geoffrey Scott, *Ethics After Babel* (Boston, Mass.: Beacon Press, 1988), 109–23.

5. Rodger Beehler, "Religion v. Militant Atheism," 131–42; Rodger Beehler, "Hounding Heaven: A Reply to Kai Nielsen," 159–66; and Barry Allen, "Atheism, Relativism, Enlightenment and Truth," all in *Studies in Religion* 23, no. 2 (1994). I respond to Allen and Beehler in chapter 16 and see, as well, my distinct response to Beehler in my "God and the Crisis of Modernity," *Studies in Religion* 23, no. 2 (1994): 143–158.

6. John Rawls, *Political Liberalism* (New York: Columbia University Press, 1993). See also, for an extensive utilization of the concept, his "Reply to Habermas," *Journal of Philosophy* 92, no. 3 (March 1995): 132–80.

7. Stuart Hampshire, "Liberalism: The New Twist," *New York Review of Books* (August 12, 1993): 45.

8. Ibid.

9. Ibid.

10. Alan Gibbard, "Constructing Justice," *Philosophy and Public Affairs* 20, no. 1 (Summer 1991): 264–79.

11. On thick contextuality see Michael Walzer, *Thick and Thin* (Notre Dame, Ind.: University of Notre Dame Press, 1994). See also his *Interpretation and Social Criticism* (Cambridge, Mass.: Havard University Press, 1987).

12. Thomas McCarthy, "Kantian Constructivism and Reconstruction: Rawls and Habermas in Dialogue," *Ethics* 105, no. 1 (October 1994): 62.

13. Walzer, *Thick and Thin*.

14. There is no doubt some redundancy in the lists. Rather than to make the lists as short as possible, I sought, by tolerating different phrasings, though with differing nuances, of what may come, in some instances, to much the same thing, to capture in its thickness what liberal reasonability comes to.

15. Rawls, *Political Liberalism*, 50.

16. Ibid., 49–50. Rawls follows Thomas Scanlon here.

17. Ibid., 43.

18. Ibid., 53–54.

19. Ibid., 123, 157, 163.

20. Ibid., 217.

21. Ibid., 58.

22. Joshua Cohen, "Moral Pluralism and Political Consensus," in *The Idea of Democracy*, ed. David Copp et al. (Cambridge, England: Cambridge University Press, 1993), 282.

23. Ibid., 284.

24. Ibid., 285; Rawls, *Political Liberalism*, 217–18.

25. Alvin Plantinga quotes with approval John Calvin's remark:" 'There is within the human mind, and indeed by natural instinct, an awareness of divinity.' *This we take to the beyond controversy*" (italics added). Alvin Plantinga, "Belief in God," in *Perspectives in Philosophy*, ed. Michael Boylan (Fort Worth, Tex.: Harcourt Brace Jovanovich, 1993). See John Calvin, *Institutes of the Christian Religion*, trans. Ford Lewis Battles (Philadelphia: Westminster Press, 1960), bk. 1, ch. 3, 43–44.

26. Stuart Hampshire, "A New Philosophy of the Just Society," *New York Review of Books* 18, no. 3 (February 24, 1972): 39.

Chapter Fourteen

Perceiving God

I

There are many (including myself) who believe that where the God in question is the God of developed Judeo-Christianity and Islam, no experiential cognition of God is a real possibility. Anything that could be perceived would not be the God of those traditions. William Alston carefully argues that this is not so.* He seeks "to show that it is possible that in at least some of the cases in which people take themselves to be directly aware of God, they are in fact perceiving God."[1] He sets out "a minimally controversial view of the basic nature of sense perception" and then tries, for the alleged awareness of God, "to show that it is possible that the experiences in question (or some of them) should exhibit the same generic structure . . ." (50). As careful as Alston's argumentation is, I do not think he has made his case, or has even come very close to doing so. Indeed, I think he has set himself an impossible task. Yet, to my knowledge at least, his account is the most careful and sophisticated on record of such an endeavor. Its failure, if indeed it is a failure, would be of not inconsiderable significance.

I shall follow out Alston's arguments, critiquing them as I go along. I shall conclude by pulling the strands together and drawing a few lessons. He, as we have noted, wants to show, or at least go some way toward showing, "that a genuine experiential cognition of God is a real possibility . . . if God exists" (25). Against chaps like myself, he argues that the very idea of such cog-

---

*Parenthetical references in the chapter refer to William P. Alston, "The Perception of God," *Philosophical Topics* 16, no. 2 (Fall 1988): 23–52.

nition, while not without its difficulties, is still intelligible and, more than that, coherent (25). When he speaks of a God who is supposedly so cognized, he means minimally "a supreme or ultimate personal agent that acts in the light of knowledge, purposes, and intentions" (25). What he wants to establish is that at least in some instances it is not incoherent for a person to believe that God is presenting Himself to that person's experience. These will include experiences (putative experiences) of God doing something vis-à-vis human beings. This includes people who are aware (think they are aware) of God as speaking or otherwise communicating a message to them. But, perhaps even more basically, or at least paradigmatically, there are the claimed situations in which people are just experiencing God as being present and displaying certain features. At least this is the claim.

There are many types of alleged experience of God, including the type reported by William James as follows: "God was present though invisible; he fell under no one of my senses. Yet my consciousness perceived him" (23). But Alston wisely concentrates on, given the extensive problematicity of the above, those experiences in which the awareness of God is mediated by sensory content (26). He is concerned with "those experiences in which it seems that God 'appears' or 'presents Himself' to one as so and so."[2]

II

I will first describe Alston's minimally controversial account of the nature of sense perception. "What is distinctive about the perception of something in the physical environment," Alston remarks, "is that it involves a 'presentation' or a 'givenness' of the object to experience, to consciousness where the object appears (looks, feels, . . .) as bearing certain phenomenal qualities (configurations of colored shapes, soundings of varying pitches and intensities, rough or smooth, hot and cold, and so on)" (28). This is what gets added when, for example, one first just thinks about a cloud or a face, but then after that one opens one's eyes and looks at the cloud or face. "This is what, most basically, distinguishes perceiving an object from thinking about it, or reasoning about it" (28). For me to see an apple is for me to have the apple presented to my awareness as bearing certain sensory qualities.

The kind of alleged direct awareness of God that Alston is interested in and that, arguably, is the central paradigm of such awareness, if there is any, is what he calls *mediated immediacy*. In ordinary sense-perception cases, mediated immediacy comes to this: "ordinarily normal vision of objects directly before one's eyes" (29). My awareness that I am writing this with a pencil, to make clear what this comes to by a translation into the concrete, is mediated by a state of visual consciousness of which I am in turn aware in a different way, but of which I am not, unless "I deliberately attend to it, ordinarily focally aware, and which is distinct from the external physical object that I perceive" (30). In applying this to an awareness of God (if such there be), people, having the experience, are prepared to say that they are "*directly aware of the presence and/or activity of God*" (30). Here there is the undergoing of a distinctive state of consciousness through which—by virtue of which—we take ourselves to be directly aware of God. In being directly aware of an apple or of a tree, we are aware of it by means of our senses, of which in turn we may in the perception of the apple or the tree, not be directly aware, or attend or advert to at all. Similarly, a direct awareness of God must come to us by means of some state of consciousness that we may in turn not be aware of or be attending or adverting to at all. We have or are in a certain state of consciousness, but in our perception of God, as in our perception of the tree, we typically are not at all aware, or are only peripherally aware, of that state of consciousness that we are in.

On Alston's conception, "God will have to be directly presented to the subject's experience as bearing certain phenomenal qualities" (31–32). But to be a direct awareness of God an experience must meet another crucial requirement: in all cases of object perception, the object must make a causal contribution to the occurrence of the experience in question. What we need to ascertain is whether the putative experience of God exhibits "the basic phenomenological structure of sense perception of objects" (35). People, who have these religious experiences, do typically take themselves "to have been in an experiential cognitive relation to God" that has that structure. God presents Himself as goodness and power and as communicating certain messages. Angela of Faligno, for example, "identifies her state as one of directly 'seeing' God, rather than as being filled with effects of God's activity" (37). It is this claim that I think makes no sense and concerning which Alston tries, knowing how problematic it is, to tease out a sense. He seeks to make what appears at least to be incoherent, coherent.

III

So much for how people claiming to have religious experience tend to see things. Still, as Alston remarks, an individual's own understanding of his or her experience should not be regarded as infallible. (Here he is, reasonably I believe, far more concessive to modernity, in arguing from religious experience, than such eminent predecessors as Friedrich Schleiermacher or Rudolph Otto or, for that matter, John Calvin, who all claim that religious experience gives us an indubitable grasp of God.) It is, as Alston goes on to remark, "conceivable that one should suppose that a purely affective experience or a strongly held conviction should involve the experiential presentation of God when it doesn't, especially if there is a strong need or longing for such a direct awareness" (37). In other words, powerful affective dispositions can lead one unwittingly to cook the books.

Alston is aware that there is a whole barrage of conceptual problems about whether any such direct cognition of God is even possible or intelligible. The very idea of an "infinite Creator and Lord of the universe being directly perceived" is not, to understate it, a pellucid one. Still, Alston rather lightly puts this issue aside, remarking that it involves considerations concerning the *ontology* and not the *phenomenology* of the experience. He claims that what is at issue here is the phenomenological character of the experience and not whether the agent having the experience has got the ontology right, to wit, whether she actually has an experience of God. Phenomenologically, one can be directly aware of a unicorn or King Arthur even while being mistaken about the existence of unicorns or King Arthur. What one, in such a circumstance, is directly aware of is not what one thinks it is, rather, one is directly aware of something one mistakenly identifies as a unicorn or as King Arthur. But—or so it seems to me—that is not to the point in the case of God, for we could not phenomenologically, or otherwise, be directly aware of what it is not even possible to be directly aware of. Such, however, is the challenge being made to claims of religious experience. Thus, to translate into the concrete again and to argue first by analogy, if someone says they saw a colorless, shapeless figure we know that they could not have seen such a figure any more than someone can draw a round square. *This is not a matter of ontology but of what makes sense.* What we have in such instances is an incoherent attempt at a phenomenological characterization of an experience. As we shall see (*pace* Alston)—or so at least my argument shall go—perceiving God is in the same boat. God is an infinite individual transcendent to the universe, but such a being could not possibly be directly experienced any more than someone could draw a round square or *see* a shapeless, colorless figure. It is not, Alston to the contrary notwithstanding, at all like whether someone could see what appears to be a unicorn. The issue in the case of God, as in my two examples, is logical or conceptual and not ontological. Trudeau may talk faster than Clark, but he cannot sleep faster than Clark. If nonetheless Trudeau reports phenomenologically that he really does or that he now sleeps faster than he used to, we will not accept his "reports" at face value, for it makes no sense to say that y sleeps faster than x or that y now sleeps faster than y formerly did. Similarly, it makes no sense to speak of perceiving an infinite individual transcendent to the universe.

IV

My remarks about what is conceptually possible may seem to some to be a little too quick. (However, too quick or not, if they are justified they undermine Alston's central claims.) We will return to that issue in section 7. But for the nonce let us put it aside and continue to conduct the argument as Alston does. Let us try to see, the above notwithstanding, if we could be directly aware of God as bearing certain phenomenal qualities. By hypothesis, these qualities are not sensory. But then what could they be? How could they then be phenomenal qualities? We have—or so at least it seems—no understanding of what it is for something to be a phenomenal quality, which is not a sensory quality. Have those claiming direct awareness of God given us any intelligible possibilities as to their identity? The trouble here is compounded by the fact that the qualities God is thought to have, and of which we are said to be directly aware, are not phenomenal qualities. They are things like power, love, goodness, beauty, plenitude. God, that is, is not present in experience in the same way that something is experienced as red, round, acrid, or bitter. But why, Alston asks, must one be directly aware of only qualities of that latter type? Why is it not possible to be *directly aware* of something being powerful, supremely good, and infinitely strong? The answer often given is that such characteristics cannot be read off the phenomenal surface of experience like something looking red or feeling soft. Where we are sticking to the phenomenal quality, as when we say something looks red, we are simply recording the qualitative distinctiveness of the way a thing visually appears, and that is all. We are saying nothing, the claim goes, about its causal powers, its entanglements with other things. But in actual life when we say how something looks or otherwise appears, we typically do not restrict ourselves to just recording some phenomenal distinctiveness of the appearance. Sometimes, to take one of several possibilities, we are making comparisons. If I say that the mango looks yellow to me now, that could be to say that the mango looks to me now as a yellow mango would under normal conditions. But that is not to make a phenomenal report, and I am not using "yellow" here simply as a vehicle for a phenomenal concept. I am, rather, saying something about how something looks under *normal* conditions. I am making a comparison. There are similar doxastic and epistemic uses of "yellow" that are not purely phenomenal. These are, along with the comparative one, different ways of conceptualizing or identifying appearances.

However, Alston, with his characteristic candor, makes an admission damaging to the analogy with God when he says that, for the various ways of conceptualizing appearings, "a phenomenal concept is, so to say, always in the background even if not explicitly employed" (39). When I say that the mango will look yellow under normal conditions, "I am really presupposing that there is some qualitative distinctiveness to the appearance that could be captured by a phenomenal concept, even though I am using no such concept at the moment" (39). This, Alston stresses, is something important to note (39).

When believers make claims to a direct awareness of God, they typically do not appeal to phenomenal concepts, but to such concepts as love, goodness, or power. But we have seen that in many, indeed, in typical, ordinary nonreligious contexts, phenomenal concepts are not appealed to either. So there is, in this respect, nothing anomalous in the believer's direct reports. They are not reporting how God appears to their experience by using phenomenal concepts but, as I just remarked, that is also typically true in many nonreligious cases. Believers will say that they are "aware of God as presenting the kind of appearance it would be reasonable to expect a supremely powerful (good, loving, beautiful) being to present. And so from the premise that they are not using phenomenal concepts, it does not follow that they are not reporting how God appears to their experience" (41). Still, in speaking of power (plainly a nonphenomenal concept), we all the same assume—and this is crucial—that the perceiver knows what power or the exercise of power looks like. But where this is seriously questioned an appeal to some phenomenal concepts emerges, for they are concepts that Alston says must *always* be there in the background for us to be able directly to perceive anything. They are essential for us to find our feet here; that is, for us to achieve an understanding of power, or its exercise, there must be phenomenal concepts in the background. What are "the basic phenomenal qualities of the sphere of divine perception, analogous to color and shape for the visual modality, temperature, and texture for the tactile, and so on" (41–42)? Alston flatly admits that he, and we as well, "are quite incapable of enumerating the basic phenomenal qualities of which 'divine phenomena' are configurations" (42). To explain *why* this is so (*pace* Alston) is of no help, given *the fact, admitted by him, that it is so*, because in all those situations where we can be tolerably confident that we have a direct awareness of something, there is there to orient us this background of sensory awareness. If we do not have this in the case of God, or any other case, we are at sea. We have noted already that Alston insists on this sensory background in all other cases. How then can he believe that without it we know where we are vis-à-vis God? Why should we, when the case of God is so exceptional—so radically different—believe that there even can be anything like perceiving God?

There is a further worry. Where we try to supply something like the sensory background for a direct awareness of God, what we get, it seems at least, are wholly *affective* qualities, namely, "various ways the subject is *feeling* in reaction to what the subject takes to be the presence of God" (42, emphasis added). But feelings are not thought to be the basis of a direct knowledge of, or some mode of direct cognition of, anything other than feelings or conative dispositions. We do not *directly* cognize nonfeeling states *via feelings*. That I feel sad at the thought of the demise of working-class culture or depressed by male violence to women does not mean that I have by my sadness or depression gained an understanding of these phenomena or some added direct awareness of the phenomena, though my affective responses presuppose that I have in some other way some understanding of the phenomena. But the affective response itself is not a further element in that understanding by a kind of knowledge by acquaintance. Feeling sad gives me an understanding of sadness; feeling dependent may give me an understanding of what it is to be dependent (in both cases an affective state), but not of an utterly other, totally nondependent being transcendent to the world.

Alston resists the idea that restriction of phenomenal content in such cases to affect rules "out the possibility of an objective reality's appearing to the subject therein" (43). He rightly notes that affective qualities are subjective in a way similar to sensory qualities or (if you will) to nonaffective sensory qualities. But that subjectivity is not what is at issue here. What is at issue, and what is to the point here, comes out in the following contrasts. That I see the blood on the floor is one thing, that I am shocked by it is another; that I feel the green mold under the carpet is one thing, that I feel disgusted by it is another; that I smell the rotting whale on the beach is one thing, that I am nauseated by it is another. One—the seeing (tactile), feeling, smelling—is a form of knowledge by direct awareness. The other is an *affective response* to that knowledge, but it is not itself a new form of direct knowledge of anything other than feelings or conative dispositions. If "the whole phenomenal content of the experience of God" is affective, we have very good reason indeed (*pace* Alston) for doubting that we can possibly have a "veridical perception of God" (43). But it seems at least to be just that.

V

Alston, mistakenly thinking he has gone around the above problems, then says something that seems at least to square badly with remarks made earlier in "The Perception of God," namely, remarks about (1) phenomenal concepts always being at least in the background and (2) of there being no possibility of direct awareness of God without them (39). He says in a later passage that "one does not have to be able to isolate and identify basic phenomenal qualities in order to have experience and use it as a vehicle of perception" (44). I think—and if this is so it defuses the conflict—that in speaking *here* of phenomenal concepts not always being in the background, he is thinking of the old reductionist program of analyzing more complex structures into their constituent elements of phenomenal qualities; that is, he is thinking of the old phenomenalist program. That, as the history of the critique of reductionism has made clear, is surely a justified critique.[3] No such reduction can be carried out. But from that it does not follow that we would understand what the direct awareness of anything could come to without understanding something of the sensory awareness that the perceiver would have to have to be aware of anything. "Children," no doubt, "learn to recognize people, buildings and toys without having any conception of the way in which sensory appearances of things are built up from elementary phenomenal qualities" (39). But Janet could hardly learn to recognize Uncle Ben without coming to recognize that man with the large red nose, the hoarse voice, the dark horn-rimmed glasses, the whiskey breath, and the like: that is, without having certain sensory experiences. Some such sensory acquaintance is going to be necessary for her to be able to recognize Uncle Ben at all. (If this be empiricism, make the most of it. Sometimes empiricism, properly constrained, is neither a metaphysical view nor an ideology, but just solid common sense.) She, of course, does not have to have a *theory* or even a *conception* of these sensory experiences, but she needs to have them to be aware directly of anything at all, whether it is Uncle Ben, yellow mangos, Socratic philosophers, or God. Yet in the alleged awareness of God case, all we have by way of phenomenal qualities are the *affective reactions* of the putative direct knower. They give us some direct knowledge of the emotional life of the alleged knower, but nothing at all in the way of knowledge of God; they do not show that we are or could be directly aware of God. We need not say that "human sense perception constitutes *a priori* limits on what is possible by way of direct experiences of objective beings by cognitive subjects" (44). There is no need to employ any conception of the *a priori* at all, to say nothing of attempting to set *a priori* limits. (It is not clear in any event what that would come to.) But when we reflect on what perception comes to—where, that is, we know our way around with such things, including talk of them—we realize that, aside (perhaps) from our awareness of ourselves, being directly aware of things involves certain sensory qualities: sensory experiences in the background such as being aware peripherally or focally of some sensory characteristics. If there is to be any literal encountering or direct awareness of God, this must be in a visible, auditory, or other sensible form.[4] But this cannot be, given what God is, and thus we have no understanding of what it would be to encounter God. Some people talk of a nonsensory direct experience of God, but no more sense has been given to that than has been given to my claim that I sleep faster than Norman Malcolm. (There are indeed mystical experiences but whether they are cognitive is another thing again.[5])

VI

Near the end of his "The Perception of God," Alston asks a question that I have in various writings centered some considerable of my attention on:

"How does a person," he asks, "identify what is appearing to her at a given moment as God, the source of all being other than Himself, judge and redeemer of mankind?" (47).[6] Alston tries to deflect that question by trotting out a general epistemological/conceptual consideration. It is not necessary for an experience's being a case of perceiving God that the subject know, or even be able to tell, that it is God she is perceiving. This point holds quite generally for perception: "I can be seeing the Louvre while supposing that it is the *Palais Royale*" (47). But if in directly perceiving God the perceiver is not cognizant that it is God she is perceiving, the fact (if it is a fact) that she in fact, though unwittingly, is perceiving God is cold comfort to her and to us. We would like to know whether we can *sometimes* ascertain, albeit fallibilistically, that it is God we are perceiving. We would also like to know whether our perceiving God can provide us with a justified belief that God exists. So we should not avoid the question of "whether, and how, one can identify what is appearing as God"[7] (46). But what Alston utterly fails to do, as far as I can ascertain, is to give us good reasons for believing that anything that *could appear* to us even *could be* the God of the Judeo-Christian-Islamic traditions; that it is even *possible* to perceive such a God.[8] I shall in the next sections give some reasons for believing that no such perception, no such direct awareness, is possible.

VII

Alston makes it clear in *Divine Nature and Human Language* that the conception of God for which he wishes to provide a philosophical elucidation and defense is the God of traditional Judeo-Christianity. He uses techniques of analytical philosophy in carrying out that elucidation and defense of this religious tradition. That is, he uses contemporary analytic techniques to defend traditional Judeo-Christian religious and theological propositions or stances. It is, it should be reiterated, the philosophically (conceptually or cosmologically) at-risk articulations of that tradition that he wishes to defend, and not some pared-down revisionist rewriting of the tradition and its canonical concepts as, say, in the writings of R. B. Braithwaite, R. M. Hare, and D. Z. Phillips, where a shift occurs in the very use of "God," a shift designed to square more readily with modern sensibilities.[9] Alston, by contrast, like Plantinga and Wolterstorff, seeks to deploy, what they take to be, the best techniques of analytic philosophy in defense of *traditional* Christianity, not some revisionist rational reconstruction.[10]

I have maintained against Alston that, given the concept of God embedded in traditional Judeo-Christianity, there is no coherent possibility that the God of that tradition, if He indeed exists or even could exist, could be perceived or be encountered or could be the object of any kind of direct awareness. I shall now make good my promise to more extensively argue that central consideration.

Alston gives no full characterization of the God he claims that some believers at least could possibly perceive, but the God he must be talking about—the God of the developed forms of Judeo-Christianity—is, as we have seen in earlier chapters, to be characterized thus: "A person without a body (that is, a spirit, present everywhere), the creator and sustainer of the universe, able to do anything (that is, omnipotent), knowing all things, perfectly good, a source of moral obligation, immutable, eternal, a necessary being, holy, and worthy of worship."[11]) This is the God of traditional Judaism, Christianity, and Islam. Such a God is a person, though an extraordinary person, for he is also the creator and sustainer of the universe, bodiless (nonmaterial and nonphysical) yet everywhere while still being a nonphysical person who acts in the world; indeed, He is the person who brought the very universe into existence from nothing, yet being the person He is, He, while remaining a person (an individual acting in the world), is an infinite, wholly other individual, transcendent to the very universe itself. This, if such a being could exist, or be a being, that being is a very extraordinary being indeed. It is a conception, to understate it, that, if we attempt to think about it in a literal way, is utterly baffling. It is difficult to see how it could add up to a coherent conception; it is not clear that we can string those words together in such a way so as to make sense.[12]

It is drastically unclear what an infinite bodiless individual could be, to say nothing of an infinite individual who is transcendent to the universe. The first is conceptually opaque, the second adds insult to injury concerning such an opaqueness. But that, all the same, is the God of The Tradition. There could be no literal seeing, perceiving, or encountering of such a being. He is transcendent to the universe and is thus in some sense beyond or outside of the universe itself, but we human beings are in the universe with no conception even of what it would be like to be outside of the universe, or to perceive beyond the universe, or to perceive something outside of the universe (assuming we can give any sense at all to that). Something that is transcendent to the universe could not be seen or be otherwise observed by us (or by anything else in the universe). If a being was seen or otherwise observed, that being would be in the universe, but any being who was in the universe and not transcendent to the universe would thereby not be the God of The Tradition: the God of The Tradition being transcendent to the universe.

Even if we somehow—to me inconceivably—set all that aside, we, God being transcendent to the universe or not, have no coherent conception of what it would be like to see or perceive, in or out of the universe, a bodiless and shapeless (odorless, tasteless) person (even assuming such a conception makes sense). How could we pick out—identify—such a person through observation and thus, distinguishing Him from other persons, locate Him? We could, of course, be directly aware of a discrete embodied individual, even of a rather large individual, only a part of which we could in fact observe at any one time from our position in space-time. (Nobody, as I argued extensively in part 3 of this book, has, or can have, a view from nowhere.) We could make definite observations of certain parts of Him at a given time and then, at a later time, from different positions, make further observations of other parts of him. But for such perceivings to be possible, He must have a body. This, to say something very obvious, is so even if the being is rather large. Large or small, for it to be the case that we could be observing or perceiving Him, He must have a body. For observation to be possible, He must somehow be bounded— even though very large—so that we could have some conception of what it was not, as well as what it was, to be perceiving Him. We need, to be able to perceive Him, to have some conception of what counts as not perceiving Him. But God—this infinite individual—is said to be not only an individual, but everywhere (utterly unbounded); but then there is no possibility of perceiving Him, for we are without a conception of misperceiving Him or seeing something else that is to be contrasted with Him, as when one meets Kohl while searching for Clinton. A bodiless, shapeless, odorless, tasteless person is not a person we could possibly directly perceive or be directly aware of.

When we add omnipresence (being everywhere) and being infinite, we have a conceptual clash with the very notion of a person (an individual). An unbounded, infinite individual is a very curious kind of individual indeed. A "discrete person" seems, at the very least, to be pleonastic.[13] Moreover, with "infinite, omnipresent person," even if we allow such a jumble of words, we have something concerning which we have no conception of what it would be like to observe, see, perceive, or be directly aware of such an alleged reality. We do not understand what it would be like for there to be such a reality. Anything we could see and identify would have to be finite and discrete, though, of course, it could be very big.

It might be said in response that within the Christian tradition God is said to be *immanent* as well as *transcendent*. Suppose it is said, in the face of my above arguments, that it is only God in His immanency that is encountered. There is still, of course, the difficulty about the bodiless part, as we saw in some detail in part 1 of this volume, but *perhaps* there is here some way around the bog that I do not see. Be that as it may, if we encounter (see, perceive) God *only* in His immanency, we could hardly have anything like even an approximately adequate knowledge (understanding) of God.[14] For God's transcendency is central to our conception of Him. But there is no experiential awareness of that, for there is no perceiving (at least from a non-transcendent perspective which is all we can have) a transcendent being and thus there is no perceiving God as The Tradition portrays Him.

VIII

Alston, however, does not always portray God in such abstract and metaphysical terms as such an austerely transcendent being. In fact, in "The Perception of God" he travels metaphysically lighter. There he characterizes God, in one instance, as "the source of all being other than Himself, judge and redeemer of mankind" (47) and, in another instance, as we have already seen, as "a supreme or ultimate personal agent that acts in the light of knowledge, purposes, and intentions" (25). Take the latter description leaving aside initially "ultimate" in the characterization of God as a personal agent. It is not at all evident that it could not be possible—and (as we have seen) Alston claims no more—to perceive a being so characterized. It is not, of course, so evident how we could know we are perceiving a supreme personal agent, but by comparison with "infinite individual transcendent to the world," the very idea of such a perception, though unclear, does not seem to be clearly incoherent. Even "ultimate" is not an utter stumbling block, though what an ultimate personal agent might be is, to put it mildly, a conception which is not clear. Perhaps Alston means nothing more, in talking as he does, than to speak of an uncreated personal agent who created everything else other than himself. That may be the sense he is giving to "ultimate." It is not clear how we could identify such an agent by observation, but it is also not utterly clear that no such observations could be made either. Where the burden of proof lies concerning possibilities here is not evident, but Alston might say that at least the issue is left open: we do not know that there could be no experiential direct awareness of God *so characterized.* Similar things could be said about the first of his characterizations quoted above. Of course, "the source of all being other than Himself" is vexingly problematic, but perhaps that problematicity is containable. It can perhaps be kept from collapsing into outright incoherence. In any event, it is not crystal clear that *such a being* is imperceptible.

Such an Alstonian response, as far as it goes, seems to me fair enough. But it does not go nearly far enough. His definitions or characterizations of God, that we have just discussed, are meant to be informal and are not designed to capture in as full a way as possible what traditional Christianity takes God to be. As such, they are what Paul Edwards has aptly characterized as low redefinitions.[15] They fail to catch the sense of the transcendency of God, the utter otherness of God, something that is essential to that tradition, a tradition that Alston wishes to defend. Of course, if we make our God anthropomorphic enough, Zeus-like enough, there will be no *conceptual* problem about perceiving or observing such a cosmic superman. Whether such a being has in fact ever been detected is, of course, another matter altogether. But such a god would hardly be an adequate object of religious worship, and it is clear in *Divine Nature and Human Language* that that is not the kind of

God in whose service Alston places his philosophical theology. And if it were, it would then be clear that Alston was no longer defending the tradition in which God is conceived to be a wholly other, ultimate spiritual reality, ultimate and still a person, wholly distinct from the world and (if this doesn't come to the same thing) transcendent to it.

This, as I and others have argued, is a very opaque reality indeed (if a reality at all): perhaps so opaque as to be an incoherent conception.[16] Jews, Christians, and Moslems can fairly enough respond that the God of their traditions could not fail to be mysterious. *A reality that was not an ultimate mystery would not be their God.* That should be granted; and that granted, the crucial point at issue is whether this conception of God we have is so opaque as to be not only mysterious but also, as I believe it to be, incoherent. More accurately, what is at issue is whether what appears to be, or at least is claimed, by religious believers, to be, an ultimate mystery will be seen on careful inspection to be instead an incoherency. That is the crucial issue.

One way to show that the God of The Tradition is mysterious, but not incoherent is to show that some people, perhaps only some people of deep faith, have a direct awareness of God, though they see now only through a glass darkly. Against people like myself who argue that such awareness is not possible, even through a glass darkly, Alston argues, not for its reality (which he neither affirms nor denies), but for its *possibility*. This is, of course, a necessary prolegomena in the establishment that there is indeed such direct knowledge. Where the God in question is the transcendent God of The Tradition, I have argued that Alston fails to show that is a genuine possibility. If I am right here, and if Alston's case for the experiential path is about as good a case for such a claim as could be made (something I believe it to be), then one crucial avenue to making sense of belief in God has been blocked, namely *the experiential path*. At the very least, as careful an argument for it as we are likely to get has been undermined, and we are left with the very general skeptical arguments for believing that no such direct awareness is possible standing unrefuted.

NOTES

1. William P. Alston, "The Perception of God," *Philosophical Topics* 16, no. 2 (Fall 1988): 23–52. That, of Alston's various writings, shall be the central text for my critique. Page references *to this article* will be given in the text. Other relevant writings of Alston's include his "Religious Diversity and Perceptual Knowledge of God," *Faith and Philosophy* 5, no. 4 (October 1988): 433–48; "Religious Experience as a Ground of Religious Belief," in *Religious Experience and Religious Belief,* ed. Joseph Runzo and Craig Ihara (New York: University Press of America, 1986), 31–51; "The Christian Language-Game" in *The Autonomy of Religious Belief,* ed. Frederick Crossan (Notre Dame, Ind.: University of Notre Dame Press, 1981), 128–68; and *Divine Nature and Human Language*

(Ithaca, N.Y.: Cornell University Press, 1989), particularly 103–20. Since this chapter was written, William Alston has expanded the arguments developed in the articles cited above into a book. William Alston, *Perceiving God* (Ithaca, N.Y.: Cornell University Press, 1991). As far as I can see, my arguments, developed in response to the above-mentioned articles, apply equally well to this book.

2. Classic contemporary critiques of appeals to religious experience have been given by Ronald W. Hepburn, *Christianity and Paradox* (London: Watts, 1958), 24–90; and by C. B. Martin, *Religious Belief* (Ithaca, N.Y.: Cornell University Press, 1959), 64–94. For a response to Hepburn here see John Hick, "A Philosopher Criticizes Theology," *London Quarterly* 31 (1962): 103–10. I have defended views similar to Hepburn's and Martin's briskly in my *Reason and Practice* (New York: Harper and Row, 1971), 195–203, and in a somewhat more nuanced and expansive way in my *Skepticism* (London: Macmillan, 1973).

3. J. L. Austin, *Sense and Sensibilia* (Oxford: Clarendon Press, 1962); Paul Marhenke, "Phenomenalism" in *Philosophical Analyses,* ed. Max Black (Ithaca, N.Y.: Cornell University Press, 1950), 299–322; and J. L. Mackie, "What's Really Wrong with Phenomenalism," *British Academy Proceedings* (1969). For powerful, more generalized critiques of reductionism, see Hilary Putnam, *Realism and Reason* (Cambridge: Cambridge University Press, 1983), and Richard Rorty, *Objectivity, Relativism and Truth* (Cambridge: Cambridge University Press, 1991).

4. Unless we are going to say, wildly implausibly, that being directly aware of God is like being directly aware of ourselves. God, the utterly other, on such an account, is to be known like we know ourselves and not like we know others or other things. Moreover, such a direct knowledge, even if it is a coherent conception, is utterly unlike perceptual knowledge. It is not what we would think of a perceptual knowledge of God coming to. But Alston is talking of *perceptual* knowledge of God. It is here where he most essentially rests his case. For someone trying to push the above analogy, Hepburn's criticism of Martin Buber could be usefully noted here. Hepburn, *Christianity and Paradox*, 28, 48–59. It should also be said that if it is *direct awareness* of God, it cannot be an *inferring* of God from our experience of sensible things. That would not be direct awareness and, if we did appeal to that, we would in effect be attempting some crude version of one of the traditional proofs. But, as Schleiermacher and Otto were well aware, as well as more recent defenders of the claim that religious experience can give us knowledge of God, such as Emil Brunner, H. H. Farmer, John Baillie, H. D. Lewis, and W. D. Glasgow, our philosophical and theological concern with such alleged direct awareness emerges as an *alternative* to the traditional proofs or indeed to proofs *sans phrase*. If we abandon *direct* awareness, we are back in the old trap of natural theology. The appeal to religious experience was made by philosopher-theologians who were convinced that the proofs would not work and who were trying to provide the believer with other assurances. Hepburn and Martin are perfectly aware that that is the name of the game here.

5. See here Williams James, *The Varieties of Religious Experience* (New York: Modern Library, 1929); W. T. Stace, *Mysticism and Philosophy* (Philadelphia: Lippincott, 1960); and Ninian Smart, *Reasons and Faiths* (London: Routledge and Kegan Paul, 1958). Terence Penelhum gives a balanced and fair-minded account of the claims of religious experience in his *Religion and Rationality* (New York: Random House, 1971), 163–84.

6. Kai Nielsen: "On Speaking of God," *Theoria* 28 (1962): 110–37; *Contemporary Critiques of Religion* (New York: Herder and Herder, 1971); *Skepticism* (London: Macmillan, 1973); *An Introduction to Philosophy of Religion* (London: Macmillan, 1982); *Phi-*

losophy and Atheism (Amherst, N.Y.: Prometheus Books, 1985); and *God, Skepticism and Modernity* (Ottawa: University of Ottawa Press, 1989).

7. It should be noted that this commits me to neither semantic nor epistemic verificationism. Though to say this is not even to give to understand, let alone to assert, that verificationism in either or both of these senses may not *in some fairly attenuated sense* be a good thing. The rather wholesale rejection of verificationism needs looking at with a skeptical eye.

8. It could, of course, be an anthropomorphic embodied God.

9. Where we get the dividing line between revisionism and traditional Christianity is not easy to decide. Alston sees himself as a fairly conservative Christian explicating and defending traditional doctrines. But from a Christian fundamentalist position, he is a revisionist. What a philosopher can do is look at various conceptions of God and see what can be said for them. Still, a conception at great distance from something recognizable as the Judeo-Christian-Islamic traditions would be of little interest. It is considerations of this sort, among other things, that makes process theology so uninteresting.

10. Shabbir Akhtar, *The Light in the Enlightenment* (London: Grey Seal Books, 1990), 8 and chapters 5 and 6, reasoning from a rather orthodox Islamic perspective, but a perspective that shares much in common with orthodox Christianity, develops with care a conception of revisionism, applying it to (among others) Terence Penelhum, Richard Swinburne, and John Hick. It is a moot point whether it would apply to Alston as well. But we must be careful here that we do not so circumscribe "believer" that we end up identifying Christian, Jewish, and Islamic believers with what Alvin Plantinga called "standard theists," making all the rest, and not just reductionists such as D. Z. Phillips or R. Braithwaite, disguised secularists or secularists in spite of themselves. For further remarks on revisionism see Shabbir Akhtar, *Reason and the Radical Crisis of Faith* (New York: Peter Lang, 1987), 134–206. Akhtar is perfectly prepared to confront and affront modern sensibilities.

11. Richard Swinburne, *The Coherence of Theism* (Oxford: Clarendon Press, 1977), 110.

12. Many of the central considerations come out in a neglected but crucial exchange between John Skorupski and Robin Horton. Horton, "A Definition of Religion and Its Uses," *Journal of the Royal Anthropological Institute of Great Britain and Ireland* 90 (1962): 201–26; Horton, "African Traditional Thought and Western Science," *Africa* 37 (1967): 131–71; Skorupski, "Science and Traditional Religious Thought I and II," *Philosophy of the Social Sciences* 3 (1973): 209–30; Horton, "Paradox and Explanation: A Reply to Mr. Skorupski," *Philosophy of the Social Sciences* 3 (1973): 289–312; Horton, "Levy-Bruhl, Durkheim and the Scientific Revolution" in *Modes of Thought*, ed. Robin Horton and Peter Finnegan (London: Farber and Farber, 1973), 249–305; Skorupski, "Comment on Professor Horton's 'Paradox and Explanation,' " *Philosophy of the Social Sciences* 5, no. 1 (1975): 63–70; and Skorupski, *Symbol and Theory* (London: Cambridge University Press, 1976). See also Robin Horton, *Patterns of Thought in Africa and the West* (Cambridge, England: Cambridge University Press, 1993).

13. For an argument that it is pleonastic see Axel Hägerström, *Philosophy and Religion*, trans. Robert T. Sandin (London: Allen and Unwin, 1964), 175–305.

14. Christians and Jews will, of course, say that we can have no adequate conception of God at least "in this life." But such a radically inadequate conception, where we can have no understanding *at all* of "transcendent individuals," moves too much in the direction of incoherence to be reflectively acceptable.

15. Paul Edwards characterizes low-redefinitions well in his *The Logic of Moral Discourse* (Glencoe, Ill.: Free Press, 1955).

16. Paul Edwards, "Difficulties in the Idea of God," in *The Idea of God,* ed. Edward H. Madden et al. (Springfield, Ill.: Charles C. Thomas, 1968), 43–77; and Paul Edwards, "Notes on Anthropomorphic Theology," in *Religious Experience and Truth,* ed. Sidney Hook (New York: New York University Press, 1961), 241–50.

Chapter Fifteen

Is Religion the Opium of the People?: Marxianism and Religion

Is there a viable materialist conception of religion? This is a less simple question than it appears to be. Plainly, there are materialist conceptions of religion, from Epicurus through Marx and Engels, which explain religion as a function of material needs, and of the material conditions of human life which give rise to these needs. The question is: Are such theories viable or adequate to explain the phenomenon of religious belief? A viable conception of religion is one which doesn't simply explain religion away, but rather explains its origins, its distinctive cultural and historical forms, its persistence in various institutional contexts, its changes and development, its continuing and present existence in the modes of belief and action of individuals. The question of whether there is a viable materialist conception of religion is therefore a question of whether any of the presumptively materialist theories meet these requirements. What would it take for a materialist theory of religion to do so adequately?

Marx W. Wartofsky

INTRODUCTION

I shall first describe in unnuanced terms the canonical core of Marxian social theory, that part of the theory which makes it a distinctive social theory and must remain, though perhaps in some rationally reconstructed form, for Marxianism to continue to be a distinctive social theory. I shall then turn to a characterization of the proper sense of "ideology" to be utilized in giving a Marxian account of religion as ideology.[1] In doing this I will argue that there is an important distinction to be made between claiming that beliefs (in-

467

cluding religious beliefs) are ideological and claiming that they are false or incoherent. Like Freud, Marx, Engels, and the other classical Marxists, as well, presupposed that the cognitive errors of religious beliefs (their falsity or incoherence) have been firmly established by previous thinkers (e.g., Hume and Bayle); they took it as their task, not to repeat or update those old arguments, but to reveal religion's ideological functions: to show the role that religion plays in our life and to show that that role is usually an ideological one.

In sections 3 and 4, I shall characterize the core of Marx's and Engels's account of religion (principally Engels's, for he wrote more extensively than did Marx about such matters). I shall, that is, characterize their materialist conception on religion. I show how they conceived of religion's origins, its distinctive historical cultural forms, its changes and how these changes match with, and are functional for, modes of socioeconomic production. I then ask whether we have good grounds for believing that that conception, taken as a sociological generalization about religion in class societies, is true or at least a plausible candidate for being true. After some initial disambiguation and a locating of the proper scope and claims of the theory, I argue that it is a very plausible account indeed. It does not show us what the sole function of religion is—there is no such thing—but it does give us a compelling account of certain key functions of religion. It yields, I argue, a viable materialist conception of religion.

I

What is central to Marxianism is *historical* materialism and the conception that societies are divided into antagonistic classes with ideologies which, standardly, without such an awareness on the part of the agents involved, function to answer to the interests of one or more of the classes in the societies in which the agents live. The master claim of historical materialism is that "it is in the nature of the human situation, considered in its most general aspects, that there will be a tendency for productive power to grow."[2] What Joshua Cohen has called *minimalist* historical materialism "is simply an elaboration of that master claim, it would only be defeated by what defeats the master claim, and so it is the final fall-back position for the defender of historical materialism."[3] Such a minimalist account is not committed to the claim that all phenomena, not even all phenomena of great cultural significance, can be explained by historical materialism, but only phenomena which (directly or indirectly) are economically significant.

Minimalist historical materialism is also a *restricted* form of historical materialism. By this is meant that "it restricts itself to explaining those noneconomic phenomena which possess economic relevance."[4] Classical historical materialism, the historical materialism defended by Marx, Engels,

Lenin, and Trotsky, claimed that all phenomena of great cultural significance, including, of course, all such religious phenomena, were economically relevant phenomena and were explained by historical materialism. This is *unrestricted* historical materialism and it is a stronger claim than the minimalist needs to make. But centrally historical materialism in any form is an attempt to provide a theory of epochal social change. For *restricted, minimalist* historical materialism, this is limited to explaining the rise and fall of whole systems of economic relations such as capitalism, feudalism, and relatedly, directly or indirectly, economically important phenomena. For *inclusive unrestricted* historical materialism, by contrast, there is an attempt to explain the emergence of all major changes in society such as the emergence of Catholicism, Protestantism, pietism, and the like and to explain them as being *required* to unfetter the productive forces at a given epoch. But to claim that Christianity is required for the unfettering of the productive forces at a certain stage of their development, let alone to claim that Protestantism is required for capitalism to arise and be sustained, is to make a very strong claim concerning the predominance of material factors in explaining social evolution. Protestantism, particularly Calvinistic Protestantism, *facilitated* the development of capitalism (was functional for it), but to claim that it was *necessary* for its development is problematical. It is not clear whether Marx was committed to making such a strong claim or that (what is more important) whether contemporary Marxians should make such a strong claim. I am inclined to think not. But, be that as it may, the weaker claim about Protestantism's facilitating the unfettering of capitalist productive forces, and thus being functional for capitalism, will suffice for my purposes. That, more generally, the various religions tend to facilitate different productive forces, and that religion is in this way functional for them, is what I am claiming for a Marxian conception of religion.

Class is a conception of equal importance to that of historical materialism for Marxianism. Class, for Marxians, is not a matter of a person's consciousness of her position in society, but, whether the person is conscious of it or not, it is a matter of her relationship to the means of production in the society in which she lives. In our society, the principal classes are capitalists and workers. A capitalist owns and controls the means of production in the society in question and buys labor power as a commodity and puts that power to work under his direction (whether direct or indirect) typically in his enterprises. It is workers who sell their labor power and, as they enter the production process, they are dominated by the capitalist or his managers. A worker, without ownership or control of means of production, or at least any significant means of production, sells her labor power in a commodity market for a wage and works, under these contracted conditions, for the owner of the means of production, directly or indirectly, under his direction.

In our societies the capitalists constitute the dominating class and workers, constituting a class themselves, are members of a dominated class. It is, however, in the interests of the capitalist class that workers are not aware that they are dominated or even that they constitute a class with interests of their own that are distinct, or partially distinct, from capitalist class interests. Socialist political struggle centrally consists in the struggle for workers to attain consciousness of themselves as a dominated class, to see what their interests are, to see that they are importantly antagonistic to that of capitalists, to become aware of their power to break capitalist class domination and for them to proceed to struggle to break that domination and control, and to gain a state where they collectively own and control the means of production.

In this class struggle ideology plays an important role. It is capitalist class ideology in our societies which works to keep workers from being aware of their position in the world and of their own interests. (This is not to say that the *production* of ideology is always or even typically deliberate.) In speaking of an ideology Marxians are speaking of a general outlook or belief system about human beings and society, about some sort of world outlook, with an associated set of practices; about how people cannot, so the ideology claims, but live in certain ways; about how, in those small areas where there is any choice in the matter, people should live; and about how society should, or even must, be ordered. These outlooks, beliefs, and associated practices, where they are ideological, answer to the interests of a determinate class or classes in a particular society or cluster of related societies during a certain epoch.

This being so, "class ideology" is pleonastic. Without classes, on a Marxian conception of ideology, there would be no ideology. Standardly, but not invariably, ideological beliefs are false beliefs and also standardly, but again not invariably, people in the grip of an ideological belief are not aware that their beliefs are false. Indeed, they typically think they either are or presuppose deep truths about the human condition. It is because of this that Marxians speak of ideological illusions and false consciousness. But false consciousness should not be taken as a defining feature of an ideology, but as something that normally goes with having an ideology or thinking or acting ideologically, but what is a defining feature of an ideology is that *an ideology answers, or takes itself to be answering, to class interests.*[5]

Religion, all religion—Judaism, Christianity, Hinduism, Islam, and the lot—is taken by Marxians to be ideological. Religious beliefs are said by Marxians to be ideological illusions, expressive of the false consciousness of the religious believer in the grip of a religious ideology. That is to say, the religious beliefs of believers are at best false and not infrequently incoherent. But Christians, Hindus, and the like, suffering from false consciousness, take them to be deep, mysterious, sometimes ineffable truths about ultimate reality. Moreover, they are taken to be beliefs essential to sustain and to make sense of their lives, lives which, without these religious beliefs, would, the people in the grip of the ideology believe, lack all significance. But this, Marxians contend, is ideological illusion, standardly, but not invariably, used in various ways, some subtle, some not, to further or protect the interests of the dominant class. Thus, in capitalist societies, Christianity, typically, but not invariably, functions to support capitalism, and it does so by giving people a false or incoherent conception of their nature and destiny.

II

I have stated here, crudely and unqualifiedly, and with no attention to nuance, a central part of the canonical core of Marxian social theory, a theory which I think is, in its sophisticated articulations, the most plausible holistic social theory available to us at present. Be that as it may, this is not the place critically to examine historical materialism or a Marxian conception of class or ideology, though, I will remark in passing that I think a much stronger case for Marxianism can be made, and indeed has been made, by analytical Marxians such as G. A. Cohen, Andrew Levine, John Roemer, Richard Miller, Erik Olin Wright, Rodney Peffer, Debra Satz, Joshua Cohen, Philippe van Parijs, and David Schweickart, than has usually been thought. But that for another day. I will assume here, what I have argued for elsewhere, namely that some rational reconstruction of Marx's social theory shows it to be a sound, or at least a plausible and attractive, social theory, and see what, given that assumption, should be said for a rather standard Marxian account of religion as ideology in the sense of "ideology" that I have outlined.[6] Indeed, its treatment of religion might be one of the places where Marxian theory needs revision. And, whether this is so or not, there is the sociological fact that not a few theologians have thought of themselves, perhaps confusedly, as being both Marxians and Christians or Jews and have taken the militant atheism of Marx and Engels to be inessential to their theories and revolutionary practice. Most Marxians believe that that conjunction rests on a mistake, even if, in some circumstances, it is a humanly and practically useful mistake. That is to say, Marxians could agree, that it may be a very good thing indeed that there is a red Archbishop in Brazil, that there are working-class priests who are Marxist militants and that there are liberation theologians and radical Christians.

Be that as it may, not a few have thought that Marxian explanations and critiques of religion are powerful as explanations of religion and as a critique of religion. Indeed, explanation and critique run tandem here, for if a Marxian explanation of religion is on the mark, that very kind of explanation is also a critique. Marxian explanation explains religious beliefs as ideological illusions mystifying, for the person taken in by them, his social relations and his conception of the world in a way that supports the socioeconomic structure, the relations of production, of his society. Moreover, it supports it in a manner that in reality does not, in most instances, answer to his interests or meet his needs. He (to concretize it for a moment to our epoch) is taken in by capitalism in a way that conflicts with his own human flourishing and his leading as good a life as he could live. So explanation and critique run together here. They are *conceptually* distinct, but in this case you cannot do the first without doing the second. If the explanation is on the mark, religion has, in being explained, been *ipso facto* criticized. (This is not, of course, to give to understand that it has been explained away. See the final section of this chapter.)

However, what is often not noticed is that Marxian explanation and critique of religion, like Freudian explanation and critique, is dependent for its soundness on the soundness of secular nonideological critiques of religion such as those of Holbach, Hume, Bayle, or contemporary atheistic or agnostic critiques such as those of Bertrand Russell, Axel Hägerström, J. L. Mackie, Richard Robinson, Antony Flew, Michael Martin, Wallace Matson, or my own. Marxian accounts assert that religious beliefs, as expressive of false consciousness, are either false or incoherent. But they do very little by way of arguing for that, but, taking it to be obvious, seek rather to show that religious beliefs are ideological beliefs. But that ideological part by itself is not enough for their critique of religion, for ideological beliefs could be true. Most of them are not, but are rather false or incoherent beliefs, expressive of false consciousness, but there is at least conceptual space for ideological beliefs being true or well warranted. And what shows they are false or incoherent is not that they are ideological. What makes them ideological is rather that they belong to a system of beliefs or an outlook concerning persons and society which answers to, or takes itself as answering to, class interests. Marx's *Capital* is as ideological as is Smith's and Ricardo's political economy. They supported capitalism, they helped sustain the class interests of capitalists, and, while making some important at least putatively true claims (claims on which Marx built), they made as well some importantly false claims, but both their true and false claims were often genuinely scientific claims which, at the very same time, were also ideological claims, e.g., they supported capitalist class interests. And their theories as a whole, while being genuinely social scientific theories, were also ideological theories in support of capitalist class interests. The same thing is true of Marx's *Capital*. It is both an ideological theory and a scientific theory. It is deliberately designed to support working-class interests and was plainly also believed by Marx to be true ("objectively true" being pleonastic) and it indeed could be true, or, on some rationally reconstructed account such as G. A. Cohen's or John Roemer's, it is at least a plausible candidate for being a true, or at least an approximately true, theory with its linked practices. Louis Althusser to the contrary notwithstanding, ideology and science, and ideology and truth, do not need to stand in conflict. They often, indeed even typically, do, but they need not and perhaps sometimes do not.

What Marx and Engels and Marxian accounts generally show, if true, is that religion is ideology and that religious beliefs are ideological. But it is a further step to show that they are false or incoherent and are expressive of false consciousness. That they are false or incoherent is not shown or, even in any remotely careful way, argued for by Marx or Engels or by the other major figures in the Marxian tradition. They rather reasonably, I believe, presuppose it and take it as something evident to anyone with a reasonable education and not beguiled by ideology. That such beliefs are false or incoherent, they argue, has been well shown by Enlightenment thinkers such as Holbach, Hobbes, Hume, and Bayle. Marxians, even such historicist Marxians as Antonio Gramsci, were children of the Enlightenment, building on and extending in new and striking ways, as did Freud as well (though very differently), the tradition of the Enlightenment.[7] Marx and Engels just assumed that philosophers such as Holbach and Hobbes had it basically right about the *grounds* for religious belief. A contemporary Marxian, who is more philosophically sophisticated about the logical status of religious beliefs than were the classical Marxists, will shy away from Holbach and Hobbes on such issues and turn instead more to Hume and Bayle or in our time to J. L. Mackie, Axel Hägerström, or Antony Flew, the latter's rather fanatical conservatism not withstanding. Marx and Engels, in an interesting little narrative in *The Holy Family* about the history of philosophy (including its discussion of religion) from Descartes to Hegel and Feuerbach, argue that Hume and Bayle have shown that religious beliefs are at best false.[8] That critical task, that is, was carried out, they believe, by classical Enlightenment thinkers. Building on that, the distinctively Marxian contribution, vis-à-vis religion, is, by contrast, to show religion's ideological functions: to show how in this domain false consciousness functions ideologically to support particular modes of production.

So it is in this way, a way that is utterly different than, but still complementary to, a Humean, Hägerströmian, or Mackian critique, Marxian accounts of religion become important. If one is justified in setting aside a broadly Humean skepticism over religion, then the Marxian critique of religion would be less interesting, for, even if it shows that religious belief is ideological, that in itself would not show that religious believers are afflicted with false consciousness or (what is something else again) that religious beliefs are false or incoherent. Indeed, their being ideological might diminish a bit their moral attractiveness, but there it would not be impossible to believe that, with some alterations, the ideological dimensions might, on the one hand, be excised or in some way neutralized or, on the other, even without alteration, they might be justified because the class interests they support should be supported. However, if a broadly Humean and Baylean skepticism about religion is in place, then the Marxian explanations and critiques of religion gain an added interest. If, that is, religious belief—belief that God exists and belief in God—is in error, indeed unexcisable error, then religious beliefs are at best false and further, if for a very long time, as Marx and Engels believed, this has been tolerably evident, then the question naturally arises, why has religious belief has been so tenaciously persistent? This is also a question Freud, with similar beliefs about the cognitive import of religion, addressed, that Feuerbach wrestled with, and that Marx and Engels considered as well. Let us see what Marx and Engels have to say about that.

III

Following Ludwig Feuerbach, both Marx and Engels regard "the Christian God," as Engels put it, as "a fantastic mirror image of man"[9] (290).* In fact all religious entities in all the various religions are, they believe, such projections of human attributes and wishes. Where religion developed beyond animism, these human projections were turned into what in the imagination of human beings were thought to be supernatural entities. But such conceptions are incoherent; belief in them is, as Engels put it, nonsensical[10](194). That the dominated have these religious beliefs answers to the interests of the ruling class, but, these projections of human feelings also answer, though in a deceptive and illusory way, to the interests of the dominated, despised people in class society, people with little hope that their needs in such societies could be met, their earthly aspirations satisfied, their lives here on earth made decent, or, in some instances, even tolerable. If their lives contained even the possibility of becoming tolerable, Engels maintains, religion would not answer to their interests, but since their tangible, genuine needs and interests cannot be met, such an eschatological religion gives them an illusory hope and in that way goes some way toward answering to something in their lives. Moreover, for them religion, and a certain kind of religion at that, was sociologically speaking inevitable. In perhaps what is his most famous passage on religion, Marx remarks in his *Contribution to the Critique of Hegel's Philosophy of Right* (1844) that

> *Religious* distress is at the same time the *expression* of real distress and the *protest* against real distress. Religion is the sigh of the oppressed creature, the heart of a heartless world, just as it is the spirit of a spiritless situation. It is the opium of the people. (42)

---

*Page references to Marx *or* Engels or to Marx *and* Engels will be given in the text and will be taken from Karl Marx and Friedrich Engels, *On Religion* (Moscow: Foreign Languages Publishing House, 1957).

Both the remark "it is the opium of the people" and "it is the sigh of the oppressed creature, the heart of a heartless world" have been quoted again and again, but while they are compatible with each other, they cut in rather different directions. A religious person could enthusiastically accept that "religion is the sigh of the oppressed creature, the heart of a heartless world," but not—or at least much less easily—that it is the "opium of the people." A Christian, for example, could very well see the condition of human beings in such stark terms, as the remark about the sigh of the oppressed creature gestures at. This in part is what brings us to sickness unto death: to despair of the world as it is, and indeed as, even in the most favorable conditions, it could be, and of our lives in it.

However, as, say, with liberation theology, but not only with it, Christians could see the Christian message, as Moslems see their religion, as one demanding a struggle against those conditions, as a call to resistance to conditions of oppression and heartlessness, even while not blinking at the fact, but fully taking it to heart, that this is the way the world is and indeed may always be. But when Marx goes on to say that religion is the opium of the people, he adds something, namely, that this sigh of the oppressed creature, this protest against real distress, takes the form of, with one or another attitude, of an acceptance of this dreadful world, an acceptance of one's lot, of one's station and its duties, no matter how harsh. And instead of placing one's faith, as did the anti-Baptists, in the coming to be of the Kingdom of God on earth, and struggling to attain it, one places one's faith in another better world, a "Spiritual World," beyond the grave, where all the terrible woes of this life will be a thousand times recompensed in a life of bliss with God. What we have to look forward to is not a better earthly condition, but a life, after one's bodily death, in God's Spiritual Kingdom. This has been thought by some people of a secular disposition to be a heavenly swindle and has been crudely called "pie in the sky by and by." Life, for many people, is hell now, in almost every sort of way, and there is no escaping this earthly hell, or even significantly ameliorating it, but, on such a religious conception, by a commitment to Christ, and a living in righteousness, we can be sure that we shall enter, after our death, the heavenly kingdom of God and live, forever, in a blissful state.

Engels and Marx—most fully Engels—trace how this conception, and related conceptions, works itself out in Christianity, though they are not denying that broadly similar things obtain for other religions, particularly for religions which have the status of what Engels calls world religions (193–203). But the stress is on Christianity, given Engels emphasis on its ideological role in the Western world: how it facilitated, and continues to facilitate, the rise, stabilization, and development of capitalism. But this account is also a narrative about the origin and development of religion. I think it is clear that Engels, a pure child of the Enlightenment, gives us a rationalistic narrative, which, as Wartofsky puts it, is also a materialist conception of the origin and development of religion in general and of Christianity in particular. But it may be none the worse for all of that.

IV

I will give some of the core bits of it and then, in the light of this narrative, and looking critically back at it, try to say something about the import of Marxian claims about religion as the opium of the people and particularly about Christianity, as an ideological mask to help sustain capitalist class society as it, though in different forms, earlier helped sustain the slave society of Rome and after that feudal society both with their distinctive modes of production.

I would like first to make a disclaimer. I am neither a historian nor a biblical scholar and am too much of a *fachidiot* to know whether Engels's historical narrative, particularly in the light of what has been discovered since his time, is a reasonably accurate telling it like it was, concerning that period and those developments, or whether instead, it is what anthropologists like to call "a just so story." *Perhaps* it is something in between, namely a reasonable account of the origin and development of Christianity, given what was known during Engels's time, but still somewhat one-sided and inaccurate in important details. I just do not know about such things. *Perhaps* there is no reasonable prospect of telling it like it was?

What I will assume, and I think not unreasonably, is that it is a plausible narrative, a (if you will) reasonable just so story, and then, on safer philosophical ground, see where we can go with it. If, I shall ask, this was the way it was, or something approximating that, what does this tell us about the ideological functions of religion at least in such a world and about the viability of religion in general and Christianity in particular? Things could have been as Engels portrays them, and perhaps they were, and indeed still are. If they were and are, what should we think about Christianity and about religion more generally?

Before turning to Engels's narrative, there is still a further preliminary to which I should attend. What goes on in Marx and Engels and most Marxian writings about religion is, for the most part, not philosophy as we have come to know it at least in an Anglo-American and Scandinavian philosophical ambience. In the *philosophy* of religion we run across claims such as "If God exists, His existence is necessary," "God is eternal," "God is the perfect good," "God is said to be an infinite individual but the very idea of an infinite individual is self-contradictory," "'God created the world out of nothing' is incoherent," "What is good cannot be identified with what God commands," "God's existence can be proved," "God's existence cannot be proved," "The very idea of taking it that the attempt to prove God's existence is a religiously serious or important matter reveals an incipient atheism." These claims and claims like them are the stuff of the philosophy of religion and philosophers, who deal at all with religion, and if they are at all competent know how to argue for or against them in ways that are clearly recognizable as philosophical.

Marx and Engels do not engage in such arguments. Indeed, I think that it is fairly evident that they would regard concern with such arguments as by now fatuous. From the narrative they gave in *The Holy Family* about the development of philosophy, we can see (as I remarked in the previous section) that they think that what is to be said here has been well said by philosophers such as Holbach, Locke, Hume, Kant, and Bayle and that there is no need to repeat their work (59–68, 289–96). In this way they believe that there can be established results in philosophy or in intellectual history.

What Engels gives us, as will become evident in what follows in the next several paragraphs, is social and psychological description (a heavily interpretive description all the same) and an explanation embedded in a narrative resulting in a critique wedded to that description and explanation. But there is little in the way of argument or conceptual elucidation. Thus, as we philosophers in the analytical tradition have come, perhaps in a too *parti pris* manner, to view philosophy, there is little *philosophy* in their accounts of religion. Their claims are, for the most part, empirical: sociological, broadly economic, historical, and psychological and are establishable or disestablishable by empirical investigation and careful reflection on that investigation. Philosophical argument and elucidation, as we have come to understand these things, have little presence here. Apart from the fact that I realize I cannot argue for them or against them in the way I am accustomed to argue for philosophical claims, I do not care in the slightest whether they are philosophical or not.[11] What I am interested in is their plausibility, whether we should accept them and the import of their acceptance or rejection. What is important is whether it is reasonable for us to believe that their central claims, at least on some rational reconstruction, are true.

However, *enfin*, to Engels's narrative of the origin, development, and function of religion. Engels remarks that our conceptions of the gods first arose through the personifications of natural forces (225). As he put it in *Anti-Dühring* (1878): "All religion . . . is nothing but the fantastic reflection in men's minds of those external forces which control their daily life, a reflection in which the terrestrial forces assume the form of supernatural forces" (146). In the most primitive societies, religion so reflected the forces of nature. But, as societies grow more complex, and particularly as a social division of labor becomes embedded in the social fabric of people's lives and classes come into existence, "social forces begin to be active—forces which confront man as equally alienated and at first equally inexplicable, dominating him with the same apparent natural necessity" as the forces of nature themselves. "The fantastic figures, which at first only reflected the mysterious forces of nature, at this point acquire social attributes, become representatives of the forces of history"[12] (147).

The religions of more complex societies—religions which have become more elaborately socialized—quickly took various forms among different peoples, differently socialized. In the general culture area from which Christianity sprang, among the Egyptians, Persians, Jews, Chaldeans, for example, we had what Engels calls "national religions" with their distinctive ceremonies, with their particular gods, with their distinctive chosen people, with rites so distinctive and demanding that "people of two different religions . . . could not eat or drink together, or hardly speak to each other" (202). Christianity emerged from this world of exclusively national religions—entering "into a resolute antithesis to all previous religions" as, in that culture area at least, "the first possible world religion" (201–202). Christianity, Engels remarks, "knew no distinctive ceremonies, not even the sacrifices and processions of the classic world. By thus rejecting all national religions and their common ceremonies and addressing itself to all peoples without distinction it becomes the *first possible world religion*" (202).

However, and that fact (if it is a fact) notwithstanding, just as with the previous national religions, Christianity arose under and reflected certain distinctive socioeconomic conditions. It emerged in the Near East during the ruthless hegemony of the Roman Empire and spread rapidly over the whole Empire. At first savagely persecuted by successive emperors, reaching its epitome with Nero, in some three hundred years it came to be the state religion of the Roman Empire. In short, things so evolved that eventually Christianity brought "the Roman Empire into subjection and dominated by far the larger part of civilized humanity for 1,800 years"[13](194). Why, Engels asks, did the "popular masses in the Roman Empire" come to prefer, as Engels puts it, "this nonsense" (194)? And why did "the ambitious Constantine," Engels also asks, finally see "in the adoption of this religion of nonsense the best means of exalting himself to the position of autocrat of the Roman world" (194)? Engels here seeks to explain the origin and development of Christianity "from the historical conditions under which it arose and reached its dominating position" (194).

Engels argues that we can "get an idea of what Christianity looked like in its early form by reading the so-called Book of Revelation of John" (197). This book, Engels claims, can be definitely dated as having been written in either 68 or 69 A.D. Engels remarks of it, that it is "the oldest, and the only book of the New Testament, the authenticity of which cannot be disputed"(207). And in it, we have Christianity in the crudest form in which it has been preserved to us. There is only one dominant dogmatic point: "that the faithful have been saved by the sacrifice of Christ" (206).

What Engels is principally interested in here is the character of that Christianity and the socioeconomic conditions under which it arose and the people who became its adherents and their life conditions. "Christianity," Engels asserts in his "On the History of Early Christianity" (1894–95), "was originally a movement of oppressed people: it first appeared as the religion of slaves and emancipated slaves, of poor people deprived of all rights, of peoples subjugated or dispersed by Rome" (313). It emerged at a time when in the Greco-Roman world, and especially in Asia Minor, Syria, and Egypt, there was "an absolutely uncritical mixture of the crassest superstitions of the most varying peoples . . ." (323). It was indiscriminately accepted and complemented by pious deception and downright charlatanism; [at] a time in which miracles, ecstasies, visions, apparitions, divining, gold-making, cabbala, and other secret magic played a primary role. It was in that atmosphere, and, moreover, among a class of people who were more inclined than any other to listen to these supernatural fantasies, that Christianity arose" (323).

The Book of Revelation—this authentic depiction of early Christianity, the earliest Christianity of which we have any knowledge—consists in a series of apocalyptic visions which make up almost the whole of the book. Christ—the lamb—appears in the garb of a high priest. Christ is depicted as the son of God, but "by no means God or equal to God," though, as an emanation of God, he is said to have existed from all eternity. But, as important as he is, he remains subordinate to God. And, crucially, the Christ of this book "has been sacrificed for the sins of the world and with whose blood the faithful of all tongues and nations have been redeemed to God" (325).

What is revolutionary here is that we get a universal religion, a religion applying fully to all the oppressed, exploited, and despised elements of society (themselves often very different people) of which in the Roman world there were very many. In a "social Darwinian" struggle for the survival of the fittest among competing religions, the vital and deeply appealing message of Christianity, which enabled it to win out, was that in Christ, by "one great voluntary sacrifice of a mediator the sins of all times and all men were atoned for once for all—in respect of the faithful"[14] (325).

The first Christians were mainly slaves, but not exclusively so; they were also in the towns impoverished freemen, living nearly as badly as slaves, with no hope of escaping their destitution, and "in the rural districts of the provinces" they were, as well, peasants "who had fallen more and more into bondage through debt" (331). They were people who had been utterly crushed by the iron fist of the Roman Empire. They were, in addition to their differing class status, also culturally speaking diverse people coming from many different societies. It was these people who became the first Christians. After the crushing defeat of the slave revolt led by Spartacus, the slaves had no hope at all of earthly (worldly) emancipation. Similar things obtained for the impoverished freemen and peasants. Moreover, their social units (tribes and unions of kindred tribes) had been destroyed by the Roman military juggernaut and its accompanying system of government. Their social systems, their systems of ownership and ways of life "had been smitten down by the levelling iron fist of conquering Rome" (331). And "Roman jurisdiction and tax-collecting machinery completely dissolved the traditional inner organization" (331). They were plundered and pillaged, savagely treated in all sorts of appalling ways, and, like many people in the Third World in our time, they were growing steadily more and more destitute. "Any resistance of isolated small tribes or towns to the gigantic Roman power was hopeless" (332).

To such people (the mass of slaves, impoverished freemen, and peasants), the Christian message of salvation fell on fertile ground. It provided a heart in a heartless world by promising freedom from bondage and misery in a life beyond, after their earthly death, in God's Spiritual World, in heaven, if only they would live righteously now. (This, remember, was the message that Nietzsche scorned.) Given their material and intellectual resources, it was a message of salvation that made sense to them and that they could take to heart. There was for them absolutely no hope of earthly emancipation. Misery and destitution was for them inescapable. So for any hope to be there at all, it must be a hope for a "world beyond this world." So their way out—their only way out—was salvation "not in this world," but in a "new world," a "Spiritual World," the world prophecized by Christianity in which the faithful would live with God in his heavenly kingdom after their bodily death.

Against the religious conceptions and conceptions of *Weltanschauung* of the Judaic world, which put little stock in such beliefs, the Christian vision (starting from a splinter in the Judaic world) magically answered to the desperate hopes of such people in such appalling socioeconomic circumstances. Christianity won out in the cultural struggle, and belief in life after death, and the desirability of life after death, gradually became "a recognized article of faith throughout the Roman world" (332). Christianity, taking "recompense and punishment in the world beyond seriously," created "heaven and hell, and a way out was found which would lead the laboring and burdened from the vale of woe to eternal paradise" (332).

Here we see clearly how, in a particular circumstance, religion can be the opium of the people and, as well, to return to that famous passage from Marx's *Contribution to the Critique of Hegel's Philosophy of Right* previously discussed, "the sigh of the oppressed creature, the heart of a heartless world, the spirit of a spiritless situation" (42). It is evident why people so situated should flock to such an eschatological religion.

Marx goes on, in a passage following the one cited above, to remark that "the abolition of religion as the illusory happiness of the people is required for their real happiness" (42). Traditional criticism of religion limits itself to showing (trying to show) the falsity or incoherence of religious beliefs. But this kind of critique is not sufficient, though it is necessary. It is necessary because it is through such a critique of religion that people become disillusioned and are made to think and to shape reality as people who have been disillusioned and have "come to reason" (42). But we must not only learn, Marx argues, that religious beliefs are illusory, even necessary illusions for people caught in certain life conditions, we must also, from careful economic and social study, establish, what Marx called the "truth of this world" (42). We need to learn about the conditions which need illusions and, as well, how we could come to have a world which did not need religious illusions or any other kind of illusion and learn, as well, how to struggle (a struggle informed by theory) to gain that world. But, of course, in certain circumstances (for example, for slaves during Nero's time), we would also see (if we were at all clearheaded) that any advance was a long way off. It was not something that was at all possible for them.

The early Christianity Engels describes fits well with the mode of production that we had in the Roman Empire: a mode of production based on slave labor. But modes of production change as the epochs go by and the forces of production develop. And, with these changed, and indeed developed, modes of production, Christianity also changes. Indeed, as long as we have class societies, Christianity, along with these changes, changes in ways that match better and serve better these changed modes of production. Thus, with the feudal mode of production, we get Catholicism with its hierarchies; with the capitalist mode of production, Protestantism, most particularly and effectively, Calvinist Protestantism or in England an Anglicanism, resulting from a political compromise fueled by an economic struggle, that yielded an Anglicanism which was a blend of Puritanism, on the one hand, and Catholicism, on the other hand, with the king as in effect a rather constrained pope. In France the violent bourgeois revolution, going hand in hand with the beliefs of the Enlightenment, moved, in a way at first favorable to capitalism, to both materialism and social ferment and, with that, to a great tossing off of tradition. While initially liberating, affording the bourgeoisie a free hand unencumbered by feudal residues, this was also unstable, given that it unleashed the rising proletariat. As principally a matter of expediency, there was eventually a return to a rather chastised Catholicism as the ruling classes, recognizing that they "had come to grief with materialism," came to stress, instead of Enlightenment values, that "religion must be kept alive for the people," for "that was the only and the last means to save society from utter ruin" (310). Even for a ruling class with little in the way of faith and for some intellectuals with a stake in the *status quo*, religion came to seem a useful device to keep the working class in line. Sometimes they were not that clearheaded, but, clearheaded or not, they saw the social indispensability of religion, if *their* civilization was to be saved.

Central to Marxism, as we already have remarked, is historical material- ism which, as Engels puts it, designates "that view of the course of history which seeks the ultimate cause and the great moving power of all important historic events in the economic development of society, in the changes in the modes of production and exchange, in the consequent division of society into distinct classes, and in the struggles of these classes against one an- other" (296). In accordance with this grand empirical hypothesis (for that is what it is), we have Engels's empirical claim that with the changes of eco- nomic development of society, with the changes in the mode of production and exchange, a society will get the form of religion that is most functional for that mode of production. But in doing so, since we are talking about class societies, that religion, to be so functional, will work to keep the dominated classes in line, to accept in one way or another their station and its duties, and to regard this as, all things considered, necessary and proper, or at least in- escapable. In that way religion is the opium of the people, and usefully so, for the dominate classes and sometimes, when their situation is very hopeless, even, in a mystifying way, for the dominated classes as well, for it gives them a consoling illusion of a heart in a world that is actually heartless.

V

Is this view true or a reasonable approximation of something that is true? If it is true, it is true as a *sociological generalization*, a generalization across all class societies. It is not a claim about what religious belief *must* be for every individual. It is a claim about how religion functions, or, more weakly, tends to function, in class societies. I am now asking whether we should believe that such a claim, so understood, is so.

If the claim is made as strong as a claim that this is the *sole* function, or even the sole social function, of religion, we have very good reason indeed for believing that it is false. Even with a basically Feuerbachian projection- ist theory of religion, which in its essentials is Marx's and Engels's as well, we have the Freudian alternative which is also a projectionist theory, only the image we project in believing in God is that of a perfect but also an almighty father, a figure who is projected as a heavenly father but also as both a feared and revered father, and different psychological mechanisms are invoked. We need, if we are making such a strong claim, to be given reasons for thinking the Freudian account is false and the Marxian one is true. Actually I think sometimes, that is in certain circumstances, one account is true and sometimes the other. And sometimes both are arguably true together. The image we project in our imagination could be that of both a heavenly father and a distorted image of our social relations functioning to lead us to accept this vale of tears. As has often enough been argued, the Freudian accounts and the Marxian accounts are both compatible and complementary, if not pressed dogmatically. Neither is very plausible as yielding the sole account of the psychosocial functions of religion. And Emile Durkheim's account, which tells us that what people worship is really society itself, though ideology leads them to misrecognize the object of their worship, is another rival materialist functional account of religion. But then no theory, neither Durkheim's, nor Freud's nor Marx's, yields the *sole* viable functional account of religion. Moreover, for projectionist accounts of the status of religious belief, Frankfurt School social theorists such as Erich Fromm, Max Horkheimer, and Theodor Adorno have pointed out that there are still other social psychological functions of religion not covered by the classical Marxian accounts and only inadequately so by the Freudian and Durkheimian ones, which are humanly speaking very important indeed. We need religion not only to make intolerable social conditions psychologically tolerable, we also need, besides opium—or at least some people need in certain determinate circumstances—religion to make sense of their (our) tangled lives and (if we live long enough) to come to grips with the decline (often a radical decline) of our powers. Whether we are rich or poor or somewhere in between, whether we are dominated or dominating, we need in some way to come to grips with the inevitability of our own death and with the deaths of others, particularly with the deaths of those we love. We know that we must die, but we need, or at least very much want, an account of its significance and with that an account of the significance, both singly and together, of our lives. (If our lives have no significance, our deaths would have no significance either.) We have, as well, to gain something of such an account, to learn to come to face, and in some way understand and come to grips with, the failures in our lives and face all the standardly wrenching face-to-face problems between intimates such as those between lovers, between parents and children, between siblings, between friends, and between acquaintances at our workplaces.

These problems not infrequently leave us as individuals in a tangled mess, and sometimes with a feeling that we do not know how to act or to try to be and with a sense that these problems are intractable and inescapable and that somehow we must just learn to live with them. It is not impossible, when confronted with such things, to come to feel that life makes no sense at all and that even the posing of these questions is a senseless activity. Many of us here experience a deep alienation and feelings of despair. And the alienation in question, as Fromm has argued, is a different kind of alienation than the alienation of which Marxists speak, but it is real for all of that.[15] In the face of this, religion functions to help us, or at least some of us, to make sense of, or at least to face and come to grips with, our own tangled lives. This is not just, or perhaps even at all, for religion to be an opiate of an oppressed people or an opiate for anyone.

These existential functions of religion, as I shall call them, so as to have a shorthand way of referring to them, would remain in any kind of society, including a classless society. They might be less pressing in societies which are less harsh, less replete with injustice and domination of one class or gender or strata by another. But still they would remain. Marx, Engels, Lenin, and Trotsky thought that as societies moved toward classlessness, religion would begin to wither away. With the coming to be of a completely classless society, which, if such a society would ever come into being, would be an egalitarian society of considerable abundance and with high levels of universal education, religion would in time completely wither away. They are, however, forgetting about what I have called the existential problems of religion. They will remain in any society, even societies as classless as you like. These societies are supposed to be truly human societies where social relations, including our face-to-face relations, will generally become clear. We will, at last, understand the truth about our world and about ourselves and finally we will have a just society, or *perhaps* even a society "beyond justice," of equals. In such a world, if anything like this could come to be, some of these existential problems, it is reasonable to believe, would become more tractable, perhaps some would even disappear, but death, declining powers, and human estrangement (something we see graphically depicted in the fictional world of Edna O'Brien) would remain. The latter might not be as frequent or perhaps so often so severe. But that estrangement, personal conflict, and the like would disappear in a classless society is, to put it conservatively, very unlikely. So some of the needs related to our existential problems, needs that fuel religion, would remain. The idea that religion would wither away with classlessness is, to put it conservatively, problematical.

Injustice, destitution, lack of control over one's life surely do exacerbate those existential problems. But death, failing powers, damaged relations, deep human conflicts will remain in those classless societies. Death and failing powers are plainly not things that are going away and there is no good reason to believe that the other existential problems would all wither away in a classless society. They are part of the human condition. Some of them—particularly the problems between human beings—*might* even be intensified with greater clarity about our lives, our being freer of domination, and our having greater leisure and more options. The burden (if such it be) of choice of life plans would in such a circumstance be greater.

I think, however, that it is unlikely that this, or anything very like it, would obtain. The greater stress of life of a class society of limited abundance and opportunity is arguably still more damaging to such relations. But that is an open question and I do not intend to beg it here. The crucial point, however, is that these existential problems, though perhaps in a moderated form, would remain in any society, including any classless society.

Existential problems will remain, but it is not obvious that our responses to them must take a religious form. Unless the use of "religion" is eccentrically extended, as Feuerbachians, Frommians, Braithwaiteians, and Wittgensteinian fideists do, so as to cover many things that would not standardly be covered by "religion," there could, in such classless or near classless societies, as there can be now for some privileged few in the rich capitalist democracies, be, more or less society-wide, a nonreligious, broadly secularly ethical response to such existential problems.

Still, as a matter of fact, such existential problems, and the responses to them, have traditionally remained firmly, except for a privileged few, in the domain of religion. Moreover, this has, culturally speaking, been very persistent, and we need to be given very good reasons indeed for believing that this function will wither away or take a nonreligious form. Still, it may not be unreasonable to expect that, as the level of social wealth and security rises, as well as the general educational level of a society (if indeed anything like this ever happens), religion will very likely become *optional* for increasingly large numbers of people in that society, as it has already increasingly become optional for the privileged, educated few in rich capitalist democracies. But that is not to say, that it will wither away or even that it should wither away. We need evidence for the first contention and arguments for the second.

VI

I think Marxians can and should accept this. They should say that these existential functions are functions of religion that might very well persist even with the demise of class societies. But they should also respond by saying that the recognition of this does nothing to undermine their claims about the ideological function of religion, claims about how it serves as an opiate to reconcile the oppressed to their condition. This is a pervasive fact of life in class societies. It is massively with us now. It is not just a function of religion in early Christianity in the Roman Empire or for a medieval serf or for German peasants during Luther's and Munzer's time or for the English peasantry during the Wars of the Roses or for a Russian serf or peasant of the nineteenth century or for the slaves in the American South. It is pervasive in popular religion today. Protestant missionaries of a more or less fundamentalist sort carry this opiating of society out with a vengeance in the Third World. Whether they aimed at it consciously or not, they, where successful, as they often are, in bringing religion to such destitute people, also bring them an opiate. Religion there is an opium of the people. The religion they bring so functions for destitute peasants, primitive peoples whose cultures arc in the process of being destroyed, and the masses of *lumpen-proletariat* crowding into the huge cities of the Second or Third World, e.g., Sao Paulo, Mexico City, Lagos, Lima, Cairo, and Manila. It also functions this way for both many poor blacks and whites in the American South as is graphically portrayed by Bertrand Tavernier and Robert Parrish in their documentary film *Mississippi Blues* (1984). These proselytizing religions lead these various impoverished down-and-out people into a hope for a heavenly by-and-by and it leads them to be quiescent before capitalist powers that savagely exploit them and rule their lives. The Religious Right is aggressive against liberalism, which it sees completely unrealistically as disguised socialism or worse, but teaches uncritical acceptance of the capitalist order. Indeed, it celebrates that order.

Here what might become revolutionary or at least radically reformative activity on the part of such destitute people is diverted into fantastic religious beliefs in many ways not unlike the beliefs of the original Christians suffering under the Roman fist or the German peasants in Luther's time suffering under the oppression of the German princes with Luther's blessing. Like schnapps introduced dirt cheap to the workers of Northern Germany, such religion works to keep the dominated class passive, accepting without question the capitalist status quo. Popular religion—consider TV evangelists in Canada and the United States—serves a similar function, though perhaps a little less obviously. People are turned away from thinking critically about their society and from looking for real options for change. Set to roll back the more progressive elements in their society, e.g., feminism and some forms of liberalism, caught up with issues which are both trifling and reactionary—issues which should not even be issues—such as (in the United States) homosexuals in the armed forces or women members of the clergy, capitalism, and indeed its rightness, is not only accepted but celebrated in its supposedly "pure form," though care is taken to agitate against, and to seek to aid in the excising of, any "socialistic" (social democratic, welfare state) danglers that some liberals add, or try to add, to a "really genuine capitalism." So here, as in the times of the Roman Empire, as in the Middle Ages, as in Luther's time, and again in Marx's time, popular religion—the vast mass of religious activity—has, however unwittingly, served the ruling, or, if you will, the dominant, classes by supporting, and sometimes adroitly, their socioeconomic order.

There have, of course, throughout history, as part of the class struggles going on, been exceptions, even in popular religion: the Albigensians in Southern France during the Middle Ages, the Levellers in England, and the anti-Baptists in Germany and Central Europe during Luther's time. But these movements have been comparatively short-lived and have repeatedly been defeated. While Martin Luther was eventually glorified and became the founder of an important branch of Protestantism, his great contemporary Thomas Munzer, for leading the peasant rebellion and preaching the Kingdom of God on earth, was rewarded by being hounded all over Central Europe until he was finally cornered and hanged, drawn and quartered.

Still, it might be responded, that for our time at least, I have been one-sided and partisan: militant atheism once more raising its ugly head. There is, it can be continued, the phenomena of Martin Luther King, Jr., in the United States, Beyers Naudé and Desmond Tutu in South Africa, the "Red Archbishop" in Brazil, militant Marxist priests in Italy, Gregory Baum in Canada, Dorothea Sölle in Germany, and the whole movement (to speak more generally) of liberation theology. In a more reformist manner, there have been movements in the United Church of Canada and some of the mainline Protestant churches in the United States to aid refugees, to provide sanctuary for some of those political refugees declared illegal by the state, to struggle for the protection of the rights of gays and lesbians, and the like. And while the Catholic church is massively, and sometimes dangerously, reactionary on many issues, there was the stand of the Catholic bishops of Canada for social justice for workers and against nuclear proliferation. In short, while there are massively and pervasively in religions the ideological functions that Marxists have specified, religion is not always an ideological dike for the status quo. Sometimes religion is a force for social change. Sometimes, as in liberation theology, for example, it is even a force for radical social change, involving a commitment to a radical transformation of society.

That religion sometimes plays this role should be acknowledged and Engels's discussion of Thomas Munzer makes it perfectly evident that he, as did Marx, recognized that. But they also recognized that this transformative stream is a minor strand of religious thought and practice which has always been either defeated or gradually absorbed into large religious groups better fitting with the mode of production of the time. Thomas Munzer's movement failed. Gradually, after his assassination, Martin Luther King's movement lost much of its distinctiveness and thrust for progressive change. Beyers Naudé and Desmond Tutu were effective as aids to the ANC, but there they were aids to a powerful secular political movement. There are transformative elements in the Catholic church, but they exist in the interstices of a very conservative, and presently, and indeed for a long time, a capitalist sustaining church hierarchy, as was exemplified by Cardinal Spellman and, somewhat more subtly, is now exemplified by the present (1996) pope. Indeed, it is even possible to believe that, the good intentions of the Catholic progressives and radicals to the contrary notwithstanding, that they in effect aid in sustaining the legitimacy and authority of "The Church" (a generally very conservative church) by showing that it has room for many mansions—can be all things to all, or almost all, people. So by ideological lights "The Church" stands vindicated, yet remains a church which, as a whole, and particularly where it is secure, usually defends very reactionary policies. (Think of Catholicism in Ireland or in Québec thirty years ago.)

The situation is somewhat different with the mainline Protestant churches. With a membership which increasingly largely comes from the more educated and affluent strata of society, these denominations often have reasonably progressive social policies, though hardly policies that try to challenge the system. But, without such policies, its more educated membership would tend to drift into secularism with, à la Max Weber, the increasing disenchantment of the world. But it also, by advocating such policies, has paid the price of losing much of its working class and really impoverished (*lumpen-proletariat*) members to more popular religions which tend to be out and out reactionary, both in socioeconomic and theological terms. So, conveniently for the established order, we have one kind of church for one strata of society and another kind for another.

There is a lot more to be said here, including perhaps qualifications to what I have said above. Some of it would require more detailed and accurate knowledge than I have. But it seems to me that my descriptions are close enough to the mark to make the Marxian sociological hypothesis a good one. Religion is in fact massively the opium of the people. Intentionally or unintentionally—presumably most of the time unintentionally—religion supports the dominate mode of production, which in our societies is capitalism, and with that the usually conservative cultural accoutrements that go with and are generally functional for it. That sometimes religion does not take that path, does not play that role, does not refute that hypothesis, for it is a sociological generalization about *tendencies* and not an attempt to state an exceptionless law sustaining contrary-to-fact conditional, something that would, at best, have a very small place in most social science in any event.

VII

I want to return to something I merely gestured at earlier. Could one be a *historical* materialist, a communist, a believer in class struggle and accept as well much of the substance of the Marxist critique of religion as ideology, while remaining in a reasonably Orthodox sense a Jewish, Christian, or Islamic theist? My argument shall be that this is at least a logical possibility and *perhaps* a reasonable possibility as well. Recall, as we have seen, that while Marx and Engels were materialists in a roughly similar sense to the way that Holbach and Hobbes were materialists (what we would now call physicalists), they did not argue for their materialism, or develop it, but simply assumed it as something that had been firmly established by these Enlightenment thinkers.[16] And with this, they accepted, I think rightly, as a corollary, atheism and the denial of immortality. Here they were good Feuerbachians. Moreover, with this they also, of course, rejected the Judeo-Christian-Islamic worldview. But this rejection was not original and was not, in any very extended or careful way, argued for by them. But what they did argue for and what they were original about was historical materialism; a theory of ideology; the labor theory of value; and a theory of classes, class conflict, and class struggle. However, in the present context, at least, the phrase "historical materialism" is misleading, for, while it is compatible with materialism understood as physicalism (the thesis that matter—physical realities—alone exists or at least the claim that nothing else has a nonderivative and independent existence), it has, at best, only a tenuous relationship with materialism (physicalism). It neither affirms nor denies that matter alone exists or that all reality, or at least all independent reality, is physical. It says, rather, as an account of epochal social change, that the ways the forces (the powers) of production develop are the fundamental determinants of major long-range social change, or at least of such change when socioeconomically important. It is the claim that, as we have already quoted Engels as saying, "the great moving power of all important historic events is in the economic development of society," is "in the change in the modes of production and exchange" (296). But this is not materialism (physicalism). Indeed, it has very little, if anything, to do with it. It just so happens that Marx and Engels were materialists in both senses. But a dualist (whether religious or not) or a theist (Christian or otherwise) could accept *historical* materialism. A Christian, Jew, or Moslem could also be a socialist or communist, believing in both the desirability and immanent feasibility of such a socioeconomic ordering of society. A certain kind of Christian radicalism or egalitarianism might aid her in that. She might be a kind of contemporary Thomas Munzer. But her communism or socialism might just be held independently, but without being in conflict with her Christian beliefs. Similar things could be said for her belief in classes, class conflict, and the importance of class struggle. Not all Christians have been pacifists or politically quiescent by any means, to say nothing of Moslems or Jews. The stumbling block for the theist might perhaps be in the Marxian belief that religion is ideology. She could not, of course, say with Engels that all "religion is *nothing but* the fantastic reflection in men's minds of those external forces which control their daily life . . ." and she could not accept the claim that God was *merely* a projection of our emotions (146). She could not accept such a reductionist, projectionist, error-theory conception of God. Such an account is a semantical account about what "God" means or "belief in God" means that is incompatible with Christian, Jewish, or Islamic belief, or at least theism, and, in articulating their accounts of religion as ideology, Marx and Engels do indeed articulate it in such Feuerbachian terms and they make it perfectly plain, and perhaps in this they are right, that Feuerbach was not only deeply insightful, but that as well they believe that the general structure of his projection theory is correct. (What they object to is his going from there to articulate a new humanist religion of man, instead of rejecting the society in which it is necessary to have religious beliefs.) They claim that religious belief systems and practices generally tend to function to support and sustain the dominant socioeconomic structure of the society. Religious institutions (Catholicism, Calvinism, Judaism) generally function to reconcile people, and most particularly the dominated and oppressed people in the society, to the social order in which they live no matter how much the social order is a vale of tears for them. In this way religion is, or pervasively tends to be, the opium of the people.

These claims mentioned in the last three sentences are the core claims of the Marxian theory of religion as ideology and these claims could be true even if the projectionist semantical or ontological claims are false or the projectionist claims could be true while this account of religion as ideology is false. Freudians and Feuerbachians have a projectionist theory, but not the Marxian account of religion as ideology. And a Christian believer could accept the Marxian theory of religion as ideology while rejecting, as she must, the projectionist theory of religion with its utterly naturalistic account of what it means to speak of God and to believe in God. Marxians, as we have seen, are also projectionists about religious belief. But their projectionism is distinct from their account of the ideological functions of religion. The latter, which is distinctive of a Marxian account of religion, could be accepted without the former. *In fine, a Christian theist (if that is not pleonastic), or indeed any kind of Christian at all, could accept what is distinctive of, and canonical for, Marxianism, without abandoning her Christianity.* She could accept, and unqualifiedly, historical materialism; the account of ideology; the labor theory of value; the theory of class, class conflict, and class struggle; the Marxist conception of *praxis;* and communism. She could not, of course, accept Marx's atheism and his materialism (physicalism), but that is not distinctive of Marxianism. Holbach, Hobbes, W. V. O. Quine, Richard Rorty, Daniel Dennett, J. C. C. Smart, Peter Strawson, Stuart Hampshire, and Donald Davidson all accept physicalism, in one form or another, and with that they must, to be consistent, accept atheism. But they could do this—and indeed all of the above do—and still be utterly distant from Marxianism. They might even, as is the case for Quine, be very conservative and positively hostile to it. And, while atheism and materialism (physicalism) was indeed important for Marx and Engels, and Lenin and Gramsci as well, it was arguably not canonical for their theories, for all of the elements listed above as canonical get along quite well without it, while materialism (physicalism) and atheism, as say in Holbach or

Quine, do not at all require these canonical Marxian doctrines for their support or further rationalization.

A Christian could even consistently accept the opium conception of religious ideology and could either be a Christian quietist or a liberation theologian. She could believe, to consider the first alternative first, that, given the sinfulness and corruption of humankind, Christians should have nothing to do with politics or the secular ordering of society. That religion makes people pacific or quiescent before Caesar is just as it should be. In that way it is a good thing that religion is an opiate. Render unto Caesar what is Caesar's and unto God what is God's. The important thing is to attain purity of heart, to spread the Word, and prepare for, and contentedly and confidently await, the coming of the Kingdom of God in heaven. This is a "Spiritual World" that we will come to after our bodily death. Focus on purity of heart and "these last things" and forget about politics. It cannot, given what we sinful human beings are like, but be a dirty business anyway. We should turn away from it and strive to develop what some Germans under Hitler called an attitude of inner immigration.

This quietist, pietistic response is not the only, and I certainly do not think (to put it mildly) the best, Christian response to a Marxian theory of the ideological functions of religion, and it is certainly not compatible with a Marxian theory of class struggle. A better Christian response, accepting class struggle as well as a Marxian account of the ideological functions of religion, is that of liberation theology. Such a Christian could, and I believe should, say that Christianity almost invariably functions as such an opiating ideology. But, as we have seen, Marxianism does not say that religion always functions this way, let alone that it *must* do so. Such a radical Christian could say that Marxian theory does us—including religious believers—a very considerable service in pointing out that this is the pervasive role that religion has played in history and that it continues very powerfully and effectively to play this role today. Our task, such a radical Christian could remark, as Christians, aware of this ideological function, is to align ourselves with atheists, or anyone else with a similar political awareness and human commitment, to struggle to bring an end to class society and the exploitation of one human being by another and to create a socialist society of equals to bring about, if you want to use religious terminology, the Kingdom of God on earth, where exploitation and injustice would be at an end and where human beings would finally form a genuine community. It would be a community where they would at long last stand together as equals in caring relations. Jesus' identification with the poor and downtrodden and his injunction for us to love one another gives us a religious rationale for so acting and for so being.[17]

Thus, I think, that there are Christians, and not Christians in any phony sense either, as in (for example) the Braithwaite-Hare conception of what it is to be a Christian, who could consistently be Marxians or Marxists, if to be a Marxian or Marxist is to hold most of the things that I have claimed to be distinctive of, and canonical for, Marxianism or Marxism.[18]

VIII

Many Marxists or Marxians will be uneasy about what I have argued in the previous section. Are there any good reasons why they should be? Should we, if what I have called the canonical portions of Marxianism are approximately true, be militant Marxian atheists?

Most Marxians, in addition to seeing Marxianism as a emancipatory social theory, have also seen it as a *worldview*. Moreover, they have attached considerable importance to it being a coherent and rationally sustainable worldview. As Wilfrid Sellars and Richard Rorty took philosophers to be doing, and legitimately so, Marxians as well want to see how things hang together in the broadest and most inclusive sense of that term. They want to establish, in doing this, that talk of a Spiritual or Supernatural World is nonsense, or at least a mistake, and, as Marx put it grandly, to establish "the truth of this world" (42). Some of them were what we now call historicists (Gramsci most clearly), but none of them, not even Otto Neurath, were relativists, skeptics, or what some now call postmodernists, who think that there is no truth of this world, or of any world, to be established. They might, if they could have studied Quine and Davidson, and could have read their Putnam and Rorty, have come to be convinced that there is and can be no one uniquely true description of the world. But that would not lead them to relativism or skepticism or to a Mannheimanish sociology of knowledge-orientation anymore than Quine, Davidson, Putnam, and Rorty are so inclined or so entrapped (so conceptually imprisoned). It is one thing to say that there is no uniquely true description of the world and it is another thing again to say that there are no true accounts of what goes on in the world that can be warranted. Science, including social science, and careful commonsense description—aware of ideological snares—will give us knowledge, much of which is cumulative, and an increasingly more adequate grip on the world (including the social world). While remaining, as were Marx and Engels, resolutely anti-metaphysical, Marxians thought, and contemporary ones continue to think, that we can gain an increasingly more adequate thoroughly naturalistic world outlook (58–68, 289–96). But this excluded religion as a source of truth and required us (a) to regard it as a cluster of human projections and (b) to treat it as a mystifying ideology, though some thought, in certain circumstances, as with Munzer, as, all the same, and (a) and (b) notwithstanding, a useful instrument (mythical as it is) to use in achieving emancipation. But, more typically, as we have seen, it functions as an instrument for conservatism: an instrument for sustaining the hegemony of the ruling classes, impeding the coming into existence of a genuinely democratic society, where we would live in a world of equals.

However, could we not reject the Marxian naturalistic worldview while still accepting what I have called the canonical parts of Marxianism, i.e., the emancipatory social science or critical theory perspective, that arguably really turns the machinery, if anything does, on the theoretical side of the struggle for socialism and a classless exploitation-free society?[19] The answer is yes: a Christian or a Jew or a Moslem could consistently reject such a naturalistic worldview while wholeheartedly accepting the canonical parts of Marxianism. Would it not, however, be a *reasonable* thing—or perhaps even the most reasonable thing—to stick with the naturalism *and* the cannonical parts of Marxianism? That, I believe, depends on your estimate of the intellectual strength of naturalism. If, on the one hand, you think, as Marx and Engels evidently do, that a materialistic or naturalistic antimetaphysics on the Holbach-Hobbes-Hume-Bayle continuum has plainly and unassailably, or even with just a considerable degree of plausibility, established a naturalistic view of the world, then you will conclude that building anything on the mere fact that canonical Marxianism and some forms of Christianity are not logically incompatible is not a reasonable thing to do.[20] If, on the other hand, you think that naturalism is a mistaken, problematic, or at least a rationally unmotivated, worldview, indeed perhaps even itself an unwitting metaphysics, revealing more about our *Weltgeist* than anything else, then you will not, or at least should not, think that that is so. You may be more hospitable to a Christian-Marxian possibility.

IX

The reason that this is the way that things stand in Marxian discussions of such issues, and that there is little argument for naturalism in Marxianism, is that Marxians, like George Santayana, who, politically speaking, was very conservative, just take it as obvious that physicalism and atheism are true. I think this is so too, but I realize that a good number of knowledgeable people do not, so I have in my writing about religion, my Marxianism notwithstanding, *argued* for naturalism. If one does not, one just side-steps argument and discussion with theists or Wittgensteinian fideists. That, for good or for ill, is where it is at in "the philosophy of religion game." I wish the *philosophy* of religion game would wither away.[21] It seems to me to pose no intellectually challenging problems, but that notwithstanding, like Gramsci and Durkheim, I think religion is a very important cultural phenomena indeed. Religion is not just superstition or just a bunch of intellectual blunders or cognitive mistakes. I agree with Marx Wartofsky's remarks, quoted at the beginning of this chapter, that an adequate materialist conception of religion could not so treat religion. But, as Wartofsky does too, I wish we would come to look at religion in good Durkheimian fashion as *just an important cultural phenomena* and orient ourselves, and orient our understanding of the world and our struggles in the world, in accordance with that perception. But, alas, we cannot just start there, if we wish to engage in the deliberations about religion going on in our society. As long as there are thoughtful and informed Christians, Jews, and Moslems in our midst, we cannot, if we wish to carry on a discussion of religion which includes them too, *just assume naturalism.* So we must, in trying (perhaps hopelessly) to gain some reasonable consensus about the truth about our world, engage in the whole dreary discussion again (mopping up after Hume, as I call it) and write about religion as J. L. Mackie, Antony Flew, Wallace Matson, Michael Martin, Ronald Hepburn, and I have, hoping that someday we can push discussion on to the purely cultural territory on which Feuerbach, Marxians, Freudians, and Durkheimians have placed it: to come to ask *not* whether its doctrines are true, or reasonably to be believed to be true or rationally to be accepted solely on faith, but instead to consider questions concerning religion solely as questions about what role religion plays, should play, can come not to play, and should come not to play in society and in the lives of human beings. Can human beings—not just a few relatively privileged individuals in a sea of religious people, but whole cultures of human beings—live without religion? And, if they can, should they? These are some of the questions that we should be asking: these are questions that should be on our intellectual and moral agenda. Looking at things this way, among other things, provides common ground for discussion between physicalists-materialists-naturalists, on the one hand, and Jews, Christians, and Moslems, on the other. Here we have something that, standing where we stand now in cultural history, no thoughtful and informed person should think she has a good answer to.

Many Marxians—most notably Marx, Engels, Lenin, and Trotsky—thought they had good answers to these questions. Human beings, they believed, could, and indeed will, attain a classless society, and when they do, they will no longer need religion. They will also not need religion when they are self-consciously traveling on the road to a classless society, as many will be, near the end of the bourgeois era with late capitalism. When, that is, they are close to it, and self-consciously struggling for it, they also will not, in such a circumstance, need religion and indeed should not have it, for it generally stands in the way of their emancipation (including their resolutely acting) and of their flourishing. Religious beliefs, they believe, are at best false and generally have harmful effects. In this they are one with Hume, though Hume, for prudentially understandable reasons, was more circumspect about this than were the classical Marxists. Thus religion, when the circumstances are right, can, and also should, gradually disappear from the cultural life of human beings, except as a cultural memory: an artifact, though a very important record of how human beings in the trying circumstances of class societies came to grips with their lives. And religion, they believed, will so gradually disappear with the stable achievement of first, socialism and then communism. Even if some form of liberation theology is coherent, it, truth being a not inconsiderable value too, is not something to be believed in and it should only be regarded as desirable as a *tactical* measure in certain circumstances: circumstances in which it would be useful in the progressive movement of society.

The atheism of Marxists is not the wistful atheism of Santayana or the resigned atheism of Freud or the ironical atheism of Hume, but, like Holbach's, a militant atheism. (Indeed, with Lenin it takes an extreme form of militancy.) Marxians want a true view of the world and our place in it (if such can be had) to be available to as many people as possible and for it to become a part of their lives; and they want, as well, people, themselves included, to be able to live without illusions and opiates and that means, they believe, *doing without religion*. This would come to a liberation of humankind from both the illusion of religion and the conditions that make that illusion necessary.

X

That Marxian vision of things is more problematical for us now, standing where we are in history, than it was for the classical Marxists. This is so for at least two reasons. We can no longer reasonably share the optimism of Marx, Engels, and Lenin that a classless society is plainly achievable. We seem as far from it as ever, perhaps even farther. The Soviet Thermidor was a bad thing, but when what replaced it was not a demystified democratic socialism, or at least social democracy, but the violent mess, lawless and corrupt we have now, for a time at least, a great hope went out of the world.[22] It can come to seem to us, looking at what was once the Soviet Union and what once was Yugoslavia, a hopeless ideal, as unworldly as Christian ideals. To take socialism and then communism as being something to be taken to be reasonably on the historical agenda can come to seem like a bad joke, something out of line with the world we know or can reasonably expect to come into being. I hope that that skepticism is an overreaction to our recent history. But it very well may, as "common wisdom" has it now, run deeper than that. Perhaps socialism and a Marxian vision of the world are dead. That is a reason, a reason that Marx did not have, to rethink questions about the import of religion as a *cultural phenomenon*, the truth of atheism (if indeed it is true) to the contrary notwithstanding. Perhaps it is both an opiate and a saving *myth?*

Perhaps, but only perhaps, if we are naturalists, we should have either the wistful atheism of a Santayana or the resigned atheism of a Freud and *not* the militant atheism of a Marx.

The second reason for greater pessimism than Marx and Engels and the other classical Marxists had is the neglect by classical Marxists of what I have called the existential problems of religion (our tangled lives, the inevitability of death, failing powers, and the like). These problems are not going to go away in any kind of society, no matter how classless and enlightened. Even if religion functions ideologically in the manner characterized by Marxists, it also, and even looked at just as a cultural phenomena, functions as a set of be‍liefs and practices which provide if not an answer, at least a response to and a stance to be taken toward these existential problems. Is there a secular al‍ternative that is as adequate or even more adequate than Jewish, Christian, Is‍lamic, or otherwise religious responses? Some of us can, as Hume and Freud did, face our death, our pain, and the destruction and madness, cultural and otherwise, all around us, stoically, and with a measured stance, not availing ourselves of the consolations of religion. Indeed, some of us *could not*, given our beliefs about what is and can be the case, so avail ourselves of the con‍solations of religion even if we wanted to. But should we, and can we, rea‍sonably, expect this to be the response of more than a very few resolute and clearheaded intellectuals fortunately situated? Should we want it generally to be the response of human beings to religion—particularly human beings in conditions of reasonable security and abundance?

Both Hume and Freud thought such an atheistic option was a live option for only a very few. Perhaps they were too pessimistic and elitist here. But perhaps not. And perhaps even Freud had his substitutes for religion? Some, of course, would say that the same obtains for Marx. Still, if we can, assum‍ing we have had the good fortune to be soberly educated, learn, as did Hume, Freud, Marx, Lenin, Gramsci, and a host of others, to face these existential problems without benefit of religion, should we? The standard answer is that we should because truth, though surely not the only good thing in the world, is one of the very important good things. But we should also not forget Niet‍zsche's and Foucault's reminders of the tricks we play on ourselves here.[23] But that notwithstanding, to overcome self-deception, other deception, cul‍tural deception, and to come to see things, as close as we can come to see them, rightly is something of not inconsiderable value. If the cumulative ar‍guments and ways of viewing things of the Holbachian-Hobbesian-Humean-Feuerbachian-Marxian continuum are on the mark, or near to it, then, given the very great value that truth has for us, we should be led away from a reli‍gious response to these existential problems.

However, we should not forget that truth—though a very great good—is one good among others and it might, in this context, be outweighed by other considerations. A Kierkegaardian might respond to the taking of such an atheist stance by saying that only self-deception, or at least a not reflecting long enough and hard enough or responding nonevasively enough to such existential problems, can lead us to think that we can overcome despair and utter hopelessness without a commitment to Christ. To do so, we must indeed crucify our intellects, believe in what is utterly absurd, but without such a leap, if we are cursed with being reflective and nonevasive about ourselves, we will find our lives utterly meaningless.

However, such a claim, at least if taken straightforwardly, is false and, taken unstraightforwardly, question-begging. People in many cultural situations have made sense of their lives without such a religious leap and it is, moreover, hardly conducive to self-respect to believe, or try to believe, what we also believe to be absurd or, what comes to much the same thing, to crucify our intellects. If faith really requires that, perhaps we can make sense of our lives, face death and the madness around us, without that Kierkegaardian blind leap of faith.

Human beings rather more generally (or so we like to think), and not just philosophers and other intellectuals, wish to see life as a whole and to see how things hang together as a whole, so that they can come to have something of a coherent view of the world they live in. And with this, they wish to make sense of their lives. They often, as well, have some hopes (perhaps unrealistic ones) of making this world of ours a little more human: a better world with less injustice, more trust, caring, and flourishing. Moreover, they also, if these hopes are serious, will want to know what must be done for that to be in some measure achieved, if indeed it can be achieved or even approximated.

An Enlightenment view of the world, say the view resulting from a coherent amalgamation and rational reconstruction of the core conceptions, arguments, and narratives of Enlightenment thinkers, for example, the Holbach-Hobbes-Hume-Feuerbach-Marx continuum, provide something of that. Perhaps the greatest weakness in such naturalism has been in grappling with what I have called the existential problems of life. Its attitude here has often been too rationalistic, but here some progress is being made. Antonio Gramsci, Kare Korsch, Richard Robinson, Erich Fromm, Max Horkheimer, Theodor Adorno, and Walter Benjamin in different ways have shown how those existential problems can be treated from a thoroughly naturalistic but still a thoroughly nonscientistic and nonrationalistic perspective.

XI

Let me see, with that in mind, if I can pull together some of the strands of my discussion and produce something that bears some resemblance to a conclusion to this chapter. Marx and Marxians see religion as a collection of at best false beliefs and, as well, of beliefs that are through and through ideological. Religious beliefs and practices function most typically as a support for the dominant class structure. That is their typical ideological function. They very often do that by consoling and mystifying the downtrodden with a belief in a glorious afterlife in God's Kingdom in heaven. There can be no doubt that religion so functions, but, in a way little noticed by Marxians, it also has what I have called existential functions. It helps us to make sense of our lives and to face our deaths, various human trials, and even the tragedies and horrors that may very well be our lot: the various ills that Simone de Beauvoir has described so starkly and so powerfully. It helps us to face things such as the loss of our powers and the death or disability (such as a decline into senility or to be wracked with cancer) of ourselves and, as well, of those we love. And it helps us come to grips with the seeing of all our hopes for a more humane world defeated.

Marxianism, as a militant atheism, with a firm belief in the desirability of the disappearance of religion, when the situation warrants, must, to yield a fully plausible materialist conception of religion, supply secular substitutes for the religious ways of meeting those existential problems. It, as I have remarked, has traditionally had little to say here, but, I think, consistently with its naturalistic and historical materialist framework (with its related materialist conception of religion), it can make a good response. Let me broach this first by a little social description followed by concocting a couple of possible scenarios for the future and then by commenting on them. First, the social description. The advent of socialism, and after that of communism, and the achievement of a classless society would have to bring with it with high levels of material abundance for all, with security, leisure, and educational opportunities for all human beings to develop their capacities, to follow out their interests and to have the wherewithal to live decently together. It would also be the coming to be of a democratic society of equals, where people together would control and order their own lives. There would in such a world also be the achieving of justice and conditions where people could live with dignity. But these things have not been achieved anywhere. Instead, particularly when we consider it at all globally, we live in a horrible world indeed—a world which seems rather steadily to get worse. Multitudes of people live in conditions which in some key respects are not so different from that of the slaves, destitute freeman and peasants in the Roman Empire at the time of the origin of Christianity or the peasants in Germany during Luther's and Munzer's time. People starve to the tune of fifty thousand a day and many, who manage not to starve, are so malnourished in childhood that for the rest of what in all likelihood will be their rather short lives, they are incapable of functioning normally. More generally, multitudes of people live desperate, marginalized lives in utter poverty and without any reasonable expectation or even hope that their lot will substantially change for the better. And that obtains in a world where the wealth of the world's 358 billionaires is greater than the combined incomes of countries with 45 percent of the world's people. In such circumstances, just as Marxians expect, religions flourish in fantastic forms and plainly, and understandably, function as opiates, as an *ersatz* heart in a heartless world. The existential problems just add an even greater overload to the problems mentioned above that weigh them down. They are not only impoverished, their face-to-face relations with their intimates go all to hell as well. It is the world of the film *Shortcuts* together with general poverty. In the face of things like this, the capitalist world might just be rolling on to what looks like a condition of utter inhumanness for vast numbers of people. In such circumstances, neither Marxians nor anyone else, if they are at all reasonable, will expect religion to disappear. The conditions that make it necessary remain firmly in place.

Suppose, however, to turn more to my scenarios, instead, after a bit, either of two things happen. Suppose, first, that social democracy gains a new lease on life with neo-liberal and libertarian market romanticism disappearing, so that we can finally get capitalism with a human face (something similar to what we have in Scandinavia now), and suppose further, on this first scenario, this gradually, with steady improvements along the way, becomes global. Globally, that is, we gradually come to have security, reasonable material well-being, reasonably high levels of education and leisure, and some reasonable measure of equality. There, if such a situation ever comes about, we can reasonably expect religion to wither away as it in fact has in Scandinavia, a few Bergmanesque frettings aside. The existential functions of religion in such circumstances will be replaced by secular ones, the practice probably proceeding the theory. We will have Weberian disenchantment of the world without despair or *angst* being pervasive in our societies.

Suppose, alternatively, no such humanizing of capitalism is possible, social democratic ways to abundance and equality do not work. We might in such a circumstance stay mired, for a not inconsiderable time, in the same old horrible world. If that obtains, then there will be plenty of ideological work for religion to do and it will flourish in the doing of it. It will remain an opiate and its existential functions will not be replaced by secular existential functions. But suppose, to go to our second scenario, in the face of the collapse of such social democratic hopes, a new militancy emerges among the *proletariat* and the *lumpen-proletariat* (the great mass of poorly off or relatively poorly off or destitute people —if you do not like Marxian categories). Suppose, in addition, that among the poorly off, which is now most of the society, there exists an often reasonably well-educated workforce (including here professional workers). But their lives, let us further suppose, like the lives of the unemployed (functionally unemployable), become very vulnerable and their material conditions, including their workplace conditions and job security, steadily worsen. Suppose further that these are conditions that obtain, among other places, pervasively in the advanced industrial societies (the great capitalist democracies). Eventually, in such a circumstance, let us further, and not implausibly, assume, becoming militant, many of these workers, together with the unemployed, so act as to topple capitalism and begin the construction of, and eventually set in place, a socialist socioeconomic order (probably now some form of market socialism). In doing this they also gradually bring about a democratically ordered, roughly egalitarian society of abundance and security. Again we can reasonably expect, as in the social democratic scenario, religion to wither away. The memory of religion's ideological support for capitalism will be in the awareness of the people making the revolution. Moreover, given the changed material conditions, and given the Marxian worldview that would go with such a socialism, religion's existential functions would, or so at least it is reasonable to expect, be gradually replaced by purely secular ones. Given its actuality and the interests it answers to, it is not unreasonable to expect of that world with that worldview that secular existential functions would replace the religious ones rather more readily than in the social democratic scenario.

Here are two ways to a world without belief in God or any other religious conceptions. If they are unfeasible, it is not because of the thought that religion in such societies (if they should ever come to be) would not be given up without life being adversely affected. If they are unfeasible, it is rather because we think that it is very unlikely that either of these socioeconomic orders will ever come into being, let alone be sustained, on anything even like a worldwide scale. It is easy to believe that either conception is as badly utopian, or at least nearly so, as pie in the sky by and by. Without speculating on the likelihoods here, what I think we can and should say is this: given the truth of naturalism, there are describable circumstances, and *perhaps* feasible circumstances (circumstances which would be good to have in any case), where it would be possible (if the circumstances obtaining are possible) to have a Godless world where it would, as well, be a good thing to live in such a world. (Suppose Iceland, with its fish stocks still in place, were the world.) It surely would be a much better world than anything we have now.

In the world we have now, it is, of course, *unthinkable* that religion would disappear or even that it would disappear as an opiate keeping only its existential functions. Is it a good thing that people are religious in such situations (that is, in our real-life situations)? The answer is both yes and no. Yes, in that it gives something of a heart in a heartless world; no, in the sense that it diminishes, with its opiating and obfuscating effects, the capacity of such exploited and degraded people to struggle against the conditions of their existence or even to see clearly their condition and the possibilities for its alteration. The obfuscating and opiating effects of religion—social effects of religion which are both pervasive and persistent—stand in the way of their seeing the possibility of, the desirability of, and the necessity for, struggle to make it the case that the conditions where religion is a need no longer obtain. However, the crucial point here is that it is pointless to ask if it is good or bad for them to have religious beliefs when they cannot but have them in their actual circumstances. Munzer plausibly claimed that struggle against such conditions, for the very down-and-out, can only take form in the garb—the vocabulary and the conceptualizations—of religion, hence his stress on the Kingdom of God on earth. In circumstances of poverty; ignorance; hopelessness; relentless, exacting domination—conditions where life is intolerable—we cannot but have religion and religion, at least in the first instance, as an obfuscating opiate.

In life situations not so severe, but still bad, as is the situation for most middle strata people in Canada and the United Sates now, we get things in between such as the mushiness and mindless blandness of much popular religion in such countries, but mindless and mushy as it is, it still continues to play both an obfuscating and opiating function in such societies. (I do not speak of the Religious Right, which, though mindless and opiating, is not in all instances bland and, in all ways, mushy.) Here Gramsci's stress is important on Marxism as a worldview taking on, though in an utterly naturalistic spirit, many of the cultural functions of religion. Perhaps such a worldview, if Marxian intellectuals could socialize the masses into accepting this "secularized religion," might come to effectively replace religion. But again we should not fail to take to heart the fact that nothing like this has happened. Moreover, given our historical experience, the idea of "The Party" replacing "The Church" does resonate with us.

These Gramscian considerations aside, where security levels of work, wealth, and education are considerable and democratic institutions are in place and stable, it is plausible to expect, where this persists for sometime, that we will get, and valuably so, a move to a greater secularization of society and a diminution of religion. And where in such a circumstance religion persists for some, we can also reasonably expect it to lose more and more of its doctrinal substance and for it, for the individuals involved, to become more and more an optional matter. Given the truth of naturalism, that, in such circumstances, is a good thing. There is no more need for opiates or for crucifying or even an obfuscating of the intellect. And the existential functions of religion, even without Gramsci's "secularized religion," can be meet in purely secular ways. Sometimes it is cloaked in a traditionally religious garb, but, where it is, it has come to have a *secular substance*. (Think here of the Braithwaite-Hare stuff or of Wittgensteinian fideism.) To be in such a situation, Marx took to be a very great good for human beings. And the things human beings would have in such a situation would also be good—indeed great goods—and about both of these matters Marx was right.

XII

Finally, I want, as a kind of coda to my conclusion, to return to the passage from Marx Wartofsky that I cited at the beginning of this chapter.[24] Wartofsky pertinently asks, "Is there a viable materialist conception of religion?" I take it that here, Wartofsky means 'materialist' in both the historical materialist sense and the physicalist sense. And, as we have seen, while these conceptions are conceptions which fit well together—they have a kind of *Weltanschuungish* affinity—still, not being logically or conceptually linked, they do not entail each other. It is, that is, very natural for someone who is a historical materialist to also be a physicalist. They are, for a historical materialist, in the same cultural space.

I have argued that, more than that, we can reasonably be both physicalists and historical materialists. Though independent, the case for both, particularly when historical materialism is given a minimalist reading and the physicalism is of a nonreductive sort, is very strong. It is not just that they conventionally go together, though they do that. Moreover, if we are consistent physicalists, we will also be atheists. That many who are physicalists (i.e., materialists) do not so label themselves—say they are atheists—reveals much about the evasive fastidiousness, even the finickiness, of many intellectuals with their characteristic fear of being thought to be anything that might be taken to be obvious or vulgar.[25] If, moreover, we are nonreductive physicalists (roughly à la Davidson, Rorty, or Strawson) and we are atheists of a broadly Humean sort (Humean as updated, vis-à-vis religion, by a consistent amalgam of J. L. Mackie, Antony Flew, and Bernard Williams) and we are as well minimalist historical materialists, then, if we turn to an account of religion's ideological functions similar to that of Engels, we will have come to have a viable materialist conception of religion, or at least have a good candidate for such a viable conception, if these accounts taken together are on independent grounds in the ballpark for being plausible candidates for being true.[26] But these things taken independently are good candidates for being true. Moreover, these things hang together in a plausible way, contributing to our reflective and rational desire to see, if we can, how things hang together: to get a coherent overall view of our situation.

Assuming—plausibly, I think—some nonreductive physicalism (the exact form for my purposes is unimportant) and assuming as well a broadly Humean atheism, I have set out, and argued for, a Marxian account of religion, an account which is essentially that of Engels. I have, after setting it out, also argued that it is plausible to believe that the story it tells, particularly if supplemented, as I have argued it can be, by a materialist account of the existential functions of religion, is a good approximation to the truth (to the most plausible way for now of seeing how things hang together). Moreover, it seems to me to be also true that we have no alternative materialist account which is more plausible, though it plainly is an account which builds on Feuerbach's impressive materialist account and that, in some ways, Feuerbach's account should be seen, though subject to Marx's and Engels's strictures, as filling in their accounts.[27] A Marxian account, or a Marxian-Feuerbachian account, explains religion, without explaining it away, as a function of our needs. It specifies some of those needs and, meeting what in effect are Wartofsky's criteria of adequacy for a viable materialist conception of religion, it explains religion's "origins, its distinctive and historical forms, its persistence in various institutional contexts, its changes and development, its continuing and present existence in the modes of belief and action of individuals."[28] It could, of course, be both more nuanced and filled in much more fully than Engels does, or than even Engels and Feuerbach taken together do, and it is likely to be mistaken in some of its details. But this—nuancing, filling in, and minor correcting—is something which can be done while using that very materialist conception of religion. We have, as is often the case in science as well, a bootstrapping operation here.

Viewing philosophy, as Wilfrid Sellars and Richard Rorty do, as an attempt to see how things hang together in the broadest sense of that term and applying this conception of philosophy here, with (a) a physicalism of a nonreductive, nonmetaphysical variety (à la Rorty and, in effect, Davidson), with (b) a broadly Humean atheism, and with (c) with a Marxian conception of the ideological functions of religion, we have (taking them together), and particularly if supplemented by a Durkheimian conception of the function of religion (an equally naturalistic conception of the function of religion), a very plausible accounting of how things in some areas central to our lives hang together and, we have, as well, a very plausible candidate for a viable materialist (naturalist) conception of religion.

Suppose it is responded that no viable *materialist* conception of religion is possible, for to be a materialist one it must explain religious beliefs as being at best false, and this, the response goes, is to explain religious phenomena away, rather than to explain the phenomena. But, as Wartofsky well insists himself, the response continues, an account which explains religion away cannot be an adequate account of religion. However, it is question-begging to claim that a conception of religion which takes key religious beliefs, such as God exists and providentially cares for humankind, to be false or incoherent, must, by making that very claim, be explaining the *phenomena* of religion away. An account which explains how religion arises, how it is sustained, what deep human needs and interests it answers to, how it is crucial under certain material conditions to give meaning to the lives of human beings and to supply, or partially supply, the social cement of society (the bonding between human beings), certainly does not explain the phenomena of religion away, but explains it, and that is exactly what a Marxian account does.[29]

NOTES

1. Andrew Levine, "What is a Marxist Today?" in *Analyzed Marxism*, ed. R. X. Ware and Kai Nielsen (Calgary: Alberta: University of Calgary Press, 1989), 29–58; and Kai Nielsen, "Analytical Marxism: A Form of Critical Theory," *Erkenntnis* 39 (1993): 1–21; Kai Nielsen, "Elster's Marxism," *Philosophical Papers* 21, no. 2 (1992): 83–106; Kai Nielsen, *Marxism and the Moral Point of View* (Boulder, Colo.: Westview Press, 1989); and Joe McCarney, *The Real World of Ideology* (London: Harvester Press, 1980).

2. G. A Cohen, *Karl Marx's Theory of History: A Defense* (Princeton, N.J.: University of Princeton Press, 1978), 158

3. Joshua Cohen, "Minimalist Historical Materialism," in *On the Track of Reason: Essays in Honor of Kai Nielsen*, ed. Rodger Beehler et al. (Boulder, Colo.: Westview Press, 1992), 161. See also G. A. Cohen, *History, Labor, and Freedom* (Oxford: Clarendon Press, 1988), 3–108.

4. G. A. Cohen, *Karl Marx's Theory of History*, 173.

5. Kai Nielsen, *Marxism and the Moral Point of View*, 98–116; and Kai Nielsen, "Some Marxist and Non-Marxist Conceptions of Ideology," *Rethinking Marxism* 2, no. 4 (Winter 1989): 146–74.

6. Nielsen, "Analytical Marxism,"1–21; Nielsen, "Afterword: Remarks on the Roots of Progress," in *Analyzing Marxism,* 497–539; Nielsen, "Elster's Marxism"; Nielsen, "On Taking Historical Materialism Seriously," *Dialogue* 22, no. 2 (June 1983); and Nielsen, "Historical Materialism, Ideology and Ethics," *Studies in Soviet Thought* 29 (January 1985): 47–64.

7. Gramsci might seem out of step here with the Marxist tradition, for he argued for a "secular Marxist religion." However, like Braithwaite and Fromm, he uses "religion" in an extended sense to connote a worldview, a *Weltanschauung,* with affective practices and commitments, whether naturalistic or not. Antonio Gramsci, *Quademi del Carcere,* ed. V. Gerrantana (Turin: Einaudi, 1975) 2185–86. See also Nielsen, "Reconceptualizing Civil Society for Now: Some Somewhat Gramscian Turnings," *Arena Journal,* n.s., no. 2 (1993/94): 159–74; and Kai Nielsen, "Marx and the Enlightenment Project," *Critical Review* 2, no. 4 (Fall 1988): 59–75.

8. See the selection from *The Holy Family* in Karl Marx and Friedrich Engels, *On Religion* (Moscow: Foreign Languages Publishing House, 1957). This is a useful collection of their writings on religion from Marx's doctoral dissertation (1841) to Engels's late writings on the history of early Christianity (1894–95). The selection from *The Holy Family* is from chapter 6 of *The Holy Family.*

9. Engels, *On Religion*, 290. Future references to Marx *or* Engels or to Marx *and* Engels will be given in the text and will be taken from *On Religion.*

10. Engels does not say what he means by calling them "nonsensical." He could simply have meant that they were plainly absurd. There is no reason to attribute to him the strict logical positivist sense of "nonsensical" as "being without sense."

11. There is here the "demarcation problem." From at least Kant to Husserl, to Wittgenstein and to ordinary language philosophy, there has been a concern to demarcate philosophy from other activities and to isolate for it something purely conceptual. Even with a Quinian rejection of that very enterprise, a rejection, that is, of any attempt at a demarcation that would isolate something pure and distinctive for philosophy to be, "uncontaminated by the empirical," the actual *practice* of analytic philosophy (Quine's included) is as if such a demarcation has been made and sustained. Given that practice, what Marx and Engels are doing in discussing religion is, for the most part, not philosophy. In considering that, we can go either of two ways. We can simply say "So what!" and go on with our business or we can argue that we should reject such essentialism over and in philosophy and claim instead that concern with demarcation is just that. Whichever way we go, I think it is important to keep hold of the fact that it is truth that we are after in discussing the issues Marx and Engels raise. Concerning demarcation, see both the introduction and the contribution by John Passmore in *Méta-Philosophie: Reconstructing Philosophy?* ed. Jocelyne Couture and Kai Nielsen (Calgary, Alberta: University of Calgary Press, 1993), 1–55 and 107–25.

12. I think it is quite mistaken to assume, as Engels does, that religion was at first simply personifications of the forces of nature and that only later did religion become involved with the personification of social forces. From what we know about primitive religions, both the personification of natural and social forces are involved in the religion of primitive societies. But that Engels is mistaken here, if he is mistaken, has no effect on the general viability of his account of religion as ideology.

13. Engels is plainly, as almost everyone was during that time, Eurocentric here. It is not the Western world, where Christianity reigned, which constitutes "by far the larger part of civilized humanity." There were many other great centers of civilization as well.

14. "Social Darwinism" goes in scare quotes because it is unclear whether "Social Darwinism" makes much sense. See Morton White, *Social Thought in America: The Revolt Against Formalism* (Boston: Beacon Press, 1957), 6–162, 206–22; and Richard Hofstadter, *Social Darwinism in American Thought*, rev. ed. (Boston: Beacon Press, 1955). It is very doubtful that sociobiology has made any difference to these analyses and appraisals of the viability of Social Darwinism.

15. Erich Fromm, *Marx's Conception of Man* (New York: Frederick Ungar Publishing Co., 1961), 24–57. See also his *Psychoanalysis and Religion* (London: Victor Gollancz Ltd., 1951) and his *The Dogma of Christ and Other Essays on Religion, Psychology and Culture* (London: Victor Gollancz Ltd., 1963).

16. They, however, no more than Hume, are mechanistic materialists. In that their materialism differed from that of Holbach. But very few physicalists nowadays are also mechanists.

17. However, as Engels makes clear in his critique of Feuerbach, it is a mistake to put "literary phrases in place of scientific knowledge, the liberation of mankind by means of 'love' in place of the emancipation on the *proletariat* through the economic transformation of production" (Engels, *On Religion*, 224).

18. One of the things that I think should be dropped from the canonical core of Marxianism is the labor theory of value. Historically speaking, of course, it has been a central part of Marxism, but it also has been an albatross around its neck and many Marxists with impeccable credentials, e.g., G. A. Cohen, Andrew Levine, and John Roemer, have dropped it.

19. Gramsci would be one Marxist who would not accept that. While being a materialist in both the senses we have discussed, he also very much thought that Marxism needed to articulate a total worldview that could and would be diffused throughout whole

societies. He agreed with Croce that *the great problem of the modern age*—perhaps here reflecting too much the particular situation of Italy of their time—*was to learn to live without religion, that is without traditional confessional religion.* Croce thought the central political task was to establish an utterly *secular* "religion of liberty," what we would now call a secular humanism. Gramsci dismissed that as "an atheism for aristocrats" and argued that we need a unified and culturally pervasive *proletarian atheism.* Societies, such as Italy, needed a coherent, unitary, society-wide diffused conception of life and of human nature. He called this a "lay philosophy" (something some now call a "public philosophy") and, as it gripped a whole culture, it would generate an ethic, a way of life, a civil and individual form of conduct. This "lay philosophy" was, in his terms, to come to function as a "secularized religion" and it would be a functional replacement of traditional religion. It was, as he put it, to be an "absolute secularization and earthiness of thought, an absolute humanism of history." He thought that "Marxism was the only religious faith that is adequate to the contemporary world and can produce a real hegemony" (Gramsci, *Quademidel Carcere,* 1854–64). It is not only, on his conception, that Marxism is a scientific theory, a political strategy, an understanding of history, a philosophy, it is also a new secularized religion which would make in an integrated way this worldview and practical ethic into a distinctive and total culture pattern. To so speak of religion and faith is a similar extension of the use of "religion" as we find it in Feuerbach, Fromm, Braithwaite, and Wittgensteinian fideists. But it is very plain that for Gramsci this religion was a Marxian atheistic *Weltanschauung.* His concern is with the dynamics by which it would become an integrated part of modern culture and come to be hegemonic in society. Indeed, it would provide a deep and holistic transformation of society. When we attend to the content of what he is saying, the phrase "secularized religion" ceases to be misleading. The key question for us to ask now, standing where we stand, is to ask of his conception the question that Rawlsian social democratic liberals ask of communitarians. Given the *de facto* intractability of pluralism in the societies of the capitalist democracies, is such an integrated total *Weltanschauung* achievable and sustainable without a morally unacceptable use of force? Indeed, is it even stably achievable with the use of such force? Our historical experience in recent decades should incline us to think not. See the references in note 7, and see W. Adamson, "Gramsci and the Politics of Civil Society," *Praxis International* 7, nos. 3–4 (1987–88): 327–28. See also W. Adamson, *Hegemony and Revolution: Antonio Gramsci's Political and Cultural Theory* (Berkeley, Calif.: University of California Press, 1980).

20. Relying, it could be further replied to the Christian, on such purely logical possibilities and setting aside what makes a good claim to be a more plausible conception of things (here naturalism) because it is not *conclusively* established is just the quest for certainty all over again.

21. Where I discussed such traditional philosophical matters most traditionally and extensively was in my *Reason and Practice* (New York: Harper and Row, 1971), 135–257.

22. G. A. Cohen, "The Future of Disillusion," in *Psychoanalysis, Mind and Art: Perspectives on Richard Wollheim,* ed. Jim Hopkins and Anthony Savile (Oxford, England: Blackwell's, 1992), 142–60.

23. Barry Allen, *Truth in Philosophy* (Cambridge, Mass.: Harvard University Press, 1993).

24. Marx W. Wartofsky, "*Homo Homini Deus Est*: Feuerbach's Religious Materialism," in *Meaning, Truth, and God,* ed. Leroy S. Rouner (Notre Dame, Ind.: University of Notre Dame Press, 1982), 154–55.

25. For example, see Barry Allen, "Atheism, Relativism, Enlightenment and Truth," *Studies in Religion* 23, no. 2 (1994). For a forthright expression of atheism by a philoso-

pher whose methodology is very similar to Allen's, see Richard Rorty, "Religion as Conversation-Stopper," *Common Knowledge* 3, no. 1 (Spring 1944): 1–6. See my reply to Allen in the same issue of *Studies in Religion*. See also the next chapter.

26. J. L. Mackie, *The Miracle of Theism* (Oxford England: Clarendon Press, 1982); Antony Flew, "The Burden of Proof," in *Knowing Religiously,* ed. Leroy S. Rouner (Notre Dame, Ind.: University of Notre Dame Press, 1985), 103–15; and Bernard Williams, "Review of *The Miracle of Theism,*" *Times Literary Supplement* (March 11, 1983). See also my *Philosophy and Atheism* (Amherst, N.Y.: Prometheus Books, 1985), 211–31

27. See here Wartofsky, *"Homo Homini Deus Est,"* and as well his *Feuerbach* (London: Cambridge University Press, 1977).

28. Wartofsky, *"Homo Homini Deus Est,"* 154.

29. I would like to thank Jocelyne Couture for her assistance in preparing this chapter. She is not, of course, in anyway responsible for its contents.

Chapter Sixteen

Atheism without Anger or Tears

I

1. APOLOGIA

My atheism squares with my—to engage in a fine fit of self-labeling—antifoundationalist, antirationalist, nonscientistic, historicist, contextualist, naturalistic pragmatism.[1] It is very distant from the Enlightenment rationalism Barry Allen inexplicably ascribes to me. Rather, in the course of what I like to think of as my philosophical development, and not my philosophical shilly-shallying, my atheism has come to be housed (perhaps only temporarily) in the metaphilosophical stance expressed in chapter 5 and succinctly in my "Philosophy as Critical Theory" quoted at length by Rodger Beehler in his "Hounding Heaven."[2] (See, for the passage Beehler quotes, the first paragraph of part 4 of this chapter.)

Having elsewhere had the opportunity to respond to Beehler, I shall here only very briefly respond to some of Beehler's thoughtful criticisms in his "Hounding Heaven."[3] I shall concentrate in this section on the central issue between us and then turn to an extended discussion in part 2 of Michael Langford's critique of me and in part 3 to an even more extended examination of Barry Allen's detailed rejection of even starting to look at the issues in the way I do. Atheism, he has it, should be characterized and regarded in a very different way than I have. The very idea of being an atheist, he also has it, rests on a mistake. To get a foretaste of the distance that stands between us, in spite of the closeness of our metaphilosophical views, I shall argue, without any irony at all, that, given a straightforward and untendentious characterization of atheism, Allen is himself an atheist.

Allen stands outside some characteristic philosophy of religion issues and ways of viewing things and argues that these issues and the discussions they engender should come off the philosophical agenda. (I am not suggesting that he thinks that we should have a "philosophical police" do it, but that he thinks it would be a good idea if philosophers could come to see the virtue of not going on about such things.) Langford, by contrast, argues inside traditional disputes and in their familiar terms. Hence the differing titles for parts 2 and 3. I devote more time to Allen than to Langford because Allen's critique, as does Beehler's, strikes at the very heart of what I am doing and raises general issues about the belief/unbelief discussion that very much need to be addressed. (It is also the case that some of the responses I make to Langford are similar to the arguments I make in some detail against Alston's views in chapter 19.)

2.

I am very grateful indeed for Rodger Beehler's two probing examinations of my views published in *Studies in Religion* (1994). Beehler tries to show how in thinking about religion I am not on the track of reason or sufficiently sensitive to what religion is and why people are religious. He also tries, in the course of criticizing my account, to give us a glimpse of what would be a better way of looking at religion. He is also perceptively ironical about some of my ways of going about things. I am, he remarks, about religion something like "some aggressively worrying sheepdog" hounding believers relentlessly "toward the heroic positivist paddock of atheist 'tough-mindedness.'" Indeed, as I first reread Beehler's two essays in preparation for this response, I said to myself, Yes, yes, he is for the most part right. I've been far too rationalistic here. I've got to look at these matters in a rather different way. But first thoughts are not always the same as second and considered thoughts. I shall stay my course as I shall with Langford and Allen as well, though I shall, of course, give my reasons for doing so, hoping that they are sound and do not reflect dogmatism settling in with a hardening of the intellectual arteries.[4]

I shall stick to the most essential issues in responding to Beehler. The most central one is what Beehler calls my irrationality thesis. It is the claim of mine, developed in this volume as well as extensively elsewhere, that has been the most extensively repudiated of any of my claims and arguments. Some simply regard it as absurd; others think that it is not only mistaken (whether absurdly or not), but, as well, reveals a militant atheism and perhaps not a little more than a touch of fanaticism and with that a drifting away from reasonableness. Both Beehler and Allen think that or at least something rather like it.

My irrationality thesis would plainly be absurdly *parti pris* if it were taken to be the thesis that all scientifically and philosophically sophisticated present-day Christians, Jews, or Muslims are irrational or unreasonable or even less reasonable than plainly reasonable and similarly sophisticated atheists such as John Mackie, Simon Blackburn, Richard Robinson, and A. J. Ayer. Such notions are simply false. All of us know of believers who are very sensitive and sophisticated intellectuals, sophisticated in all the ways I consider, and are, as well, very reasonable human beings indeed. (Reasonable in the senses I elaborated in the introduction to part 4.) I initially thought that that would be so obvious as to not need saying, but, given the ways I have been misunderstood, I went out of my way, both in *God, Skepticism and Modernity* and in *Search for Community in a Withering Tradition,* to assert this commonplace and to make clear that my irrationality thesis was no denial of it.[5] But I did claim, and would continue to claim, that many rational and indeed generally reasonable people, both believers and atheists, can have irrational beliefs. One does not have to be a Freudian to believe that. Even a Davidsonian can do so.

3.

Beehler correctly identifies my irrationality thesis as involving a complicated hypothetical. What I am claiming is that *if* it has been shown that anthropomorphic God-talk results in false or probably false truth-claims and is religiously inappropriate as well and *if* it has also been shown that the nonanthropomorphic God-talk of mainstream Judaism, Christianity, and Islam, while religiously appropriate, is actually incoherent, and *if* it has been shown that we can make at least as adequate sense of our lives (including, of course, our moral sensibilities) without recourse to religion, *then* it is irrational for someone in a good position to know these things to believe in God.

This thesis of mine, as I remarked above, has caused offense or, offense or not, has seemed to many deeply counterintuitive. I think these reactions result from its being, perhaps understandably, misunderstood. Properly understood it should, as the hypothetical that it is, be obvious, almost commonplace, but true nonetheless. (Truisms can be true.) What is controversial are the *antecedents* (or at least the second one, which indeed is very controversial), but, *if* they are true, then the consequence is almost obviously secure. I have always realized that the antecedents—and most particularly the second one—are controversial and recognized that I had to argue for them. But that is precisely what I have done in my writings about religion. I have in particular realized that the claim about incoherency is controversial and that the burden or proof is on me to establish it, if indeed it can be established. I have been at considerable pains to try to do so. I may have failed and indeed the claim itself may even be mistaken. (Even if I have failed to establish it, it could, of course, be true.) But all I have been concerned to claim for the irrationality thesis *itself* is that if the incoherence antecedent, and the other antecedents as well, hold and if most of the background conditions characterized in the cumulative argument hold, then it is irrational for a person, who is in a good position to know these things, to believe in God.[6] Beehler, however, seems at least to be saying that a person can know, firmly know, these things (these antecedents together with their background conditions) to be true, and still reasonably believe in God. That is, so to say, the official line of his argument, but, as I shall attempt to show, his actual arguments do not even attempt to do that, but challenge instead the truth or warrantability of some of my antecedents. But to refute my irrationality thesis, given, as Beehler himself recognizes, that it is a complicated hypothetical, he must show that there is no such logical connection. Refuting the antecedents, even if successful, will not refute the irrationality thesis itself, though it would render it less significant.

I was, and still am, concerned to argue for the truth of the antecedents, but with the irrationality thesis I was simply concerned to show an important consequence of these antecedents being true, if indeed they are true. This was a way of trying to induce a serious consideration of the antecedents by showing what appears at least to be a humanly and religiously important consequence of them. Beehler, as far as I can see, has done nothing to show that that consequence does not obtain *if* these antecedents are true.

It isn't—to argue for my above claim—that Beehler's believers actually agree that the concept of God is incoherent or that believing in God necessarily leads to inconsistent beliefs and then go on to say that that does not matter to the reasonability of religious belief as long as religion enables us to cope.[7] Rather, Beehler characterizes believers as having a reasonable strategy for setting aside *apparent* inconsistencies or incoherencies as being only apparent and for not considering the issue of their actual coherence. And indeed a believer may very well not be able to show a claimed incoherency is only an apparent inconsistency and not be any the worse for all of that. What is the case here may be very difficult to establish. He may not have the foggiest idea what to say here. But, given his recognition

that God's being *is a mystery,* that His ways exceed the wisdom of human beings, that He is to be trusted in, not challenged to produce his credentials, that He is to be waited on faithfully, no matter what adversity befalls the believer,

all of which go with being a knight of faith, then the believer's epistemic posture will, and should be, "always to give first priority to reconciling the claims of belief against *allegedly* contrary facts or [*alleged*] inconsistency" (italics and bracketed addition added). It is also true, Beehler claims, that

> the believer is supported in this both by the affective commitment involved in believing in God . . . *and* by our wider rational procedure of reserving judgment when confronted by inconsistent and inconclusive data.

This does seem to me an accurate description of what it is to be a person, or at least a perceptive person, of faith. (It, note in passing, is very distant from the fundamentalist fanatic. One has the spirit of reasonableness, the other does not.) It also seems to me to reasonably accurately characterize the epistemic posture of many believers. Moreover, with one modification, it seems to me a posture that believers *should* have. The modification is that, if in their data they have two propositions not both of which can be true, that, while they should initially not abandon crucial beliefs in the face of that, but should try instead to see if, after all, they really are inconsistent with each other, or if with some acceptable adjustments somewhere in the system of belief, they could be rendered mutually consistent. Only if, after repeated tryings—trying not just by an individual but broadly in the intellectual community—neither of these things can be satisfactorily done, should the belief be modified or abandoned. But, if these things cannot be done, and this becomes apparent after considerable trying, it is not reasonable to stick with both beliefs. But the first move should be a persistent attempt at reconciliation. That makes good Quinean methodological sense. But, if, after the most careful inspection, the propositions continue to certainly seem inconsistent by all those competent to make such observations, then that calls for some modification in the belief system in question.

Subject to the above, not unimportant modification, my critique of religion took its departure from such an understanding of faith and from an acceptance of that epistemic stance. But from there I went on to argue that such a reconciliation project breaks down in the face of the repeated, varied, and sometimes very profound probing that religion has received since the Enlightenment. There are just too many falsehoods, unsound arguments, and at least apparent inconsistencies and incoherencies that resist resolution into an account which is free of them. Merely apparent incoherencies, believers can reasonably live with, but an incoherency that resists repeated attempts to explain it away as apparent *only* and, as well, is a central part of a web of belief and practice that contains crucial falsehoods and unsound arguments, is a incoherency that shows us a belief system, even when linked with an associated set of attractive practices, that it is not reasonable to accept for someone who knows these things. But that appears at least—or so I have in some detail argued—to be what Judaism, Christianity, and Islam all yield.

Here the effect of my cumulative argument, and the place of my arguments about incoherency in it, become crucial; they are matters that Beehler mentions, but then ignores. It is, to recall the core conclusions of the cumulative argument, by now fairly evident that we cannot prove or give sound grounds for believing that God exists, religious experience though real shows nothing of God's reality, the very idea of a miracle is problematic, the problem of evil is intractable, (*pace* Kierkegaard) we do not need faith to make sense of our lives or to sustain morality or to show the way to a more adequate morality than otherwise would be available to human beings; there are as well radically different religions (some, as the Lesser Vehicle, without any belief in God at all) and we have no way of knowing which (if any) is "the true religion" or even whether that very idea makes much sense; putative revelations are many and not infrequently conflicting with there being no way of ascertaining which of these putative revelations is *the* or even *a* genuine revelation, and finally, as a *candidate* for inclusion in the core, conclusions of the cumulative argument, the very concept of God in developed forms of Judaism, Christianity, and Islam is not only problematic, it is actually incoherent.[8] (It will widely be admitted to be problematic.)

The last claim about incoherency aside, the other considerations have, in the intellectual culture of societies such as ours at the present time, a very wide acceptance. By now, by contrast with Locke's time or Hume's, a large number of informed people, including not a few religious people, take it as a fairly evident matter that these core claims are true. This probably in part explains the attraction of fideism among reflective and informed believers. This, of course, fits well with Wittgenstein's slenderist-support-imaginable-theme. Such things in effect attest to the force of the cumulative argument. In fine, the core claims of the cumulative argument are becoming increasingly hard reasonably to set aside. There continues to roll on the relentless disenchantment and demystification of the world. Many, perhaps most, sophisticated believers by now think very much like secularists. (Indeed, that may be partially definitive of what it is to be a sophisticated believer.)

My tendentious appeal to incoherence arguments functions here as a late and controversial proposed addition to the cumulative argument. Belief in God in societies such as ours is very difficult to sustain, let alone to justify. The very concept of God is problematic. We are helped to see why, when we reflect on the fact that the God of developed religions is claimed to be an infinite individual, omnipresent, yet still an individual, a bodiless person, who, though still a person, is transcendent to the world. My point, to put it bluntly, is that such a string of words makes no sense. Neither the believer nor anyone else understands *what* they are talking about here, *what* they are trying to take on faith. I say "trying to" because one can only take on faith something that one can *to some extent* understand, so that one can understand what it is that one is accepting on faith.[9] Such a conception of God is incoherent.

Beehler does nothing to show that this at least seemingly manifest incoherency is not a real incoherency. Without all the other previous considerations of the cumulative argument, the reconciler might reasonably follow Beehler's recipe and say, "Though such talk certainly does appear to be incoherent, after all God is said to be mysterious: His being a mystery." This being so, he will go on believing in God and not allow himself to be bamboozled by skeptical philosophers. And, if this believer is also a philosopher, with a little intellectual curiosity about religion, he will try to develop arguments (though his belief in God will not wait on that) to show the alleged incoherency is only apparent. His attitude here is similar to the attitude of Anselm toward proving the existence of God.

Such a stance would be reasonable one for a medieval philosopher. But—or so I think and so I have argued—it is not so for a contemporary person who understands and turns over and takes to heart the force of the cumulative argument. Moreover, what I have called the cumulative argument, though so labeled and so articulated by me, is certainly not my creation or the creation, let alone the fabrication, of a little band of atheist philosophers, but something with deep roots in the history of Western culture. It is an ever growing wave arising from a number of more or less secular (though not only secular—think of Kant and Herder) thinkers, who have been writing about religion and related matters since the emergence of the Enlightenment.

4.

I shall set out the following challenge (to cut short, as I must, what could be a long discussion of Beehler's response to me). The challenge claims that (1) the core claims of the cumulative argument are true and (2) the incoherence argument is actually sound and not just plausible. If, the challenge continues, (1) and (2) are true, and a knowledge of their truth is readily available to us, then is it not unreasonable to believe in God? If it is in turn responded—and rightly, I believe—that (2) isn't (to put it mildly) *certainly* true, and, then the responder goes on to ask, "So isn't the reconciliation project, after all, a reasonable project?" I will, then, in turn, respond, "Not if (1) is true and we can know things—as we can—that are not *certainly* true." But is not (1) true and do we not have very good grounds for believing it to be true?

I think the *burden of proof*, given the development of our thought since the Enlightenment, is very much on the believer to show that (1) is not substantially true. And, given the above burden of proof, (2) becomes a pertinent claim far less easily turned aside than Beehler believes. Without (1), (2) could be, as Beehler argues, fairly enough set aside, but (1) is massively there setting a very considerable challenge to religious belief, rendering both belief that God exists and belief in God problematic. And thus, against such a background, (2) becomes a powerful *additional* challenge to faith. It gives us, among other things, an explanation of why (1) could not but be so and then goes on to in effect assert that belief in *God* is so problematical that there is nothing there but unintelligible verbal formulae for the believer to try to believe in. It is, if we ignore for the moment the hot-context background, like someone's trying to take procrastination drinks melancholy or Clinton sleeps faster than Bush on trust. If "There is a bodiless infinite individual transcendent to the universe" is such a senseless verbal formulae or collocation of words, then belief in God, resting as it does on belief that God exists, must be deeply illusory.

Neither Beehler nor Allen do, or even try to do, anything at all to meet that challenge or to show that (1) is not so. Langford, somewhat after the manner of Alston, tries to meet (2), but, as I shall argue in the next section, his arguments fail. If that is so, then the irrationality thesis is very much on the agenda.

I agree with Beehler, as indeed this book has made abundantly evident, about the importance of contextuality and historicity. I repeatedly rely on that, as we have seen, not only in social philosophy but in thinking about religion as well. Hegel is right in thinking that no one can overleap history. I also agree that there is a domain of rationality that is grounded in practice. But when, being as contextual as your like, we look closely at the very practice or cluster of practices that Judaism, Christianity, and Islam are, we will see that these practices carry with them, *as nonexcisable elements*, cosmological beliefs. We will further see, if we are attentive, that certain crucial ones are either false (and readily known to be so) or so problematical as to be very good candidates for incoherency. We should also see that this messes up the rationality of continuing with these metaphysics-encased practices for someone who is aware of the falsity of anthropomorphic religious beliefs and also concludes that the problematicity really does add up to incoherency.[10] If the practices help the believer cope with life, he will reasonably walk the tightrope and discount the apparent falsities and inconsistencies, taking it as a part of his faith that they are only *apparent* falsities, inconsistencies and incoherencies. But there comes a point, I argue, where the intellectual and, as well, the moral impediments to belief pile up and become too great for belief to remain reasonable. When this obtains (there is no algorithm here) *and* it is also realized that other sources of living meaningful lives are available, it becomes irrational to continue to go on believing.[11]

Rationality is indeed tied to wants, or at least to interests, but one of our interests is an interest in truth and to not crucify our intellects. Truth is not our only interest, the only thing we both strongly and reflectively want, nor is it our supreme interest (nothing is), or always our overriding interest (nothing is), but it is a strong and persistent interest. That interest in such a circumstance exerts pressure until there comes a point where the tightrope should break, and will break, if the countervailing forces to our interest in truth are not too great. If we can hold on to our brains *and* to our hearts, and keep them in tandem, it not only will snap, it should snap.

II

QUESTIONS INTERNAL TO THE FRAMEWORK

1.

Michael Langford's response to me is internal to the framework for he seeks, playing the philosophy of religion game, to provide a defense of theism, to show for us how, standing where we stand, knowing what we intellectuals know or think we know, that Christianity and its sister religions are, or at least should be, *live options* for us. He believes that he can show that Christian belief is, even for we twentieth-century critical intellectuals, reasonable; that it is rationally respectable for us to be, for example, Christian believers. He wants to show, against my arguments, that at the present time a scientifically and philosophically sophisticated intellectual, in societies such as our own, can reasonably believe in the God of Christianity, Judaism, and Islam.

What are his arguments and how does he attempt to counter my arguments? He agrees with me, against Wittgensteinian fideists, and implicitly against Beehler, that it is not enough that religious utterances have a grammar, and are embedded in a cluster of social practices, to show that they are coherent. To show they are coherent, he has it, we must also show something of the propositional content of sentences like "God created the heavens and the earth" or "Humankind lives within the providence of God" or "The universe has a creative and loving source beyond the universe itself." Rather surprisingly, and to my mind rightly, he takes certain rather positivistic questions to be in order. We rightly ask how we test these religious propositions, how we ascertain either their truth-conditions or their assertability-conditions, so that we could understand the conditions under which it would be correct to say that they are true or warrantedly asserted or false or unwarranted, he has it, we must not, however, begging the question, as Langford thinks I do, be demanding criteria appropriate for *discrete objects* rather than for the *universe as a whole*.

However, we, of course, must not, as Langford actually does, beg the question in another way by simply assuming 'universe' stands for some kind of entity, stands for some very, very big thing, rather than being a label—an umbrella term—for the very different things, events, and processes there are. It is only by thinking of the universe as some kind of gigantic thing or some kind of entity or totality that we can have a shot at intelligibly speaking of the universe as a whole. But 'universe' may be just an umbrella term for the various things, events and processes there are. It is at least plausible to believe, as Hilary Putnam has argued and as I argued in part 3, that we have no criteria for counting the number of objects there are in a room, let alone how many objects there are, period. Look around you and try to count the number of objects in the room in which you are. Convention governs what you will say here, if indeed you take the request as making sense at all, not anything in the facts of the case. This being so, we cannot sensibly speak of the number of objects there are in a room, let alone of the number there are in the universe and which supposedly make up the totality of the objects there are in the universe. We cannot do this and thus we cannot go on to say intelligibly that that totality is the universe. (Again, by that very way of talking, we are trying to treat the universe as a mysterious kind of entity. It is, to echo John Wisdom, the manner and not the matter here that stultifies.) We cannot intelligibly speak of the sum of things so that we could intelligibly speak of them as a whole and ask if, and, if so, how, this universe was created and is sustained. Moreover, since the universe is not an object, event, process—not any kind of entity at all—there is no such thing as the universe itself for "universe" to stand for. Rather the term "universe" is an umbrella term standing for the objects, events, and processes there are. But there is no sense to trying to count the number that there are and to come to speak of the universe as a whole. "Universe" does not stand for some mysterious entity, but indifferently for those various discrete things. Things of which, since "object" is not a count word, we cannot count the sum. There is, that is, no way of summing them up and fixing the number of them there are. This being so, we cannot coherently speak of the universe itself—that totality—being caused, created, sustained, and the like. To ask for the cause of the universe is to make what in the good old Ryleian days would have been called a category mistake.

Still, whether the universe-as-a-totality is a coherent conception or not, Langford believes that when we come to speak of the universe as a whole, we must use analogical reasoning and not the literal language of univocity that I use in speaking of objects. "God" is not the name of even a possible genus of which there could be species. He is not, as Paul Tillich stressed, and as Aquinas did much earlier, an object or being—even an "eternal object" or "eternal being"—among objects or a being among beings. God, if anything, is Being or Being *as such*. In speaking of God's understanding or awareness, just as in speaking of Being, we must, Langford has it, be using these terms analogically, if we are to speak properly. Here, Langford avers, following Thomists, that 'understanding' and "awareness," when applied to God, do not have a completely different sense than when applied to us; but the terms are not being used univocally either. There is, of course, a very great difference between God's understanding and ours, but it is not a difference in kind, but a very considerable difference in degree. Yet to conceive of God's understanding, awareness or love as just something which is very much greater than ours, but still the same sort of thing, makes God too much like a kind of supreme superman. God, on such a conception, can solve chess problems or prove theorems or understand people's personalities and problems or know about epochal social change much, much better than we can, but He is still in the same sort of thinking business. He does what we do, only He does it much, much better. But to talk that way plainly shows no understanding of God at all. That is not how we, if we have any *religious sensibility*, speak of God's understanding.

Similar things should be said about God's love. And sure enough—analogical reasoning or not—we have Langford in reality dropping his talk of degrees of difference. He remarks: ". . . God can be said to have infinitely more of the things we are familiar with. In this matter, there is an 'infinite gap' with respect to degree, but not with respect to substance." But this talk is utterly obscure; we have no understanding of what we are asserting when we are trying to assert (1) "There is an infinite gap with respect to degree" or (2) "There is not an infinite gap with respect to substance." What is being talked about here? What, if anything , do (1) and (2) say? They are rather strange English sentences and—or so at least is seems—we do not understand what their propositional content is. What are the truth-conditions or assertability-conditions for saying either of these things, so that we could have even the faintest idea of whether they are true or false or what it would be like for them to be true or false or about how to go about gaining some grasp of whether they are one or the other and thereby getting some grip (even the slightest grip) on what we are trying to say when we utter such utterances. Langford gives us no directions. I suppose that here I am like Beehler's sheepdog driving the believer toward the "positivist paddock." But isn't such hounding justified *here*?

Similar things obtain when Langford begins to talk of a bodiless person—a pure spirit—who might have affections. We understand what it is to have a physical body; but we have no understanding of "spiritual body" or "bodiless person with feelings." We have, as I argued in detail in part 1, no idea at all how to identify such an alleged person or how to ascertain or to determine the referent of such terms. We just do not understand *what* we are talking about here. Yet Langford rightly insists that it is crucial that we understand here *what* we are talking about.

However, he does remark, anticipating my above remarks, that the

> possibility of there being nonphysical bodies that house the consciousness of the departed, and, *a fortiori*, the possibility of a reality that has nothing corresponding to a body, are, of course, ruled out by an empiricist philosophy, but it is precisely the adequacy of this philosophy that is being called into question.

However, while it is true that most empiricists have thought this way, not all have. H. H. Price and Curt Ducasse, for example, both took seriously the possibility of disembodied existence. Yet they are thoroughly empiricist philosophers and indeed distinguished ones at that.[12] So such a possibility is not, of course, or even at all, ruled out by an empiricist philosophy. I think (*pace* Price and Ducasse), that empiricists *should* reject such notions as incoherent, but that is an entirely different matter. The immediately relevant point here is that some of them did not and yet they remained empiricists. Indeed, it is anything but clear that they were inconsistent empiricists in the way Locke arguably was. Moreover, and even more crucially, it is not necessary to be an empiricist or adopt any *theory* or meaning or *theory* of reference to reasonably believe that we do not know *what* we are talking about when we speak of "bodiless persons," let alone speak of "an infinite bodiless person transcendent to the world." We know how to determine, without a theory, whether Jane is in the room or whether Jane is a loving person, but we have no idea at all of whether there is or is not a pure spirit in the room or whether this pure spirit is or isn't loving. In recognizing this to be so we are not invoking a philosophical *theory*, empiricist or otherwise, of meaning or reference or any other kind of *theory* of meaning or reference.

The above is a familiar enough point, and Langford, with his robust defense of theism, has done nothing to meet it or even to deflect it. And the making of it is not the making or expressing of an empiricist dogma. Someone as antiempiricist as Ludwig Wittgenstein or Richard Rorty would find such talk of "bodiless persons" as senseless as would many, indeed most, empiricists. We need not say, *a priori* that such a bodiless person cannot be conceived, but simply ask, without relying ourselves on a *theory* of meaning, the person, who claims that it is possible to conceive of a bodiless person, to explain or describe what it would be like to conceive it: to show the propositional content (the truth-conditions or assertability-conditions) of "There is a bodiless person in the room." Just, comes the request, describe them or state them clearly or, for that matter, even unclearly. And remember what can't be described cannot be conceived either. Neither is there a powerful theory, or indeed any theory at all, at work here nor need there be one. (It is in driving home this notion that the work of Ludwig Wittgenstein, and building on his work, the work of Cora Diamond and Hilary Putnam, have been so very important.)

The same considerations apply in full force, and even more obviously, to "The ground of the universe as a whole is a creative intelligence beyond the universe itself" or "Being as such is eternal" or "The universe is such that its loving providential order reveals itself." We have no idea of what would or could count for or against the truth or warrantability or such putative propositions. With them language has gone on a holiday. We need sheepdogs here. But the sheepdogs need not be positive ones.

2.

Finally, let me turn to a different consideration in my examination of Langford's views. It is probably right, though perhaps not very helpful, to say, as Langford does, that God is an interpretative concept. We may, as he remarks, not be able to point to specific things that a believer expects to happen that an atheist does not. But in taking up a religious standpoint one will give a different reading to one's experience than one will if one is an atheist. For example, a believer, who is at all reflective, will, of course, know very well that in ordinary ways she can be harmed, but she still may think that no harm can *really* come to her, for God is always with her and that, with her faith in God, she must gratefully accept her life whatever it is, whatever befalls her, as being in accordance with God's sovereign and gracious will. But these attitudes of hers, no matter how powerfully governing they are of her life, do not reflect, surface appearances to the contrary notwithstanding, differences in belief from those of an atheist. She knows as well as an atheist does that her son may get cancer and die, that her friends may betray her, or that she may become senile and lose all her creativity. She does not blink, turn her face away, from these possibilities, possibilities that very well may become actualities. Such a believer and an atheist do not disagree—or so at least it seems—about the facts at all.[13] Yet, as a person of faith, she also believes that everything is in God's hands, that, however it goes, all goes well, that what befalls her, whatever it is, is in accordance with God's Providence. But this does not show that she has different beliefs about what the facts are from that of the atheist. They do not differ about what the world and what life (mundanely, discretely, plainly) are like. But she surely does have a different attitude toward the facts, toward the world: she gives the same facts a different reading. They have a *different significance* for her.

Treating God as an interpretative concept in that way reveals not a difference in knowledge or even of beliefs about the world, but reveals a difference *in* attitude but not *in* belief.[14] On such a reading, atheists and believers differ only *in their feelings, in their sensibilities;* there is no difference of substance between them. Such a believer cannot actually manage to believe anything that the atheist does not.

3.

Perhaps Langford is right and it is reasonable for philosophers and other intellectuals to be Christians. Perhaps theism is even true. But he has done very little to make either of these things plausible things to believe. Forms of fideism—powerfully articulated in Pascal, Hamann, Kierkegaard, and Barth—have seemed to me the most profound ways we have of articulating religious faith. They do not try to make religious belief rational or to provide philosophical or any other kind of foundations for Christian faith. They rather try to show, as does Wittgenstein with much greater *conceptual* sophistication, that talk of rationality, reasonability, or philosophical justification will come to nothing here. Indeed, it will just get in the way of faith. The acceptance of Christianity, and Judaism and Islam as well, are straight matters of faith. Philosophy and so-called natural theology will just take us down the garden path.

Langford's modified or moderate fideism is in reality no *fideism* at all, for it relies on philosophical and theological claims—a defense of analogical predication, for example—that genuine fideists set aside as neither conducive to enlightenment nor salvation. Langford's very reliance on the philosophy of religion—his very much remaining internal to the framework—would surely provoke not only Nietzschean scorn but Kierkegaardian irony. Perhaps, even from the standpoint of faith, fideism should be rejected and we should accept Langford's modest proposal, but, before leaping, we first should face the fact that Langford's very way of going about things is very vulnerable to both Humean and Kierkegaardian critique: vulnerable, that is, to the arguments of both the atheist and the fideist.

III

QUESTIONS EXTERNAL TO THE FRAMEWORK

1.

One very central place where I am at odds with Barry Allen is over the characterization of atheism and over the assessment of its import. (The two matters, as will become evident, are linked.) In his characterization of atheism Allen is *très parti pris*, in effect, treating "militant atheism" and "rationalistic atheism" as pleonasms and so characterizing atheism—that a type of atheism the militant rationalistic Enlightenment atheism of Condorcet, Diderot, and Holbach—becomes atheism *sans phrase*. My atheism gets, without any justification at all, thrown into that rationalistic hopper. But there are militant atheists, James Joyce, Simone de Beauvoir, Jean-Paul Sartre, and Friedrich Nietzsche, for example, who were anything but Enlightenment rationalists or rationalists of any sort. Moreover, there is the thorough, but utterly nonmilitant, atheism of George Santayana. His atheism, though certainly unhesitant and unyielding, was a nostalgic, even wistful, atheism. Santayana, who strongly empathized culturally with Catholic culture, thought, as much as Holbach, belief in God, or even belief that God exists, a childish fantasy. Indeed, he found it difficult to believe that anyone, even Christians, could really believe in God. He thought that deep down they really knew better. But, for all of that, he remained immersed in the way of life of Catholicism. There is also the historicized, culturally sensitive atheism of Antonio Gramsci. Gramsci in deeply examining Italian culture and society understood very well indeed the human importance of religion. Then, of course, there is the stark pessimistic, rather resigned atheism of Sigmund Freud and Max Weber, both of whom, though in different ways, had a very sensitive understanding of religion, but lacked altogether a Condorcetian hope for the attainment of an enlightened and flourishing social order. And so we could go on and on. There are many sorts of atheists and many of them (*pace* Allen) are very distant indeed from any conception of the Platonic good of enlightening truth. They have no such faith in truth, though they recognize that truth is one of our great goods, though by no means always, anymore than any other good, an overriding good. Moreover, while there are truths ("objective truth" is pleonastic), some think , including this atheist among others, there is, literally speaking, no such thing as *the* truth, let alone there being something called the truth which will transform our lives. Treating atheism as a Platonic heresy says more about Allen's own philosophical agenda than it does about atheism.[15]

A central thing that is mistaken in Allen's understanding of atheism comes out in his brief concluding paragraph where he remarks:

> I doubt the continuing relevance of atheism not because I believe in god or
> believe such belief to be more reasonable than the atheist allows, but because
> I do *not* believe what philosophical atheists believe is a necessary step on the
> historical road to universal enlightenment and human self-perfection.[16]

Only some "philosophical atheists" believe that, namely such *philosophes* of the Enlightenment as Holbach and Diderot and, turning to a later time,

Friedrich Engels and V. I. Lenin and perhaps Karl Marx, Ludwig Feuerbach, and George Eliot, but certainly not Hume, certainly not Nietzsche, certainly not Santayana, Freud, or Weber, certainly not Sartre, certainly not Axel Hägerström, Bertrand Russell, Ingemar Hedenius, A. J. Ayer, Rudolph Carnap, B. A. Farell, W. V. O. Quine, John Mackie, Ernest Nagel, Paul Kurtz, Antony Flew, Paul Edwards, Richard Robinson, Russell Norwood Hanson, Walter Kaufmann, Michael Scriven, or myself.[17] Leaving me aside, for a minute, all the other contemporary philosophers mentioned in my last sentence think that it is a very considerable confusion indeed to believe that there is any historical road we are traveling which is leading us in some determinate direction, let alone there being anything inexorable here so that we could speak of the necessary steps we are taking on destiny's course. And all of them think, along with Hume and Nietzsche, that belief in such universal enlightenment and human self-perfection is itself religiose and certainly not "the truth of atheism." It is precisely such nonfallibilistic metaphysical conceptions that these atheists reject. Some of them, as do some non-atheists as well, modestly *hope* that, if social wealth, levels of education, and liberal tolerance increase in the world, human flourishing and human self-understanding might, just might, be somewhat enhanced. But they would agree with Isaiah Berlin about the logical absurdity of historical inevitability.[18] Their moderate whiggish hopes are a far cry from the heavenly city of the *philosophes*.

My atheism is in this respect like Hume's, Ayer's, Robinson's, and Nagel's. We certainly see eye-to-eye about the absurdity of an atheism that believes that atheism, or anything else, is a necessary step on the historical road to universal enlightenment and human self-perfection. Such conceptions are mythological and are in effect very much like religious notions. They do not square at all with the fallibilistic, utterly secular thought of a thoroughgoing atheism. Because the *philosophes* had some religiously inverted residues linked to their atheism, their atheism, their intentions to the contrary notwithstanding, was not thorough. An atheism that was thorough, fully in tune with our secular world, would be fallibilistic and without the religiose rationalistic belief that we are necessarily marching anywhere, let alone that we are marching to some blessed world of universal enlightenment and human self-perfection.

What, at most, some fallibilistic, nonrationalist atheists could hope for, if they are also either Deweyan pragmatists or analytical Marxians, would be that it is perhaps, just perhaps, possible to construct a plausible *empirical* theory of epochal social change, à la G. A. Cohen, Andrew Levine, or Debra Satz, and that this theory will give us some reason to expect that a noncapitalist socialist society will, if certain circumstances obtain, come into being, sustain itself, eventually become a classless society, and that in such social circumstances there will be considerably more human flourishing than there is now.[19] It is possible, and I believe desirable, to take that fallibilistically as an *empirical* hypothesis and, in addition, remembering that one is also a social agent, to work for the bringing into being of such a world. As such an agent, one will hope that such a situation will prevail even though one may be very pessimistic about its prospects. It may well be too much like pie in the sky by and by.

A skeptical Marxian who is also an atheist will think like that. But that is still a far cry from Enlightenment rationalism's belief in universal enlightenment and human self-perfection. Moreover, most fallibilistic atheists are not Marxians. Instead they share the atheoreticism of most historians about accounting for social change and they do not allow themselves even my modest hope.[20] (Think here of the deep, though in each case differently rooted, pessimism of Freud, Santayana, and Weber.)

2.

What then is the "truth of atheism," if indeed it has any truth? To see what is at issue here we need first to characterize atheism, something Allen hardly obliges us with. There are more and less adequate characterizations of atheism, but what is common to all of them is the claim that an atheist is a person who believes that there is no God and, as well, atheism involves a rejection of all belief in spiritual beings. This, if one thinks about it for a second, makes it evident that atheism rejects Judaism, Christianity, and Islam with their common belief, at least as ordinarily understood, that there is a God who created the universe out of nothing and who has absolute sovereignty over His creation. Human beings for these religions are taken to be sinful, utterly dependent on God and they can only make adequate sense of their lives by accepting without question God's ordinances for them. Atheism, as we will see in detail in the next chapter, rejects that conception of human beings as well as the distinctively religious side of the morality that goes with it. (Recall Hume's impatience with monkish virtues.) Atheists typically, but not invariably, believe that people can make good sense of their lives, including their lives as moral beings, without any belief in God or any other spiritual realities.

Rather standardly, but I think mistakenly, or at least inadequately, it is said that to be an atheist is simply to believe, either, on the one hand, that it is false or at least probably false that God exists or, on the other hand, that it is unreasonable to believe that God exists.[21] (Of course such a belief could be both false and unreasonable.) But, considering the way much discussion of religion has gone in the last two centuries, it is better to characterize an atheist as someone who *rejects* belief in God for one or another of the following reasons (which rejection applies, will depend on how God in that instance is being conceived). *First*, for an anthropomorphic God, even an attenuatedly anthropomorphic God, atheists reject belief in that God because they believe that it

is false, probably false, or unreasonable—depending on how that anthropomorphic God is conceived—to believe that there is such a God. *Secondly*, for
a nonanthropomorphic transcendent God (the God of Maimonides and
Aquinas, of Luther and Calvin), atheists reject belief in such a God on the
grounds that, on the one hand, such a belief is false, unwarranted, or unreasonable or, on the other, that that concept of God is either meaningless, unintelligible, contradictory, incomprehensible, or incoherent. (Which, applies,
depends on two things: [1] on just how this God is being conceived and [2]
on the meta-account doing the examining.) *Thirdly*, where "God" is simply
construed, as "God" is sometimes now construed, as a term standing for love,
trust, ultimate commitment, or morality touched with emotion, atheists join
with many believers in rejecting such a belief in God because such conceptions of God merely mask an atheistic substance. Such conceptions of God,
as in the writings of Richard Braithwaite, R. M. Hare, or D. Z. Phillips, are
atheistic in reality (in substance) but sugar over and sometimes as well mys-
tify things with soothing and not infrequently—as in Phillips's case, but not
in Braithwaite's or Hare's—syrupy obscurantist talk and conceptualizations.[22]

All forms of atheism have in common a *rejection* of a belief in God, but,
as conceptions of God differ, the form the rejection takes will differ as well,
but all these atheistic rejections will agree that in rejecting belief in God, they
are doing so because such belief rests on a mistake. (The remark about "mistake" is essential, for a prideful or sinful person [to speak internally to religion
for a moment] could reject God by rebelling against Him while still believing
that God exists. That such behavior is irrational does not mean that it does not
occur. But that rebellion, of course, is not any kind of an atheistic rejection.)

The above, though a somewhat more expanded characterization of atheism than the usual one, is still relatively untendentious. It captures the different forms of atheism that are part of our Western tradition and, the third type
aside, does not let anything in that would not very generally be regarded as
atheism.

Diderot and Holbach are, of course, atheists, but of a distinctive sort.
While they reject belief in God either because they think it is false that God
exists or that the very concept or conceptualization of God is incoherent, what
Allen fastens on as essential to their atheism and objects to, namely their Platonic conception of enlightening and transforming truth, is actually a dangler
on their atheism, a fortuitous and inessential feature, easily excisable. It is not
what makes their accounts *atheistic* and is not an essential part of atheistic belief for nonatheists could very well have such eschatological beliefs as well
and, as we have seen, many atheists utterly reject such an eschatology. Having such beliefs is not what makes Diderot and Holbach *atheists*.

Given the above characterization of atheism—a reasonably nontenden-
tious one—Allen is himself an atheist, for he announces he does not believe

in god (he, without explanation, puts it in the small *g*). He also remarks that he does not "believe such belief to be more reasonable than the atheist allows." Many, through and through secularly minded people, including philosophers who call themselves naturalists, physicalists, or materialists, are plainly also in reality atheists. They probably do not call themselves atheists for they may think it sounds too vulgar, too *ordinaire*, too tub-thumping, too *engagé*, or nonfallibilistic, and the like. But naturalists or physicalists such as Dewey, Hook, Quine, Strawson, Davidson, Armstrong, Smart, and Rorty cannot, if they are to be consistent, but be atheists. If you are a naturalist, physicalist, or materialist, you are *thereby* an atheist whether you like to make such a self-ascription or not.

There are, of course, troubled atheists, atheists like some of the characters in Dostoevsky's novels, who suffer because they cannot believe in God, but there are also untroubled atheists (atheists that religious people not infrequently think, quite question-beggingly, are superficial people) such as John Dewey, Sidney Hook, and Richard Rorty, who happily concern themselves with the problems of life, perfectly free of the need for religious or metaphysical comfort. Some, as Quine probably is, are just rather indifferent and perhaps somewhat bemused by such matters. *But being physicalists or naturalists there is nothing else for them to be but atheists.* They cannot (*pace* Hook) even, as naturalists or physicalists, be agnostics, for the agnostic claims we cannot be in a position to either justifiably affirm or deny that God exists for the evidence here, one way or the other, is always insufficient, so the agnostic neither believes nor does not believe that God exists.[23] He remains in doubt for he believes evidential and other rational considerations are always insufficient to go one way or the other here. But that is not an option for the naturalist or physicalist, for they, as naturalists and physicalists, are saying, or giving to understand, that there are no spiritual or supernatural beings.

They are, of course, if they have absorbed anything of the spirit of modernity, fallibilists, but that just means, as we have seen, that, like many believers as well, they do not think we can gain *certain* knowledge, or knowledge that is not, at least in principle, revisable, about any matter of substance. But that is not at all enough to make them agnostics. They are not certain that there is no God, but that merely signifies for many atheists—certainly for this atheist—little more than something flowing from the belief that we cannot be certain about any matter of substance. *But that is fallibilism, not agnosticism.*

So what Allen rejects is not atheism, but an inessential metaphysical side of a very particular atheism with "an absolute animus toward religion," the atheism, that is, of the French Enlightenment of Condorcet, Diderot, and Holbach as well as, in certain respects, but the inverted Platonism aside, that of Engels and Lenin. What he sets himself against is an atheism born militant, born a 'project' of universal ambition . . . a concise and polemical formulation for the determination of intellectuals to rid natural knowledge of theological direction. An absolute god had to be excluded absolutely from the field of evidence and explanation in natural philosophy.

Then, Allen goes on to say, making a bit of a logical leap, that, on such a conception,

there is only one good in terms of which such an absolute proscription can be framed: the classical (Platonic) good of enlightening reason.

Allen avers, that such a metaphysically inverted Platonism is as pointless as the Platonism from which it flows. Platonic heresy and Platonism are both without justification and by now without any rationale. But (*pace* Allen) Platonism and Enlightenment rationalism are not *equally* besides the track, for the latter does not have a theory of forms and remains physicalistic. That seems at least something of an advance. All metaphysics may be bad but some metaphysics is worse than other metaphysics. "The atheism of the Enlightenment and the theology it sought to displace from the domain of knowledge" may form "a dialectical duo," but one partner may be more hobbled than the other.

3.

Following his discourse on the atheism of Enlightenment rationalism, Allen writes of me:

Kai Nielsen's atheism seems to be a variation on Enlightenment Platonism. His animus toward religion is inspired by its errors, the falsehoods and "unclear representations" upon which religious belief depends. Like the Platonist, he calls for us to "throw" off the shackles of ideology and see the world as clearly as possible. We must renounce metaphor and metaphysical comfort in the name of the literal truth. We must, if we are struggling to see the world rightly in the teeth of centuries of religious talk, force ourselves to think literally. If we see the world rightly we will see the truth of atheism. Religion has no literal truth. The key concepts of Judaism, Christianity, and Islam are (not) legitimate concepts capable of sustaining truth-claims.

However, as we have already seen, seeing the truth of atheism (if it is indeed true) is not seeing all, or indeed any, of that Platonistic and utopian metaphysical stuff to which Allen refers. Rather, it is simply to come to a soundly reasoned conclusion, if indeed that can be done, that there is no God, that our lives as moral beings need not collapse because of this and *perhaps* could even more adequately flourish. Some atheists, A. J. Ayer, Paul Edwards, and Antony Flew, and, classically, Karl Marx and Friedrich Engels, had, the confidence Allen does not share "that our society is not harmed . . . but made better, more rational, by the withering of religion." But that is surely not *the* atheist's confidence, but *some* atheist's confidence. Certainly Santayana, Weber, Durkheim, and Rorty do not share this confidence. I, speaking for myself, am of divided mind about it. It is true, as Allen points out, that *some* churches—it is important to keep in mind that they are only certain ones—are in many very concrete ways in the forefront of humane and liberating social action. They clearly show by their protective deeds how deeply they value human life, how they seriously treat life as sacred. There is plainly good in the world that would not be there but for their strenuous and often fearless efforts. More generally, religion has often been a humanizing force in the world. People would be even more brutish than they in fact often are without the *sometimes* civilizing influence of religion. Or at least so it is not implausible to believe.

I wrote in 1985,

> . . . since I think a belief in God is either a false belief or an incoherent one, depending on how one construes the term 'God', it makes me an atheist, but, while that is compatible with being irreligious, it does not make me irreligious. To be irreligious is to be scornful of religion or religious people and while I am scornful of some religions—the Mooney religion, for example, or of Christian Science—and some religious people, Ian Paisley, for example, or the late Cardinal Spellman, I am generally not scornful of religions or religious people. And some religious people, Father Daniel Berrigan, Gregory Baum, Dorothee Sölle, or Beyers Naudé, to take some outstanding examples, I regard as my comrades in a common struggle, while I am totally out of sympathy with the reactionary conservatism defended by such professional atheists or agnostics as Antony Flew, Wallace Matson, or Sidney Hook. And I am much more in sympathy with much of the social outlook of the World Council of Churches than I am with the generally conservative and overly rationalistic social outlook of many, but by no means all, secular humanists.[24] [I think now that it was a mistake to include Hook in that trio, but that does not touch the force of the above paragraph.]

Whether life in our century and the century to come would be better or worse without religious belief is not easy to know. Whatever we say concerning this will be no more than speculative guessing. There is the humanizing phenomena Allen points to and I have mentioned above. But there is evidence and considerations that cut the other way as well. Iceland, Denmark, Norway, Sweden, and Finland, which are all wealthy, or relatively wealthy, very secular societies, seem to be far better places in which to live than societies where religion is strong. Think of Ireland (North and South), Bosnia,

North Africa, Iran, Israel, India, Indonesia, Afghanistan, Pakistan, and parts of what once was the Soviet Union. Religion in those places, and some others as well, seems to breed fanaticism, intolerance, and extensive brutality, while the secular Scandinavian societies are just the opposite. We need to ask whether, in any, culturally speaking, very extensive way, there can be intense religious conviction without fanaticism. Though, against the worry that religion is fanaticism-prone, we need to keep in mind that some religious people in the rich liberal societies and as well *some* of the religious institutions in such societies show none of that fanaticism. But is that due more to their being in rich *liberal* societies, or perhaps just rich societies, or to something about the religious response itself? I do not think we can be very confident about what to say here. But contrasting Scandinavia with Ireland and Bosnia (to stay within European countries), we need to recognize that there are factors at work here other than religion. Among other things, there is the difference in wealth between the societies. The Swedish are much better off than the Irish. Still the religious factors are very prominent and it is not unreasonable to wonder if these societies, i.e., Bosnia and Ireland, wracked as they are by fanaticism, would not be a lot better off if they were more secular.

There are matters of degree here. Ireland is not Bosnia, but it is certainly not Denmark either. And even in some of the wealthy capitalist democracies— the United States and Canada very plainly—with issues such as abortion and euthanasia, which are difficult enough anyway, their reasonable and humane consideration has been made very much more difficult by entrenched, and often not very reflective, religious views. Similar things should be said about attitudes toward divorce, gender, and homosexuality.

So I think it is hard to balance things up and come up with a reasonable view about what to say about the human value of religion. Fortunately we do not have to agonize through that. Where religion is stable and secure, wrestling with the above question, given the entrenched state of religion, is all rather hypothetical. What we need to ask instead is what kind, if any kind, of truly human morality can go with it, since we are going to have religion in place anyway. What I have directed my attention to is neither of these questions, but, in my writings about ethics and religion, I have considered the question of whether in a disenchanted world, where more and more people just cannot believe in God, whether such people, in such a world, can make firm sense of their moral lives.[25] I have also in that context struggled with the question of whether religious moralities have any ground for a claim to superiority over purely secular ones. I have argued that we can make sense of our lives and find moral orientation even in an utterly godless world and that there is no justification for the belief that religious moralities are superior to purely secular ones. But (*pace* Allen) my argumentation here in no way leans on anything even like a Platonic heresy.

4.

What, I think, Allen holds against atheists, and thus holds against me, is rooted in his belief that atheists must be radical *Aufklärers* bent on sustaining in their conceptions of a good and just world-order a universality and unconditionality that cannot be obtained. In that they are no better—or so he believes—than the religions they seek to replace. There are no, Allen believes, true interests which human beings, *just in virtue of being human beings*, must have, no matter where they are placed or what their particular socialization has been. There is no one true description of the world which will just tell us, independently of our particular human interests, what the world is really like in itself. We have no way of understanding what it would be like to have "the truth of nature" and thus or so Allen believes "the truth of atheism."

In showing (*pace* Aquinas or Scotus) that there is no natural theology which could just tell us what nature and supernature are and must be like, Enlightenment atheology did not finally replace theology with the one true description of the world. As Allen puts it, that "final discreditation of theology for the production of scientific knowledge was not a step in the direction of greater global rationality." Indeed, Allen has it, there is no such thing. "Reason is a fine thing," he tells us,

> but it is not *one* thing. If you can talk you can reason; there is nothing more to reason "itself" than to language (or communication) "itself." Just as there is no essential unity to everything that is called "language" neither is there one dimension of "reason" in respect of which historically different styles of reasoning can be compared and ranked.

Allen's *assumption* is that atheists must reject such Wittgensteinian contextualism and claim instead that there is and must be a single true description of the world which, in an interest-irrelevant, particular-position, and purpose-irrelevant way, will just tell us how things must be: give us the one true—indeed necessarily true—description of the world. He just seems to assume—inexplicably and arbitrarily—that there can be no Wittgensteinians who are atheists as there are Wittgensteinians who are Christians. The reason, presumably, that atheism must go rationalist and cannot go pragmatist or Wittgensteinian and contextual, is atheism's claim that Christian, Jewish, or Islamic discourses cannot be rationally sustained, that in the twentieth century they can be recognized to be incoherent belief systems that it is not reasonable for a twentieth-century philosophically and scientifically sophisticated person to accept. Allen's point against such an atheistic conception is that reasonability and reason are too contextual for such a grand claim to be something which can be intelligibly made. There is no Archimedean fulcrum from which philosophers or other intellectuals can pass judgment "on the supposedly fundamental cognitive claims of religion." There is no coherent place for philosophers or anyone else to stand in making such a judgment.

Pace Nielsen, to speak of the irrationality, or for that matter the rationality, of religion has no grip at all in our social world. What is reasonable to do, to believe, or to commit yourself to, goes with some particular styles of reasoning. Our criteria and conception of reasonableness are therefore very context-dependent and particular social practice-dependent. There is no coherent conception of what is rational or reasonable *überhaupt*. It is reasonable to sometimes say that the moon is pink on a given autumn evening when our interests are roughly aesthetic or practical and we are making casual observations concerning what we see. But when we are doing physics and giving physical descriptions of the moon, such remarks about its color are irrelevant. But there is no one interest-free true description, somehow closer to reality than the others, which tells us what the moon is really like. We can make many true statements about the moon, but there are no elite entities and we have no elite concepts yielding elite descriptions which just tell us, independently of our interests and purposes, what the moon or anything else is like in itself.

If we accept this point about "the one true description of the world," as Hilary Putnam, Richard Rorty, Barry Allen, and I all would, then the ground, Allen has it, has been yanked out from under atheism, as well as (presumably) from theism, for then there can be no one true description of the world, no global rationality, and no interest-independent, interest-free criteria for what it is reasonable to believe and do. From a religious perspective or from within religious language-games and forms of life, such and such is reasonable, while from a nonreligious perspective it is not. But there is no such thing as the one true perspective which will tell us what it is, *sans phrase*, rational or reasonable to believe or to do. The atheist, Allen has it, thinks there is such an Archimedean fulcrum, but his thought here is at best mythological and perhaps it would be more accurately described as being incoherent.

Religious culture as much as scientific culture or moral culture can have an intellectual integrity of its own that philosophy can perhaps perspicuciously represent or helpfully articulate, but it is and can be in no position to judge or assess such cultures with their distinctive practices. It is an illusion—and an arrogant one at that—for an atheist (professing a "philosophical atheism" or for that matter any kind or atheism) to think that she has a doctrine by the use of which she can make such an assessment of religion. It makes no sense to think that she can so stand in judgment of the rationality or reasonability of belief.

5.

I do not think that we general critical intellectuals, we pragmatist philosophers or Marxian social theorists, are so fettered. To see what I have in mind here let me first bring out some ways in which I agree with Allen. I agree, as has been made very clear and explicit in this book, with his arguments that urge an acceptance of something like Rorty's nonscientistic, historicized contextualist pragmatism; and, I further agree with him, that this does not conceptually, or in any other way, imprison Rorty or us in a relativism (conceptual, metaethical, ethical, or cultural), but provides Rorty, and the rest of us, with the resources, both intracultural and intercultural, to make sense of our lives and assess our lives in an open-ended process where we endlessly repair the ship at sea.[26] We do not have, and cannot get, as I argued in part 3, an Archimedean fulcrum or (*pace* Bernard Williams) an Absolute conception of the world.[27] We, of course, start from our own culture, our own traditions, our own considered convictions—where else could we possibly start?—but we are also in a position to listen to others, sometimes very different others, and to relate and set alongside each other our own beliefs and theirs.[28] Noting what the results of doing so are, and, depending on what the result is, we accordingly revise or sometimes even jettison some of our beliefs concerning what is to be thought and done. We endlessly, though with temporary closures, correct ourselves as we go along, sometimes gaining, in this trial-and-error manner, a better sense of how we should go on. We can in this way gain, for a particular time and place, a somewhat better understanding of what it makes sense to do and believe. We sometimes, at some particular junctures, will fail in these endeavors, but we sometimes will also succeed. There is neither *a priori* blockage here nor, of course, a guarantee of success.

We have our various interests and purposes and we set them, if we are reasonable, in trying to get a coherent package, in relation to those of others, including sometimes culturally very different others. This is what I have called the method of reflective equilibrium, but it could also be called the pragmatic method, where, in a completely open-ended process, we correct our beliefs—factual, normative, conceptual, what you will—in the light of our other beliefs or beliefs from other cultures and other times, without ever *per impossible* standing free of our own culture or gaining an Archimedean fulcrum, but still without being imprisoned by or in our culture either.[29]

There are religious language-games, scientific ones, political ones, legal ones, culinary ones, basketball ones, literary ones, and the like. They all have criteria *in part* particular to themselves, but the criteria are also in part aligned with the criteria of other language-games. There is overlap and much reinforcement and, as well, sometimes strain, between different language-games. Some, of course, are more closely related to each other than others. But they are all rooted in natural languages (French, English, Chinese, German, Russian, etc.) and in various traditions. In following the style or reasoning of a particular language-game, we have something which is not balkanized such that the various language-games are like windowless monads with their own utterly local and utterly language-game-dependent conceptions of reasonability, intelligibility, and criteria for what is taken to be true and what is not. (We have in the introduction to part 4 seen this in some detail for reasonability.) Thus, if in morality, I ought to impartially consider the interests of all those involved in a moral situation, I will also, if I think for a moment, realize that to do this I must be able to determine what their interests are and how they can be satisfied and that this involves factual and at least rudimentary scientific styles of reasoning. The moral styles of reasoning, as Dewey stressed, do not stand free from the factual and scientific ones.[30] Similarly the scientific ones do not stand free of the moral ones either. In taking account of evidence in science, if we are to do it in a scientifically proper way, we must consider the evidence impartially. We cannot cook the books in doing science anymore than we can simply consider the interests of our friends and ignore the interests of others in morality. The appropriateness and indeed the necessity of impartiality cuts across contexts here.

In establishing the identity of persons—to switch to another example of the general point I wish to make—bodily criteria, as we saw in part 1, play an essential part in identifying individuals, in determining who they are. "Discrete individual" seems at least to be pleonastic.[31] "Infinite" cannot be conjoined with "individual" in the language-games we play in talking about persons.[32] There is no use for "infinite individual" or "infinite person" in such language-games. In engaging in *religious* language-games, utilizing what are the practices and styles of reasoning of religion, if I try to speak of a bodiless person or try to take it as a background assumption that there are such mysterious persons, and if, in attempting to do this, I try to identify such an alleged bodiless person in such a context, I will end up, as we saw in part 2 of this chapter, being, to understate it, rather baffled. There will be even more bafflement if we try to speak of "infinite individual" or of an "infinite person." And, as far as comprehensibility is concerned, I add insult to injury when I speak of such an infinite individual being transcendent to the universe. Such ways of talking do not go together with our familiar ways of talking and of conceptualizing things in the language-games in which we speak of persons, in the language-games in which such talk is at home. Perhaps, by weaving and reweaving our web of thought and belief, we can put things together so as to achieve sense here, so as to make sense here, but perhaps we cannot, and perhaps we will continue to find such a way of putting words together incoherent.

There can be no *a priori* claims here one way or the other. If we end up on the atheist side saying that "talk of an infinite individual transcendent to the universe" and of "a person who is pure spirit and, as such, utterly bodiless" are incoherent strings of words, as I argued in this chapter in discussing Langford and I have argued in more detail in part 1 and, from a different perspective, in chapter 14, we say this because we find that we can make nothing of such a way of putting words together.[33] We could, of course, stipulatively *give* them a sense, but they do not *have* a sense. We cannot figure out—come to discover—what is meant by them or even what we mean by them: what we are trying to say. They are bizarre collocations of words. Moreover, we cannot fit them together with the other ways we speak and think in the nonreligious language-games we play. All we have are some strange pictures, pictures we do not know how to apply.

We may say then either that for these reasons such talk is incoherent or, alternatively, in a more Quinean spirit, that such baffling utterances are false. They say things that are false because they are not only baffling, but they are, as well, incompatible with other ways we speak and think, ways that are pervasive in our thought and speech. In either case, we cannot get our beliefs and conceptions into reflective equilibrium. We find the religious ones out of sync with others, even after taking to heart the fact that as religious utterances they have to be mysterious. (A God who was not mysterious would not be the God of Judaism, Christianity, or Islam. This, note, is what Wittgenstein would call a grammatical remark.) Still, even after acknowledging that, they remain *so* mysterious that we can make nothing of them. We either simply do not understand them or, looking at things differently, we understand them sufficiently well to recognize that we have very good reasons to think that they are false because they are so out-of-joint with the other things we think, say, and believe. In that way they are incomprehensibly false.

So in either case we cannot, keeping the religious beliefs, get our beliefs and conceptions into reflective equilibrium; we find the religious ones the odd man out: they do not fit with the rest of what we believe and think. And this in turn leads us either to the belief that these key religious beliefs are either incoherent or incomprehensibly false. Either way of looking at things is, of course, atheistic, but in both instances it is an atheism that fits perfectly well with a Rorty-Putnam pragmatist antifoundationalist, antirepresentationalist metaphilosophical stance and does not at all commit the atheist to a nonhistoricist, noncontextualist belief in the one true description of the world or to some obscure, and no doubt obscurantist, notion of a substantial reason marching through history.

In short, while there remains in such an atheist a loyalty to the Enlightenment, as there is in Rorty, Putnam, and Foucault as well, there remains nothing of Enlightenment *rationalism* or Platonism, heretical or otherwise. The critique of the cognitive claims of religion and of the rationality of religious beliefs—here much too abrupt, the dialectic of argument is more complex than that—come from *within our forms of life* and require no appeal to some Absolute conception of the world or some view from nowhere. It requires no belief that there can be such a thing as the one true description of the world. I can, and do, that is, share Allen's, Rorty's, and Putnam's views that such Absolutistic conceptions make no sense. But I can, and do, do this without abjuring naturalism and physicalism and thus without rejecting atheism. In this respect my views and Rorty's are identical.

6.

I would like to see, as would Rorty as well, the practice fade away of suckering beginning undergraduates in philosophy courses into taking seriously "the problem of the external world" and "the problem of other minds." In the same spirit, Allen would like to see discussions of whether we can in any sense at all prove the existence or nonexistence of God, and, more generally, discussions of atheism versus religious belief, come off the philosophy curriculum and to cease to preoccupy philosophers. That such things still get discussed, he seems to think, is a kind of intellectual and cultural disgrace.

To take such issues off the philosophy curriculum seems to me a bad mistake, though as a philosopher actively engaging in philosophy I find such discussions wearisome: through and through unchallenging and unrewarding. But such issues, as we have seen (*pace* Plantinga), are rather different than the problem of the external world or the problem of other minds. These latter "problems" are entirely artificial, hothouse products resulting from the reading of certain philosophical texts (i.e., certain texts of Descartes, Locke, Berkeley, Hume, Reid, and Kant). Students have to be suckered into taking these arguments in these texts seriously and sometimes they, to my mind quite rightly, resist. Worries about whether there is a God, and whether we could come to know that there is, by contrast, well up out of our culture more generally. In that way they are more like moral skepticism then epistemological skepticism.[34] Similarly with atheism. People, sometimes very young people, particularly in our culture, wonder whether there is a God or whether they should be atheists; they wonder whether all that religious talk is not just nonsense or somehow just mythical or whether it answers to something deep within ourselves and perhaps as well about our universe or perhaps even about what is "beyond the universe." They did not have to read any philosophers or theologians at all to have such thoughts and sometimes to be deeply perplexed and engaged by such questions. We would rob them of something very precious in their and our culture if we did not make readily available to them the most careful and refined discussions of these issues that we have, namely those of Augustine, Scotus, Ockham, Aquinas, Hume, Kant, and Feuerbach.[35]

The pedagogical situation will have changed if in the next few decades or so a Weberian disenchantment of the world becomes so pervasive and so deep, that in time—let us hypothesize (probably unrealistically)—we will come to live in a postreligious, or at least a posttheistic, culture and that these questions concerning religion will fall into benign neglect, so much so that even atheism loses its sense of being a live option from having no opposition. We would then come to read Augustine and Aquinas and those parts of Hume and Kant dealing with God as I hope sometime reasonably soon we will come to read those parts of Hume and Kant dealing with the problem of the external world and of other minds. We would, that is, come to read all these things as set historical pieces, as rather quaint parts of our intellectual and, in the religious case, of our cultural history. Though again, given what religion has been, these questions about the existence of God would remain something to be more serious about than about the problem of the external world.

If we came to live in such a postreligious culture, we would say something like this to our students: Once people believed in God—believed in a supernatural being who was said to have created the world—and, at that time, some people were deeply committed to those beliefs, some devoting their lives to them and sometimes even to fighting wars against those they took not to have the proper belief in God. We would, knowing as we do about the old beliefs, try to convey to our rather bemused students how important these issues were for such people. And, I submit that, we on reflection would want to do this, for we do not want an Orwellian world in which we lose a sense of our own history. Still, both sets of questions would in such an ambience become purely questions in the history of ideas rather than being live philosophical or religious questions.

Like Allen, I wish philosophy would move on to other things: things I regard as both more humanly useful and more intellectually challenging. I share Dewey's conception of the way philosophy should be transformed.[36] But that is a metaphilosophical issue about where philosophy should go and what it should try to be and not a pedagogical point about what should be in a university curriculum. (I do not say there is no significant relation between the two, but they still are distinct issues.) I am, as I remarked, thoroughly bored by the discussions of the proofs for the existence of God. I think Hume and Kant together essentially settled those issues. Wallace Matson, Michael Scriven, Michael Martin, and John Mackie, in returning to those issues, are just carrying out mopping-up operations. But others—reflective and informed others—are not so bored and some few philosophers, Hugo Meynell and Richard Swinburne, for example, to mention able defenders of a very old tradition, think that such issues are still very much alive and should remain so. Moreover, there are not a few reflective and intelligent students and people in the community beyond the university who care very much about such issues and care, as well, and connectedly, about the options atheism or religious belief. Because of these various people, we should keep these questions on the philosophical agenda. There should—and it seems to me that this point *should* be a commonplace—be forums left open for giving these issues the most intelligent, informed, and dispassionate airing we can muster. That Allen and I wish to go on to other things, and that we believe that the philosophy of religion is not at the cutting edge of philosophy, is a very different matter.

IV

CONCLUDING UNSCIENTISTIC POSTSCRIPT

1.

I want now to turn to Beehler's perceptive point about the clash or at least the tension between my broadly positivist attitude toward religion and my metaphilosophical stance which is that of a nonscientistic contextualist pragmatist.[37] First, a note of explanation: the positivist side comes out most starkly in my earliest writings on the philosophy of religion; later, as my metaphilosophical views gradually developed, my extensive reliance on verificationism as a general criterion of *factual* significance (not significance *sans phrase*) changed and my beliefs about what philosophy could and should try to do changed as well.[38] I certainly do not rely as heavily on verificationist arguments as I once did and my central argument about the incoherence of the concept of God has been stated independently of it.[39] Still, it might be thought that even there I am giving philosophy an overseer and adjudicator role that on my own metaphilosophical view it cannot properly have. Philosophy cannot, on that view, stand in judgment of, or even provide the foundation for, or a critique of, a form of life.[40] As I have said myself, and Beehler quotes,

> philosophy cannot be the arbiter of culture, distinguishing between what is rational or reasonable and what is irrational and unreasonable to believe and do. Philosophers cannot tell us what makes our ideas really clear, what we really mean, or what we are justified in believing. We are not able in general to say anything very enlightening about what meaning, truth, knowledge, or rationality is.[41]

Yet, Beehler goes on to remark, that when Nielsen talks about religion—quite contrary to this metaphilosophical stance—he goes around laying down the law, left and right, about what can rationally be believed, what makes sense, what is indefensible nonsense, and so on—all the imperial 'foundationalist' transgressions he delights in declaring *verboten* when, in the avowed company of Rorty and Habermas, he sweeps fiercely through the philosophical stables in a metaphilosophical mood.

My own metaphilosophy, Beehler contends, should allow no such judgments about what it makes sense to say or what is coherent and what is not.[42]

So what am I to say for myself here? Should I not just admit that either my "positivism" or contextualist pragmatism should go or both? I cannot, it seems evident, reasonably hold onto both. I think, however, that I can hold on to both with some rather minimal adjustments and with a careful attention to how a pragmatist understands what it is to do philosophy. This sounds like a classic case of wanting to have your cake and eat it too. I will try to show, though with less confidence than the following argument suggests, that that is not so.

In *After the Demise of the Tradition,* and in this volume as well, I follow Rorty in distinguishing between *p*hilosophy and *P*hilosophy.[43] And to keep this distinction firmly in mind is crucial for what I argue for here. The former, that is *p*hilosophy, is arguably quite unproblematic, and, as practiced by pragmatists such as John Dewey, *p*hilosophy can do useful critical work, including work in the examination and critique of religion. In the metaphilosophical passage, Beehler cites, and I have just quoted, I was talking about *P*hilosophy, something conceived of as an autonomous discipline, and not *p*hilosophy, which claims no such autonomy or such a disciplinary status.

What I have in mind here surely needs to be explained. What Rorty calls *p*hilosophy is "the attempt to see how things, in the broadest sense of the term, hang together, in the broadest sense of the term."[44] *P*hilosophy, by contrast, is the attempt, either in the grand metaphysical tradition, in the tradition of foundationalist epistemology or in the philosophy of logic or language, to construct a systematic *a priori* theory which, as part of an autonomous discipline, would, in one way or another, critique the various forms of life. Plato, Descartes, and Kant (with varying degrees of purity) gave different, but in each case classical, articulations and defenses of *P*hilosophy.

*P*hilosophy I regard as an impossibility as does Rorty as well. It is something to be set aside as a house of cards. It was part of the genius of Wittgenstein to show how this can be done without erecting, in a paradoxical self-refuting way, another *P*hilosophy. It is *P*hilosophy, as such an autonomous discipline, that both Rorty and I argue should come to an end. But *p*hilosophy should go right on rolling along, as an attempt, common to all critical intellectuals, and rooted in no discipline, to see how things hang together. Pragmatists, as Rorty avers, recognize "that one can be a *p*hilosopher precisely by being anti-Philosophical. . . ."[45] One steps back from the issues of Perennial Philosophy, of foundationalist epistemology, and of metaphysics. One does not try to show the rational *foundations* of science, religion, morality, politics, or of everyday life: the underlying truth about these practices and forms of life. The various articulations by Philosophy are taken to be illusory. There are no such foundational truths, no such 'rational foundations' or even a need for them; and there is no genuine discipline called Philosophy which could articulate and justify such "foundations." There is no such knowledge and Philosophy cannot play such a foundational and critical role. This is what Beehler rightly notes, in my metaphilosophical thinking, is my not setting Philosophy up as a critic or overseer of culture, including of course, of religion. But to say that Philosophy cannot play that role is not to deny that philosophy can. It is, however, to deny that there is some one discipline or *superdiscipline* that can do it.

I think that philosophy can play a demythologized form of that role. But just how it can, if it can, and what "the it" is here, surely needs elucidation and explanation. Without that my remark at the end of the last paragraph is so obscure as to be completely unhelpful. Indeed, stated just like that, it sounds like an evasion on my part. So let me explain. With philosophy we do not have some specialized discipline with some special knowledge—some *Philosophical* knowledge—so that there is something a Philosopher as such can know that no one else can know so well. But philosophy is not that sort of thing at all. If we limit ourselves to doing philosophy, our activity so construed, will take roughly a Deweyan pragmatist turn, for which Wittgenstein in effect supplies a good meta-account. What I have called philosophers, on such a construal, are general all-purpose critical intellectuals (among other things, critics of society) including in their ranks all sorts of scientists (from both the natural and the human sciences), historians, scholars in cultural studies and religious studies, former Philosophers (reformed into philosophers), novelists, poets, dramatists, literary critics, literary theorists, legal theorists, and the like.

So construed philosophy is not an *a priori* purely conceptual investigation. It will be broadly empirical and historicist and rooted in a consideration of the problems of the epoch in which the philosopher philosophizes. In doing philosophy, such all-purpose critical intellectuals (philosophers), coming from all over the place, with a heterogenous bunch of skills, notions, and sensibilities, will be starting with their traditions, their own preconceptions, and their considered convictions. Some of them will, as well, sometimes use, in a pragmatic manner, certain Philosophical notions or conceptual analyses, where philosophy, now as conceptual elucidation, functions purely as an elucidatory *second-order* discourse.[46] But these things will be used with caution by the philosopher and only where they have a chance of working. And in being so used pragmatically, they will not be taken as contributing to or as presupposing a foundational theory or any kind of *a priori* theory or perhaps any theory at all. They will just be something which such philosophers (critical intellectuals) use in their attempts to see how things hang together *and* in looking with a critical eye for a conception of how things might better hang together. These philosophers—these critical intellectuals—will try to see how things hang together and they will, in doing so, and quite properly, ask critical questions concerning religion or any other practice, including philosophy itself. (That is why we have such a thing as metaphilosophy.[47]) They will most particularly ask questions about how these beliefs fit together with our other beliefs, if indeed they do. Repairing the ship at sea, including sometimes throwing overboard some rotten planks, they will try for a time, but only for a time, and thoroughly fallibilistically, to see how things hang together. In doing so, the philosopher will not infrequently reject certain beliefs and conceptions—and indeed sometimes, though rarely, very fundamental ones—as not being conducive to our being able to forge a coherent picture of how things hang together and thus to a gaining of a better understanding of our lives and perhaps, as well, to a coming to understand a little more adequately how we might best live our lives both together and as individuals.

What I characterized in section III.5 of this chapter, with my use of wide reflective equilibrium, was just such an attempt to articulate how to do that and something of a conception of what this would come to. It was not an attempt to articulate a foundational theory or indeed any kind of *theory*. And it most certainly was not an attempt to articulate an autonomous Philosophical theory. But it was an attempt to do *philosophy*. It pragmatically used a few Philosophical notions coming principally from positivist and other analytical traditions, but, in my utilization, they were not systematically tied to those traditions or to any Philosophical view. Like any good carpenter, pragmatists use whatever tools and materials that come in handy for the problem at hand. There is, in such work, a Deweyan pragmatist philosophy and a roughly Wittgenstein therapeutic metaphilosophy. The latter has the purely negative task of making the world safe *from* Philosophy. It is in this contextualist way in which we, without the "aid" of some superdiscipline, can critically appraise our practices, including sometimes showing that certain ones should be put out to pasture as in the past we put out to pasture our astrological and magical practices.

This pragmatist conception of philosophy, where it takes a somewhat more theoretical turn than in Dewey, as in Quine, Rorty, Davidson, and Putnam, is an account which does not work with any firm analytic/synthetic distinction, trying to capture a hard logical must or to provide us with the *a priori* foundations of anything, but urges a conception of philosophy, and as well works with that conception, as an empirical critical theory, in which theory,

metatheory, evidence, inferential norm, or alternatively, content and framework are not sharply distinguished.[48] The fence, as Quine likes to put it, is really down.

There is no seeking out of foundational conceptual truths, but pragmatically deployed conceptual analyses can sometimes play a useful role in articulating a critical theory which in turn might, though not without caution and
skepticism, be used in trying for a time, but only for a time, to get a better understanding of how things hang together. Grammatical remarks, to switch to
Wittgenstein's idiom, are not always out of place in such an endeavor.

That was the role of my arguments about the coherence of God-talk. It
was not an attempt (*pace* both Beehler and Allen) to lay down the law about
what it makes sense to say or to articulate *a theory* of meaning or even, in my
later writings, to give a criterion of factual significance (as I attempted in earlier writings).[49] What I did try to do was to establish that when we look at
God-talk in an attempt to see how things hang together, we can see, *without
any theory at all*, that certain religious notions make such a bad fit with other
things that are very pervasive in our lives that we can see no sense in them.
And the "them" here is God-talk, including centrally *first-order* God-talk.
That is not a laying down of the law, but an attempt to get people to reflect
on what this strange talk comes to, if anything, in the context of our actual
practices, and to suggest that it looks like such talk comes to nothing that we
can make out as coherent.

Rorty, who thinks positivism a retrograde philosophical movement,
caught up in *Philosophy* as much as the Platonism or Cartesianism it rejects,
remarks, in line with what I argued above,

> . . . the positivists were absolutely right in thinking it imperative to extirpate
> metaphysics when 'metaphysics' means to give knowledge of what science
> cannot know. For this is the attempt to find a discourse which combines the
> intersubjective security of objective truth . . . with the edifying unjustifiable
> but unconditional moral claim.[50]

I can understand why someone—myself included—would, in certain moods,
want something like this metaphysical comfort, but we can also see how
such conceptions do not fit with our seaworthy practices. Again, it is more
nostalgia for the Absolute and a seeking for a kind of incoherent security that
we cannot have and do not need.

Perhaps there is too much, particularly in my earlier writings on religion
and the philosophy of religion, Carnapian scorn and Ryleian joshing, themselves uneasily combined. *Perhaps* I should not have spoken of certain philosophical problems as pseudoproblems or of certain, sentences, concepts, or beliefs as incoherent, senseless, or meaningless. With the fence down between

the analytic and synthetic, it would have *perhaps* been better to argue that belief in God is so incomprehensible as to be a belief that should be rejected as false—incomprehensibly false—rather than as incoherent. Such religious beliefs are false because religious sentences expressive of those beliefs express beliefs that are so extremely problematic that we cannot make out anything of what is being claimed when they are used. I am still inclined, fence down or not, to utilize conceptual remarks about God-talk (Wittgenstein's conception of grammatical remarks), keeping in mind that conceptual distinctions can be made in a pragmatic spirit as distinctions we try on for fit and utility, in trying to get the best empirical and normative account we can get of how things hang together. And this still inclines me to say that God-talk is incoherent rather than talk which at key points makes false assertions.[51] But whether we say that these beliefs are incoherent or false, the result is still atheism. Without (*pace* Langford) engaging in *Philosophy* or what might be called the metaphysics of empiricism or logical positivism, I articulated and defended a *foundationless* form of atheism to go with my foundationless naturalism.

The dominant, largely implicit, meta-account in my earlier writings was broadly positivistic; my later explicit meta-account is Wittgensteinianly therapeutic and pragmatist. But what I actually did (my *first-order* doings) in arguing about religion, as distinct from how I represented what I did, has remained much the same. In my later more pragmatic turn, where this became an issue, as Beehler brings out clearly, I do not, for the reasons I have given above, think that I am trying to have my cake and eat it too.

2.

Allen, and perhaps Beehler as well, seem to regard "militant atheism" as a redundancy. Presumably I share with the *philosophes*, on Allen's view, "an absolute animus toward religion." Beehler doesn't put it that strongly, but the very titles of Beehler's two essays betray his belief that I am a militant atheist, i.e., "Religion v. Militant Atheism" and "Hounding Heaven"; and we have already noted the aggressive worrying sheep-dog analogy. Moreover, Beehler also remarks, much in the spirit of Allen, that "atheism has long had its own proselytizing agenda aimed at sweeping the gods from their altars and setting up reason in their place." I surmise that he believes that I have that proselytizing agenda.

So I ask myself, Am I a militant atheist and if so should I continue to be? What, of course, is important here is not what I think, but whether someone arguing for atheism, as I do, and with roughly the views about atheism that I have, should be, or perhaps even necessarily is, if he or she is at all consistent, militant about it. In speaking of being a militant atheist I take it that we are talking of someone who tries, more or less relentlessly, to persuade people to be atheists and tries to do his or her best to bring about an atheistic world: a world in which people no longer believe in God or even believe that God exists because they know (think they know) or believe with sound warrant (what they take to be sound warrant) that God does not exist and they further know (think they know) that the having of this knowledge or warranted belief is a good thing. The aim of a militant atheist is to have a culture in which, so viewing the world, is secular through and through. Their task, as individuals, is to do their bit in the achieving of that.

This is what they as militant atheists believe and this is how they believe they should act. We have seen, however, in earlier sections of this chapter, that atheists, though they often—perhaps even rightly—are militant need not be militant: Santayana being the most striking example of an utterly nonmilitant atheist but still a very thorough atheist nonetheless. So "militant atheist" is not a redundancy. Moreover, Santayana, without any shift in *first-order* beliefs or normative attitude, could have adopted my theoretical articulation of atheism, e.g., have accepted my cumulative argument and my irrationality thesis with the gloss that I give it. This, of course, is a way of giving to understand that my theoretical articulation of atheism does not commit me to militancy.

Still the question remains, though there is no logical entailment there, am I, on more particular grounds, a militant atheist and should one be, if my theoretical conception of atheism is on the mark? Put more simply, should an atheist be a militant atheist? I think, for Allen and Beehler, there can be no question that I, or for that matter anyone else who is really an atheist, must, to remain consistent, be committed to such militancy. It should also be noted in passing that "militant" for them has a negative emotive force. But I would not make their implicit *persuasive* definition. It is an open question for me whether militancy is a good or bad thing. I believe that sometimes it is and sometimes it is not. Relatedly, I believe some forms of militant atheism in some contexts are good and some bad.

We have to see in what way, if in any way, I am a militant atheist and then assess that particular militancy. Certainly it is perfectly clear that I have no "absolute animus toward religion." Indeed, generally I have no animus at all toward religion. Sometimes Judaism, Christianity, and Islam all take forms—say, the fundamentalist versions of all these religions—that I do have an animus toward, though it does not follow that I have an animus toward individuals who are fundamentalists. It all depends on how they behave. But I do have an animus toward fundamentalism itself as well as (even where they are distinct) toward the Religious Right. But so do many very thoughtful *religious* people as well. So the animosity is not rooted in the fact that fundamentalists and religious reactionaries believe in God or have a doctrine of salvation. Rather the reason for the animus is in certain particular things they do (attacking abortion clinics, for example) and advocate, including very fundamentally their intolerance, narrowness, and doctrinaire claims to certainty: their through and through unreasonability. But, let me repeat, my animus here is certainly not a general animus toward religion, or toward Judaism, Christianity, or Islam, and it is not dependent on my atheism or even on my more generalized secularism. Karl Barth, no doubt, would have a very similar animus.

However, Allen claims that my "animus toward religion is inspired by its errors, the falsehoods and 'unclear representations' upon which religious belief depends." I, along this line, whether it is an animus or not, argue for the setting aside of metaphysical beliefs, including the beliefs that God exists and that we are immortal. Like Rorty and the positivists, I seek, but, as they do, through rational argumentation, to extirpate claims to some factual or "superfactual" knowledge (which metaphysics purports to yield) that science cannot know.[52] In so arguing against such metaphysical beliefs, a background assumption of mine, in so reasoning, is that the attainment of true beliefs is *an* important good. We should put aside the search for metaphysical comfort and try to see the world as clearly as we can, as free as possible from ideological distortion. I argue, as Allen notes, that we "must, if we are struggling to see the world rightly, in the teeth of centuries or religious talk, force ourselves to think literally." And, if we do this with persistence and care, I further argue, we will see that the key religious claims are at best false and that atheism is true. Is just to believe this, as Allen thinks and perhaps Beehler as well, in itself militancy?

As we have seen (*pace* Allen) this view, if true at all, is no doctrine, not even a heretical doctrine, of Platonic truth. But in the present context, its truth or falsity is not at issue, but its alleged militancy. If *any normative* view arguing for a normative position is taken, just in virtue of its very normativeness, to be militant, then the view is plainly militant and I am, without doubt, a perfectly unrepentant militant atheist. But that view of militancy, in effect, rests on a *persuasive* redefinition of "militancy": a redefinition that makes many things which are ordinarily not thought to be militant, militant by implicit stipulative definition. It reveals, if you will, a kind of positivist or Wittgensteinian fear of, or at least skittishness about, the normative, at least when we are doing philosophy. But philosophers have argued normatively and with rigor, care, and ingenuity. John Rawls, Ronald Dworkin, Robert Nozick, David Gauthier, Richard Norman and G.A. Cohen are striking examples. Such skittishness is unjustified. So I have no hesitation about arguing normatively or about making normative claims.

I, to take a normative turn, care about truth—though it is surely not the only thing I care about—and it seems to me that to believe in God is a mistake, for it is to have a belief which is at best false and that it is at best false is by now reasonably obvious. Moreover, though less obviously so, to think that we need to believe in God to make sense of our lives is to have another false belief and, as well, to engage in a form of self-deception. (I shall return to this in the next and final chapter.) Moreover, to the extent that we prose-lytize this need to believe, we, usually unwittingly, deceive others as well, if our proselytizing is successful. But believing things that are false, self-de-ceptive, or other-deceptive is normally, but not utterly invariably, a bad thing. In some very unusual situations, it may be a good thing to have irrational be-liefs. When, for example, one is lost miles from anyone in the frozen North in winter, it may be a very good thing indeed to believe, against all the prob-abilities, that, if one can hold on to one's brains, keep one's nerve, and try very hard, one can survive. Maybe such an irrational belief is necessary here to have any chance of survival at all. But these are very rare exceptions and cer-tainly not the rule. If I am right in my arguments that there is usually, and very generally, no need for this self-deception to make sense of our lives, then be-lief in God is a bad thing for people in a good position to know that. But, right or wrong, I argue for this dispassionately and not in the spirit of proselytiz-ing zeal. I do not just fanatically proclaim it or insinuate it without argument.

Struggling to see the world rightly is, as I construe it, on the pragmatist's way of doing things, the attempt to see how things hang together and is no metaphysical search for some foundationalist truths or for "ultimate realty." We are in so proceeding engaging in philosophy and not in Philosophy. *In try-ing to see the world rightly we are not searching for the one true description of the world.* That is something which I think is an utter impossibility. Indeed, I think—and I argued for it in part 3—the very idea is incoherent. We are in-stead trying to get the best understanding we can get, standing where we are, of how things hang or fit together. We are not in search of the holy grail, to wit a perspectiveless Absolute conception of the world. Again, with an Ab-solute conception of the world we have something which is at least arguably an impossibility and perhaps actually incoherent.[53] But to try to see in the pragmatist's way how things fit together, and how we might even forge a bet-ter fit, is plainly a desirable, and at least seemingly an intelligible, thing to do.

However, it might be asked of me, would you like, if this could be done without force or propaganda, for religions to go away and for people to live nonevasively in accordance with reason? You believe, the questioning could continue, that our central religious claims are at best false and you also be-lieve that it is good to be reasonable and, usually at least, to act in accordance with what we have the best reasons for believing to be true. But what do you say to a believer's remark that he is not so sure about truth, but he does care very much about coping with life? Such a believer does not want to be un-reasonable, but he does not want to make a fetish of reason or truth either. For him, what is more vital than discovering or constructing what is "the point of view of reason" (if indeed there is such a thing) is for people generally to be able, as well as for it to be possible, to cope with their tangled and, not infrequently, miserable lives. *To reply that truth is more important than coping is just to be rationalistically dogmatic.* It is to be caught up in a "faith in reason," the very faith that Allen, Beehler, and Hendrik Hart believe that you, Nielsen, commit yourself to.[54] You are, after all, more like the *philosophes* than you are willing to acknowledge.

Well, if it were just a straightforward choice between *coping* and *truth*, then I would not know what to say in response. There might be nothing nonarbitrary that we could *in general* say. Certainly I would not say, "Let truth prevail come what may!" That seems to me an absurd thing to say. So, I do not see how it is that I am such a great worshipper or fetishizer of reason. What I have argued in my writings about ethics and religion—something I returned to briefly in the introduction to part 4—is that we are not faced with that stark choice. Indeed, so viewing things is pure unrealistic romanticism. We, or at least many of us, can and do cope at least as well without religion as with it. If we examine moral matters with reasonable care, and also take them to heart, we can come to see that morality has a rationale and life makes sense even in an utterly Godless world. Even those who now think they need religion to cope can come to see, if they can and will reflect carefully, that that is not so. There are purely secular resources available to them for coping.

However, the recognition of that would not lead me to make a claim so strong as the claim that I would wish that religion in all forms would wither away, that I want to see an utterly postreligious culture come into being. I honestly do not know what I want here or what I should think. In one way at least it may be a rather unreal question, for, given the ubiquity of religion over cultural space and historical time, it is rather unlikely, even with the relentless disenchantment of the world, that religion will wither away. There will always be a need for social bonding. And we human beings will find ways of reenchanting our world. It is more likely that religion will transmute. And, normatively speaking, one should be rather cautious about the wish for the end of something that has at all times and places played such a humanly important role. Here Emile Durkheim's reminders deserve very careful consideration. (Though we should not forget here how very different religions have been. Some forms of Buddhism, for example, have neither God nor worship. There is simply in these religions no belief in God at all.[55]) So I would be cautious about wishing for the end of religion.

However, I remain, nonetheless, ambivalent here. There is virtue, as W. D. Falk has powerfully argued, in living nonevasively and religion does involve, if my atheism is justified, falsity and illusion and it is not, for people in the relatively fortunate circumstances of most readers of this volume, a necessary saving myth crucial for their human flourishing or for overcoming alienation.[56] It is not that with a "proselytizing agenda" I wish to sweep "the gods from their altars" and set "up reason in their place." But, like Falk and many others, I do think that there is something admirable about living nonevasively. We are creatures of sentiment, as well as of reason, but one very strong human sentiment is to keep our integrity, both intellectual and moral, and not to crucify our intellects and not to believe, or try to believe, fearing sickness unto death, what is not believable. But belief in God seems to me to be just such an incomprehensibly unbelievable thing. But for destitute people, in horrible conditions of life, with little chance of a change in condition, thoughts of living nonevasively may be an unaffordable, even a frivolous, luxury.

So, if the above is true, as I think it is, religion (or at least Judaism, Christianity, and Islam) is not an unmixed blessing. So there is for me ambivalence here, but what I do argue with confidence, and without any ambivalence at all, is that there are purely secular moral and similarly existential resources here which enable people in a disenchanted world of moderate abundance and security to cope. People in such circumstances, I argue, can reasonably and effectively cope even if they find that they just cannot believe in God. What I am trying to show is that they are not bereft or adrift, even if they inhabit a Godless world. Coping need not break down or even become attenuated in such a circumstance.

What I have argued for is that, for people so situated, atheism is more reasonable and more attractive from the moral point of view than religious belief. We can, as Simone de Beauvoir and Jean-Paul Sartre near the end of their lives described themselves as doing, and as having done throughout their adult lives, lead fully productive, fulfilling, happy, and *engagé* lives even in the complete absence of any belief, or even temptation to believe, in God.[57] The idea that without God nothing matters, or nothing matters very deeply, is simply false. Perhaps de Beauvoir and Sartre, and many less famous people like them, were mistaken, perhaps even somehow self-deceived; and, perhaps I am mistaken as well, in thinking that such living without God or God substitutes is possible and, if possible, a good thing for at least some people. But neither Simone de Beauvoir's detailed account of her life, in her massive four-volume autobiography, nor Sartre's briefer remarks, bear the marks of self-deception at least on this topic. Whatever we may think of their *Philosophy*, on these matters, and in describing how they lived and their rationale for living, their remarks carry conviction.[58] Moreover, what they say is utterly sane, relaxed, thoughtful, and for the most part convincing. And their *Philosophy* hardly enters here at all. A similar thing is true of the much more well-known account of Hume's meeting his end, though here we have in addition the pleasure of encountering Hume's superb irony. I argue, doing a bit of *philosophy*, for such a secure living in a disenchanted world. I try to do this with some attention and care and, I believe, I do it in a nonpartisan manner. So mistaken or not, unless I cannot see the mote in my own eye, this is neither fanaticism nor militancy, but it is to argue from *conviction*. But it is not to argue from a conviction which is so unshakable that I am not willing to put it to question. I do not say, like Calvin and Plantinga, that these things are beyond controversy. Whether or not I am self-deceived here is for others to judge.

NOTES

1. My self-labeling was, of course, in earnest, but is was also deliberately turned against Rodger Beehler's remarks against labeling and self-labeling. Beehler believes that "the whole practice of fastening labels like 'Wittgensteinian', 'Marxist' and so on, upon ideas and arguments, needs to be got rid of." He thinks such labeling tends to close down thought. For the persons labeled it can lead to their pigeon holing and with that to an easy and automatic dismissal. Similarly, self-labeling "constrains the self-labeler constantly to tailor and monitor his or her thinking to that of the 'master'." These things, of course, can happen and I agree that when they do they are bad. But with serious thinkers, and who else should we care about in these matters, labeling and self-labeling usually does not work this way. G.A. Cohen, whom I admire as much as Beehler does, is, in company with Richard Rorty, Isaiah Berlin, Andrew Levine, Hilary Putnam, John Roemer, Charles Taylor, and Jon Elster, one of the most accomplished labelers and self-labelers around, as can be seen from the essays in the very book of Cohen's from which Beehler quotes. Far from shutting down thought, it serves for such thinkers to facilitate it by giving it an initial orientation and context. It lets one's readers know where one is coming from, as they used to say in California; and it provides a geography of thought, an initial rough map, which, though it may upon occasion misguide, will generally enable us to see where we are so that we do not constantly have to be beginning at the beginning. Take, for example, the masterful, certainly not shallow or *parti pris*, review article of present-day ethical theory written jointly by Stephen Darwall, Allan Gibbard, and Peter Railton, "Toward *Fin de siècle* Ethics: Some Trends," *Philosophical Review* 101, no. 1 (January 1992): 115–89. In setting out the issues they do a good bit of labeling and self-labeling. I would like to ask Beehler how he could write an article trying to say where we are now in ethical theory and, as well, to hint where we might best go without the use of labels. If he tried to do so without their use, he would be just pointlessly tying his own hands. And *if* he says such essays are pointless, then he is just being *parti pris*. Similarly, Charles Taylor's attempt to set his own communitarian views off from liberalism, while taking on board what is valuable in liberalism, have helped us to understand better political and moral thought even when, and indeed because of, its leading us to a sustained examination of what liberalism and communitarianism are and of whether they necessarily conflict. It is by now (*pace* Alasdair MacIntyre) not at all clear whether a communitarian liberal is a contradiction. And what is more crucial is that in thinking about these isms, if you will, we are led to more carefully think about community and our choices and possibilities as human beings and of what a good life for human beings would look like. In this vein, I would like to think (or at least hope) that the present chapter, and the essays it is responding to, taken together, do not close down thought, but in probing atheism—putting atheism to stress— they help us better to understand what is involved in the choice between belief and unbelief. No biologists, to shift focus on the same general theme, today are Darwin*ists*, but most, if not all, are Darwin*ians*, meaning by that, though they reject or greatly modify many of Darwin's particular conceptions, they see their thinking as growing out of the tradition that Darwin initi-

ated and to which he gave a striking articulation. Jon Elster writes similarly about Marx, as I have and as has Andrew Levine. Our relation to Marx is like that of contemporary biologists to Darwin. We are, and so in effect are G.A. Cohen and John Roemer, Marx*ians* and not Marx*ists,* just as biologists are Darwin*ians* and not Darwin*ists*. Though we reject a lot—in Elster's case most—of what Marx thought, we see Marx as someone who has initiated and powerfully articulated a tradition that deeply effects our ways of thinking and whose continuing importance we recognize. Beehler rejects, to my mind quite properly, many things in Wittgenstein. Yet Beehler's very method, his way of thinking and conceptualizing is saturated with the spirit of Wittgenstein. Hence the label—and quite appropriately so—Wittgensteinian, just as Cohen is a Marxian, Rorty a Deweyan, and Taylor a communitarian. Such labels do not shut down thought, they facilitate it by showing where various thinkers are coming from and something of the importance of history and tradition. Kai Nielsen, "Analytical Marxism: A Form of Critical Theory," *Erkenntnis* 39 (1993): 1–21; Andrew Levine, "What Is a Marxist Today?" in *Analyzing Marxism,* ed. Robert Ware and Kai Nielsen (Calgary, Alberta: University of Calgary Press, 1989), 29–58; and Kai Nielsen, "Elster's Marxism," *Philosophical Papers* 21, no. 2 (1992): 83–106. Isaiah Berlin in his study of Johann Georg Hamann well illustrates what I have in mind about the adept use of labels. He refers to Hamann initially as "the pioneer of anti-rationalism in every sphere" (64), giving powerful resistance to the eighteenth-century march of enlightenment and reason, the resistance to "which in time culminated in Romanticism, obscurantism, and political reaction . . ." (64). But then we are led to see the complexity and force of Hamann's antirationalism and its depth. We come away from a reading of Berlin's essay with a better understanding of the counter-Enlightenment and of a whole way of resisting, on the one hand, atheistic rationalism, as well as rationalism more generally, and, on the other hand, mere sentimental pietism. We start with labels to help fix our thought, but then move, as we follow his narrative, to a deeper understanding of the history of ideas and, as well, of the struggles between belief and unbelief and between the Enlightenment and counter-Enlightenment. Isaiah Berlin, "The Magus of the North," *New York Review of Books* 11, no. 17 (October 21, 1993): 64–71.

2. All quotations from Allen, Beehler, and Langford are taken from their essays in examination of my views on religion published in *Studies in Religion* 23, no. 2 (1994).

3. There are a host of other issues where I would take issue with Beehler. I discuss two more in the concluding section of this chapter, another in the first footnote, and, in my response to Allen in section III.5. Much of what I say vis-à-vis Allen could be applied to Beehler as well. See, as well, my response to the first of Beehler's essays in my "God and the crisis of modernity," *Studies in Religion* 23, no. 2 (1994): 143–58.

4. Simone de Beauvoir in *Old Age* (Harmondsworth, Middlesex, England: Penguin Books, 1977) gives a rather persuasive account of how very frequently even very intelligent older people are intellectually blocked: capable of working well within their own paradigms or frameworks but not in responding intelligently to new ideas.

5. Beehler was not one of those who so misunderstood me nor was Hendrik Hart.

6. A little more than the bare conditionals are needed. To bring out the full force of my claim, we need as well the conclusions I mentioned as being the core propositions—the incoherence argument aside—of the cumulative argument. They need to be included and to have been established as well. This illustrates how formulae cannot contain all we want to say on any tolerably complicated substantial matter. I think one of the weaknesses of traditional analytical philosophy is in its obsessional search for canonical formulae for our understanding of knowledge, morality, rationality, science, God, or what you will. But to recognize this is not to embrace, à la Hamann, and against Hume, obscurantism and illusiveness.

7. I give above in the text one case of Beehler's believers *not really accepting*, full stop, that belief in God is incoherent and then going on to argue that all the same it is reasonable to believe. But others occur as well, particularly in his first essay. He needs, to be effective in the way he wishes to be against me, a case in which his believer accepts without any hedging at all the belief that the concept of God is incoherent, but continues to claim that it doesn't matter, for all the same, incoherent or not, it enables the believer to cope. But Beehler doesn't give us that kind of case. But that is what he needs or his argument is no counter to mine.

8. The arguments and narratives that make up the cumulative argument come from many sources. A bibliography giving some of the crucial sources is in J. P. Moreland and Kai Nielsen, *Does God Exist?* (Amherst, N.Y.: Prometheus Books, 1993), 308–12. In my *Reason and Practice* I try to lay out many, by a way of continuous development, of the central considerations in this cumulative argument. See Kai Nielsen, *Reason and Practice* (New York: Harper and Row, 1971), 135–326.

9. Kai Nielsen, "Can Faith Validate God-talk," *Theology Today* (July 1963); "Religious Perplexity and Faith," *Crane Review* 8, no. 1 (Fall 1965); and *Philosophy and Atheism* (Amherst, N.Y.: Prometheus Books, 1985), 145–58.

10. Wittgensteinian fideists, such as D.Z. Phillips and Ilham Dilman, though they regard themselves as nonreductionists, try to set aside this cosmological or metaphysical element. I understand their motivation, for with such cosmological claims incoherency lies. But still these claims are a part of religious language-games and not just theological or metatheological additions or danglers which can stand apart from them. Without them religious practices would be very different than they are now and have been throughout history.

11. In a taped discussion toward the end of their lives, Simone de Beauvoir and Jean-Paul Sartre show a firm and good-natured atheism, which, for all their philosophical differences with him, is reminiscent of Hume's. They show something of the many sources of purpose and happiness that remain for utterly nonanguished atheists. Simone de Beauvoir, *Adieux Sartre* (Harmondsworth, Middlesex, England: Penguin Books, 1981), 433–45.

12. H. H. Price, *Essays in the Philosophy of Religion* (Oxford, England: Clarendon Press, 1972), 78–122; H. H. Price, *Belief* (New York: Humanities Press, 1969), 435–88. Curt Ducasse, *Nature, Mind and Death* (La Salle, Ill.: Open Court Publishing Company, 1951); *A Philosophical Scrutiny of Religion* (New York: Ronald Press Co., 1953); *A Critical Examination of the Belief in a Life after Death* (Springfield, Ill.: Charles C. Thomas Publishers, 1961).

13. For such a way of looking at things see John Wisdom, "The Modes of Thought and the Logic of God," in *The Existence of God,* ed. John Hick (New York: Macmillan, 1964), 275–98. I argue against such conceptions in my *God, Skepticism and Modernity* (Ottawa, Ontario: University of Ottawa Press, 1989), 134–59.

14. Charles Stevenson, *Ethics and Language* (New Haven, Conn.: Yale University Press, 1944).

15. This is not to say that Allen's agenda is not a significant one. Indeed it is, as should become apparent from reading his striking book, *Truth in Philosophy* (Cambridge, Mass.: Harvard University Press, 1993). It is just that in discussing the present issue it gets in his way and blurs his vision.

16. The very notion of '*philosophical* atheism' is far from clear. There are many philosophers, as well as others, who are atheists, but I do not know that anything sensible is added by calling their atheism *philosophical* anymore than anything sensible is added by saying of a philosopher who is a socialist that his socialism is a philosophical

socialism. I wanted my *Philosophy and Atheism: In Defense of Atheism* to be simply entitled, after its lead essay, *In Defense of Atheism*. But this conflicted with another Prometheus title. My publisher proposed as a title *The Philosophy of Atheism,* which I rejected out of hand, and quite correctly so, for there is no philosophy of atheism, though atheism can have a philosophical articulation and defense.

17. Allen contests that Hume and Nietzsche are atheists. In the case of Nietzsche this boggles the mind for he is plainly an atheist, though as much out of sorts with rationalism, as is Hamann. Allen gives the game away when he remarks that like "Voltaire and Hume, Nietzsche is not an atheist, not if that means laying a claim to know the Platonic truth about god." But, as we have seen, this is precisely what being an atheist does not mean for most atheists. Identifying atheism with an absurd rationalism, Allen makes it the case that, by stipulative redefinition of "atheism," neither Nietzsche nor Hume are atheists. But this is just conversion by an arbitrary *stipulative redefinition*. However, Allen apart, Hume is a more complicated case for classification in this respect than Nietzsche. Hume's posthumously published elegant *Dialogues Concerning Natural Religion*, which he worked on for many years and concluded only on his death bed, has, as a dialogue, characters taking different positions about religion and Hume, speaking clearly for himself, does not add any commentary independent of the dialogues. There has long been a scholarly dispute about which of the characters most closely expresses Hume's own views. But, if we can use evidence from his other writings as well as biographical and contextual evidence, it seems perverse to identify him with anyone but Philo and this puts Hume into the atheist camp. More exactly, he is, what Antony Flew, following Pierre Bayle, calls a Stratonician atheist. Antony Flew, "David Hume," in *The Encyclopedia of Unbelief,* ed. Gordon Stein, vol. 1 (Amherst, N.Y.: Prometheus Books, 1985), 325. See as well Antony Flew, *David Hume: Philosopher of Moral Science* (Oxford, England: Basil Blackwell, 1988); and Terence Penelhum, *Hume* (London: Macmillan, 1975).

18. Isaiah Berlin, *Historical Inevitability* (London: Oxford University Press, 1954).

19. G. A. Cohen, *Karl Marx's Theory of History: A Defense* (Oxford, England: Oxford University Press, 1978); G. A. Cohen, *History Labor and Freedom* (Oxford, England: Clarendon Press, 1988); Andrew Levine, *The End of the State* (London: Verso, 1987), 87–130; Andrew Levine, *The General Will: Rousseau, Marx, Communism* (Cambridge, England: Cambridge University Press, 1993). Kai Nielsen, "On Taking Historical Materialism Seriously," *Dialogue* 22, no. 2 (1983); and Debra Satz, "Marxism, Materialism and Historical Progress," in Ware and Nielsen, *Analyzing Marxism,* 393–424.

20. Andrew Levine, "What Is a Marxist Today?" in Ware and Nielsen, *Analyzing Marxism,* 45–48.

21. Kai Nielsen, *Philosophy and Atheism,* 9–31, 55–106, 211–31; and Kai Nielsen, *God Skepticism and Modernity,* 220–52. I am also the author of the articles on atheism in the current editions of the *Encyclopedia Britannica* and *Collier's Encyclopedia.* If I go wrong here, misinformation will be rather widespread.

22. Richard Braithwaite, "An Empiricist's View of the Nature of Religious Belief," in *The Logic of God: Theology and Verification,* ed. Malcolm L. Diamond and Thomas V. Litzenburg (Indianapolis, Ind.: Bobbs-Merrill, Co., 1975), 127–49; R. M. Hare, "The Simple Believer," *Religion and Morality,* ed. Gene Outka and John Reeder, Jr. (Garden City, N.Y.: Anchor Books, 1973), 393–427; D. Z. Phillips, *Faith and Philosophical Enquiry* (London: Routledge and Regan Paul, 1970). See my critique of such Godless Christianity in my *God, Skepticism and Modernity,* 172–89.

23. For the exchange see Kai Nielsen, "Religion and Naturalistic Humanism: Some Remarks on Hook's Critique of Religion," in *Sidney Hook and the Contemporary World,*

ed. Paul Kurtz (New York: John Day Company, 1968), 257–79; Kai Nielsen, "Secularism and Theology: Remarks on a Form of Naturalistic Humanism," *Southern Journal of Philosophy* 13 (Spring 1975): 109–26. Sidney Hook, "For An Open-Minded Naturalism," *Southern Journal of Philosophy* 13 (Spring 1975): 127–36; and Hook's *The Quest For Being* (New York: St. Martin's Press, 1960), 115–35, 145–95.

24. Kai Nielsen, *God and the Grounding of Morality* (Ottawa, Ontario: University of Ottawa Press, 1991), 136.

25. Kai Nielsen, *Ethics Without God* (Amherst, N.Y.: Prometheus Books, 1990); Kai Nielsen, *God and the Grounding of Morality;* and Kai Nielsen, "Atheism," in *Encyclopedia of Ethics,* ed. Lawrence C. Becker, vol. 1 (New York: Garland Publishing Inc., 1993), 60–64. See also the second section of the next chapter.

26. Allen is justified in claiming that I misread Rorty in ascribing relativism to him. But Rorty certainly wrote in a misleading way concerning such matters. Almost all of his critics, to say nothing of his casual readers, including among his critics Hilary Putnam, so misread him. It seemed to many people that, whether he liked it or not, his views committed him to relativism. But Rorty has by now made it clear how his views are not relativistic. Richard Rorty, "Putnam and the Relativist Menace," *Journal of Philosophy* 90, no. 9 (September 1993): 443–61.

27. I have criticized such conceptions in my "Perspectivism and the Absolute Conception of the World," *Critica* 25, no. 74 (August 1993).

28. Charles Taylor, *Philosophy and the Human Sciences* (Cambridge, England: Cambridge University Press, 1985), 116–51.

29. Kai Nielsen: *After the Demise of the Tradition* (Boulder, Colo.: Westview Press, 1991), 195–248; "Reflective Equilibrium and Relativism," *Monist* 76 (1994): 316–31; and "Philosophy Within the Limits of Wide Reflective Equilibrium Alone," *Iyyun* 73 (1994): 3–41; and "Going for the Widest: Wide Reflective Equilibrium without Uniqueness," *Iyyun* 45 (January 1996): 23–35.

30. John Dewey: *Intelligence in the Modern World* (New York: Modern Library, 1939), 761–94; *Theory of the Moral Life* (New York: Holt, Rinehart and Winston, 1960); *Problems of Men* (New York: Philosophical Library, 1948), 211–49 (the essay cited here was written in 1903); and *Human Nature and Conduct* (New York: Modern Library, 1936).

31. Axel Hägerström, *Philosophy and Religion*, trans. Robert T. Sandin (London: Allen and Unwin, 1964), 175–305.

32. Kai Nielsen, "Perceiving God," in *Faith, Skepticism and Personal Identity,* ed. J. J. MacIntosh and Hugo Meynell (Calgary, Alberta: University of Calgary Press, 1994), 1–6. See also chapter 14.

33. Kai Nielsen, *Skepticism* (New York: St. Martin's Press, 1973), 41–48.

34. David Copp, "Moral Skepticism," *Philosophical Studies* 62 (1991): 203–33. See also Kai Nielsen, *Transforming Philosophy: A Metaphilosophical Inquiry* (Boulder, Colo.: Westview Press, 1995), chapter 6.

35. I also have in mind those philosophers of religion, typically analytical philosophers, who have rationally reconstructed, refined, and critically examined these classical arguments and conceptions.

36. Kai Nielsen, "Dewey's Conception of Philosophy," *Massachusetts Review* 1, no. 2 (Autumn 1960): 110–34; and Kai Nielsen, "Transforming Philosophy," *Dalhousie Review* (1989).

37. I develop my metaphilosophical views most extensively in my *After the Demise of the Tradition* and in my *Transforming Philosophy.* But note also the reference in note 46.

38. My most extensive reliance on verificationism occurs in my "On Speaking of God," *Theoria* 28 (1962); in my "Religion and Commitment," reprinted in my *Philosophy and Atheism*, 107–28; and in my *Contemporary Critiques of Religion* (London: Macmillan, 1970). But even in these earlier writings my reliance was not just on verificationist arguments. "On Speaking of God," (verificationist or not), I have always regarded as one of my key essays in the philosophy of religion and regret that less attention has been paid to it than to essays of mine I regard as being of lesser importance. It has been reprinted in *Analytical Philosophy of Religion in Canada,* ed. Mostafa Faghfoury (Ottawa, Ontario: Ottawa University Press, 1982), 75–96.

39. For places, indeed key places, where I do not principally rely on verificationism, see Kai Nielsen: *Philosophy and Atheism*, 77–106, 211–31; *God, Skepticism and Modernity*, 15–26; and *An Introduction to the Philosophy of Religion* (London: Macmillan Ltd., 1982), 140–70.

40. Rodger Beehler cites appropriately my "Philosophy as Critical Theory," *Proceedings of the American Philosophical Association* (1987): 89–108, as rejecting any appeal to an Archimedian fulcrum. And that is right. I am not sneaking, in spite of what some have thought, something like foundationalism back in through the back door. See also my "Reflective Equilibrium and the Transformation of Philosophy," *Metaphilosophy* 20, no. 3–4 (July/October 1989): 235–46; and my *After the Demise of the Tradition*.

41. Richard Rorty forcefully makes the point that we cannot say anything very enlightening or helpful *in general* about meaning, truth, rationality, coherence, reasonability, and the like. But it does not follow from that that in specific contexts a lot that is useful cannot be said about those notions for those contexts. So I could stick with my point that we cannot say anything, or anything very helpful, about meaning, truth, knowledge, rationality, or reasonability *in general* and *sans phrase,* while also sticking to my point that we can say a lot about the rationality or reasonableness of belief in God. Richard Rorty, *Objectivity, Relativism and Truth* (Cambridge, England: Cambridge University Press, 1991), 126–50; and Richard Rorty, "Putnam on Truth," *Philosophy and Phenomenological Research* 52, no. 2 (July 1992): 415–18. My remarks about "reasonability" in the introduction to part 4 point to ways in which I would now wish to qualify the remarks Beehler cites above. We can have no thick context-independent criteria of reasonability and the like, but still, in the Western tradition (itself, of course, a context), we can say some general only mildly platitudinous things about reasonability.

42. Hugo Meynell has made a somewhat similar critical point. But while Beehler, I would surmise, thinks I should suppress the positivist side of my thought and go more in a Wittgensteinian-Rortyan contextualist direction, Meynell, out of fear of relativism, thinks I should suppress the Wittgensteinian-Rortyan side and return single-mindedly to my positivism only to work through it, by examining its paradoxes and presuppositions, to a solid metaphysical realism (here his views are like C. B. Martin's). I think from what I say in the body of the text, it should be obvious why I would decline that gambit. One can and should be, in my view, a good commonsense realist without being a *metaphysical* realist. The realistic spirit and any metaphysics are at odds. Cora Diamond, *The Realistic Spirit: Wittgenstein, Philosophy and the Mind* (Cambridge, Mass.: MIT Press, 1991), 13–72.

43. Kai Nielsen, *After the Demise of the Tradition*, 1–8; Richard Rorty, *Consequences of Pragmatism* (Minneapolis, Minn.: University of Minnesota Press, 1982), xiii–xxi. Michael Williams, "The Elimination of Metaphysics," in *Fact, Science and Morality*, ed. Graham MacDonald and Crispin Wright (Oxford: Basil Blackwell's, 1986), 21–23, challenges the idea that even philosophy is unproblematic. We may have no coherent conception of what it is to see how things hang together. See here my wrestling with

this and related matters in my *After the Demise of the Tradition*, 91–122, and in chapter 1 of the present volume.

44. Rorty, *Consequences of Pragmatism*, xiv. He, in this famous remark, is quoting, with acknowledgment, Wilfrid Sellars, *Science, Perception and Realty* (London: Routledge and Kegan Paul, 1976), 19.

45. Rorty, *Consequences of Pragmatism*, xvii.

46. Jocelyne Couture and Kai Nielsen, " On Construing Philosophy," in *Méta-Philosophie: Reconstructing Philosophy?* ed. Jocelyne Couture and Kai Nielsen (Calgary, Alberta: University of Calgary Press, 1993), 1–50; and Kai Nielsen, "An Un-Rortyan Defense of Rorty's Pragmatism," *Inquiry* 39 (1996): 71–95.

47. See the metaphilosophical essays in Couture and Nielsen, *Méta-Philosophie*.

48. Stephen Darwall, Allan Gibbard, and Peter Railton, "Toward *Fin de siècle* Ethics: Some Trends," *Philosophical Review* 101, no. 1 (January 1992): 121–22. For an account of why Quine and Davidson, along with such self-avowed pragmatists as Putnam and Rorty, should be regarded as pragmatists, see John P. Murphy, *Pragmatism From Peirce to Davidson* (Boulder, Colo.: Westview Press, 1990).

49. In *Reason and Practice* I make a sustained attempt to show that it is a good criterion of *factual* significance. With the advent of a Quinean holism and a Wittgensteinian contextualism, there is not much interest now in articulating criteria of meaning and particularly for anything as general as a criterion of factual *significance*. Surely there are difficulties concerning such a project. I have not followed them up or pursued that line of inquiry at all in the last twenty-five years. But I am still *half-inclined*—perhaps too much out of ignorance—to think that there may be more to such criterion articulating than is usually thought. For my old, if you will, pre-Quinean, pre-Wittgensteinian arguments here, see Kai Nielsen, *Reason and Practice*, 393–491.

50. Rorty, *Philosophy and the Mirror of Nature*, 384.

51. In a carefully argued defense of atheism, J.L. Mackie treats these key religious beliefs as false rather than as incoherent. For an argument that Mackie passes over too easily questions about the coherence of religious beliefs, see Antony Flew, "The Burden of Proof," in *Knowing Religiously,* ed. Leroy S. Rouner (Notre Dame, Ind.: University of Notre Dame Press), 103–15.

52. Some might say that all metaphysics does not aim at a kind of "factual knowledge" that science cannot have. Rather there are metaphysical views that give a general description of our basic categories or offer us, or try to offer us *(pace* Davidson), new conceptual schemes. Think here of a Strawsonian or Hampshirean descriptive metaphysics or of attempted conceptual revisions of our whole conceptual scheme. These views, basically derivative from Kant, are more, on the one hand, descriptive or, on the other, stipulative, and thus redescriptive, than they are metaphysical and thus lack the robustness of the grand old paradigmatic metaphysical views (e.g., Thomism or Absolute Idealism) that seek to go beyond a systematic description of our categories and give us a deeper understanding of the "ultimate nature of reality." The descriptive and redescriptive—or at least the descriptive—stuff makes sense, but hardly seems to be metaphysics. The other is the stern metaphysical stuff all right, but is of doubtful intelligibility.

53. Bernard Williams has argued for such a conception and has *tried* to keep it apart from any commitment to metaphysical realism. Hilary Putnam and Richard Rorty have criticized such a conception, as I have as well, partly reacting to William's responses to Putnam and Rorty, in my "Perspectivism and the Absolute Conception of the World," *Critica* 25, no. 74 (August 1993).

54. Kai Nielsen and Hendrik Hart, *Search for Community in a Withering Tradition* (Latham, Md.: University Press of America, 1990).

55. Ninian Smart, "Buddhism and Religious Belief," *Humanist* 76 (1961): 47–50; and Ninian Smart, *A Dialogue of Religions* (London, England: SM Press Ltd., 1960), 70–80.

56. W. D. Falk, *Ought, Reasons and Morality* (Ithaca, N.Y.: Cornell University Press, 1986), 163–79, 198–260.

57. They showed firmly these beliefs and attitudes toward the end of their lives. See reference in note 11.

58. I am not a great admirer of much of their *Philosophy*. It seems to me to have the obscurantist defects of much Continental philosophy from the time of Hegel through their times. But in their novels, short stories, plays, their sociological and political writing, and for most of the time in their autobiographical and other descriptive writing, they write plainly with good sense and with probing reflectiveness. That even much of their *Philosophy* can be demythologized into *philosophy* comes out, though differently, in some writings of A. J. Ayer and Stanley Cavell. A. J. Ayer: "Novelist-philosophers: Jean-Paul Sartre," *Horizon* (1946); "Albert Camus, Novelist-philosopher," *Horizon* (1946); and "Philosophy at Absolute Zero," *Encounter* (1955): 24–33. Stanley Cavell, *Themes Out of School* (Chicago, Ill.: University of Chicago Press, 1983), 195–234.

Chapter Seventeen

Morality and Making Sense of Life: With God and Without

I

Ireturn in this final chapter to two related questions (more accurately in both instances a cluster of related questions). First, I shall face some plausible criticisms made of my account of a morality without God. This case for a secular conception of morality that neither requires nor needs religious beliefs or any other religious backing was made in my *Ethics Without God* and my *God and the Grounding of Morality*.[1] I not only respond here to some perceptive criticisms made of this conception, but to seek, as well, to develop it by further refining it and by showing how it does not require, and indeed should not for its most adequate articulation make, foundationalist assumptions. As I now articulate it, it is truly an ethics without God that is also an ethics without foundations, as my naturalism is without foundations.

In my *Ethics Without God,* I was not even close to being clear enough about that. But, or so I shall argue, its negative criticism of Divine Command ethics and a religiously based natural law ethics holds for all of that.[2] Secondly, and connectedly, I shall turn again, particularly in the context of trying to make sense of life, to a consideration of the existential, and other, functions of religion, to, if you will, its psychological and social "foundations" and to the claim often made that, whatever its cognitive merits or lack thereof, religion is essential for the lives of human beings to have meaning.

I shall in the present section and as well in sections 2–4 turn to the first question. In doing this I shall consider what two able, though rather different philosophers, Jeffrey Stout and Terence Penelhum, have said about my *Ethics Without God*.[3] Stout challenges it incisively at a very fundamental level and subjects it to a powerful critique. Penelhum does not challenge it, except perhaps indirectly, but seeks to show how I neglect an important way in which religious ethics can make a vital difference in our moral lives. Their accounts, as different as they are, nicely dovetail and I will examine them in the context (to use the title of Penelhum's essay) of discussing "Ethics with God and Ethics Without" and of making, in a renewed dialogue with religious ethics, a case for sticking with a secular humanist ethics: an utterly Godless morality. (This, of course, to revert for a second to two corollaries of the previous chapter, is not to in anyway advocate a morality despising of religion or an irreligious morality. Atheists need not, and indeed should not, be either cultured or uncultured despisers of religion. It can be rejected without despising it.)

In my writing about religion and morality there is, as in *Ethics Without God*, a *text* and a *subtext*. The text is more important than the subtext and could be maintained even if some, or perhaps even all, of the subtext turns out to be mistaken. The message of the text is generously stated by Penelhum in this way: Nielsen's "*Ethics Without God* contains a formidable array of arguments against the widely held view that morality, in some sense, "depends on" or "requires" religion" (107). My *text*, that is, is that we do not need religion to make sense of or to justify morality and, as well, that a justified, reasonable morality need not, and perhaps even should not, make any appeal to any religious beliefs or to any religious foundations. It is argued in my two books mentioned above that even the empirical claim made by Bronislaw Malinowski that religion is indispensable for the maintenance of morals is not justified. Neither, as a matter of human psychology, nor as a matter of logic, nor as a matter of reflection about the grounding of morality or reflection concerning the significance of life, is it the case that we need God or even a conception of God for morality. I take it that Stout, no more than Penelhum, is attaching or contesting that. So, as far as they are concerned, my *text* remains intact.

It is my *subtext* that bothers Stout. What is my subtext? It is that foundationalist religious ethical theories—"Divine Command theories" or *religiously* based "natural law" theories—rest on foundations that are in shambles. This being so we cannot reasonably appeal to them either in defending a religious morality or in showing—and here is a link with my text—that morality, if it is to be adequately grounded, requires religion.

Before I turn in section 3 and 4 to Stout's and Penelhum's arguments respectively, I will in the next section briefly, but I hope incisively, make the case again for my text, laying out in bald terms its essential claims and arguments. For me the text is the most important thing at issue here and is not, as I have already remarked, contested by either Stout or Penelhum, but, in our popular culture, and by some apologists, and even by some theologians and philosophers, it is, not infrequently, fiercely contested. I will make my case here by recycling in a slightly altered form an encyclopedia article of mine that I wrote before I read either Stout's or Penelhum's accounts.[4] I do this recycling because I think that that article is a forceful articulation of the case for an ethics without God and, as well, because, even if all the criticisms made of me by Stout—criticisms I shall state and then examine in section 3—are sound, the arguments I make in section 2 are not adversely affected. They are not held captive to anything like even the implicit foundationalism with which Stout taxes me. After section 3, where I state and then examine Stout's criticisms, I turn in section 4 to Penelhum's account of the important difference that a religious ethics can make.

So in sections 2–4, my case for a Godless morality is at least tentatively made. I can then turn to my other major consideration in this last chapter, namely to a renewed consideration of the social and psychological functions of religion, an issue which, in another way, threatens to raise again the issue of the adequacy, moral and otherwise, of an utterly secular stance. That issue I shall discuss in sections 5–6.

II

Atheism (the belief that God or no other supernatural reality exists) was once thought to be a form of madness. As late as the eighteenth century even such a progressive thinker as John Locke, rather characteristically for his time, thought atheism to be beyond the pale of intellectual and moral respectability. By now, particularly among the intelligentsia, atheism is a commonplace. There is no distinctive ethical theory that goes with atheism though atheists will tend to have the spectrum of values characteristic of the Enlightenment. Atheists have not infrequently been utilitarians, but some have been deontologists or perfectionists. In metaethics atheism fits well with ethical naturalism or noncognitivism while religious thinkers *tend* to be nonnaturalistic cognitivists and intuitionists. The link, however, is not tight. Henry Sidgwick, G. E. Moore, and C. D. Broad are distinguished intuitionists, one might say the most distinguished intuitionists. Yet they were either atheists or agnostics. (Indeed, Moore was a resolute atheist.)

The key problem for atheists vis-à-vis morality is not to work out a distinctive ethical theory providing the unique fit for atheism, but to meet the challenge thrown out by religious believers and even by some existentialist atheists (Camus and the youthful Sartre) that if God is dead nothing matters, or at least nothing really ultimately matters. Or, more moderately, the claim that a secular ethic must be inadequate when compared with at least a properly nuanced religious morality.[5]

In our societies moral perplexity runs deep and cynicism, or at least ambivalence about moral beliefs, is extensive. Recognition of this is common ground between reflective and informed atheists and similar believers. Atheists will argue that there is no reason to lose our nerve here and to claim we must have religious commitments to make sense of morality. Torturing human beings is wrong, exploiting and degrading human beings is vile, cruelty to human beings and animals is wrong, treating one's promises lightly or being careless about the truth is wrong, treating people merely as means is wrong. If we know anything to be wrong, we know these things to be wrong and to be just as wrong in a Godless world as in a world with God.

There is, of course, a *philosophical* problem about *how* we know these things to be wrong, but that is as much a problem for the believer as for the atheist. Still, for anyone, believer and nonbeliever alike, if that person has an understanding of the concept of morality, has an understanding of what it is to take the moral point of view, that person will *eo ipso* have an understanding that it is wrong to harm others, that promises are to be kept and truth is to be told. This does not mean that such a person will be committed to the belief that a lie can *never* be told, that a promise can *never* be broken, or that a human being in *no circumstance* whatsoever can rightly be harmed. (Remember here the discussion in part 2 of the problem of dirty hands.) But if there is no understanding that such acts always require special justification and that the presumption of morality is always against them, then there is no understanding of the concept of morality. But this understanding is not logically bound up with a belief in God or the taking of a religious point of view.

Defenders of Divine Command Theory, one of the major types of religious ethical theory, maintain that such an understanding does imply a knowledge of or at least a belief in the reality of God because we only know these things to be wrong because we know they are against God's will. Something is good or morally required only because God wills it and only wrong because He prohibits it. That is the central claim of the Divine Command Theory.

Setting aside skeptical questions—questions which in reality are very real—about how we can know what God does and does not will, the old conundrum arises —something as old as Plato—whether something is good simply because God wills it or does God will it because it is good? Leaving aside *God* for the moment, what is evident is that something is not good simply because it is willed or commanded. A military officer can command his troops to take no prisoners or a father can command his son to lie to his mother. Neither of these things become good or in any way morally acceptable, let alone required, just because they are commanded. Indeed, something is not even morally speaking a good thing to do simply because it is willed or commanded by an omnipotently powerful and perfectly intelligent being. Unless we wish to reduce morality to prudence, to take the will of such a being as your moral law is to reduce morality, as Peter Geach does, to power worship.[6] Might, even omnipotence, doesn't make right and a perfectly intelligent being could be through and through evil.

However, to this criticism of the Divine Command Theory, it is not implausible to respond that it is *God's* commanding that makes all the difference, for God, after all, is *the supreme, perfect* good. But it, in turn, can be asked how we know that, if indeed we know it. If we say we know it through studying the Scriptures and through the example of Jesus where His goodness is manifest, then we know it only in virtue of our own quite autonomous (vis-à-vis religion) moral appreciation of His goodness. We see exemplified in the Bible stories behavior which we take to be morally exemplary. But it is because of having our own appreciation of what goodness is, our own at least rudimentary conception of goodness, that we can appreciate that this is so. We feel, understanding something of what morality is, the moral force of the story of Jesus dying on the cross to save humankind. Moral understanding is not grounded in a belief in God; just the reverse is so. An understanding of the religious significance of Jesus and the Scriptures presupposes a moral understanding on the part of human beings. Our moral understanding is logically independent of any belief we may have that God exists.

If alternatively we claim that we do not come to understand that God is the supreme and perfect good in that way, but claim that it is a necessary truth like "Puppies are young dogs" (something which is true by definition), then we still should ask: how do we understand that putatively necessary proposition? But again, we should recognize that it is only by having an understanding of what goodness is that we come to have some glimmering of the more complex and extremely perplexing notions of supreme goodness or perfect goodness. Only if we understand what a good meal is could we possibly have any inkling of what a wonderfully good meal is. Only if we understand what a sacrifice is can we understand what a supreme sacrifice is.

The crucial thing to see here is that there are things which we can come to appreciate on reflection to be wrong, God or no God. Whatever foundational account of morality we give, or whether we can give one, or need to give one at all, we can be far more confident that we are right in claiming that torturing, lying, breaking faith with people, or treating them as mere means are wrong than we can be in claiming any rational belief in God or knowledge of His order or what He requires of us. There are primitive *moral* certainties that are vastly more certain than that and these certainties are not at all undermined by "the death of God."

Someone might respond to the above critique of Divine Command theory by saying that God, if there is a God, is the cause of everything there is and could be. Thus, if the Judeo-Christian-Islamic cosmological story is true, there would be no goodness or anything else if there were no God. Without God, given the truth of that account, there would be nothing and thus there would be no valuable or morally required somethings. But this confuses *causes* and *reasons*: confuses questions about *causally* bringing something into existence and *sustaining* it in existence, on the one hand, and *justifying* its existence, on the other. If God exists and He is what the Scriptures say He is, then everything *causally* depends on Him. However, even if there were no God who made the world, it still would be vile to torture little children. That is, that would remain so even though there were no one to do it. Similarly, even if, since God had not created them, there were no people and thus no people to be kind, it would still be timelessly true that human kindness would be a good thing and that the goodness of human kindness does not become good or cease to be good by God's fiat or anyone else's or even because of the fact that there just happen to be kind people. In terms of its *fundamental rationale*, morality, in its most basic aspects, is utterly independent of belief in God. Atheists should respond to the religious claim that if God is dead nothing matters by asserting in turn that to make sense of our lives as moral beings there is no need to make what may be an intellectually stultifying blind leap of religious faith. Such a moral understanding, as well as a capacity for moral response and action, is available to us even if we are human beings who are utterly without religious faith. There is no reason why the atheist should be morally at sea.

There are religious moralists who would acknowledge this and still maintain that there are religious moralities which are superior moralities (morally speaking more adequate moralities) to anything available to atheists. We are religious beings in need of rituals and saving myths. Without belief in God and immortality, our lives will remain fragmented, anxiety ridden, and meaningless. A secular morality can afford us no sense of a cosmic providential care while a Jewish, Christian, and Islamic morality can. God, on such conceptions, is taken to be a creator who is the supreme source of care, protection, and moral guidance and, if we are Christians at least, we believe that we know that we live or will come to live in God's Kingdom. At least in certain vital respects we will be, if our faith is strong, free of anxiety and fear. (We will critically examine Terence Penelhum developing that conception with considerable care in section 4.) With a firm belief in God, we have the reassurance that, if we will orient our will to God, we will be saved and that evil will not *ultimately* triumph and our moral struggles will not be in vain because the evil in the world will prevail and overwhelm us. In belief in God we can find peace and reassurance that all is not hopeless. Jews, Christians, and Muslims can, if their faith is strong, have a confident future-oriented view of the world where they firmly believe that there is a purpose *to* life, that we are creatures of God made *for* a purpose in which ultimately there will be salvation, at least for those who believe, in a life of eternal bliss. There is, the claim goes, a hope and moral promise there that no secular morality can match.

At this stage in the argument the viability of the truth-claims of religion become important in a way that is not the case in arguing about Divine Command Theory or religious natural law theories. If, as atheists claim, we cannot know, or even reasonably believe, what religious people claim we know or can reasonably take on faith, we should not crucify our intellect and try to rely on a religious morality. Moreover, the religious moralist portrays things in a Godless world as being much grimmer than they actually are. There is no good reason to think life is senseless or without point without God. There are purposes *in* life even if there is no purpose *to* life.[7] And to be made for a purpose as the religious story maintains is not so morally unproblematic, for it seems at least to rob us of our autonomy. Moreover, an atheist need not be limited to small rather personal purposes in life. There are also larger rather impersonal things that can perhaps be realized through political and social struggle that she can make, by her own deliberate acts, her own purposes. At a minimum we can fight the plague and more maximally we can struggle to transform the world. Such things will plainly afford sufficient meaning in life to halt the threat of meaninglessness.

Morality, it should be added, still has one of its very fundamental functions in a godless world, just as much as in any kind of other world, namely, its function to adjudicate in a fair way the conflicts of interests between persons. In seeking this, atheists, as well as religious people, might very well come reflectively to desire that something like a kingdom of ends come to obtain. An atheist can, just as well as a religious person, respect persons just because they are persons and never treat people as means only. Atheists, as others, will, as well, recognize self-respect to be a fundamental good. But this will, very likely, lead them to a respect for persons, for each moral agent, if she thinks at all carefully, will recognize that if self-respect is a good for her it will be a good for anyone else as well. We human beings do not differ in that respect. Self-respect is for all of us a very fundamental good. Universalizability and fairness require us to go beyond ourselves and at least acknowledge the appropriateness of a world in which respect for persons plays center stage. Similar things should be said for the relief of human suffering. If we can know anything to be bad we can know that suffering is bad. (It *may* sometimes be *instrumentally* good but it is never *intrinsically* good.) Where there is some reasonable expectation that we can, at least without extensive sacrifice, do something about it we have, God or no God, an obligation to relieve it. That is bound up with our very understanding of morality.

Again, a religious moralist can acknowledge the truth of at least much of that and still respond that there are morally relevant needs that religious morality answers to that no secular morality can. But it is also true that there are needs that a secular morality answers to that religious morality does not. So there is a question of choices here and of trade-offs. With a religious morality—or, more accurately, with some religious moralities—there is a hope for immortality and a belief in a world of providential care in which we can have the at least putative guarantee that our moral efforts will not be defeated. If religious beliefs, including belief in immortality, were reasonably plausible, that might be enough to tip the scale in favor of a religious morality, but if, as atheists believe, belief in the existence of God and immortality are highly implausible, as has been argued extensively in this book, then a religious ethic becomes less attractive for it appears that to hold to it there must be a crucifixion of the intellect and that, *pace* Kierkegaard, is not such a plainly desirable thing. Moral *integrity* is a threat to, or at least a problem for, a religious morality in such a circumstance. There is something to be said, atheists will argue, for the person who can hold steady on the course in the moral world without telling herself fairy tales or feeling the need to believe things which are wildly implausible, perhaps even incoherent. Moral integrity, fraternity, and love of humankind (though not a turning of the other cheek to all individuals irrespective of how they behave) are worth subscribing to without a thought to whether or not such virtues will be rewarded in heaven or even whether they will be dominant in our world, though again this should not require us to be suckers.

There are such trade-offs here and the trade-offs atheists will make are not, to put it circumspectly, obviously mistaken or indicative, as some believers believe, of a shallow worldview with a shallow morality and conception of life. There is no need to make an arbitrary Kierkegaardian leap of faith and believe in what one admittedly takes to be absurd to make sense of one's life, including one's moral life. What should be had by way of moral belief and commitment is not independent of the probabilities here. Atheists believe, and not unreasonably, that the probabilities go very much against religious belief. To have a robust moral conception of life one need not go against those at least putative probabilities.

III

Stout criticizes, as I have remarked, what I call the subtext of my *Ethics Without God*. His arguments are sophisticated, careful, detailed, and deserve close attention. They may be divided into two general kinds. The first is a relatively internal critique focused on the *Euthyphro*-dilemma that I and others seek to foist on Divine Command theory. Stout maintains that a person concerned to defend such an account can rightly grasp one of the horns of the dilemma and break it. I shall argue that Stout's arguments here, careful as they are, fail, and in effect bring out one of the key points that I was concerned to make, namely, that religion, in a very fundamental way, is dependent on a moral understanding that is logically and conceptually independent of religion. Stout's second major argument is that in *Ethics Without God*, I, without argument or even any clear awareness, assume a *foundationalism*, both for my own account and, without warrant, for a religious ethics. Furthermore, with that foundationalism, I deploy a mistaken deductivist linear model of justification, rather than a more realistic coherentist horizontal model of justification. It is, he contends, only on such a mistaken deductivist model of justification, with its linked foundationalism, that my critique of Divine Command ethics and theological natural law ethics could possibly be justified. But since that conception of justification rests on a mistake, my critique of Divine Command and natural law conceptions of ethics has not been vindicated.

I believe that *part* of this second criticism is justified. When I wrote *Ethics Without God,* and most particularly in the first edition (the edition Stout examines), I was not cognizant of the dispute between foundationalism and anti-foundationalism and I, along with many other philosophers, just unwittingly made foundationalist assumptions at least at the programmatic level. I also (part of the time) used, in criticizing Divine Command ethics and natural law ethics, the mistaken deductivist *model* of justification. Stout also rightly points out that later in *Ethics Without God* I deploy, though unself-consciously, what is in effect a coherentist conception of justification. Certainly, as my present antifoundationalism, contextualism, and my use of the method of wide reflective equilibrium make abundantly clear, by now I have come to think foundationalism is indefensible and deductivism a mistaken model of justification at least in ethics and social theory. I should have been clearer about that when I wrote *Ethics Without God.*

However, at least as classically articulated, Divine Command ethics and natural law ethics are foundationalist and deductivist. Reasoning in this traditional manner—playing their own game, so to speak—I argue that their accounts fail. Stout has done nothing to show, or at least so I shall argue, that my arguments here are unsound or not to the point, given the structure of Divine Command ethics and a religiously based natural law ethics. Moreover, we have no clear picture of what Divine Command ethics or natural law ethics would look like shorn of their foundationalism. They just are foundationalist accounts and without that foundationalism it is very unclear what, if any, rationale they have.

Before examining in detail Stout's arguments, I shall provide a more exacting statement of my subtext: the account Stout seeks to show is through and through mistaken, not just in its detail but in its very conception. My *subtext* is that Divine Command ethical theories and even theologically or religiously based natural law theories (the key foundational accounts of religious ethics) are in shambles—are not sound accounts—because it is at best false that we can come to recognize or acknowledge what is morally required of us by knowing, or at least believing, that God exists and what His ordinances are. Moreover, it is not true that by knowing, or at least believing, that God exists and that He commands such and such that we also know that we must, if we are to act rightly, accept *whatever* God commands as what, morally speaking, must be done and as what we must commit ourselves to to act and live rightly.

We cannot know this or justifiably believe this, if we can know it at all, my sub-text runs, without recourse to some understanding of what is good that is logically and conceptually independent of religious beliefs. Put otherwise, we need for moral agency some understanding of what it is desirable or fitting to do or think that is itself not derived from or based on a knowledge that, or a belief that, God exists and of what He commands us to do. In that key respect, morality is not based on religion, but religion on morality. Without some logically prior understanding of what is good or fitting, we cannot know that we ought to do whatever God commands; we cannot even recognize something to be God (a being supremely worthy of worship) as He is depicted in the high Judaic-Christian-Islamic tradition without a prior understanding of good. A core bit of my subtext, as Stout correctly quotes me as saying, is the claim "that the fact that God wills something—if indeed that is a fact—cannot be a fundamental criterion of its being morally good or obligatory and thus it cannot be the only criterion or the only adequate criterion for moral goodness or obligation"[8] (111).*

My argument for the subtext relies on the posing, *Euthyphro-style*, of what Stout calls an unpleasant dilemma for the defender of Divine Command ethics, in effect saddling her with a *reductio* which will, I argue, force her to abandon her position, if she will be reasonable. The dilemma, as Stout puts it, is this. You must either provide a purely theological or religious foundation for morality or not. But, if you take the first alternative and try to provide a purely religious or theological foundation for ethics, you will, the claim goes, be impaled on the first horn of the dilemma. You say, taking the first alternative, that whatever it is that God wills you must do, for what must be done is defined in terms of being in accordance with God's will and, indeed, that all distinctively moral concepts are defined in terms of what God wills. If you do that, to state the first horn of the dilemma, you not only have the *reductio* that if God commands you to torture innocent children that is what you must do, but, to rub salt in your wounds, you cannot even give *content* to your praise of God as the being supremely worthy of worship or "even justify awarding the title *God* to a being who deserves it" (112). To so define or characterize what must be done and what is good in terms of obeying God's commands, no matter what He commands, is to be subject to such *reductio* arguments.

If, on the other hand—to set out the other horn of the dilemma—you do not propose a purely theological or religious foundation for morality, then you

---

*Stout here, and throughout this chapter, is citing me from the first edition of *Ethics Without God* (Amherst, N.Y.: Prometheus Books, 1973).

have in effect granted that we are, after all, capable of exercising moral judgments which are independent of religion. Indeed, we must so exercise our own judgment in ascertaining which being, if any, deserves the title "God." But then morality does not, and indeed cannot, depend on a theological or religious foundation for its justification. When, in getting to a solid ground or to bedrock, in ascertaining whether there is, or isn't, a supremely good being, worthy of worship, whose commands we must obey, we must, inescapably must, rely on our own moral insight and understanding, fallible as it is. But then God cannot, logically cannot, be the foundation of our morality.

"Either," Stout remarks, "you propose a purely theological foundation for morality or you do not. The dilemma poses an exhaustive and exclusive choice with no chance of slipping between the horns of the dilemma" (112). Stout then asks whether, after all, we can break one of the horns. He claims that we can. And he tries to show that we can by seeking to establish that we can and should break the second horn (112–13). He asks why cannot the theologian or religious moralist simply say that religious moralists need have no stake in defending a purely theological foundation for morality? Stout puts these words into the mouth of a hypothetical theological or religious interlocutor with me and to my posing of the *Euthyphro*-dilemma.

> The theologian who grasps the second horn can admit that if morality has a foundation it isn't purely theological. But that leaves open the possibility that the most adequate morality includes theological elements. Such a morality would be partly but not entirely theological. The nontheological part would suffice to help us recognize the real God. It would also give content to our praise of God's moral perfection. We wouldn't have to say, for example, that "God is good" means simply that God conforms to the will of God. But the theological part, it might be argued, needs to be included to make our morality more adequate. In this case, morality would not require a purely theological foundation, but, if it is to be adequate, theological judgments would be essential to it. (113)

However, this is to break the second horn of the dilemma by the expedience of caving in: by, that is, simply abandoning the *heteronomy* (to use Emil Brunner's Kantian phrase) of a Divine Command ethics or of a theological conception of natural law, for an *autonomous* ethics which takes it that certain very fundamental moral beliefs and moral principles are independent of religion: moral beliefs, that is, which do not require God or a belief in Him for their justification. To make matters even worse for a religious ethics, these autonomous moral conceptions are even required to intelligibly speak of God, for we need some way of ascertaining what, if anything, is supremely worthy of worship before we can even intelligibly speak of God. For, given a Jewish, Christian, or Islamic, but not a Deist, conception of Him, He, by definition, is said to be something supremely worthy of worship. But to speak with understanding here requires at a very fundamental level an autonomous moral understanding, not, logically or conceptually speaking, rooted in religion. We need some such understanding of what it is to be worthy and beyond that what it is to be *worthy of worship* and still beyond that what it is for anything to be *supremely worthy of worship*. But these are all with respect to religion autonomous moral judgments that we need to make to even have any understanding of what it is to speak of God in the Judeo-Christian-Islamic sense. Our very religious understanding must, at a very crucial point, be dependent on—logically dependent on—our moral understanding. It is that which is the more basic even if nothing is basic "absolutely speaking." (We may very well have no understanding of the latter.)

This implicit appeal to an autonomous moral understanding, that is to an understanding that is logically and conceptually independent of religious belief, shows itself in several places in the above quotation from Stout, a statement intending to show how the second horn can be broken, the *Euthyphro*-dilemma escaped. To speak of "the possibility that the most adequate morality includes theological elements" implicitly appeals, with its little give-away normative term *adequate,* to, with respect to religion, independent moral judgments, judgments we need to make to ascertain what is or isn't "the most adequate morality" here. The same is true for "essential" in "if it is to be adequate, theological judgments would be essential to it." We must make out here on normatively and logically autonomous nonreligious, nontheological grounds whether a religious ethics—an ethics with theological elements—would be a more adequate or a less adequate ethics than a purely secular humanistic ethics. The initial point in appealing to such a religious ethics was to show, *by its very religious appeal,* that (a) no morality could be adequate that did not include belief in God and (b) that morality is groundless and arbitrary without a religious foundation. But now we see that such an appeal has been abandoned and that we are using secular moral criteria, or, if you will, nonreligious moral criteria, to assess the adequacy and essentialness of religious morality. If we are to say that a morality with religious elements is more adequate than any purely humanistic morality, we must use secular moral criteria—religiously autonomous moral judgments and assessments—to establish that. So again we see an important way in which religion is founded on morality and not vice versa. We have not been shown how the second horn can be broken. (Note, further, that this holds no matter what we say about foundationalism.)

This can also be seen, in a somewhat different way, by examining the detailed argument attributed to what Stout calls my theological opponent (a hypothetical opponent he appropriately manufactures) who seeks to break the second horn of the dilemma. His argument runs this way, though the italics are added by me.

1. God wills what he does because it is *right*.
2. "X is right" does not mean "X is willed by God."

and

3. We do in fact have to use some nontheological [*evaluative* or *normative*] judgments in determining which if any being is the true God.
4. God's revealed will is nonetheless *the best* criterion of *rightness* available to us, given our finitude and his perfection.

and therefore

5. The *best* available or *most adequate* morality for us must incorporate theological elements.

This would mean

6. The most *adequate morality* would in some significant sense depend on theological beliefs.

even though

7. Theology would not be said to supply, all by itself, that foundation for morality. (113)

But in propositions 1, 4, 5, and 6 the italicized expressions, and the bracketed expressions added by me in 3, all make an appeal to moral or normative notions that are purely secular. That is to say, they are not, logically or conceptually, rooted in religion and are *required to even make sense of a religious morality*. Moreover, they are all ground floor, rock-bottom, "foundational" (if you will) notions for this religious morality. This shows, once again, how religion depends on secular moral insight and judgment and not the other way around. (I should add, parenthetically, that the bracketed phrases added in 3 are essential to give 3 the sense that Stout wishes to give it, as can be seen from his argument in the paragraph previous to the one in which the above-cited argument occurs.)

Stout asks how his argument 1–7 relates to my major thesis, which he says is my denial "that God's will can constitute a fundamental criterion of moral goodness or obligation" (113). He responds that 1–7, including 4, do not conflict with my denial, for they say nothing about *fundamental* criteria. But that, I think, is a mere playing with words, for in 4 "the best criterion of rightness available to us" needs to be understood as referring to fundamental criteria. What would be *the best* criterion available to us if it would not be our fundamental criterion? That is what we mean by saying that it is the best. The same is true for, in 5, "the *best* available or most *adequate* morality" or in 6 "the most *adequate* morality" or, most likely, in 1, the reference to right, in that context, shows that what is under cognizance are fundamental criteria. If that is not so, it would be very difficult to ascertain what claim that proposition makes.

In response to what I have just argued, it could be replied that a religious moralist can still go in either of two ways. Either conformity to God's will constitutes one fundamental moral criterion and thus one part of the foundation of morality or we should simply avoid "mention of fundamental criteria and foundations altogether, insisting only that this criterion is *essential*" (113–14, italics added). But the appeal to something being *essential* is again to make a moral judgment not logically dependent on religion concerning the importance of an appeal to God's will. And it is surely a very close relative to something being fundamental. How else are we to understand "essential" here? If a given criterion is essential and another not, then the essential criterion is the more fundamental criterion. Whatever, if anything, is the most essential, like whatever in this context is the most adequate, is the most fundamental criterion we have in a particular domain. Again, we in effect show, vis-à-vis morality, that certain secular claims are more fundamental than religious claims and indeed the very religious claims that are taken by religious people themselves to be very fundamental.

To the alternative claim that God's will is one part of the foundation of morality, my arguments in the paragraph above have shown that it is not even *a* fundamental criterion, and thus not a foundational criterion, but a derivative criterion that is dependent on, for its very intelligibility, accepting still more fundamental secular moral criteria. Still, Stout concludes that the theologian escapes my dilemma: the second horn is broken. But, if my above arguments here have been near to the mark, he has established nothing of the kind.

Stout makes a further point, as a transition to his second general argument, that should be examined. When it is affirmed or denied that God's will, or whatever, constitutes a fundamental moral criterion, how, Stout asks, are we to understand what it is for something to be a fundamental criterion (115)? After finding some difficulties with my conceptualization of what it is, he goes on to give what seems to me to be a perspicuous and useful characterization of "fundamental criteria," and, beyond that, of what it is to be the most fundamental criteria and even the most fundamental criterion (if there is one). Stout writes:

A proposition, p, is more fundamental than another proposition, q, if and only if, you'd have to be justified in accepting p before you could justify accepting q. If we then take "fundamental moral criteria" to mean the *most* fundamental criteria we employ in moral judgment, they would be such that you could and must be justified in accepting them first—that is, before you proceed to justify other moral beliefs and criteria on that foundation. *The* fundamental moral criterion, if there is one, would then be the most fundamental of all, the criterion on which all others depend. (115–16)

My argument was that, in the sense specified in the above quotation from Stout, God's will could not be the most fundamental moral criterion. Stout is prepared to grant that, but the claim that God's will is the fundamental moral criterion, in a way Stout does not notice, is precisely the claim that a paradigmatic Divine Command theorist such as Emil Brunner is making in his attempt to show that we must ground morality on religion[9] (116). Brunner is claiming, as do other Divine Command theorists as well, that what is commanded or willed by God is the fundamental moral criterion in just the sense that Stout specified. But this was the position I was concerned to criticize. The position, Stout leaves the religious moralist with, if she is to break one of the horns of the dilemma, gives no such pride of place to religion over morality. It allows in reality for a morality independent of religion and insists on, as well, that a religious morality must accept autonomous, *vis-à-vis* religion, moral judgments at the base of the religious moral system.

In effect changing the subject, Stout claims that another kind of religious morality, seeking to break the second horn of my dilemma, need not make that strong claim of a Divine Command ethics. It still could be the case, he remarks, that a criterion connecting moral goodness or obligation to God's will could be as fundamental as many other moral judgments "and even so fundamental that God's will could belong to the foundation of morality—the level of criteria and beliefs on which the bulk of moral judgments depend for their justification" (116). But this, and in accordance with his own conception of fundamental moral criteria, fails to meet my argument that God's will could not be even *a* fundamental moral criterion, for we can only know that God's will should be morally decisive for us, if we can know that God is all powerful, omniscient, and *perfectly good*. But we can only know that the being—the necessary being, if you will—people refer to as "God" is perfectly good, if we can know what it is for a person to be good. And to understand that, we would, in turn, have to know what it is for something, anything at all, to be good. And, this, of course, is one of our (logically speaking) most primitive normative judgments. But then, on Stout's own criterion, for one thing being more fundamental than another thing, our judgments that something is good and indeed that that which religious believers call "God" is good are more fundamental than the judgment that God's will must be done, for that latter judgment could be justified only if these other judgments are justified and not the other way around. That whatever God wills must be done depends, that is, for its justification, on the other two judgments. But they do not depend for their justification on God's will or on God's existing or anything that requires a reference to religion. "God's will must be done" could not, *on Stout's own conception*, belong to the foundations of morality (if there are such), for it depends for its justification on the normative judgments that there is, or even could be, something that is good, a being that is perfectly good and that some persons are good persons as well as the moral judgment that there is, or even can be, a person who is supremely worthy of worship. These moral and normative judgments, two perfectly banal, are, logically speaking, still more fundamental, in the very sense of "fundamental" Stout specified, than the judgment that God's will must be done.

It should further be noted that all of this can be soundly argued without our deciding what is *the* most fundamental criterion or even whether there is or even could be one. But we do know that "God's will must be done," however important it is for theists, depends for its justification on these other nontheistic normative judgments, though still judgments that theists themselves make and must make to make their own characteristically theistic judgments. The judgments that "God's will must be done" are dependent on, and include, among others, such mundane but unproblematic ones as our capacity to make judgments, however fallible, about the goodness of persons. Thus, appeal to God's will could not be at the most fundamental level, even if it is plausible to believe, as I think that it is, that there is no single fundamental moral criterion, but rather a cluster of mutually dependent fundamental moral and otherwise normative criteria. The judgments that some things are good while others are not, that there are good persons, that there is or isn't a perfectly good person, that there is or isn't a being worthy of worship do not depend on God's will being something that must just be acted in accordance with. There is a dependence of the latter moral judgment on the former ones, but, *pace* Stout, no relations of *mutual* dependency.

I shall now turn to Stout's second cluster of criticisms—criticisms which I believe have more force. They turn, as I noted earlier, on a rejection of what he takes to be my foundationalism and on my appeal to a deductive model of justification. They are two things that go very naturally together. Stout begins this part of his critique by remarking:

> Once the idea arises that there might be relations of mutual epistemic dependence, of course, we may begin to entertain doubts about references to "foundations" and "fundamental criteria" as such. We may ask, for example, whether we have any good reason to believe that relations of mutual epistemic

dependence are confined to a single, most basic level of moral criteria. To pursue this thought would be, as it were, to uproot the second horn of Nielsen's dilemma completely by calling into question the foundationalist imagery it employs. (117)

In proceeding as I do in *Ethics Without God,* I say that to justify specific moral beliefs—religious moral beliefs or otherwise—we must move to more general moral beliefs from which, with the help of other premises, factual or otherwise, we derive the more specific moral propositions or beliefs. The more general moral belief will in turn be justified only if it is a basic, underived belief that we just commit ourselves to or if it, in turn, is justified by some still more basic belief from which it can be derived. Again, where the second alternative obtains, we, examining this still more general belief, look to see if there is some still more basic belief from which it can be derived or whether it is itself a basic underived belief from which the other nonbasic beliefs are derived. We keep, on this deductivist model of justification, repeating this until we arrive at some basic underived belief or beliefs from which all the other beliefs are derivable. In this way we discover the foundation or basis of all the other moral beliefs in these basic underived moral beliefs.

In so reasoning morally, we finally reach a point, as I put it in *Ethics Without God,* where we "can give no further justification for our claim—having arrived at basic beliefs which are not only underived but are underivable—and we must simply, by our own deliberate decision or subscription, simply resolve to take a certain position. In the end we must simply decide"[10] (57, 118). Moreover, on my account, there is no intuiting "moral truth"—just coming to appreciate that the basic moral propositions are true—or deriving them from nonmoral propositions either factual or metaphysical (including bits of natural theology). We must, as I then argued, in the end just *decide* what, if any, moral propositions we are going to accept and commit ourselves to. Decision and commitment rule the roost here.

If this is how we must reason morally, then, Stout claims, we end up with an utterly arbitrary basis for ethics (118). He believes that the secular humanist, if this model of moral reasoning is correct, is no better, though no worse off, than is the religious or theological moralist. We all end up, if this is what "the logic of moral reasoning" comes to, with something like Camusian arbitrary moral commitment[11] (118).

However, Stout responds, rightly it seems to me, that this deductivist, foundationalist model of moral reasoning is both an unrealistic and an otherwise mistaken conception of moral reasoning and justification. He points out that in other passages I show that I do not really believe "that justification is relative to arbitrary decisions of principle" (118). I remark, he points out, that "we do justify moral claims by an appeal to factual claims"[12] (118). And he further, correctly and aptly, quotes me as saying: "We cannot deduce moral statements from factual ones but we all repeatedly use factual statements to back up our moral statements"[13] (118–19). But, if that is so, Stout also correctly remarks, "justification, then, must not consist essentially in deduction" (118).

What I in effect do, without a clear awareness of what I am doing, is to move from the classical deductivist model of justification of foundationalism to a coherentist model, the model, more fully fleshed out and more self-consciously and carefully articulated, that in my later thinking came to be that of wide reflective equilibrium. Stout puts it well when he remarks:

> Responsible moral agents, Nielsen now seems to be saying, must shape their moral principles in the light of the best available understanding of what nature, history, and humanity are like. As our beliefs about the way things are undergo change, especially as they bear on human desires and needs, we struggle to bring our beliefs into line. Our moral beliefs are not deducible from nonmoral beliefs, but they are responsive, in a rational way, to changes in our beliefs about the way things are. (119)

But, as Stout is fully aware, such a view, if consistently thought through, carries with it a contextualist, antifoundationalist coherentism. Stout says that with such a view we should drop talk of fundamental criteria or of some conception of the foundations of morality. "If justification is not essentially deductive," as he remarks, "then highly general moral criteria may very well be responsive to strong convictions about specific cases as well as to beliefs about the way things are" (119). He then points out that that is the way I actually reason in the later chapters of *Ethics Without God*, in practice utilizing reflective equilibrium before I had articulated to myself an account of it, indeed, before I realized, methodologically speaking, what I was doing. (One can, of course, perfectly well do something without being able to perspicuously represent to oneself what one is doing.) But this means, as he correctly sees, that I do not *in practice* "treat general moral criteria as fundamental in any strong sense" (119). Sometimes, as I have repeatedly argued in this book and elsewhere in my later writings, the justification of general moral principles "depends upon their coherence with relatively certain convictions about what one ought to do in specific cases" (119). This being so, it is at best misleading "to say that general criteria are the foundation on which more specific convictions depend, as if the relation of epistemic dependence didn't go, much of the time in the other direction" (119). Sometimes, indeed much of the time, this is so. But, as he also says, in a good Rawlsian spirit, sometimes but not always. Sometimes we do, and rightly, come to give up certain of our moral convictions or intuitions about specific cases because they conflict with an especially important and deeply embedded moral principle, something which itself will be a firm moral conviction of ours. We have considered moral convictions or judgments at all levels of generality. But again sometimes we will not stick with the general principle, but instead with a particular considered conviction. We, in the neverending process, of coming to an understanding of what we should think and do, shuttle back and forth here. Stout in this context quotes with approval a remark of J. B. Schneewind's which is an early and insightful partial statement of reflective equilibrium. Schneewind writes:

> Moral philosophers, whatever their theoretical programs, have in practice always recognized that allegedly basic moral principles depend no less on fairly specific moral propositions than on other sorts of grounds that have been offered for them. A principle that led to the conclusion that truth-telling was usually wrong, and torturing children normally permissible would be rejected, no matter what kind of proof it might have. But if general principles may sometimes depend on particular moral judgments, and particular judgments sometimes on general principles, then there is no impersonal necessary order of dependence within the realm of moral knowledge.[14] (119–20)

Pace David Gauthier, and with John Rawls and Thomas Nagel, we should not, trying to set aside considered convictions, place such trust in moral theory and in the philosopher's penchant for generalization. It is vital that we come to learn to see what is on the ground. We must learn, that is, to do our reflecting in accordance with what Cora Diamond calls the realistic spirit, something which has nothing to do with either metaphysical or moral realism.[15]

A religious moralist who accepts this conception of moral reasoning, Stout has it, should respond to me "by saying: No, God's will is not the fundamental criterion of morality, but the problem you pose has more to do with foundationalist theories of knowledge than with theological ethics" (120). A good moral theory or account of morality, religious or secular, should abandon talk about *the foundations of ethics or morality.* Religious ethics, if properly done, should have no stake in foundationalism at all, neither epistemological foundationalism nor normative ethical foundationalism nor ontological foundationalism. They are all houses of cards.

To this I should respond by remarking that my critique of religious ethics was directed at foundationalist religious ethics and, most particularly, at a distinctive species of foundationalist religious ethics, widely accepted in religous circles, namely Divine Command theories. If the theologian tries for such foundations, his account will fail and he has no grounds for trying to saddle, as Brunner, for example, does, secular moralists with needing such grounds to have an adequate account of morality or to articulate a sound ethic.[16] Neither Divine Command theories nor religiously based natural law theories—both foundationalist theories—give a good rationale for religious ethics nor show that we should ground our ethical theories religiously or else treat them as arbitrary. Nothing Stout has said affects those considerations: considerations which were essential to both my text and subtext.

However, there is still the matter of what should be said about religious morality that is neither foundationalist nor works with foundationalist assumptions only to undermine them. We have seen in part 1 of this volume how it is possible for both the religious person and the secularist to utilize wide reflective equilibrium. Where this is done, discussions of religious ethics become more realistic. The specific content of what divides religious moralists and secular humanists will in such a circumstance get into the discussion in more than a tangential way. There will, if such a method is used, be no way of discussing the reasonableness or warrant of religious ethics or the choice between a religious ethics and a purely secular ethic without bringing in the cosmological and doctrinal elements of religion, and often of a particular religion at that. We must, in attempting to articulate a sound moral view, consider everything we know or can reasonably believe that has a bearing on questions concerning how we should live—on how we should relate to each other and to how, as individuals, we should orient our own lives. And it is there, as the proper methodology of such an approach, where wide reflective equilibrium comes in with its commitment to maximizing the coherence over many domains of our various beliefs, concepts, convictions, and practices.

If what I argued in part 1 is on the whole justified, Jews, Christians, and Muslims, as well as other religious believers, cannot, *as a matter of fact*, get their beliefs into wide reflective equilibrium. Their doctrinal commitments conflict with too many of their other beliefs and convictions, not only in other domains but in morality as well. Moreover, they are beliefs and convictions that are not only theirs but are a firm part of the web of belief and conviction of the very culture in which they live. And this, of course, is our world, our deeply and intractably pluralistic world.

IV

I want to illustrate something of what is at issue here by turning to a consideration of Terence Penelhum's reflective and sensitive essay "Ethics With God and Ethics Without." Penelhum agrees with the position I have articulated that in a certain very fundamental sense morality is independent of religion and that there is at least "one obvious way in which religion (or at least religious conviction) depends on morality, rather than the reverse" (107). But he goes on to remark, correctly, I believe, that "it does not follow from this that the adoption of a Christian religious stance has no influence on one's moral judgment or one's moral life, even though there is often a congruence between the moral programs that Christians and non-Christians choose to pursue" (107). Penelhum tries to say "what difference Christianity makes to morality in a world where morality without religion is an acknowledged reality" (108).

In doing this, the moral impact of Jesus' preaching, understandably, is important for him. He takes as his source "for comment on Christian ethics the teaching that we find in the Synoptic Gospels about the presence of the Kingdom and its implications for conduct" (108). In Jesus' preaching about the coming of the Kingdom of God, which Jesus tells us is near at hand, he "clearly seeks to bring about changes in the moral objectives and attitudes of his hearers; and he does this in order to make them prepare themselves for the coming of the Kingdom of God" (108). A secularist, of course, will have trouble with this talk of the Kingdom of God having, as he does, trouble with the very idea of there being a God. But for a while at least we can set that aside and consider only the attitudes and ways of acting and responding characteristic of a genuinely Christian person. Against what he takes to be a tradition of unvarying adherence to rules and a stress on rigid ritual observance, Penelhum stresses the need for inner purity—purity of heart and purity of intention. Like Socrates, Jesus stresses the need for moral agents to exercise judgment in the following of rules. They are not to be regarded as a set of rules, a set of moral Absolutes, we must obey come what may. We must not be rule-worshippers; instead, we must use moral discernment, bringing in play our moral sense, in deciding whether we should conform to the rules or not: act in a given situation as they prescribe. We have to make our own moral judgments here. *In this way* we have something very like the *weak* Consequentialism I defend and we can see, as well, how it matches nicely with a stress on the importance of intention and purity of heart. But so far we have nothing that conflicts with an utterly secular way of viewing things. We have one person— Jesus—telling his fellow human beings how they should live.

This is also true of the next thing Penelhum remarks on about the moral message of the Synoptic Gospels. While Jesus is not a rule-worshipper, his "moral preaching is in another way very rigorous and uncompromising" (110). It is not enough to avoid killing and acts of hatred and revenge, but we must free ourselves of hatred and a desire for revenge. What we must do, to have moral worth, must spring from the right inner state and the right state is one of love toward our neighbors even if they are not loveable and even if they do ill to us. We must learn, Jesus has it, to love our enemies. We are not to make our love for people conditional on how they are to us or to others. We should live with trust and without prudential calculation toward others.

Many secular moralists—David Gauthier, to take a striking instance—

would say that we should not live in this Christian manner. To do so is to be a sucker, to set oneself up for exploitation and abuse by others. Our cooperation, and acting with good will, should be conditional on others so acting as well. Where they do not so act, we should not turn the other cheek, but protect ourselves and others who are also willing to be cooperators. We should fairly cooperate with cooperators, but not with those who will not genuinely cooperate. Morality requires a genuine mutual reciprocity, not unrationalized selflessness.

Religious persons, or at least Christians, would respond that we should, uncalculatingly, love our fellow human beings irrespective of their merit because God is like this and wants us to be like this as well and because we should want what God wants. It will in turn be responded by the secularist that that is too much to expect of us, for we, unlike God, are vulnerable and are beset with needs and problems. Moreover, if we are at all realistic about life, we will recognize that we can hardly reasonably act as if there were no enemies or brutal realities out there to which we may very well be held in thrall. We just, if we take this religious route, set ourselves up, and often others as well, for abuse.

However, there is a response that religious moralists characteristically make, and Penelhum in effect makes, to this not infrequently secular critique. And here we reach a point where very problematical religiously metaphysical beliefs enter. (All metaphysical beliefs are problematical, but some are more problematical than others.) In a world, the reply goes, without God, it would, of course, be wildly unreasonable to so act: to act, that is, as Jesus advocates. But in a world where God actually exists and will care for us in such a way that no harm can befall us, it is perfectly reasonable to act as Jesus calls on us to act: to, so unstintingly and uncalculatingly, love our neighbors no matter what they are like. As Penelhum puts it, if people "really understood that, they would not have to worry about any risks that moral regeneration brought with it, for they would enjoy the peace that comes with the knowledge that whatever the appearances, their real needs would be met by God"[17] (110). After all, in a very real sense, because of God, they are not vulnerable. They will, with such an understanding, live without anxiety and so living would be reasonable in a way that it would not be in a Godless world (111).

Here we have a clear conflict between a secular ethic and such a religious one. (Indeed, a paradigmatic religious ethic.) But the conflict, *ethically speaking,* is a *derivative* one, for the having of the different moral beliefs and attitudes that the secularist and the religious person respectively have is dependent on their differing about what in fact the world is like. And their differing, deeply and crucially here in their assessments about what the world is like, is, in turn, rooted in their differing about cosmology and metaphysics. More broadly, their differing attitudes and commitments are rooted in differing beliefs about what there is and can be. The religious person's moral beliefs and other relevant beliefs are metaphysically mediated. He takes it that his metaphysics counts, indeed decisively counts, in his determination of what there is or can be. And, even if he is fideist enough to try to construe claims that God exists and created and sustains the world somehow nonmetaphysically, he is still making at least putatively factual claims about what there is and can be that differ fundamentally from those of the secularist. Moreover, the moral conceptions of the religious moralist are rooted in those claims. We have an appeal, on the part of the religious moralist, to metaphysical beliefs or (if he is a fideist) to otherwise putatively factual claims and, in both instances, to very problematical claims at that, namely that there is, and thus can be, a god, that the God depicted in Christian teaching exists, and that we have reason to believe He is a loving God who will care for us come what may so that no harm can really come to us. Atheists, and some others as well, will believe that these beliefs are groundless and indeed unreasonable beliefs. Some will even believe, as I do, that they are incoherent. If we, as Stout well advises, are to be coherentists and, if our pattern of justification is so coherentist, we will have to consider the plausibility of such metaphysical claims and otherwise putatively factual claims in making our reflective judgments about the viability of a religious ethics. But if we do so, we will see that such a religious ethic is very problematical indeed while a nonscientistic secular morality need have no such metaphysical danglers. Or, if I am on the mark in my defense of naturalism, or, if Hume was before me, no metaphysical danglers at all.

We can easily enough see that if things were very different than they are, then we perhaps could reasonably, and desirably, live free from anxiety and unstintingly love our fellow human beings. But, given the best understanding we can get of how the world and human beings are and what our human condition is, it would be very unreasonable and undesirable indeed to try to live as Jesus recommends. Such a conception of the moral life could not be gotten into wide reflective equilibrium. To take it on faith that we should act as Penelhum accurately describes Jesus as exhorting us to act is not to have a reasonable or desirable faith. *Perhaps*, in imitation of Christ, one could set it *as a purely personal ideal for how to live oneself*, but it would be very irresponsible to advocate it as a moral code or to advocate it to others as something they must do, or even should do, if they are to live the best sort of lives. We should not advocate that people try to become such knights of faith committing themselves to what is both absurd and dangerous to themselves and others. Such advocacy is very irresponsible because, if successful, very many people would almost certainly be harmed by it, indeed very severely harmed. That is a sure way to increase the suffering in the world. It is *perhaps* all right to take that chance for oneself, but not to try to talk others into taking such chances. They, where such advocacy is successful, would have been sold what very much looks like a harmful *moral ideology*. As it is there is already enough suffering in the world. We should not do things that add to it.

There are no good reasons at all to believe that we are children of God and that He will look after us, that His providential care will shield us. It is indeed true, as Penelhum remarks, that the "Christian demand that we love one another is presented here in the context of divine love for us, not as a mere moral requirement" (111). But to believe that there actually is such divine love is for us—at least for we critical intellectuals standing where we are now in history and culture—is to have an unreasonable belief, or, at the very least, a badly mistaken belief, and thus the *agape* of Christian ethics, tied as it is to such a cosmological belief, is also unreasonable and unjustified. More than that, if its advocacy were successful and some considerable number of people, even most people, actually tried to live as Jesus advocates, a very considerable harm would be done to them. They would be taken advantage of, often tricked and exploited and sometimes cruelly harmed by those, even if they were only a few, who did not so act. If everybody were all of the time, or at least most of the time, to act as Jesus advocates, then the situation would not be so bad, though even here, with no stress on recognizing and protecting one's own legitimate interests as well as having concern for the legitimate interests of others, we would often not know what to do. Altruism is not enough, even if it were perfect, to determine what is a fair division of things. And often, in a world of scarcity, fair divisions need to be made. But the central point is that it is totally unrealistic to expect everyone to act that way or even to expect that people rather generally will act in that way and have such *agapeistic* attitudes. However innocent and high-minded the intent of its advocates is (and I do not question that *at all* in most instances), it is in reality a harmful *moral ideology*: harmful not simply because it is false but (in this context) more seriously harmful because of the effect it would have on the lives of people.

Penelhum is not claiming to be trying to establish that Christian morality is "the true morality" (whatever, if anything, that means) or that the religious morality he characterizes is more adequate or sounder than at least some secular moralities or that he even knows what it would be like to make decisions or form judgments about their comparative adequacy (112). He, as he puts it, modestly and plausibly, was *not* trying "to argue that the Christian understanding of our moral situation is true," but sought only to articulate "some parts of what it is and how it affects Christian moral choice" (117). He sought to show how Christian "teachings underlie the moral life of those who accept them" (117). And in doing this he shows how at least one religious morality (a distinctively Christian religious morality) differs from a secular morality. I think he has indeed done that, and very clearly, but, as I have in effect argued above, that in the very doing of it so clearly, he has unintentionally shown how Christian morality cannot be a morality that we, as critical intellectuals, standing where we are now in culture and history, should accept. To believe that everything is in God's hands and that, in spite of appearances to the contrary, nothing can really harm us and that if we will keep trust with God we will be saved is to have some very unreasonable beliefs, if we are critical intellectuals with a good philosophical and scientific education (as plainly Penelhum has). (Recall here, so as not to misconstrue what I have just said, the claim I made in discussing Plantinga's views, a claim which is also apposite here. It was this: reasonable people can, and almost invariably do, have *some* unreasonable beliefs. No one is free of that. I am certainly not claiming, absurdly, and with ridiculous *hubris*, that Penelhum is less reasonable than I am, but only that *this belief* of his is unreasonable, that it is unreasonable for him to have it, and, in effect, though certainly not in intention, that it is a harmful belief.) There is, moreover, no justifying or even reasonably accepting such things *just on faith*. It is not just that Christian moral beliefs are utopian, but that, rooted as they are in cosmological beliefs which are at best false, they are unreasonable and indeed, as Hume realized, harmful to our lives and to our coming to have and to our sustaining a sound morality.

Christian cosmological beliefs do not make a *direct* difference to the kind of morality we would judge it appropriate to have. But when we attend to the warrant for, and the coherence of, such beliefs, we will, if we can live nonevasively, reject the very things that make Christian morality distinctive. The "ethical teachings of Jesus in the New Testament have an irreducibly theistic character" and that, since theism is at best false, is part of what is wrong with them (114). With those cosmological beliefs—beliefs which underlie the Christian's conception of the moral life—there is just too much in the way of scandals to the intellect for them to be reasonably accepted. And this includes very centrally having the "expectation of a future life in which development toward full selflessness can continue" (117). It is difficult enough to try to make sense of a Kingdom of God which is already here, but not yet completely so, without our adding, to our understanding of what this is, some eschatological belief with some robust conception of the immortality of the soul. It is, of course, easy enough to appreciate the psychological dynamics of such an eschatological hope. Penelhum brings them out very clearly. The believer, who firmly has such beliefs, is not only free from despair about the world, but he is, as well, freed from despair about his own anything-but-perfect moral capacities and powers. But the price of such freedom from despair is very high, as Kierkegaard saw. To gain it we have to crucify our intellects. And, as Hume saw, the ethics proclaimed, if really lived, would be the cause of extensive utterly needless human suffering.

Penelhum, I am confident, would not see things this way. He, no more than Alston, Wolterstorff, or Plantinga, believes that such beliefs are unreasonable. And he indeed argues for them in a reasonable way. But, *if* my arguments in this volume, where I have discussed such cosmological beliefs and where I have discussed the parity argument, are sound, such cosmological beliefs, together with their defenses, are mistaken. They are not even beliefs we can just take as *properly basic* (if indeed there is such a thing), setting aside as irrelevant all questions of proving them or giving evidence for them. If these things have been reasonably established, then we cannot get religious beliefs into wide reflective equilibrium. (Maybe we can't anyway, but we certainly cannot if my arguments there are sound.) So, unless my arguments in part 1 and again in the previous chapters of part 4 are thoroughly mistaken, these antitheistic claims have been established.

I shall now take stock of what I have so far argued in this chapter. I have argued that the claim made by many believers that without belief in God we can make no sense of the moral life or have anything like a sound moral point of view is through and through mistaken. Indeed, exactly the reverse is true. Without some moral understanding, logically prior to any theistic belief, we could have no understanding of what it is to believe in God or indeed even an understanding of the Judeo-Christian-Islamic conception of God. In these very important respects religion depends on (religiously speaking) an autonomous morality rather than, popular belief to the contrary notwithstanding, of morality on religion. Put somewhat differently, religion, in a very crucial respect, depends on an autonomous, vis-à-vis religion, moral understanding. Both Stout and Penelhum accept that and they accept as well what I have called the *text* of my *Ethics Without God*, namely that we can have reasonable and sound moral beliefs in a Godless world and without any appeal to religious beliefs or any grounding of ethics or morality from or on religious beliefs. But, as we have seen, Stout resists what I have called my *subtext*, namely my arguments that Divine Command ethical theories and religiously based natural law theories are impaled on the horns of a *Euthyphro*-type dilemma. Stout argues, as we have seen, that my argument fails. Religious moralists, he has it, can legitimately break the second horn of the dilemma and, moreover, my argument uncritically assumes foundationalism and the standard deductivist conception of justification, neither of which religious moralists need accept. I respond that his arguments fail to show that the second horn can be broken. In doing this, I, among other things, argue that Divine Command theories and natural law theories accept foundationalist conceptions and attempt to show that morality requires such foundations and, indeed not only foundations, but religious ones at that. Playing their own game, for the sake of the argument and to find the maximal common ground with them, I attempt to show that their arguments fail. Stout, as far as I can see, has not been able to establish that those arguments of mine are unsound. Without retracting anything of that, I agree with Stout that (a) we should be antifoundationalists, or at least nonfoundationalists, utilizing a coherentist, contextually sensitive conception of justification (for me wide reflective equilibrium); (b) I further agree with him that religious moralists can be antifoundationalist coherentists; and (c) that in doing so, if they allow (vis-à-vis religious conceptions) autonomous moral conceptions into their web of belief, they can develop an account of religious morality different from Divine Command theories, or theologically or theistically based natural law theories, which are not subject to my criticisms of those foundationalist theories. But I then argue in turn that such religious moralists jump from the frying pan into the fire, for using a coherentist model of justification they must, as John Hick and Terence Penelhum do, in their articulations and defenses of religious ethics, appeal to and be able to defend central cosmological conceptions of a very problematical kind in setting out the distinctive nature, rationale, and appeal of a religious ethics. But these cosmological claims, I have argued in detail in this volume and elsewhere as well, are at best false and cannot reasonably be believed by critical intellectuals in our societies at our time. We, as Penelhum, Stout, and Hick all agree, do not need God to be moral and indeed reasonably and justifiably so. But we have no parity here, for religious ethics are in shambles tied as they are to an unbelievable and unreasonable cosmology.

V

I have argued in the previous sections that even—indeed most particularly—when we look at all the relevant considerations, turn them over carefully and take them to heart, we have no good reasons to believe that a religiously based ethics, even the most sensitively nuanced religious ethics, is superior to, or even as adequate as, a similarly nuanced purely secular ethics. Indeed, we have good reasons to prefer the secular humanist ethics to the religious one.

Someone might respond, however, by arguing that if we look more broadly than simply looking at ethics or morality, but look at our human lives as a whole—what is sometimes called grandly "the human condition"— both at our lives as individuals, and our lives together in society—religion, at least in some form—cannot but play an important part, indeed, an indispensable part, in our lives. If we go back to what I called in chapter 15 the existential functions of religion and as well to what for Emile Durkheim are the social bonding functions, the way religion provides the social cement of society, the sense of its moral unity, we will come to see, the argument goes, how humanly indispensable religion is. We can, perhaps, ascertain what a just social order is, how we, more generally, should relate to each other, and what a good life for human beings is without reference to religion, but we require the rites, the symbolic structures of religion, to make us feel vividly those bonds that bind us together, that make us a *moral community*. So we need to look at those two social functions: the existential or coping function and the social bonding function.

People very generally, though certainly not all individuals, need—or so it seems—religion to cope with life, to face death, estrangement, defeat of hopes, moral failure, loss of those they love, prolonged illness, various psychological incapacitations, and the like. I have argued in chapter 15 that, where life goes very badly, as it does for many people now and as it did in the past as well: where whole strata and classes of people, or distinct races, or women are pushed against the wall without any realistic hope of overcoming or even significantly ameliorating their oppression and degradation, where there can be no realistic hope for their human flourishing or for their even leading a decent life, most people, in one way or another, and in one form or another, turn to religion in such a circumstance. Religion, sociopsychologically speaking, is *there* indispensable for most people. To say that in so turning to religion they are being unreasonable is not only cruelly harsh, it is itself unreasonable. What else have they to turn to? Could we expect anything else of them or, for that matter, of ourselves if we were so circumstanced? (There by the grace of our social circumstances go we.) Perhaps some of the most clear-sighted, the strongest, the most resolute and tough-minded could fight free of the chains of illusion? But they would be few in number. Could there more generally speaking in such circumstances be anything other than an illusory meeting of needs? Illusions here are what Marx called necessary illusions: necessary for most people in such desperate conditions devoid of all reasonable hope.

In such circumstances, religion, and typically very unreasonable and reactionary ones at that (even by religious standards), will flourish and the coping with life functions will continue, whether we intellectuals like it or not, to be provided by religion and, indeed, typically by such Neanderthal religions. The needs of people—their most ordinary reasonable desires for a decent life—cannot be meet in such a society. So religion comes in to provide them opiates to give them the illusion of human possibilities, to give them hopes— albeit illusory hopes—for a flourishing life beyond the grave, and, in doing this, it will also pacify them, lull them into an acceptance of their dreadful social world, to accept, depending on where they are, some version (a version for their particular society and usually a reactionary one) of the orthodox religious system, Jewish, Christian, Islamic, Hindu, Buddhist, Confucian, as the case may be. And with that they will be led to accept, as inevitable and natural, or at least as inescapable, the socioeconomic system to which the religious system in question is related. Where the conditions of life of people are so ghastly (as they certainly are for very many people in very many places), so alienating, and so destructive of human potential, religious attachment, in some form or another, is *inescapable* for most people.

The question I pressed in chapter 15 is whether, in a society of abundance equitably distributed, of security, of high levels of education widespread in the society, and in a society still having some sense of common unity as a people, whether religion would continue to flourish and whether religion's existential or coping functions would not, quite widely in that society, be met secularly. It is not, I argued, obvious that they cannot and, if they can, it is at least arguable that such a secularization would be a desirable thing, given the fact that religion is not truth tracking and the further fact that truth, while not the only good, is a very great good.

The social-bonding function occasions somewhat different problems than does the coping (existential) function. Religion functions symbolically, on the Durkheimian conception, to provide the sense of moral unity of society—its social cement or social glue, depending on the metaphor you prefer—and it is essential, it is almost routinely claimed, for the health of a society that it have that *moral unity*. (This is a great theme of communitarians.) But it is anything but evident that our modern societies, intractably pluralistic and conflicting as they are, can give us anything like the basis for *such a moral unity*. It seems no longer possible, in modern societies, for religion, or for that matter for anything else, to provide *such* a social bonding, to give us in the public sphere a sense of moral unity, so that we can see ourselves as a people. It can, under circumstances favorable to their continued existence, work for small groups, for example, for Pentecostals, Quakers, Amish, Hutterites, Orthodox Jews, some Muslim groups, committed communists, and socialist anarchists. There is among both these particular religious and nonreligious groups a sense of moral unity. It is somewhat more doubtful whether in present conditions among large denominations, such as Lutherans, Roman Catholics, Calvinists, or across the Jewish community as a whole, there will be much of a sense of that moral unity. Where such a bonding actually exists and a generalized liberalism, penetrating deeply into the society, has not withered it away, religion will function in this Durkheimian way. Among rather isolated, rather marginalized, and partly self-isolating groups, there plainly is such a sense of moral unity, though with more conflict than is usually recognized. We see exemplified, for these small groups, as subcultures forming kinds of quasi-societies, what Durkheim took to be the most fundamental function of religion. But in our modern pluralistic societies (*gesellschaften*, not *gemeinschaften*), it does not, as MacIntyre well stresses, function society-wide, but only among isolated, rather marginalized small groups of people such as I mentioned above. But where they exit and have not been undermined by liberalism or, as well, in the case of the religious sects, by modernization, they often, but not invariably, in our societies, exacerbate the already deep conflicts between groups in the society. So even when religion has this social function, it will not, in modern large-scale societies, be society-wide and will be a mixed blessing. *It* will not yield a sense of moral unity for us as a society, as a people, but only for us as Amish, Hutterities, Quakers, Trotskyists, and the like, not for us as citizens of any of the vast modern nation-states. (I am thinking here of the United States as compared to, say, Iceland.) The social bonding that Durkheim took to be the most essential function of religion, its very *raison d'être,* does not exist for us as citizens of the great capitalist democracies. Think particularly of countries like the United States, the United Kingdom, Canada, or France. The fact (or at least apparent fact) that we must now face is that we now seem at least to have no basis for a society-wide sense of moral unity. So, in such an intractably pluralist world, religion loses one of its deepest rationales.

We should also realize that in having to live in a society that, propagandistic State rhetoric aside, has no moral unity, we have lost something. We pay for our liberal pluralism, even though it may be the expected result of certain pervasive socioeconomic circumstances. There is not only nostalgia for the Absolute, there is, among not a few, nostalgia for a lost moral unity as well, though perhaps it is a nostalgia—a thought that shoots right past communitarians—for what in reality is only an *imagined* past moral unity? Perhaps there never were any *gemeinschaften,* but, as Marx thought, only *gesellschaften* sometimes parading as *gemeinschaften*?

I have argued in earlier chapters that we might have, or come to have, a broadly Rawlsian, society-wide consensus on primary social and natural goods, on social justice, and on what Rawls calls public reason, together with a consensus on the role that such conceptions play in the governing of our political life. This could, I believe, serve as a functional replacement for this lost moral unity. I am confident that someone like Alasdair MacIntyre would think it a pale replacement for a lost, whether just imagined or not, moral unity. But, still, for us, given our intractably pluralistic situation, it is perhaps a perfectly adequate replacement or, at least, the only one that we stand any chance of coming to have. This would not in any full sense give us the moral unity of a united moral community, for there is no agreed-on underlying comprehensive conception of the good, and thus, of course, there is no sense of unity rooted in an internalized comprehensive conception of the good that binds all the people in the society together. We do not have, and are not going to get, such a community in modern societies. (And, whether we like it or not, there seems to no alternative to such a pluralistic modern society in the foreseeable future.)

Still, the Rawlsian social democratic thing would give us the core of a reasonable consensus enabling us to see ourselves as a people (as citizens of a given country to which we are loyal), to have some reasonable basis for cooperation, and with that to have a kind of minimal moral unity *sans* any mutually accepted comprehensive conception of the good. This could very well be the best thing for such pluralistic societies with very different compre-hensive conceptions of the good, where there can be no expectation at all, short of being there as a result of force and domination, of one comprehen-sive conception winning out and being heralded as the one true comprehen-sive conception of the good. Indeed, it is at least arguably a good thing that there is in the society no one comprehensive conception of the good that is taken to be *authoritative*, for everyone in the society.

Even (*pace* the above) if it could somehow (magically somehow) come about benignly, still, such an authoritative comprehensive view would be confining. It would not answer to the diverse interests, aspirations, and hopes of the very different people differently situated that make up our modern plu-ralistic societies. Moreover, as long as there is a solid agreement (rooted in a society-wide social consensus) about primary goods, social justice, and pub-lic reason, the having of some comprehensive conception of the good is not necessary for a decent life, for human flourishing, and for us to have a sense of ourselves as a people. Many comprehensive conceptions of the good can flourish side by side, *if none are taken to be socially binding (authoritative) and as constituting the social cement of the society.* Justice and the like is enough for a society-wide source of normativeness and requiredness. We are, at least arguably, better off without the social cement of religion. And (*pace* MacIntyre) such a world with its greater autonomy, not at all in conflict with equality, is a better world than a world in which there is the insistence that some particular comprehensive conception of the good is the one true comprehensive conception of the good for all to follow. There is solidarity enough in seeing ourselves, and in being as well, a people bound by a com-mon sense of justice with its related notions and with a conception of our-selves as citizens.

However, the pluralism, as we have seen, could not, to be humane and just, just be any old pluralism, but would have to be a *reasonable* pluralism, by which I mean that all the different groups which constitute that pluralism would have to have reasonable views—"reasonable" as partially specified in the introduction to part 4—and for the most part to act in accordance with them. It is, however, anything but clear that in our societies we have such a reasonable pluralism or even much in the way of prospects of gaining one. But, if we did, or could plausibly come to expect the coming into existence in favorable circumstances of such a pluralism, it would be a pluralism, though *compatible* with a religious orientation, that would not, and indeed could not, *require* one. But it could not *require* a secular orientation either. There can be no acceptable state-mandated atheism or agnosticism.

This scaled-down (if you will, minimal) moral unity for a pluralist soci-ety—tolerantly pluralist between religions and tolerantly pluralist between secular and religious orientations and organizations—would not yield the strong moral unity that Durkheim took it to be the function of religion to pro-vide.[18] One of the deepest rationales for religion, something that fuels the religious yearnings of communitarians, cannot function in its properly society-wide basis in our societies. This leaves us, Alasdair MacIntyre believes, in a moral wilderness.[19] But (*pace* MacIntyre) it is not evident that a broadly Rawlsian liberal social democratic option, with a deeply secular orientation at its base, but still tolerant of religions that do not make theocratic, illiberal demands or claims, would not be possible and indeed, as well, a desirable option for us, if through political action we can bring about the existence of a reasonable pluralism. (Something that, to put the best face we can on it, if it exists anywhere at all, perhaps exists in the Scandinavian societies and in Holland.) It would be a society with a moral unity, though without any consensus on a comprehensive conception of the good, and thus without religion supplying the social cement for this unity (on a society-wide basis) and *perhaps* in time without any religion at all. At least, in such a society, religion would not be necessary to symbolize its moral unity. It would neither have nor need *that kind of unity*, a unity they could only be gained by a society-wide consensus on some particular comprehensive conception of the good.

I should add, parenthetically, so as to not be misunderstood in what I say above about religions which are illiberal and theocratic in intent, that, when they actually and realistically have the potential for control and domination of the society, as, say, in Israel or in Ireland, then they should be opposed. They, in such circumstances, actually present a clear and present danger to the social fabric of a liberal society. And on those grounds their actions should not, where it is possible to check them, be tolerated for, unchecked, they would force their vision and version of the world on all others. But, where they are just talking to little effect, where there is no realistic reason to think they present a great danger to the society, then they too should be tolerated. It is even arguable, free speech being the great value that it is, that they even should be tolerated when the threat they pose is real, though still plausibly containable, should they begin to act effectively. It is in these senses that we should tolerate the intolerant. Here the standard liberal distinction between *words* and *deeds* is important. Freedom of thought and freedom of speech being very great goods, we should be very wary of limiting them. This carries certain risks, but a liberal society in reasonably secure circumstances (say the present-day circumstances of France or the United States) should be prepared to take these risks.

VI

Let us from another angle consider some of the psychological and sociopsychological functions of religion. Here the issue of immortality we discussed in some detail in part 1 returns like the return of the repressed. And here I want to turn briefly to another naturalistic account of the function of religion, namely to that of social anthropologist Bronislaw Malinowski.[20] He gives an account of the psychological functions of religion claiming that religion is psychologically rooted in two "twin needs" and that it gives us, and more generally people at all times and places, a sense of purpose and well-being. (Presumably though, he did not need it himself, for he was an agnostic.) Like Durkheim, he recognizes that religion is a tribal affair involving a whole culture and, as critical as he was of Durkheim in certain respects, and while claiming that religion had its deepest sources in individual experience, he also, like Durkheim, thought that the public rituals of religion had an important social function, for they were, on his view, as on Durkheim's, the very cement holding a society together and the existence of this "social cement" was, he thought (contrary to what we have argued above), "indispensable for the maintenance of morals."

Still, religion, Malinowski thought, arises to a great extent and powerfully from purely individual sources. Human beings are religious animals whose most deeply religious moments come not during public religious rituals which provide the social cement of society, but in solitude and with a sense of detachment from the world. For Malinowski religion was very fundamentally and crucially linked to life-cycle rituals and most essentially to those concerned with death. These rites answer to what, in various circumstances, we intensely feel in solitude, when we try to come to grips with our lives and to face what Malinowski calls "the final crisis of our lives": death, and the keen and distressing recognition of its inevitability. It is over this "final crisis of our lives" and how human beings respond to it where religion most forcefully comes onto the scene. Phenomena linked with the fear of death, he believed, are intimately connected with the emergence and staying power of religion. We—that is, almost all human beings—are intensely afraid of death: of complete cessation, of annihilation, when we simply, and forever, will be no more. This is a thought, he has it, that we can barely tolerate. Religion with it funerary ritual functions provides us with psychological safeguards here. They, as well as their associated religious conceptions and beliefs, are essential, Malinowski maintains, in helping people to meet that final crisis of life.

The belief in immortality and in spirits, which together, Malinowski has it, form the very essence of religion, have a psychological origin and psychological function. Psychologically speaking, they yield an illusory but fervently held belief that we will be "saved from surrender to death and destruction." Something will persist, most people cannot help but believe, after our bodily death, something which will somehow preserve our identity. The need, Malinowski argues, is very great to believe that somehow we will continue to exist after bodily death.

Malinowski, naturalist that he was, thought that there was no nonpsychological, nonsociological truth in these religious claims and beliefs, or indeed in any other religious claims, but still, psychologically speaking, these particular religious beliefs are, he thought, universal and, humanly speaking, indispensable. They give us a sense, albeit an illusory sense, of a mastery of our fate that science cannot give us. They enable us to refuse, psychologically speaking, to capitulate to death. Our lives, we are illusorily led to believe, will not cease with the death of our earthly bodies. (I am most inclined to put shudder quotes around "earthly bodies," as if we had any conception of what another kind of body could be.) We shall, the universal "saving myth" of religion has it, be preserved and in such a way that our identities and our own awareness of our identities will not be lost. Death will not, appearances to the contrary notwithstanding, be a final annihilation. This, Malinowski has it, is an essential "saving myth" that people in every culture at every epoch need. Without it life would simply be intolerable.

If Malinowski is right about this psychological fact about human beings and if my arguments were sound in part 1 that belief in immortality, depending on how it is construed, is either false or incoherent, then many of us are in a fine pickle. We either have to crucify our intellects—try to make ourselves believe something that is manifestly unreasonable—or to go around with a pervasive sense of the meaninglessness and horror of our lives: lives which will sooner or later simply and irrevocably come to an end. Our options seem to be to either somehow to manage to deceive ourselves about how things are or to stoically accept that we will be annihilated, knowing that there is nothing else that we can reasonably believe, and taking some very small comfort in our being able to be reasonable in spite of the dreadfulness of it all.

I will consider two ways of responding to this. First, *a* (but not *the*) Wittgensteinian way, defended by D. Z. Phillips, which I take to be a mistaken way of responding, and secondly, the ethical and naturalistic response I shall give to it. I turn first to Phillips's Wittgensteinian response.[21] To such a Malinowskian psychologizing treatment of the belief in immortality, a notion which is generated and sustained—or so Malinowski believes—by an instinct for self-preservation, Phillips responds as follows: ". . . the thought that we shall cease to exist is intolerable to us." The promise of immortality allays this fear. But allaying it, Phillips has it, robs us of what death can teach us. The traditional theistic conception of immorality keeps us from saying farewell to life and from understanding the significance of saying such a farewell. A genuinely religious person will see, what any nonevasive person will see, namely, that death is no respecter of persons. This will further show, for a religious person, "that life is given and taken away, that we are not the center of the universe. The religious expression of this fact is to say that we are in God's hands." The coming of death is seen by the genuinely religious person as the "culmination of a life of spirituality." We need to come to see and to take to heart that our whole life is answerable to God. The believer, with all her weakness, if grace is hers, becomes more than she could ever become by her own efforts. This is what happens at death, if she genuinely offers herself to God.

Religious belief, Phillips has it, promises that where God is there we will also be. "God is a spiritual reality. We become more than ourselves at death when we become part of that spiritual reality." Saying farewell to life is part of what is meant by giving glory to God. It is in this way that the believer becomes more than he or she is; it is in this way that the mortal, as Phillips opaquely has it, "puts on immortality, and the corruptible puts on incorruption."

The standard philosophical conception and belief in immortality—what Phillips calls temporal eternity—is rightly seen, he avers, by atheistic critique as both at best false and as well as an ethical failing in being an inability to say farewell to life. The genuinely religious person, Phillips believes, will side with the atheist here. But what the atheist critique does not see in the religious response "is a mode of saying farewell to life" in which, to repeat his opaque, as well as his strange saying, "the mortal puts on immortality and the corruptible puts on incorruption." We have here a picture of immortality *without metaphysics* which claims, in contrast to the traditional accounts I have examined in part 1, to, in its account of immortality, be sensitive to the natural habitat of the words used to express these beliefs. It purports to capture, in a way traditional philosophical and theological accounts do not, as Phillips puts it, again providing us with another opacity, "the "soul" in the words of religious belief."

I think it is right to say that to make sense of the uses of our terms and our forms of speech, we must see how they function in their natural habitat, in the practices in which they are embedded and have their life. Wittgenstein in his later writings has certainly so stamped that in that only the most stubbornly bloody-minded could fail to see it. Phillips is also right, in good Wittgensteinian fashion, in saying that philosophers frequently ignore that and, in doing so, they misconstrue the uses of words. Philosophers, sometimes only in practice, but sometimes both in theory and practice, are so bloody-minded. Moreover, often, even when they do attend to the habitat of words—and this is a subtler mistake—they are still, not infrequently, dominated by a *mistaken* picture of the workings of their language, and in being so dominated, they misdescribe the uses of words when they try to give a clear account of them. (This is not to say that we can do without pictures here.[22]) But that this *must* be the case is not at all evident. And, in particular, it is not evident that the philosopher is misdescribing our uses of words when he says that when we consider what is at issue in speaking of "immortality" that an important part of what is at issue is the alleged persistence of some strange identity preserving something after the death of our earthly bodies.

We have our forms of life, and when we do philosophy one of the things we want to do—and it is a very important thing for a philosopher—is to give a perspicuous representation of them and of the words and sentences which give expression of them. Moreover, a form of life will involve *beliefs* as well as *concepts* and *attitudes,* with all of these things standing in mutually supporting relations. Concerning beliefs, and not only in scientific forms of life, but in all forms of life, questions can relevantly arise about how such beliefs can be supported or grounded. This applies to talk about God and the soul and not just when the engine is idling but as well when these concepts with their linked beliefs are working away in their natural habitat. Attitudes are indeed important, as Phillips shows, in understanding what talk of immortality comes to, as does, as well, a consideration of what sort of concepts we have embedded in what sort of content and context. But in considering the practice-embedded use of "immortality," *pace* Phillips, considerations concerning the *belief* that there is a persistence of something after the death of our present bodies is also very centrally at issue. Indeed, that is itself a religious-practice embedded belief. Moreover, as we have seen, claims about incoherence come up here and, connected with this, issues about the warrant for a belief in immortality arise. We are not dealing here just with attitudes and the concepts that go with these attitudes, but with beliefs as well.

Moreover, we should not assume, as Phillips and other Wittgensteinian fideists do, that beliefs which form part of even the core of a form of life cannot be incoherent. Only, such Wittgensteinians believe, the philosopher's and other intellectuals' construals of the beliefs can be incoherent; philosophically innocent people, by contrast, cannot have incoherent beliefs, including incoherent *first-order* beliefs. *Au contraire* to find out what language-game we play with "immorality" need not be to come to see that the belief is in order without any cognitive defect. It may be, but then again it may not. We have to look and see, and that looking and seeing must be sufficiently holistic to see how different language-games connect with other language-games. Where a part of a language-game is philosophically suspect (perhaps, of course, mistakenly so), as is the case with talk of "immortality," this is particularly important. We should not, if we wish to command a clear view of the workings of our language at a particular point, try to balkanize our language-games.

Perhaps Phillips's picture of immortality without metaphysics is in order. But, if it is, it would only seem to be so by giving an account of immortality which differs from utterly secular and reductive accounts of immortality—while still showing "the "soul" in the words of religious belief"—by taking the notion that the soul is immortal to be something which cannot be true or false, because in reality such talk is expressive of an attitude towards life and death rather than being, as well, linguistic expressions of a belief that something of us will persist after our present bodily death. (The lesson from the old debates about "independent emotive meaning" and "quasi-independent emotive meaning" should not be forgotten here. An upshot, agreed to by all parties to the debate, was that something cannot just be an attitude or attitude-expressing without also being a belief or belief-expressing as well.[23])

There, to give Phillips his due, is in Phillips's account with his distinctive way of talking, for all its vagueness, an articulation of deep attitudes and admirable ones as well, a cluster of attitudes which will enable a believer to overcome temptations that may assail her as death approaches. But, as John Hyman well puts it, this figurative but religiously attractive way of speaking of immortality has not been shown to be what "outside the philosophy of religion . . . is meant by immortality of the soul."[24] It has not been shown how in its natural habitats this is how the language-game of soul-talk goes. Indeed, I think that Hyman's suspicion is justified that "on the contrary, that this is what is meant by the immortality of the soul only *within* a philosophy of religion, albeit an unorthodox one." It is, I would add, so unorthodox as to come to an almost a complete reconceptualization of the Judeo-Christian-Islamic tradition's talk and conception, including the plain believer's talk and conception, of God and the soul.

What Phillips gives us, like John Wisdom before him, is an account of religion, including immortality, which is *naturalistic in substance, but religious in its vocabulary*, though this is often not seen. It is only where a careful reading of the vocabulary is given, as it only sometimes is, that the implicit naturalism, though only rather opaquely, shows itself. Where, as we frequently do in Phillips's writings, we have a rich religious vocabulary, which in complex ways is figuratively construed, we do not know what is being literally claimed. We often do not know what he is trying to assert or deny. (There can be a distinction, and a useful one, between the figurative and the literal, even though there is *no sharp line of division* between them or perhaps any sentences at all which are "purely literal" or "just figurative." Here we have something which is perhaps similar both to Putnam's treatment of the analytic and the synthetic and to, à la Putnam, what lessons we should draw from a distinction there that does not mark a *dichotomy* or a *dualism*, generating pragmatist and neopragmatist rejection.) Phillips's talk of immortality, while saying, through misleading language, the very opposite, is in reality showing us how to live without a belief in immortality. That is what—or so at least it seems—an important part of what Phillips's talk of immortality without metaphysics comes to. The same is true of his talk of God. Again, it is atheistic in substance while being Christian in rhetoric.

So, if plain religious people, for their very psychological security, need, as Malinowski avers, a robust belief in immortality, where something of their persons are believed to persist after the death of their present bodies, then

Phillips's demythologized account, however ethically attractive to some secular-minded, but still religiously involved, elites, will not answer to this fundamental and pervasive religious need. It is just a morally sensitive form of the old atheistic talk clothed in a religious vocabulary and placed in a narrative that is in some ways morally attractive.

However must we have such a "saving myth"? Do we really need it, as Malinowski avers? Some people no doubt do, but not all people. It is not, moreover, just that Malinowski himself and a few other intellectual elites do not need it, but, far more importantly, cultures have existed and still exist without such a belief and without such a craving. Some Buddhist cultures have a doctrine of spiritual enlightenment, but no doctrine of salvation. *Nirvana* is extinction and there is no God in their religion to which we can return. There is nothing to worship in their religion and there is no salvation or escape from extinction, though there is spiritual enlightenment. Indeed, this religion, in such an austere form, as Max Weber points out, has been the Buddhism of the elites in the culture and mass Buddhism (the religion in that culture of the masses) is much less austere, though still something of its structure trickles down.[25] Still, in such a religion, there is a critical mass of rather educated people, existing stably over time, who affirm it in its austere form: a form in which there is neither immortality, God, nor worship.[26] This culture has a long and stable history, so there is good reason to deny that belief in immorality, as personal survival after present bodily death, is a belief rooted in a universal need, as Malinowski takes it to be. Here we have the strange phenomena of a distinguished anthropologist being himself unwittingly ethnocentric.

Moreover, in our culture, with its steady disenchantment of the world, more and more people, including some Jews and Christians, have come to learn to live, and without any diminution of their flourishing, without a belief in, or even a hope for, immortality. With an increase in security, education, and with flourishing life-conditions for all (if ever that comes to be), it is not unlikely that this "saving myth" will become less of a need for more and more people. Such needs may slowly wither away. And, given the value of a life of integrity where people do not (if they can avoid it) tell themselves mythical stories that do not track truth (except, of course, as plain fictions to exercise their imaginations), the setting aside of this pervasive "saving myth" will be seen as a good thing and indeed will be a good thing. We can come to face death unblinkingly; the recognition that we will not live forever need not be intolerable or something we cannot live with and still flourish. The world portrayed in Leo Tolstoy's *The Death of Ivan Ilych* need not be the way we all are, unless we deceive ourselves, in facing death. No doubt we will always bamboozle ourselves about somethings, but the illusory nature of a belief in immortality is just too obvious to not be a scandal to the intellect. It is so plainly a matter of wish fulfillment that it will, with an increase in education, be harder and harder to give any credibility to it at all for more and more people. We can, particularly if our circumstances are not horrible, come to face death squarely, without evasion: the recognition that we will not live forever need not be intolerable. It need not be the case that in all circumstances most people, to keep from feeling that their lives are meaningless, must simply block out the thought of utter annihilation and tell themselves consoling fictions. Its steady recognition is something we can live with and still flourish. We can, and should, learn both to live in a certain way and still say farewell to life, but we can do both of these things without either creating myths or subscribing to those myths we find pervasive, but certainly not ubiquitous, in our cultural space. We should want our lives to have certain structure, including a narrative structure, but in that structure nonevasiveness and intellectual integrity should not have a negligible part. We should not be like children who tell ourselves fairy tales, even consoling fairy tales.

Perhaps the repeated "we" in the last part of the above paragraph should be replaced with an "I" and, by doing so, to draw attention to what surely is the case, namely, that I am here giving expression to where I stand and to what I deeply believe and feel. I, in so speaking, nail a part of my manifesto to the masthead. I am indeed certainly speaking for myself here, but I am also exhorting, in this last bit of my account, my readers to take, over these matters, careful thought, to turn the matter over and take it to heart, consulting both their intelligence and their feelings: their heartbeat, as Hendrik Hart puts it. I am trying to get people to put it to themselves, with the full weight of *both* deliberation and a taking to heart, whether this living without a belief in God and immortality is not something that they, and we as well, should do—a firm attitude we should take toward life. It is certainly so for me and I think it should be so for you as well. This is indeed advocacy, but it is not advocacy without supporting argument and without a supporting narrative. I do not think, and I also do not think that Wittgenstein thought, in spite of his famous remark to that effect, that philosophy should leave everything just as it is. Sometimes, of course, but not always. Sometimes we should say with Marx that the point is not merely to describe and explain the world, however accurately and perspicuously, but also to change it.

NOTES

1. Kai Nielsen, *Ethics Without God,* rev. ed. (Amherst, N.Y.: Prometheus Books, 1990); and Kai Nielsen, *God and the Grounding of Morality* (Ottawa, Ontario: University of Ottawa Press, 1992).

2. I speak of a religiously or theologically based natural law theory because Alan Donagan has deftly argued that even traditional natural law conceptions can be uncoupled,

though with a certain loss, from their theological or religious foundations. I consider them where they are, as they are in Aquinas, Jacques Maritain, or F. C. Copleston, together. Alan Donagan, "The Scholastic Theory of Moral Law in the Modern World," in *Aquinas: A Collection of Critical Essays,* ed. A. Kenny (London: Macmillan, 1969), 325–39.

3. Jeffrey Stout, *Ethics After Babel* (Boston: Beacon Press, 1988); and Terence Penelhum, "Ethics with God and Ethics Without," in *On the Track of Reason: Essays in Honor of Kai Nielsen,* ed. Rodger Beehler et al. (Boulder, Colo.: Westview Press, 1992), 107–18. Further references to them will be given in the text.

4. Kai Nielsen, "Atheism," in *Encyclopedia of Ethics,* ed. Lawrence C. Becker, vol. 1 (New York: Garland Publishing, Inc., 1992), 60–64.

5. Such an ethic is not only articulated by Penelhum but, as well, by John Hick, "Belief and Life: The Fundamental Nature of the Christian Ethic," *Encounter* 20, no. 4 (1959): 494–516. I critically examine Hick's account in chapter 4 of my *Ethics Without God.* (This criticism is given in chapter 2 of the first edition.)

6. Peter Geach, *God and the Soul* (London: Routledge and Kegan Paul, 1969), 117–29, and most particularly 127–29.

7. Kurt Baier, "The Meaning of Life," and Kai Nielsen, "Linguistic Philosophy and the 'The Meaning of Life' " both in *The Meaning of Life,* ed. E. D. Klemke (New York: Oxford University Press, 1981), 81–117 and 177–204 respectively.

8. Stout there, and throughout, is citing me from the first edition of *Ethics Without God* (Amherst, N.Y.: Prometheus Books, 1973), 2.

9. Emil Brunner, *The Divine Imperative,* trans. Olive Wyon (London: Lutterworth Press, 1947), chapter 9. A very useful collection of essays on the ethics of Divine Commands is given by Janine Adziak, ed., *Divine Command Morality: Historical and Contemporary Readings* (New York: Edwin Mellen, 1979).

10. Nielsen, *Ethics Without God,* 1st ed., 57.

11. Albert Camus, *Letters to a German Friend,* and Jean-Paul Sartre, *Existentialism,* trans. B. Frechtman (New York: Philosophical Library, 1947). In spite of being austerely metaethical, some of the emotivists realized that they had certain affinities with existentialists. See A. J. Ayer, "Novelist-Philosophers: Jean-Paul Sartre," *Horizon* (1946); and A. J. Ayer, "Novelist-Philosophers Albert Camus," *Horizon* (1946). More generally, and from other perspectives, the notion that the basis of ethics is arbitrary once had a considerable philosophical appeal. See Charner Perry, "The Arbitrary as a Basis for Rational Morality," *Ethics* 43 (January 1933); and D. C. Williams, "Ethics as Pure Postulate," *Philosophical Review* 42 (1933). The wheel of even contemporary history, as far as ethical theory is concerned, has turned.

12. Nielsen, *Ethics Without God,* 1st ed., 56.

13. Ibid., 31.

14. J. B. Schneewind, "Moral Knowledge and Moral Principles," in *Revisions,* ed. Stanley Hauerwas and Alasdair MacIntyre (Notre Dame, Ind.: University of Notre Dame Press, 1983), 118–19.

15. Cora Diamond, *The Realistic Spirit* (Cambridge, Mass.: MIT Press, 1991). For its application to ethical theory, see most particularly her last chapter, 367–80.

16. Brunner, *The Divine Imperative,* chapters 9 and 11.

17. This is John Hick's view as well. John Hick, "Belief and Life."

18. Michael Walzer is very astute with his conceptions of thick and thin, minimal and more maximal, moralities. Michael Walzer, *Thick and Thin: Moral Argument at Home and Abroad* (Notre Dame, Ind.: University of Notre Dame Press, 1994).

19. Alasdair MacIntyre, *After Virtue* (Notre Dame, Ind.: University of Notre Dame Press, 1981).

20. Bronislaw Malinowski, *Magic, Science and Religion and Other Essays* (London, Souvenir Press, 1974); Bronislaw Malinowski, *A Scientific Theory of Culture* (Chapel Hill, N.C.: University of North Carolina Press, 1944); and Brian Morris, *Anthropological Studies of Religion* (Cambridge, England: Cambridge University Press, 1987), 144–51.

21. D. Z. Phillips, "Dislocating the Soul," in *Can Religion Be Explained Away?* ed. D. Z. Phillips (London: Macmillan, 1996). All quotations are taken from the conference paper given and circulated at the Claremont Graduate School, February 4, 1995.

22. On the necessity of pictures see Hilary Putnam, *Words and Life* (Cambridge, Mass.: Harvard University Press, 1994), 276–77; and James Conant, "Introduction" to *Words and Life*, xlvi–lviii

23. Max Black, "Some Questions About Emotive Meaning," *Philosophical Review* 57 (1948); and R. B. Brandt, "The Emotive Theory of Ethics," C. L. Stevenson, "Brandt's Questions About Emotive Ethics," Brandt, "Stevenson's Defense of the Emotive Theory," all in *Philosophical Review* 59 (1950); and William Frankena, "'Cognitive' and 'Noncognitive'" in *Language Thought and Culture,* ed. Paul Henle (Ann Arbor, Mich.: University of Michigan Press, 1958), 146–72.

24. John Hyman, "Immortality Without Metaphysics: A Reply to D. Z. Phillips," in *Can Religion Be Explained Away?* ed. D. Z. Phillips. All quotations are taken from the conference paper given and circulated at the Claremont Graduate School, February 4, 1995.

25. Max Weber, *Ancient Judaism,* ed. H. H. Gerth and D. Martindale (New York: Free Press, 1958); Max Weber, *Economy and Society,* vol. 1, ed. Guenther Roth and Claus Wittich (Berkeley, Calif.: University of California Press, 1978), 399–634; *From Max Weber: Essays in Sociology,* ed. H. H. Gerth and C. Wright Mills (New York: Oxford University Press, 1958), 267–359; Ahmad Sadri, *Max Weber's Sociology of Intellectuals* (New York: Oxford University Press, 1992), 33–68.

26. Ninian Smart: "Buddhism and Religious Belief," *Humanist* 76 (1961): 47–50; "Numen, Nirvana and the Definition of Religion," *Church Quarterly Review* (April–June 1959): 216–25; and *A Dialogue of Religions* (London: SCM Press, Ltd., 1960).

Index